ShaderX²: Shader Programming Tips & Tricks with DirectX 9

Edited by

Wolfgang F. Engel

Wordware Publishing, Inc.

Library of Congress Cataloging-in-Publication Data

ShaderX^2 : shader programming tips and tricks with DirectX 9 / edited by
   Wolfgang F. Engel.
     p. cm.
   Includes bibliographical references and index.
   ISBN 1-55622-988-7 (paperback, companion CD-ROM)
   1. Computer games--Programming. 2. Three-dimensional display systems.
   I. Title: ShaderX squared. II. Engel, Wolfgang F.
   QA76.76.C672S48 2003
   794.8'16693--dc22   2003018871
                               CIP

© 2004, Wordware Publishing, Inc.

All Rights Reserved

2320 Los Rios Boulevard
Plano, Texas 75074

Printed in the United States of America

ISBN 1-55622-988-7

10 9 8 7 6 5 4 3 2 1
0308

All inquiries for volume purchases of this book should be addressed to Wordware
Publishing, Inc., at the above address. Telephone inquiries may be made by calling:

(972) 423-0090

Contents

Preface

After the tremendous success of *Direct3D ShaderX: Vertex and Pixel Shader Tips and Tricks*, I planned to do another book with an entirely new set of innovative ideas, techniques, and algorithms. The call for authors led to many proposals from nearly 80 people who wanted to contribute to the book. Some of these proposals featured introductory material and others featured much more advanced themes. Because of the large amount of material, I decided to split the articles into introductory pieces that are much longer but explain a lot of groundwork and articles that assume a certain degree of knowledge. This idea led to two books:

> *ShaderX²: Introductions & Tutorials with DirectX 9*
> *ShaderX²: Shader Programming Tips & Tricks with DirectX 9*

The first book helps the reader get started with shader programming, whereas the second book (this one) features tips and tricks that an experienced shader programmer will benefit from.

As with *Direct3D ShaderX*, Javier Izquierdo Villagrán (nurbs1@jazzfree.com) prepared the drafts for the cover design of both books with in-game screen shots from Aquanox 2, which were contributed by Ingo Frick, the technical director of Massive Development.

A number of people have enthusiastically contributed to both books:

Wessam Bahnassi
Andre Chen
Muhammad Haggag
Kenneth L. Hurley
Eran Kampf
Brian Peltonen
Mark Wang

Additionally, the following *ShaderX²* authors proofread several articles each:

Dean Calver
Nicolas Capens
Tom Forsyth
Shawn Hargreaves
Jeffrey Kiel
Hun Yen Kwoon
Markus Nuebel
Michal Valient
Oliver Weichhold

These great people spent a lot of time proofreading articles, proposing improvements, and exchanging e-mails with other authors and myself. Their support was essential to the book development process, and their work led to the high quality of the books. Thank you!

Another big thank you goes to the people in the Microsoft Direct3D discussion group (http://DISCUSS.MICROSOFT.COM/archives/DIRECTXDEV.html). They were very helpful in answering my numerous questions.

As with *Direct3D ShaderX*, there were some driving spirits who encouraged me to start this project and hold on through the seven months it took to complete it:

Dean Calver (Eclipse)
Jason L. Mitchell (ATI Research)
Natasha Tatarchuk (ATI Research)
Nicolas Thibieroz (PowerVR)
Carsten Wenzel (Crytek)

Additionally, I have to thank Thomas Rued from DigitalArts for inviting me to the Vision Days in Copenhagen, Denmark, and for the great time I had there. I would like to thank Matthias Wloka and Randima Fernando from nVidia for lunch at GDC 2003. I had a great time.

As usual, the great team at Wordware made the whole project happen: Jim Hill, Wes Beckwith, Heather Hill, Beth Kohler, and Paula Price took over after I sent them hundreds of megabytes of data.

There were other numerous people involved in this book project that I have not mentioned. I would like to thank them here. It was a pleasure working with so many talented people.

Special thanks goes to my wife, Katja, and our daughter, Anna, who spent a lot of evenings and weekends during the last seven months without me, and to my parents, who always helped me to believe in my strength.

— Wolfgang F. Engel

P.S.: Plans for an upcoming project named *ShaderX³* are already in progress. Any comments, proposals, and suggestions are highly welcome (wolf@shaderx.com).

About the Authors

Dan Amerson
Dan graduated from North Carolina State University in 2001 with a bachelor's degree in computer science. During his undergraduate studies, he focused on artificial intelligence research for automated camera control and positioning. After graduation, Dan joined NDL in late 2001 to work on the NetImmerse and Gamebryo engines. He works primarily on console rendering technologies and most recently served as lead programmer for the Gamebryo shader demo Eturnum.

Marwan Y. Ansari (mansari@ati.com)
Marwan is a member of the 3D Application Research Group at ATI Research. He received a master's degree in computer science from the University of Illinois at Chicago and a bachelor of science degree in computer science and mathematics from DePaul University. Prior to moving to ATI's 3D Application Research Group, he worked on OpenGL drivers for Number Nine Visual Technology before joining ATI's Digital TV group. In addition to his image space contributions to *ShaderX²*, Marwan has also contributed to *Game Programming Gems 4* and spoken about real-time video processing using shaders at the Game Developers Conference.

Kristof Beets (kristof.beets@powervr.com)
Kristof took his first steps in the 3D world by running a technical 3D fan site, covering topics such as the differences between traditional and tile-based rendering technologies. This influenced his electrical engineering studies in such a way that he wrote his thesis about wavelet compression for textures in Direct3D, a paper that won the Belgian Barco Prize. He continued his studies, obtaining a master's degree in artificial intelligence, while working as a technical editor for Beyond3D and writing various technical articles about 3D hardware, effects, and technology. As a freelance writer he wrote the "FSAA Explained" document for 3Dfx Interactive to explain the differences between various types of full-screen anti-aliasing. This document resulted in a full-time job offer at 3Dfx. Currently he is working as a developer relations engineer for PowerVR Technologies, which includes research into new graphical algorithms and techniques.

Flavien Brebion (f.brebion@vrcontext.com)
Flavien has had a passion for video games since he got an Amstrad CPC at the age of 12. He still remembers typing in hundred-page listings just to see a small sprite appear on-screen. He studied computing science at the University of Nantes, France, where he graduated with both bachelor's and master's degrees in 2000. He has also done a lot of research and developed many small games and rendering engines on his own. Currently he works at VRcontext, a virtual reality company

in Brussels, where he develops software designed to display industrial models made up of millions of triangles. He works on amateur games and graphical demos in his spare time, trying to get the most out of the new, powerful video cards. His web site is http://www.fl-tw.com/opengl/SoftShadows/.

Chris Brennan (cbrennan@ati.com)

Chris graduated with bachelor's degrees in computer science and electrical engineering from Worcester Polytechnic Institute in 1997 and joined Digital Equipment Corp.'s Workstation Graphics group doing hardware design and verification. When Digital died, Chris joined ATI as a 3D ASIC designer for the Radeon line of graphics chips and then moved over to the 3D Application Research Group where he tries to get those chips to do things that were not originally thought possible.

Kevin Buchin

Kevin received his master's degree from Hasso Plattner Institute for Software Engineering in Potsdam, Germany, in 2003. He wrote his thesis on real-time non-photorealistic terrain rendering. He has studied math, logic, and computer science in Muenster, Germany, and Leeds, England, and is involved in the 3D rendering engine VRS (www.vrs3d.org) and the 3D-map software system LandExplorer (www.landex.de).

Aaron Burton (aaron.burton@powervr.com)

Aaron has been a developer relations engineer at PowerVR Technologies since he received his Honours degree in information systems engineering in 1998. His first computer was a VIC 20, though his fascination for 3D graphics began with the Atari ST. At PowerVR he has been able to indulge this interest by developing a variety of demos, benchmarks, and debug/performance tools, and supporting developers in creating faster and better games. When he's not climbing, he spends his spare time working on ray-tracing and real-time 3D demos.

Dean Calver

Games are fun! Dean figured that out at age 2 and has spent the ensuing years working on how to make better games. For the last seven years, people have even paid him to do it. Having no real preference for console or PC has meant a mixed career switching between them for every project. Professionally, he has worked on a war game, racing games, an X-COM style game, arcade classic updates and the port of Silent Hill 2 to the PC. He is currently working on an Xbox RPG called Sudeki at Climax Solent.

Nicolas Capens (sw-shader.sourceforge.net)

Nicolas is a master's student in civil engineering in computer science in Ghent, Belgium. He became interested in graphics programming after discovering some Quake mods, and he quickly learned C++ and x86 assembly by himself. His main interest is software rendering and optimization. For more than two years he has been developing his own software renderer in his spare time. He is currently focusing on implementing shader emulation using the MMX and SSE instruction sets and dynamic code generation.

Francesco Carucci

Francesco has been a professional game programmer for three years and currently works on Black&White 2 for Lionhead Studios. He studied graphics programming-related subjects at university for five years before that. His passion for video games and 3D graphics help him spend many sleepless nights after long days of writing shader code.

Roger Descheneaux

Roger has been working on 3D graphics since the late 1980s, and he has a vaguely uncomfortable feeling that he should somehow be better at it by now. In 1991 he graduated to working on 3D graphics device drivers for IBM. The first driver he worked on was for a five-card graphics solution that sold for $30,000 and couldn't do texture mapping. The graphics hardware is slightly faster and somewhat cheaper these days. He currently works on OpenGL device drivers for ATI Research in Marlborough, Massachusetts, for graphics chips that can definitely do texture mapping.

Sim Dietrich

Sim manages the U.S. Technical Developer Relations team at nVidia Corporation. Sim has written chapters for *Game Programming Gems 1* and *2* and served as editor of the Graphics Display section of *Gems 2*. He was a key contributor to the CgFX effort, bringing real-time shaders to Max, Maya, and SoftImage for the first time. Sim's interests include new shadow techniques and improving graphics workflow through efforts like Cg and CgFX.

Wolfgang F. Engel (wolfgang.engel@shaderx.com)

Wolfgang is the editor of *ShaderX²: Introductions & Tutorials with DirectX 9*, the editor and a co-author of *Direct3D ShaderX: Vertex and Pixel Shader Tips and Tricks*, the author of *Beginning Direct3D Game Programming*, and a co-author of *OS/2 in Team*, for which he contributed the introductory chapters on OpenGL and DIVE. He spoke at GDC 2003 and at Vision Days 2003 in Copenhagen, Denmark. He has published articles in German journals and on www.gamedev.net, www.gamasutra.com, and his own web site, www.direct3d.net. During his career in the game industry he built up two small game development units.

Tom Forsyth (tomf@muckyfoot.com)

Tom has been obsessed by 3D graphics since seeing Elite on his ZX Spectrum. Since then he has always tried to make hardware beg for mercy. Tom has written triangle-drawing routines on the Spectrum, Sinclair QL, Atari ST, Sega 32X, Saturn, Dreamcast, PC, GamePark32, and Xbox, and he's getting quite good at them now. Tom's coding past includes writing curved-surface stuff for Sega and graphics drivers for 3Dlabs. Currently he works in Guildford, England, at Mucky Foot Productions, where past projects include Urban Chaos, StarTopia, and Blade2.

Eli Z. Gottlieb

Eli is a self-taught programmer attending ninth grade at Bethlehem Central High School in Delmar, New York.

Matthew Halpin

Matthew started programming before he was 10 and has continued to hold an interest in the areas of graphics and physics. Starting with 2D vector and sprite rendering, he quickly moved onto software 3D rendering and later 3D hardware accelerated rendering combined with rigid body and particle physics systems. He has been working in the games industry since receiving a BA in computer science from Cambridge University.

Shawn Hargreaves

After finishing a degree in music, Shawn has been writing games for the last six years, most recently as lead programmer on Climax's MotoGP bike racing game. Having started out coding 2D graphics by hand in DOS (where he created the popular Allegro library (http://www.talula.demon.co.uk/allegro/index.html) and then spending time on the N64 and PS2, he is still in awe of the sorts of things that are possible with programmable shaders on Xbox and modern PC cards.

Evan Hart

Evan is a software engineer with ATI's Application Research Group where he works on technology evangelism and adoption. He is a graduate of Ohio State University.

O'dell Hicks

O'dell has been a professional game programmer since 1998 and a hobbyist several years longer than that. He has done work on both the PC and Xbox. One day he hopes to finish a game that he is working on by himself in his spare time. His web site can be found at http://odellworld.com/.

Oliver Hoeller

Oliver currently works as senior engine programmer at Piranha Bytes, which developed the RPGs Gothic I and II. He started programming at age 10 on his Commodore VIC20, working his way through 6502(VIC20), 6510(C64), and 68000(Amiga) Assembler. His first game project was with 15, a jump and run game named Platou (Kingsoft, C64). He was an active member of the German demo scene in the '80s and early '90s. After a detour — during which he developed music software, created a security program, and worked as a consultant for web services — Oliver returned to his roots and developed his first 3D engine (Warrior Engine, 1995-98). He was lead programmer and director of development at H2Labs/Codecult and was responsible for development of the Codecreatures game system.

Takashi Imagire

Takashi has been a professional game programmer for five years, mainly working with the PlayStation and PlayStation2. Currently, he is programming real-time 3D graphics in his spare time, while focusing on the newest shader technology. A number of articles and demos on shader programming can be found on his web site at http://www.t-pot.com/. His goal is to publish his demos immediately after the release of new shader technology.

John Isidoro

John is a member of the 3D Application Research Group at ATI Technologies and a graduate student at Boston University. His research interests are in the areas of real-time graphics, image-based rendering, and machine vision.

Greg James

Greg is a software engineer with nVidia's technical developer relations group where he develops tools and demos for real-time 3D graphics. Prior to this, he worked for a small game company and as a research assistant in a high-energy physics laboratory. He is very glad to have avoided graduate school, and even happier to be working in computer graphics, which he picked up as a hobby after his father brought home a strange beige Amiga 1000.

Jeffrey Kiel

Jeff started his work in graphics as an undergrad at the University of North Carolina doing volume rendering research. After a stint in the corporate world, he moved on to work at Interactive Magic as a lead programmer on Destiny (one of the first 3D strategy games), iF18, and WarBirds. Then he joined Sinister Games to work on Shadow Company (3D squad-based strategy game) and the Dukes of Hazzard I and II on PS1. Jeff returned to his passion for graphics by joining nVidia, where he has worked on a couple of 3D engines, incorporating shader technology into real-world applications. His shader experience covers standard transform/lighting/shading, special effects, mesh animation, and particle systems.

Shaun Kime

Shaun is a software engineer at NDL where he is the lead developer on the 3ds max tools pipeline. Prior to working at NDL, he worked on the Mimesis project at North Carolina State University doing research on integrating narrative planning into virtual worlds. When he isn't at work, he can be found reviewing local pubs at http://www.drinktheworld.com.

Jakub Klarowicz

Jakub is an engine programmer at Techland where he works on all low-level aspects of game engine development. His biggest interest is, of course, real-time 3D graphics. He received an MS in computer science from Wroclaw University of Technology in 2001, and has been programming computers since he was 10. Jakub always wanted to push hardware to its limits so he started learning assembler while his friends were still playing games. In his work with 3D graphics, Jakub has gone all the way from software rendering to shader programming. He has been playing with hardware-accelerated rendering for five years, using Glide, OpenGL, and Direct3D. For the last three years he has worked with 3D graphics professionally.

Jesse Laeuchli

Jesse is a self-taught programmer who now makes his home in Budapest, Hungary. As the child of a Foreign Service officer, he has lived in such places as China, Taiwan, Africa, and Saudi Arabia. He has written for several computer magazines, books, and web sites, and is also an avid epee fencer. His web site is www.laeuchli.com/jesse/.

Sylvain Lefebvre

Sylvain is a Ph.D. student in the iMAGIS team at the French National Institute for Research in Computer Science, working on the rendering of natural scenes. He is also interested in many aspects of game programming and real-time graphics. He is currently focusing on developing new approaches with vertex and pixel shaders to handle the complexity of natural scenes. His home page is at http://www.aracknea.net.

Jean-Sebastian Luce

Jean-Sebastian has been a professional game programmer specializing in computer graphics for three years in the Nadeo studio where he worked on the games Virtual Skipper 1 and 2. He is currently working on improving their graphic engine quality by using more complex shaders for the recent games TrackMania and Virtual Skipper3. He has also studied applied mathematics, computer science, and image synthesis in a French National Institute (ENSIMAG).

Dean Macri

Dean is a software engineer with Intel Corporation where he works with software developers in optimizing the processor-specific aspects of their titles. He wrote his first graphics application, a line and circle drawing program, in TMS9900 assembly language in 1984 on a Texas Instruments 99/4A. Since then he's been hooked on graphics and programming, majoring in computer science as both an undergraduate and a graduate student. Starting in 1992, he spent five years developing high-speed assembly routines for 2D graphics transition effects at a multimedia kiosk development company. In 1998 he joined Intel where he continues to evangelize the benefits of new processors and technologies to software developers and provide their feedback to the processor architects.

Jason L. Mitchell (JasonM@ati.com)

Jason is the team lead of the 3D Application Research Group at ATI Research, makers of the Radeon family of graphics processors. Jason has worked with Microsoft on the Microsoft campus in Redmond for several years to define key new Direct3D features. Prior to working at ATI, Jason did work in human eye tracking for human interface applications at the University of Cincinnati, where he received his master's degree in electrical engineering in 1996. He received a bachelor's degree in computer engineering from Case Western Reserve University in 1994. In addition to this book's article on advanced image processing, Jason wrote about HLSL programming in *ShaderX²: Shader Programming Tips & Tricks with DirectX 9*, and has written for the *Game Programming Gems* books, *Game Developer* magazine, Gamasutra.com, and academic publications on graphics and image processing. He regularly presents at graphics and game development conferences around the world. His home page can be found at http://www.pixel-maven.com/jason/.

Ádám Moravánszky

Ádám is a recent graduate of the Swiss Federal Institute of Technology. After finishing his thesis in the field of real-time 3D graphics, he co-founded NovodeX (www.novodex.com), a company providing game physics middleware, where he is the chief software architect.

Christopher Oat

Christopher is a software engineer in the 3D Application Research Group at ATI, where he explores novel rendering techniques for real-time 3D graphics applications. His focus is on pixel and vertex shader development for current and future graphics platforms. Christopher has contributed as an original member of the RenderMonkey development team and as a shader programmer for ATI's demos and screen savers. He has been published in *Game Programming Gems 3* (Charles

River Media, 2002) and *Direct3D ShaderX: Vertex and Pixel Shader Tips and Tricks* (Wordware, 2002). Christopher is a graduate of Boston University.

David Pangerl

David's addiction to computers and games started early in his life, and the vision to create virtual worlds continues to be a strong force in his life. He has been involved in the production of several games, including Crash, Casanova, Hitchcock, Hannibal, and most recently Mistmare. His main interests are computer graphics, artificial intelligence, and compilers.

Kurt Pelzer

As a senior programmer at Codecult, Kurt developed several real-time simulations and technology demos built on CC's high-end 3D engine Codecreatures (e.g., a launch demo for nVidia's GeForce4 Ti generation and the well-known Codecreatures-Benchmark-Pro). He designed the innovative fx systems of Codecreatures and was involved in creating a simulation of the Shanghai TRANSRAPID track for SIEMENS AG. Kurt also worked on Piranha Bytes' PC game Gothic and the top-selling Gothic II—which were named RPG of the Year in Germany in 2001 and 2002. In prehistoric times Kurt started programming on C64 and Atari's ST; later on he studied mathematics, always focusing on computer graphics. When he's not scribbling down equations or reading the book of seven seals, Kurt works at Piranha Bytes to guarantee a high level of visual quality for the company's future products.

Emil Persson

Emil recently graduated from Luleå University of Technology in Northern Sweden after studying computer science and engineering. Over the years Emil has gathered experience from early software rendering attempts to advanced techniques in the Glide, OpenGL, and Direct3D APIs. His web site at http://esprit. campus.luth.se/~humus/ focuses on real-time 3D graphics. In the future you'll probably find Emil working as a game developer working on the next generation of game engines.

Tim Preston

Tim is a software engineer working on the Direct3D sections of the Gamebryo game engine at NDL. He graduated from Princeton University in 1997 with a degree in chemistry and a desire to do pretty much anything but chemistry. He went to the University of North Carolina for a master's in computer science, where he did a lot of molecular modeling work that led to an interest in 3D graphics. When he graduated in 1999, the game industry was a good match for his experience and his goal of not doing anything too important.

Maurice Ribble

Maurice graduated in 2001 from the Milwaukee School of Engineering with a bachelor's degree in computer engineering. During his junior year he had the opportunity to take part in a summer internship at Los Alamos National Labs. He was somewhat disappointed that other people worked on million-dollar workstations while he worked on consumer-level hardware, but after writing an application that performed lighting calculations for volume textures on first-generation consumer fragment shader hardware, he realized that consumer-level hardware was in for exciting changes, and he wanted to be part of the action. He currently works on the OpenGL device driver team at ATI Research.

Guennadi Riguer

Guennadi is a software developer at ATI Technologies, where he is helping game engine developers to adopt new graphics technologies. Guennadi holds a degree in computer science from York University and previously studied at Belorussian State University of Computing and Electronics. He began programming in the mid-80s and worked on a wide variety of software development projects prior to joining ATI.

Thomas Rued (rued@digitalarts.dk)

Thomas started his programming career at the local mall in 1983, doing small graphics programs in BASIC until an angry salesperson turned the computer off and he had to start all over. Later he programmed multimedia programs for InterVision in assembler and Pascal. Then he decided that education was in order and earned a degree in computer science. He moved on to Interactive Vision for several years, where he was a senior software engineer and worked on 3D applications plus the in-house frameworks for game development using C++ and DirectX. Currently Thomas works at Digital Arts (www.digitalarts.dk) where he focuses on high-end 3D visualization stuff in real time using modern 3D hardware. In his spare time he is the co-coordinator of the Danish IGDA chapter.

Scott Sherman

Scott is a software engineer at NDL where he is the lead on the Xbox version of their graphics engine. After receiving degrees in physics and electrical engineering, a short stint in the hardware side of the computer industry led to doing on-air statistics and scoring systems programming for sporting event broadcasts. Once the excitement of live television wore off, he moved over to the field of game programming, and is currently focused on real-time 3D graphics.

Peter-Pike Sloan

Peter-Pike currently works on D3DX at Microsoft. Prior to that he worked in the Microsoft Research Graphics Group, the Scientific Computing and Imaging group at the University of Utah, PTC, and Evans & Sutherland. His primary research interests revolve around interactive graphics techniques. Most of his publications are available at http://research.microsoft.com/~ppsloan.

Marco Spoerl (http://www.marcospoerl.com)

Like just about everyone else, Marco started programming way back on a C64. After buying a PC just so he could play Doom, he learned about computer graphics. He started his professional career as an engine programmer at Codecult Software, working on the Codecreatures Game Development System and the Codecreatures Benchmark Pro. After receiving his diploma in computer science, and a short walk on the wild side as a freelance software developer, he's now working in the training and simulation department at Munich-based Krauss-Maffei Wegmann.

Natalya Tatarchuk (Natasha@ati.com)

Natalya is a software engineer working in the 3D Application Research Group at

ATI Research, where she is the programming lead for the RenderMonkey IDE project. She has worked in the graphics industry for more than six years, working on 3D modeling applications and scientific visualization prior to joining ATI. Natalya graduated from Boston University with a bachelor's degree in computer science, a bachelor's degree in mathematics, and a minor in visual arts.

Nicolas Thibieroz (nicolas.thibieroz@powervr.com)

Like many kids of his generation, Nicolas discovered video games on the Atari VCS 2600. He quickly became fascinated by the mechanics behind those games, and started programming on C64 and Amstrad CPC before moving on to the PC world. Nicolas realized the potential of real-time 3D graphics while playing Ultima Underworld. This game inspired him in such a way that both his school placement and final year project were based on 3D computer graphics. After obtaining a bachelor's degree in electronic engineering in 1996, he joined PowerVR Technologies where he is now responsible for developer relations. His duties include supporting game developers, writing test programs and demos, and generally keeping up to date with the latest 3D technology.

Alex Vlachos (http://alex.vlachos.com)

Alex is a staff engineer in the 3D Application Research Group at ATI, where he has worked since 1998 focusing on 3D engine development as the lead programmer for ATI's Demo Team. He developed N-Patches (a curved surface representation introduced in Microsoft's DirectX 8), also known as PN Triangles, and TRUFORM. He has published in *Game Programming Gems 1, 2*, and *3*, ACM Symposium on Interactive 3D Graphics (I3DG), and *Direct3D ShaderX: Vertex and Pixel Shader Tips and Tricks*. He has presented at Microsoft Meltdown Seattle and UK, I3DG, GDC, and GDC Europe. Alex is a graduate of Boston University.

Daniel Wagner (daniel@ims.tuwien.ac.at)

Daniel has been fascinated by programming computer graphics since he got his first PC in 1991. In 1995 he developed the software SimLinz for the Ars Electronica Center (museum of the future) in Linz, Austria. During his study he worked for Reality2, a company that created virtual reality software. After finishing his master's thesis, "EndoView: A System for Fast Virtual Endoscopic Rendering and Registration" in summer 2001, he worked as a lead developer for BinaryBee, a company developing arcade-style web games. Daniel is currently working on his Ph.D. thesis on augmented reality at the Interactive Media Systems Group at the Vienna University of Technology.

Arkadiusz Waliszewski

Arkadiusz holds a master's degree in computer science from Poznan University of Technology and is currently a software engineer in Poland. He started his adventure with computer graphics when he got his first computer (Atari 65XE) and has become addicted. Beside real-time computer graphics, he is also interested in object-oriented programming and design. He likes good movies, dry wine, and big fluffy carpet slippers.

Maike Walther

Maike's research interests lie in computational and cognitive aspects of computer depiction. She has studied mathematics, logic, computer science, and psychology at the universities of Muenster, Germany, and Leeds, England. Maike graduated in 2003 from the Hasso Plattner Institute in Potsdam, Germany after writing her master's thesis on computer graphics and algorithms for real-time non-photo-realistic rendering of 3D city models. She is currently developing for the Virtual Rendering System (www.vrs3d.org).

Oliver Weichhold

Oliver has been a programmer and developer on a number of projects, including a software implementation of the Direct3D pipeline.

Carsten Wenzel (carsten@crytek.de)

Carsten has been passionate about computer graphics ever since he got a hold of intros and demos for Amiga and PC. Although he's never really been active in the demo scene, it's always been a big inspiration for him. As a 3D programmer at Totally Games, he developed many of the pixel and vertex shaders used for special effects in an Xbox game. At that time he also wrote a tech demo for nVidia's GeForce3. His latest demo, Meshuggah, was released in spring 2002, and he received his master's degree in computer science in December 2002. He currently works at Crytek.

Guillaume Werle (guille@free.fr)

Guillaume is a 26-year-old graphic engineer at Montecristo (www.montecristo-games.com). He joined the R&D department team last year where he is working on the next-generation 3D engine. In the game industry since 1998, he has done two PlayStation games for Infogrames and one PC game for Montecristo. Despite the little spare time he has, he is still an active demoscener (http://cocoon.planet-d.net). His last demo, Raw Confessions, was nominated for the Demoscene Awards (http://awards.scene.org/) in the "Best Demo" category and won the "Best Graphics" award.

Renaldas Zioma

Renald Zioma has been driven (mad) by computer graphics since he saw ZX Spectrum. After learning assembly and writing a Tetris clone for his ZX, he switched to PCs, finished school, wrote a couple of small non-commercial games, gained experience with object-oriented programming and design while working at a software development company, and received a bachelor's degree in computer science from Kaunas University of Technology. He has been working as a professional game programmer for the last two years. Recently he finished a demo of a 3D fighting game based on real-time motion recognition for Interamotion, LLC. In his spare time, he programs demos and games and organizes small demo/game scene related events in Lithuania.

Introduction

This book is a collection of articles that discuss ways to use vertex and pixel shaders to implement a variety of effects. The following provides a brief overview of these articles:

Section I — Geometry Manipulation Tricks

This section starts with a DirectX 9 sequel to Dean Calver's vertex compression article in *Direct3D ShaderX: Pixel and Vertex Shader Tips and Tricks*. Dean shows a number of ways to reduce vertex throughput by compressing vertex data. Carsten Wenzel points out how to use lookup tables in vertex shaders to reduce the workload of the vertex shader hardware. A feature-complete and very hardware-friendly terrain engine is explained in Daniel Wagner's article, "Terrain Geomorphing in the Vertex Shader." The speed of the example program provided with source is impressive. Creating 3D planets for a space-shooter type of game can be done entirely on the GPU, which Jesse Laeuchli shows how to do in his article "3D Planets on the GPU."

The vs_3_0 vertex shader model has a feature called vertex texturing, which Kristof Beets uses to create a very realistic-looking cloth animation in his article "Cloth Animation with Pixel and Vertex Shader 3.0." In "Collision Shaders," Takashi Imagire, who is known for the example programs on his web site (www.t-pot.com), uses shaders to calculate collisions, something that has never been shown before. The final article in this section covers using displacement mapping as a method of geometry compression. The main aim of Tom Forsyth's article is to allow people to take data from the industry's current mesh and texture authoring pipelines, and to derive displacement map data from them.

Section II — Rendering Techniques

The section starts with an article by Greg James that presents a convenient and flexible technique for rendering ordinary polygon objects of any shape as thick volumes of light scattering or light absorbing material with ps_1_3. O'dell Hicks shows in his article, "Screen-aligned Particles with Minimal VertexBuffer Locking," how to create screen-aligned particles with a vertex shader, bringing us one step closer to the goal of having almost everything done by the GPU. "Hemisphere Lighting with Radiosity Maps," written by Shawn Hargreaves, shows a lighting model that was designed for fast moving objects in outdoor environments. Its goals are to tie in the moving objects with their surroundings, to convey a sensation of speed, and to be capable of rendering large numbers of meshes at a good frame rate on first-generation shader hardware. The companion movie on the CD includes jaw-dropping effects.

Jesse Laeuchli has contributed two additional articles. In "Galaxy Textures," he uses a procedural model to generate easy-to-vary galaxies that can be implemented almost entirely on hardware using pixel shaders. "Turbulent Sun" demonstrates how to implement a sun using a 3D noise function. The example program runs solely on the GPU using shaders. A complete implementation of Phong lighting, together with a cube shadow mapping implementation, is shown in Emil Persson's article, "Fragment-level Phong Illumination." Getting a nicely distributed specular reflection on ps_1_1 hardware is a challenge, but Matthew Halpin shows a new and very efficient way to achieve this in "Specular Bump Mapping on Pre-ps_1_4 Hardware." With the advent of pixel shader 3_0, graphics hardware has become capable of rendering hardware-accelerated voxels. Aaron Burton's article, "Rendering Voxel Objects with PS_3_0," shows how to implement real voxels on third-generation graphics hardware. Current DirectX 9 hardware is not capable of alpha-blending between floating-point render targets, but Francesco Carucci shows a way to simulate alpha-blending on this hardware in his article, "Simulating Blending Operations on Floating-point Render Targets."

Eli Z. Gottlieb's article, "Rendering Volumes in a Vertex & Pixel Program by Ray Tracing," shows how to render volumes by using ray tracing and a volume texture on ps_2_x hardware. Using bump maps to create bump mapping effects increases the amount of data necessary in memory. Jakub Klarowicz's article, "Normal Map Compression," shows how to compress bump maps with a common DXT format. Sylvain Lefebvre discusses how to implement pattern-based procedural textures in "Drops of Water and Texture Sprites." These kinds of textures are not procedural in the sense of classic marble or wood textures, but they combine explicit textures (patterns) in order to create a larger texture with the desired appearance. Kurt Pelzer explains how to implement a realistic water simulation that is extensively usable in his article "Advanced Water Effects." If you ever wondered how this was done in the CodeCreatures engine, don't look any further.

Peter-Pike Sloan uses irradiance environment maps to render diffuse objects in arbitrary lighting environments in "Efficient Evaluation of Irradiance Environment Maps." He presents a method that uses spherical harmonics to efficiently represent an irradiance environment map, which is more efficient to compute and uses fewer resources than diffuse cube maps. In a second article, "Practical Precomputed Radiance Transfer," Peter-Pike Sloan shows how to use precomputed radiance transfer to illuminate rigid objects in low-frequency lighting environments with global effects like soft shadows and inter-reflections. These results are achieved by running a lengthy preprocess that computes how light is transferred from the source environment to exit radiance at a point. Marco Spoerl and Kurt Pelzer discuss how to render advanced sky domes in "Advanced Sky Dome Rendering." This article describes the implementation of a basic vertex color sky dome, which computes the correct position of both the sun and the moon depending on time of day, changes its color depending on the position of the sun, renders a projection of the sun at its correct position, and renders a projection of the moon at its correct position including the moon's current phase.

Nicolas Thibieroz shows how to implement deferred shading in "Deferred Shading with Multiple Render Targets." Contrary to traditional rendering algorithms, deferred shading submits the scene geometry only once and stores per-pixel attributes into local video memory to be used in the subsequent rendering passes. Carsten Wenzel explains how he created the effects in his Meshuggah demo in "Meshuggah's Effects Explained." It is impressive what he has done on DirectX 8.1-capable hardware and on the Xbox. John Isidoro, Chris Oat, and Natalya Tatarchuk explain how they created a two-tone, suspended microflake car paint shader in "Layered Car Paint Shader." Motion blur effects as shown in the Animusic demo Pipe Dream are described in "Motion Blur Using Geometry and Shading Distortion" by Natalya Tatarchuk, Chris Brennan, Alex Vlachos, and John Isidoro. "Simulation of Iridescence and Translucency on Thin Surfaces" by Natalya Tatarchuk and Chris Brennan focuses on simulating the visual effect of translucency and iridescence of thin surfaces such as butterfly wings.

Arkadiusz Waliszewski describes in "Floating-point Cube Maps" how to use floating-point cube maps to get a much more visually pleasing cube mapping effect. Thomas Rued compares three different kinds of stereoscopic rendering and provides shader implementations for each of them in his article "Stereoscopic Rendering in Hardware Using Shaders." The article "Hatching, Stroke Styles, and Pointillism" by Kevin Buchin and Maike Walther shows how to implement hatching by combining strokes into a texture. These compositions of strokes can convey the surface form through stroke orientation, the surface material through stroke arrangement and style, and the effect of light on the surface through stroke density. Guillaume Werle explains a technique that achieves a realistic-looking layered fog in "Layered Fog." It computes the height on a per-vertex basis and uses the texture coordinate interpolator to get per-pixel precision. Ádám Moravánszky's article, "Dense Matrix Algebra on the GPU," shows how to use shaders to solve two common problems in scientific computing: solving systems of linear equations and linear complementarity problems. Both of these problems come up in dynamics simulation, which is a field drawing increasing interest from the game developer community.

Section III — Software Shaders and Shader Programming Tips

Dean Macri's article, "Software Vertex Shader Processing," explores optimization guidelines for writing shaders that will use the software vertex processing pipeline. Additionally, the techniques described in this article should also apply to vertex shaders written for graphics hardware. Emulating pixel shaders efficiently on the CPU might be the first step in writing a software 3D engine with shader support that runs only on the CPU. In "x86 Shaders-ps_2_0 Shaders in Software," Nicolas Capens shows how to create a fast-performing software emulation of ps_2_0 shaders by using a run-time assembler. Oliver Weichhold has created a software implementation of the Direct3D pipeline. His article, "SoftD3D: A Software-only Implementation of Microsoft's Direct3D API," describes how he did it. Jeffrey Kiel shows a very handy trick for using named constants in shader development in "Named Constants in Shader Development."

Section IV — Image Space

Jason L. Mitchell, Marwan Y. Ansari, and Evan Hart describe in their article "Advanced Image Processing with DirectX 9 Pixel Shaders" how to perform color space conversion using an edge detection filter called the Canny filter, separable Gaussian and median filters, and a real-time implementation of the Fast Fourier Transform with ps_2_0 shaders. The article "Night Vision: Frame Buffer Post-processing with ps.1.1 Hardware" describes how to implement an efficient night view on ps_1_1 hardware. Guillaume Werle uses a three-step approach to achieve this, first rendering the scene into a texture, converting this texture to grayscale, and using the luminance value of each pixel as the index into a gradient texture. Shawn Hargreaves shows the non-photorealistic post-processing filters he used in the game MotoGP 2 for ps_1_1 hardware and the Xbox in "Non-Photorealistic Post-processing Filters in MotoGP 2."

Marwan Y. Ansari discusses in his article "Image Effects with DirectX 9 Pixel Shaders" how to achieve transition, distortion, and posterization image effects in a video shader. Roger Descheneaux and Maurice Ribble show how to achieve a mosaic-like effect via post-processing in "Using Pixel Shaders to Implement a Mosaic Effect Using Character Glyphs." The article "Mandelbrot Set Rendering" by Emil Persson shows how to implement a Mandelbrot set in a ps_2_0 pixel shader. Guennadi Riguer, Natalya Tatarchuk, and John Isidoro present two variations of a two-pass approach for depth of field simulation in their article "Real-Time Depth of Field Simulation." In both variations, the scene is rendered in the first pass with some additional information such as depth, and in the second pass some filters are run to blur the result from the first pass.

Section V — Shadows

In the article "Soft Shadows" by Flavien Brebion, a soft shadows algorithm that works as an extension of the shadow volumes algorithm is explained. This is achieved by using two volumes, the first from the standard point light (inner volume) and the second from a jittered point light position (outer volume). This second volume defines the outer contour of the penumbra. The inner and outer volumes are next rendered to the shadow map, each in one color component channel, and then blurred. Sim Dietrich shows in "Robust Object ID Shadows" how to prevent the depth aliasing problem of shadow maps by using object IDs instead of storing depth in the light view texture. In his article "Reverse Extruded Shadow Volumes," Renaldas Zioma suggests a solution for dealing with shadowing artifacts using stenciled shadow volumes that allow proper self-shadowing while using occluder geometry.

Section VI — 3D Engine and Tools Design

Tom Forsyth shows in "Shader Abstraction" how to abstract shaders by specifying a description of an ideal shader, but then in code the shader is allowed to degrade gracefully in quality according to both platform and distance from the camera. In an additional article, Tom Forsyth discusses how to generalize many of the common effects in current games into a unified framework, where multiple effects can be added, tried out, and combined at run time without replicating shared code, in order to keep speed and memory use optimal when only a few of the effects are visible. The article "Shaders under Control (Codecreatures Engine)" by Oliver Hoeller describes the base architecture used in the Codecreatures engine. Scott Sherman, Dan Amerson, Shaun Kime, and Tim Preston describe how they integrated shaders into the Gamebryo Engine. A complete high-level programming language vertex shader compiler with source is given in David Pangerl's article "Vertex Shader Compiler." The final article in this book, "Shader Disassembler," by Jean-Sebastian Luce covers the creation of a shader disassembler that can disassemble all available shader versions in DirectX 9.

Section I

Geometry Manipulation Tricks

1

Using Vertex Shaders for Geometry Compression

Dean Calver

This article is a follow-up to an article I wrote in *Direct3D ShaderX: Vertex and Pixel Shader Tips and Tricks*. DirectX 9 has introduced new data types and added new capabilities to the vertex stream model. This, combined with more complex and faster vertex shaders, allows us to explore more advanced forms of vertex and geometry compression.

What's New in DirectX 9?

Vertex Shaders

In most cases I still use vertex shader version 1.1, as this is executed in hardware on the greatest number of machines. The new cards do benefit in the extra constant space available. This improves the amount of batching that can occur. Static branching also makes it easier to use different compression methods on different models. Vertex shader version 3.0 potentially offers a number of new capabilities, the most prominent being vertex texturing. This will offer a new range of compression methods but isn't explored here due to current lack of hardware support.

New Vertex Stream Declaration Format

The vertex stream declaration system from DirectX 8 was completely overhauled to make it both easier to use and add new capabilities. From a compression point of view, the most interesting items are the new vertex data types and the extra control over where each element comes from in the stream (stream offset).

Limitations

When under DirectX 8 drivers (you can check via the D3DDEVCAPS2_STREAM-OFFSET cap bit), most new capabilities of the DirectX 9 vertex stream declarations can't be used. Under DirectX 7 drivers, you must stick to FVF-style declarations. Also, if a declaration's stream offsets produce overlapping vertex elements, then even on DirectX 9 drivers, the D3DDEVCAPS2_VERTEXELE-MENTSCANSHARESTREAMOFFSET cap bit must be set. Another limitation is that stream offsets must align on DWORD boundaries (4 bytes).

The new vertex data types now have cap bits for each new type that DirectX 9 introduced (and UBYTE4 from DirectX 8); you must check these before using them. If the cap bit for the data type that you want is set, use it; otherwise, you will have to emulate the functionality via vertex shader code or change the vertex data to a format that is available on this hardware.

NOTE The DirextX 9 documentation states the following about each new vertex data type: "This type is valid for vertex shader version 2.0 or higher." This appears to be a documentation bug; if the cap bit is set, you can use it with any vertex shader version. There is already hardware that supports this, even on hardware that doesn't support vertex shader version 2.0. (ATI supports some of the new data types on all its vertex shader-capable hardware.)

New Vertex Data Types

Most of these new types are signed, unsigned, and normalized versions of the existing DirectX 8 data types, but a few add new capabilities. The following table lists data types sorted by bits per channel.

Data Type	Number of Channels	Bits Per Type	Bits Per Channel	Range in Vertex Shader Register	Cap Bit?	Notes
D3DCOLOR	4	32	8	[0,1]	N	a
UBYTE4	4	32	8	[0,255]	Y	
UBYTE4N	4	32	8	[0,1]	Y	
UDEC3	3	32	10	[0,1024]	Y	b
DEC3N	3	32	10	[−1,1]	Y	b
SHORT2	2	32	16	[−32768,32767]	N	
SHORT4	4	64	16	[−32768,32767]	N	
USHORT2N	2	32	16	[0,1]	Y	
USHORT4N	4	64	16	[0,1]	Y	
SHORT2N	2	32	16	[−1,1]	Y	
SHORT4N	4	64	16	[−1,1]	Y	
FLOAT16_2	2	32	16	[−6.55e4,6.55e4]	Y	c
FLOAT16_4	4	64	16	[−6.55e4,6.55e4]	Y	c
FLOAT1	1	32	32	[−3.48e38, 3.48e38]	N	d
FLOAT2	2	64	32	[−3.48e38, 3.48e38]	N	d
FLOAT3	3	96	32	[−3.48e38, 3.48e38]	N	d
FLOAT4	4	128	32	[−3.48e38, 3.48e38]	N	d

a)   D3DCOLOR also reorders elements as it enters the vertex shader. ARGB becomes RGBA.

b)   The two top bits are unused and are lost without explicit vertex stream programming.

c)   float16 is an OpenEXR standard, a new standard created by nVidia and PIXAR. Use D3DXFLOAT16 to manipulate (or the library in the OpenEXR SDK).

d)   float is an IEEE754 standard, corresponding to C type float.

This is quite a rich set of data types with all data type multiples of 32 bits (this is the reason for losing the two bits on the DEC3 formats). The cap bits to check are under D3DCAPS9.DeclType, the specific bit is D3DTCAPS_datatype, and the type to use is D3DDECLTYPE_datatype (where the data type is from the list above).

Reclaiming Two Bits

When DEC3N or UDEC3 formats are used, we seem to have lost two bits, but even two bits can be used quite effectively, so we want them back (e.g., if you have per-vertex branching, you could store the number of bones here). By causing two different vertex elements to point to the same memory in the vertex buffer, we can get access to our two bits (this requires the overlapped stream offset cap bit to be set).

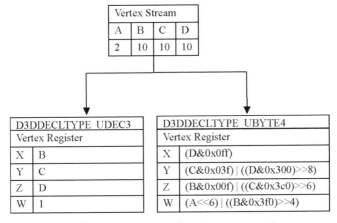

Figure 1: Data from vertex stream element to vertex register

The vertex stream declaration for a single stream if we stored normals (a common use) as UDEC3 and wanted to reclaim our two bits is below. The vertex shader can now bind NORMAL0 to access the data as UDEC3 and NORMAL1 as UBYTE4.

D3DVERTEXELEMENT9 decl[] =

```
{
    // first element, a 'normal' UDEC3 declaration
    {   0,                          // stream number
        0,                          // stream offset in bytes
        D3DDECLTYPE_UDEC3,          // vertex type for this access
        D3DDECLMETHOD_DEFAULT,      // not used so leave at default
        D3DDECLUSAGE_NORMAL,        // usage (used to bind in the vertex shader)
        0                           // usage number (you can have n normals)
    },
    // second element, a UBYTE4 that accesses the same memory as the normal above
    {   0,                          // stream number, same as first element
        0,                          // stream offset, same as first element
        D3DDECLTYPE_UBYTE4,         // vertex type for this access
        D3DDECLMETHOD_DEFAULT,      // not used so leave at default
```

```
            D3DDECLUSAGE_NORMAL,    // usage (used to bind in the vertex shader)
            1                       // usage no (so you can have n normals)
        },
        D3DDECL_END()
};
```

To get our two bits in a usable form, we need to divide by $2\char`^6$ (64) and then floor the result. This has the effect of shifting the extraneous data to the right of the decimal point and only keeping the integer part, which will be our reclaimed two bits in the range 0 to 3. The floor can be removed if you are going to use the two bits as a constant address register (the mova instruction rounds to zero).

```
struct VS_INPUT
{
    float4    normal    : NORMAL0,
    float4    enc2Bit   : NORMAL1
};

void main( VS_INPUT input )
{
    // access normal as usual
    float3    normal = input.normal;
    // decode our 2 bits (0-3)
    float     two_bits = floor(input.enc2Bit.w / 64.0);
}
```

A Better Compression Transform Data Type

The new DEC3N data types allow us to easily design a format with three channels with 10, 10, and 12 bits precision. This is a useful format for compression transformed positions. (Compression transform is discussed in my "Vertex Decompression in a Shader" article in *Direct3D ShaderX*; briefly, it compresses positions by solving the eigen-system of the covariant matrix of the mesh positions and transforming the positions into this basis before quantization. Decompressing a matrix vector multiple in the vertex shader restores the original position.)

Many natural and man-made objects have a dominant axis (e.g., along the spine of many animals, etc.). By giving that axis the extra two bits, we are able to use a 32-bit format for some objects that would have required switching to a 64-bit format (SHORT4). For simplicity in the vertex shader, we arrange the compressor to always make z the longest axis and then append the extra two bits to it before uncompressing.

```
struct VS_INPUT
{
    float4    position : POSITION0,
    float4    enc2Bit  : POSITION1
};

void main( VS_INPUT input )
{
```

```
// get the 10,10,10 portion of the position
float3 cpos = input.position;
// decode our 2 bits (0-3)
float  two_bits = floor(input.enc2Bit.w / 64.0);
// factor in the extra bits and convert back into the 0-1 range
cpos.z = (cpos.z + two_bits) * 0.25;
// transform by the inverse compression matrix
float4 pos = mul( float4(cpos,1), InvCompressionTransform );
}
```

Displacement Compression

My previous article covered the use of vertex shaders to render displacement maps. This capability can be extended to a very powerful technique that Tom Forsyth has termed "displacement compression." It's a complete family of techniques that includes patch rendering, displacement mapping, and subdivision surfaces that any vertex shader-capable hardware can do and is a powerful form of geometry compression.

Usually tessellation levels are decided by the CPU, as we currently have no programmable tessellation hardware, but there are a few fixed-function hardware tessellation systems that you may be able to use. This is the technique's major limitation — to a limited degree, we can remove triangles (by sending the vertices to be clipped), but we cannot add triangles.

By using the vertex shaders as a function evaluator with the vertex stream bringing in the function parameters, we can render many geometrical surfaces. For the surfaces we use here, this consists of a barycentric surface function with an additional displacement scalar, but other surfaces' parameterizations are possible.

There are two components that are needed for displacement compression.

- **Displacement mapping:** A method of retrieving a scalar displacement along the surface normal. Without it, your displacement compression becomes standard surface patch evaluation.

- **Surface basis:** Every displacement compression shader requires a basis system that defines the base surface before displacement. The simplest is just planar, although it could be as complex as a subdivision surface.

Displacement Mapping

There are at least four ways to get the displacement value into the vertex shader. The more advanced methods require explicit hardware support and are not covered here. Refer to presentations from Mike Doggett and Tom Forsyth for details [2]. Also, Tom Forsyth's article covers actual generation of displacement data in detail [1].

The technique presented here works on any vertex shader hardware by treating the displacement map as a 1D vertex stream. It's a generalization of the technique that I presented in *Direct3D ShaderX*, which had an implied planar basis that with a few minor modification works for any surface basis.

The displacement value is stored explicitly in a vertex stream. If kept in a separate stream, it can be accessed via the CPU as a standard displacement map, or you can choose to pack it with other vertex elements. Packed will usually save space, but a separate stream can be more convenient, especially for dynamically updated displacement maps.

As there is only one one channel vertex data type (FLOAT1), you will probable store your displacement map in another data type that will have spare channels. For 8-bit displacement map data, UBYTE4 is the obvious choice. This may appear to waste a lot of space, but in practice, enough other data has to be provided so that if space is a concern, it can be reclaimed to store other surface parameters.

NOTE Unfortunately, DirectX 9 has no GPU-powered way of transferring or sharing data between render targets and vertex streams. This is purely an API issue, but it makes GPU-based dynamic displacement maps difficult (if not impossible) under DirectX 9. Mike Doggett's OpenGL uber-buffer render-to-vertex-array demo shows what GPU modification of vertex data can do.

Pre-Filtering Displacement Maps

One form of filtering that can be used with vertex stream displacement is to store the displacement value that would occur at the lower tessellation levels with the usual displacement value. This is similar to mipmapping in that the filter is run before the actual rendering. As with mipmapping, you can use either point sampling (just select the appropriate displacement value) or linear filtering (select two displacement values and linearly interpolate). The main difference with mipmapping is that there is no easy way to access the texture derivatives in vertex shaders, so you will probably have a global blend factor or base it on distance from the camera.

If you store displacement values in UBYTE4, you could pack three lower levels in the other three channels, which gives you an effective linear mip filter (but with point min/mag filter).

Surface Basis

The key to displacement compression is reversing the standard relationship between the vertex stream and the constant registers. A vertex shader for indexed triangles can only access the data of one vertex at a time, but each vertex shader can access more than one vertex constant. Thus, if you put mesh data into constant memory, each vertex shader execution has access to multiple vertices, etc. We upload vertices or control points to constant memory and feed normalized barycentric coordinates (aka areal coordinates) and surface indices in via the vertex stream. (For some surface bases we may need other parameters — i.e., subdivision surfaces require surrounding surface indices as well.)

The normalized barycentric coordinates and surface indices uniquely define where in the mesh (stored in constant memory) the vertex shader is currently evaluating the surface basis function.

Points Inside a Triangle

A unique point inside a triangle can be computed via the three vertices defining the triangle and the barycentric coordinates of this interior point. The three vertices for each triangle are placed into constant memory, and we store two of the barycentric coordinates in the vertex stream (k can be computed from i and j). A vertex stream triangle index is used to select which set of three vertices in constant memory makes up the triangle with which we are currently working.

Here we hit a small issue: Some vertices belong to more than one triangle. We have to duplicate each vertex attached to more than one triangle and give each one a separate index.

```
//HLSL code for calculating interior points of a number of triangles.
float3 VertexPos[3 * NUM_BASE_TRIANGLE];

void main(float3 vertexStream : POSITION0)
{
    float i =  vertexStream.x;
    float j =  vertexStream.y
    float k = 1.0 − i − j;
    float baseIndex =  vertexStream.z * 256; // un-normalize index
    float3 pos =       i*VertexPos[ (baseIndex*3) + 0 ] +
                       j*VertexPos[ (baseIndex*3) + 1 ] +
                       k*VertexPos[(baseIndex*3) + 2 ];
}
```

N-Patches

N-Patches (Curved PN Patches [3]) are a type of bicubic patch where the control points are determined from a triangle's vertex positions and normals. N-Patches come in two variations, both with cubic interpolated position, but they differ in whether the normal is interpolated linearly or quadratically. The algorithm calculates the control points for the patch and then evaluates at each point on the base triangle.

Effectively, there are two frequencies at which this vertex shader needs executing; the control points need calculating only once per patch, whereas the evaluation needs running at every vertex. Some consoles can execute this pattern on the GPU, but on current PC architectures you can either generate the control points on the CPU and upload them to vertex constant memory or recalculate the control points at every vertex. The first uses CPU power per patch, and each patch uses more constant memory (for linear normal N-Patches, 39 floats versus 18 for vertices), whereas recalculating at every vertex uses a lot of vertex shader power but allows better batching and has lower CPU overhead.

```
float3 VertexPos[3 * NUM_BASE_TRIANGLE];
float3 VertexNormals[3 * NUM_BASE_TRIANGLE];

// bicubic control points
float3 b300,b030,b003, b210,b120,b021, b201,b102,b012, b111;
```

Using Vertex Shaders for Geometry Compression

```
float3 n200,n020,n002;
void generateControlPointsWithLinearNormals(float baseIndex);
{
    float3 v0 =  VertexPos[ (baseIndex*3) + 0 ];
    float3 v1 =  VertexPos[ (baseIndex*3) + 1 ];
    float3 v2 =  VertexPos[ (baseIndex*3) + 2 ];
    float3 n0 =  VertexNormal [ (baseIndex*3) + 0 ];
    float3 n1 =  VertexNormal [ (baseIndex*3) + 1 ];
    float3 n2 =  VertexNormal[ (baseIndex*3) + 2 ];
    // For the book I'll do one bicubic patch control point here, for the rest
    // see example code on CD/Web or reference ATI's Curved PN Patch paper [3]
    float3 edge = v1 - v0;
    // E - (E.N)N
    float3 tangent1 = edge;
    float tmpf = dot( tangent1, n0 );
    tangent1 -= n0 * tmpf;
    b210 = v0 + (tangent1 * rcp3);
}


void evaluateNPatchLinearNormal(float i, float j, out float3 pos, out float3 norm)
{
    float k = 1 - i - j;
    float k2 = k * k;
    float k3 = k2 * k;
    float i2 = i * i;
    float i3 = i2 * i;
    float j2 = j * j;
    float j3 = j2 * j;

    // bicubic position
    pos = (b300*k3) + (b030*u3) + (b003*v3) +
          (b210*3*k2*i) + (b120*3*k*i2) + (b201*3*k2*j) +
          (b021*3*i2*j) + (b102*3*k*j2) + (b012*3*i2*j) +
          (b111*6*k*i*j);

    // linear normal
    norm = (w * n200) + (i * n020) + (j * n002);
}


void main(float3 vertexStream : POSITION0)
{
    float i =  vertexStream.x;
    float j =  vertexStream.y
    float baseIndex =  vertexStream.z * 256;
    float3 pos, norm;

    generateControlPointsWithLinearNormals(baseIndex);
    evaluateNPatchLinearNormal(i, j, pos, norm);
}
```

Making It Fast Using a Linear Basis

Evaluating N-Patches via a vertex shader can be quite expensive. If you are also using a displacement map, the inherent surface curve usually isn't very important anyway. Usually when using displacement compression, we would like a basis that has a smooth surface normal but relies on the displacement map to handle the position. A linear basis has all these properties: The surface normal is smooth between patches (assuming the vertex normals are smooth), but the position before the displacement is planar. The surface normal is generated from the linear interpolation of the vertex normals (in a similar manner to how Phong shading interpolates the lighting normal).

A linear basis only requires the mesh vertex data, and as these can be shared between patches, it's usually better to store vertex indices rather than a triangle index at every interior point. This usually increases the number of vertices that can be stored in constant memory, which increases performance as more patches can be evaluated per call at the expense of slightly larger per-vertex data.

```
//HLSL for a displaced linear basis surface with indexed vertices
float MAX_DISPLACEMENT_HEIGHT = 100;    // this is just an example value
float3 VertexPos[NUM_BASE_VERTICES];
float3 VertexNormal[NUM_BASE_VERTICES];
float2 VertexUV[NUM_BASE_VERTICES];

struct VS_IN
{
    float2 barycentric;
    float3 indices;
    float displacement;
};

void main( VS_IN input )
{
    float i = input.barycentric.x;
    float j = input.barycentric.y
    float k = 1.0 - i - j;
    float i0 = input.indices.x * 256;
    float i1 = input.indices.y * 256;
    float i2 = input.indices.z * 256;

    float3 pos = i*VertexPos[i0] + j*VertexPos[i1] + k*VertexPos[i2];
    float3 normal = i* VertexNormal[i0] + j* VertexNormal[i1] + k* VertexNormal[i2];
    float2 uv = i* VertexUV[i0] + j* VertexUV[i1] + k* VertexUV[i2];

    normal = normalized( normal );
    pos = pos + input.displacement * normal * MAX_DISPLACEMENT_HEIGHT;
}
```

Barycentric coordinates are in the range [0,1] and are the same for each triangle at a particular subdivision. Indices only require a maximum of 256 values (there are currently only 256 constants). So a byte per index is enough. For the triangle indexed version, this is 1 byte + 1 byte displacement and a shared 8 bytes (two floats), and for the vertex indexed version it is 3 bytes + 1 byte displacement and a shared 8 bytes (two floats). A good approach is to place the barycentric coodinates in one stream and the indices and displacement in another. The barycentric stream can be reused by all meshes at the same subdivision level.

Lighting Normal

As getting a perturbed lighting normal proves to be difficult, the best option is not to bother at run time. If the displacement map is fixed, you can just create a normal map off-line that encodes the lighting normal. Even if you are vertex lighting, you can feed the normal map values into the vertex shader in the same manner as the displacement values.

If you really have to derive a sensible lighting normal in the vertex shader, it is possible with some preprocessing. If we could access the local surface points around us (perturb i and j by a small amount) and look up the displacement maps at those points, we could calculate the local post-displaced tangent plane. The only way of doing this in a vertex stream is by using a process similar to prefiltering, by storing at every interior point the displacement values around us. By storing all surrounding displacement values at every interior point, we could run the surface evaluator (including the displacement) on each perturbed point and calculate the lighting normal. In practice, only storing a couple of displaced values (usually left and down) is enough to get a reasonable lighting normal.

Conclusion

Vertex shaders can be used as effective geometry decompressors; with tight packing of vertex data and techniques like displacement compression, we can save considerable memory and, more importantly, bandwidth. The cost of using extra vertex shader instructions is usually not a problem, as in most cases this isn't a bottleneck; by using this "spare" vertex throughput to save bandwidth, it may make things run faster.

Displacement compression requires changes to the tools (these are described elsewhere [2]) but are an important future technique that you should be thinking about implementing in the near and long term.

References

[1] Forsyth, Tom, "Displacement Mapping," *Shader X²: Shader Programming Tips & Tricks with DirectX 9*, Wolfgang Engel, ed., Wordware Publishing, Inc., 2004, pp. 73-86.

[2] Doggett, Mike and Tom Forsyth, "Displacement Mapping," GDC 2003.

[3] Vlachos, A., J. Peters, C. Boyd, and J. Mitchell, "Curved PN Triangles," http://www.ati.com/developer/CurvedPNTriangles.pdf.

Using Lookup Tables in Vertex Shaders

Carsten Wenzel

Crytek

When writing vertex shader code, you almost always want to squeeze out a few instructions. Maybe you have to do it in order to stay within the instruction limit, which can easily be reached when doing complex animation and lighting calculations. Or maybe you simply want to speed up your code to gain some extra frames per second. Both goals can be achieved by encoding functions and terms in your vertex shader that consume a lot of instructions (and thus time) to evaluate. Another potential scenario would be the use of empirical data for certain calculations. This is where lookup tables can come in handy.

A table lookup can be implemented quite easily using the address register a_0 to index an array of constant registers $c_{tableBase} \cdots c_{tableBase + tableSize - 1}$ containing the actual table data. Generally, you want to keep the table as small as possible. Therefore, it is often necessary to interpolate between consecutive table values. Here's an example. Say your lookup table stores values of a continuous function $f(x)$ for all integers x in the range [0, 10]. Now it happens that you need to look up the value for $f(3.25)$. The exact value isn't stored in the lookup table. To get an estimated result, we could use the fractional part of the index value as the blend factor for a linear interpolation, i.e.:

$$f(3.25) = f[3] + 0.25 \cdot (f[4] - f[3])$$

Do not forget about the Nyquist theorem[1] when representing continuous functions via lookup tables, or else you'll face aliasing. That is, make sure the table is not too small — which implies that encoding terms and functions by means of lookup tables is not feasible if the range you're interested in exhibits high frequencies. Also note that the table size directly affects the precision of the interpolated result.

To demonstrate how a table lookup translates into actual shader code, let's start with a description of a sample application. Imagine you'd like to write a particle effect that simulates stars in a galaxy. They are placed in clusters on the x/z plane with some variation in y and spin around the y axis with the galaxy center being the pivot point. Rotation speed is based on the squared distance $(0 = d^2 =$

---

1   The Nyquist theorem describes one of the most important rules of sampling. To fully reproduce a continuous signal one needs to sample it with a frequency at least twice that of the highest frequency contained in the original signal. For example, to reproduce a full 20 kHz audio signal it has to be sampled at least 40,000 times a second.

1.0) to the center. Further assume that the vertex shader version used is 1.1, which means there are no cosine and sine instructions at your disposal, but you still want to do the animation entirely on the GPU. The following matrix M_{rot} describes how much a star should be rotated after *time* seconds:

$$a = \frac{time}{0.1 + 1000 \cdot d^2}$$
$$c = \cos(a)$$
$$s = \sin(a)$$
$$M_{rot} = \begin{pmatrix} c & 0 & -s & 0 \\ 0 & 0 & 0 & 0 \\ s & 0 & c & 0 \\ 0 & 0 & 0 & 1 \end{pmatrix}$$

This shows the rotation matrix that should be built per vertex on the GPU.

Some of you might say that cosine-sine pairs can be calculated at the same time using a Taylor-series expansion — such as the code written by Matthias Wloka, which takes nine instructions and three constant registers to execute. But you'd also need to determine *a* to pass it to the cosine-sine evaluation code. Since we intend to use a lookup table anyway, all these calculations can be baked together there, thus saving instructions in the vertex shader. Here is how to set up the lookup table:

```
const unsigned int TABLE_SIZE(64);
const unsigned int TABLE_BASE(10);

for(unsigned int uiI(0); uiI < TABLE_SIZE; ++uiI)
{
    float d2(uiI / (float) (TABLE_SIZE - 1));
    float alpha(time / (0.1f + 1000.0f * d2));
    float c(cosf(alpha));
    float s(sinf(alpha));

    D3DXVECTOR4 vLookup(c, s, 0.0f, 0.0f);
    pD3DDev->SetVertexShaderConstant(TABLE_BASE + uiI, &vLookup, 1);
}

float fIndexScale((float) (TABLE_SIZE - 1));
float fIndexOffset(0.0f);
D3DXVECTOR4 vIndex(fIndexScale, fIndexOffset, 0.0f, 0.0f);

const unsigned int TABLE_INDEX(9);
pD3DDev->SetVertexShaderConstant(TABLE_INDEX, &vIndex, 1);
```

This way, to look up *c* and *s*, we only need to find d^2, which is as simple as dotting the position of a star with itself — the center of the galaxy is at (0, 0, 0). The previous pseudocode also sets all constants required to properly index the lookup table, as we see very soon.

What remains to do is write the vertex shader to animate each particle. The code will be split into several pieces showing all necessary steps to get the stars spinning on the GPU. The following part computes the table index.

```
#define srcPos          v0          // (x, y, z, 1)

#define temp0           r0
#define temp1           r1
#define temp2           r2
#define worldPos        r3

#define TABLE_INDEX      9
#define TABLE_BASE      10

vs.1.1

#ifdef DX9
dcl_position0 srcPos
#endif

// calculate d^2 and table index
dp3    temp0, srcPos, srcPos
mad    temp1, temp0, c[TABLE_INDEX].x, c[TABLE_INDEX].y

// get fraction of table index
expp temp0.y, temp1.y

// set table index for relative addressing of lookup table
#ifdef DX9
add  a0.x, temp1.y, -temp0.y
#else  // DX8
mov  a0.x, temp1.y
#endif
```

The first section of the vertex shader determines the table index for the lookup table. It calculates d^2 and applies the index scale and offset constant. Why mad can be used to evaluate the table index in a single instruction and how to set up the index scale and offset constant for lookup tables covering arbitrary intervals is shown in the appendix to this article.

When copying the table index to a_0, care must be taken. According to the DirectX 8.1 specs, moving a value into the address register automatically computes the floor of that value — exactly the behavior we are after. Quite the contrary if you use DirectX 9. Here you have to do the floor calculation yourself because a value moved into the address register gets rounded to the nearest integer. This would obviously break the interpolation code due to a possibly incorrect index in a_0.

The following part of the shader calculates the linearly interpolated table lookup value. It fetches the values for $a_0.x$ and $a_0.x + 1$ from the lookup table. Then it takes the already-computed fraction of the table index to blend between them.

```
// fetch two consecutive values from lookup table
mov   temp1, c[a0.x + TABLE_BASE]
mov   temp2, c[a0.x + TABLE_BASE + 1]

// lerp them using fraction of index
add   temp2, temp2, -temp1
mad   temp2, temp2, temp0.y, temp1
```

The third section starts off with a trick. Knowing that $\cos(x)^2 + \sin(x)^2 = 1$, we can renormalize the linearly interpolated table lookup values to feed the rotation matrix with proper ones, which is important for rotations. Now we can build the matrix and transform each particle into world space.

```
// renormalize cos/sin
dp3   temp1.w, temp2, temp2
rsq   temp1.w, temp1.w
mul   temp2, temp2, temp1.w

// build y rotation matrix
mov   temp0, temp2.xzyw         // 1st row: cos 0.0 -sin 0.0
mov   temp0.z, -temp0.z
mov   temp1, temp2.yzxw         // 3rd row: sin 0.0  cos 0.0

// rotate particle
mov   worldPos, srcPos
dp3   worldPos.x, srcPos, temp0
dp3   worldPos.z, srcPos, temp1
```

Once the particle is in world space, you can apply the view-projection matrix as usual, calculate the point size for the particle, set its color, etc. The following screen shot shows the result of our efforts.

Figure 1: Screen shot of vertex shader in action

Appendix

Say you'd like to create a lookup table containing *tableSize* entries for a function $f(x)$ in range $[x_{min}, x_{max}]$. The values stored in an array of constant registers $c_{tableBase}$ ... $c_{tableBase + tableSize - 1}$ look like this:

$$0 \leq i < tableSize$$

$$c_{tableBase+i} = f\left(x_{min} + i \cdot \frac{x_{max} - x_{min}}{tableSize - 1} \right)$$

To do a lookup you now need to map a value x from $[x_{min}, x_{max}]$ to $[tableBase, tableBase + tableSize - 1]$:

$$index = \frac{x - x_{min}}{x_{max} - x_{min}} \cdot (tableSize - 1) + tableBase$$

This can be decoupled to:

$$index = \frac{x}{x_{max} - x_{min}} \cdot (tableSize - 1) - \frac{x_{min}}{x_{max} - x_{min}} \cdot (tableSize - 1) + tableBase$$

In the equation above, everything but x is invariant. Taking a closer look reveals that it can be expressed in terms of a mad:

$$index = indexScale \cdot x + indexOffset$$

$$indexScale = \frac{tableSize - 1}{x_{max} - x_{min}}$$

$$indexOffset = -\frac{x_{min}}{x_{max} - x_{min}} \cdot (tableSize - 1) + tableBase$$

Since *tableBase* can be used as a fixed relative offset when fetching values from the lookup table (as can be seen in the vertex shader sample code above), *indexOffset* can be rewritten as:

$$indexOffset = -\frac{x_{min}}{x_{max} - x_{min}} \cdot (tableSize - 1)$$

Terrain Geomorphing in the Vertex Shader

Daniel Wagner

daniel@ims.tuwien.ac.at

Introduction

Terrain rendering has heretofore been computed by a CPU and rendered by a combination of CPU and GPU. It is possible to implement a fast terrain renderer that works optimally with current 3D hardware. This is done by using geo-mip-mapping, which splits the terrain into a set of smaller meshes called patches. Each patch is triangulated view-dependently into one single triangle strip. Special care is taken to avoid gaps and t-vertices between neighboring patches. An arbitrary number of textures, which are combined using multiple alpha-blended rendering passes, can be applied to the terrain. Since the terrain's triangulation changes over time, vertex normals cannot be used for lighting. Instead, a precalculated lightmap is used. In order to reduce popping when a patch switches between two tessellation levels, geomorphing is implemented. As we point out later, this splitting of the terrain into small patches allows some very helpful optimizations.

Why Geomorphing?

Terrain rendering has been an active research area for quite a long time. Although some impressive algorithms have been developed, the game development community has rarely used these methods because of the high computational demands. Recently, another reason for not using the classic terrain rendering approaches such as ROAM [Duc97] or VDPM [Hop98] emerged: Modern GPUs just don't like CPU-generated dynamic vertex data. The game developers' solution for this problem was to build very low-resolution maps and fine-tuned terrain layout for visibility optimization. In contrast to indoor levels, terrain visibility is more difficult to tune, and there are cases where the level designer just wants to show distant views.

The solution to these problems is to introduce some kind of terrain LOD (level of detail). The problem with simple LOD methods is that at the moment that vertices are added or removed, the mesh is changed; this leads to very noticeable popping effects. The only clean way out of this is to introduce geomorphing, which inserts new vertices along an existing edge and later moves that vertex to its final position. As a consequence, the terrain mesh is no longer static but changes ("morphs") every frame. It is obvious that this morphing has to be done in hardware in order to achieve high performance.

Previous Work

A lot of work has already been done on rendering terrain meshes. Classic algorithms such as ROAM and VDPM attempt to generate triangulations that optimally adapt to terrain given as a heightmap. This definition of "optimally" was defined to be as few triangles as possible for a given quality criteria. While this was a desirable aim some years ago, things have changed.

Today, the absolute number of triangles is not as important. As of 2003, games that render up to 200,000 triangles per frame have been released, including games such as Unreal 2. An attractive terrain triangulation takes some 10,000 triangles. This means that it is no longer important if we need 10,000 or 20,000 triangles for the terrain mesh, as long as it is done fast enough. Today "fast" also implies using as little CPU processing power as possible, since in real-life applications the CPU usually has more things to do than just drawing terrain (e.g., AI, physics, voice-over, IP compression, etc.). The other important thing today is to create the mesh in such a way that the graphics hardware can process it quickly, which usually means the creation of long triangle strips. Both requirements are mostly unfulfilled by the classic terrain meshing algorithms.

The work in this article is based on the idea of geo-mipmapping described by de Boer in [Boe00]. Another piece of work that uses the idea of splitting the terrain into a fixed set of small tiles is [Sno01], although the author does not write about popping effects or how to efficiently apply materials to the mesh.

Building the Mesh

The terrain mesh is created from an 8-bit heightmap that has to be sized 2^n+1 * 2^n+1 (e.g., 17*17, 33*33, 65*65, etc.) in order to create $n^2 * n^2$ quads. The heightmap (see Figure 1a) can be created from real data (e.g., DEM) [Usg86] or by any program that can export into raw 8-bit heightmap data (e.g., Corel Bryce [Cor01]). The number of vertices of a patch changes during rendering (see view-dependent tessellation), which forbids using vertex normals for lighting. Therefore, a lightmap (see Figure 1b) is used instead.

In order to create the lightmap, the normals for each point in the heightmap have to be calculated first. This can be done by creating two 3D vectors, each pointing from the current height value to the neighboring height positions. Calculating the cross product of

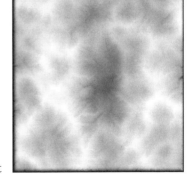

Figure 1a: A sample heightmap

these two vectors gives the current normal vector, which can be used to calculate a diffuse lighting value. To get better results, including static shadows, advanced terrain data editing software such as Wilbur [Slay95] or Corel Bryce should be used.

Figure 1b: Corresponding lightmap created with Wilbur

The heightmap is split into 17*17 values-sized parts called patches. The borders of neighboring patches overlap by one value (e.g., value column 16 is shared by patch 0/0 and patch 1/0). Geometry for each patch is created at run time as a single indexed triangle strip. A patch can create geometry in five different tessellation levels, ranging from full geometry (2*16*16 triangles) down to a single flat quad (two triangles; for an illustration see Figure 2). Where needed, degenerate triangles are inserted to connect the sub-strips into one large strip [Eva96].

In order to connect two strips, the last vertex of the first strip and the first vertex of the second strip have to be inserted twice. The result is triangles that connect the two strips in the form of a line and are therefore invisible (unless rendered in wireframe mode). The advantage of connecting small strips to one larger strip is that less API calls are needed to draw the patch. Since index vertices are used and a lot of today's graphics hardware can recognize and automatically remove degenerate triangles, the rendering and bandwidth overhead of the degenerate triangles is very low.

Figure 2: The same patch tessellated in different levels ranging from full geometry (level 0) to a single quad (level 4)

Calculating the Tessellation Level of a Patch

Before a frame is rendered, each patch is checked for its necessary tessellation level. It's easy to see from Figure 2 that the error of each patch increases as the number of vertices is reduced. In a preprocessing step, for each level the position of the vertex with the largest error (the one that has the largest distance to the corresponding correct position, called "maxerror vertex" later on) is determined and saved together with the correct position.

When determining the level at which to render, all saved "maxerror vertices" are projected into the scene and the resulting errors calculated. Finally, the level with the largest error below an application-defined error boundary is chosen. In order to create a specific level's geometry, only the "necessary" vertices are written into the buffers. For example, to create level 0, all vertices are used. Level 1 leaves out every second vertex, reducing the triangle count by a quarter. Level 2 uses only every fourth vertex, and so on.

Connecting Patches

If two neighboring patches with different tessellation levels were simply rendered one next to the other, gaps would occur (imagine drawing any of the patches in Figure 2 next to any other). Another problem is t-vertices, which occur when a vertex is positioned on the edge of another triangle. Because of rounding errors, that vertex will not be exactly on the edge of the neighboring triangle, and small gaps that are only a few pixels in size can become visible. Even worse, when moving the camera, these gaps can emerge and disappear every frame, which leads to a very annoying flickering effect.

To solve both problems, it is obvious that each patch must know its neighbors' tessellation levels. To do so, all tessellation levels are calculated first without creating the resulting geometry and then each patch is informed about its neighbors' levels. After that, each patch updates its geometry as necessary. Geometry updating has to be done only if the inner level or any of the neighbors' levels has changed. To close gaps and prevent t-vertices between patches, a border of "adapting triangles" is created that connects the differently sized triangles (see Figure 3). It is obvious that only one of two neighboring patches has to adapt to the other. As we can see in the section "Geomorphing," it is necessary for the patch with the finer tessellation level (having more geometry) to adapt.

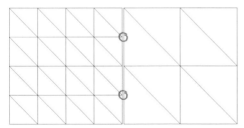

Figure 3a: T-vertices at the border of two patches

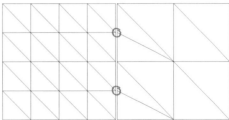

Figure 3b: T-vertices removed

Figure 3a shows a typical case of where t-vertices occur. In Figure 3b those "adapting triangles" at the left side of the right patch are created to avoid t-vertices. Although these triangles look like good candidates for being created by using triangle fans, they are also implemented using strips, since fans cannot be combined into bigger fans, as can be achieved with strips.

Materials

Our terrain has no shading or materials yet. Applying dynamic light by using surface normals would be the easiest way to go but would result in strange effects when patches switch tessellation levels. The reduction of vertices goes hand in hand with the loss of an equal number of normals. When a normal is removed, the resulting diffuse color value is removed too. The user notices such changes very easily — especially if the removed normal produced a color value that was very different from its neighboring color values.

The solution to this problem is easy and well known in today's computer graphics community. Instead of doing real-time lighting, we can use a precalculated lightmap, which is by its nature more resistant to vertex removal than per-vertex lighting. Besides solving our tessellation problem, it provides us with the possibility to precalculate shadows into the lightmap. The disadvantage of using lightmaps is that the light's position is now fixed to the position that was used during the lightmap's generation.

In order to apply a lightmap (see Figure 4), we need to add texture coordinates to the vertices. Since only one lightmap is used for the whole terrain, it simply spans the texture coordinates from (0,0) to (1,1).

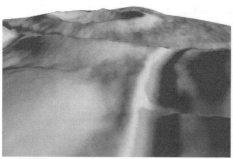

Figure 4a: Lit terrain

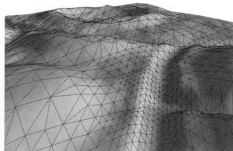

Figure 4b: Same terrain with wireframe overlay

Figure 4c: Terrain with overlaid triangle mesh

Figure 4d: Getting close to the ground, the highly detailed materials become visible.

Now that the terrain's mesh is set up and shaded, it's time to apply some materials. In contrast to the lightmap, we need far more detail for materials such as grass, mud, or stone to look good. (See Figures 4c and 4d.) The texture won't be large enough to cover the complete landscape and look good, regardless of how high the resolution of a texture might be. For example, if we stretch one texture of grass over a complete terrain, the grass wouldn't even be recognizable. One way to overcome this problem is to repeat material textures.

To achieve this, we scale and wrap the texture so that it is repeated over the terrain. By setting a texture matrix we can use the same texture coordinates for the materials as for the lightmap. As we see later, this one set of (never-changing) texture coordinates, together with some texture matrices, is sufficient for an arbitrary number of materials (each one having its own scaling factor and/or rotation) and even for moving faked cloud shadows (see below).

To combine a material with the lightmap, two texture stages are set up using modulation (component-wise multiplication). The result is written into the graphics buffer. In order to use more than one material, each material is combined with a different lightmap containing a different alpha channel. Although this would allow each material to use different color values for the lightmap too, in practice this hardly makes any sense. This results in one render pass per material, which is alpha blended into the frame buffer. As we see later, a lot of fillrate can be saved if not every patch uses every material — which is the usual case (see the section titled "Optimizations"). Figure 5 shows how two materials are combined with lightmaps and then blended using an alpha map. (For better visualization, the materials' textures are not repeated in Figure 5.)

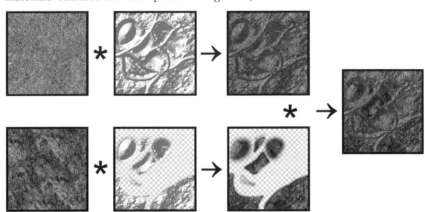

Figure 5: Combining two render passes

In the top row of Figure 5, the base material is combined with the base lightmap. Since there is nothing to be drawn before this pass, no alpha map is needed. In the bottom row, the second pass is combined with another lightmap. This time there is an alpha channel (invisible parts are drawn with checkered boxes). The resulting image is finally alpha-blended to the first pass (the right image in Figure 5).

It is important to note that this method allows each material pass to use a free scaling (repeating) factor for the color values, which results in highly detailed materials, while the lightmap does not need to be repeated since lighting values do not need as much detail. Only two texture stages are used at once, which allows combining an arbitrary number of passes. Most applications will not need more than three or four materials.

After all materials have been rendered, another pass can be drawn in order to simulate cloud shadows. Again, we can repeat the shadows in order to get more detailed-looking shadows. As we are already using a texture matrix to do scaling, we can animate the clouds easily by applying velocity to the matrix's translation values. The effect is that the clouds' shadows move along the surface, which makes the whole scene look far more realistic and "alive."

Geomorphing

One problem with geometry management using level of detail is that at some point vertices will have to be removed or added, which leads to the already-described "popping" effect. In our case of geo-mipmapping, where the number of vertices is doubled or halved at each tessellation level change, this popping becomes very visible. In order to reduce the popping effect, geomorphing is introduced. The aim of geomorphing is to move (morph) vertices softly into their position in the next level before that next level is activated. If this is done perfectly, no popping but only slightly moving vertices are observed by the user. Although this vertex moving looks a little bit strange if a very low detailed terrain mesh is used, it is still less annoying to the user than the popping effect.

It can be shown that only vertices with odd indices inside a patch have to move and that those vertices on even positions can stay fixed because they are not removed when switching to the next coarser tessellation level. Figure 6a shows the tessellation of a patch in tessellation level 2 from a top view. Figure 6b shows the next level of tessellation coarseness (level 3) and that the vertices 1, 2, and 3 do not have to move since they are still there in the next level. There are three possible cases in which a vertex has to move:

■ Case A: The vertex is on an odd x- and even y-position. Vertex has to move into the middle position between the next left (1) and the right (2) vertices.

■ Case B: The vertex is on an odd x- and odd y-position. Vertex has to move into the middle position between the next top-left (1) and the bottom-right (3) vertices.

■ Case C: The vertex is on an even x- and odd y-position. Vertex has to move into the middle position between the next top (2) and the bottom (3) vertices.

Things become much clearer when taking a look at the result of the morphing process: After the morphing is done, the patch is retessallated using the next tessellation level. In Figure 6b it becomes obvious that the previously existing vertex A had to move into the average middle position between the vertices 1 and 2 in order to be removed without popping.

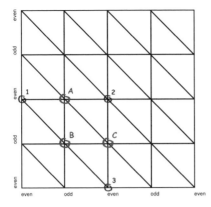

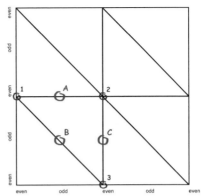

Figure 6a: Fine geometry with morphing vertices

Figure 6b: Corresponding coarser tessellation level. Only odd indexed vertices were removed.

Optimizations

Although the geometry's creation is very fast and we are rendering the mesh using only a small number of long triangle strips (usually about some hundred strips per frame), there are quite a few optimizations that we can do to increase the performance on the side of the processor as well as the graphics card.

As described in the section titled "Materials," we use a multi-pass rendering approach to apply more than one material to the ground. Generally, most materials will be used only in small parts of the landscape and be invisible in most others. The alpha channel of the material's lightmap defines where which material is visible. Of course, it's a waste of GPU bandwidth to render materials on patches that don't use that material at all (where the material's alpha channel is zero in the corresponding patch's part).

It's easy to see that if the part of a material's alpha channel that covers one distinct patch is completely set to zero, then this patch does not need to be rendered with that material. Assuming that the materials' alpha channels won't change during run time, we can calculate for each patch which materials will be visible and which won't in a preprocessing step. Later at run time, only those passes are rendered that really contribute to the final image.

Another important optimization is to reduce the number of patches that need to be rendered at all. This is done in three steps. First, a rectangle that covers the projection of the viewing frustum onto the ground plane is calculated. All patches outside that rectangle will surely not be visible. All remaining patches are culled against the viewing frustum. To do this, we clip the patches' bounding boxes against all six sides of the viewing frustum. All remaining patches are guaranteed to lie at least partially inside the camera's visible area. Nevertheless, not all of these remaining patches will necessarily be visible because some of them will probably be hidden from other patches (e.g., a mountain). To optimize this case, we can finally use a PVS (Potentially Visible Sets) algorithm to further reduce the number of patches that need to be rendered.

PVS [Air91, Tel91] is used to determine, at run time, which patches can be seen from a given position and which are hidden by other objects (in our case, also patches). Depending on the type of landscape and the viewer's position, a lot of patches can be removed this way. In Figure 7 the camera is placed in a valley and looks at a hill.

Figure 7a: Final image

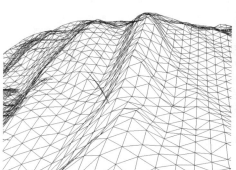

Figure 7c: With PVS

Figure 7b: Without PVS

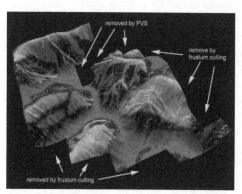

Figure 7d: View from camera's position

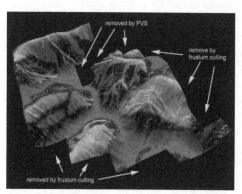

Figure 7e: Same scene as 7d from a different viewpoint with same PVS and culling performed (See Color Plate 1.)

Figure 7b shows that a lot of triangles are rendered that do not contribute to the final image because they are hidden by the front triangles forming the hill. Figure 7c shows how PVS can successfully remove most of those triangles. Figures 7d and 7e show the same PVS optimized scene, as seen from the camera's view and as seen from above. The nice thing about PVS is that the cost of processing power is almost zero at run time because most calculations are done offline when the terrain is designed.

In order to (pre-) calculate a PVS, the area of interest is divided into smaller parts. In our case it is obvious that we should use patches for those parts. For example, a landscape consisting of 16x16 patches requires 16x16 cells on the ground plane (z=0). To allow the camera to move up and down, it is necessary to have several layers of such cells. Tests have shown that 32 layers in a range of three times the height of the landscape are enough for fine-graded PVS usage.

One problem with PVS is the large amount of memory needed to store all the visibility data. In a landscape with 16x16 patches and 32 layers of PVS data, we get 8,192 PVS cells. For each cell we have to store the 16x16 patches that are visible from that cell. This means that we have to store more than two million values. Fortunately, we only need to store one-bit values (visible/not visible) and can save the PVS as a bit field, which results in a 256Kbyte data file in this example case.

Figure 8 shows an example image from the PVS calculation application where the camera is located in the center of the valley (the black part in the middle of the green dots (the lighter dots at the top center)). All red dots resemble those patches that are not visible from that location. Determining whether a patch is visible from a location is done by using an LOS (line of sight) algorithm, which tracks a line from the viewer's position to the patch's position. If the line does not hit the landscape on its way to the patch, this patch is visible from that location.

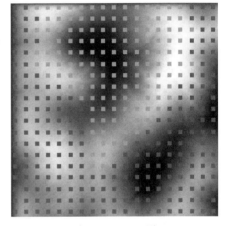

Figure 8: PVS from top view. The camera sits in the valley in the middle of the green dots.

To optimize memory requirements, the renderer distinguishes between patches that are active (currently visible) and those that aren't. Only those patches that are currently active are fully resident in memory. The memory footprint of inactive patches is rather low (about 200 bytes per patch).

Geomorphing in Hardware

Doing geomorphing for a single patch basically means doing vertex tweening between the current tessellation level and the next finer one. The tessellation level calculation returns a tessellation factor in the form of a floating-point value, where the integer part means the current level and the fractional part denotes the tweening factor (e.g., a factor of 2.46 means that tweening is done between levels 2 and 3 and the tweening factor is 0.46). Tweening between two mesh representations is a well-known technique in computer graphics and easily allows an implementation of morphing for one single patch (vertices that should not move simply have the same position in both representations).

The problem becomes more difficult if a patch's neighbors are considered. Problems start with the shared border vertices, which can only follow one of the two patches but not both (unless we accept gaps). As a consequence, one patch has to adapt its border vertices to those of its neighbor. In order to do correct geomorphing, it is necessary that the finer patch allows the coarser one to dictate the border vertices' position. This means that we do not only have to care about one tweening factor as in the single patch case but have to add four more factors for the four shared neighbor vertices. Since the vertex shader cannot distinguish between interior and border vertices, these five factors have to be applied to all vertices of a patch. So we are doing a tweening between five meshes.

As if this wasn't already enough, we also have to take special care with the inner neighbor vertices of the border vertices. Unfortunately, these vertices also need their own tweening factor in order to allow correct vertex insertion (when switching to a finer tessellation level). To point out this quite complicated situation more clearly, we go back to the example of Figure 6b. For example, we state that the patch's left border follows its coarser left neighbor. Then the tweening factor of vertex 1 depends on the left neighbor, whereas the tweening factor of all interior vertices (such as vertex 2) depend on the patch itself. When the patch reaches its next finer tessellation level (Figure 6a), the new vertex A is inserted. Figure 9 shows the range in which vertices 1 and 2 can move and the range in which vertex A has to be inserted. (Recall that a newly inserted vertex must always lie in the middle of its preexisting neighbors.) To make it clear why vertex A needs its own tweening factor, suppose that the vertices 1 and 2 are both at their bottom position when A is inserted (tweeningL and tweeningI are both 0.0). Later on when A is removed, the vertices 1 and 2 might lie somewhere else and A would now probably not lie in the middle between those two if it had the same tweening factor as vertex 1 or vertex 2. The consequence is that vertex A must have a tweening factor (tweeningA) that depends on both the factor of vertex 1 (tweeningL — the factor from the left neighboring patch) and on that of vertex 2 (tweeningI — the factor by which all interior vertices are tweened).

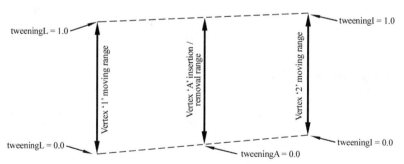

Figure 9: Vertex insertion/removal range

What we want is the following:

Vertex A should:

■ be inserted/removed in the middle between the positions of vertex 1 and vertex 2

■ not pop when the patch switches to another tessellation level

■ not pop when the left neighbor switches to another tessellation level

The simple formula `tweeningA = (1.0-tweeningL) * tweeningI` does the job. Each side of a patch has such a tweeningA that results in four additional tessellation levels.

Summing this up, we have nine tessellation levels that must all be combined every frame for each vertex. What we actually do in order to calculate the final position of a vertex is the following:

```
PosFinal = PosBase + tweeningI*dI + tweeningL*dL + tweeningR*dR + tweeningT*dT + ...
```

Since we only morph in one direction (as there is no reason to morph other than up/down in a heightmap-generated terrain), this results in nine multiplications and nine additions just for the geomorphing task (not taking into account any matrix multiplications for transformation). This would be quite slow in terms of performance on the CPU. Fortunately, the GPU provides us with an ideal solution. The vertex shader command dp4 can multiply four values with four other values and sum the products in just one instruction. This allows us to do all these calculations in just five instructions, which is only slightly more than a single 4x4 matrix multiplication takes.

The following code snippet shows the vertex data and constants layout that is pushed onto the graphics card.

```
; Constants specified by the app
;
;    c0      = (factorSelf, 0.0f, 0.5f, 1.0f)
;    c2      = (factorLeft, factorLeft2, factorRight, factorRight2),
;    c3      = (factorBottom, factorBottom2, factorTop, factorTop2)
;
;    c4-c7   = WorldViewProjection Matrix
;    c8-c11  = Pass 0 Texture Matrix
;
;
; Vertex components (as specified in the vertex DECLARATION)
;
;    v0      = (posX, posZ, texX, texY)
;    v1      = (posY, yMoveSelf, 0.0, 1.0)
;    v2      = (yMoveLeft, yMoveLeft2, yMoveRight, yMoveRight2)
;    v3      = (yMoveBottom, yMoveBottom2, yMoveTop, yMoveTop2)
```

We see that only four vectors are needed to describe each vertex, including all tweening. Note that those vectors v0-v3 do not change as long as the patch is not retessellated; they are therefore good candidates for static vertex buffers.

The following code shows how vertices are tweened and transformed by the view/projection matrix.

```
;-----------------------------------------------------------------
; Vertex transformation
;-----------------------------------------------------------------
mov r0, v0.xzyy          ; build the base vertex
mov r0.w, c0.w           ; set w-component to 1.0

dp4 r1.x, v2, c2         ; calc all left and right neighbor tweening
dp4 r1.y, v3, c3         ; calc all bottom and top neighbor tweening

mad r0.y, v1.y, c0.x, v1.x  ; add factorSelf*yMoveSelf
add r0.y, r0.y, r1.x        ; add left and right factors
add r0.y, r0.y, r1.y        ; add bottom and top factors

m4x4 r3, r0, c4          ; matrix transformation
mov oPos, r3
```

While this code could surely be further optimized, there is no real reason to do so, since it is already very short for a typical vertex shader.

Finally, there is only texture coordinate transformation.

```
;-----------------------------------------------------------------
; Texture coordinates
;-----------------------------------------------------------------

; Create tex coords for pass 0 – material (use texture matrix)
dp4 oT0.x,  v0.z, c8
dp4 oT0.y,  v0.w, c9

; Create tex coords for pass 1 – lightmap (simple copy, no transformation)
mov oT1.xy, v0.zw
```

oT0 is multiplied by the texture matrix to allow scaling, rotation, and movement of materials and cloud shadows. oT1 is not transformed, since the texture coordinates for the lightmap do not change and always span (0,0) to (1,1).

Results

The following table shows frame rates achieved on an Athlon-1300 with a standard GeForce3. The minimum scene uses just one material together with a lightmap (two textures in one render pass — see Figure 10a). The full scene renders the same landscape with three materials, plus a cloud shadow layer, plus a skybox and a large lens flare (seven textures in four render passes for the terrain — see Figure 10b).

The following are frame rates achieved at different scene setups and LOD systems:

	Static LOD	Software Morphing	Hardware Morphing
Minimum Scene	587 fps	312 fps	583 fps
Full Scene	231 fps	205 fps	230 fps

The table shows that geomorphing done using the GPU is almost as fast as doing no geomorphing at all. In the minimum scene the software morphing method falls back tremendously since the CPU and the system bus cannot deliver the high frame rates (recall that software morphing needs to send all vertices over the bus each frame) achieved by the other methods. Things change when using the full scene setup. Here the software morphing takes advantage of the fact that the terrain is created and sent to the GPU only once but is used four times per frame for the four render passes and the skybox and lens flare slow down the frame rate independently. Notice that the software morphing method uses the same approach as for hardware morphing. An implementation fundamentally targeted for software rendering would come off far better.

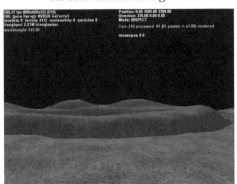

Figure 10a: Terrain with one material layer

Figure 10b: Same as 10a but with three materials (grass, stone, mud) + moving cloud layer + skybox + lens flare

In this article I've shown how to render a dynamically view-dependent triangulated landscape with geomorphing by taking advantage of today's graphics hardware. Splitting the mesh into smaller parts allowed us to apply the described optimizations, which led to achieved high frame rates. Further work could be done to extend the system to use geometry paging for really large terrains. Other open topics are the implementation of different render paths for several graphics cards or using a bump map instead of a lightmap in order to achieve dynamic lighting. The new generation of DX9 cards allows the use of up to 16 textures per pass, which would enable us to draw seven materials plus a cloud shadow layer in just one pass.

References

[Air91] Airey, John, "Increasing Update Rates in the Building Walkthrough System with Automatic Model-Space Subdivision and Potentially Visible Set Calculations," Ph.D. thesis, University of North Carolina, Chapel Hill, 1991.

[Boe00] de Boer, Willem H., "Fast Terrain Rendering Using Geometrical MipMapping," E-mersion Project, October 2000, http://www.connectii.net/emersion.

[Cor01] Corel Bryce by Corel Corporation, http://www.corel.com.

[Duc97] Duchaineau, M., M. Wolinski, D. Sigeti, M. Miller, C. Aldrich, and M. Mineev-Weinstein, "ROAMing Terrain: Real-time Optimally Adapting Meshes," *IEEE Visualization*, Oct. 1997, pp. 81-88, http://www.llnl.gov/graphics/ROAM.

[Eva96] Evans, Francine, Steven Skiena, and Amitabh Varshney, "Optimizing triangle strips for fast rendering," 1996, pp. 319-326, http://www.cs.sunysb.edu/evans/stripe.html.

[Hop98] Hoppe, H., "Smooth View-Dependent Level-of-Detail Control and its Application to Terrain Rendering," *IEEE Visualization*, Oct. 1998, pp. 35-42, http://www.research.microsoft.com/~hoppe.

[Slay95] Slayton, Joseph R., Wilbur, the latest version can be retrieved at http://www.ridgenet.net/~jslayton/software.html.

[Sno01] Snook, Greg, "Simplified Terrain Using Interlocking Tiles," *Game Programming Gems 2*, Charles River Media, 2001, pp. 377-383.

[Tel91] Teller, Seth J. and Carlo H. Sequin, "Visibility preprocessing for interactive walkthroughs," *Computer Graphics* (Proceedings of SIGGRAPH '91), July 1991, 25(4):61-69.

[Usg86] U.S. Geological Survey (USGS), "Data Users Guide 5 — Digital Elevation Models," Earth Science Information Center (ESIC), U.S. Geological Survey, 507 National Center, Reston, VA, 1986.

3D Planets on the GPU

Jesse Laeuchli

www.laeuchli.com/jesse/

Rendering planets in a 3D application is a difficult task. Previously, if a programmer wanted to include planets, the CPU had to juggle planet rendering and any other tasks the program might have. Now it is possible to perform almost the entire task on the GPU using vertex and pixel shaders. Moreover, the procedural model presented here allows a near infinite number of different planets to be rendered. This article examines rendering planets entirely on the GPU using nVidia's Cg. (See [nVidia] for more information about Cg.)

The most important task in rendering planets is to generate the geometry. This is usually done by first generating a sphere and then deforming the points on the sphere with some type of fractal. The sphere can be generated using the parametric equation:

$$X = \sin(u) * \sin(v)$$
$$Y = \cos(u) * \sin(v)$$
$$Z = \cos(v)$$

Evaluating this equation on the GPU is fairly simple. It can be done by passing the u,v values in position.xy and then calling the sincos function. Using the sincos function (as opposed to separately calling the sin and cos functions) can make the code cleaner and faster. The code below achieves this.

```
float fxsin;
float fxcos;
float fysin;
float fycos;
sincos(In.pos.x,fxsin,fxcos);
sincos(In.pos.y,fysin,fycos);
Sphere.x= fxsin* fysin;
Sphere.y= fxcos* fysin;
Sphere.z= fycos;
```

After the sphere has been generated, it must be deformed to create the planet geometry. A function is needed that can be called at each point of the sphere, which will then return a scalar value that can be used to modify the sphere's geometry. We can obtain this function by using noise to create a fractal. The fractal shown here is a hybrid multifractal [Ebert98] and is created by calling 3D noise several times and then scaling the noise by the product of the frequencies. This creates a fractal with smooth planes, rounded hills, and tall mountains. See

[Ebert98] for more types of fractals. Below is the code to implement the multifractal:

```
float MultiFractal(float3 pos, float octaves, float offset,float freqchange,float h,
      float4 pg[B2])
{
    float result;
    float signal;
    float weight;
    float freq=1;
    result=(noise(pos,pg)+offset)*pow(freq,-h);
    freq*=freqchange;
    weight=result;
    pos*=freqchange;
    for(int i=0;i<octaves;i++)
    {
        clamp(weight,0,1);  //Clamp used to get rid of a conditional and keep weight
                            // within [0:1]
        signal=(noise(pos,pg)+offset)*pow(freq,-h);  //Get noise value and multiply it
        freq*=freqchange;   //Update frequency each octave.
        result+=weight*signal;
        weight*=signal;
        pos*=freqchange;
        i++;

    }
return result;
}
```

Note that this code is only usable with a vertex profile because it uses looping to keep the instruction count down. It would be possible to use the code in a pixel shader (to generate a planet texture, for example), but then the loop would need to be unrolled.

It is also possible to use a 2D noise function, but doing so would introduce artifacts around the poles of the planets by crowding too much detail around them and too little around the middle. However, using a 2D noise function has the benefit of being faster then a 3D noise function. In the example program, a 3D noise function is used, specifically Perlin's noise function [Perlin], which works by taking the dot product between several vectors and interpolating between the results. Below is the Cg code used:

```
float noise(float3 v, float4 pg[B2])
{
v = v + float3(10000.0f, 10000.0f, 10000.0f);   // hack to avoid negative numbers

float3 i = frac(v * BR) * B;   // index between 0 and B-1
float3 f = frac(v);            // fractional position

// lookup in permutation table
float2 p;
p[0] = pg[ i[0]     ].w;
p[1] = pg[ i[0] + 1 ].w;
```

```
p = p + i[1];

float4 b;
b[0] = pg[ p[0] ].w;
b[1] = pg[ p[1] ].w;
b[2] = pg[ p[0] + 1 ].w;
b[3] = pg[ p[1] + 1 ].w;
b = b + i[2];

// compute dot products between gradients and vectors
float4 r;
r[0] = dot(pg[ b[0] ].xyz, f );
r[1] = dot(pg[ b[1] ].xyz, f - float3(1.0f, 0.0f, 0.0f));
r[2] = dot(pg[ b[2] ].xyz, f - float3(0.0f, 1.0f, 0.0f));
r[3] = dot(pg[ b[3] ].xyz, f - float3(1.0f, 1.0f, 0.0f));

float4 r1;
r1[0] = dot(pg[ b[0] + 1 ].xyz, f - float3(0.0f, 0.0f, 1.0f));
r1[1] = dot(pg[ b[1] + 1 ].xyz, f - float3(1.0f, 0.0f, 1.0f));
r1[2] = dot(pg[ b[2] + 1 ].xyz, f - float3(0.0f, 1.0f, 1.0f));
r1[3] = dot(pg[ b[3] + 1 ].xyz, f - float3(1.0f, 1.0f, 1.0f));

// interpolate
f = s_curve(f);
r = lerp(r, r1, f[2]);
r = lerp(r.xyyy, r.zwww, f[1]);
return lerp(r.x, r.y, f[0]);
}
```

Perlin noise works well with vertex profiles but is less suitable for pixel profiles, where other (albeit lower quality) noise functions can be written that use fewer texture accesses and require fewer instructions.

By passing the x,y,z coordinates of the sphere to the multifractal function, it is possible to create the planet geometry. Figure 1 is a screen shot of the generated geometry.

After the geometry has been generated, the planet needs to be textured. This can be done in a pixel shader by first creating a one-dimensional texture containing the various colors that the planet will use. In the example program, a simple texture containing just a few

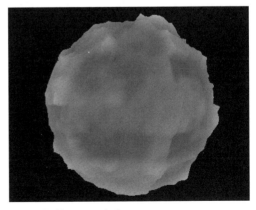

Figure 1: Untextured planet geometry

shades of green, brown, and white is used, but different textures and textures containing different colors are also possible. If, for example, a planet resembling Mars is required, then the texture could be filled with reddish colors. To index into the texture, the vertex shader passes the height used to modify the sphere geometry, scaled to the range [0,1], to the pixel shader. The pixel shader then uses this to access the texture. However, this leads to a fairly unrealistic color distribution. In nature, height is not the sole basis for the terrain color. Snow does uniformly appear on the tops of mountains, and sometimes it falls lower down. The same applies for grass and other types of terrain. To account for this, noise can be used to modify the index into the texture. This makes the distribution of terrain types more random and visually pleasing. Below is the code used to achieve this:

```
float height=In.dif.x;                              //Height passed from vertex shader
float modifyindex=(2*noise(normalize(In.tex1.xyz*10,BaseTexture2)-1)/10;  //scale noise
height+=modifyindex;                                //modify height.
float4 color=tex1D(BaseTexture, height);  //index into buffer.
```

The noise function used here is a type of value noise. It works by indexing into an array of random variables, then linearly interpolating the results and smoothing those results with an ease curve. It uses fewer texture accesses than Perlin noise and typically requires fewer instructions. However, another noise function may be substituted for this one without a significant change in the results.

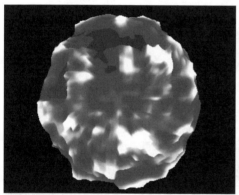

Figure 2a: Planet texture generated using noise

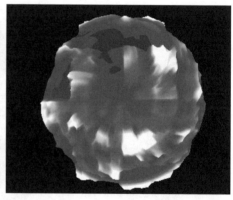

Figure 2b: Planet texture generated using just height value

```
half random(float x,float y,float z,sampler1D g)
{

    half index=(x*6.6)+(y*7.91)+(z*8.21);
    index=index*0.001953125;
    index=h1tex1D(g,index);
    return index;

}
half3 scurve(half3 v)
{
    return v * v * (3 - 2 * v);
}
```

```
half noise(float3 v,sampler1D g)
{

    half3 LatticePoint=floor(v);
    half3 fracl=scurve(frac(v));
    half4 v1;

    v1.x = random(LatticePoint.x,LatticePoint.y,LatticePoint.z,g);
     v1.y = random(LatticePoint.x + 1, LatticePoint.y,LatticePoint.z,g);
       v1.z = random(LatticePoint.x, LatticePoint.y + 1,LatticePoint.z,g);
         v1.w = random(LatticePoint.x + 1, LatticePoint.y + 1,LatticePoint.z,g);

    half2 il = lerp(v1.xz , v1.yw , fracl.x);

    half a=lerp(il.x , il.y , fracl.y);

        v1.x = random(LatticePoint.x,LatticePoint.y,LatticePoint.z+1,g);
        v1.y = random(LatticePoint.x + 1, LatticePoint.y,LatticePoint.z+1,g);
        v1.z = random(LatticePoint.x, LatticePoint.y + 1,LatticePoint.z+1,g);
        v1.w = random(LatticePoint.x + 1, LatticePoint.y + 1,LatticePoint.z+1,g);
         il = lerp(v1.xz , v1.yw , fracl.x);

    half b=lerp(il.x , il.y , fracl.y);

    return lerp(a,b,fracl.z);


}
```

It is also possible to use this noise function to create a cloud layer for the planet. To do this, another slightly bigger sphere needs to be drawn around the planet, and then several octaves of noise need to be summated, each octave with successively higher frequency and lower amplitude.

```
color.w=noise(input,BaseTexture)+noise(input*2,BaseTexture)*.5+noise(input*4,BaseTexture)
    *.25+noise(input*8,BaseTexture)*.125;
color.w=1-color.w;
```

This could be improved by drawing several cloud spheres, with each sphere being slightly larger than the last. This gives the clouds a volumetric look.

Oceans can easily be added to the planet by rendering a semitransparent sphere with a radius less than that of the planet sphere. Then, any land that has a low enough height value will be below water level.

The last step in rendering the planet is lighting it. It is quite

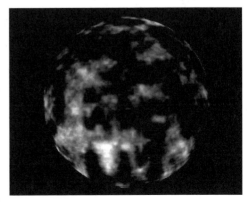

Figure 3: Clouds rendered with five octaves of noise

difficult to achieve accurate per-pixel lighting on the planet. To do this, it is necessary to either recompute the sphere normals when the sphere is deformed or generate tangent space for the planet. Unfortunately, due to the current instruction count of the program, it is impossible to regenerate the normals. However, it is easy to generate tangent space for the sphere by taking the partial derivative with respect to u,v, giving:

$$\partial u = \cos(u)*\sin(v), -\sin(u)*\sin(v), 0$$
$$\partial v = \cos(v)*\sin(u), \cos(v)*\cos(u), -\sin(v)$$

It would then be possible to use the amount that the sphere geometry is perturbed by to generate normals and would work for lighting the clouds. However, as we generate the sphere geometry for the planet, the sphere equation changes, and so it becomes much more difficult to generate the tangent space by taking the derivative of the parametric sphere equation. The total equation is:

$$X = \sin(u)*\sin(v)*Multifractal(\sin(u)*\sin(v), \cos(u)*\sin(v), \cos(v)) + 1$$
$$Y = \cos(u)*\sin(v)*Multifractal(\sin(u)*\sin(v), \cos(u)*\sin(v), \cos(v)) + 1$$
$$Z = \cos(v)*Multifractal(\sin(u)*\sin(v), \cos(u)*\sin(v), \cos(v)) + 1$$

Because the partial derivative for this function is difficult to find and the vertex program is already reaching the maximum instruction limit, the example program simply uses the sphere normals to generate per-pixel lighting. This means that the planet lighting is not accurate, as the changes to the geometry of the sphere are not reflected; however, it does allow some lighting to be performed. This is done with the following code in the planet pixel shader.

```
Out.dif.xyz= color.xyz*dot(normalize(In.tex1.xyz), In.tex2);
//Light position in In.tex2, sphere normal in In.tex1
```

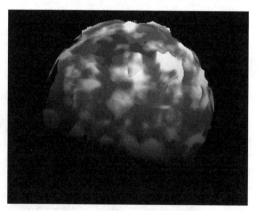

Figure 4: Planet with cloud cover, noise texture, ocean, and per-pixel lighting (See Color Plate 2.)

Conclusion

This article examined how to generate 3D planets using only the GPU to perform the required rendering by evaluating the multifractal, value, and Perlin noise functions almost entirely on the graphics card and using these functions to generate the planet geometry, textures, and atmosphere. This provides a good starting point for developers seeking to implement planets using the latest hardware and for further experimentation with 3D planets.

References

[Ebert98] Ebert, David S., et al., *Texturing and Modeling: A Procedural Approach* (Second Edition), San Diego: Academic Press, 1998.

[nVidia] Cg Language information available online at http://www.cgshaders.org and http://developer.nvidia.com/view.asp?IO=cg_about.

[Perlin] Perlin, Ken, "Improved Noise reference implementation," http://mrl.nyu.edu/~perlin/noise/.

Cloth Animation with Pixel and Vertex Shader 3.0

Kristof Beets

PowerVR Technologies

Introduction

In computer graphics, simulating cloth has always been a topic of much research [UCL02]. In everyday life we observe cloth behavior without realizing the complexity of the physics involved. The model and shaders introduced in this article attempt to simulate cloth using a simplified massless spring model, which can be executed completely by next generation graphics hardware. The spring model is used to generate the position and normal of a cloth's control points, which are then stored into "geometry textures" using an advanced pixel shader 3.0. Finally, the vertex texturing capabilities of the vertex shader 3.0 model allows us to render the deformed cloth using the position and normal data stored in these geometry textures.

Basic Cloth Model

Before attempting to simulate cloth behavior using shaders, it is important to understand the underlying cloth model that we will be implementing [Elias01]. Our cloth surface is modeled using a network of nodes linked together by massless springs. A first-level approximation is to connect every node to its four direct neighbor nodes, thus creating a simple grid; however, this results in an extremely flexible cloth that fails to retain its area and shape. This can be improved by connecting each node to its eight direct neighbor nodes, thus adding diagonal springs that work against shearing deformations. A final optimization is to add four or eight more connections to neighbor nodes that are two steps away; these connections again battle deformation of the original cloth shape and also avoid excessive bending of the cloth surface. Ultimately, it is possible to connect each node to all the direct neighbors and those two steps away, resulting in 24 spring connections. Figure 1 shows a central node with the various spring configurations as described.

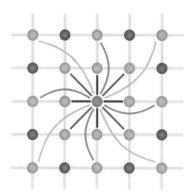

Figure 1: The interconnection of cloth springs

Now let's introduce an actual model for these interconnecting springs. A property of springs is that they will fight against any force that attempts to compress or stretch them. This behavior can be translated into the following formula:

$$SpringForce = SpringConst \times \frac{DefaultSpringLength - SpringLength}{DefaultSpringLength}$$

This formula calculates the relative deformation of the spring. If the spring is stretched, the relative deformation will be negative and result in a force counteracting the stretching. If the spring is compressed, the relative deformation will be positive and result in a force counteracting the compression (see Figure 2). If the spring is untouched, the relative deformation is zero and results in no force. SpringConst translates the relative deformation into an actual force. This constant can be used to modify the power of the spring: A high number will result in a strong counteracting force, while a low number will result in a small counteracting force. It is possible to further modify the spring behavior by changing this formula. For example, we could take the square of the relative deformation, which

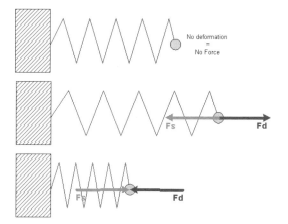

Figure 2: An example of springs with a Deformation Force (Fd) and the resulting Spring Force (Fs)

means that the force would behave in a nonlinear way to deformations. Effectively, this is how the cloth material type can be changed.

To translate this force into a movement, we have to dig out Newton's second law:

$$Force = Mass \times Acceleration$$

Or, reorganized:

$$Acceleration = \frac{Force}{Mass}$$

Acceleration is the change of velocity over time, and velocity is the rate of change of the position over time. This can be translated to:

$$Velocity_{NEW} = Velocity_{OLD} + Acceleration \times \Delta t = Velocity_{OLD} + \frac{Force}{Mass} \times \Delta t$$

$$Position_{NEW} = Position_{OLD} + Velocity_{NEW} \times \Delta t =$$
$$Position_{OLD} + Velocity_{OLD} \times \Delta t + \frac{Force}{Mass} \times \Delta t^2$$

In summary, the new position (after a period of time) is dependent on the old position, existing velocity, the force acting on the object, and the mass of the object. Our aim is to have a very simple model, so we will ignore velocity and acceleration and just reduce this to:

$$Position_{NEW} = Position_{OLD} + ForceScaleConst \times Force$$

Basically, we flatten all of the above factors into a single constant. The main property that we maintain is that the movement is related to the total force acting upon the nodes of the cloth. Combining this with our SpringForce equation, we get:

$$Position_{NEW} = Position_{OLD} + Const \times \frac{DefaultSpringLength - SpringLength}{DefaultSpringLength}$$

In other words, in this highly simplified model, the change of position is dependent only on the deformation of the spring multiplied by a constant.

To recap, we first chose the basic model for our cloth: A grid of nodes represents the cloth surface with the nodes interconnected by a network of springs. The second step was to build a model for these springs that describes how the node will move under the impact of its neighboring nodes.

Finally, we bring all of this together into one complete model that also takes into account external factors, such as gravity and collisions with objects; I'll introduce this model using easy-to-understand pseudocode:

Variables

```
VECTOR ARRAY: ClothOld (0 to X, 0 to Y) (init. with start positions)
VECTOR ARRAY: ClothNew (0 to X, 0 to Y) (target for result of model)

VECTOR: MovementVector
```

```
VECTOR: SpringVector
VECTOR: ForceVector
VECTOR: Gravity  (init. to (0, 0, g, 0) where g is gravity)

SCALAR: Length
SCALAR: ForceScaler

CONSTANT SCALAR: NormalLength (undeformed length of spring)
CONSTANT SCALAR: SmallAmount (const translates force to movement)
```

Functions

```
CheckConstraints (checks for collision, intersection, etc.)
DisplayCloth (displays the cloth)
```

Main Processing Loop

```
For every node (x,y) on the cloth:
    MovementVector = Gravity
    For each of the 4/8/12/16/... neighboring points
        SpringVector = (position of neighbor) - (position of node)
        Length       = length of SpringVector
        NormalLength = undeformed length SpringVector
        ForceScaler  = (Length - NormalLength) / NormalLength
        SpringVector = (SpringVector/Length)
        ForceVector  = SpringVector * ForceScaler
        ForceVector  = ForceVector * SmallAmount
        MovementVector += ForceVector
    End of loop
    ClothNew (x,y) = ClothOld(x,y)+ MovementVector
    CheckConstraints (ClothNew (x,y))
End of loop
DisplayCloth (ClothNew)
Copy all the values in ClothNew to ClothOld (double buffering)
```

Repeat Main Processing Loop forever

The pseudocode above shows an iterative loop that processes the input to create updated output positions. These output positions are then fed back into the system as input to create the next position and so on. The code uses a vector array to store the node positions; this array is initialized with the start positions of the nodes (cloth) before executing the main loop. For each node, the code looks at a certain number of neighboring nodes and, based on the distance between the current node and its neighbors, calculates the corresponding forces. The sum of these forces is then converted into a translation, which is added to the original position of the node along with some motion due to a static gravity. The conversion from forces to motion is done using a constant. This constant has to be chosen carefully: If the value is too big, the motion will be too large and the network will become unstable; if the constant is too small, the model will take forever to evolve. The new position finally undergoes a constraint check that involves checking collisions with objects. Specifically, if the new node position is within a constraining object, the node position has to be updated so the cloth will drape correctly on top of the object rather than sit inside it.

Implementation Using Shaders

Now that we have a model to simulate cloth, we can start to convert it to the world of pixel and vertex shaders so that full hardware acceleration can be used.

The model uses a double-buffered vector array to store the position of each node; this is implemented using textures. This storage needs to support both reading and writing, which is possible with textures created with the D3D-USAGE_RENDERTARGET flag. This position (x, y, and z) needs to be stored with sufficient accuracy — at least a 16-bit float per component should be used. This can be achieved by using either a 64-bit texture format (such as D3DFMT_A16B16G16R16F) or Multiple Render Targets (MRTs, such as 2 x D3DFMT_G16R16F). Our goal is to use these values to create the final geometry on screen. If vertex lighting is required, a normal vector will also be needed for each vertex. This brings the number of components to six: x, y, z and Nx, Ny, Nz. These can be stored easily and efficiently in three render targets with format D3DFMT_G16R16F. Because the texture data contains positions and normals, it effectively contains geometry; for this reason, these textures are referred to as *geometry textures*. The size of these geometry textures matches the number of nodes in our cloth grid (tessellation). For example, if we want a 32x32 grid of nodes forming the cloth, we need a 32x32 texture. Now that we have decided on our storage format, we can start to use it to implement our algorithm, which we will split into the following six phases: initialization, depth, cloth, constraint, normal map, and display.

Initialization Phase

The initialization phase is only run once at the start of the program or when we want to restart the cloth simulation. This phase fills the geometry textures (MRTs) with their initial startup values and clears the buffers. To keep things simple, we restrict our scene to a unit cube. The cloth starts at the top of the cube and falls down (possibly colliding with objects causing constraints) until it reaches a stable position or the bottom of the cube that is effectively the floor. This is illustrated in Figure 3.

The initial values for our MRT are (x, y, start height of cloth). Since we are working in a unit cube, the x and y positions can be generated quite easily using a trivial vertex and pixel shader program. All we

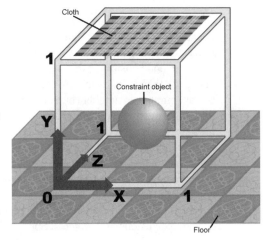

Figure 3: The scene containing cloth and objects within the unit cube

need to do is render a full-screen quad with texture coordinates interpolating from 0 to 1 along both the x and y-axes. We then store the interpolated texture coordinate for each pixel using the pixel shader, since each interpolated coordinate matches the position of a node.

Vertex shader code:

```
vs_3_0

; Input registers
dcl_position0 v0        ;Position in NORMALIZED SCREEN COORDINATES
dcl_texcoord0 v4        ;Texture coordinates = base node position

; Output registers
dcl_position0 o0.xyzw   ;Vertex position
dcl_texcoord0 o1.xy     ;Texcoord

; C8 contains scaling constants that influence the cloth size

mov r0, v0
mov r0.w, c21.w
mov o0, r0              ;Output Position

mad r1, v4, c8.x, c8.y  ;Scale cloth – change init positions
mov o1.xy, r1;          ;Output Texture Coord = node position
```

Pixel shader code:

```
ps_3_0

; Input
dcl_texcoord0 v0.xy     ;Tex Coord = node position

; Output results
mov r0.rg, v0.xy
mov oC0, r0             ;Node (X,Y) = interpolated texcoord

mov r0, c12             ; = (<initial cloth height>, 0.0f, 0.0f, 0.0f)
mov oC1, r0             ;Write Initial Depth
mov r0, c12.y
mov oC2, r0             ;Init to Zero
```

At the end of this phase, we have initialized all our buffers and they are ready for processing by the following phases.

Depth Phase

So far, we have not discussed how to handle constraints. The main aim for this implementation is to have cloth draping realistically over a collection of objects. When the objects are simple, it is easy to use a mathematical constraint. For example, it is quite trivial to detect if the new position of a node is inside a sphere. However, when working with more complex objects, such as a human body, a teapot, a table, etc., it becomes considerably more difficult to use mathematical constraints. To handle cloth draping over complex objects, we use depth maps (height field). Since we have cloth falling down, we need at least a depth value for every vertical column within the unit cube. Using the (x, y) position of a node, we can then do a dependent read within the depth map to detect if a collision has occurred.

Having only a top depth map does impose some limitations. For example, cloth might drape over a table, and during this process a tip of the cloth might flap down and move slightly underneath the table. If this happens, the tip of the cloth could suddenly be affected by the constraint (i.e., the table surface), and the tip will be moved instantly to the top of the table surface by the constraint, creating a cloth loop. Obviously this behavior is incorrect and can cause severe instability within the node-network. To solve this problem, a range is placed on the constraints. Specifically, it only applies the constraint if the depth value of the node is within a certain range of the constraint depth value. This issue and the solution are illustrated in Figure 4.

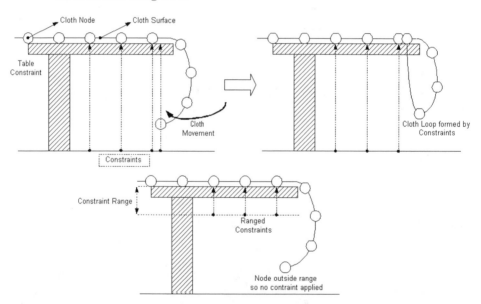

Figure 4: The cloth loop problem and its solution using ranged constraints

An even better constraint system is to use a "cube" depth map, meaning we create a depth map for all the surfaces of our unit cube; this allows us to do true volumetric testing. This can be illustrated using a sphere as the constraining object: The top and bottom depth maps will contain depth values that indicate the start of the sphere volume (the top depth map contains the depth of the top half of the sphere) and the end of the sphere volume (the bottom depth map contains the depth of the bottom half of the sphere). It is quite easy to fetch both of these depth values and do a comparison, and only if the node is between the top and bottom constraint points (that is, inside the volume along the z-axis) does it need to be moved to the value stored within the closest map. The same principle can be applied to the other faces of the depth cube map. Essentially, we check if a node is within the volume along each of the x, y, and z-axes, and only when a test along an axis indicates the point is inside the volume would the node position be corrected. This technique is illustrated in Figure 5.

The resolution of the depth map(s) should be high enough to avoid jagged artifacts in the geometry; for static scenes, these depth map(s) only have to be calculated at the start of the simulation, so there is no reason not to use a sufficiently high resolution. For dynamic scenes, the situation is different because whenever the constraints change (i.e., objects move), the depth map(s) need to be regenerated, which incurs a fillrate cost.

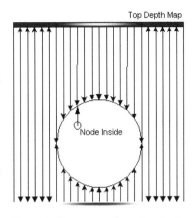

Figure 5: The usage of a cube depth map along one axis

The following vertex shader code is used with an orthographic projection (as perspective distortion is unwanted in these depth constraint maps) to store the world space linear depth into the texture:

```
vs_3_0

; Input registers
dcl_position0 v0        ;Position in NORMALIZED SCREEN COORDINATES

; Output registers
dcl_position0 o0.xyzw   ;Vertex position
dcl_texcoord0 o1.x      ;Texcoord

; C0-3 contains World+View+Proj Matrix
; C4-7 contains World+View Matrix
; C9 contains scene scaling and translation values

m4x4 r0, v0, c0         ;Transform by view/projection/world matrix
mov  o0, r0             ;Output position

dp4 r1.z,  v0, c6       ;Transform by world+view Z
mov r1  ,  r1.z
;Convert to world space depths rather than camera relative depths:
add r1  , -r1, c9.x
mul r1  ,  r1, c9.y     ;Scale to unit cube depth sizes
mov o1.x, r1            ;Move scaled world depth result into tex coord
```

The pixel shader simply stores the depth value, created in the vertex shader and passed on through a texture coordinate field, in the render target.

The current demonstration application implements a single top depth map with constraint range; a full cube depth map version might be added at a later stage.

48

Cloth Phase

The cloth phase is where the real action occurs. The pixel shader used in this phase will need to read the node's position and apply a step of the earlier described iterative cloth model to generate a new position. To create this shader, we need to translate our previous pseudocode into pixel and vertex shader code. Our pseudocode involves operations on the center node position using the position of several neighboring nodes as input. These positions need to be fetched from textures (filled during the initialization phase or during previous cloth phases), which requires texture coordinates that we will set up in the vertex shader. The following code sets up 16 2D texture coordinates; this is achieved by storing two sets of 2D coordinates in a single 4D coordinate register.

```
vs_3_0

; Input registers
dcl_position0     v0
dcl_texcoord0     v4

; Output registers
dcl_position0     o0.xyzw      ; Vertex position
dcl_texcoord0     o1.xyzw      ; center texcoord
dcl_texcoord1     o2.xyzw      ; 1 of 8 dual 2D Coords
dcl_texcoord2     o3.xyzw      ; 2 of 8 dual 2D Coords
dcl_texcoord3     o4.xyzw      ; 3 of 8 dual 2D Coords
dcl_texcoord4     o5.xyzw      ; 4 of 8 dual 2D Coords
dcl_texcoord5     o6.xyzw      ; 5 of 8 dual 2D Coords
dcl_texcoord6     o7.xyzw      ; 6 of 8 dual 2D Coords
dcl_texcoord7     o8.xyzw      ; 7 of 8 dual 2D Coords
dcl_texcoord8     o9.xyzw      ; 8 of 8 dual 2D Coords

; VERTEX POSITION
; ---------------
mov r0, v0
mov r0.w, c21.w
mov o0, r0

; MODEL TEXTURE COORDINATES
; -------------------------
; Copy base XY into both sections to generate two 2D coords per vector
mov o1.xy, v4          ; Center position
mov r1, v4.xyxy        ; Copy Base into both sections
; c10-c17 contain the delta for each neighbor position - set in code
add r0, r1, c10
mov o2.xyzw, r0        ; 1 out of 8 dual 2D Coords
add r0, r1, c11
mov o3.xyzw, r0        ; 2 out of 8 dual 2D Coords
add r0, r1, c12
mov o4.xyzw, r0        ; 3 out of 8 dual 2D Coords
add r0, r1, c13
mov o5.xyzw, r0        ; 4 out of 8 dual 2D Coords
```

```
add  r0, r1, c14
mov  o6.xyzw, r0       ; 5 out of 8 dual 2D Coords
add  r0, r1, c15
mov  o7.xyzw, r0       ; 6 out of 8 dual 2D Coords
add  r0, r1, c16
mov  o8.xyzw, r0       ; 7 out of 8 dual 2D Coords
add  r0, r1, c17
mov  o9.xyzw, r0       ; 8 out of 8 dual 2D Coords
```

After generating these texture coordinates, we can use them efficiently in our pixel shader. (Note the following code is written so it is easy to compare with the pseudocode — it is not performance optimized.)

```
ps_3_0

; Samplers
dcl_2d   s0            ;Input Textures MRT0 (x,y)
dcl_2d   s1            ;Input Textures MRT1 (Z,Nx)


; Input registers
dcl_texcoord0 v0.xyzw  ;Base Pos
dcl_texcoord1 v1.xyzw  ;Neighbor Dual Coord Set 1/8
dcl_texcoord2 v2.xyzw  ;Neighbor Dual Coord Set 2/8
dcl_texcoord3 v3.xyzw  ;Neighbor Dual Coord Set 3/8
dcl_texcoord4 v4.xyzw  ;Neighbor Dual Coord Set 4/8
dcl_texcoord5 v5.xyzw  ;Neighbor Dual Coord Set 5/8
dcl_texcoord6 v6.xyzw  ;Neighbor Dual Coord Set 6/8
dcl_texcoord7 v7.xyzw  ;Neighbor Dual Coord Set 7/8
dcl_texcoord8 v8.xyzw  ;Neighbor Dual Coord Set 8/8

; Constants
; c1..4 Set in code to weight to translate force to translation
; c7..10 Set in code to default spring length constants
defi i0, 4, 1, 1, 0    ;Used for loop

; Init Movement vector
mov r0, c0             ;Init movement vector with gravity

; Sample Main Position
texld r1, v0.xy, s0    ;Main Pos (x,y)
texld r2, v0.xy, s1    ;Main Pos (z,Nx)
mov r1.z, r2.x
mov r1.w, r2.y         ;Main Pos (x,y,z,Nx)

; Main processing loop for 16 neighbor nodes split up in 4 cases each 4 nodes
; Case A + C : Length of "1.0" and "2.0" for undeformed springs (Axis Springs)
; Case B + D : Length of "1.4" and "2.8" for undeformed springs (Diagonal Springs)

loop aL, i0            ; for (aL=1; aL<5; aL+=1)

  ;Case A
    texld r2, v[aL].xy, s0   ;Sample Neighbor (X,Y)
    texld r3, v[aL].xy, s1   ;Sample Neighbor (Z)
```

```
mov r2.z, r3.x          ;Neighbor (X,Y,Z) = R2
add r2, r2, -r1         ;Spring Vector = Neighbor - Main
dp3 r3.x, r2, r2        ;Sum of Squares
; Is it an edge pixel ? - if we clamp to the same value then don't do maths
if_ne r3.x, c0.x
    rsq r4.x, r3.x      ;RSQ of Sum of Squares = for Normalization
    rcp r5.x, r4.x      ;RCP of RSQ of Sum of Squares = Length = R5
    add r5.x, r5.x, -c7.x  ;Create Force scale using default lengths
    mul r5.x, r5.x, c7.y   ;R5 is Force Scale
    mul r2, r2, r4.x    ;Normalized Spring Vector
    mul r2, r2, r5.x    ;r2 is Force Vector
    ;Convert Force Vector to translation and add it to final movement vector
    mad r0, r2, c1, r0
endif


;Case C
texld r2, v[aL].zw, s0  ;Sample neighbor (X,Y)
texld r3, v[aL].zw, s1  ;Sample neighbor (Z)
mov r2.z, r3.x          ;Neighbor (X,Y,Z) = R2
add r2, r2, -r1         ;Spring Vector = Neighbor - Main
dp3 r3.x, r2, r2        ;Sum of Squares
; Is it an edge pixel ? - if we clamp to the same value then don't do maths
if_ne r3.x, c0.x
    rsq r4.x, r3.x      ;RSQ of Sum of Squares = for Normalization
    rcp r5.x, r4.x      ;RCP of RSQ of Sum of Squares = Length = R5
    add r5.x, r5.x, -c9.x  ;Create Force scale using default lengths
    mul r5.x, r5.x, c9.y   ;R5 is Force Scale
    mul r2, r2, r4.x    ;Normalized Spring Vector
    mul r2, r2, r5.x    ;r2 is Force Vector
    ;Convert Force Vector to translation and add it to final movement vector
    mad r0, r2, c3, r0
endif


;Case B
texld r2, v[aL+4].xy, s0  ;Sample neighbor (X,Y)
texld r3, v[aL+4].xy, s1  ;Sample neighbor (Z)
mov r2.z, r3.x          ;Neighbor (X,Y,Z) = R2
add r2, r2, -r1         ;Spring Vector = Neighbor - Main
dp3 r3.x, r2, r2        ;Sum of Squares
; Is it an edge pixel ? - if we clamp to the same value then don't do maths
if_ne r3.x, c0.x
    rsq r4.x, r3.x      ;RSQ of Sum of Squares = for Normalization
    rcp r5.x, r4.x      ;RCP of RSQ of Sum of Squares = Length = R5
    add r5.x, r5.x, -c8.x  ;Create Force scale using default lengths
    mul r5.x, r5.x, c8.y   ;R5 is Force Scale
    mul r2, r2, r4.x    ;Normalized Spring Vector
    mul r2, r2, r5.x    ;r2 is Force Vector
    ;Convert Force Vector to translation and add it to final movement vector
    mad r0, r2, c2, r0
endif


;Case D
```

```
    texld r2, v[aL+4].zw, s0    ;Sample neighbor (X,Y)
    texld r3, v[aL+4].zw, s1    ;Sample neighbor (Z)
    mov r2.z, r3.x              ;Neighbor (X,Y,Z) = R2
    add r2, r2, -r1            ;Spring Vector = Neighbor - Main
    dp3 r3.x, r2, r2          ;Sum of Squares
    ; Is it an edge pixel ? - if we clamp to the same value then don't do maths
    if_ne r3.x, c0.x
        rsq r4.x, r3.x         ;RSQ of Sum of Squares = for Normalization
        rcp r5.x, r4.x         ;RCP of RSQ of Sum of Squares = Length = R5
        add r5.x, r5.x, -c10.x ;Create Force scale using default lengths
        mul r5.x, r5.x, c10.y  ;R5 is Force Scale
        mul r2, r2, r4.x       ;Normalized Spring Vector
        mul r2, r2, r5.x       ;r2 is Force Vector
        ;Convert Force Vector to translation and add it to final movement vector
        mad r0, r2, c4, r0
    endif
endloop

;Write Out Final Values
add  r2, r1, r0
mov  r3, r2.z
mov  oC0, r2      ; (X, Y)
mov  oC1, r3      ; (Z, X)
```

The pixel shader code contains three large sections. The first section handles the initial setup, such as initializing the movement with a fixed gravity factor and reading the main node position. The second section is the main processing loop, which contains four subsections. These subsections correspond to different spring groups, as described in our model (see Figure 1). The code within each subsection calculates the force created by the spring between the central node and its neighbors, based on the distance between the nodes and the original undeformed spring length. This last element is a constant, which is different for nodes along the diagonal (relative length of $\sqrt{2}$ and $2 \times \sqrt{2}$) and nodes along the axis (relative length of 1.0f and 2.0f); this is the main difference between the subsections. The final and third section adds the movement vector to the original node position and writes the result out to the render targets. This shader can be adapted to use more or fewer neighbor positions; for details, check the shaders included with the demo application, which support 4, 8, 12, 16, 20, and 24 neighbor nodes.

Performance Considerations

The cloth shader code contains a loop, but while a loop makes the code easy to understand and read, it might not be optimal for hardware execution. If the hardware supports enough instructions, it might be better to unroll this loop, since by unrolling the loop no cycles would be wasted on actually executing the loop instructions (i.e., the compare and jump operations). However, in most cases a developer should not have to worry about this, since the driver's compiler should automatically handle it according to the capabilities of the host 3D device.

To handle cloth border cases correctly, where there are fewer neighbor nodes to consider, the shader contains a conditional dynamic branch (if_ne). By using branching, it is possible to jump over some instructions that do not need to be executed. For example, in the above shader the branch stops seven instructions from being executed in *some* cases; however, this comes at the overhead of executing the conditional branching instruction itself in *all* cases. Depending on the cost of the branching instruction (which is hardware dependent), it might be better to implement a different (cheaper or faster) mechanism to handle the border cases correctly, such as a cmp or setp instruction.

At first glance, this shader might look very complex and one might expect poor or non-real-time performance; however, it is important to understand that this shader is only executed on a very small set of pixels — a 64x64 grid is equivalent to rendering a 64x64 pixel texture and results in a network with 4,096 vertices. A render target of 64x64 pixels (or even 128x128, which results in a network with 16,384 vertices) is negligible compared to a default 1024x768 screen resolution. So even though the shader is complex, it is only being applied to a very small number of pixels, and hence real-time performance is still achieved.

Constraint Phase

During the constraint phase, we check all the new node positions and verify whether they have collided with an object. If they have, the node has to be moved so it sits on top of the object. As described before, this will be implemented using a depth compare using the depth map that we have created during a previous phase. All we need to do is use the (x, y) position of the node as a texture coordinate to do a dependent texture read into the depth map. We can then compare the node's current z position with the depth value stored for that column in the unit cube, and if the new depth value is smaller (i.e., closer to the floor) than the value of the depth map, we replace the node's z value with the depth map's value. To avoid instability, we add a safety margin to this compare so that we only constrain nodes that have a depth value within a certain range of the stored depth value. This way, if the tip of the tablecloth moves under the table, it is not suddenly jerked to the top of the table. This can be achieved using the following pixel shader code:

```
ps_3_0
; Declare inputs
dcl_2d      s0      ; X ,Y
dcl_2d      s1      ; Z ,Nx
dcl_2d      s2      ; Ny,Nz
dcl_2d      s3      ; Depth Map
dcl_texcoord0 v0.rg   ; Base Tex Coord

def c0, 0.05, 0.0, 0.0, 0.0   ; Controls range of the constraint

texld r0, v0, s0      ; Fetch (X,Y) of Node
texld r1, r0, s3      ; Read Depth Map at (X,Y) = Z Constraint
texld r2, v0, s1      ; Fetch (Z,Nx) of Node
```

```
add r4.r, r1.r, -r2.r    ; Subtract Cloth and Constraint Z
if_gt r4.r, c0.x         ; Compare with range
    mov r1.x, r2.r       ; keep cloth (e.g., cloth tip under table)
else
    max r4, r1.r, r2.r   ; Constrain cloth to largest value
    mov r1.x, r4.x       ; Update the output
endif

mov oC0, r0              ; output (X, Y)
mov oC1, r1              ; output (Z, Nx)
```

Different kinds of constraints can be introduced in this phase. We could have implemented a mathematical constraint, or we could simply use this shader to lock certain vertices in place (e.g., cloth hanging from two hooks, elastic cloth in a frame, etc.). The possibilities are endless and easy to implement.

Normal Map Phase

This phase calculates a normal for each node based on the neighboring nodes' information. This concept alone is probably worth a complete article; the current implementation creates two vectors (using a cross shape) from the four neighboring nodes and calculates the cross product to generate the normal. This is a very basic implementation; while more advanced solutions are possible, which would probably result in better image quality, they also come with increased sampling and processing costs. The sampling positions are set up in the vertex shader (similar to that illustrated in the cloth phase section) and processed as follows by the pixel shader:

```
ps_3_0

; Samplers
dcl_2d s0                ; MRT0 (X ,Y )
dcl_2d s1                ; MRT1 (Z ,Nx)

; Inputs
dcl_texcoord0 v0.xy      ; Main Node Sample Coord
dcl_texcoord1 v1.xy      ; Right Node Sample Coord
dcl_texcoord2 v2.xy      ; Top Node Sample Coord
dcl_texcoord3 v3.xy      ; Left Node Sample Coord
dcl_texcoord4 v4.xy      ; Bottom Node Sample Coord

texld r0 , v0, s0        ; Center Node (X,Y)
texld r11, v0, s1        ; Center Node (Z)
mov oC0, r0              ; Output (X,Y) to MRT0

texld r0, v1, s0         ; Right Node (X,Y)
texld r1, v1, s1         ; Right Node (Z)
mov   r3.xy, r0
mov   r3.z, r1.x         ; Right Node (X,Y,Z)
```

```
texld r0, v2, s0        ; Top Node (X,Y)
texld r1, v2, s1        ; Top Node (Z)
mov   r4.xy, r0
mov   r4.z, r1.x        ; Top Node (X,Y,Z)

texld r9 , v3, s0       ; Left Node (X,Y)
texld r10, v3, s1       ; Left Node (Z)
mov   r5.xy, r9
mov   r5.z, r10.x       ; Left Node (X,Y,Z)

texld r9 , v4, s0       ; Bottom Node (X,Y)
texld r10, v4, s1       ; Bottom Node (Z)
mov   r6.xy, r9
mov   r6.z, r10.x       ; Bottom Node (X,Y,Z)

; create vectors for cross product
add r0.xyz, r3.xyz, -r5.xyz
add r1.xyz, r4.xyz, -r6.xyz

; cross product and normalization
crs r7.xyz, r0, r1
nrm r0, r7.xyz          ; Vertex Normal

; Output results to MRT1 and MRT2
mov r11.y, r0.x
mov r9  , r0.y
mov r9.g, r0.z

mov oC1, r11            ; (Z, Nx)
mov oC2, r9             ; (Ny,Nz)
```

Display Phase

The final phase is the display phase, which will render our deformed cloth on the screen. To achieve this, we need to read every node's (vertex's) position and normal from the texture, rescale from the unit cube space into world space, transform, and display them on screen. All of this is achieved using the following vertex shader code:

```
vs_3_0
; Input Registers
dcl_position0    v0
dcl_texcoord0    v4

; Output Registers
dcl_position0    o0.xyzw  ; Final Vertex Position
dcl_color0       o1       ; Diffuse color for lighting
dcl_texcoord0    o2.xy    ; Texture Coordinates

; Samplers
dcl_2d    s0  ;   (X ,Y)
dcl_2d    s1  ;   (Z ,Nx)
```

```
dcl_2d    s2  ;    (Ny,Nz)

def c10, 120.0, 240.0, 100.0, 0.0        ; Scale Factor
def c11, 0.4267,-0.853,0.298,0.0         ; LIGHT
def c12, 0.0, 0.0, 0.0, 1.0              ; Init value

; Sample Vertex Textures
texldl r1, v4, s0   ; Read Node (X , Y)
texldl r2, v4, s1   ; Read Node (Z , Nx)
texldl r3, v4, s2   ; Read Node (Ny, Nz)

; Create XYZ in r4
mov r4.xy, r1        ; Grab XY
mov r4.z, r2.x       ; Grab Z

; Create NxNyNz in r5
mov r5.x, r2.y       ; Grab Nx
mov r5.yz, r3.xxy    ; Grab Ny, Nx

; Create Final Node/Vertex Position
mov r6, c12
mad r6.x, r4.x, c10.y, -c10.x     ; Rescale [0 -> 1] => [-120 -> 120]
mul r6.y, r4.z, c10.y             ; Rescale [0 -> 1] => [0 -> 240]
mad r6.z, r4.y, -c10.y, c10.x     ; Rescale [0 -> 1] => [-120 -> 120]
m4x4 r2, r6, c0                   ; Transformation (c0 set in code)
dp3  r4, r4, c11                  ; Simple Lighting Model

mov o0, r2                        ; Output Position
mov o1, r4                        ; Output Diffuse Color
mov o2.xy, v4                     ; Output Texture Coordinate
```

The above vertex shader should be easy to understand, as vertex texturing is the only exciting new feature used. Vertex texturing is virtually identical to texture accesses done in the pixel shader. It is, however, essential to understand the impact of vertex texturing on performance. All texture accesses come with high latencies, meaning that the period between fetching a value from a texture and being able to use the result can be quite long. There will be a lot of clock cycles spent moving the data from external memory into the chip (on a cache miss), through the cache, through texture filtering calculation, and eventually into the vertex shader. For this reason, throughput when using vertex texturing can potentially be quite low; however, it also means that if the shader has instructions that do not rely on the result of the texture fetch, the texture fetch can be "free," since non-dependent instructions can be executed while waiting for the texture data to arrive. On the other hand, if there are no non-dependent instructions, the hardware may stall while waiting for the texture data, and valuable processing power will be lost. Given this potential high per-vertex cost, it is essential to maximize vertex cache usage (e.g., using D3DX's Mesh Optimize functions).

The pixel shader used during the display phase applies a simple base texture with diffuse lighting; this is to maintain acceptable performance on the Direct3D reference device given the lack of 3D hardware supporting the 3.0 shader model.

NOTE   Vertex texturing should never be referred to as displacement mapping, as displacement mapping is only a very small subset of the millions of possibilities that can be brought to life by the ability to read texture data from within the vertex shader. The algorithm and the geometry textures presented here are just one such case: Geometry is stored as a position (and normal) within a texture, and the massive parallel processing power of the pixel shader can be used to modify that geometry using complex physics or simulation models. In this case, a simple physics-based model is implemented, but other interesting possibilities include fluid dynamics, metaballs, and chemical simulations.

Overview

Figure 6 shows an overview of the various shaders and buffers as they work together to bring cloth animation to life:

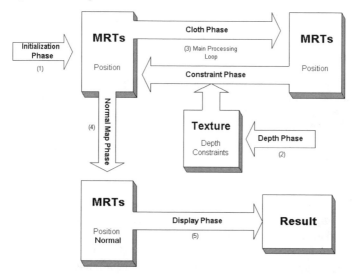

Figure 6: Shader interaction overview

The initialization phase writes the default node positions into the MRTs, and the depth phase writes the results of the depth render to a texture. The main processing loop then executes the cloth phase on the node positions, and the result undergoes the constraint phase. At this point, the cloth phase can start another iteration followed by another constraint phase. After looping through the cloth and constraint phases for a certain number of iterations, the normal map phase creates a new MRT, which contains the position and normal, and these are fed into the display phase, which creates the final on-screen result.

Color Plate 3 illustrates the contents of the position and normal map MRTs as well as the final result in wireframe and solid mode.

Sample Application

A sample application and a movie can be found on the companion CD. Updated versions are available at www.pvrdev.com and www.shaderx2.com.

Conclusion

This article described a method of bringing real-time cloth simulations to life using the high performance and flexibility of pixel and vertex shader 3.0. A simple physics model was introduced together with various methods to apply constraints. This was then translated into a number of advanced shaders making use of advanced new functionality only found in the 3.0 shader model, such as dynamic branching and loops within the pixel shader, and texturing from within the vertex shader.

References

[Elias01] http://freespace.virgin.net/hugo.elias/models/m_cloth.htm.

[UCL02] http://www.cs.ucl.ac.uk/research/vr/Projects/3DCentre/cloth_simulation_links.htm.

Collision Shaders

Takashi Imagire
www.t-pot.com

Introduction

It is well known that GPU power is evolving at a rate far exceeding the expectations of Moore's Law for general CPU power growth. However, this does not necessarily mean a simple speedup of the GPU. The GPU processes data at a much quicker speed than the CPU because of the parallel nature of the vertex and pixel pipelines. Rendering is a special process that is easy to parallelize. Although general-purpose calculations cannot always be carried out by the GPU, if processes are well suited to parallelization, they can likely be processed at high speeds using the GPU.

In games, collision detection is one of the most processor-demanding processes. Collision detection is a complicated process that tends to be divided into many calculations because of the difference among many situations and is difficult to create as a single routine. For collision detection between objects, there is a "brute-force" algorithm that is simple but has a high processing load. The geometry of objects is mapped to a two-dimensional depth texture, and collision detection is performed for each texel of the texture. Since this method calculates in a parallel fashion, calculation time is reduced, each texel is processed independently, parallel processing is possible, and processing can be calculated at a high speed by the GPU. This article discusses this method of calculation by the GPU.

Calculation by the GPU not only brings about an improvement given its incredible evolution speed, but it also lessens the load on the CPU, which can therefore assign more time to other processes (e.g., AI). In some game situations the CPU is busy, whereas in others the GPU is. The situation may change quickly depending on the scene. If it is possible to predict which processor carries the higher load, the calculation can be assigned to the other and the application will attain more efficient processing. (Of course, in order to be able to always perform this, the the CPU and GPU must be able to perform identical processing. This will probably be difficult. Additionally, this process of changing over to the GPU will only be used for specific scenes.)

As another advantage, if calculating only by the GPU is possible, we do not have to wait for data to be locked in video memory before the CPU accesses it. For example, when analyzing a rendering result by the CPU, we have to wait for the GPU to finish a rendering. Generally, when processing using the CPU and the

GPU simultaneously, blocking often occurs since the data cannot be used by the other processor until processing is completed. The performance will improve, since we no longer have to wait for the other processor to be able to access the results.

Visibility Test

In performing the collision detection by the GPU, we first consider a simple case: that of a scene with a wall. Although an object will be rendered when it lies in front of a wall, it will not be rendered when it is placed behind a wall because it has not passed the z test. That is, the front or back relationship between objects can be judged by the number of pixels rendered.

Let's now consider the case where we transpose this wall to the ground and set a camera pointing upward from underneath the wall, which we think of as the earth's surface. When an object is above the surface, the object is not rendered, since it is on the other side of the wall. But if the object is moved below the ground, it is rendered. Since the rendering of the object takes place after the rendering of the surface, it can be deduced that the object collided with the surface.

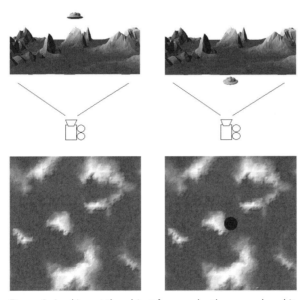

Figure 1: Looking at the object from under the ground and its rendered images

We will now consider a concrete implementation. In order to detect whether the rendering was carried out, it is easiest to use an asynchronous notification mechanism introduced in DirectX 9. If an asynchronous notification is used, the number of rendered pixels can simply be measured. When using asynchronous notification, the object needed by the application side is a pointer to an IDirect3DQuery9 object.

```
IDirect3DQuery9*        m_pQuery;
```

The initialization of the IDirect3DQuery9 object is performed by IDirect3D-Device9::CreateQuery. In order to count the number of pixels rendered, D3DQUERYTYPE_OCCLUSION is specified as the argument of IDirect3D-Device9::CreateQuery.

```
m_pd3dDevice->CreateQuery(D3DQUERYTYPE_OCCLUSION, &m_pQuery);
```

m_pQuery is used twice, before and after rendering the object. As opposed to normal rendering, the sub-surface camera must be prepared when preparing to render for collision detection. In order to prepare this camera, it is necessary to set a viewpoint on the bottom of the ground and make an observing point directly above. Since the direction of the camera's target is along the Y-axis, the up direction of the camera must be set along the direction of the Z-axis so that it is not parallel to the direction of the camera's view.

```
D3DXVECTOR3 vEye      = D3DXVECTOR3(0.0f,-1.0f, 0.0f);
D3DXVECTOR3 vLookatPt = D3DXVECTOR3(0.0f, 0.0f, 0.0f);
D3DXVECTOR3 vUp       = D3DXVECTOR3(0.0f, 0.0f, 1.0f);
D3DXMatrixLookAtLH(&mView, &vEye, &vLookatPt, &vUp);
m_pd3dDevice->SetTransform(D3DTS_VIEW, &mView);
                    // width height min_z max_z
D3DXMatrixOrthoLH(&mProj, 10.0f, 10.0f, -10.0f, 10.0f);
m_pd3dDevice->SetTransform(D3DTS_PROJECTION, &mProj);
```

In the rendering loop of each frame, the z-buffer that records the geometry of the ground is generated by rendering the ground first. Since the camera looks at the underside of the ground, it is extremely important that the culling mode be set to none or reverse. Otherwise, the rendering will not be performed. Moreover, if it finishes rendering the ground, it is necessary to restore the original culling mode.

```
m_pd3dDevice->SetRenderState(D3DRS_CULLMODE, D3DCULL_CW);
Rendering of the ground
m_pd3dDevice->SetRenderState(D3DRS_CULLMODE, D3DCULL_CCW);
```

Next, the asynchronous notification that measures the written-in number of pixels is started, and the rendering of the object that detects collision is carried out. After finishing the rendering, we must stop counting the rendered pixels.

```
m_pQuery->Issue(D3DISSUE_BEGIN);
Rendering of the object
m_pQuery->Issue(D3DISSUE_END);
```

The number of rendered pixels is counted by calling m_pQuery->Issue with the D3DISSUE_BEGIN argument before rendering is performed and passing the D3DISSUE_END parameter after rendering is complete.

If a rendering is completed, the result of the asynchronous notification is receivable. The number of rendered pixels can be determined by calling IDirect3DQuery9::GetData. The argument of IDirect3DQuery9::GetData is a pointer to a variable of the DWORD type which receives a result and the size of the variable (sizeof (DWORD)) and a flag specifying the query type. If the function is successful, S_OK is returned as the result. If the rendering is not yet completed, an error is returned.

```
DWORD pixels;
while(S_OK!=(hr=m_pQuery->GetData(&pixels, sizeof(DWORD), D3DGETDATA_FLUSH ))){
    if(D3DERR_DEVICELOST == hr) break;
}
if(1000<=pixels){       // When 1000 or fewer pixels are drawn, it is determined that no
                        // collision has taken place
    The response to a collision is performed.
}
```

Since asynchronous notification does not return an S_OK result until the rendering is complete, we must take caution so that it will not fall into an infinite loop. A method that should be avoided is waiting for rendering to finish while calling IDirect3DQuery9::GetData in an infinite loop. It is good practice to proceed without blocking the program, even though the function will fail and succeed, and to check a collision only when it returns S_OK.

The algorithm introduced here is simplified. In order to actually use it, a little improvement is required. Since the asynchronous notification mechanism does not immediately return a result, it is better to prepare two or more IDirect3DQuery9 interfaces, changing the interface every frame and waiting for the result of a previously called interface.

Also, if the number of the rendered pixels is not zero, it means the object was rendered. However, simply checking that zero pixels were rendered is often too strict in collision testing, as the object may have just grazed the other one. In many cases, the count should be set for more than a designated number of pixels for a more natural effect.

In the above example where collision detection was performed between objects and the ground, the camera was placed below the ground and the rendering was carried out upward. This method can be extended to collision detection between objects of more complicated geometry than the ground. For example, in the case of a convex type object, we can do collision detection using a cube map. The surface of an object can be mapped with a pixel of a cube map if a camera is put inside the convex type object and we render the object six times, once for each direction, with culling reverse. Collision detection of objects is possible by recording the depth value of the convex type object on the z-buffer first, rendering another object after that, and counting the number of rendering pixels. We can decompose non-convex objects into multiple convex objects and apply this cube map rendering to each of these sub-objects. For convex type objects, since the same processing can handle any rendering target that encloses the object from the surroundings, a dual paraboloid map and a sphere map as well as an environmental map can be used for collision detection. Generally, if a one-to-one correspondence exists between a rendering target and the object surface, it is possible to use this method in any coordinate space.

Collision Map

When performing collision detection, after a collision is detected, we want to find out the area with which the object collided. Although we can find out where an object currently is by asynchronous notification when objects penetrate, we do not know the point of collision. Moreover, a collision cannot be detected when an object moves too quickly and jumps through the area between the ground and camera. We will now explore more detailed collision detection by examining the path that the object moved along.

The "path volume" is introduced to detect any collisions with the moving object. This is an object similar to the well-known "shadow volume." Just as the shadow volume is a mesh that includes the object that casts a shadow as well as the object that is extruded in the direction away from the light, the path volume is a mesh that includes the object of the present position and the object of the past position about a certain object.

Since the path volume is determined by the same method used to create shadow volumes caused by parallel light sources, many different methods exist for generation [Brennan]. For example, another mesh that embeds degenerate polygons about all the edges of an original mesh of the object is prepared. The polygons are degenerate quadrangles and the vertices of such polygons are specified to be every two vertices of both ends of an edge. The normal vectors of two faces that share an edge of the original mesh are assigned to the normal vector of two overlapping vertices, respectively. The path volume is dynamically created at the time of rendering. The normal vector of every vertex is compared with the velocity of an object. (Specifically, the dot product of each vector is calculated, and the sign determines the position, past or present, to which the vertex goes.) The prepared mesh is drawn in the present position when its direction of movement equals the direction of the normal vector. If not suitable, it will draw in the past position. For the portions of the mesh where the dot product of the normal and velocity vectors changes sign, the edge is filled with a degenerate quadrangle.

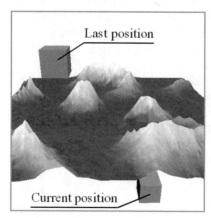

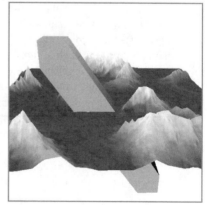

Figure 2: Meshes shown at the present position and at the last position

Figure 3: Path volume

There is a simpler method of using the original mesh as is without introducing additional degenerate polygons. For each vertex, the normal vector of the original mesh is compared with the direction of movement using the dot product, and the vertex is rendered in the present position when the dot product is greater than 0. The past position is rendered when the directions differ by more than 90 degrees (dot product < 0). Although this method can be processed by half vertex data compared with the first method, the result is not exact. With this method, the *edge* where the move direction and the direction of a normal vector change is not extended, but the *face* with normal vectors that gives the value of positive and negative both about the mark of the dot product of the move direction and direction of normal vector is extended. Since the original mesh changes shape through this enlargement, the generated path volume will be smaller than the "correct" one, although it will still be a subset of it. (See Figure 4.) Therefore, it can be used only as a simple approximation. However, when actually used in a game, this method of determining path volume is not a bad idea, as it makes the processing load lighter.

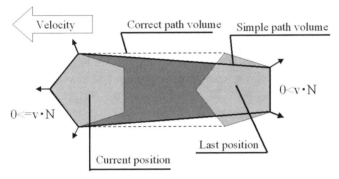

Figure 4: Simple but incomplete path volume

Although the path volume that connects the present position and the past position was introduced here as a linear path, it can also be created when the movement lies along a curve. When the movement of an object is as complicated as a parabolic movement by free-fall, etc., a path volume by the curved surface surrounding the volume that moved can be used. (In fact, a curved surface will be finely divided using a tessellator unit, etc.)

Next, we explain how to determine the area of collision using a path volume. This is very similar to the calculation of a shadowed area using a shadow volume. The rendering target for collision detection will be referred to as a "collision map" here. First, it is initialized by applying black to the collision map. (Although any color is sufficient for collision detection, the color black is convenient for special effects.) Next, a camera is put on the bottom of the ground and turned upward, and the rendering of the earth's surface is carried out. It is not necessary to write anything to a color component at this time. Rather, the purpose is just to write the depth value of the ground in the z-buffer. The next step is rendering the path volume. The rendering of the path volume is carried out twice. In the first pass, only the polygons of the path volume that face the camera are drawn with white (in fact, any color is sufficient as long as it is different from the color of the ground). In the second pass, only the polygons that face the reverse side of the camera are drawn with the same black color as the ground. In both passes of the path volume rendering, it is necessary to set the rendering states so that the z-buffer will *not* be written in but color components will be (we have to perform the z test still). Consequently, the area that was drawn by the first pass but not by the second (i.e., failed the z test) remains white in the collision map. This white area is exactly the domain where the ground and object contacted. (In Figure 5, for clarity, the ground is seen from across, whereas when actually performing the test, a camera is set just under the ground and a collision map that corresponds to a one-to-one relationship with the ground plane is created.)

  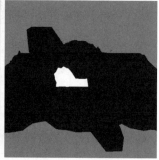

Figure 5: Rendering the front surface and the back surface and taking the difference between two images

When using a collision map along with a path volume to determine whether an object has collided, we need to handle the use of the asynchronous notification a bit differently. Because the path volume will have rendered pixels without a collision necessarily occurring, we need to count both the number of rendered pixels of the front-facing polygons and the number of rendered pixels of the back-facing polygons and take the difference between the two numbers.

This method of creating a collision map returns the right result only when rendering the path volume for a convex object. In the case of a concave object, if the indented portion has become sideways when drawing the front of the path volume, we have pixels that have been drawn to multiple times. At this time, the actual area of collision will be overwritten by the front polygon. When dealing with complicated objects that are not convex, it is necessary to find the difference between the rendering targets. A stencil buffer is often used for this more exact method. First, the value of a stencil buffer is filled with 0. When drawing the front surface of the path volume, the increment of the value of the stencil buffer is carried out; when drawing the back, the decrement of the value of the stencil buffer is carried out. The area where the back was not drawn by a z test failure but the front surface was is the area where the final value in the stencil buffer is not 0. (In some GPUs supporting the features of DirectX 9, such as the Radeon 9700 Pro, the rendering of the path volume can be completed by one drawing pass using the function of a two-sided stencil feature.) Since two or more objects can be processed repeatedly when a stencil buffer is used (without clearing a stencil buffer), there are many merits to using a stencil buffer. The only problem is that it is difficult to use asynchronous notification for the two-sided stencil buffer.

The created collision map can be used for special effects by the application. In Figure 6, a special effect that puts "flares" in the collision area is demonstrated.

Figure 6: Using a collision map, we draw "flares" in the areas where bullets hit the ground.

The collision map is a map that records an instantaneous collision and is updated with each frame. Since we want to burn all the places where the ground and the object have collided up until now, the created collision map is rendered to another map by addition composition. Initially, the accumulated map is completely black. If the collision maps are drawn one after another, at the end they will become pure white. That is, everyplace on the ground will blaze up.

Although flaring on this accumulated collision map is a problem completely different from collision detection, it is still an important visual problem. The method involves post-processing, which applies an effect in screen space. First, the accumulated collision map is transformed to coincide with the ground and then rendered to a screen-aligned texture. This makes the "burning" areas of the screen become white. Next, we combine this texture via multiplication composition with a random animated texture that we call "the seed of fire." This random animation means a wooden bit burns. However, with simple multiplication, the areas where the bullet collided with the ground only become bright on and off. In order to express the way the flame moves upward, a technique using an "afterimage" is used [James]. In order to make a flame, two screen-aligned textures are prepared for accumulation. We take the accumulated texture of one frame ago, reduce the intensity of its color, shift it upward in space a little, and render it to another accumulated texture. The current burning texture is drawn by addition composition as is. If the amount of color reduction is changed, this will affect the size of the flames. Since a flame slowly disappears when the color is reduced a little bit, a flame goes up high. Conversely, if the color is reduced greatly, it will quickly fade to 0 and a flame will hardly rise. If the created texture is drawn by addition composition on the whole screen at the end, the ground will blaze up red. This technique is a two-dimensional one and has a fault in that it does not account for areas where the flame should be obscured, such as those beyond a mountain.

Furthermore, in order to give additional realism, still another texture consisting of a blurred version of the accumulated collision map is created; using this, the ground darkens to represent the scorched areas. When rendering this texture on the ground, after blurring it in two dimensions, we transform it so that it coincides with the ground, like we did for the burning texture. In order to darken the area, we use subtractive composition with black.

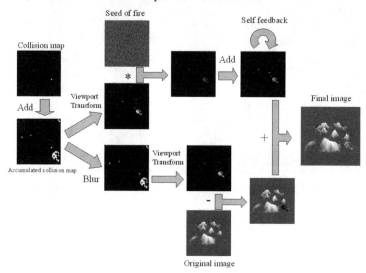

Figure 7: Rendering steps

Reflection by the Interaction

If the area of collision between two objects is known, it is natural to want to know how to calculate the interaction between them. Here, as one example, we consider an interaction from which a bullet rebounds from the ground.

If the incident velocity vector to the ground is set to v_{in}, and the normal vector of the ground is n, the velocity vector v_{out} after rebounding from the ground is set to $v_{out} = v_{in} - 2*(n, v_{in})n$.

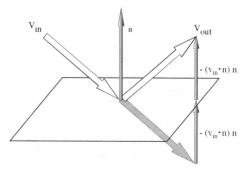

Figure 8: Vectors for velocity reflection

Therefore, an object can be reflected if the normal vector of the ground and the velocity before reflection are known.

Here, the problem is to determine the normal vector in the place where the bullet reflected. As long as a collision map is used, the place that collided can be determined only as an area rather than a single point. In order to find the normal, it is necessary to choose one point that collided by averaging the pixels of the area (i.e., find the centroid of the collision area). The alternative — averaging normal vectors over the collision area — can lead to anomalies. Consider the case where a bullet collides in the center of the sharp mountain. Although the place where the bullet hit may become level as an average of normal vectors, the summit of a mountain is not necessarily level. Thus, where a change of the normal vector in a nearby place is big, when the normal vector in the domain that collided is averaged, the normal vector that came out may become the value of a normal vector not existing in the original ground. Therefore, it is more reliable to choose specific coordinates and calculate the normal vector about the point.

In order to calculate the centroid, it is necessary to prepare two textures beforehand. One texture, called the coordinate map, is based on the image of the ground when seen from the bottom. Here, the texture coordinate values are output to the red and green color components of the texels, creating a linear ramp. Moreover, in the blue component, the value of 0.0f is written in the areas where the ground does not exist and 1.0f where it does. Another texture is the normal map, which maps screen coordinates to the texture coordinates. By using texture coordinates based on screen coordinates, it becomes possible to do a direct lookup in the normal map texture for the value of a normal vector directly.

In the preceding example, since only the normal vector was used in the collision response calculations, only the normal map was prepared. Sometimes we may also want to use the position of the model of the ground, such as when moving a bullet to the position of the surface of the ground so that it doesn't sink into the ground when it contacts. In this case, it is necessary to prepare another texture, which contains the value of the height or the geometry of the ground, that maps screen coordinates to the texture coordinates.

When a model without a texture is used (in other words, the model does not have texture coordinates), a suitable coordinate system should be chosen for the screen coordinate of a normal map and a height map of the ground, such as a world coordinate. It derives a normal vector from the place that collided without a texture coordinate.

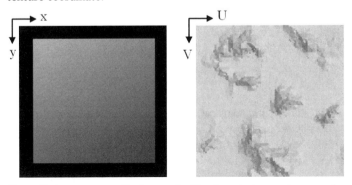

Figure 9: A texture coordinate map looking from below and a normal map

At each rendering cycle, the texture coordinates of the center of the collision area are calculated using the collision map and the coordinate map. We compute this efficiently by using hardware texture bilinear filtering, since we can think of filtering as computing the average of the values contained in a given area. First, we multiply our collision map texture with the coordinate map texture. However, the right result will not be obtained if we simply filter the composite texture consisting of the collision and coordinate maps. Since the domain in which we compute our average is the collision area, not the entire texture, we need to divide by the relative extent of the collision area.

We prepare a rendering target with a small size, similar to creating a mipmap. About the prepared rendering target, all texels to which the original texture corresponds are filtered — in effect, "averaging" the values contained in their color components. The blue component of the texture coordinate map is used for derivation of the collision area. Since a 1.0 is written where the ground exists for the blue component of a texture coordinates map, the blue component of the "averaged" texture represents the area of collision, where 0.0 would mean no collision area whatsoever and 1.0 would mean that the area of collision covered the entire ground plane.

When composition is performed together with the average operation, it is efficient. The final result, the texture coordinates of the centroid of the collision area, equals the xy (red and green) components of the filtered compound texture divided by the z (blue) component. Although the whole texture is multiplied by the constant, the result does not change. Therefore, efficient calculation of average values over an area can be performed if a sampling point is set as the center of four texels and the four texels are read by one sampling using a bilinear filter. Furthermore, the result will be valid even for a 2x2 rendering target. By sampling the center of the created texture, the average value of a texture can be calculated, and this can be used as a final result.

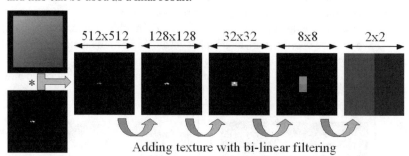

Adding texture with bi-linear filtering

Figure 10: Multiplying a texture coordinate map and collision map and subsequent averaging using bilinear filtering

If the normal map is sampled using the texture coordinates determined above, the normal vector of a point of collision is obtained.

In order to change direction of an object using a normal vector, we have to pass the derived normal vector to the collision response calculation. For a CPU-based calculation, we can access this data from the GPU by locking texture memory and doing a texture read or by using asynchronous notifications as described earlier. However, such methods are very slow and cannot be considered practical. It is hard to imagine that feedback of the data from the GPU to the CPU will become high speed in the future. Therefore, it is necessary to redesign an application so that these calculations normally performed by the CPU may be performed by the GPU.

The most important thing is memory that saves information. In terms of particle calculations, the CPU and the GPU are capable of almost the same thing. However, the memory that each can access directly is different. The CPU acquires information from the main memory, while the GPU acquires information from the video memory. We can use a texture as a means to read and write data in video memory. Thus, in order to replace particle calculation from the CPU to the GPU, the position and velocity of an object are recorded on a "particle map" texture. For example, the position of an object is saved in the top row of a texture and velocity is saved in the second row. When treating two or more objects, each object's attributes are arranged horizontally and indexed via the x-coordinate. Furthermore, the acceleration that acts on each particle is written in the row under the velocity. This storing of data in a texture is well suited for our purposes, since the row under each texel of a texture is the time derivative of the value represented by that texel. Similarly, the row above each texel represents the time integral of the values. If we denote position, velocity, and acceleration by x, v, and a, respectively, the operation that compounds by shifting a texture can be written with the following expression:

$$x = x + v$$
$$v = v + a$$

This formula represents the movement of the object over a unit of time, assuming constant acceleration. Processing, in which a texture is shifted and rendered, consists of only a one-pass rendering about the polygon of the size of the texture, which can be done very fast.

Particle index

0 1 2 3 ...

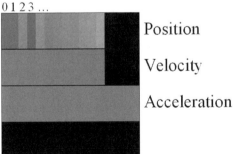

Position

Velocity

Acceleration

Figure 11: Particle map

The problem that remains is the calculation of acceleration. The acceleration value is what allows us to change the movement of an object in the scene. Although it is 0 at the time of a uniform straight-line motion when it reflects with the ground, we need to determine the proper acceleration to change the velocity to that represented by the reflected vector. The formula to use is 2*(n·v)n, which yields the expected behavior for reflection. Here, n is the normal vector calculated using the collision map. The HLSL program for deriving acceleration using a particle map is as follows.

```
float4 ReflectPS ( REFLECT_VS_OUTPUT In ) : COLOR0
{
    float4 acceleration;

    float4 coord = tex2D( CoordSamp, In.Tex0 );
    float4 velocity = 2.0f*tex2D( VelocitySamp, In.Tex1 )-1.0f;
    float  pixels = coord.z;
    coord /= pixels;
    float4 normal = 2.0f*tex2D( NormalSamp, coord )-1.0f;

    if(pixels<0.0000001f) {
        acceleration = 0; // no collision occurred
    } else {
        acceleration = -2.0f*dot(normal.xyz, velocity.xyz) * normal;
    }

    return 0.5f* acceleration + 0.5f;
}
```

The mapping of the interval [–1.0 to 1.0] into [0.0 to 1.0] centered on 0.5 is done for the value of the particle, or normal, map so that we can store them in a texture. This is unnecessary when using the floating-point format like D3DFME_A32B32G32R32F, which can save a sign to those textures. In addition, when a particle does not touch the ground or, in other words, when the drawn collision area is 0 (in this program, since it uses floating-point format, it considers this to be the case when pixels<0.0000001f, taking calculation error into consideration), since there is no reflection of a particle, it sets acceleration to 0, causing the motion of the particle to remain unchanged. Although this HLSL program is considering only the acceleration induced by reflection with the ground, external forces may exist as well, such as gravity. When calculating an external force, the additional acceleration contributed by this force should be added to the acceleration of the particle map by rendering using additive composition. Since +0.5 has already been carried out by reflective calculation with the ground at this time, it is not necessary to take an additional +0.5 when rendering external force.

When rendering the object, we need access to the particle map texture data in the vertex shader. In DirectX 9, there are two kinds of methods by which this can be done: displacement mapping and texture reads introduced by vs_3_0. For the displacement mapping method, it is necessary to add the D3DDECLUSAGE_ SAMPLE declaration, which maps the position data contained in the particle map texture to the vertex declaration.

```
D3DVERTEXELEMENT9 decl[] =
{
    {0,  0, D3DDECLTYPE_FLOAT3, D3DDECLMETHOD_DEFAULT, D3DDECLUSAGE_POSITION, 0},
```

```
    {0, 12, D3DDECLTYPE_FLOAT3, D3DDECLMETHOD_DEFAULT, D3DDECLUSAGE_NORMAL, 0},
    {0,24, D3DDECLTYPE_FLOAT2, D3DDECLMETHOD_DEFAULT, D3DDECLUSAGE_TEXCOORD, 0},
    {0, 32, D3DDECLTYPE_FLOAT2, D3DDECLMETHOD_LOOKUP, D3DDECLUSAGE_SAMPLE, 0},
    D3DDECL_END()
};
```

The texel coordinates of the position map are contained in this newly added vertex data. For example, if the width of the position map is defined as MAP_WIDTH, the texture coordinates about the i-th object are set to (i/MAP_WIDTH, 0). Since each instance of an object in a scene may refer to a different position of the texture, a solution would be to create additional copies of the mesh that differ in the position map texture index. However, since we can set the source of the displacement map-related vertex data to be another stream in DirectX, if only the data of texture coordinates differs about each mesh, we can save memory by avoiding redundant vertex data.

There can be a maximum of one texture used for displacement mapping that can be referred to in this manner as a variable from a vertex shader program. Here, position coordinate is used for this variable to refer to. However, we also need the velocity of the object for generating and extruding the path volume. When using the displacement mapping method, it's not possible to refer to multiple values in the particle map per vertex, and so we need to set the initial velocity through the CPU.

At the time this sample program was written, the vs_3_0 standard was not yet supported by existing DirectX hardware. Therefore, only the displacement mapping technique is demonstrated here. In addition, GPUs supporting floating-point textures and displacement mapping in hardware did not exist yet. The displacement mapping technique is a provisional one, and in the future, texture reads in vs_3_0 shaders will be the preferred method.

Conclusion

In this chapter, methods of collision detection and response by the GPU using an asynchronous notification and collision map were discussed. Both methods involve checking whether the rendering of the object has been carried out and judging if it has collided or not.

Since the sample program using this method is included on the companion CD, I encourage you to play with the source. (These programs have been checked on GeForce FX 5800 Ultra and Radeon 9700 Pro cards.)

One example that can use this method immediately is recording bullet marks as a texture in an FPS. As another example, in a race game, accurate depths of dents due to collisions could be recorded as a texture using a displacement map.

Currently, for an actual game, the GPU is insufficient for general processing, and the performance of the GPU can be used only for drawing. However, it is expected that using the GPU for purposes other than rendering, such as collision detection, will become possible in the future.

References

[Brennan] Brennan, Chris, "Shadow Volume Extrusion Using a Vertex Shader," *Direct3D ShaderX: Vertex and Pixel Shader Tips and Tricks,* Wolfgang Engel, ed., Wordware Publishing, Inc., 2002, pp. 188-194.

[James] James, Greg, "Operations for Hardware-Accelerated Procedural Texture Animation," *Game Programming Gems 2,* Charles River Media, Inc., 2001, pp. 497-509.

Displacement Mapping

Tom Forsyth
Mucky Foot Productions

Principles

Displacement mapping is essentially a method of geometry compression. A low-polygon base mesh is tessellated in some way. The vertices created by this tessellation are then displaced along a vector — usually the normal of the vertex. The distance that they are displaced is looked up in a 2D map called a displacement map.

The main aim of this article is to allow people to take data from the industry's current mesh and texture authoring pipelines and derive displacement map data from them. There will also be some discussion of rendering techniques on past, current, and future hardware.

It is worth mentioning that the problems and restrictions inherent in authoring for displacement maps are the same as those that occur when authoring for normal maps because they are essentially two different representations of the same thing. Generating normal maps has recently come into fashion, and there is plenty of hardware around to support it. If you are going to be generating normal maps, generating and using displacement map data is a relatively simple enhancement to the tool chain and rendering pipeline. As shown later, there is already widespread hardware support for at least some form of displacement mapping, new and faster hardware has been released recently, and there is, no doubt, even more direct support for displacement maps on the way.

Advantages

Using displacement maps reduces the amount of memory required for a given mesh level of detail. Bulky vertex data is replaced by a 2D array of displacements — typically 8 or 16 bits in size, with most attributes such as texture positions, tangent vectors, and animation weights implicit. This reduces storage requirements and the bandwidth needed to send that data to the rendering hardware, both of which are major limits on today's platforms. Alternatively, it allows much higher detail meshes to be stored or rendered in the same amount of memory space or bandwidth.

Reducing the mesh to a far simpler version (typically around a few hundred vertices rather than tens of thousands) means operations such as animation and morphing are cheaper. They can therefore be moved from the GPU back onto the

73

CPU, which is a much more general-purpose processor. Because of this, the range of possible operations is expanded — more complex animations are possible and different techniques used, such as multi-target morphing (for facial animation), volume-preservation (for bulging muscles), and cloth simulation. One other advantage is that the animation algorithms used are no longer tied to the specific GPU platform or to the lowest-common-denominator of platforms. Indeed, the animation programmer no longer needs to know the core details of the graphics platform to experiment with and implement new techniques.

A more abstract advantage is that using displacement maps turns meshes — tricky 3D entities with complex connectivity — into a few 2D entities. 2D objects (i.e., textures and images) have been studied extensively, and there are a lot of existing techniques that can now be applied to meshes. For example:

■ Mesh simplification and LOD becomes mipmap generation.

■ Compression can use frequency-based methods such as Fourier transforms or wavelets.

■ Procedural generation of meshes can use existing 2D fractal and image-compositing methods.

■ Morphing becomes a matter of blending 2D images together.

■ End-user customization involves 2D grayscale images rather than complex meshes.

Using graphics hardware and render-to-texture techniques, many of the above features can be further accelerated.

Disadvantages

Displacement maps place some restrictions on the meshes that can be authored and are not applicable everywhere. Highly angular, smooth, or faceted objects do not have much fine or complex surface detail and are better represented either by standard polygonal mesh data or some sort of curved surface representation, such as the Bezier family of curves or subdivision surfaces.

Highly crinkled or fractal data such as trees or plants are not easy to represent using displacement maps, since there is no good 2D parameterization to use over their surfaces.

Meshes that overlap closely or have folds in them can be a problem, such as collars, cuffs, or layers of material like jackets over shirts, or particularly baggy bits of material. This is because a displacement map can only hold a single height value. Although this is a problem at first, if artists can author or change the mapping of displacement maps, they can map each layer to a different part of the displacement map and duplicate each layer in the low-polygon base mesh. Automated tools are also easy to modify to do this correctly.

Authoring displacement maps almost always requires specialized tools — it is very hard to directly author the sort of maps discussed here (large-scale ones that cover a whole object). However, the amount of work required to write, adapt, or buy these tools is small compared to the benefits. The recommended tools are discussed below.

At first glance, hardware support is slim for displacement mapping. Currently, only two PC graphics cards support it natively (the Parhelia and members of the Radeon 9x00 series) and none of the consoles. However, with a bit of thought, displacement mapping methods can be applied to a much wider range of hardware. On the PC, anything using any sort of vertex shader can use them, including software VS pipelines used by many people for animation or bump-mapping on older cards. On the consoles, the VU units of the PS2 can use displacement maps directly, and any CPU with a SIMD-style instruction set (such as the GameCube's) can efficiently render displacement map data. On the consoles, the reduction in memory use and memory bandwidth is well worth the extra effort.

Required Source Data

To use displacement mapping in hardware or software, you eventually need the basic ingredients:

- A low-polygon base mesh
- A "unique" UV texture mapping for the base mesh
- A heightfield displacement map for displacement of vertices
- A normal map for lighting

Typically, displacement maps are lower resolution than normal maps, though they may demand more precision. Additionally, displacement maps and normal maps usually share the same mapping, since the same problems must be solved by both — filtering (especially mipmapping), representation of discontinuities, texel resolution at appropriate places on a mesh, and assigning each texel a unique position on the mesh.

How you get these basic ingredients is almost entirely up to the art team and the available tools. They are available from many sources in many combinations.

For reference, all vertex numbers given are for a human figure that would normally take around 10,000 vertices to represent with a raw mesh with around 40 bones. Typically, there are twice as many triangles as vertices in a mesh.

Low-Polygon Base Mesh

As a guide, this mesh is around 100 vertices for a human figure, depending on the quality of animation required and the complexity of the clothing. The artists can directly author this mesh, or it can be derived from higher-polygon meshes by using a variety of mesh simplification techniques. These may be completely automatic, or they may be semiautomatic with visual checks and tweaks by artists.

There are many methods to automatically reduce meshes in complexity. Those based on half-edge collapses are popular, especially as they can also be used to directly author progressive mesh sequences, which are useful for rendering continuous levels of detail on older hardware. Other options include using Delaunay-style parameterization and remeshing and also voxelizing the mesh and remeshing from appropriately filtered voxel data.

Unique Texture Mapping

Displacement and normal maps generally require a mapping over the mesh, which ensures that each texel is used no more than once. Although not strictly necessary in some specialized cases (for example, when an object has perfect left/right symmetry), in general the extra flexibility is well worth the effort.

The unique mapping can be authored directly, using a spare mapping channel in the mesh. Automated generation is possible using the variety of "texture atlas" methods that exist, including the same Delaunay-style parameterization as the above remeshing or using the technique in Gu's "Geometry Images" [1] of a minimal number of cuts to unfold and flatten a mesh onto a square plane.

There are also existing unique mapping solutions in 3D authoring tools, such as 3ds max's "flatten" mapping. However, it is important to note that it is not the high-polygon mesh that needs the unique mapping but the low-polygon version. Unique-mapping the high-polygon mesh can work in some cases, but it tends to introduce a lot of unwanted discontinuities, which hinder many of the polygon-reduction techniques used to produce the low-polygon base mesh. If the mesh simplification is a plug-in for the authoring package, that can be performed first, before unique mapping. Alternatively, the mesh can be exported, simplified by external tools, and reimported for unique mapping. Although clumsy, this does have the advantage that the artists can tweak the automated unique mapping — sometimes a useful ability.

The unique mapping can also be used for lightmap generation or procedural textures, if required.

Heightfield Displacement Map and Normal Map

Displacement maps can be authored directly using grayscale textures and suitable art tools. However, 8 bits per pixel is generally not sufficient for a high-precision displacement map, and few if any art packages handle 16-bit grayscales. Even when they do, since they are designed for visual use rather than heightfield authoring, the control over the values is relatively coarse, and it is hard for artists to achieve anything but an approximation of the correct shape. In practice, this leads to "caricatures" of the object.

A better choice is to author most or all of the data using a high-polygon mesh. Using the unique mapping above, each texel on the displacement and normal maps has a single position on the low-polygon base mesh. A ray is cast from that position along the interpolated low-polygon normal and the intersection found with the high-polygon mesh. The normal of the high-polygon mesh is written into the normal map, and the distance along the ray to the point of intersection is written into the displacement map. Remember that these distances may be negative — the ray needs to trace both outward and inward from the low-polygon mesh, as shown in Figure 1.

When creating the high-polygon mesh, the artists still need to be aware that they are indirectly authoring a heightfield. Folding or overlaps of geometry will not be recorded well by a heightfield. In practice, we find it is better to have the ray-caster report difficult or ambiguous intersection cases and have the artists fix

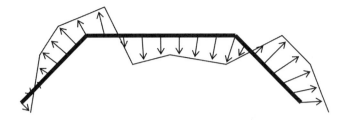

——— High-polygon mesh

████ Low-polygon mesh

——→ Displacements stored in map

Figure 1: A displacement map applies scalar offsets along the interpolated normals of a base mesh.

the mesh (either the high- or low-polygon ones as appropriate) than to attempt to make the ray-caster very intelligent. These tricky cases are rare, and this method highlights them rather than trying to hide them, reducing unwanted surprises.

Normal maps (either object-space or surface-local space) are almost impossible to author directly but are easily generated from displacement maps or bump maps. Although a bump map is actually a heightfield and is essentially the same thing as a displacement map, since absolute scale is far less important when generating normal maps than when displacing positions, they are routinely generated by hand.

High-frequency displacement and normal maps are fairly easy to author by using bump maps. These are used to provide texture to a surface or add small ridges or creases, such as those between panels of a car body. These are often applied to medium-polygon meshes to add fine details, rather than to the low-polygon mesh that is used in displacement mapping. It is easy to apply them to existing or generated displacement and normal maps, as long as there is already a unique texture mapping. The high frequency implies small displacements, so the lack of a well-controlled scale for those displacements is not as much of a problem. Having a crease in clothing twice as large as desired is not a major problem, unlike having a character's nose twice as long as it should be. Note that the mapping of these high-frequency maps is kept flexible on the artist's end. They do not need to be uniquely mapped, and it is perfectly acceptable to tile a small bump map over a larger surface to provide noise and detail. They will be rendered into the normal and displacement maps by the ray-caster, and it is those that are uniquely mapped.

Mucky Foot Choices

At Mucky Foot we tend to author medium-polygon meshes (around 3,000 vertices for humans) with high-frequency bump maps. It is more efficient for the artists to put small creases and surface texture into a bump map than it is to generate them with polygonal creases, and it is just as visually effective. It also reduces the problem of high-frequency polygon data confusing the ray-caster and causing multiple intersections.

For some objects, we author the unique mappings directly. Manual unique mapping is typically used on objects such as people, since they are already mapped fairly uniquely, except for left/right symmetry. This is easily fixed by selecting the right half of the part of the object that has been mapped this way (typically everything below the neck) and adding 1 to either the U or V value of the texture coordinates. Since these meshes use texture wrap address mode by default (as opposed to clamp-to-edge), this does not affect the diffuse, specular, etc., texture maps, but it does create a unique mapping for use by the displacement map. This mapping is then packed (see below) for better texel efficiency.

For other objects, we generate unique mapping automatically using fairly standard "texture atlas" creation techniques. In some cases, such as buildings, 3ds max's "flatten" tool mostly does a good enough job and has the benefit that the artists can directly tweak any problem areas. In other cases, this produces too many seams (or takes too much time to fix up by hand), and we first reduce the mesh to the low-polygon base mesh version and then uniquely map the object using our own texture atlas code.

To produce a low-polygon base mesh, Mucky Foot uses a quadric error metric-based semiautomatic edge-collapse sequence that is visually checked and manually tweaked where necessary. Fully automated reduction is generally acceptable down to around 500 vertices, and then manual tweaking can be required in a few places to reduce to around 100 vertices. The tweaking is generally required to collapse features that are visually less important, such as the feet, or prevent collapse of perceptually important features, such as the face, elbows, knees, and hands. Automation of these (for example, taking bone weights into account) was attempted with mixed results. It seems generally quicker and better simply to allow the artists full control by this stage; frequently, the extra "intelligence" of the tool gets in the way. Production of a low-polygon mesh typically takes around 30 minutes per human mesh, which compares well with the initial authoring time.

As well as producing the low-polygon base mesh, this process also generates a view-independent progressive mesh, which is useful when rendering the mesh on some hardware (see below). The same tool also produces VIPM sequences for objects that do not use displacement maps — simple or smooth objects such as coffee mugs, dustbins, chairs, and tables.

The high- or mid-polygon meshes that the artists author are only used as input to the offline ray-caster; they are not used directly at run time. Because of this, the limits imposed by the rendering pipeline on polygon counts are almost totally removed. The new limit on polygon count is simply whatever the artists have time to author. The limits on connectivity, large or small polygon sizes, and mesh complexity are also largely removed — as long as a sensible low-polygon base mesh can be produced. Games are getting bigger and becoming more limited by what we have the time, talent, and manpower to author, rather than by the hardware, and this extra flexibility allows the artists to optimize for their time rather than for the peculiarities of a graphics engine.

Although we use our own VIPM and texture atlas libraries, it should be noted that they are fairly standard algorithms, and many of the tools mentioned later would do just as good a job. We use our own code simply because it was already written and is now well integrated with our tool chain.

Art Tools

We found a number of tools handy when authoring displacement maps. Many of these tools have other uses, such as the QEM-based edge collapser which also generates view-independent progressive mesh data. Some of them already exist in various forms, and experimenting with these off-the-shelf solutions is a very good idea. Many produce readily usable data, while others make useful test cases before committing to writing custom tools.

Displacement Map Previewer

If displacement maps are authored directly, some sort of preview tool is usually needed. Some 3D packages may have displacement map renderers included, but if not, it is fairly simple to write a brute-force previewer that simply tessellates the base mesh to the resolution of the displacement map — one quad per texel. Although it is a lot of triangles to draw, it is not unreasonable if done on a single object at a time. A 512x512 map requires half a million triangles to render, which can be done at acceptable speeds on most decent PC graphics cards.

If displacement maps are extracted from a high-polygon mesh, this previewer is usually not necessary.

Unique Mapping Checker

When creating unique texture mappings manually, it is easy to accidentally map two areas of mesh to the same bit of texture. This is easily solved by rendering the mesh to a texture using the UV mapping as XY coordinates, counting each time a particular texel is touched. Where a texel is touched more than once, render an opaque red texel. Otherwise, render a translucent blue texel. When the mesh is loaded back into a 3D modeling package and the texture applied to it, any red/opaque texels show where the problem spots are. As there will be red texels in both places that conflict, it is easy to spot and correct the overlap.

This tool is usually a special mode of the ray-caster, since both rasterize base-mesh polygons onto a uniquely mapped texture. The difference is that the ray-caster does a lot more work to decide what data to write to the texels.

Ray-caster

The ray-caster rasterizes base-mesh triangles to the displacement and normal maps. For each texel, it casts a ray from the texel's position on the base mesh (after interpolation by whatever basis is used — linear, N-Patches, subdivision surface, etc.) along the normal, looking for the best intersection with the high-polygon mesh. "Best" is defined by various heuristics. It is usually the nearest intersection to the base mesh, though if multiple intersections are close together, this often indicates a high-frequency part of the mesh that folds back on itself or a mesh "decal" where smaller polygonal details have been added over a coarser part of the mesh. Usually, the furthest of these bunched intersections is used. This heuristic will take some tweaking — alternatively, it is often wise to highlight problem areas so that the artists can manually check and tweak them.

The ray-caster takes the normal of the high-polygon mesh, modifies it by any applied bump map, and writes it to the normal map.

It takes the distance along the ray from the base mesh to the intersection and writes that value into the displacement map. Any high-frequency bump map applied to the high-polygon mesh will also modify the displacement at this stage as a "detail" displacement map. In theory, a bump map should perturb the high-polygon mesh and alter where the ray intersects it. However, we have found that simply adding the bump map height onto the intersection distance produces perfectly acceptable results, as long as the bump map has a small displacement scale and is only used for creases and small bumps, rather than major features.

After the ray-caster has written texel data to the normal and displacement maps, the maps are usually sent through a dilation filter, which spreads written values outward to any neighboring unwritten texels. This fills in the gaps between mapped areas with sensible data and ensures that filtering still brings in sensible data, especially when mipmapping.

ATI's Normal Mapper [2], nVidia's Melody, and Crytek's PolyBump [3] all do this ray-casting, though at the time of publication all only output normal maps. It would be simple to modify them to output displacement data as well, and this support is planned for them. All include a variety of heuristics to decide the "best" ray intersection to use for various cases.

Unique Mapping Packer

There are two problems in unique mapping. One is to get a unique mapping so that no texel is used in two places, and the other is to pack the many small areas of connected triangle "patches" together on the texture in the most efficient way. The first can be solved by automation, but human intervention is frequently necessary, and it involves some judgment calls. Fortunately, these decisions are usually easy and quick for humans to make.

The second part — equivalent to the problem of packing odd shapes in a box — is tedious for humans. But because it involves no perceptive judgment calls, it is simple to leave a computer crunching away through possible solutions (possibly overnight) until it finds a good one. To reduce "bleeding" between patches due to filtering (especially mipmapping), patches must be separated by certain minimum numbers of texels. After packing, these texels are filled with the value of the nearest used texel (again so that filtering does not bring in undefined values).

Where unique texturing is generated or tweaked by hand, this automatic packing allows artists to concentrate on the task of uniquely mapping an object. They do not have to simultaneously keep all the bits optimally packed — they can scatter them all over the UV domain and arrange them for easier mental labeling (all the parts of one type together, etc.).

A further enhancement is to analyze the frequency of the displacement and normal map data in each triangle patch and scale them up or down to allocate more texture space to the areas with the higher frequency data. By packing the patches together after this scaling, a given size of displacement or normal map will be spread over the object with more texels applied to detailed areas.

It is important to not completely remove the artist-determined scales. A maximum grow/shrink factor of two in each UV axis is sufficient to ensure good use of available space but allows artists to deliberately allocate extra texel space to areas of high importance, such as the face and hands of people, and reduce perceptually minor parts, such as the undersides of cars, which are very crinkly but not very visible (unless it's that sort of game, of course!).

Note that this scaling implies a slightly more complex pipeline. First the patches are packed together without scaling. This is just to get them all onto a single map of reasonable size — the packing does not need to be very efficient. Then the ray-caster is run to produce a first approximation of the displacement and normal map data. For quick previews, that data is then used directly for display.

For final artwork, the frequency of the data in each patch is determined, and the patches are scaled accordingly and repacked — possibly with a more expensive or thorough algorithm. Then the ray-caster is run again with this new optimal mapping, usually with a very high-resolution map. The large map is then filtered down to the actual size stored on disk. This second pass is typically run on a batch job overnight, which means it can devote a lot of time to finding near-optimal packing and use really big maps for the ray-casting phase, removing as many sampling artifacts as possible.

Alternative methods of optimizing texture space for signal frequency are given by Sander et al. [4].

Mesh Reduction

Mesh reduction is probably the trickiest tool to get right since it usually needs to have an interactive element to it and it relies on a lot of heuristics.

The most common mesh-reduction techniques are based on incremental edge or half-edge collapses. This technique produces a progressive mesh [5] as it works, which can be used for rendering continuous level of detail meshes. Many heuristics exist to decide the order of edge collapses, most based on the quadric error metric by Garland and Heckbert [6] or modifications of it by Hoppe [7].

An increasing number of existing tools can be used for this:

- The Direct3DX library PMesh interface
- Melody tool by nVidia [8]
- Galaxy3 source library by Charles Bloom [9]
- Source code to my article "Comparison of VIPM Methods" in *Game Programming Gems 2* [12]

The above all use edge-collapse methods. Alternatively, there are various styles of remeshing using Delaunay triangulation [10] or voxelizing and remeshing.

Rendering

Once the basic data of a low-polygon mesh, a displacement map, a normal map, and a mapping for the maps is obtained, the data can be processed for the capabilities of the target hardware. Much of the details are either proprietary (in the case of consoles) or have been discussed elsewhere (in the case of my "displacement compression" techniques [11]), so only brief outlines are given here. Fortunately, this processing rarely requires any human intervention and is fairly simple number crunching. I address each platform separately.

The techniques for rendering normal maps are fairly standard between most of these platforms. The exception (as always) is the PlayStation 2, but again these details are proprietary.

Adaptive Displacement Mapping

■ Matrox Parhelia, future hardware

Make mipmaps of the displacement map and render the low-polygon mesh with the displacement map. If necessary, feed some distance-related or perceptual biases into the adaptive tessellator. The hardware does the rest.

Pre-sampled Displacement Mapping

■ ATI Radeon 9700, maybe PlayStation 2, and GameCube

Offline, regularly and uniformly tessellate the base mesh in software and sample the displacement map at the generated vertices. This produces an array of $n(n+1)/2$ displacements for each triangle on the base mesh. These values are swizzled in a hardware-specified manner into a linear stream fed to the vertex shader unit. At run time, the vertex shader unit performs this tessellation itself, reads the values from the displacement stream, and draws the final displaced vertices.

To perform level of detail transitions, repeat the above process for a variety of different tessellation amounts (generally the powers of two), giving an effective "mipmap chain" of displacement streams. This allows discrete LOD transitions, though with some popping as the mesh switches from one tessellation level to the next.

To remove the popping, each displacement stream entry holds two displacements rather than one. The first holds the standard displacements, and the second holds the upsampled displacements from the lower LOD tessellation. In the vertex shader (or equivalent), a per-mesh scalar interpolates between the two sets of displacements. Just using these upsampled values should give a mesh that is visually identical to the lower LOD version. As an object goes away from the camera, this allows the high LOD version to smoothly morph into the low LOD version and then the low LOD version swaps in with no visual popping but reducing the triangle and vertex count.

Because this method samples the displacement map in a predictable manner, you may get some improvement in quality by ray-casting at the required positions directly rather than going via a displacement map. This also means that a unique mapping is not required for displacements, since there is no actual 2D displacement map but simply a displacement stream for each triangle of the base mesh. However, a unique mapping is still required for the normal map.

The Radeon 9500-9800 series are currently the only cards to explicitly support this method, though it seems possible that the PlayStation 2 and GameCube could also implement it with a bit of work. As with all things on the PS2, it depends heavily on the rest of the rendering pipeline being used.

Displacement Compression

■ All PC cards with hardware vertex shader support (nVidia GeForce 3 and better, ATI Radeon 8500 and better, and others), GameCube, Xbox, PlayStation 2, software vertex shader pipelines on DX6 or better cards

The base mesh vertices are uploaded to the memory of the vertex unit rather than in a standard mesh/vertex stream. This may need to be done in multiple sections because of limited vertex unit memory, with each section drawn before the next is uploaded.

Tessellation of the mesh is performed offline to whatever degree required, and the tessellated vertices and/or indices are fed in as a standard mesh. The difference is that rather than holding a raw vertex position, normal, texture coordinates, etc., each vertex stores only the following data:

■ Three indices to three base-mesh vertices

■ Two barycentric coordinates that interpolate between the base-mesh vertices

■ A displacement value

This reduces the size of a vertex to 6 bytes (though many systems require padding of the vertices up to 8 bytes). The vertex unit interpolates position, normal, texture coordinates, tangent vectors, and so on from the given three base-mesh vertices and the two barycentric coordinates. The vertex is then displaced along the interpolated normal.

It is important to realize that this method does not require the hardware to tessellate the mesh. All tessellation is performed offline, and a fairly standard mesh renderer is used. The difference is that the vertices are compressed using the data from the displacement map.

Interpolation can be performed using any basis, but linear and bicubic are common. Linear interpolation is fine for most objects, though highly animated objects may benefit from using an N-Patch-style basis because it is relatively smooth, even under heavy mesh distortion.

As with presampled displacement mapping, there is no actual 2D displacement map (the displacements are held by the vertices themselves), so the displacement for each vertex can be sampled directly using the ray-caster if desired.

Level of detail transitions can be done using the same trick as with presampled displacement mapping — storing two displacements per vertex and lerping between them — or using view-independent progressive meshes. Mucky Foot currently uses the lerping method on the PlayStation 2; on other platforms with indexed primitive support, we use "sliding window" VIPM [12].

In some cases, the interpolated texture coordinates (used for the diffuse and normal maps) are slightly distorted from the desired coordinates. The simple solution is to add 2 bytes to the vertex format that offset the UV values from the interpolated ones. This brings the vertex size up to 8 bytes. On the PC, vertices are required to be multiples of 4 bytes anyway, and on other platforms, the larger vertices are still a substantial improvement on traditional mesh data. The other option is to distort the diffuse maps slightly to correct for this effect — this fits in easily with some pipelines.

It is possible to reformulate this method so that instead of sending base-mesh vertices to the vertex unit, base-mesh triangles are sent. Each displaced vertex then only needs a single index to determine which triangle it is on. This reduces the possible size of vertices down to 4 bytes. However, since there are typically more triangles then vertices in the base mesh, more information is required to store a triangle, and vertex unit storage space is typically at a premium, this may be slower except for highly tessellated objects with simple base meshes.

Start-of-Day Tessellation

■ Slow CPUs with DX5 or earlier graphics cards, software rasterizers, laptops, PDAs, mobile phones

These devices do not have enough polygon throughput and/or CPU power to use run-time displacement mapping to any useful extent. However, you can tessellate and displace the data using software either at installation time or at start of day. By tessellating according to the CPU speed of the machine and tessellating multiple versions of each mesh, you still gain the advantages of adapting polygon count to the scene complexity, machine capability, and the size of each mesh on the screen without having to author them directly.

If the data is delivered on a format with reduced bandwidth or size (for example, over a modem or on a multi-game "sampler" disk) you gain the excellent compression and space savings that come with using displacement and normal maps.

On really slow hardware, the low-polygon base map is just used directly with no tessellation at all.

Some software rasterizers may be able to do normal mapping, and some hardware may be able to use the displacement map data to do emboss bump-mapping. Otherwise, it is easy to do a prelighting phase applied to the normal map with the mesh in its default pose and light coming from above to give lights and shadows in appropriate places. While not strictly correct, it produces images easily acceptable by the standards of the available hardware but does not cost any extra authoring time to produce.

Summary

Displacement mapping reduces memory use and increases mesh detail. Once displacement maps are authored, highly scalable content is easy to generate automatically, allowing an application to use very long view distances, more complex scenes, a wide variety of platforms, and (to an extent) future-proof itself and the art assets for future hardware.

The difficulties of authoring displacement maps directly are reduced to a far more manageable pipeline with a few simple tools and a small amount of artist training. Previously, greater effort was frequently taken when authoring and re-authoring different levels of detail for different platforms or to rebalance processing load for specific scenes. Almost all of the difficulties with displacement maps are shared by the generation of normal maps — if generating one, you can frequently get the other with very little effort.

Despite appearances, there is already wide hardware support for displacement maps — all the current consoles and almost all "gamer" PC hardware. Newer hardware allows more efficient implementations of displacement mapping, but any of the methods listed give speed and size advantages over raw mesh rendering.

References

[1] Gu, X., S. Gortler, and H. Hoppe, "Geometry Images," ACM SIGGRAPH '02, pp. 355-361.

[2] ATI Normal Mapper tool, available from http://mirror.ati.com/developer/index.html.

[3] Crytek PolyBump package, http://www.crytek.com/.

[4] Sander, P., S. Gortler, J. Snyder, and H. Hoppe, "Signal-specialized parametrization," Eurographics Workshop on Rendering 2002, http://research.microsoft.com/~hoppe/.

[5] Hoppe, H., "Progressive meshes," ACM SIGGRAPH '96, pp. 99-108.

[6] Garland, M. and P. Heckbert, "Surface simplification using quadric error metrics," SIGGRAPH '97 Proceedings, Aug. 1997.

[7] Hoppe, H., "New quadric metric for simplifying meshes with appearance attributes," *IEEE Visualization* 1999, October 1999, pp. 59-66.

[8] Melody tool by nVidia, www.nvidia.com.

[9] Galaxy3 source library by Charles Bloom, http://www.cbloom.com/3d/galaxy3/.

[10] Eck, M., T. DeRose, T. Duchamp, H. Hoppe, M. Lounsbery, and W. Stuetzle, "Multiresolution analysis of arbitrary meshes," *Computer Graphics*, 1995.

[11] Forsyth, T., "Where Have All the Bumpmaps Gone" (Meltdown 2000) and "Highly Scalable Character Rendering" (Meltdown 2001), available at http://www.tomforsyth.pwp.blueyonder.co.uk/.

[12] Forsyth, T., "Comparison of VIPM Methods," *Game Programming Gems 2*, Charles River Media, 2001.

Section II

Rendering Techniques

Rendering Objects as Thick Volumes

Greg James
nVidia

Introduction

This article presents a convenient and flexible technique for rendering ordinary polygon objects of any shape as thick volumes of light-scattering or light-absorbing material. Vertex and pixel shaders are used in multipass rendering to generate a measure of object thickness at each pixel. These thicknesses are then used to produce the colors of the object on screen. For example, we can render a volumetric shaft of light by creating a simple polygonal model of the light shaft. Each frame, new thickness information for this object is rendered from the current point of view, and the thicknesses are converted to colors. The result is a true volumetric rendering of the object suitable for interactive dynamic scenes.

The technique can be implemented on hardware that supports Microsoft's pixel shaders version 1.3 or higher and runs at real-time frame rates in complex scenes. No preprocessing or special treatment of the volume object geometry is required, making it trivial to animate and distort the volume objects. An efficient and simple method is given to properly render any volume objects, convex or concave, and handle complex intersection cases where opaque objects of any shape penetrate the volumes. This article also introduces a new method of dithering to eliminate the effects of aliased thickness information. The dithering is accomplished using texture data, and it does not complicate the rendering or require additional passes.

This article focuses on rendering based on the thickness visible from the current viewpoint. This is suitable for volumes of single-scattering material. In this case, each bit of light arriving at the viewpoint is the result of only one scattering interaction within the object, and the total amount of light is a function of the total thickness. As the visible thickness increases, the number of scatterers or the chance of scattering increases. The scattering can both add light and attenuate light as a function of thickness. More sophisticated models of scattering could be employed but will not be presented here. Hoffman and Preetham have a good demo and introduction to various types of scattering [Hoffman02].

The appearance of the volume objects is easy to control, and an artist-created color ramp can be used to map object thickness to color. While the technique treats objects as volumes of constant density, the color ramp allows us to map increasing thickness to an exponential ramp, overbright saturated colors, or any

89

arbitrary colors. The technique is being used in several upcoming games and has great promise for bringing practical volumetric effects to interactive real-time rendering.

The Big Picture

This technique is a significant departure from traditional 3D rendering. It involves rendering to off-screen textures, rendering depth information as RGBA colors, using simple vertex shader programs and textures to encode information, and using alpha blending to add and subtract high-precision encoded depth information. Rather than jump into detailed discussion right away let's begin with an overview of the complete rendering process, so you can clearly see what's involved and how the technique compares to other approaches.

The full implementation of the technique is illustrated in Figure 1. These steps render any volumetric shape, handle all solid objects intersecting the volumes, dither the thickness information, and handle any camera position in the scene, whether the camera is inside or outside of the volumes or solid objects. Rendering proceeds as follows and is covered in greater detail later in the article:

1. Opaque objects are rendered to the ordinary back buffer. See Figure 1a.

2. The view-space depth of opaque objects that might intersect the volume objects is rendered to a texture that we label O. Depth is encoded as RGBA colors. See Figure 1b.

3. All volume object back faces are rendered to texture B using additive RGBA blending to sum the depths. A pixel shader samples O while rendering each triangle in order to handle intersections. See Figure 1c.

4. All volume object front faces are rendered to texture F while sampling O to handle intersections. See Figure 1d.

5. Textures B and F are sampled to compute the volume thickness, convert this to color, and blend the color to the scene rendered in Step 1. See Figure 1e.

One of the advantages of this technique is that the rendering does not have to change in order to handle various intersection cases and camera positions. No extra passes or knowledge about the objects is required as long as the depth complexity of the volume objects remains below a certain adjustable limit. A later section presents this in greater detail, but the depth complexity limit depends on the precision of the thickness information. This can be adjusted from frame to frame. A depth complexity of 16 or 32 volume object faces can be rendered at high precision with no additional passes.

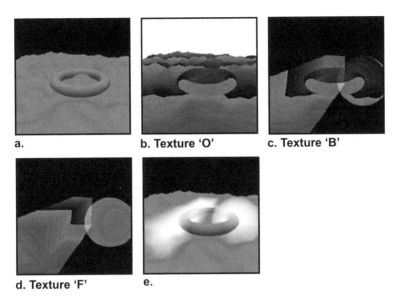

a.   **b. Texture 'O'**   **c. Texture 'B'**

d. Texture 'F'   **e.**

Figure 1: Overview of the rendering steps. Five rendering passes produce correct results for all cases where volume objects intersect opaque objects and for all camera locations inside or outside of the objects. One additional pass (not shown) is required for hardware that does not support pixel shaders 2.0.

Computing Thickness

First, we need a way to get thickness information from ordinary polygon hulls. Dan Baker presents a technique for this in the Microsoft DirectX 8.1 SDK VolumeFog example [Baker02]. His approach can be extended in a number of ways, but the basic approach is to calculate thickness by subtracting the view-space depth of an object's front faces from the depth of the back faces. The depths of an object's faces are rendered to off-screen render targets, and the thickness is computed from information in the render targets. At any given pixel, if we sum the depths of all of an object's front faces at that pixel and sum the depths of all back faces, the thickness through the object is the back face sum minus the front face sum. This is illustrated in Figure 2.

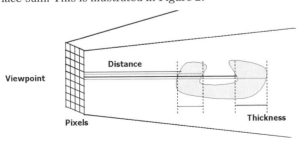

Figure 2: For a given pixel on screen, the thickness through the object is the sum of the depths of all front faces at that pixel subtracted from the sum of the depths of all back faces at that pixel.

Depth is calculated at each vertex as part of the standard 3D view transform. This is interpolated for standard Z-buffer rendering, but the Z-buffer information is not practical to use for this technique. It is too costly in terms of performance, and the graphics APIs have no flexibility for summing and differencing the Z-buffer information. Attempting to manipulate the information on our own would require decompressing and copying the GPU data across to the CPU for processing. This would break the parallelism of the two processors, stall the GPU, and burden the CPU unnecessarily.

Instead, we can use standard RGBA 8-bit color rendering and additive blending to accomplish the thickness calculations entirely on the GPU. A high-precision depth value can be split up and encoded across the color channels of an RGBA-8 color. I'll refer to this as RGB-encoding of the depth information. Standard blend operations can then sum the encoded values. This allows us to process and sum, for example, 12-bit or 18-bit depth information using commonplace RGBA-8 render targets.

The latest generation of consumer GPUs (the GeForce FX and Radeon 9800 series) has introduced support for rendering high-precision color information with up to 32 bits per color component for a total of 128 bits per RGBA color. Unfortunately, these chips do not support additive blending of these high-precision colors, so they are not capable of performing the depth sums as efficiently or quickly as with RGBA-8 additive blending.

RGB-Encoding of Values

A standard RGBA-8 render target can do a fantastic job of storing and accumulating high-precision scalar (1D) values. The bits of a number can be split across the 8-bit red, green, blue, and alpha color channels using any number of the low bits of each channel. When the bits of a number are split across the R, G, and B colors, I call it an RGB-encoded value. A particular case is illustrated in Figure 3, where a 15-bit number is split into three 5-bit color values. The precision at which we can encode values is given by the number of low bits, L, that we use in each color channel multiplied by the number of color channels. For example, if we use four low bits (L=4) from each R, G, and B channel, we can encode 12-bit values (3*4).

It's important to note that we use only a few of the lowest bits of each color channel to encode any single value. The remaining high bits are left empty so that when two or more values are added, the low bits can carry over into the unused high bits. RGB-encoded values can be added together using standard RGBA blend operations until all the bits of any color channel are full. At that point, any further additions will be lost because the bits of one color channel do not carry into the other channels. The number of high "carry" bits in each color channel is (8-L), and the number of RGB-encoded values we can add together without error is 2^{8-L}. There is a tradeoff between the precision that we can encode and the number of encoded values that can be added together. For our case of encoding a 15-bit value (L=5), we have three carry bits, so we can sum at most eight values into any given RGBA-8 color. Figure 3 includes a table relating precision to the number of values that can be safely added.

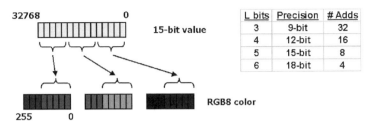

Figure 3: Encoding a 15-bit value using five low bits (L=5) of each 8-bit R, G, and B color channel. The diagram on the right relates the number of low bits, L, to the precision of each value and the number of encoded values that can be added into an RGB-8 color before error occurs due to saturating all of the bits of a particular color channel.

Figure 4 illustrates the RGB-encoding applied to a steadily increasing value. The RGB-encoded value is the sum of the R, G, and B ramps at a point along the axis. Only two bits per color channel are used to better illustrate the relationship of the colors, and a scheme is used where blue holds the least significant bits, green holds the middle significant bits, and red holds the most significant bits. Thus, the green values go through one cycle each time red increases by one bit, and blue cycles once for each green increment.

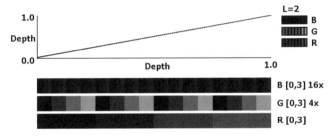

Figure 4: Encoding 6-bit depth values using two low bits (L=2) of each channel of an RGB-8 color. Depth varies from 0 to 1 from the near clipping plane to the far clipping plane and is encoded by adding the blue, green, and red color ramps shown. At a depth of 1.0, the color is RGB=(3,3,3) out of the full (255, 255, 255) range, and at 0.75, the color is (3,0,0).

Applying this RGB-encoding of depth to the simple scene in Figure 5a gives the result shown in Figure 5b. Here, four bits are used from each color channel. The RGB colors are displayed overbright because in practice the low bit values of each color would appear mostly black. Red values are too low to be noticeable in Figure 5b, but if the objects extended farther toward the far clip plane, the red values would become noticeable. In practice, the RGB-encoded depths are rendered to an off-screen texture render target. This allows us to read back the depths in later rendering operations, which is important for handling solid objects that intersect the volumes of fog.

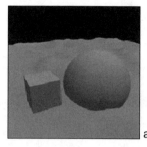 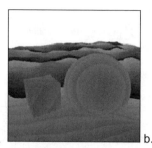

a.   b.

Figure 5: Objects rendered with a) traditional shading and b) RGB-encoded depth rendering at 12 bits of precision (L=4). The RGB-encoded colors are shown overbright, as their actual range, in this case from [0, 16] out of [0, 255], would appear mostly black.

RGB-encoding is easy to achieve using programmable vertex shaders and small color ramp textures. The encoding can be applied to any per-vertex scalar that we compute in a vertex shader, but here all we care about is the per-vertex depth. The vertex shader computes a depth value at each vertex as part of the standard 3D transform from object space to homogenous clip space (HCLIP space), as shown in the following vertex shader assembly code VS 1:

```
DP4 r1.x, V_POSITION, c[CV_WORLDVIEWPROJ_0]                    (VS 1)
DP4 r1.y, V_POSITION, c[CV_WORLDVIEWPROJ_1]
DP4 r1.z, V_POSITION, c[CV_WORLDVIEWPROJ_2]
DP4 r1.w, V_POSITION, c[CV_WORLDVIEWPROJ_3]
MOV oPos, r1
```

V_POSITION is the input vertex position in object space, and CV_WORLD-VIEW-PROJ_<N> are the elements of the standard 4x4 transform-and-project matrix used in 3D rendering. The r1.w component is the vertex's distance to the camera plane (not the radial distance to the camera and not the distance to the near clip plane), so it behaves correctly when linearly interpolated in rasterization. This W component is easily turned into three texture coordinates that can access small color ramp textures to achieve the encoding of Figure 5. All we have to do is scale the W component so it varies from 0 to 1 from the near to far plane and scale that value by the number of times each color ramp repeats.

The color ramp textures are typically small with one texel per color value, and they are created to match our choice of the number of low bits, L, that we are using from each channel. The color value at each texel of the color ramps is simply an integer, L-bits in size, corresponding to the texel location. For example, if we choose a 12-bit encoding, then L=4 bits from each color channel, so we use R, G, and B ramps 16 texels long (16 being 2^L), with values ranging from 0 to 15 over the 16 texels. The lowest coordinate texel, which is at (0,0), has the value 0 out of 255, the second texel has the value 1 of 255, the eighth is 7, etc.

Texture repeating or wrapping is enabled so that one color ramp can repeat many times over the range of depths. The texture coordinate for the red texture ramp is the W depth scaled to [0,1] from the near to far clip plane. (The range notation [n,m] denotes all numbers from n to m, inclusive of the limit values n and m.) The coordinate for green is this same coordinate multiplied by the number of values in the red color ramp, which is 2^L, so that the green color ramp repeats 2^L times, or once for each bit increment of the red color. The texture coordinate for the blue color ramp is the red coordinate scaled by $2^L * 2^L$, or 2^{2L}, so that the blue ramp repeats once for each increment of the green color ramp. For the case of Figure 5, where L=2, the texture coordinate for green ranges from 0 to 4, and the blue coordinate spans [0,16]. These texture coordinates are calculated and output by the vertex code fragment listed in VS 2, where "near" and "far" denote the distances to the near and far clip planes.

```
// CV_RAMPSCALE = ( 1.0, 2^L, 2^(2L), 0 )                               (VS 2)
// CV_NEARFAR = ( 1/(far-near), -near/(far-near), 0, 0 )
// Scale r1.w to [0,1] from near to far clip planes
MAD r1.w, r1.w, c[CV_NEARFAR].x, c[CV_NEARFAR].y
// oT0 = ( [0,1], [0,2^L], 0, 0 ) + ( 0, 0, 1, 1 )
MAD oT0.xyzw, r1.w, c[CV_RAMPSCALE].xyww, c[CV_RAMPSCALE].wwxx
// oT0 = ( [0,2^(2L)], 0, 1, 1 )
MAD oT1, r1.w, c[CV_RAMPSCALE].zwww, c[CV_RAMPSCALE].wwxx
```

Three separate color ramp textures could be used, but it is better to combine the red and green ramps into a single texture, where red is accessed with the X coordinate and green is accessed with the Y coordinate. This saves a texture fetch and math operation in the pixel shader that fetches the color ramps. The blue ramp is not merged with red and green because that would entail using a 3D volume texture. For simple color ramps, such a texture is wasteful. As we see later, the blue bits are special, and we can use a larger 2D dithered color ramp to dither the least significant bit of depth information. To form the RGB-encoded depth value and output it to a texture render target, we use the following pixel shader code, PS 1, which adds the red-green color from T0 to the blue color from T1:

```
ps.1.1                                                                  (PS 1)
TEX     t0          // read red+green texture ramp
TEX     t1          // read blue texture ramp
ADD     r0, t0, t1  // output RGB-encoded value
```

These simple shader fragments and the small RGB ramp textures are all we need to render functions of depth and distance for any object. Vertex positions can be animated in software or in a vertex shader, and the depth-encoding behaves correctly in all cases. In practice, more operations are added to these shaders to compare depth-encoded objects to previously rendered RGB-encoded values, but there's more about that later.

Decoding RGB-encoded Values

There are several advantages to this scheme of encoding high-precision values. Unlike exponentiation (RGBE) or multiplicative (RGBM) encoding, RGB-encoded values can be added by simply adding each color channel. An offset can be added to each color channel in order to store negative values in a biased state, and decoding the values can be done in a single dot product operation. Hardware that supports Microsoft's D3D8 pixel shaders version 1.1. or higher can perform the decode in one shader instruction.

The RGB-encoding scheme spreads the bits into each color channel by dividing the middle and high bit ranges by a scale factor or shifting the bits down to begin from zero. Decoding the values is simply a matter of multiplying each color channel by that same scale factor (shifting the bits back up to their original values) and adding the shifted values together. This is accomplished by a single dot product, as illustrated in equation 1.1, where $V_{Decoded}$ is the decoded value, T0 is the RGB-encoded value, C is a constant vector of scale values for each channel, and scale is an arbitrary scale factor that can be used as a convenient control to adjust the output to some meaningful or more pleasant visual range.

$$
\begin{aligned}
(C.x, C.y, C.z) &= \text{scale} * (1.0, 1/2^L, 1/2^{2L}) \\
V_{Decoded} &= C.x * T0.\text{red} + C, y * T0.\text{green} + C.z * T0.\text{blue} \\
V_{Decoded} &= C \text{ DOT } T0
\end{aligned}
\tag{1.1}
$$

The multipliers, C, for each channel depend on the number of bits, L, we chose from each channel to encode the values. Typically, four or five bits are used from each channel, so the values $1/2^L$ and $1/2^{2L}$ may be small. For example, with L=5 we have C = (1, 1/32, 1/1024). Since the values may be small, the dot product must be executed at high precision in the pixel shader.

Pixel shader versions 1.1 to 1.4 have two classes of operations: texture addressing operations and arithmetic operations. Arithmetic operations can be executed at 9-bit precision per color component. This is not sufficient to hold small-scale values like 1/1024, so we should use the texture addressing operations, which must be performed at floating-point precision. If we're working with pixel shaders 2.0 and higher, all operations are executed at floating-point precision, so the ps.2.0 arithmetic operations can be used. Shader program fragments to perform the decode for ps.1.3 and ps.2.0 are shown in listings PS 2 and PS 3. In these shaders, a dot-product operation generates a texture coordinate, which we use to access a color ramp texture. This maps the RGB-encoded values (depth, thickness, etc.) to any colors we like, and it provides a convenient way for artists to control the look of the volume objects.

```
// vertex shader pseudocode to set up values
// for the pixel shader below
vs.1.1
MOV     oT0, SCREEN_COORDS  // map texture to the screen
MOV     oT1, scale * ( 1, 2^(-L), 2^(-2L) )
```

```
ps.1.3                                                      (PS 2)
TEX     t0              // read RGB-encoded value
TEXDP3  t1, t0          // decode and output color from t1 texture
MOV     r0, t1          // output the color value
```

```
ps.2.0                                                      (PS 3)
// c0 = scale * ( 1, 2^(-L), 2^(-2L) )
dcl         t0.xyzw
dcl_2d      s0          // A texture with RGB-encoded values
dcl_2d      s1          // A color ramp mapping value to color
```

```
TEXLD     r0, t0, s0      // read the RGB-encoded value
DP3_SAT   r0, r0, c0      // decode the RGB-encoded value
TEXLD     r0, r0, s1      // convert value to color
MOV       oC0, r0         // output the color
```

These shader fragments work for RGB-encoded values with both positive and negative values in the color channels. They also work for RGB-encoded values that result from adding or subtracting two or more encoded values. As you'll see in the next section, two sums of RGB-encoded values are easily subtracted and decoded. The result of decode(A) – decode(B) is identical to the result of decode(A – B), which is very convenient! At each pixel we can easily calculate the front face and back face depth sums, subtract them to get an RGB-encoded thickness value, and convert this into a color for the volume object.

Rendering Thick Volumes

With Nothing Intersecting the Volumes

Applying RGB encoding to the method of computing an object's thickness gives us a way to render ordinary polygonal objects as thick volumes of material. This section gives a step-by-step discussion of the rendering for volumes in free space where no opaque objects intersect the volumes. A few issues related to each step are also presented, and I focus on the ps.2.0 implementation. The ps.1.3 implementation is almost identical, and information about the differences is included in the demo source code. Situations where objects intersect the volumes are far more common; these are covered in the next section.

To render volumes in free space, two off-screen texture render targets are needed. These render targets could be a lower resolution than the ordinary back buffer, but if the rendered volumes have high-contrast edges, the render targets should match the back buffer size to reduce aliasing. These color render targets may or may not need an associated depth buffer. It depends on whether or not the solid objects in the scene can occlude the volumes, and it depends on the geometry used to render the final volume object color into the back buffer. A simple approach that handles occlusion is to use a depth buffer and render the final color with a large quad covering the entire screen. In that case, rendering proceeds as follows:

1. Render the scene to the color and depth buffers as you normally would with no volumetric objects.

2. Switch to an off-screen texture render target, which I call the "back faces" target. In Direct3D, the depth buffer can be shared between the back buffer and the texture render target if they are the same size and multisample type. Otherwise, the depth of occluders in the scene needs to be rendered again into a separate depth buffer that matches the texture render target. Clear the render target to black, set the cull mode to render volume object back faces, set the depth test to less-equal, and disable depth writes. Render the RGB-encoded depth of all back faces of the volume objects with additive blending

to the color target. Where several back faces overlap, the encoded depths will be added to form a sum of all back face depths at each pixel. The result will be similar to Figure 1c, where colors are shown overbright to better illustrate their values.

3. Switch the color render target to the other off-screen render target, which I call the "front faces" target. Clear it to black and render the RGB-encoded depth of all volume object front faces to create the front face depth sum. The result will be similar to Figure 1d.

4. If using hardware that supports pixel shaders 2.0, switch to the ordinary color and depth back buffers from step 1. Disable depth testing. Render a single quad covering the entire back buffer with the pixel shader listed in PS 4. This shader builds on the shader from listing PS 3. It samples the depth sums in the "back faces" texture, samples the "front faces" texture, computes the object thickness, and converts the thickness to the volume object color. It converts the thickness to a color value using an arbitrary color ramp texture bound to the D3D S2 sampler. The color ramp can be created by an artist or computed from a mathematical model of light scattering. For hardware that supports only pixel shaders 1.3, an extra pass and texture render target are needed to compute the RGB-encoded thickness value and supply this to the shader PS 2 listed above.

```
ps.2.0                                                            (PS 4)
// c0 = scale * ( 1, 2^(-L), 2^(-2L) )
dcl        v0.xyzw
dcl        t0.xyzw
dcl_2d     s0        // back face depth sum
dcl_2d     s1        // front face depth sum
dcl_2d     s2        // color ramp

TEXLD    r0, t0, s0    // back face depth sum
TEXLD    r1, t0, s1    // front face depth sum
ADD      r0, r0, -r1   // RGB-encoded thickness = back - front
DP3_SAT  r0, r0, c0    // decode to floating-point coordinate

TEXLD    r0, r0, s2    // convert thickness to fog color
MOV      oC0, r0
```

An alternate approach is to use the volume object geometry instead of a full-screen quad to drive the computation of volume object color and rendering to the back buffer. The choice depends on the coverage and complexity of the volume objects, and you can switch between methods, depending on the viewpoint and performance. This geometry provides the appropriate pixel coverage on screen. It creates pixels over an area so the pixel shader receives input and can perform the computations. If we use a simple full-screen quad, we waste fill rate rendering pixels where there is no volume thickness. If we use the volume objects themselves, we might reduce the fill rate by drawing pixels only where the volumes are, but we could spend more time transforming vertices or passing over pixels more than once where the depth complexity of the volume objects is greater than one. Since alpha blending is used to blend the volume's color into the scene, the depth complexity is important. If we use the volume object geometry, we need to enable a stencil or destination alpha test to avoid blending the volume color more than once at each pixel where the depth complexity might be greater than one.

If we use the volume objects to drive the processing, we need a shader that projects the front and back face depth sum textures from steps 2 and 3 onto the volume object geometry so that the pixel shader receives the correct values for each point on screen. This is simply a matter of turning the screen-space position into a texture coordinate from [0,1] across the full screen. A Direct3D vertex shader code fragment for this is listed in VS 3. This code is also used in handling solid objects that may intersect the volumes, since it can project rendered texture information at each pixel onto the same pixels as they are rendered again, regardless of the shape of the geometry. The code is useful in many multipass approaches, so it's good to keep in mind for other effects.

```
vs.1.1                                                          (VS 3)
// Transform position to clip space and output it
DP4 r1.x, V_POSITION, c[CV_WORLDVIEWPROJ_0]
DP4 r1.y, V_POSITION, c[CV_WORLDVIEWPROJ_1]
DP4 r1.z, V_POSITION, c[CV_WORLDVIEWPROJ_2]
DP4 r1.w, V_POSITION, c[CV_WORLDVIEWPROJ_3]
MOV oPos, r1
    // Convert geometry screen position to a texture coordinate,
    // so we can project previously rendered textures to the same
    // pixels on screen for any geometry.
    // CV_CONSTS_1 = ( 0.0, 0.5, 1.0, 2.0 )
MUL r1.xy, r1.xy, c[CV_CONSTS_1].yyyy
    // Add w/2 to x,y to shift from (x/w,y/w) in the
    //   range [-1/2,1/2] to (x/w,y/w) in the range [0,1]
MAD r1.xy, r1.wwww, c[CV_CONSTS_1].yyyy, r1.xy
    // Invert y coordinate by setting y = 1-y
    // Remember, w!=1 so 1.0 really equals 1*w
    //   and we compute y = 1*w - y
ADD r1.y, r1.w, -r1.y
    // Add half-texel offset to sample from texel centers
    //   not texel corners (a D3D convention)
    // Multiply by w because w != 1
MAD r1.xy, r1.wwww, c[CV_HALF_TEXEL_SIZE], r1.xy
    // output to tex coord t0
MOV oT0, r1
```

The steps above work for any camera position in the scene. The camera can move through the volume objects and the rendering remains correct, with a volume thickness contribution from only the part of the volume in front of the near clip plane. This is a consequence of choosing our RGB depth-encoding to start from 0 at the near clip plane. Without this, the volume object's polygons would have to be clamped or capped at the near plane so their depth values are not clipped away.

These steps require the volume objects to be closed hulls. There can be no back face without a corresponding front face, and vice versa. The depth complexity of the volume objects must also be kept below the limit for adding the RGB-encoded values together. The front and back faces are summed to separate render targets, so the depth complexity limit is for only the number of back or front faces, not for the total of front and back faces. In practice, using 12-bit encoding (L=4) allows 16 front and back faces (see the table in Figure 3), which is more than enough for interesting scenes. The approach also sums the thicknesses of overlapping volumes, so where two volumes intersect, the thickness will be greater. Everitt's technique of depth peeling [Everitt02] could be applied to eliminate the overlapping areas, but this would require several more passes and might be too costly in terms of performance.

Handling Solids Intersecting the Volumes

Often, we want opaque objects to pass through the volume objects, or we want to place the volumes in a scene without having to worry about their polygons being clipped away by solid objects. Handling the areas where solid objects intersect the volumes is key to making the technique easy to use. Fortunately, even complex intersection cases are easy to handle using one additional render target texture and a comparison of RGB-encoded values in the pixel shader.

If an opaque object cuts through a volume object's hull, we have to use the depth to the opaque object instead of the depth to the volume object faces that are occluded by the opaque object. This ensures that we get thickness contributions for only the part of the volume that is visible in front of the opaque object. This can be accomplished by doing a comparison of depth values in the pixel shader as each face of the volume objects are rendered. The pixel shader that created the RGB-encoded depth value (as in listing PS 1) can also sample a texture containing the solid object depth. This texture holds the RGB-encoded depth of the solid object closest to the near plane. The pixel shader compares the RGB-encoded depth of the volume object pixel being rendering to the encoded depth of the nearest solid object and outputs whichever value is the lesser depth. This allows both the back faces and front faces of volume objects to be occluded by the solid objects. It is an efficient way to handle any and all solids that might penetrate the volumes, and it handles complex volumes of any shape or depth complexity. Where a volume object face goes inside or behind a solid object, its depth contribution becomes the depth of the solid object. The volume object is effectively clamped to always begin from the solid object, and the varying depth complexity of concave or folded volume objects is handled correctly in all cases. This is illustrated in Figure 6 (on the next page).

To implement this approach, first render a texture to hold the RGB-encoded depth of the nearest part of any opaque objects that may penetrate or occlude the volume objects. There is no need to render all the opaque objects in the scene to this texture, and the regions of intersection do not have to be computed. Next, render the volume object faces according to steps 2 and 3 from the previous section, but in the pixel shader, sample the solid object depth texture, perform the depth comparison, and output the lesser depth. The depth is either the opaque object depth read from the texture or the depth of the volume object face at that pixel. Shaders to perform this on ps.1.3 and ps.2.0 hardware are shown in listings PS 5 and PS 6.

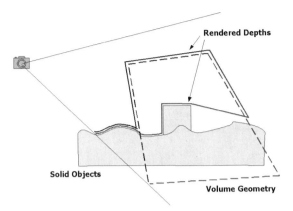

Figure 6: Handling opaque objects intersecting the volume objects. The volume geometry is shown with a dotted line. A pixel shader compares the volume object depth to the solid object depth read from a texture and outputs the lesser depth value. This results in depth information being taken from the geometry shown with solid lines. The depth comparison clamps the occluded volume object pixels to the nearest solid object depth, effectively limiting the volume object thickness to the proper amount for all intersection cases.

The depth comparison barely fits within the limits of a ps.1.3 shader. Unfortunately, Direct3D API restrictions require an additional instruction slot for the CMP instruction on ps.1.1 hardware, so this comparison can't be expressed in a ps.1.1 shader. Also note that the ps.1.3 shader can't decode the RGB-encoded values to a high-precision scalar, so it relies on comparing each R, G, and B channel separately. It scales and clamps each R, G, and B difference to [–1,1]. The ps.1.3 comparison will not work for RGB-encoded values where the high carry bits are used, but this doesn't present a problem. Additional comments are provided in the demo's shader source code. Since the ps.2.0 shader operates at floating-point precision, it is simpler and can handle values where the carry bits are on.

```
ps.1.3                                                        (PS 5)
    // RGB-encoded depth comparison.
    // Outputs the lesser RGB-encoded value
    // Requires saturation to [-1,1] range
    // Weight for each of the RGB channels
DEF c7, 1.0, 0.66, 0.31, -0.66
    // CMP uses >= 0.0, so use this small bias to get a
    // "less than zero" comparison
DEF c6, -0.01, -0.01, -0.01, -0.01

TEX t0          // red+green ramp texture
TEX t1          // blue ramp texture
TEX t3          // depth of solid objects
ADD t2, t0, t1  // Add R + G + B to make depth value

    // Difference between pixel depth and solid object depth
    // Use *4 to increase the contrast.  The goal is to saturate
```

```
   // each R,G,B channel of the signed number the values
   // -1, 0, or +1.
ADD_x4 r1, -t3, t2      // diff * 4
ADD_x4 r1, r1, r1       // diff * 32
ADD_x4 r1, r1, r1       // diff * 256
   // DP3 the saturated difference with the c7 weights.
   // The result is positive, negative, or zero depending on the
   // difference between the high precision values that t3 and t2
   // represent
DP3_x4 r1, r1, c7
   // Subtract a small value from r1
ADD r1, r1, c6
   // Compare r1 decision value to 0.  If r1 is positive,
   // output t3, otherwise output t2
CMP r0, r1, t3, t2
```

```
ps.2.0                                                          (PS 6)
// Comparison of RGB-encoded depths
// Outputs the lesser RGB-encoded value
// c0 = scale * ( 1, 2^(-L), 2^(-2L) )
dcl        t0.xyzw
dcl        t1.xyzw
dcl        t3.xyzw
dcl_2d  s0        // red+green ramp texture for depth encode
dcl_2d  s1        // blue ramp texture for depth encode
dcl_2d  s3        // RGB-encoded depth value of nearest solid

TEXLD   r0, t0, s0   // red+green part of depth encoding
TEXLD   r1, t1, s1   // blue part of depth encoding
ADD     r0, r0, r1   // Depth of volume object's pixel
TEXLDP  r1, t3, s3   // RGB-encoded depth from texture at s2
   // RGB-encoded difference
ADD     r2, r0, -r1
   // Decode to positive or negative value
DP4     r2, r2, CPN_RGB_TEXADDR_WEIGHTS
   // Choose the lesser value:  r2 >= 0 ? r1 : r0
CMP     r3, r2.xxxx, r1, r0
MOV     oC0, r3
```

Dithering the Low Bit

In this technique, depth is represented by discrete values, so aliasing can appear in the thickness values. This aliasing is always present. Even at high precision, it can be noticeable, especially if thin objects have their thickness multiplied by a large scale factor in order to generate some visible contribution. Depth aliasing appears as sharp transitions between light and dark in the color of the rendered volume, and its shown in Figures 7a and 7b. Luckily, there is a painless way to dither the lowest bit of depth information, which breaks the sharp bands into dithered transitions that appear smooth. The results are shown in Figures 7c and 7d.

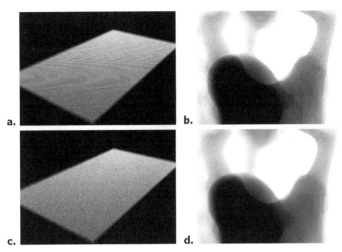

Figure 7: Artifacts of depth aliasing in severe cases are shown in a and b. Low depth precision is used to accentuate the effects. Dithering the depth information breaks the artifacts into gradual noisy transitions, which appear smooth, as shown in c and d.

The dithering is very easy to implement. The lowest bit of depth, held in the blue color channel, is read from a small color ramp texture, as described above. To dither the depth information, all we have to do is dither the color ramp texture! As long as the texture coordinate used to access the color ramp is not aliased, this approach works very well. The texture coordinate is a high-precision floating-point value with more precision than the 12 or 15 bits of depth precision typically used. The demo source code has a few functions to create dithered color ramps. To access the dither pattern, a 2D texture coordinate is used instead of the 1D coordinate oT1 (.x only) of listing VS 2. The dither pattern varies in the second (.y) coordinate direction, so the Y coordinate can vary randomly to create gradual dithered transitions. There is some subtlety involved in wrapping the dither pattern in the X direction from one end of the texture to the other so that dithering continues where the color ramp repeats. This involves using the alpha channel of the blue ramp to hold a value that represents a negative increment to the next highest (green) bit.

The dithered depth information can be used to create interesting noise effects in the volume rendering. As the depth precision is lowered, the dithered thickness becomes progressively noisier. At just a few bits of depth precision, the volume shape and thickness remain recognizable, and the rendering appears as though it were coming from a noisy video source. An example is shown in Figure 8.

a.   **b.**

Figure 8: A curious volume noise effect is produced by an object spanning only three bits of depth precision. The depth-aliased rendering is shown in a, where only a few bit-increments of thickness occur. Dithering the least significant bit of depth during depth encoding gives the result in b, which is a close but noisy match to the actual volume.

Negative Thicknesses

Objects can be treated as contributing negative thickness to the volume rendering. This could be used to render shafts of shadow cutting through a volume or modulate the thickness of objects. It is accomplished by simply reversing the front and back faces for negative objects. To render an object as subtracting from the total thickness, its front-facing triangles are rendered to the "back faces" depth sum texture, and the back-facing triangles are rendered to the "front faces" depth texture. This approach is not robust and works correctly only if the negative objects lie entirely within a positive thickness. If two negative volumes overlap or if a negative volume extends outside of a positive volume, they will still subtract from the total thickness. This would create areas of over-subtraction, where the total thickness ends up being too thin. For some situations, the effects of this are not problematic, but to properly handle such cases, Everitt's technique of depth peeling [Everitt02] could be used. This requires several more rendering passes and would have a substantial impact on frame rate.

Additional Thoughts

For slower hardware, you may want to use a single texture for both the front faces and back faces depth sums. This texture would begin from a mid-range value, such as RGB=(128,128,128). The back face depths are added to this, and the front face depths are subtracted using subtractive frame buffer blending. The advantage is that one less non-power-of-2 texture needs to be read. The disadvantage is that the depth complexity that can be handled in a single pass for a given choice of RGB-encoding precision is half of what it is when two separate render target textures are used.

The method of RGB-encoding can be extended to higher precision and depth complexity by spreading the bits across multiple render targets. For example, you could use two RGBA-8 surfaces to encode 64-bit values. Older hardware will run out of precision in the texture coordinate interpolation used to read the color ramp textures, but newer hardware can calculate the color ramp values in the pixel shader itself.

The method of rendering RGB-encoded depths to a texture and projecting these back onto objects can be used to implement shadow mapping. Depths can be rendered from the point of view of a light, and any number of passes can be used to implement complex and customizable filtering of the shadow map comparisons. This could provide high-quality hardware-accelerated shadow mapping for near-real-time applications.

Going a step further, the thickness through an object to a light source can be computed and used to render translucent materials like jade or approximate the appearance of sub-surface scattering. It is also possible to render shadows from semitransparent objects, where the shadow darkness depends on the thickness through objects.

Conclusion

Programmable shaders and a few render-to-texture passes are all that is needed to render ordinary polygon objects as thick volumes of light-scattering material. This article presented an efficient and direct means to render and accumulate high-precision values using 8-bit-per-component render targets, handle objects intersecting and occluding any volume object shape, and eliminate aliasing artifacts. The approach works for any viewpoint in the scene, and it is trivial to animate the volume geometry. The technique can be used on the large installed base of Direct3D8 ps.1.3 hardware. When hardware supports additive blending to floating-point render targets, the method of RGB-encoding can be abandoned to simplify the implementation.

Using thickness to determine the appearance of objects offers exciting new possibilities for real-time interactive rendering. Scenes can be filled with dynamic wisps of fog, clouds, and truly volumetric beams of light that are easily created and controlled. Intuitive controls and color ramps govern the appearance of the volume objects, though more sophisticated treatments of scattering could also be employed.

Example Code

Example code and additional images for this technique and others are available from nVidia's developer web site:

http://developer.nvidia.com

http://developer.nvidia.com/view.asp?IO=FogPolygonVolumes

References

[Baker02] Baker, Dan, VolumeFog D3D example, Microsoft D3D8.1 and D3D9 SDKs, http://www.microsoft.com.

[Everitt02] Everitt, Cass, "Order Independent Transparency," http://developer.nvidia.com/view.asp?IO=order_independent_transparency.

[Hoffman02] Hoffman, Naty and Kenny Mitchell, "Photorealistic Real-Time Outdoor Light Scattering," *Game Developer* magazine, CMP Media, Inc., Vol. 9 #8, August 2002, pp. 32-38.

Screen-aligned Particles with Minimal VertexBuffer Locking

O'dell Hicks
http://odellworld.com

Terminology

A particle is the smallest component of a *particle system*, or group of common particles. A spark in a spark shower, a snowflake in a blizzard, and a puff of smoke from a campfire are examples of particles. The puff of smoke is a good example of a particle being the smallest component. In real life, smoke consists of microscopic particles floating in the air. Unless you are doing an extremely complex simulation of smoke, this is obviously too small, so we need to make a reasonable approximation. A single, wispy puff often works as the smallest element. In this article, particles are treated as screen-aligned planar geometry (in our case, quads composed of two triangles), but they can also be geometrically complex objects.

A *particle system* is basically a common behavior pattern for particles. In general, it will define texture, color, size, motion, and other attributes. A particle system binds particles into functionality, such as campfire smoke or a blizzard.

A *particle emitter* is an object that initializes new particles (or recycles old ones that have gone through their life cycle), usually with physical data from the emitter. For example, a particle emitter attached to the tail of a missile would pass along the current position and direction of the missile for a more realistic emitting of smoke.

Aligning to the Screen

Screen-aligned particles, or *billboards*, always face the viewport in the same way so that a different perspective of them is never seen, regardless of view orientation. This gives the illusion of the particles having a three-dimensional volume. A circle appears to be a sphere (solid of revolution), and a 2D image of smoke becomes a 3D cloud. At this point, you may be thinking that a solution already exists in recent video cards — point sprites. While they can be useful in limited examples from hardware vendors, at the time of publication, they leave something to be desired. The biggest issue, in my opinion, is that the largest they can be is 64x64 pixels in screen space. Imagine playing a game in a resolution of 1280x1024 pixels. In the distance, smoke from the campfire will look good, but, as you get close, the smoke will begin to look weird. When near enough to walk through the

107

smoke, it will appear as odd-looking, sparse puffs. Another limitation is that particles can't be rotated about the view's forward axis.

So, how do we go about manually aligning our billboards? The answer lies in the view transformation matrix.

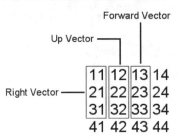

Figure 1: The orientation vectors of the view transformation matrix

As Figure 1 shows, the orientation vectors of the view transform can be directly retrieved from the matrix.

NOTE You may wish to reference a general-purpose 3D text to better understand why we can use these components of the view matrix directly. Such an explanation is beyond the scope of this book.

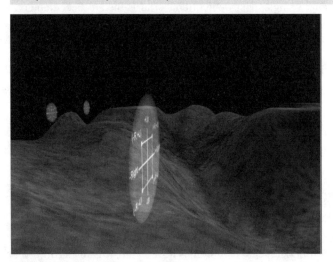

Figure 2: Billboard drawn normally

Of interest are the Right and Up vectors, the first three components of the first and second column, respectively. Screen-alignment is a two-axis operation not requiring the forward vector, as it would only affect the distance from the camera and not alignment.

NOTE This applies to row-major matrices as used by Direct3D. Other graphics APIs may use column-major matrices, so the orientation extraction must be changed accordingly.

If each of the four billboard vertices (in world space) were offset from the center of the billboard along the Up and Right axes, they would form a square, as shown in Figures 3 and 4.

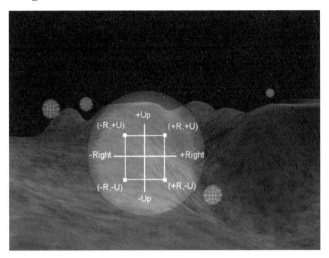

Figure 3: Billboard drawn aligned to the viewport

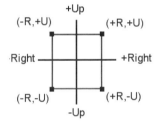

Figure 4: Four vertices of a billboard projected along the view's Up and Right vectors

The unused forward vector can be used for a test, just to prove alignment. If the normal of the plane formed by the four projected vertices were calculated, the dot product of it and the forward vector would show that they are parallel for any view orientation.

The Particle Vertex Shader

Unless your particles are static and the camera never moves, this alignment will have to be recalculated every frame. Particles are generally very active, thus various attributes such as color and size are also likely to change. Before vertex shaders, all of this required locking the vertex buffer and modifying vertices for every frame. But with a bit of planning and special use of vertex data, we can greatly reduce the amount of locking. Very complex particle systems will require locking more often, but many effects can simply be driven by a time set in a vertex shader constant. For now, we focus on the alignment. The following is a simple vertex structure for a particle:

```
struct ParticleVertex
{
    float x, y, z;                    // vertex position
    unsigned int diffuse;             // color
    float tu, tv;                     // one texture coordinate set
    float rightFactor, upFactor;      // custom data for projecting vertices
};
```

The members rightFactor and upFactor are both a combination of two values — half the width and half the height, respectively, of the billboard and the direction (positive or negative; see Figure 2) along the Right and Up vectors that the vertex is projected. It is half the width and height because on each axis, vertices are projected along a unit vector positively and negatively, resulting in a doubled width and height. Alternatively, you could multiply the Up and Right vectors by 0.5f.

Each particle has four vertices, and all vertices must be set up properly, as demonstrated by the following pseudocode:

```
For each particle
{
    For all four vertices in this particle // set common vertex data
    {
        vertex.xyz = particle.center;      // all vertices are set to center of particle
        vertex.diffuse = color;
    }
    // now set unique data
    Set Uvs
    // vertices are referred to as upperLeft, upperRight, lowerLeft, and lowerRight
    // to indicate their position relative to the particle's center
    vertex[upperLeft].rightFactor = -1.0f * halfBillboardWidth;
    vertex[upperLeft].upFactor = 1.0f * halfBillboardHeight;
    vertex[upperRight].rightFactor = 1.0f * halfBillboardWidth;
    vertex[upperRight].upFactor = 1.0f * halfBillboardHeight;
    vertex[lowerRight].rightFactor = 1.0f * halfBillboardWidth;
    vertex[lowerRight].upFactor = -1.0f * halfBillboardHeight;
    vertex[lowerLeft].rightFactor = -1.0f * halfBillboardWidth;
    vertex[lowerLeft].upFactor = -1.0f * halfBillboardHeight;
}
```

With this vertex data set up properly, we then set some constants and our shader (as well as appropriate render states). I have my vertices in world coordinates, but you may have them in a local object space if desired. Just remember to first transform the position by the world matrix before projecting along the view vectors. In my shader, c0 through c4 contain the concatenated, transposed view and projection transformations. c20 is the view's Right vector, and c21 is the Up vector. The fourth float (w-component) of both constants is set to 0.0f.

```
vs_1_1 ; vertex shader 1.1
#define VIEW_PROJECTION_TRANSPOSED c0
#define VIEW_RIGHT_VECTOR c20
#define VIEW_UP_VECTOR c21
dcl_position v0 ; vertex position in register v0
```

```
dcl_color v1 ; vertex color in register v1
dcl_texcoord v2 ; vertex texture coordinates in register v2
dcl_texcoord1 v3 ; custom data, albeit declared as a texture coordinate (see DX9 SDK)
; right: r0 = view.Right * vertex.rightFactor
mul r0, VIEW_RIGHT_VECTOR , v3.x
; up: r1 = view.Up * vertex.upFactor
mul r1, VIEW_UP_VECTOR , v3.y
; final world position = position + up projection + right projection
add r2, r0, r1
add r2, v0, r2
; transform to homogenous clip space
m4x4 oPos, r2, VIEW_PROJECTION_TRANSPOSED
; set diffuse and texture coordinates
mov oD0, v1
mov oT0.xy, v2
```

We now have particles that are aligned properly every frame, without having to touch the vertex buffer! But since they are static, they are rather dull and nearly useless. Let's look at a more complex particle structure:

```
struct DynamicParticleVertex
{
    float x, y, z;                         // vertex position
    float tu, tv;                          // one texture coordinate set
    float rightFactor, upFactor;           // custom data for projecting vertices
    float velocityX, velocityY, velocityZ;
    unsigned int beginningColor, endingColor;
};
```

A non-looping particle effect driven on a normalized timer ranging from 0.0f to 1.0f is easy to create. Once an event, such as a grenade exploding, triggers the need for the effect, the vertex buffer is locked once at the very start to initialize the effect. Vertex positions will be set, as well as velocityX, velocityY, and velocityZ and beginningColor and endingColor. The velocity can be treated as a texture coordinate set with three components, just as upFactor and rightFactor are defined through a two-component texture coordinate set.

 NOTE Don't forget to scale the velocity and to the actual time. If the effect plays over 30 seconds, then the velocity should be scaled by 30. Also, all four vertices of a particle should have the same velocity.

The beginningColor would be the color at the start of the effect. In a fiery blast, some particles may be white hot, while others might be a cooler orange or red. The endingColor would be the color at the end of the effect, usually RGBA (0,0,0,0) for additive blends and RGBA(255,255,255,0) for most other types of blending, resulting in a totally transparent, faded-out particle.

Applying this data in the shader is easy. Another constant is needed to pass along the normalized time. Since there will be an interpolation between colors, one constant's values should be the complement of the time (1.0 – current time).

For the velocity, just multiply the vertex's velocity by the current time constant, and add that to the position before transforming to homogenous clip space:

```
;v3 is the vertex velocity, c22 is the time constant, and r2 is the vertex aligned to the
;viewport, before the transform to clip space
#define TIME c22.x
#define ACCELERATION c22.y; 0.5f * acceleration * time2
mul r3, v3, TIME; r3 = velocity * time
add r3.y, r3.y, ACCELERATION ; apply gravity along the up axis
add r4, r2, r3; r4 = position + velocity and acceleration offset
;then transform r4 to homogenous clip space
```

The color can easily be linearly interpolated. The complement of the current time is multiplied by the beginning color and added to the ending color multiplied by the current time:

```
diffuse = ( complement of time * beginning color ) + (time * ending color)
c22.x is the time, c22.y is the complement, v4 is the start color, v5 is the end color
mul r1, v4, c22.y;
mul r2, v5, c22.x;
add oD0, r1, r2;
```

Most particle effects can be done very easily in this manner. However, a more complex particle simulation, such as a tornado, would require more touching of the data between frames — not every single frame, if done cleverly, but more than just the start of the effect.

Wrapping It Up

Be sure to check out my sample on the CD to see some cool examples of particle effects. One major issue that I haven't touched is sorting. Obviously, alpha-blended objects should be drawn last in the scene. A very useful thing to know is that additively blended particles (Source = D3DBLEND_ONE, Destination = D3DBLEND_ONE) do not have to be sorted amongst *each other*. Since they are all simply added to the frame buffer, any order will give the same results. For effects with a different blend type, you will have to sort, but you don't have to mess with the vertex buffer. If you keep a system memory copy of your particles and track the centers, you can sort them and modify the index buffer, which would touch far less memory than adjusting the vertex buffer.

Summary

In this chapter, we learned how to do screen-aligned particles with a vertex shader, bringing us one step closer to the big goal of having almost everything done by the GPU. With a little cleverness, you can make vertex shaders for almost any basic type of particle effect.

Hemisphere Lighting with Radiosity Maps

Shawn Hargreaves
Climax Brighton

This lighting model was designed for fast-moving objects in outdoor environments. Its goals are to tie the moving objects in with their surroundings, convey a sensation of speed, and be capable of rendering large numbers of meshes at a good framerate on first-generation shader hardware.

It combines a crude form of radiosity lighting with world-to-object shadowing, using just one texture lookup and four pixel shader blend instructions. Approximation is the name of the game here, with performance being by far the most important consideration!

Figure 1a: Diffuse (dot3) sunlight plus radiosity hemisphere lookup (See Color Plate 4.)

Figure 1b: With the addition of specular and Fresnel contributions, using a static cube map holding an image of typical surroundings

Hemisphere Lighting

There is an apocryphal story that in the early days of color television, someone pulled off a successful scam selling kits that claimed to upgrade existing black and white TVs to display a color picture. This was done using a bit of plastic that fitted over the TV screen and tinted the top third of the display blue, the middle green, and the bottom brown, on the assumption that most things in life have sky at the top, trees in the middle, and soil underneath. This was not perhaps the most robust of solutions, and I suspect the people who bought this kit were not terribly happy, but it would have worked okay — at least for a few carefully chosen images!

Hemisphere lighting is basically just a shader implementation of the same concept.

Most conventional lighting models evaluate some sort of equation for the more important few lights in a scene and then add in a constant ambient term as an approximation of all the leftover bits and pieces. This works nicely for scenes with many complex light sources but is less than ideal for outdoor environments where all the direct light is coming from the sun. With only a single light source available, fully half of every object will be in shadow and will thus be illuminated only by the ambient term. This gets even worse in overcast or rainy weather conditions because as the sun is obscured by clouds, its direct contribution becomes less, and almost all of the light in the scene ends up being provided by the catch-all ambient constant. A constant amount of light results in a constant color, which makes things look flat and boring.

This is clearly wrong because you only have to step outside on a foggy morning to notice that even though the sun itself may by entirely hidden, there is still enough variation in light levels that you can easily make out the contours of whatever you are looking at.

The problem with conventional lighting models is that in the real world, the majority of light does not come directly from a single source. In an outdoor setting, some of it does indeed come straight from the sun, but more comes equally from all parts of the sky, and still more is reflected back from the ground and other surrounding objects. These indirect light sources are extremely important because they will often provide a much larger percentage of the total illumination than the sun itself.

Hemisphere lighting is a simple way of emulating the indirect light contributions found in a typical outdoor scene. Any kind of complex radiosity lighting could be modeled by encoding the surrounding light sources into an HDR (high dynamic range) cube map, but it is impractical to update such a cube map in real time as large numbers of objects move around the world. So we need to approximate, cutting down the complexities of the real world into a more efficient real-time model.

The sun is easy: A per-vertex dot3 can handle that quite nicely. With this taken out of the equation, we are left with a pattern of light sources that can be roughly divided into:

- Sky: Usually blue, emits lots of light, located above your head

- Ground: Some other color, darker than the sky, located underneath you

This is trivial to evaluate in a vertex shader; just set your sky and ground colors as constants, and use the y component of the vertex normal to interpolate between them!

Radiosity Maps

Hemisphere lighting avoids the flatness that can result from a constant ambient term, but it also poses a question: What should you use for the ground color? Bearing in mind our goal of making moving objects fit in with their surroundings, it would be good if this could change appropriately depending on your location in the world.

The solution is obvious: Encode the ground color into a texture as a large, top-down image of the landscape. This map can then be sampled at a position corresponding to the location of the object or, even better, offset some distance (a meter or so works well) along the vertex normal. Adding this offset stretches the sample area to include a larger region of the ground image and introduces some horizontal lighting variation in addition to the vertical ground to sky transition.

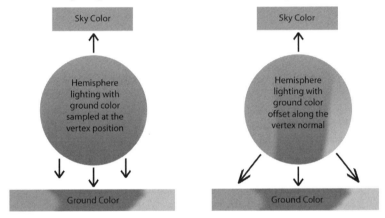

Figure 2: Hemisphere lighting with and without a vertex normal offset

The results may not be exactly what a high-end renderer would describe as radiosity lighting, but it can be a remarkably good approximation. The underside of an object picks up color from the ground directly beneath it, while the sides are influenced by the scenery slightly off to each side, and the top is affected entirely by the sky color.

Making the Map

Ground color maps can easily be generated by taking a screen shot of your level viewed from above with an orthographic projection. The results can be improved if you preprocess the mesh by removing polygons that are too high above the ground surface and rotating vertical polygons to face upward so elements like the sides of fences will contribute to the radiosity colors.

I also found it useful to add about 10 percent of random noise to the resulting texture, as this introduces a subtle speed-dependent flicker that gives an effective sense of motion as you move around the world.

A 1024x1024 texture (only half a megabyte when encoded in DXT1 format) is sufficient to represent a couple of square miles of landscape with enough precision to make out details such as alternating colors along the rumble strip at the edge of a racetrack or dappled patterns of light and shadow in a forest scene.

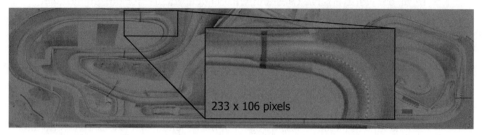

233 x 106 pixels

Figure 3: The images in Figures 1, 4, and 5 were created along the zoomed-in section on this 2048x512 radiosity map. (See Color Plate 5.)

Shadowing

Once you have the ground color encoded in a texture, it seems that static environment to object shadows ought to "just work" if you put a dark patch in the relevant portion of the radiosity map. Compared to other shadowing techniques, this is highly approximate but also incredibly cheap, and it can be very effective especially for complex shadow patterns, such as a forest floor.

Unfortunately, it doesn't "just work." The problem with using the radiosity map to encode shadows is that even if you darken down the ground color, the sky color is still a constant and so will not be affected.

There are several possible solutions:

■ Use one texture to encode the ground color and another to encode shadows. This is the highest quality and most controllable approach, but it burns two texture units and requires double the amount of storage for the two textures.

■ You could encode the shadow amount into the alpha channel of the radiosity texture. In this case, your ground color would be (radiosity.rgb * radiosity.a), while the sky color would be (sky_color_constant * radiosity.a). This works well, but using alpha in the radiosity map requires at least an 8-bit texture format, such as DXT5. For such a large image, storage space is a serious concern.

■ At the risk of excessive approximation, it is possible to collapse the ground color and shadow data into a single RGB texture, thus allowing it to be stored in 4-bit per-texel DXT1 format. The process is:

1. Convert your radiosity map into an HSV color space.

2. Find the average V (brightness) value.

3. Normalize the map so that all texels have this same constant brightness level, except for areas shadowed by static environment geometry, for which the brightness is left at a lower level. Hue and saturation are not affected by this process.

4. Convert back into RGB format.

5. Work out a scaling factor that will turn the average radiosity brightness into your desired sky color, and set this as a shader constant.

At run time, the ground color can be looked up directly from the modified radiosity map. Except for areas of shadow, this will now be lacking any variation in brightness, but the changes in hue are enough for the technique to remain effective.

To calculate the sky color, dot the ground color with (1/3, 1/3, 1/3) in your pixel shader, thus converting it to grayscale. Because of the brightness normalization, this will produce a constant value for all non-shadowed areas, or a darker shade of gray if you are in shadow. Multiplying this value by the sky color scaling constant gives a correctly shadowed version of the sky term.

Combining the ground color and shadow information into a single texture creates one final dilemma: Where should this texture be sampled? The radiosity lighting works best if the sample position is offset along the vertex normal, but that is blatantly incorrect for shadowing, where the map should be sampled directly at the vertex position.

A hacky compromise is to apply an offset along the left-to-right component of the normal but not in the front/back direction, so polygons facing forward or backward will sample the radiosity map at their exact position, while side-facing polygons use an offset sample point. Since objects usually travel roughly along their forward axis, this maintains a nice solid transition as they move in and out of shadow, while still allowing radiosity tints to be picked up from either side of their exact location.

Figure 4: These images show the hemisphere lighting on its own, using a single DXT1 format radiosity map that encodes both shadow and ground color information. (See Color Plate 6.)

The Shaders

The complete lighting model combines four elements:

■ Base texture

■ Radiosity texture combining ground color and shadow information. The vertex shader calculates the sample location and ground-to-sky tweening factor, while the pixel shader generates a shadowed version of the sky color based on the grayscale of the ground color and performs the hemisphere tween.

■ Environment cube map containing a static image of a typical area of the level along with a specular highlight in the alpha channel. The envmap intensity is calculated in the vertex shader, combining a per-vertex reflectivity amount (mapped by artists) with a 1-cos Fresnel approximation.

■ The direct sun contribution is calculated per vertex using a straightforward infinitely distant dot3 light.

```
vs.1.1


// vertex inputs:
#define iPos       v0          // vertex position
#define iNormal    v1          // vertex normal
#define iDiffuse   v2          // reflectivity amount
#define iTex0      v3          // base texture coordinates

dcl_position       iPos
dcl_normal         iNormal
dcl_color0         iDiffuse
dcl_texcoord0      iTex0



// constants:
def c0, 0, 0, 0, 1

#define VS_CONST_0          c[0].x
#define VS_CONST_1          c[0].w

#define VS_EYEPOS           1   // object space eye position

#define VS_CAMERA1          2   // 4x4 object to screen matrix
#define VS_CAMERA2          3
#define VS_CAMERA3          4
#define VS_CAMERA4          5

#define VS_ENVMAP1          6   // 3x3 object to world matrix
#define VS_ENVMAP2          7
#define VS_ENVMAP3          8

#define VS_FOG              9   // fog transform vector
```

```
#define VS_AMBIENT          10  // ambient light color
#define VS_LIGHT_COLOR      11  // diffuse light color
#define VS_LIGHT_DIR        12  // object space light direction

#define VS_RADIOSITY_U      13  // radiosity U mapping
#define VS_RADIOSITY_V      14  // radiosity V mapping

#define VS_RADIOSITY_SIDE   15  // object sideways offset

#define VS_RADIOSITY_SAT    16  // ground vs. sky vector


// outputs:
//
//  oPos    = position
//  oFog    = fogging
//
//  oT0     = base texture coordinates
//  oT1     = radiosity map sample location
//  oT2     = environment cube map coordinates
//
//  oD0.xyz = dot3 sunlight
//  oD1.xyz = radiosity ground to sky tween factor
//  oD0.w   = fresnel term
//  oD1.w   = specular intensity



// transform the vertex position
mul r0, c[VS_CAMERA1], iPos.x
mad r0, c[VS_CAMERA2], iPos.y, r0
mad r0, c[VS_CAMERA3], iPos.z, r0
add oPos, c[VS_CAMERA4], r0

// calculate the fog amount
dp4 oFog, iPos, c[VS_FOG]

// output the base texture coords
mov oT0.xy, iTex0


// *************** RADIOSITY HEMISPHERE ***************

// stretch the radiosity lookup area to either side of the model
dp3 r0.x, iNormal, c[VS_RADIOSITY_SIDE]
mad r0.xyz, r0.x, c[VS_RADIOSITY_SIDE], iPos

// planar map the radiosity texture
mov r0.w, VS_CONST_1

dp4 oT1.x, r0, c[VS_RADIOSITY_U]
dp4 oT1.y, r0, c[VS_RADIOSITY_V]
```

```
// calculate the ground to sky radiosity tween factor
dp4 oD1.xyz, iNormal, c[VS_RADIOSITY_SAT]


// *************** FRESNEL / SPECULAR CUBE MAP ****************

// calculate and normalize the eye->vertex vector
sub r0.xyz, iPos, c[VS_EYEPOS]
dp3 r0.w, r0, r0
rsq r0.w, r0.w
mul r0.xyz, r0, r0.w

// dot the vertex normal with eye->vert
dp3 r1.x, r0, iNormal

// fresnel term = (1 - r1.x) * reflectivity amount
mad oD0.w, r1.x, iDiffuse.x, iDiffuse.x

// also output a non-fresnel version of the reflectivity amount
mov oD1.w, iDiffuse.x

// reflect the view direction through the vertex normal
add r1.x, r1.x, r1.x
mad r0.xyz, iNormal, -r1.x, r0

// transform the environment map sample location into worldspace
dp3 oT2.x, r0, c[VS_ENVMAP1]
dp3 oT2.y, r0, c[VS_ENVMAP2]
dp3 oT2.z, r0, c[VS_ENVMAP3]


// *************** DOT3 SUNLIGHT ****************

// let's do a boring old school per vertex diffuse light, too...
dp3 r0.x, iNormal, c[VS_LIGHT_DIR]
max r0.x, r0.x, VS_CONST_0
mul r0.xyz, r0.x, c[VS_LIGHT_COLOR]
add oD0.xyz, r0, c[VS_AMBIENT]
```

```
ps.1.1

// inputs:
//
//   v0.rgb = dot3 sunlight
//   v1.rgb = radiosity ground to sky tween factor
//   v0.a   = fresnel term
//   v1.a   = specular intensity
//
//   c1     = sky color
```

```
def c0, 0.3333, 0.3333, 0.3333, 0.3333

tex t0                          // base texture
tex t1                          // radiosity texture
tex t2                          // environment cube map

// envmap + specular
lrp r0.rgb, v0.a, t2, t0        // fresnel tween between envmap and base
mad r0.rgb, t2.a, v1.a, r0      // add the specular component

// radiosity hemisphere
dp3 r1.rgb, t1, c0              // grayscale version of the ground color
mul r1.rgb, r1, c1              // calculate sky color
lrp r1.rgb, v1, t1, r1          // tween between ground and sky
mul_x2 r0.rgb, r0, r1           // apply the radiosity color

@codebg = // per vertex sunlight
mul_x2 r0.rgb, r0, v0           // output color * diffuse
+ mov r0.a, t0.a                // output base texture alpha
```

Figure 5: The complete lighting model, combining a base texture, radiosity hemisphere, Fresnel cube map, and dot3 sunlight (See Color Plate 7.)

Additional Considerations

This form of lighting can easily be simplified, using cheaper versions to implement shader LOD on distant objects. Most significantly, the per-pixel radiosity lookups and sky color calculations can be replaced by a single CPU texture lookup at the center of the object, with the resulting sky and ground colors set as vertex shader constants, the hemisphere tween evaluated per vertex, and no work at all required in the pixel shader.

Doing single-texel CPU lookups into the radiosity map is extremely fast, and this data can be useful in many places. For instance, a particle system might do a ground color lookup when spawning a new dust particle, to see if it should be in shadow and also so it can be tinted to match the hue of its surroundings.

The radiosity maps can easily become very large, but they are also highly compressible. Large areas of the map will typically contain either flat color or smooth gradients, so good results can be obtained by splitting it into a grid of tiles and adjusting the resolution of each tile according to how much detail it contains. At run time, a quick render to texture can expand the area around the camera back out into a continuous full resolution map.

Because the radiosity map is only a two-dimensional image, there will obviously be problems with environments that include multiple vertical levels. Such cases can be handled by splitting the world into layers with a different radiosity map for each, but this lighting model is not well suited to landscapes with a great deal of vertical complexity.

References

Philip Taylor (Microsoft Corporation) discusses hemisphere lighting at: http://msdn.microsoft.com/library/default.asp?url=/library/en-us/dndrive/html/directx11192001.asp

The non-approximate version: Image Based Lighting, Cunjie Zhu, University of Delaware: http://www.eecis.udel.edu/~czhu/IBL.pdf

Videos demonstrating various elements of the shaders presented above can be found on the companion CD.

The lighting model presented in this article is used in the game MotoGP 2, on PC and Xbox, developed by Climax and published by THQ. MotoGP 1 used a similar radiosity technique but without the Fresnel term on the environment cube map.

Galaxy Textures

Jesse Laeuchli
www.laeuchli.com/jesse/

In many space simulations, it is useful to be able to render galaxies to provide some background settings. Galaxies are a good effect to generate using a procedural model, as there are many different types and variations of galaxies, and so it is useful to be able to vary the generated galaxies. In this article a procedural model is presented that can be implemented almost entirely on the GPU using Cg pixel shaders.

Cluster Galaxies

The simplest type of galaxy to render is the cluster galaxy. A cluster galaxy is a group of stars clustered together. This is fairly easy to simulate using a single quad and a pixel shader. First, a quad is drawn and a texture filled with values from [0,1] assigned to it. Then, for each pixel the distance from the center of the quad needs to be found. To do this, the Cg function distance() can be used to find the Euclidian distance between two points:

```
float4 center;
center.x=.5;
center.y=.5;
center.z=.0;
center.w=.0;
float d=distance(center,In.tex);
```

After the distance d has been obtained, the star density of the current point can be found with the following equation:

$$stardensity=(1-(2*d))*(randomtexture \char`^ (d*10))$$

This equation moves d from the range [0,.5] to [0,1] and then multiplies that by randomtexture to the power of d times 10. This causes the star density to fall off away from the center of the galaxy.

Note that the constants 2 and 10 can be modified to adjust the appearance of the galaxy. In addition, if the texture coordinates used to fetch the random variables are changed over time, the galaxy structure will appear to change. While this may not be very realistic (real galaxies take many years to change drastically), it looks nice and can provide the application with more visual interest.

Cg Cluster Galaxy code:

```
float random(float2 xy,sampler2D BaseTexture)
// Index into texture filled with random values
{
    float color=tex2D(BaseTexture,xy);
    return color;
}
Pix Out;
float2 InputTest;
float4 center;
center.x=.5;
center.y=.5;
center.z=.0;
center.w=.0;
float d=distance(center,In.tex);
float randomtexture=random((In.tex.xy*10)+Time.xx,BaseTexture);//Random texture

d=(1-d*2)*pow(randomtexture,d*10);
Out.dif.x=d;
Out.dif.y=d;
Out.dif.z=d;
```

Figure 1: Real cluster galaxy

Figure 2: Procedural cluster galaxy

Spiral Galaxies

These equations can easily be modified to create another type of galaxy — a spiral galaxy. Spiral galaxies are galaxies with swirls of stellar matter emanating from their center. The amount, thickness, and length of the spirals vary greatly in real galaxies, so any procedural model should be easily modifiable.

The first step in modifying the equation to support spirals is to find out the angle at which the current pixel is being shaded. In other words, as the galaxy is circular in shape, we need to find which angle of the circle the point being shaded lies in.

We can do that by finding the inverse tangent of the point, like this:

```
float angle=atan((In.tex.y-.5)/(In.tex.x-.5));
```

However, as atan's range is [–π/2, π/2], it is necessary to move it so that its range is positive. It is also helpful to convert the output into degrees.

```
float angle=atan((In.tex.y-.5)/(In.tex.x-.5)); //find angle

angle=degrees(angle); //convert angle

angle+=270;        //Move angle to (0,360)
```

Next, the galaxy needs to be split into spiral sections. This can be done by performing a modulus operation on the angle.

```
Angle%(360*d)
```

The amount that the angle is modulated by increases as the point being shaded is farther away from the center of the galaxy. Spirals only result if the amount that the angle is modulated by is increased with the distance. If the amount used to modulate the angle is constant, the galaxy will be split into straight sections. This calculation can be skipped if the point is too close to the center of the galaxy, as the center of the galaxy does not swirl.

```
if(d>.15)
    {
        angle=fmod(angle,360*d);
        dense=(dense)*(angle);
        dense/=25;//scale the density

    Out.dif.x=dense;
    Out.dif.y=dense;
    Out.dif.z=dense;
```

It is easy to change the appearance of the galaxy by changing a few of the constants used here. For example, lowering 360 will change the structure of the galaxy by changing the number of spirals. Changing the amount that dense is divided by will change the galaxies' overall brightness.

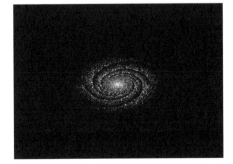

Figure 3: Two procedural spiral galaxies

Figure 4: Two real spiral galaxies

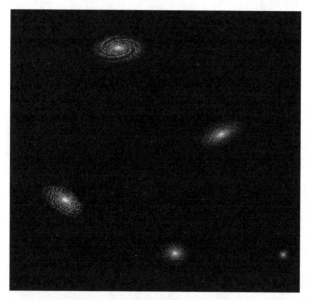

Figure 5: Space background, showing galaxies generated
with the methods shown here

Summary

This article examined a procedural galaxies model used to generate various types
of animated galaxies, which can be used to generate a space background.

Turbulent Sun

Jesse Laeuchli

www.laeuchli.com/jesse/

Many 3D engines today have situations where the sun needs to be rendered. Whether the engine is being used to create a space simulation, flight simulation, space conquest game, or even just a shooter, the sun needs to be displayed. Many developers solve this by taking a sphere, texturing it bright yellow, and whitening out the user's view, but this is visually boring. By using the latest pixel shaders and Cg, the sun can be rendered and animated entirely on the GPU. This article examines how this can be done using nVidia's Cg and shows several styles of suns that can be generated by tweaking the shader.

The most important part of the sun shader is a noise function. As of publication, Cg does not yet have a noise function implemented, so a large part of the code is spent implementing one. In this shader, a 3D value noise function is used. This takes a 1D table (stored in a 1D texture), looks into the table for the random values surrounding each pixel, and then interpolates between them using an ease curve and linear interpolation. Vnoise is used here because it only uses one channel of one texture unit and reduces the number of texture lookups used. On the downside, it uses a few more instructions than a gradient noise implementation. Using a different noise function will not affect the way the final image looks significantly, so another noise function may be substituted as desired. Below is the code for vnoise:

```
half random(float x,float y,float z,sampler1D g)
{
    half index=(x*6.6)+(y*7.91)+(z*8.21);
    index=index*0.001953125;
    index=h1tex1D(g,index);
    return index;
}
half3 scurve(half3 v)
{
    return v * v * (3 - 2 * v);
}

half noise(float3 v,sampler1D g)
{

    half3 LatticePoint=floor(v);
    half3 frac1=scurve(frac(v));
    half4 v1;
```

```
vl.x = random(LatticePoint.x, LatticePoint.y, LatticePoint.z,g);
vl.y = random(LatticePoint.x + 1, LatticePoint.y, LatticePoint.z,g);
vl.z = random(LatticePoint.x, LatticePoint.y + 1, LatticePoint.z,g);
vl.w = random(LatticePoint.x + 1, LatticePoint.y + 1, LatticePoint.z,g);

half2 il = lerp(vl.xz , vl.yw , fracl.x);

half a=lerp(il.x , il.y , fracl.y);

//
vl.x = random(LatticePoint.x, LatticePoint.y, LatticePoint.z+1,g);
vl.y = random(LatticePoint.x + 1, LatticePoint.y, LatticePoint.z+1,g);
vl.z = random(LatticePoint.x, LatticePoint.y + 1, LatticePoint.z+1,g);
vl.w = random(LatticePoint.x + 1, LatticePoint.y + 1, LatticePoint.z+1,g);

il = lerp(vl.xz , vl.yw , fracl.x);

half b=lerp(il.x , il.y, fracl.y);

return lerp(a,b,fracl.z);

}
```

For each pixel, the function random is called eight times to index into the table for the random values (if animation is not desired, this can be reduced to four) and then lerps between them. The artifacts generated by using lerps instead of a better interpolation function are surprisingly small in this instance, and in any case they are masked by using an ease curve to smooth it. Half variables are used instead of floats to improve the performance, as the visual difference is not noticeable in this instance. The texture is a 1D texture containing values from –1 to 1 in the red channel.

To generate a sun texture, this function should be called several times per pixel with different frequencies each call, using the texture coordinates as the x and y parameters and time for the z parameter, if animation is desired. The output is then applied to the final color. Calling noise more times makes the image have more detail, but calling it past certain levels dependent on the display resolution is useless, as there will be more detail than a single pixel can capture. Also, calling noise more times increases the length of the program, so it is desirable to call it fewer times. In the example below, it is called four times.

```
ninput.x=(IN.TexCoord0.x)*10;
ninput.y=(IN.TexCoord0.y)*10;
ninput.z=Time.x;

float suncolor= (noise(ninput,texture1)+(noise(ninput*2,texture1)*.5)+
    (noise(ninput*4,texture1))*.25) )+(noise(ninput*8,texture1))*.125);
```

When setting the output color, giving added weight to the red component makes the sun look better. In Figure 1, the red is set to twice the value of green, and the blue component is set to 0.

A more interesting look can be achieved by using a turbulence function. Turbulence is the same as the sum of the noise functions used above, but instead of using normal noise, the absolute value of signed noise is used. Signed noise is usually created by:

```
2*noise(x,y,z)-1;
```

This scales the output to (–1,1).

Note that it is not required that the value 2 be used and that other values can sometimes yield more interesting results. In Figure 2, a value of 1.5 was used. This of course changes the value to which noise is scaled.

Figure 1: Sun generated using noise   Figure 2: Sun generated using turbulence

The change to the shader is simple:

```
Noise function...
.....

    return 1.5*lerp(a,b,fracl.z)-1;
}

float test=abs(noise(ninput,texture1))+abs((noise(ninput*2,texture1))*.5)+
    abs((noise(ninput*4,texture1))*.25) +abs((noise(ninput*8,texture1))*.125);
```

This looks better than just the sum of normal noise, but one other interesting form is possible. Instead of getting the absolute value of every call to snoise, add all the values of snoise and then take the absolute value. (See Figure 3.)

```
float test=abs(noise(ninput,texture1)+(noise(ninput*2,texture1)*.5)+
(noise(ninput*4,texture1)*.25) +(noise(ninput*8,texture1)* .125).);
```

After the sun has been rendered, a flare can be drawn using vertex shaders to give the impression of light rays being emitted from the sun. The basic idea is to render a circle around the sun, then deform the uppermost vertexes of the circle by a constantly updated random value. This shader can be used even on graphics cards that support only DirectX 8 functionality or even a software implementation of vertex shaders. To generate the vertex coordinates, the number of triangles to use must be decided on. Obviously, the more triangles used, the closer the approximation is to a true circle, and the better it looks. In the following example,

1000 triangles are used. After the number of triangles has been chosen, the vertex number must be passed for each vertex, as well as the random number used to deform the vertex position. The vertex shader then uses the sincos Cg function to generate the vertex positions. The following code is used to do this. Position.x contains the number of the vertex being rendered, and position.y is used to deform the flare and control the size. AmountOfVertexes is the uniform parameter passed to the shader containing the number of vertexes in the flare:

```
float4 temppos=IN.position;
float step=IN. position.x*(6.283185307179586476925286766559)/AmountOfVertexes;
sincos(step, temppos.x, temppos.y);
temppos.x = (temppos.x * IN. position.y);
temppos.y = (temppos.y * IN. position.y);
```

To animate it, position.y should be updated with new random values periodically.

Figure 3: Sun generated with moderate turbulence

Figure 4: Sun with corona

It is important when passing the parameters that a value of 1 be specified for the innermost vertexes so they stay connected to the sun. Also, the flares should become more transparent the farther they reach from the sun:

```
OUT.cColor.x = 1;        // Flame-like color
OUT.cColor.y = .7125;    // Flame-like color
OUT.cColor.z = 0;
OUT.cColor.w = 1-(In. position.y-1)*2
```

Summary

In conclusion, this article has examined how to generate value noise in a Cg shader and then use it to produce turbulence, which can be applied per-pixel to create animated sun textures. Also, a method for displaying and animating a light flare around the sun has been shown. The entire source code for the shaders and the example code can be seen on the companion CD.

Fragment-level Phong Illumination

Emil Persson
http://esprit.campus.luth.se/~/humus/

Introduction

Phong illumination really isn't anything new. The Phong illumination model has been around for almost three decades now. First introduced by Phong Bui-Tuong in 1975, this model is still frequently used in both the offline rendering world and the real-time graphics world. Due to the complex math behind the model, it has until recently only been used for vertex lighting in the real-time rendering world. Both the Direct3D and OpenGL illumination models closely follow the Phong model with some small variation. Doing it on a vertex level often causes visible artifacts and a less-than-convincing look, unless you use a very high tessellation. With advances like the dot3 operation in the fixed function pipeline, we came a step closer to getting lighting on a per-pixel level. Unfortunately, the limitations of the fragment processing pipeline meant a lot of compromises had to be made, even in DirectX 8 level pixel shaders. With a limited range of [–1,1], or [–8,8] in PS 1.4, and with the limited precision that the DirectX 8 level graphic cards offers, much of the required math is simply not possible to do. Further, the fact that there are no advanced math instructions in these graphics solutions is another obstacle on our way toward advanced lighting, not to mention the instruction limit. For these reasons, tricks like packing attenuation into a 3D texture, using cube maps for normalization, and using textures as lookup tables for exponentiation of the specular component has been the norm for the past generation.

Fortunately, this will sooner or later be nothing but a bad memory. With DirectX 9 level hardware, we not only have the close-to-infinite range of floating-point components and much higher precision, we are also able to do advanced math and have a lot more instructions to play with before reaching the hardware limits. This means that for the first time ever, we are able to truly evaluate the Phong illumination model for each pixel completely in a pixel shader. I will state, however, that even though we are finally able to evaluate the whole Phong illumination model in the pixel shader, there are still considerations and limitations that need to be addressed. The number one consideration to take into account is, of course, performance. Even with the top high-end graphics cards of today, the full equation can be quite demanding on the fragment pipeline, and if care is not taken, performance will suffer. We address some of these issues later in this article.

131

The Phong Illumination Model

Let me start by introducing the Phong illumination model:

$$I = A_{coeff}A_{color}D_{color} + \sum_i (Att \cdot L_{color}(D_{coeff}D_{color}(N \bullet L_i) + S_{coeff}S_{color}(R \bullet V)^{S_{exp}}))$$

So what does all this do? Let's consider every component and their purpose. The first component, I, is of course the resulting color or intensity. The other components, A, D, and S, represent three different attributes of light and are called ambient, diffuse, and specular.

The Diffuse Component

We begin with diffuse, as it's the most intuitive (though not the simplest) of these. To understand what diffuse lighting is, take a piece of paper and point a light toward it (or just imagine it). The paper may represent a polygon in our little world. When the paper faces the light, it receives a lot of light and looks bright white. Now slowly turn the paper around until the edge faces the light instead. As you can see, it fades with the angle as the paper faces away from the light. This phenomenon is what diffuse lighting represents. The actual math behind this is what we see in the middle of the equation above, $N \cdot L_i$. N is the normal of the surface, and L_i is the light vector. The light vector is a vector that points from the point we're lighting toward the light. The light vector should be normalized (that is, being of length 1). The same should of course be true for the normal too. The dot product factor will thus be a number between –1 and 1. We don't want negative light contribution, so all dot products in this article are assumed to be clamped to the [0...1] range. Why does this expression give us the desired result? See Figure 1 for an illustration.

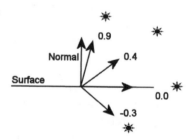

Figure 1: The diffuse component

A dot product between two perpendicular vectors will return 0. That's the case with light lying in the surface plane in the illustration above. Anything behind the surface will return a negative number and thus be clamped to 0. A light shining perpendicularly toward the surface from above will return 1, and anything lighting the surface from an angle will get a higher contribution as the light vector approaches the surface vector. Quite intuitive, but this is of course no proof of correctness. At this time, it's better to spill the beans: The Phong model isn't correct. It's just an approximation of how light tends to behave but nowhere near acceptable for studying optics. However, in graphics we don't need correctness; our main concern is to please the eye. Thus, the motto is: If it looks good, then it is good. Phong illumination looks good and consequently is good. That it can't predict how photons interact with matter is not going to concern us a whole lot.

If we go back to the equation, you can see that the diffuse contribution is multiplied with two other variables, D_{coeff} and D_{color}. D_{color} is the color of the material of the surface, commonly represented by a texture or a constant color. We use a texture, which is the normal base material texture used in many applications and games and should not need any further introduction. D_{coeff} is simply a variable telling how much the diffuse component is going to contribute to the whole lighting equation. You'll notice that there's also an A_{coeff} and an S_{coeff} variable, which control how much ambient and specular we want. For performance, we do not necessarily need to care about all of these. In fact, it can be beneficial to just bake the D_{coeff} into the base texture. If you want less diffuse contribution, you can just use a darker texture, similar to ambient and specular. So we can do the same thing with that in mind and consequently have a somewhat simpler expression. Here the components A, D, and S have their coefficients and colors pre-baked into single entities.

$$I = AD + \sum_i (Att \cdot L_{color}(D(N \bullet L_i) + S(R \bullet V)^{S_{exp}}))$$

The Specular Component

So far we have only discussed diffuse lighting. Diffuse lighting works well for materials like wood, stone, fabric, etc. But it won't work that well for materials like plastic, metal, and porcelain. Why not? These materials have a property that rough wood, for instance, lacks — they are shiny. Shininess is the property that the specular component tries to resemble. For rough wood you could do without any shininess, and it would look pretty good. But even for rough wood, a small specular component can enhance the image. There's a saying in graphics: "If you can't make it good, make it shiny." But be careful; with Phong illumination, you can make it good, so you shouldn't need to resort to making it overly shiny. Unless you're trying to make it look like polished wood, you should use a low specular component. The best images are created by carefully balancing specular and diffuse properly according to the properties of these materials in real life.

So how is the specular component calculated? The idea is similar to that of the diffuse component. To begin with, compute the dot product between the reflection vector R and the view vector V. The view vector is similar to the light vector, except the view vector is the vector from the camera to the lit point rather than from the light to that said point. This reveals a significant property of specular lighting. While diffuse lighting is viewpoint independent, specular is by its nature very viewpoint dependent. If you navigate around in your little computer graphics world, it doesn't matter from where you observe a piece of rough wood; it'll look the same regardless of where you view it from. That's not true for materials like plastics though; as you move around, you'll see the reflection of the light in the surface, and as the viewpoint changes the reflection will move around. Figure 2 (on the following page) illustrates the behavior of the specular component.

You, of course, get maximum reflected light if you view the surface from somewhere along the reflection vector. As you move away from this vector, you

see less and less reflected light. If you were
to use the dot product of the view vector
and reflection vector, the surface still
wouldn't look particularly shiny; rather it
would just look bleached. Why is that?
Think of a perfectly reflective surface — a
mirror in other words. A mirror will only
reflect light in the exact direction of the
reflection vector. That is, if you viewed it at

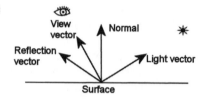

Figure 2: The specular component

a slight angle off from the ideal reflection angle, as in Figure 2, you wouldn't see
any reflected light at all. Thus, in that case the dot product alone obviously does-
n't work. Also think of a dull surface. It will reflect light in all possible directions,
so reflections should be visible from pretty much everywhere, even though you
don't see a sharp reflection but rather just a uniformly lit surface. The difference
is the spread. The mirror doesn't have any spread, while the dull material has a
significant spread. In other words, the more reflective the material, the faster the
light falls off as you move away from the reflection vector. Enter the specular
exponent. As you can see in the Phong equation, the dot product of the view vector and the reflection vector is raised to a power. This exponent represents the
shininess of the material. The higher the exponent, the shinier the material. A
specular exponent of infinity is a mirror, and a specular exponent of 0 is a completely dull surface where light is spread equally in all directions. If you didn't
raise the specular to a power, basically using a specular exponent of 1, you still
have a pretty dull surface. Normal values of the specular exponent tend to be
around 8 to 64. We will use a constant specular exponent of 24, something I
choose because it looks pretty good. Remember, it if looks good, then it is good.
With pixel shaders 2.0, nothing really prevents us from changing the shininess of
the surface by storing the exponent in a texture and using that as a lookup table
for specular exponents for each pixel. This can be used to let rusty parts of metal
be non-shining while letting the intact parts shine as appropriate. A dark region in
this texture represents a non-shiny area, while bright regions are those that are
shiny. I'll leave this as an exercise for the interested, however, and instead focus
on a more important part by which we can create a quite similar effect — gloss.

Gloss is basically just another word for the specular coefficient. As you
remember, we baked the coefficients together with the colors for each of the components — ambient, diffuse, and specular. One often leaves the specular color as
white, which basically reduces the S component to be nothing but the specular
coefficient, or the gloss. This is because most shiny materials don't significantly
change the color of the light as it reflects off the surface. Some material does
though, and if you're going to simulate this behavior you should of course keep
the specular color component. Gloss is an important part of the equation, however, and should generally be left in the equation. It often gives better results to
just alter the gloss instead of the specular component across a surface to do
effects like rusty parts of a metal surface. So we will use a texture containing the
gloss, a so-called gloss map. If you want to use a specular color, you can bake it
into the gloss map, but in our case we will take advantage of the fact that we only

have a single property to take care of and use a single channel texture to store our gloss map, which reduces the bandwidth need.

Attenuation

In real life, light fades as the lit surface gets farther from the light. The falloff is roughly a $1/r^2$ function (think of the area of a sphere with the light in its center). In real life, light sources aren't really a dimensionless point in space either. A lightbulb, for instance, while not particularly large, is still not exactly infinitesimal either. So if we applied an attenuation factor of $1/r^2$, we wouldn't get very realistic results. To better capture the behavior of light, a slightly more complex function is commonly used:

$$Att = \frac{1}{c + 1 \cdot r + q \cdot r^2}$$

We have constant, linear, and quadratic attenuation — c, l, and q in the formula above. It's not necessary to use all components; I usually drop the linear component, since it doesn't add a whole lot and places the heaviest load on the fragment pipeline because it requires a square root. Usually it's enough to just offset the inverse square function with a constant. Setting this constant to 1 will usually suit us well. So the attenuation function we use is:

$$Att = \frac{1}{1 + q \cdot r^2}$$

The Ambient Component

If we were to implement the lighting equation as discussed so far, we would get quite good results. However, there's still something that will hurt the impression of reality. Polygons in our little virtual world that face away from our light will be black. This may sound natural, as no light would hit it. However, experience tells us otherwise. If you're in a decently lit room, you'll have a hard time finding a surface that's so dark you can't see its details and texture. Nothing really gets black. Why is that? When light hits a surface, some of it scatters back. Some of that light hits our eyes, which is the sole reason we can see anything at all. Not every photon scattering off from a surface will hit the eyes of the viewer though; some will bounce away and hit other surfaces. Some of that light will then once again scatter back into the scene. This is called *indirect lighting* and is something that our Phong model doesn't take care of. Fortunately, there's a very cheap way to fake it. Enter the ambient component. While none of the components of Phong illumination are particularly real or physically correct, the ambient is the most fake of them all. In fact, it clearly goes against all our knowledge about light. But as always, if it looks good, then it is good. Ambient gets rid of the blackness of unlit surfaces and gives a decent impression that indirect light is present in the scene. This alone is a noble enough goal to justify its place in the Phong model, and given how cheap it is to implement, one would really have to justify the decision not to use ambient.

So what is ambient then? Basically it's nothing but a constant light that hits every surface. One assumes that the light scattered off from the surfaces in the scene is uniformly distributed in all directions and all places. This is hardly close to reality but works reasonably well for most normal scenes. With light hitting a surface uniformly from all directions, you get no reflective behavior. It's also completely angle independent, so anything like diffuse is out the window too. Basically you end up with just the texture color multiplied with a constant of how much ambient you want in the scene; very simple but quite effective. For being so effective and yet so cheap, it's easily the most worthwhile calculation your fragment shader can do.

Fragment-level Evaluation

In real life, few surfaces are really flat; this is a painful truth for the graphic artist, as it becomes so much harder to create realistic environments given the base primitives of 3D graphics. However, there are solutions, and Phong illumination on a fragment level gives you opportunities to ease the burden on the artist without the need for zillions of tiny triangles to simulate rough surfaces. Also, it would be wasteful to do all this work on every pixel without taking advantage of the possibilities this gives you. One could, for instance, just interpolate the normals and evaluate the Phong equation on each pixel. While this would certainly look better than normal per-vertex lighting, it would still look flat. Fortunately, the Phong illumination model still has room to improve this significantly. The solution is, of course, to store them in a texture and look them up on a per-pixel level instead of just interpolating the normals. This is what's commonly called a normal map, or bump map. This will let you give surfaces properties that real surfaces tend to have, like roughness, bumpiness, and fine details. However, this introduces some important issues, and the full concept can be a significant threshold for many people to get over. Let's take it from the beginning and study the issues that it raises in detail.

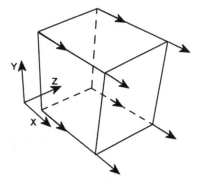

Figure 3: World space normals

So let's assume that we have a texture with the normals stored. We sample this texture in our pixel shader and do the math. Will this work? Those who have tried (including me before I understood these issues) can assure you that it'll look very odd and incorrect. It will look okay at some spots but wrong in most others. If the normal map was created exactly for the given direction of a polygon, it would work, but we can't create a separate normal map for every direction that a texture may be located in our scene. Not only would our dear artist refuse to take on this tremendous job, but even if he did, we would bring the graphic card to its knees due to the extreme memory requirements. So this is obviously not an option. Ideally, we would want a base texture, a normal map, and a gloss map to go together for each material. This is the solution I come to in the end, so why do I insist that just sampling a texture and doing the math requires a separate texture for each given possible direction? Consider a simple example: You are inside a cube. All six faces use the same texture and the same normal map. Now assume we want them all to look flat, so we store a constant normal (say for instance, (1, 0, 0)) in the normal map. Applying this to all six faces will give us something like Figure 3. Of course, you'd want the normals to point into the box. The faces of the cube obviously have different normals, and in this case only one face has correct normals. It may appear impossible at first that the faces can share the same normal map given that they are oriented differently and have very different normals. Using a separate normal map seems to be the only solution at first. Fortunately, there's a better solution.

Tangent Space

To solve the problem, we need to introduce the concept of a vector space. Imagine that we removed the axis pointers in Figure 3. How would we know which direction is the X direction? We wouldn't! Why? Because the direction of X is nothing but an arbitrary choice that we have made. There's no fundamental truth behind this choice. It's just a choice as good as any. Imagine that we put X into Y's position and vice versa. Suddenly the (1, 0, 0) normal would be incorrect for a face that it was correct for before. Not only that, but suddenly it's correct for the face in the bottom of the cube. Now imagine that we used different meanings of X, Y, and Z for each face. What would that imply? (1, 0, 0) can be the correct normal for every face; we only need to adjust our coordinate system to suit the normals. This may seem backward, but it is an extremely handy thing to do in graphics.

A vector space is basically just a coordinate system. You have three vectors defining the direction of each major axis. These are the vectors pointing in the X, Y, and Z directions, as defined by that vector space. There are two vector spaces that are important to us right now. First, the standard vector space we place all our objects into is called *world space*. This is the vector space you've been using even though you may not have realized it. As we place our objects in absolute coordinates, the world space is defined by the vectors (1, 0, 0), (0, 1, 0), (0, 0, 1). The other space that's important to us is the so-called *tangent space*. It is defined by the tangent vectors and the surface normal. Note that we still need the surface normal even though we have normals stored in the normal map. The difference though is that the surface normal is a normal normal (no pun intended) — i.e., it's defined in world space. The normal map, however, contains normals in tangent space. To better understand the concept of tangent spaces, try to think of a texture quad. The vectors that define this vector space are the ones that point in the direction of the U and V texture coordinate in world space. The normal points perpendicularly right up from the surface as usual. Figure 4 (on the following page) may help you understand the concept. The tangent space in this figure is thus defined by (0, 1, 0), (0, 0, –1), and (1, 0, 0), since the direction of the U texture coordinate points in the Y direction, V points in the –Z direction, and the normal points in the X direction.

Now that we have our tangent space, what's next? Well, we need to store the tangent space for each vertex in our geometry and pass that along with the vertex and texture coordinates to the vertex shader. The vertex shader needs to transform the light vector and reflection vector into tangent space and pass that along to the pixel shader. The pixel shader can then work as usual and use the normal from the normal map.

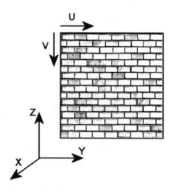

Figure 4: Tangent space

An obvious question at this point is, of course, how do we create the normal map? Unfortunately, there's no general method for creating a normal map from a base texture. Instead, the artist needs to create the normal map along with the base texture as two separate but obviously connected entities. It's quite unintuitive to draw a normal map, however; a height map is much more intuitive. It's easier to think of white as high and black as low than it is to think of pink as pointing to the right and light green as pointing down, etc. Fortunately, there's a general way to convert a height map into a normal map that can also be done at load time. All you need to do is apply a Sobel filter to every pixel. Fortunately, the concept of a Sobel filter is quite simple, but if that's still too much, you can resort to the D3DXComputeNormalMap function. Basically, a Sobel filter finds the slope of a grayscale picture. First you apply the Sobel filter in the X direction and then in the Y direction to form the the vector (dX, dY, 1). Then normalize this vector, and you're done. The filter kernels look like this:

−1	0	1
−2	0	2
−1	0	1

−1	−2	−1
0	0	0
1	2	1

If you're unfamiliar with the concept of filter kernels, just place the pixel that you're filtering right now in the middle square. Then multiply each pixel that each square covers with the number that's in that square and sum it all together. The result is your filtered value. So applying the left filter will give you dX, and applying the right one will give you dY.

Implementation

If you've read everything to this point, you are probably getting a little tired of all the theory. So without further ado, let's dive straight into the implementation. The first thing we need to define is our vertex format. As we've concluded earlier in this text, the data we need is a vertex position, a texture coordinate, and our tangent space. This gives us this vertex format:

```
struct TexVertex {
    Vertex vertex;
    float s, t;
    Vertex uVec, vVec, normal;
};
```

Now we need to feed this info into the vertex shader. Feeding the vertex and texture coordinates into a vertex shader should be pretty much straightforward. It's important to note at this time though that texture coordinates no longer need to be in any way related to textures. They are really nothing but generic interpolated properties. So we feed info into the vertex shader through texture coordinates and then pass new texture coordinates from the vertex shader into the pixel shader. So the vertex declaration looks like this:

```
D3DVERTEXELEMENT9 texVertexFormat[] = {
    { 0, 0,                                      D3DDECLTYPE_FLOAT3, D3DDECLMETHOD_DEFAULT,
                                                 D3DDECLUSAGE_POSITION, 0},
    { 0, 1 * sizeof(Vertex),                     D3DDECLTYPE_FLOAT2, D3DDECLMETHOD_DEFAULT,
                                                 D3DDECLUSAGE_TEXCOORD, 0},
    { 0, 1 * sizeof(Vertex) + 2 * sizeof(float), D3DDECLTYPE_FLOAT3, D3DDECLMETHOD_DEFAULT,
                                                 D3DDECLUSAGE_TEXCOORD, 1},
    { 0, 2 * sizeof(Vertex) + 2 * sizeof(float), D3DDECLTYPE_FLOAT3, D3DDECLMETHOD_DEFAULT,
                                                 D3DDECLUSAGE_TEXCOORD, 2},
    { 0, 3 * sizeof(Vertex) + 2 * sizeof(float), D3DDECLTYPE_FLOAT3, D3DDECLMETHOD_DEFAULT,
                                                 D3DDECLUSAGE_TEXCOORD, 3},
    D3DDECL_END()
};
```

The vertex shader needs to compute the light vector and the view vector from the provided data. Thus, we need to provide the vertex shader with the camera position and light position. This is best done with vertex shader constants, as these attributes don't change with the geometry in any way. Once the view and light vectors are done, we need to transform them into tangent space. The transformation is just a matrix multiplication, which is nothing but a set of dot products. As these are three-dimensional properties, we need only do a dp3 operation with each of uVec, tVec, and the normal. The resulting vertex shader ends up as something like this:

```
vs.2.0

dcl_position  v0
dcl_texcoord0 v1    // TexCoord
dcl_texcoord1 v2    // uVec
dcl_texcoord2 v3    // vVec
dcl_texcoord3 v4    // normal

// c0-c3 = mvp matrix
// c4    = camera position
// c5    = light position

// Transform position
m4x4    oPos, v0, c0

// Output texcoord
mov     oT0, v1

sub     r0, c5, v0        // r0 = light vector
```

```
dp3     oT1.x, r0, v2
dp3     oT1.y, r0, v3
dp3     oT1.z, r0, v4        // oT1 = light vector in tangent space

sub     r1, c4, v0           // r1 = view vector
dp3     oT2.x, r1, v2
dp3     oT2.y, r1, v3
dp3     oT2.z, r1, v4        // oT2 = view vector in tangent space
```

Everything should now be properly set up for the most important piece of code of ours, the pixel shader, which will do all the tough work. As everything is now in tangent space, we can carry on all operations as if all data, including the normal from the normal map, had been in world space. The pixel shader will be much longer, so we'll go through it step by step instead of just printing all the code right here. Let's start with the diffuse component.

```
ps.2.0

dcl t0.xy
dcl t1

dcl_2d s0
dcl_2d s1

def c0, 2.0, 1.0, 0.0, 0.0      // (2.0, 1.0, unused ...)

texld   r0, t0, s0              // r0 = base
texld   r1, t0, s1              // r1 = bump

mad     r1.xyz, r1, c0.x, -c0.y // bump[0..1] => bump[-1..1]

dp3     r7.w, r1, r1
rsq     r7.w, r7.w
mul     r1.xyz, r1, r7.w        // r1 = post-filter normalized bump map

dp3     r7, t1, t1
rsq     r7.w, r7.x
mul     r3, t1, r7.w            // r3 = normalized light vector

dp3_sat r4, r3, r1              // r4 = diffuse

mul     r4, r4, r0              // r4 = base * diffuse
mov     oC0, r4
```

This should be pretty straightforward. We begin by sampling our base texture and grabbing the normal from the bump map. We could have used floating-point textures given that normals can have components that range from –1 to 1, but that would reduce performance without a whole lot of image quality improvement. Actually, it would reduce the image quality on current hardware, since at the time of publication no hardware is available that supports filtering on floating-point textures. Instead, we take the traditional approach of packing it into a normal D3DFMT_X8R8G8B8 texture. This means that we have to unpack it in our shader though, and that's the mad (as in "multiply" and "add," not "crazy") instruction right after the sampling. Note that the linear filter on the normal map isn't really that suitable for normals, so after the filtering, the normal may no longer be of unit length but rather slightly shorter. This may not matter a whole lot for diffuse, but it does matter quite a lot for specular. If the length is 0.99 instead of 1.0 and you raise it to, say, 24, it'll end up not with the wanted 1.0 but rather something much lower, $0.99^{24} = 0.785$, which will make our specular highlights significantly less sharp. So the post-filter normalization is certainly needed, though maybe not this early, but it doesn't hurt to use a better normal for diffuse also. The normalization process is quite simple. As you may remember from linear algebra, a vector dot multiplied with itself is the squared length of that vector. So what we do is take the inverse square root of that squared length, which gives us the inverse of the length. Multiply the vector with the inverse length, and the normalization is done. The same is then done to the light vector. After the normalizations, we can just do the dot product between these vectors, multiply that with the base texture, and our diffuse is done. Note that we use dp3_sat as opposed to just dp3. This is so that all negative dot products get clamped to zero. We don't want negative light, remember?

So far, the output doesn't look particularly impressive. The most obvious drawback is the lack of attenuation. So far, only the angle matters, not how far from the light the surface is. We'll remedy the problem right away. So we'll need this piece of code inserted right after the light vector normalization:

```
// c2 = (constant attenuation, quadratic attenuation, unused ...)
mad     r5, c2.y, r7, c2.x
rcp     r5, r5.x            // r5 = attenuation
```

This will give us our wanted attenuation factor, which we can multiply with our diffuse to get a properly attenuated light. So the last step in the shader changes is as follows:

```
mul     r4, r4, r0          // r4 = base * diffuse
mul     r4, r4, r5          // r4 = base * diffuse * attenuation
mov     oC0, r4
```

Next up is our specular. To begin with, we need to sample our gloss map. It has the same texture coordinates as the base texture and normal map, so it's straightforward to add. As you may remember from our vertex shader above, we get our view vector in t2. So we normalize as we did with the light vector. We then need to compute the reflection vector. The reflection vector is illustrated in Figure 5.

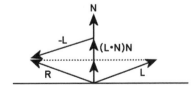

Figure 5: Reflection vector

Once the reflection vector is done, we basically just need to do the dot product, raise it to a power, and multiply with the gloss and we're done. We'll add the specular exponent to the first constant. The code ends up something like this:

```
dcl t2
dcl_2d s2
...

def c0, 2.0, 1.0, 24.0, 0.0        // (2.0, 1.0, specular exponent, 0.0)
...

texld    r2, t0, s2                // r2 = gloss
...

dp3      r7, t2, t2
rsq      r7.w, r7.x
mul      r6, t2, r7.w              // r6 = normalized view vector

dp3      r7, r3, r1
mul      r7, r7, c0.x
mad      r3, r7, r1, -r3           // r3 = reflection vector

dp3_sat  r3, r3, r6
pow      r3, r3.x, c0.z            // r3 = specular
mul      r3, r3, r2                // r3 = specular * gloss
```

Given the discussion above, there shouldn't be a whole lot of questions about this code. Now we just need to combine it with the diffuse component. The last piece of code is as follows:

```
mad    r4, r4, r0, r3             // r4 = base * diffuse + specular * gloss
mul    r4, r4, r5                 // r4 *= attenuation
mov    oC0, r4
```

The last piece of the equation that remains is the ambient, which is also the simplest to implement. So without further ado let's go right to the task. We need to pass the ambient factor to the shader. There are some unused components in our c2 constant, so we'll just use one of these. Then we only need to squeeze another instruction into the final combining code.

```
// c2 = (constant attenuation, quadratic attenuation, ambient, unused)
mad    r4, r4, r0, r3             // r4 = base * diffuse + specular * gloss
mul    r4, r4, r5                 // r4 *= attenuation
mad    r4, r0, c2.z, r4           // r4 += base * ambient
mov    oC0, r4
```

Yes, that's it. The Phong model is now complete and ready for some serious action.

Aliasing

While we already get pretty good results, there are still a couple of issues that need to be addressed. One such issue is aliasing. You probably already know why we use techniques like mipmapping. If you don't have the mathematical background, you probably at least know from experience that not using mipmapping will cause severe shimmering artifacts on objects at a distance. Why is that? The mathematical explanation is that it violates the Nyquist frequency. That probably sounds like Greek to most people; only those with a signal processing background will be familiar with it. Basically we are stating that the frequency present in the texture is higher than half the sampling rate, which may only confuse you more, but it's actually a quite easy concept to understand, even though it would take a higher degree of mathematical skills to do the reasoning from a mathematical point of view. Assume we are rendering to a resolution of 256x256, a resolution that will hardly ever be used in real life, but for this example it makes it easy to understand the issues. Assume we also have a texture of a 256x256 containing a checkerboard pattern (that is, every other pixel is black and white). Ignoring that we usually have linear filtering, it would appear that mapping this texture onto the full screen will work just fine. Every other pixel gets black and white. Now assume we map it to the upper-left 128x128 pixels. Only every other pixel from the texture will end up on screen (still ignoring filters), so we get only the black pixels by seemingly unfortunate bad luck. Obviously, information got lost in the process. It's hard to get something useful in this situation either way, but at least we would want all pixels in the texture to contribute to the final results, producing some kind of gray. Alright you say, and you point out that this is exactly what a linear filter will do for us. True — in this case using a linear filter would be enough, but then consider another checkerboard texture but with each 2x2 pixels being either white or black. Mapping this to either 256x256 or 128x128 will work just fine. Now map it to 64x64 and consider the results. We're back in the same situation — we will get nothing but black, as nothing from the white 2x2 pixel blocks will ever be touched by the linear filter. Obviously, information once again got lost. Ideally we would want every 4x4 block in the texture to contribute to each pixel. This is basically what mipmapping does. It tries to match the pixel and texel rates by using smaller down-sampled textures to better fit the spacing between where in the texture each pixel would sample. So when mapping to a 256x256 pixel area the full 256x256 mipmap would be used, while when mapping it to a 64x64 pixel area it would use a 64x64 mipmap. For anything in between, it would interpolate between the two closest mipmap levels for a smooth transition. Doing this should effectively get rid of all kinds of texture shimmer artifacts related to texture sampling.

So what's up with all this theory? The problem is solved, right? Well, I'd love that to be true. Unfortunately it's not. During the DirectX 7 era, one could pretty much state that it was a solved problem, but with the pixel shaders of today, we are basically back at square one again. Why? Well, during the DirectX 7 era, textures were combined with simple arithmetic operations like modulating a base texture with a lightmap, possibly adding an environment map onto that. Simple arithmetic operations like multiplications and additions don't change the frequency properties of the texture. So as long as you use these simple operations, you'll be fine. Unfortunately this is not the case with operations like dot products. It basically kicks all the assumptions from the reasoning behind mipmapping out of the window. This means that we once again see shimmering. Since the trend is that multisampling replaces supersampling as the preferred anti-aliasing technique, we won't get any help there either. The situation is not as horrible as it may first appear, however. We just need to be aware of the problem and carefully tackle it. While mipmapping may no longer perfectly match our source, it certainly helps us a lot. Again, what's the reason for shimmering? There are too-high frequencies in the source material. What can we do about it? Reduce the high-frequency components in our textures; in plain English, use blurrier textures. It is important to note that there's no need to use a blurrier base texture, since it will only be part of simple arithmetic operations. Our main target is instead our normal map, and to some extent the gloss map. The general advice is to avoid having sharp contrasts in the normal map. You also don't necessarily need to use the whole 0-to-1 range when creating your height map. Sharp contrasts in the gloss map are generally not desired either. Smoother transitions in the gloss map can help hide the aliasing artifacts slightly. It's also noteworthy that a high specular exponent, while giving sharper and generally better-looking specular highlights, also adds to the aliasing, so these two factors need to be balanced. Some good advice is to use a blurrier normal map the higher the specular exponent is. That is, a shiny surface will need a blurrier normal map, while a matte surface may do fine with fairly high contrasts in the normal map. Aliasing certainly occurs from diffuse too, so you can't use normal maps that are too sharp for dull surfaces either. It's also important to note that the artifacts tend to occur on lower mipmap levels, so it may help to not only downsample the previous mipmap level when creating the mipmap chain but also apply a soft blur filter.

If you work for a game or content creation company, it's important that you make sure the artist understands these issues. Unlike many other issues that can be handled graciously by the programmer, this will require awareness from the artists. The best thing the programmer can do is educate the artist and provide good tools for previewing the material.

Shadows

There is one thing left that seriously hurts the impression of reality, and that's the lack of shadows. It would be wasteful to spend all this time implementing Phong illumination and leave it in this state. There are several shadowing techniques to choose from, some of them existing in several different forms. Unfortunately, they all suck in one way or another. The two most common are stencil shadows and shadow mapping. The advantages of stencil shadows are that the shadows are pixel accurate, and stenciling is widely supported. The disadvantages are that it's slow, not particularly scalable, hard to implement, and not very general, and it may interfere with some anti-aliasing techniques. The advantages of shadow mapping are that it's reasonably fast, quite scaleable, easy to implement, and very general. The disadvantage is that the shadows are prone to aliasing. It has enough pluses though to make it my shadow technique of choice.

The idea behind shadow mapping is simple. In the first pass you render the distance to the light into a texture from the light's point of view. Then in the second pass you check the distance to the light against what's stored in the texture from pass 1. If the distance is larger than the stored value, obviously some other object is in the same line of view that covers the light, which implies that it's in shadow. Otherwise, it's lit. Quite simple, isn't it? In our case, we use omnidirectional lights, so we need to render to a cube map instead of a normal texture. As we're only interested in distance and not colors, etc., we can use a much simpler pass — no textures, just plain geometry. For that we need a pair of simple shaders.

```
vs.2.0

dcl_position  v0
// c0-c3 = mvp matrix
// c5    = light position

// Transform position
m4x4      oPos, v0, c0

sub       oT0, c5, v0      // oT0 = light vector
```

It can't be simpler; just compute the light vector — no tangent spaces or anything, just a subtraction and we're done. The pixel shader isn't any more complex.

```
ps.2.0

dcl t0

dp3    r0, t0, t0
mov    oC0, r0
```

The dot product with itself gives the squared length of the light vector. Normally, one would compare the distances, but the squared distances work just as well and give a significant speed boost. There is an issue we need to take care of for this to work well, however; when comparing with the stored distance, there will unavoidably be precision errors due to the finite resolution of our shadow map and limited number of bits. For this reason, you need to bias the distance to give some headroom for precision errors. Normally, you would just add a small number. However, if we're using the squared distances, this won't work very well due to the non-linear spacing that we have. It would effectively make our bias smaller and smaller with distance, and artifacts would soon be visible. If we use a larger bias, we would instead get problems with missing shadows close to the light. Unfortunately, there's no optimal bias in between either; rather, we could find biases that cause both artifacts. Instead, we take a different approach. We just multiply the distance with a constant slightly less than 1. This will instead define the allowed error in terms of a certain percentage, which will work much better. Only very close up on the light will there be artifacts. If this is a problem, there's still the option to use linear distance rather than the squared distance (but at a performance cost, of course).

Note that squared distances will return quite large numbers — certainly larger than 1 in general, unless we use a very small world. So we'll need a floating-point texture to store it to. We could use a normal fixed-point texture too, but then we'd need to scale it down so that we'll never get anything larger than 1. We can't allow clamping, as that will destroy our shadows. Also, floating point better suits our quadratic representation of distance. So the best choice for us is to use a D3DFMT_R32F texture. Note that some pixel shader 2.0 hardware doesn't support floating-point cube maps, but otherwise this is an ideal format, as it is single channel and floating point with high precision. If you need to support such hardware, you're better off just using the linear distance instead.

To implement shadows, we also need to change our lighting shaders. Our vertex shader will receive another line:

```
mov    oT3, -r0          // oT3 = shadow map
```

This line isn't obvious just by looking at it; instead you must take a look at the old vertex shader and see that r0 will contain the light vector from earlier computations (that is, the light position minus the vertex position). We want to look up in the cube map in the direction from the light position toward the vertex position (that is, the exact opposite direction of the light vector). So that's how we come up with –r0. The pixel shader gets more extensive additions. First we need some basic setup, and then we sample the shadow map:

```
dcl t3
dcl_cube s3
...

def c1, 0.97, 1.0, 0.0, 0.0     // (biasfactor, averaging factors)
...

texld    r8, t3, s3             // r8 = shadow map
```

Then right after we normalize the light vector, we'll squeeze in an instruction to compute the biased distance to the light. r7.x contains the squared distance to the light from previous calculations above.

```
mul     r8.y, r7.x, c1.x       // r8.y = lengthSqr(light vector) * biasfactor
```

We now need to get a shadow factor (that is, 0 if we're in shadow and 1 otherwise). So we'll compare and grab a 0 or 1 from our c1 constant, depending on the outcome of the comparison.

```
sub     r8.x, r8.x, r8.y
cmp     r8.x, r8.x, c1.y, c1.z  // r8.x = shadow factor
```

Now we only need to multiply this with our diffuse and specular components. The ambient will be left alone though, as we want ambient to be visible in shadowed areas too. So the component combining will be changed to this:

```
mad     r4, r4, r0, r3         // r4 = base * diffuse + specular * gloss
mul     r4, r4, r5             // r4 *= attenuation
mul     r4, r4, r8.x           // r8 *= shadow factor
mad     r4, r0, c2.z, r4       // r4 += base * ambient
mov     oC0, r4
```

Ta da — we have shadows! We could leave it at this and be fairly satisfied. This doesn't mean that there are no improvements left to be done, however. Sure enough, I have another trick for you. While the shadows created with the above code look fairly good, there is a problem. If the shadow map is of low resolution (say 256x256), we will get pixelation of the shadows in which the edges have obvious stair-stepping. What can we do about it? Well, we could increase the resolution of our shadow map. This will quickly kill our performance, though. Rendering to a 512x512 shadow map requires four times the fillrate of rendering to a 256x256 shadow map. Instead, let's try to anti-alias our shadows. How can we do that? By taking several samples and averaging them. So we just take the normal shadow map sampling position, add an arbitrary constant to offset it slightly, and take another sample. Take three additional samples for a total of four to get a decent smoothing of the edges. So we need to provide three additional sampling positions from the vertex shader.

```
def c8,   1.0,  2.0, -1.0, 0.0
def c9,   2.0, -1.0,  1.0, 0.0
def c10, -1.0,  1.0,  2.0, 0.0
...

sub    oT4, c8,  r0
sub    oT5, c9,  r0
sub    oT6, c10, r0
```

The pixel shader gets its fair share of additions also. The changes are pretty straightforward. First we just sample at the newly provided sample positions:

```
dcl t4
dcl t5
dcl t6
...

texld    r9,  t4, s3      // r9  = shadow map
texld    r10, t5, s3      // r10 = shadow map
texld    r11, t6, s3      // r11 = shadow map
...
```

Then we need to revise the shadow factor calculation slightly. Let's use 0.25 instead of 1.0 for obvious reasons. We accumulate the results from all sample comparisons in r8.x, so the final combining code remains the same:

```
def    c1, 0.97, 0.25, 0.0, 0.0 // (biasfactor, averaging factors)
...

sub    r8.x,  r8.x,  r8.y
sub    r9.x,  r9.x,  r8.y
sub    r10.x, r10.x, r8.y
sub    r11.x, r11.x, r8.y

cmp    r8.x,  r8.x,  c1.y, c1.z
cmp    r9.x,  r9.x,  c1.y, c1.z
cmp    r10.x, r10.x, c1.y, c1.z
cmp    r11.x, r11.x, c1.y, c1.z

add    r8.x,  r8.x,  r9.x
```

```
add     r8.x, r8.x, r10.x
add     r8.x, r8.x, r11.x
```

And that's it. The shadows should now look much smoother. If we look closely though, we can still see stair-stepping; more samples would solve that. I'll leave that as an exercise for those who are interested.

We've come a long way. We have implemented something that was hardly possible to do in real time just a year ago. It's fascinating how far graphics technology has advanced recently, and we're still moving. As mentioned several times in this article, we are still doing many things that are hardly real, but as technology goes forward, I hope we can overcome these problems also. I hope we can join up some time in the future and implement real soft shadows, real indirect lighting, and real displaced geometry instead of normal mapped simulations. See you then.

Specular Bump Mapping on Pre-ps_1_4 Hardware

Matthew Halpin

MatthewHalpin@mail.com

Introduction

This article presents a selection of techniques that can be used to improve the quality and flexibility of specular bump mapping on pre-ps_1_4 hardware. The techniques are targeted at ps_1_1 hardware, with certain optimizations presented for higher pixel shader versions. It should be noted that these techniques are strictly suitable for pre-ps_1_4 hardware; there are more efficient and elegant solutions for ps_1_4 and better hardware. There exists extensive documentation for per-pixel lighting on these higher pixel shader versions (see [1] and [2]).

The following diagrams are provided to define some terms that will be used extensively in this chapter.

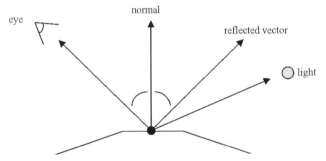

Figure 1: Phong shading terms

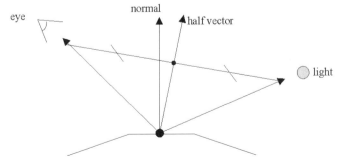

Figure 2: Blinn shading terms

The equation for the specular lighting term using Phong shading is:

$$S = C * (R.L)^P$$

Where S is the final specular value, C is the specular light value, R is the reflected eye vector, L is the light vector, and P is the surface specular power.

The equation for the specular lighting term using Blinn shading is:

$$S = C * (N.H)^P$$

Where S is the final specular value, C is the specular light value, N is the surface normal, H is the interpolated half vector, and P is the surface specular power.

All techniques discussed in this article make use of per-vertex tangent space data (tangent, normal, and bi-normal). See [2] for an explanation of tangent spaces.

There are a number of aspects that affect the quality of a given specular bump mapping technique. Here are the ones relevant to this article:

■ *Half vector or reflected eye vector.* A technique can use an interpolated half vector (Blinn shading), or it can interpolate a vertex to eye vector and calculate the reflection vector through the pixel normal (Phong shading). In the case of Blinn shading, the interpolated half vector is combined with the per-pixel normal using the dot product to find the parameter for the specular power function. In the case of Phong shading, the per-pixel reflected vector is combined with an interpolated light vector using the dot product to find the parameter for the specular power function. Phong shading generally gives a nicer-looking highlight but requires more work per pixel.

■ *Normalized half or reflected eye vector.* When interpolating a vector between vertices, the length of the vector can be shortened. This can cause problems for vectors that are meant to be of unit length (light vector, half vector, eye vector). A technique can ignore this problem on the assumption that the mesh will be tessellated enough for the vector shortening to not have a visible effect, or it can normalize the vector using a normalization cube map or shader arithmetic.

■ *Per-pixel specular power.* A technique can allow a per-pixel specular power value to be looked up from a texture, or it can allow a fixed specular power value for each primitive render. Per-pixel specular power normally imposes a fill-rate cost on the technique but allows meshes to be batched together if they normally would have been rendered separately due to requiring different specular values. Per-pixel specular power primarily provides more flexibility for the artwork.

■ *Per-pixel specular level (gloss).* This is a per-pixel value that is used to modulate the specular pass. This can be used to vary the surface material between being shiny (e.g., metal) and being dull (e.g., rust).

■ *Arbitrarily high specular exponent.* Some techniques may be limited in the range of specular power values that they are able to work with. Generally, high values will be unavailable rather than low values.

■ *Amount of banding for high specular exponents.* Raising a value to a power is not directly supported by ps_1_x hardware. There are a number of solutions that can broadly be split into two categories: texture lookups and arithmetic operations. Precision problems often occur when using arithmetic operations to raise a value to a high power (e.g., a value can be raised to a power of 16 by doing four successive multiply operations, but banding artifacts will be visible). This is because ps_1_1 hardware generally has limited precision fixed-point arithmetic units, and each multiply loses precision.

All the final solutions presented below use Blinn shading (using half vectors) rather than Phong shading.

In the following sections, techniques are presented for achieving various combinations of the aspects presented above. This includes some alternatives for the aspects that are of lower quality, as these are still useful as optimizations for rendering of objects that may not necessarily require the higher quality techniques.

Standard Shader

Here is an example standard shader that could be used to do specular (and diffuse) bump mapping:

```
; c0 – c3 = local to clip space matrix
; c4 = camera position in local space
; c5 = light position in local space
vs_1_1
dcl_position0 v0
dcl_texcoord0 v1
dcl_normal v2
dcl_tangent v3
dcl_binormal v4
m4x4 oPos, v0, c0        ; transform position into screen space
mov oT0, v1              ; output uv for diffuse texture
mov oT1, v1              ; output uv for normal map

sub r0, c4, v0          ; vertex to camera vector
dp3 r0.w, r0, r0
rsq r0.w, r0.w
mul r0, r0, r0.w        ; Normalized view dir in r0

sub r1, c5, v0          ; vertex to light vector
dp3 r1.w, r1, r1
rsq r1.w, r1.w
mul r1, r1, r1.w        ; Normalized light dir in r1

add r0, r0, r1          ; add view and light vectors
dp3 r0.w, r0, r0
rsq r0.w, r0.w
mul r0, r0, r0.w        ; Normalized half vector in r0
```

```
dp3 oT2.x, v3.xyz, r1.xyz
dp3 oT2.y, v4.xyz, r1.xyz
dp3 oT2.z, v2.xyz, r1.xyz      ; Tangent space light dir in oT2

dp3 oT3.x, v3.xyz, r0.xyz
dp3 oT3.y, v4.xyz, r0.xyz
dp3 oT3.z, v2.xyz, r0.xyz      ; Tangent space half vector in oT3

; c0 = diffuse color
; c1 = specular color
ps_1_1
tex t0                         ; Diffuse texture
tex t1                         ; Normal map
texm3x2pad t2, t1_bx2          ; u = (N.L)
texm3x2tex t3, t1_bx2          ; v = (N.H)
mul r0, t0, c0                 ; diffuse texture * diffuse light color
mul r0, r0, t3.a               ; diffuse * (N.L)
mad r0, t3, c1, r0             ; (((N.H)^p) * specular) + diffuse
```

This shader uses (N.L) as the texture u coordinate and (N.H) as the texture v coordinate. The texture contains (u) in the alpha component and (v^p) in the RGB components. The light vector and half vector are not normalized per pixel.

Per-pixel Specular Power

Techniques have been investigated that use arithmetic instructions to achieve per-pixel variable specular power (see [3]). The most significant disadvantage to this approach is the banding that occurs due to precision problems. The approach presented in this article uses texture lookups to evaluate the specular power function for a number of specular power values and then uses arithmetic instructions to interpolate the final value. For example, the specular power function may be evaluated for power values of 2, 10, 30, 60, and a value of 45 can be achieved by interpolating halfway between the 30 and 60 values. The per-pixel specular power is stored as a single texture channel with the range [0–1]. This maps directly to the range of specular powers. Hence a value of 0 means a power of 2, and a value of 1 means a power of 60.

It is possible to evaluate the specular power function at up to four values due to textures having up to four channels (alpha, red, green, blue). Each channel can store the precomputed result of each specular power value. This can be achieved by precalculating a 1D texture that stores u^p for four different values of p in each channel and then doing a texture lookup with the result of the lighting dot product (N.H) as the u coordinate.

The next step in the shader is to use the per-pixel specular power value to interpolate between these four specular results. Initially this will be achieved using another texture operation for simplicity, but this will later be converted to arithmetic instructions.

An interpolation between two values can be achieved using this equation:

$$R = (t * a) + ((1 – t) * b)$$

This is of the form of a weighted sum of a and b, where the weight for a is t and the weight for b is (1–t). Here are the graphs for these weights, given t:

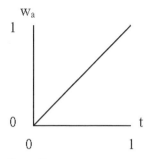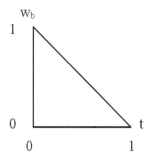

Figure 3

This needs to be extended to interpolate between four values. Value a must have a weight of 1 when t = 0, and b, c, and d must have weights of 0. Likewise, b must have a weight of 1 when t = $\frac{1}{3}$, c when t = $\frac{2}{3}$, and d when t = 1. The graphs for w_a, w_b, w_c, and w_d are given below:

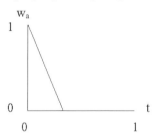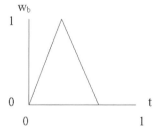

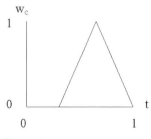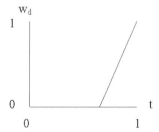

Figure 4

Texture-Encoded Interpolation

These weights can be encoded in a texture in a similar way as described above for evaluating the specular power function. In this case, w_a goes in the alpha channel, w_b in the red channel, w_c in green, and w_d in blue. This texture then needs to be read with the per-pixel specular power value as the u coordinate.

The final step is to evaluate the weighted sum:

$$R = (w_a * a) + (w_b * b) + (w_c * c) + (w_d * d)$$

This equation is the same as a 4D dot product. Certain pixel shader versions have a dp4 instruction, but where this isn't available, a dp3 followed by a mad can be used as follows:

```
dp3 r0, t1, t2
mad r0, t1.a, t2.a, r0
```

The dp3 instruction only modulates and sums the red, green, and blue components, so the alpha component must be added with the mad instruction.

Here is the final pixel shader:

```
; c0 = specular color
ps_1_2
tex t0                  ; read normal map with specular power in alpha
texdp3tex t1, t0_bx2    ; read (N.L)^p for 4 different values of p.
texreg2ar t2, t0        ; read weights for each component
dp3 r0, t1, t2          ; dp3
mad r0, t1.a, t2.a, r0  ; extend dp3 to dp4
mul r0, r0, c0          ; specular * specular light color
```

 NOTE   This shader only evaluates specular lighting, not diffuse.

The texreg2ar instruction uses the source texture alpha component as the u coordinate and the source texture red component as the v coordinate. In this case, it is being used to look up in the 1D weight's texture, so the red component is being ignored.

The pixel shader instruction texdp3tex is only available in pixel shader versions 1.2 and 1.3, so for version 1.1 the texm3x2tex instruction can be used instead, though a wasted texm3x2pad instruction must be included as well.

Here is the final ps_1_1 shader:

```
; c0 = specular color
ps_1_1
tex t0                  ; read normal map with specular power in alpha
texm3x2pad t1, t0_bx2
texm3x2tex t2, t0_bx2   ; read (N.L)^p for 4 different values of p.
texreg2ar t3, t0        ; read weights for each component
dp3 r0, t2, t3          ; dp3
mad r0, t2.a, t3.a, r0  ; extend dp3 to dp4
mul r0, r0, c0          ; specular * specular light color
```

Arithmetic Interpolation

The interpolation of the four specular values can be implemented as arithmetic instructions instead of a texture lookup. This has the advantage of reducing texture bandwidth as well as making the technique compatible with more complex specular solutions that require all four texture stages.

The graphs for w_a, w_b, w_c, and w_d need to be created using pixel shader arithmetic instructions. Here is the shader fragment that achieves this:

```
; c0 = -0.33333, 0.0, 0.33333, 0.66666
; c1 = 0.0, 0.33333, 0.66666, 1.0
; c2 = 0.75, 0.75, 0.75, 0.75
sub_sat r0, t0.a, c0      ; offset rising edges
mul_x4_sat r0, r0, c2     ; scale rising edges
sub_sat r1, t0.a, c1      ; offset falling edges
mul_x4_sat r1, r1, c2     ; scale falling edges
sub_sat r0, r0, r1        ; combine rising and falling edges
```

 NOTE The input per-pixel specular power value is in t0.a, and r0 outputs the final interpolated specular value.

This shader calculates each weight in parallel (in each component). It consists of three parts: constructing the rising edge of the triangle, constructing the falling edge of the triangle, and combining the two. The rising and falling edges have gradients of 3 and –3, but the pixel shader constants can only be in the range of –1 to 1. Hence, a _x4 modifier must be used in combination with multiplying by 0.75 to achieve a multiply by 3.

In this section, texture and arithmetic solutions have been provided for achieving an approximation of per-pixel variable specular power using segmented interpolation.

Normalized Specular Bump Mapping

The example shaders given previously all suffer from denormalized half vectors. This happens when a vector that is meant to be of unit length is linearly interpolated between vertices. When a denormalized vector is used in a dot product operation, the result will be smaller than it would be for a normalized vector. This can cause dulling of specular highlights in the middle of triangles and triangle edges. To fix this, the vector needs to be normalized after interpolation and before being used in a dot product. Usually, a normalization cube map is used to normalize the vector because the texture-addressing algorithm for cube maps is independent of vector magnitude.

Using a normalization cube map prohibits a technique from using a texture lookup to implement the specular power function. This is because the relevant instructions (texm3x2tex, etc.) do dot products between one texture result and one texture coordinate, rather than between two arbitrary texture results.

To overcome this problem, the cube map can be directly used to implement the specular power function as well. The technique is an extension of the standard environment-mapped bump mapping shader. Here is the standard shader:

```
; c0 = specular light color
ps_1_1
tex t0
texm3x3pad t1, t0_bx2
texm3x3pad t2, t0_bx2
texm3x3vspec t3, t0_bx2
mul r0, t3, c0
```

This shader transforms the per-pixel normal value in t0 into world space, calculates the eye reflection vector, and looks this up in an environment cube map (the eye vector is interpolated in oT1.w, oT2.w, and oT3.w).

The cube map will be precalculated as having a single light pointing in a fixed direction. Each texel will be calculated using the specular function with the normalized u,v,w coordinates of the texel as the input vector and a fixed vector for the light direction, e.g., (0,1,0).

Using the above shader, this will give a consistent specular highlight in the fixed direction (0,1,0), which is incorrect, as the highlight needs to point in the direction of the light. By adjusting the interpolated texture coordinates (associated with t1, t2, and t3) in the vertex shader, the cube map can be aligned with the direction of the light. To ease this process, the shader will be switched to use Blinn shading rather than Phong shading. This means that the cube map needs to be aligned with the vertex half vector, and the last texture instruction needs to be texm3x3tex rather than texm3x3vspec. This also means that the vertex shader doesn't need to output the eye vector in the w components of oT1, oT2, and oT3, as the pixel shader doesn't need this information.

In order to perform this alignment, a 3x3 matrix needs to be constructed that will transform the half vector onto the fixed vector (0,1,0). This matrix defines a world space coordinate system that will be referred to as "light space." Once this matrix has been determined, it needs to be combined with the tangent space matrix (tangent, normal, and bi-normal) so that the per-pixel normal will be transformed from tangent space into light space before looking up in the cube map.

The light space matrix consists of three vectors defining the x, y, and z axes of the light space in world space.

There is one constraint on creating the light space matrix: The y-axis must be the same as the vertex half vector because the fixed light direction was (0,1,0). Hence, the other two axes must be in the plane perpendicular to the half vector in order to form an orthogonal basis, though their specific orientation does not affect the lighting, as the cube map is symmetrical around the y-axis.

NOTE   The only difference between directional and point lights for this technique is in the calculation of the half vector (directional lights use the light direction; point lights use the normalized vertex to light vector). After the half vector has been calculated, the vertex shaders are identical and the pixel shaders are completely identical.

Light Space Interpolation Consistency

One way of generating the other two axes (x and z) is to take any fixed vector, cross it with the half vector to get the z-axis, and then cross the half vector with this z-axis to get the x-axis. Once normalized, these two vectors will form an orthonormal basis with the half vector.

Problems occur with this technique when the half vector points near the fixed vector or nearly opposite the fixed vector. This is because neighboring vertices might have half vectors that surround the fixed vector. When this happens, the x- and z-axes for neighboring vertices will point in radically different directions as the small difference between the half vector and the fixed vector defines their direction. This problem manifests itself as small highlights appearing inside triangles where there shouldn't be any. Hence, a fixed vector cannot be used to construct a light space that can be consistently interpolated.

To overcome this problem, the tangent space vectors can be used as a starting point for constructing a light space that can be consistently interpolated over the mesh. Simply cross the vertex tangent vector with the half vector to get the light space z-axis. Then cross the half vector with this z-axis to get the light space x-axis. This works because a highlight is usually only visible on the surface wherever the half vector is near to the surface normal and hence approximately perpendicular to the tangent vector. Additionally, the tangent vector can be consistently interpolated over the mesh (this is an assumption that all bump mapping techniques have to be able to make about the tangent and bi-normal vectors).

NOTE   This light space construction isn't guaranteed to be artifact free; if the mesh is so sparsely tessellated that neighboring tangent space vectors vary greatly, then the half vector could point too close to the tangent vector and risk causing small highlight artifacts.

Here are the vertex and pixel shaders to implement this:

```
vs_1_1
dcl_position0 v0
dcl_texcoord0 v1
dcl_normal v2
dcl_tangent v3
dcl_binormal v4
m4x4 oPos, v0, c0     ; transform position into screen space
mov oT0, v1           ; output uv for normal map

sub r0, c5, v0
dp3 r0.w, r0, r0
rsq r0.w, r0.w
mul r0, r0, r0.w      ; Normalized light dir in r0

sub r1, c4, v0
dp3 r1.w, r1, r1
rsq r1.w, r1.w
```

```
mul r1, r1, r1.w          ; Normalized view dir in r1

add r2, r0, r1
dp3 r2.w, r2, r2
rsq r2.w, r2.w
mul r2, r2, r2.w          ; Normalized half vector in r2

; Work out lightspace
; LightY = half vector. (r2)
; LightZ = Tangent x LightY (r6)
mul r6, v3.zxyw, r2.yzxw
mad r6, v3.yzxw, r2.zxyw, -r6
; Normalize
dp3 r6.w, r6, r6
rsq r6.w, r6.w
mul r6, r6, r6.w
; LightX = LightY x LightZ (r7)
mul r7, r2.zxyw, r6.yzxw
mad r7, r2.yzxw, r6.zxyw, -r7
; Normalize
dp3 r7.w, r7, r7
rsq r7.w, r7.w
mul r7, r7, r7.w

; Work out Tangent in lightspace
dp3 oT1.x, v3.xyz, r7.xyz
dp3 oT2.x, v3.xyz, r2.xyz
dp3 oT3.x, v3.xyz, r6.xyz
; Work out Bi-normal in lightspace
dp3 oT1.y, v4.xyz, r7.xyz
dp3 oT2.y, v4.xyz, r2.xyz
dp3 oT3.y, v4.xyz, r6.xyz
; Work out Normal in lightspace
dp3 oT1.z, v2.xyz, r7.xyz
dp3 oT2.z, v2.xyz, r2.xyz
dp3 oT3.z, v2.xyz, r6.xyz

; c0 = specular light color
ps_1_1
tex t0                    ; read normal in .rgb
texm3x3pad t1, t0_bx2
texm3x3pad t2, t0_bx2
texm3x3tex t3, t0_bx2     ; lookup specular cube map with light space normal
mul r0, t0, c0            ; multiply by specular color
```

Normalized Specular Bump Mapping with Per-pixel Power

This section combines the techniques described in the previous sections to give a shader that can render specular bump mapping with normalized half vector and per-pixel variable specular power.

Taking the normalized half vector shader described above as a starting point, the first thing to do to extend it to allow per-pixel specular power is precalculate four different specular functions, one in each channel of the cube map. Once this has been done, the final shader simply involves copying the shader fragments from the per-pixel specular power section and adjusting the register names so they fit together. The vertex shader is the same as for the normalized half vector technique, so here is the final pixel shader:

```
; c0 = -0.33333, 0.0, 0.33333, 0.66666
; c1 = 0.0, 0.33333, 0.66666, 1.0
; c2 = 0.75, 0.75, 0.75, 0.75
; c3 = Specular light color
ps_1_1
tex t0                      ; read normal in .rgb and power in .a
texm3x3pad t1, t0_bx2
texm3x3pad t2, t0_bx2
texm3x3tex t3, t0_bx2       ; lookup specular cube map with light space normal

sub_sat r0, t0.a, c0        ; offset rising edges
mul_x4 sat r0, r0, c2       ; scale rising edges
sub_sat r1, t0.a, c1        ; offset falling edges
mul_x4_sat r1, r1, c2       ; scale falling edges
sub_sat r1, r0, r1          ; combine rising and falling edges

dp3 r0, t3, r1              ; dp3 between weights and specular values
mad r0, t3.a, r1.a, r0      ; extend to dp4.

mul r0, r0, c3              ; multiply by specular color
```

NOTE Light attenuation can be added to this shader: Calculate the attenuation value in the vertex shader, modulate with the specular light color, output this in the oD1 register, and then replace the final pixel instruction with mul r0, r0, v1.

Implementation Details

The demo associated with this article provides implementation details for some of the techniques discussed. All the techniques use normalized half vectors. Pressing the S key will cycle through different specular techniques to provide a comparison between them. The "Fixed High" and "Per Pixel" options implement the techniques described in this article, while the others use standard arithmetic techniques for approximating specular power functions.

When implementing specular bump mapping on ps_1_1 hardware, it is important to use the most efficient shaders that will achieve the desired effect. For example, if per-pixel specular power is not needed (and it won't be for many surfaces), then use a more efficient and simpler shader. Similarly, if a fixed power of 8 is sufficient for a given surface and the banding is not noticeable, then use it rather than the shaders described in this article.

The demo shows how to combine a diffuse pass with the specular pass while incorporating per-pixel specular level maps (gloss maps). It is also extended to allow for multiple lights. The gloss map is stored in the diffuse texture alpha channel and written to the destination alpha channel during the first pass. In subsequent passes, alpha writing is disabled (by using the D3DRS_COLORWRITE-ENABLE render state). This means that the gloss map is permanently stored in the destination alpha channel, and specular passes can be modulated and added using the following blend mode: D3DRS_SRCBLEND = D3DBLEND_DEST-ALPHA; D3DRS_DESTBLEND = D3DBLEND_ONE.

Conclusion

In this article, two primary factors were addressed that affect specular bump mapping: per-pixel specular power values and normalized high exponent specular power functions. It has been shown how to achieve either or both of these factors in a single pass on ps_1_1 level hardware while minimizing banding artifacts.

Acknowledgments

Thanks to Oscar Cooper, Dean Calver, Andrew Vidler, and Peter Halpin for proofreading.

Thanks to Tim Mews for providing the artwork in the demo.

References

[1] ATI developer page, http://www.ati.com/developer/. Papers, http://www.ati.com/developer/techpapers.html.

[2] nVidia developer page, http://developer.nvidia.com/.

[3] Beaudoin, Philippe and Juan Guardado, "A Non-Integer Power Function on the Pixel Shader," http://www.gamasutra.com/features/20020801/beaudoin_01.htm.

Voxel Rendering with PS_3_0

Aaron Burton

PowerVR Technologies

Introduction

With the advent of pixel shader 3_0, graphics hardware has become capable of rendering hardware-accelerated voxels.

Voxel objects are stored as a three-dimensional map of matter, with each voxel (or texel in a volume map) indicating something about that "lump" of matter — its color, translucency, or "power" in the case of metaballs. In the "power" case, a threshold value is used; voxel values that are above this value are considered to be solid matter, with the rest considered to be empty space. (Alternatively, an implementation could reverse the comparison and consider matter to exist in all voxels with a value below the threshold.)

Typically, voxel objects are converted to polygons before rendering using the "marching cubes" algorithm or something similar. The method presented here submits a single eight-vertex cube and extracts the surface in the pixel shader; a ray is traced step by step through the volume, sampling the texture at each step, searching for matter.

The method requires pixel shader loops, dynamic flow control (IF, BREAK), unlimited texture reads, and unlimited dependent reads; it also makes use of function calls.

The Plan Revealed

The basic recipe is simple.

1. Take a volume texture(s) containing the voxel object. D3DTADDRESS_CLAMP should be used, although small changes to the code would allow texture repeats if that is desired.

2. Render a cube. The eight vertices have 3D texture coordinates applied that simply map the entire volume texture to the cube (i.e., one vertex has coordinates [0 0 0] and the opposite corner is [1 1 1]). If the front clip plane clips this cube, it must have capping polygons added to cover the hole created.

3. In the vertex shader, output the 3D texture coordinate and a vector indicating the direction of the line from camera to vertex.

4. In the pixel shader, start at the given texture coordinate and step along the line, deeper into the volume. Sample the texture at each step.

The length of the camera to vertex vector, which is calculated in the vertex shader, directly controls the distance stepped through the volume texture each loop; thus volume textures containing small objects will require the vector length to be no longer than the size of a voxel. For example, a 64x64x64 volume texture would require the length of the step vector to be 64^{-1}.

Note that the normal issues with vector interpolation apply: As the cube is rendered, this vector will be linearly interpolated between vertices, and so it may be shorter for some pixels — those toward the middle of polygons — than it should be. This is not likely to be a problem unless both the near clip plane and the object are very close to the camera, so the shaders herein do not attempt corrective action.

The voxels may be rendered in many ways; the three demonstrated here are accumulative (e.g., additive, such as holograms or light volumes, or multiplicative, such as smoke), solid, and lit.

The Vertex Shader

The vertex shader used is simple and the same no matter which rendering method is chosen.

```
// Constants:   c0..c3    world.View.Proj matrix
//              c4        Camera position (model space)
//              c5.x      Length of camera->vertex vector for pixel shader

vs_3_0

dcl_position    v0
dcl_texcoord    v1

dcl_position    o0
dcl_texcoord0   o1
dcl_texcoord1   o2

m4x4    o0, v0, c0      // Output: transformed position
mov     o1.xyz, v1      // Output: texture coordinate

sub     r1, v0, c4      // Camera->Vertex vector in model space...
nrm     r2, r1          // ...normalize it...
mul     r1, r2, c5.x    // ...and scale it to the right "step" length.
mov     o2.xyz, r1      // Output: Camera-direction in texture space
```

Accumulated Voxels

This is the simplest method. Accumulated voxels require a single volume texture containing the color at each voxel. The colors are summed (accumulated) as the ray traces through the volume.

Accumulated voxel rendering is most obviously applied as additive (e.g., holography or light volumes), or obscuring, as smoke or fog (i.e., multiplicative blending), or another blend type for another effect. There can be a problem with using accumulated voxels as light volumes (i.e., the light from a window shining through a dusty atmosphere) or smoke/fog volumes, which is covered later in this article in the section titled "The Problem with Depth Buffering."

1. As the ray steps through the volume, the texture is read and accumulated. The final number must be modulated by some value, or else it will likely be too bright — at least in the case of additive blending.

2. If a fixed number of steps are taken through the volume, this number can then be used to divide the total and gain the final result; this will work on pixel shader 2_0 hardware. Note that if pixel shader 2_0 hardware is used with D3DTADDRESS_CLAMP, the pixel shader will be unable to terminate the ray when it hits the edge of the volume; this will require the edge voxels to be empty, as otherwise, matter in the edges will appear to be stretched to infinity.

3. If the ray is terminated when it leaves the [0..1] texture coordinate range, then fewer texture reads will be performed, and thus pixel shader 2_0 is no longer sufficient. The number chosen to modulate the final result can be tuned to give the desired brightness or set from the maximum number of steps possible through the volume. The number must be constant across all pixels (to avoid color banding), not calculated per pixel.

```
// Constants:   c1.x    Length of step, used as scale factor for final result
//              i0      Loop enough times to step completely through object


ps_3_0


def     c0, 0, 1, 0, 0


dcl_texcoord0   v0.xyz              // Start texture coordinate
dcl_texcoord1   v1.xyz              // Ray "step vector"
dcl_volume      s0                  // "Matter map" - use alpha channel
dcl_volume      s1                  // Color map


mov     r0.xyz, v0                  // r0.xyz is current sample position
mov     r0.w, c0.x                  // r0.w is number of samples taken
texld   r1, v0, s0


rep     i0
    add     r0.xyz, r0, v1          // Step further along the ray
    add     r0.w, r0.w, c0.y        // Increment sample count
```

```
// Stop if any ray coord leaves [0..1] range
mov_sat r3.xyz, r0
sub      r3.xyz, r3, r0
abs      r3.xyz, r3
dp3      r3.w, r3, c0.y
if_ne    r3.w, c0.x
    break
endif


// Load the texture then
texld    r2, r0, s0          // Load the texture...
add      r1.a, r1, r2        // ...and add it to the total
endrep

// Scale result and output color
mul      r1.a, r1.a, c1.x
mov      oC0, r1.a
```

Solid Voxels

With solid voxels, the aim is to step through the volume texture until a non-empty voxel is found and then render its color. This requires the ray to terminate when it leaves the volume or finds matter. This is simple and should be easily understood by examining the shader code.

If point sampling is used, a special color, or color-key, can be used to indicate whether the voxel is opaque or not. If bilinear filtering is to be used, and this does improve the results, then an additional alpha channel must be used to indicate the existence of matter, as color filtering will prevent the use of a color-key. Most of the ray tracing operation will consist of sampling the information contained in the alpha channel, as the final color is only retrieved after an opaque voxel has been found. For this reason, it may be best for performance if the matter (alpha) map and color map are two separate volume textures. For the matter map, D3DFMT_A8 will do, although 1 bit per pixel might be sufficient (e.g., for a landscape). For metaballs and other surfaces that have varying densities, an 8-bit channel could be ideal. It is then possible to vary the threshold value that the pixel shader considers to be matter; this effectively changes the isosurface that is rendered.

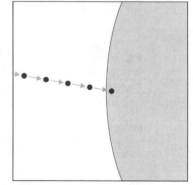

The ray traces through the matter map, sampling each step and searching for matter. When matter is found, the pixel shader can then sample the color map and write the value. In Figure 1, the circles indicate sample positions, and the arrows indicate the direction of the ray. Sampling stops and the object

Figure 1: The ray steps through the volume, sampling the texture to search for matter.

color is output as soon as matter is found, in this case by the rightmost sample, the fifth in the image.

```
// Constants:   c1.y    Threshold value to detect matter
//              i0      Loop enough times to step completely through object


ps_3_0


def    c0, 0.5f, 1, 0, 0


dcl_texcoord0  v0.xyz    // Start texture coordinate
dcl_texcoord1  v1.xyz    // Ray "step vector"
dcl_volume     s0        // "Matter map" - use alpha channel
dcl_volume     s1        // Color map


mov    r0.xyz, v0        // r0 is our ray position; it starts at v0 and adds v1 with each step
mov    r1, c0.z          // Initialize output with black


rep    i0
    texld   r2, r0, s0       // Sample the "matter map"

    // Matter detected?
    if_gt   r2.a, c1.y
        texld   r1, r0, s1       // Sample the color texture.
        break                    // Done!
    endif

    add     r0.xyz, r0, v1       // Step further along the ray

    // Stop if any ray coord leaves [0..1] range
    mov_sat r2.xyz, r0
    sub     r2.xyz, r2, r0
    abs     r2.xyz, r2
    dp3     r2.w, r2, c0.y
    if_ne   r2.w, c0.z
        break
    endif

endrep


// Output color
mov    oC0, r1
```

Lit Voxels (Calculating a Normal)

In order to light the rendered voxels, a normal must be obtained. Depending on how the volume data was extracted, another volume texture containing normal data could be accessed for visible voxels. If such data is not available, then a normal vector must be calculated per pixel; computing an accurate normal from volume data is a complex task that could make it the object of an article of its own. The techniques described below give a good approximation of normal calculation;

however, more sampling data and complex algorithms could be used to improve the visual accuracy of the results.

One approach is to trace three rays per pixel and calculate the cross product of the resulting hit points, but this is inordinately expensive — and problem-rich.

A better solution is illustrated in Figure 2 and described here:

1. The hit point is found just as with the solid voxels approach.

2. Sample a number of points on a sphere around the hit point (eight sample points are shown as diamond shapes in the diagram).

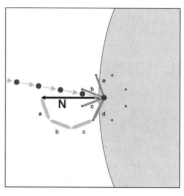

Figure 2. Additional texture samples can calculate an approximate normal.

3. Sum the offset vectors (i.e., the vector from hit point to sample point; vectors a, b, c, and d in the diagram) that do not hit matter and normalize the resulting vector (N in the diagram). This then approximates the normal.

Improvements

The points sampled in order to generate the normal can be tuned to get the best results.

1. The offset vector to each sample position on a sphere can be stored in pixel shader constants. These positions are stored for just one octant of the sphere; the sample positions for the other seven octants can be found by inverting the offset vector across each axis. Thus, three supplied offset vectors, with signs flipped and summed to the hit point, give coordinates for 24 texture samples. (Figure 3, which is 2D, would store two offset vectors per quadrant for a total of eight sample positions.)

2. Better results may be gained by sampling from several spheres of differing radii; this can be easily achieved by varying the lengths of each supplied offset vector.

There is potential for an error if the ray hits a thin sliver of matter, as shown in Figure 3. Offset vectors 2, 3, 4, 6, 7, and 8 all detect "no matter"; the summed result is a zero-length normal.

An additional check solves this problem: When calculating the normal, only perform texture samples for cases where the dot product of the offset vector and the step vector is negative (i.e., in Figure 3, sample

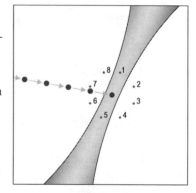

Figure 3: Thin slivers of matter can generate invalid normals unless fixed with additional code.

points 5, 6, 7, and 8 would be tested); this also has the benefit of halving the number of texture reads.

```
// Constants:   cl.x    Length of step
//              cl.y    Threshold value to detect matter
//              i0      Loop enough times to step completely through object


ps_3_0


def     c0, 0.5f, 1, 0, -1
def     c2, 0.363f, 0.363f, 0.858f, 0   // Offset vectors; 3 matter checks per octant
def     c3, 0.363f, 0.858f, 0.363f, 0   // (used for normal calculation)
def     c4, 0.858f, 0.363f, 0.363f, 0
def     c20, 0, 1, 0, 0                 // Light vector

dcl_texcoord0  v0.xyz     // Start texture coordinate
dcl_texcoord1  v1.xyz     // Ray "step vector"
dcl_volume     s0         // "Matter map" - use alpha channel
dcl_volume     s1         // Color map

mov     r0.xyz, v0        // Initialize ray position to v0; add v1 with each step
mov     r11, c0.z         // Initialize output with black


rep     i0
    texld   r1, r0, s0

    // Matter detected?
    if_gt   r1.a, cl.y

        // Zero r1; it will be used to sum the vectors contributing to the normal
        mov     r1, c0.z

        mov     r2, c2
        mul     r2, r2, cl.x      // r2 is the offset to sample around curr pos
        call    l0                // Will update r1 with normal contributions

        mov     r2, c3
        mul     r2, r2, cl.x      // r2 is the offset to sample around curr pos
        call    l0                // Will update r1 with normal contributions

        mov     r2, c4
        mul     r2, r2, cl.x      // r2 is the offset to sample around curr pos
        call    l0                // Will update r1 with normal contributions

        // If the normal is zero, use the inverse camera direction
        dp3     r1.w, r1, c0.y
        if_eq   r1.w, c0.z
        mov     r1.xyz, -v1
        endif

        // Now normalize the normal & do some lighting
        nrm     r2, r1
```

```
        dp3     r3, r2, c20
        mad     r11, r3, c0.x, c0.x


        break
    endif


    add     r0.xyz, r0, v1      // Step further along the ray


    // Stop if any ray coord leaves 0..1 range
    mov_sat r1.xyz, r0
    sub     r1.xyz, r1, r0
    abs     r1.xyz, r1
    dp3     r1.w, r1, c0.y
    if_ne   r1.w, c0.z
        break
    endif


endrep


// Output color
mov     oC0, r11


ret     // End of main


//////////////////////////////////////////////////////////////////////
// Purpose: Check for matter around a position.
// In:      r0.xyz  Hit position
//          r1.xyz  Summed normal-contributions
//          r2.xyz  Offset vector, in octant 0, to use to search around r0
// Out:     r1.xyz  Updated with new contributions (if any)
// Uses:    r3..r5
//////////////////////////////////////////////////////////////////////
label 10
    mov     r3, r2                  // Octant 0
    call    11


    mul     r3.xyz, r2, c0.yyw  // Octant 1
    call    11


    mul     r3.xyz, r2, c0.ywy  // Octant 2
    call    11


    mul     r3.xyz, r2, c0.yww  // Octant 3
    call    11


    mul     r3.xyz, r2, c0.wyy  // Octant 4
    call    11


    mul     r3.xyz, r2, c0.wyw  // Octant 5
    call    11
```

```
    mul     r3.xyz, r2, c0.wwy  // Octant 6
    call    11


    mul     r3.xyz, r2, c0.www  // Octant 7
    call    11

ret     // End of function: 10


///////////////////////////////////////////////////////////////////////////
// Purpose: Check a position for matter; sum the offset vector if no hit.
// In:      r0.xyz  Hit position
//          r1.xyz  Summed normal-contributions
//          r3.xyz  Offset vector
// Out:     r1.xyz  Updated with new contributions (if any)
// Uses:    r3..r5
///////////////////////////////////////////////////////////////////////////
label 11

    // Only check this sample point if the offset vector faces the camera
    dp3     r3.w, r3, v1
    if_lt   r3.w, c0.z
        add     r4.xyz, r3, r0
        texld   r5, r4, s0

        // If no is matter here, the offset vector can contribute to the normal
        if_le   r5.a, c1.y
            add     r1, r3, r1      // Add to the generated normal
        endif
    endif

ret     // End of function: 11
```

The Problem with Depth Buffering

Translucent, "accumulative" voxel objects will most likely be drawn after the other geometry of the scene. Figures 4 and 5 show an object inside a light volume. Ideally, a ray being traced from the front of the volume would not only terminate at the back of the volume but also when it hits an object, as shown in Figure 5. The supplied code does not demonstrate this. Thus, if an object gradually moves through the volume from behind to in front, the intensity visible in front of the object will not smoothly diminish; it will switch from full to none as the object passes through the front of the volume. Fixing this requires knowledge of the contents of the depth buffer, which currently can only be achieved by having a copy of it in a texture.

With both solid and lit voxels, it may be desirable to have the objects correctly depth buffered by calculating and outputting the correct depth value oDepth in the pixel shader. For solid objects that should never have any intersections with other objects, this is not necessary and should be strongly avoided for performance reasons, as 3D hardware typically prefers not to have the pixel shader output a depth value. However, in most other cases, correct depth buffering will likely be required. Note that unlike the accumulative case, it is not necessary to have current depth buffer values available as an input to the pixel shader.

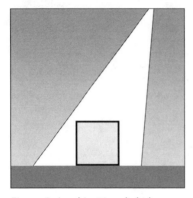

Figure 4: An object in a light beam, which is passing through a dusty atmosphere

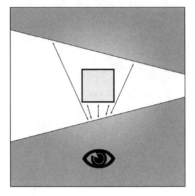

Figure 5: Top view of Figure 4, showing the eye position and ray paths

Comparison with "Stacked Quads" Method

Another method that has been used to visualize a volume texture is the "stacked quads" approach. A collection of quads is rendered, screen aligned, equally spaced in depth, and with the same screen-space size, each with 3D texture coordinates applied, which extract a different "slice" of the volume; the volume texture can be rotated by changing the texture coordinates or moved by shifting the stacked quads. Typically, additive blending is used. This can be compared to the accumulative, additive voxels; the distance between each quad is similar to the length of the step vector. One approach uses more geometry; the other uses more pixel shader power. If an alpha-test were used on the stacked quads approach, the visual result would be similar to the solid rendering approach. Lighting — that is, normal calculation — appears to be beyond the stacked quads method.

Imposters

Just as with polygonal models, "imposters" may be used to cut the processing costs of voxel objects.

In addition, voxel objects could conceivably be used as a 3D imposter. This would require code to be written to render slices of polygonal objects to the slices of a volume texture. 2D imposters must be updated when the view of the object significantly changes, for reasons including motion toward/away from the camera or when it changes (animates) or rotates. A 3D imposter would not have to be updated due to rotation.

Shadows

Voxel objects are compatible with shadow-buffer shadows but not with stencil shadows. This is because a shadow texture can be rendered containing the voxel object as easily as rendering it to the screen, but there is no geometry information from which to calculate a shadow volume for stencil shadows.

Generating Voxel Data

Voxel data can come from many sources. Physical objects can be scanned and converted to voxel data, for example, from MRI or CT scans. Polygonal objects can be rendered in slices to volume textures; an approach similar to rendering stencil volumes should work, though appropriate code was left as a "future direction." Another approach is algorithmically generating voxel data, as in the case of metaballs; the volume texture is filled with power values, and the pixel shader code considers matter to exist when the power is above a certain threshold.

CD Demo

The demo included on the companion CD requires 3D hardware supporting the pixel shader 3_0 model. If no such 3D accelerator is present, a batch file forcing the reference device is provided so that the demo can be run. Note that performance will then become a direct factor of the CPU power of the host platform.

The CD also contains movies illustrating some of the techniques described in this article.

Summary

Consumer triangle-accelerating hardware has become sufficiently advanced that it is now able to hardware accelerate voxels and metaballs. This article described how to render voxel objects using volume textures. Different implementations were proposed, which can be evaluated depending on the application required. While it might be some time before consumer 3D hardware can run anything more than a few voxel objects at acceptable speeds, this technique opens the door to a new set of possible visual effects, which, until now, were not accessible in mainstream real-time rendering.

Simulating Blending Operations on Floating-point Render Targets

Francesco Carucci
Lionhead Studios

Introduction

One of the most exciting new features introduced with DX9 class hardware (R300 and NV30) is floating-point textures, where RGBA channels are not fixed-point numbers restricted in the range from 0.0 to 1.0, as in the past, but can be expressed by 16- or 32-bit floating-point numbers, which extends both dynamic range and precision. A floating-point texture can be used both as input in a pixel shader or as a render target, storing the result coming from pixel color computation. This comes with some limitations: Current generation hardware can't do blend operations on floating-point render targets. This article introduces a technique to overcome the limitation when non-overlapping geometry is rendered.

Creating a Floating-point Texture

Direct3D 9 currently supports 16 and 32 bits per-channel formats for textures that can be used as render targets.

D3DFMT_R16F	16-bit texture using 16 bits only for the red channel
D3DFMT_G16R16F	32-bit texture using 16 bits for the red channel and 16 bits for the green channel
D3DFMT_A16B16G16R16	64-bit texture using 16 bits for each channel (alpha, blue, green, red)
D3DFMT_R32F	32-bit texture using 32 bits only for the red channel
D3DFMT_G32R32F	64-bit texture using 32 bits for the red channel and 32 bits for the green channel
D3DFMT_A32B32G32R32	128-bit texture using 32 bits for each channel (alpha, blue, green, red)

The 16 bits per-channel format is an s10e5 floating-point number with 10 bits mantissa and 5 bits exponent. The 32 bits per-channel format is an s23e8 floating-point number with 23 bits mantissa and 8 bits exponent.

Here is some code to create a floating-point texture to use as a render target:

```
LPDIRECT3DSURFACE9    gColorBufferSurface[2];
LPDIRECT3DTEXTURE9    gColorBufferTexture[2];
// create color buffer surfaces
gD3DDevice->CreateTexture(
    gWidth, gHeight,
    1,
    D3DUSAGE_RENDERTARGET,
    D3DFMT_A16B16G16R16F,
    D3DPOOL_DEFAULT,
    &gColorBufferTexture[0],
    NULL);

// get associated surfaces
gColorBufferTexture->GetSurfaceLevel(
    0,
    &gColorBufferSurface[0]);
```

Where gWidth and gHeight are the screen's current width and height.

Texture and surface (gColorBufferSurface[1] and gColorBufferTexture[1]) for the second color buffer can be created in the same way and will be used later in the code.

The following code sets the floating-point texture surface as the current render target:

```
gD3DDevice->SetRenderTarget(
    0,
    gColorBufferSurface[0]);
```

It's now possible to output the color resulting from pixel shader computation to the floating-point render target and make full use of higher precision floating-point math, for example, to accumulate results of several lighting passes without the limitations imposed by fixed-point math, both in precision and dynamic range.

Overview of the Technique

Current generation DX9-class hardware cannot perform post-pixel shader operations, such as blending, dithering, alpha testing, fogging, and masking on floating-point render targets, but blending operations with some limitations can be simulated in the pixel shader using floating-point precision.

The idea behind this technique is simple: By setting the floating-point render target both as input texture and as output in a pixel shader, we can read the color value of the currently rendered pixel and blend it with the color computed in the pixel shader and then write it again into the render target in the same pass.

An additive blending operation, for example, looks like this:

```
FinalColor = TexelColor + PixelColor
```

Where FinalColor is the color being written to the render target, TexelColor is the color read from the input texture, and PixelColor is the color computed in the pixel shader.

The idea cannot be implemented in a straightforward manner as described because having the same render target texture both as input and as output of the same pixel shader is not officially supported by current hardware and might lead to undefined and unpredictable results, due to the presence of texture and frame-buffer caches that usually do not talk to each other.

As a workaround, we can borrow the double buffering idea and create two floating-point textures; when the first one is used as input texture, the second one is used as a render target. After the pass is rendered, they can be switched for the next pass. The pseudocode for this is as follows:

```
Set i to 0
Clear texture[0]
Clear texture[1]

For each pass
    Set texture[i] as input texture
    Set texture[not i] as render target

    Render geometry

    Swap texture[0] and texture[1];
```

Reading the Input Texture in the Pixel Shader

The first step is to properly read the input texture stored by the previously rendered pass from within the pixel shader. Each fragment processed by the pixel shader corresponds to a unique texel in the input texture, which is the pixel computed in the previous pass. To compute the texture coordinates to access that texel, the vertex shader will pass the position of each vertex transformed in normalized device coordinates (x, y, and z vary from –1.0 to 1.0) through a texture coordinate interpolator, which is automatically linearly interpolated per pixel and gives the needed position of each fragment in the right space. This is implemented by the following HLSL code:

```
struct sVertexOutput
{
    float4 pos:       POSITION;
    float2 texcoord0: TEXCOORD0;
    float4 position:  TEXCOORD1;
};

sVertexOutput main(
    sVertexInput vIn)
{
    sVertexOutput o;

    // transform vertex position using the model view projection matrix
    float4 pos   = mul(vIn.position, matModelViewProj);

    // copy transformed position to output vertex position
```

```
    o.pos        = pos;

    // copy input vertex texture coordinates to the first interpolator
    o.texcoord0  = vIn.texcoord0;

    // copy transformed position to the second interpolator
    o.position   = pos;

    // return output vertex
    return o;
}
```

To compute the 2D coordinates to access the input texture, the pixel shader must now project the position in normalized device space of the fragment or, in other words, divide x and y by the w component; notice that this is exactly the same operation performed internally by the rasterizer when a pixel is projected after being transformed by the projection matrix. After the projection, x and y are in the range from –1.0 to 1.0; a simple scale and bias will give the right texture coordinates (in the range from 0.0 to 1.0) to access the color buffer texture. Here is a function in HLSL that accepts as input a sampler to a color buffer texture and a transformed position and returns the right pixel value:

```
float4 tex2DRect(
    in sampler2D s,
    in float4 position)
{
    float2 tc;

    tc.x = (position.x / position.w) * 0.5 + 0.5;
    tc.y = (-position.y / position.w) * 0.5 + 0.5;

    return tex2D(s, tc);
}
```

This function can be optimized using a projected texture access that saves the explicit division by w. The scale and bias can be moved to the vertex shader to further save some instructions in the pixel shader. While production code should use these tricks, the presented code is much more readable and easy to test during the development cycle.

Putting Everything Together

Finally, everything is put together in a simple shader that shows the technique.

```
float4 main(
    in float4 pos:        POSITION,
    in float2 texcoord0:  TEXCOORD0,
    in float4 position:   TEXCOORD1): COLOR
{
    float4 o;
```

```
// fetch the diffuse texture
float4 src   = tex2D(texture, texcoord0);

// read the previous pass' source pixel
float4 dst   = tex2DRect(ColorBuffer, position);

// additive blend!
o = src + dst;

return o;
}
```

In a real shader, the source color comes from some kind of computation (in this small example, it's just a texture fetch from a diffuse map) and is blended with the color in the destination color buffer to achieve the wanted result.

When Should One Use It?

I have used this technique to accumulate lighting passes in a high-precision color buffer with pleasing results. This is the blending equation used:

$$C_f = (A + L_1 + L_2) * T$$

Where C_f is the final color, A is the color from an ambient light pass (it is useful to fill the z buffer using an inexpensive rendering pass so as to take full advantage of the early-z rejection unit of DirectX9-class GPUs), L1 and L2 are colors from two lighting passes, and T is the final texture color blended with the content of the floating-point accumulation buffer.

The result of this computation might be greater than 1.0, which cannot be displayed directly if not saturated or properly mapped. A simple logarithmic function can be used to map the result to the [0.0, 1.0] displayable color range to avoid color saturation (a problem likely to appear in such a situation). Refer to "color mapping" techniques in high dynamic range rendering for further details on this topic.

This technique can't be used when the source color needs to be blended with a destination color computed in the *same* pass, as the requisite color has not yet been written to the destination color buffer. As an example, this is a common problem when developing a particle system. In this case I would suggest rendering the particle system in a normal color buffer after the color mapping, which reduces fillrate usage.

The last problem in using floating-point color buffers is the huge amount of fillrate used to render to a 64- or 128-bit render target, but, if the application is CPU bound or fillrate is not an issue, the use of floating-point color buffers significantly improves an application's visual fidelity at a negligable cost.

Rendering Volumes in a Vertex & Pixel Program by Ray Tracing

Eli Z. Gottlieb
egottlieb2@yahoo.com

3D graphics programmers have long strived for the most realistic graphics possible. We've used mathematical lighting models, textures, bump maps, environment maps, and now vertex and pixel shaders to achieve as much realism as possible with as much speed and interactivity as possible. And as always, we have used streams of triangle vertex data to represent shapes. Still, perfect realism can only come from one thing: ray tracing. Ray tracing simulates how photons interact with the environment by following a ray as it moves through a scene. There were always two problems with ray tracing, though; first, you need access to all the scene data at once, and second, performing ray-triangle intersections and reflections is very slow, even when done on the GPU via shaders. Volume textures are a solution to all these problems. Volumes store the entire scene as a 3D array of voxels, which in memory are xyzw floating-point vectors, just like pixels. This means we can trace rays through volumes, and we're no longer reliant on triangles that would eventually grow smaller than a pixel! In this article, an algorithm is presented for tracing rays through volume textures and using the rays for lighting implemented in v_2_x vertex and pixel shaders. The algorithm is written in Cg for readability, but you can implement it in any shading language that you want.

To Trace a Ray

In order to trace a ray through a volume, we first need to be able to render a volume. For this algorithm, we trace a ray at the same time as rendering the volume. So we just need to render a cube or another low-poly model to put the volume in.

We also need to pass the vertex's object space coordinates to the pixel shader for use as texture coordinates into the volume. To do that, we use this fairly simple vertex shader:

```
struct VertexIn
{
float3 xyz : POSITION;
};

struct VertexOut
```

```
{
float4 xyzw : POSITION;
float3 xyz : TEXCOORD0;
};

float4 Vec3To4(float3 v)
{
return float4(v.x,v.y,v.z,1);
}

VertexOut main(VertexIn vIn,uniform float4x4 mWorld,uniform float4x4 mView,uniform float4x4 mProj)
{
VertexOut fOut;
fOut.xyz = vIn.xyz;
fOut.xyzw = mul(Vec3To4(vIn.xyz),mWorld);
fOut.xyzw = mul(fOut.xyzw,mView);
fOut.xyzw = mul(fOut.xyzw,mProj);
return fOut;
}
```

In the pixel shader we use the texture coordinate to trace the ray through the volume and sample the appropriate voxels. Now we've got to start writing our pixel shader.

Inputs and Outputs of the Pixel Shader

The first thing we do to write the pixel shader is figure out what parameters we need and what data to return. We definitely need the output of the vertex shader, and this ray tracing algorithm doesn't require any depth returns or multiple render targets, so we just return a float4 for the pixel color. This pixel shader doesn't do much; it's just a starting point to work from.

```
struct VertexIn
{
float4 xyzw : POSITION;    //Clip space position for rasterizer.
float3 xyz : TEXCOORD0;    //Object space position.
};

struct FragOut
{
float4 color : COLOR0;    //Output pixel color.
};
FragOut main(VertexIn vIn)
{
FragOut fOut;
fOut.color = float4(1,1,1,1);
return fOut;
}
```

As you can see, we need a way to store our volume texture data. For ray tracing, we're going to need a per-voxel normal, a voxel color, and a voxel emissive light color.

That's too much for one voxel in any format! So we have to split it into multiple textures. We use an ARGB volume texture to contain the normal data in x, y, and z, and it also holds a 1D texture coordinate into the other two in its alpha component. That component is used to look up a 1D ARGB color texture and a 1D RGB emissive light texture. In reality, light doesn't have an alpha component, so therefore there is no alpha in the emissive light texture. After those changes, the result is this shader:

```
FragOut main(VertexIn vIn,
        uniform sampler3D tVolume,    //Normal in RGB, texcoord in A.
        uniform sampler1D tColor,     //RGBA voxel color.
        uniform sampler1D tLight)     //RGB emissive light color.
{
FragOut fOut;
fOut.color = float4(1,1,1,1);
return fOut;
}
```

Notice that we gain an advantage in working with the two 1D textures in that like voxels can lookup at the same coordinate, thus saving memory. Now we need a way to map our polygon model with the volume texture. To do this, we sample the volume and use the .a swizzle supported by Cg to lookup into the color texture and set the color. Then we lookup into the light texture and light the pixel. First, though, to get a proper coordinate into the volume texture, we must transform the object space vertex position from a space with the origin at the center, where OpenGL and Direct3D 9 place the origin, to a space with the origin at the top-left front corner.

To do this, we just multiply it by an appropriate matrix. Now our code looks much closer to rendering volume textures.

```
const float4x4 mVolumeCoords = {1,0,0,0,
                                0,-1,0,0,
                                0,0,1,0,
                                0.5,-0.5,1,0};


float4 Vec3To4(float3 v)//Converts float3 to float4 w/ w=1.
{
return float4(v.x,v.y,v.z,1);
}


FragOut main(VertexIn vIn,
        uniform sampler3D tVolume,    //Normal in RGB, texcoord in A.
        uniform sampler1D tColor,     //RGBA voxel color.
        uniform sampler1D tLight)     //RGB emissive light color.
{
FragOut fOut;
float3 texcoord = mul(vIn.xyz,mVolumeCoords);
fOut.color = tex1D(tColor,tex3D(tVolume,texcoord).a);
```

```
fOut.color.rgb *= tex1D(tLight,tex3D(tVolume,texcoord).a);
return fOut;
}
```

There's still one more thing necessary to make a shader for volume rendering. If the sampled voxel is empty, we should extrude the texture coordinate along the vector from the eyepoint to the vertex position. This is where things start to get messy. To do the extrusion, we need to use a while loop, and the Cg compiler can't compile while loops in pixel shaders. This means you'll have to translate the shader into ASM yourself. For the extrusion we need to add a new uniform parameter, a float3 containing the eye position in object space. We also need the volume texture dimensions so we always extrude one voxel. Finally, we arrive at the shader for rendering volume textures.

```
struct VertexIn
{
float4 xyzw : POSITION;    //Clip space position for rasterizer.
float3 xyz : TEXCOORD0;    //Object space position.
};

struct FragOut
{
float4 color : COLOR0;    //Output pixel color.
};

const float4x4 mVolumeCoords = {1,0,0,0,
                                0,-1,0,0,
                                0,0,1,0,
                                0.5,-0.5,1,0};

float4 Vec3To4(float3 v)                   //Converts float3 to float4 w/ w=1.
{
return float4(v.x,v.y,v.z,1);
}

FragOut main(VertexIn vIn,
             uniform float3 vDimens,      //Dimensions of the volume texture.
             uniform float3 vEyePos,      //Eye position in object space.
             uniform sampler3D tVolume,   //Normal in RGB, texcoord in A.
             uniform sampler1D tColor,    //RGBA voxel color.
             uniform sampler1D tLight)    //RGB emissive light color.
{
FragOut fOut;
bool bPixelFound = false;
float3 vVolPoint = vIn.xyz;              //Cartesian point in the volume to sample.
while(!bPixelFound)
{
fOut.color = tex1D(tColor,tex3D(tVolume,mul(vVolPoint,mVolumeCoords)).a);
if(fOut.color.a > 0)
  {
  bPixelFound = true;
  fOut.color.rgb *= tex1D(tLight,tex3D(tVolume, mul(vVolPoint,mVolumeCoords)).a);
```

```
    };
    vVolPoint += normalize(vVolPoint-vEyePos)/vDimens;
    };
    return fOut;
}
```

Okay, now how do we ray trace with that? Well, one aspect of ray tracing is finding out where the ray is going. This means that we trace it through the volume and reflect and refract it off of voxels as necessary. We can already trace a ray and reflect it in the pixel shader by storing the coordinate's voxel that we're currently sampling in vVolPoint, giving the ray a velocity, iterating through a loop to reflect vVolPoint against voxels, and at the end of every iteration adding the velocity vector to vVolPoint to trace the ray one voxel further. Here's the resulting shader:

```
const float4x4 mVolumeCoords = {1,0,0,0,
                                0,-1,0,0,
                                0,0,1,0,
                                0.5,-0.5,1,0};


float4 Vec3To4(float3 v)                //Converts float3 to float4 w/ w=1.
{
return float4(v.x,v.y,v.z,1);
}



FragOut main(VertexIn vIn,
            uniform float3 vDimens,      //Dimensions of the volume texture.
            uniform float3 vEyePos,      //Eye position in object space.
            uniform sampler3D tVolume,   //Normal in RGB, texcoord in A.
            uniform sampler1D tColor,    //RGBA voxel color.
            uniform sampler1D tLight)    //RGB emissive light color.

{
FragOut fOut;
float3 vRayPoint = vIn.xyz;             //Cartesian point in the volume to sample.
float3 vRayDir = normalize(vIn.xyz-vEyePos);
float3 vLight = float3(0,0,0);          //RGB light.
while(length(vRayPoint) <= 1)           //Once vRayPoint is > 1 we would be sampling voxels
                                        //outside the volume.

 {
 float3 vNormal = tex3D(tVolume,mul(vRayPoint,mVolumeCoords));
 if (length(vNormal) > 0)
  {
  fOut.color.rgb *= tex1D(tColor,tex3D(tVolume,mul(vIn.xyz,mVolumeCoords)).a).rgb;
  vLight += tex1D(tLight,tex3D(tVolume, mul(vRayPoint,mVolumeCoords)).a).rgb;
  if (dot(vRayDir,vNormal) > 0)         //Allow for 2-sided objects to be represented w/a
                                        //1-sided set of voxels.
   vRayDir = reflect(vRayDir,-vNormal);
  else
   vRayDir = reflect(vRayDir,vNormal);
  };
 vRayPoint += vRayDir/vDimens;
 };
```

```
return fOut;
}
```

Now there's only one thing missing: refraction. To implement it, we would have to be able to start a new loop whenever the ray is refracted. This is impossible because Cg code can't add new loops to itself at run time. We can, however, encapsulate the tracing of the ray in a function and call the function inside itself whenever we need to refract. So the next question is, how do we know when to refract? We check the alpha component of the voxel's color. If it's below 1, then the voxel is transparent to some degree and we need to refract through it. To get the refractive index, a one-component float texture is sampled. Finally, the color, light, ray position, and ray direction need to be passed to the tracing function every time it's called. All the unchanging parameters can be made global variables. We end up with this final version of the ray tracing code:

```
struct VertexIn
{
float4 xyzw : POSITION;   //Clip space position for rasterizer.
float3 xyz : TEXCOORD0;   //Object space position.
};

struct FragOut
{
float4 color : COLOR0;
}

const float4x4 mVolumeCoords = {1,0,0,0,
                                0,-1,0,0,
                                0,0,1,0,
                                0.5,-0.5,1,0};

float4 vColor;
float3 vLight;            //No alpha in light.
float3 vNormal;
float3 vDimens;
sampler3D tVolume,
 //An RGBA volume texture for normals in object space and a texcoord.
sampler1D tColors,        //An RGBA texture containing voxel colors.
sampler1D tLight,         //An RGB texture containing emmissive colors.
sampler1D tRefracts)      //A one-component texture for refractive indices.

float4 Vector3To4(float3 v)
{
return float4(v.x,v.y,v.z,1);
}

float4 TraceRay(float4 vColor,inout float3 vLight,float3 vRayPos,float3 vRayDir)
{
float4 fOut;
bool bLit = false;
if (length(vNormal) == 1)
 {
```

```
vColor = tex1D(tColors,tex3D(tVolume,mul(Vector3To4(vRayPos),mVolumeCoords)).a);
vLight += tex1D(tLight,tex3D(tVolume,mul(Vector3To4(vRayPos),mVolumeCoords)).a) .rgb;
if (dot(vRayDir,vNormal) > 0)
 vRayDir = reflect(vRayDir,-vNormal);
else
 vRayDir = reflect(vRayDir,vNormal);
fOut.color *= vColor;
};
vRayPos += vRayDir/vDimens;
while (!bLit)
{
if (vColor.a < 1)
 {
 float4 vRefractColor = TraceRay(vColor,vLight,vRayPos,refract(vRayDir,vNormal,tex1D
     (tRefracts,tex3D(tVolume,mul(Vector3To4(vRayPos),mVolumeCoords)).a).r);
 vColor = vColor.a*vColor * vRefractColor*vRefractColor.a;
 };
 vNormal = tex3D(tVolume,mul(Vector3To4(vRayPos),mVolumeCoords)).rgb;
 if (length(vNormal) == 1)
 {
 vColor = tex1D(tColors,tex3D(tVolume,mul(Vector3To4(vRayPos),mVolumeCoords)).a);
 vRayDir = reflect(vRayDir,vNormal);
 fOut *= vColor;
 };
 else
  if (length(vRayPos) == 1)
  {
  fOut *= vColor * clamp(vLight) + (vLight - 1.xxx);   //Diffuse and specular lighting.
  bLit = true;
  }
 vRayPos += vRayDir/vDimens;
 };
return fOut;
}


FragOut main(VertexIn vIn,
 uniform float3 vDimens,      //Dimensions of the volume texture.
 uniform float3 vEyePos,      //The eye position, in object space.
 uniform sampler3D Volume,
  //An RGBA volume texture for normals in object space and a texcoord.
 uniform sampler1D Colors,    //An RGBA texture containing voxel colors.
 uniform sampler1D Light,     //An RGB texture containing emmissive colors.
 uniform sampler1D Refracts)  //A 1-component texture for refractive indices.
{
FragOut fOut;
tVolume = Volume;
tColors = Colors;
tLight = Light;
tRefracts = Refracts;
float3 vRayDir = normalize(vIn.xyz-vEyePos);
float3 vRayPos = vEyePos;
vColor = tex1D(tColors,tex3D(tVolume,mul(Vector3To4(vRayPos),mVolumeCoords)).a);
```

```
vLight = tex1D(tLight,tex3D(tVolume,mul(Vector3To4(vRayPos),mVolumeCoords)).a) .rgb;
vNormal = tex3D(tVolume,mul(Vector3To4(vRayPos),mVolumeCoords)).rgb;
fOut.color = float4(0,0,0,1);
fOut.color = TraceRay(vColor,vLight,vRayPos,vRayDir);
fOut.color.a = 1;
return fOut;
}
```

Some Optimizations

Of course, there are some things that you can do to make the shader run faster or use less memory. One would be a limit on how many times the tracing function can nest. Another, obviously, would be to compress the textures. You can also make a fairly small quality sacrifice to save memory by using point lights to trace rays back to. You may even see a way to optimize the shader code (this wouldn't surprise me). As is though, I think the shader runs fast enough on most volumes to be used in real time.

What to Use It For

Probably the best current use of the shader is to render the unchanging parts of a scene as volumes so you can obtain the benefits of ray tracing. Another good use of volume ray tracing is rendering objects with complicated emissive lighting, such as fireballs, lightning, flashlights, and anything else that shines. On future hardware, you might be able to blit volume textures, allowing the rendering of the scene as volumes so you can show an entire ray-traced scene! For now, however, we don't have such OGL 2.0 type hardware. In conclusion, volume textures can have rays traced through them starting from the pixel's object space coordinates to render them with ray tracing effects such as shadowing, reflection, and refraction. This algorithm achieves that goal using hardware pixel shaders for real-time speed.

Normal Map Compression

Jakub Klarowicz

Techland

The development of new rendering techniques and the increasing popularity of per-pixel lighting make normal maps play more and more of a significant role in a texture set of any 3D project. New tools for geometry simplification that move all geometry details to bump maps (like ATI's Normal Mapper or nVidia's Melody) generate an additional amount of high-resolution normal maps. It leads to a situation where big chunks of precious video memory are consumed by normal maps.

In the past, when the number and size of textures used in graphical projects were increasing quickly, developers faced the same problem. A solution to this was a lousy texture compression standard called DXTC, which allows for memory footprints up to six times smaller for a texture without noticeable loss in image quality. Unfortunately, the direct use of the DXTC format for normal map compression leads to poor quality results. Because of the nature of data contained in normal maps, as well as the way they are used in the rendering process, all distortions and errors caused by the compression are easily noticeable. Only very subtle and soft normal maps can be compressed with an acceptable quality.

This article presents a new approach to the compression of normal maps using DXTC. The special preprocessing of a map before the compression allows for the retention of much more detail in comparison with direct compression and also results in a significantly better visual quality of renderings.

Technique

The main idea of the technique is to use all four RGBA channels of the DXT5 format to compress a three-channel normal map (RGB). The map is transformed in such a way that part of the information is moved from RGB to alpha channel A. Since RGB and A channels are compressed independently in the DXT5 format, the loss of information during compression is smaller and artifacts caused by the compression are less visible.

The transformation that has to be applied to normal maps before the compression is very simple. One channel of the normal map (R, G, or B) is copied to the alpha channel A, and it is then cleared (filled with zero values). The transformed map consists of the same components as the original map, with one of them moved into alpha channel A and one of the R, G, or B channels containing only zeroes. Normal maps preprocessed in such a way are then compressed with any application that is able to compress to the DXT5 format.

185

In order to use the compressed normal map, it is necessary to move the component stored in the alpha channel back to its original place (R, G, or B). Decoding is performed during the rendering and is also very simple. It requires one additional pixel shader instruction and one additional pixel shader constant. Here's some ps 1.1 code that does the job:

```
ps_1_1

def    c0, 1, 0, 0, 0       // 1 in red channel

tex    t0                   // read normal map
mad    t0, t0.a, c0, t0     // move alpha to red channel
...                         // use normal map
```

The code assumes that the red channel has been stored in alpha. For other cases, the only thing that is different is the value of the c0 constant. It should be 0,1,0,0 for green in alpha and 0,0,1,0 for blue in alpha. The c0 constant doesn't have to be stored in the pixel shader code directly; it can be set using the Direct3D function SetPixelShaderConstantF. This way, a proper constant can be set according to how the normal map that is being used has been prepared.

Results

The figures on this and the following page present a per-pixel lit quad with the same normal map.

Notice the "blocky" look of the directly compressed map. These blocks correspond to 4x4 groups of pixels — the basic unit on which DXTC compression operates. As you can see in Figure 3, the presented method significantly reduces the "blockiness." You can also see that much more detail is preserved in the map.

The best results are obtained with tangent space normal maps. Vectors in model space normal maps vary much, and thus compression artifacts are more visible. It is best to place a component that has the greatest variation in the alpha channel — for tangent space normal maps, it's either R or G.

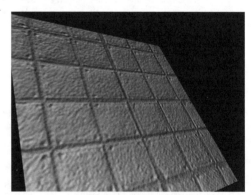

Figure 1: Uncompressed normal map

There's a small application on the CD that shows the results for various normal maps. All maps have been coded with the green in alpha method.

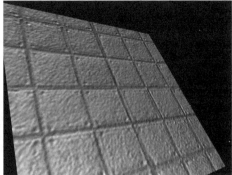

Figure 2: Normal map compressed directly to DXT5

Figure 3: Normal map compressed with described method

How to Prepare the Normal Map

Here's a complete procedure on how to prepare a normal map with the green channel copied to the alpha using Adobe Photoshop 7.0 and nVidia DDS Compression Plugin [1].

1. Load uncompressed map to Photoshop.
2. Choose Channels from the Window menu.
3. Select the green channel in the Channels tab.
4. Right-click on the green channel.
5. Select Duplicate Channel from the pop-up menu and press OK in the dialog that appears.
6. Select the green channel again.
7. Choose All from the Select menu.
8. Choose Clear from the Edit menu.
9. Save the map using Save As and the DDS format, making sure the Alpha Channels check box is selected.
10. Choose DXT5 format in the Save Format combo box.
11. Press Save.

Why It Works

This section assumes the reader's basic knowledge of the DXT5 format, especially its compression methods. Details can be found in [2].

At first sight, it may be surprising that map quality can be improved just by moving one normal component to the alpha channel. One reason for this is that the alpha channel is quantized separately from RGB channels; the other is the fact that it is quantized with an increased accuracy. In DXT5, each 4x4 block of pixels quantizes the alpha to eight separate values. These eight values are distributed uniformly in a sub-range of the [0, 1] alpha range. This way, the compressed alpha channel can represent the original content very precisely. The accuracy of the representation depends on how much the original values differ in the 4x4 block — the less they differ, the narrower the sub-range is, and thus the quantization error is smaller. Fortunately, in most normal maps the variation of the normal vector is smooth and doesn't change by a big amount in one block.

Due to removing one of the RGB components, the quantization of the RGB channels is also improved. The DXT5 format quantizes the color channel to a palette of four colors for each 4x4 block. Two of these colors are stored within the block, and the other two are derived as a weighted sum of the former two. This four-color palette can be treated as a set of four points placed on a line in 3D space. Two of these points can be chosen arbitrarily to explicitly define the line. 16 points in 3D space representing sixteen original colors in the block are replaced with four colors from the palette. It is now obvious why directly compressed normal maps look so bad — each block is represented by only four different vectors; smoothly varying normal vectors are snapped to four vectors from the palette.

By removing one of the RGB components, the dimension of the original 16 points is reduced by one. Now four points from the palette represent 16 points in 2D space — therefore, the quantization error is smaller in most cases. Further improvement follows with normal maps authored for the tangent space because such normal maps are almost 2D initially. Vectors in the tangent space maps are near (0,0,1), so if the x or y component is removed, the remaining vector is almost 1D and only one of its components varies. This makes a very good fit to the 1D color quantization of the DXT5.

Pros and Cons

Pros:

- The described method is widely available because of good hardware support for DXTC.
- Only uses 8 bits per pixel — three times less memory sizes
- Only 1 TMU used (does not require additional TMUs)
- Easy to use, does not require dedicated tools for compression
- Fast and simple decoding in the pixel shader
- It uses DXT5, so it guarantees that the color channel is decoded with full 24-bit precision on all nVidia hardware.

Cons:

- There is a small amount of additional data stored with each normal map — the constant for a pixel shader required to decode the map that has to be set in the pixel shader.
- Doesn't work as well for model space normal maps as for tangent space maps

■ Very rough normal maps still look bad when compressed; uncompressed format is required in such cases.

References

[1] DXTC texture tools: http://developer.nvidia.com/view.asp?IO=ps_texture_compression_plugin.

[2] DirectX SDK 9.0, DirectX documentation for C++.

Drops of Water and Texture Sprites

Sylvain Lefebvre
www.aracknea.net

Introduction

Textures are present in almost every real-time graphics application. They are a very convenient way of improving the appearance of a surface at low cost (in comparison to the geometry needed to obtain the same appearance). We can distinguish two main types of textures: explicit textures that consist of (potentially large) images that are loaded in memory and procedural textures that are computed on the fly at the pixel level (only the procedure needs to be stored).

While the former are supported by almost all graphics hardware, procedural textures have been limited to software renderers. Nowadays, as graphics hardware becomes more and more powerful, classical procedural textures become affordable on the GPU [1].

However, in many applications something between purely procedural and explicit textures is needed; we want textures to be created by procedurally combining explicit textures. We refer to these textures as *pattern-based procedural textures* (see [2]). They are not procedural in the sense of classical marble or wood textures [3], but they combine explicit textures (patterns) in order to create a larger texture with the desired appearance. For instance, we may need footsteps to appear on top of a snow texture, impacts to appear where a bullet hit the wall, or drops of water to fall along a surface. These kinds of dynamic textures cannot be explicit: Just imagine a game level with thousands of surfaces. Each time a bullet hits a wall, we have to update the corresponding texture. But as we do not want the same impact to appear on all surfaces, we need to create a copy of all the texture data for each surface. The required amount of texture memory would be prohibitive. Moreover, the resolution of the impacts would not be able to exceed the resolution of the original texture.

Yet there are bullet impacts on the walls in my favorite first-person shooter game. How is this done? In most games, effects like bullet impacts are created by adding a small textured geometric quad, called a *decal*, on top of the geometry. This has some inconveniences. First, the quad has to be positioned precisely and split along the edges of the model on which it is applied. Second, this introduces geometry for non-geometrical reasons; the effect is purely textural, and here we

190

have to simulate it using geometry. Third, imagine that we want to animate the decals on top of the surface; we would have to do all the positioning work at each frame for each decal. Working with complex surfaces, this would have a high computational cost.

To overcome this problem, [2] introduced a method of implementing *texture sprites* using graphics hardware. Texture sprites allow us to position and animate sprites *in* a texture. The main advantage is that we no longer have to worry about the geometry; the problem will be directly solved in texture space. Another interesting point is that the resolution of the sprites can be higher than the resolution of the underlying texture. The memory cost of this technique is low, and it can be implemented on GeForce3/Radeon 8500 (with some limitations) and on the latest programmable graphics board. The Drops of Water shader uses the texture sprites technique to render drops over the texture. It is therefore a pattern-based procedural texture, as its appearance results from the procedural combination of explicit textures (the drop and the surface texture).

In the section titled "Texture Sprites," we introduce the texture sprites technique and describe its implementation on various types of hardware. In the section titled "The Drops of Water Effect," we see how to combine texture sprites, a wet surface effect, and a magnification effect in order to create the Drops of Water shader.

Texture Sprites

The texture sprites technique relies on a new functionality of graphics hardware that was first designed to create a fake bump mapping. This functionality is called *offset textures*. It allows the encoding in a texture of an offset that is added to the texture coordinates of a second texture. We use this in order to position sprites in our textures.

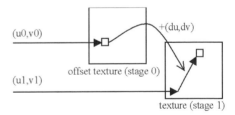

Figure 1: The value read in the offset texture (stage 0) is used to add an offset to the texture coordinates of a second texture (stage 1).

Reference Texture

First we need to store our sprites in a texture, which is called the *reference texture* in the discussion that follows. The reference texture is considered a regular grid. Each cell of this grid is a square block of pixels called a *tile*. In each tile, we can either store a sprite or leave it empty (i.e., with the background color). For implementation reasons, we need empty tiles around a tile containing a sprite. This limitation can be overcome on the latest graphics hardware, as explained in the "Implementation Notes" section.

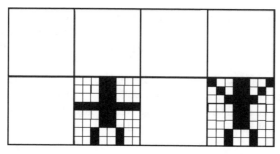

Figure 2: A reference texture containing two sprites. It consists of 4x2 tiles of 8x8 pixels each. The resolution of this reference texture is therefore 32x16 pixels. Each sprite is surrounded by empty tiles (the texture is cyclic).

Offset Map

Now we can see how to use offset textures to procedurally create a new texture from a given explicit texture. We begin with a practical case: Let's take an offset texture with a resolution of 8x8 pixels. Each pixel encodes an offset. If we apply this offset texture on a geometric quad without any filtering, we obtain a grid of 8x8 cells, one for each pixel of the offset texture. Each cell will contain one (du,dv) vector. Now we take another texture with 256x256 pixel resolution, map it onto the same quad, and use the offset texture to perturb its texture coordinates.

Each cell of the offset texture therefore applies a translation to the texture coordinates of a block of 64x64 pixels of the second texture (256/8 = 64). This way we can independently translate the content of each texture block by simply updating the corresponding cell of the offset texture (only one pixel in video memory). As the translation is applied to texture coordinates, this method can be used with any textured geometry. This type of offset texture is called an *offset map*.

Sprite Positioning

We use an offset map to procedurally create a new texture from the tiles of the reference texture. This new texture shows the sprites at their choosen position. We need each cell of the offset map to cover a tile of the reference texture. Suppose that the offset map and the reference texture are respectively in texture stages 0 and 1 and have independent texture coordinates. The idea is to compute the texture coordinates of the reference texture so that one cell of the offset map covers exactly one tile. This can easily be done in a vertex program.

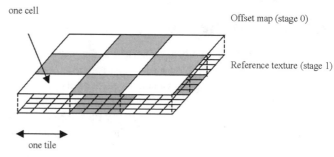

Figure 3: Each cell of the offset map covers exactly one tile of the reference texture.

Visually, the effect is as if each cell of the offset map were a window opened on the reference texture. This window has the same resolution as one tile. In each cell we can choose which part of the reference texture will be displayed. As we can choose to display only a small part of a tile of the reference texture, we need to have empty tiles around one sprite tile; we do not want a neighboring sprite to be visible if we only display a small part of a sprite.

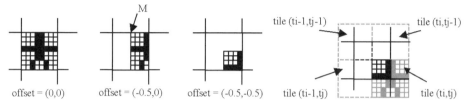

offset = (0,0)   offset = (-0.5,0)   offset = (-0.5,-0.5)

Figure 4: Adding an offset (u,v) to the texture coordinates results in a translation (-u,-v) of the sprite in the texture.

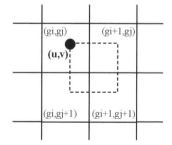

tile (ti-1,tj-1)   tile (ti,tj-1)

tile (ti-1,tj)   tile (ti,tj)

When the sprite in tile (ti,tj) is translated, the neighbouring tiles become visible.

As you can see in Figure 4, to translate the sprite by (0.5,0) we have to use an offset of (–0.5,0). It comes from the fact that the offset is added to the *texture coordinates*. Let's assume that the point at the top-left corner of the sprite is at (0,0) in the reference texture. Point M, without using the offset map, has texture coordinates (0.5,0). When we add the offset (–0.5,0) to M, the resulting texture coordinate is (0,0); that is why we can see the top-left corner of the sprite at this location. Visually, the sprite has been translated by (0.5,0).

We now have a reference texture containing some sprites and an offset map that allows us to display sprites or part of sprites in its cells. How do we position a sprite at a given texture coordinate?

Imagine that we want a sprite at texture coordinates (u,v). That is to say, we want the top-left corner of the tile containing the sprite to be at (u,v). We can easily compute in which cell (gi,gj) of the offset map the (u,v) texture coordinates lie; if the offset map has a resolution of N x N, the corresponding cell is[1]:

$$(gi,gj) = (floor(N * u) \% N, floor(N * v) \% N)$$

As the tile of the sprite has the same size as the cell of the offset map, four cells of the offset map are needed to display the sprite.

First we position the chosen sprite tile in the four concerned cells of the offset map: (gi,gj), (gi+1,gj), (gi,gj+1), (gi+1,gj+1). See Figure 6, step 1. For this purpose, we need to compute which tile (ti,tj) of the reference texture is displayed in the cell at the (u,v) texture coordinates if we were not using an offset map. If the reference

Figure 5: To display a sprite at an arbitrary position in the texture, four cells of the offset map are needed.

---

1   % is the modulo operator; *floor(x)* returns the greatest integer that is less than or equal to x.

texture contains T by T tiles[2], the corresponding tile is:

$$(ti,tj) = (gi \% T, gj \% T)$$

We can therefore compute the offset (du_{ij}, dv_{ij}) to be stored in (gi,gj) in order to have the tile containing the sprite (si,sj) displayed instead of the tile (ti,tj):

$$(du_{ij}, dv_{ij}) = (\frac{(si-ti)}{T}, \frac{(sj-tj)}{T})$$

This offset translates the tile (si,sj) on top of the tile (ti,tj).

Now we have to take into account the relative position of the sprite tile within the cell (gi,gj). See Figure 6, step 2. The relative position $(\Delta u_{ij}, \Delta v_{ij})$ of (u,v) within (gi,gj) is computed as follows:

$$(\Delta u_{ij}, \Delta v_{ij}) = (u*N - gi, v*N - gj)$$

To make the sprite appear at the correct position in tile (gi,gj), we have to translate it by:

$$\frac{(\Delta u_{ij}, \Delta v_{ij})}{T}$$

Because we work in texture coordinate space, we have to subtract[3] this vector from the previously computed offset (du_{ij}, dv_{ij}). Given $(\Delta u_{ij}, \Delta v_{ij})$, the $(\Delta u, \Delta v)$ values of the four cells are:

$(\Delta u_{ij}, \Delta v_{ij})$	$(\Delta u_{(i+1)j}, \Delta v_{(i+1)j})$	$= (\Delta u_{ij} - 1, \Delta v_{ij})$
$(\Delta u_{i(j+1)}, \Delta v_{i(j+1)}) = (\Delta u_{ij}, \Delta v_{ij} - 1)$	$(\Delta u_{(i+1)(j+1)}, \Delta v_{(i+1)(j+1)}) = (\Delta u_{ij} - 1, \Delta v_{ij} - 1)$	

The entire process of sprite positioning is summarized in Figure 6.

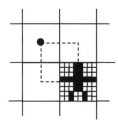 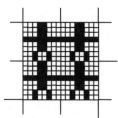 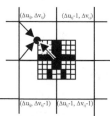 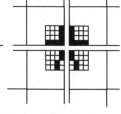

Figure 6: We want to position the top-left corner of the sprite at (u,v).

Step 1: Using the offset map and the computed (du,dv), the tile containing the sprite is placed in the four cells.

Step 2: A translation $(\Delta u, \Delta v)$ is added in the four cells in order to display only the needed part of the sprite.

Each cell displays a part of the sprite. When viewed side by side, the sprite appears to be at the chosen (u,v) coordinates.

---

2   If tile$_{res}$ * tile$_{res}$ is the size (in pixels) of a tile, the reference texture has a size (in pixels) of (T * tile$_{res}$) by (T * tile$_{res}$).

3   As explained before, translating a sprite by (tu,tv) corresponds to subtracting (tu,tv) from the offset.

Rotation and Scaling

Now that we are able to position sprites in a texture, we can go further and apply transformations on each sprite (i.e., scaling and rotation). The idea is to transform the sprite within its tile by applying the transformation to the texture coordinates before accessing the sprite texture data. To do so, we need a map of the same resolution as the offset map to store the transformation associated with a sprite (i.e., rotation angle and scaling factor). This map will be called the *transformation map*. In the same way that a sprite uses four cells of the offset map, the four corresponding cells of the transformation map will store the transformation information of the sprite.

Imagine that we are accessing a texture with (u_0,v_0) coordinates, where $(u_0, v_0) \in [0,1]\times[0,1]$. If we want the texture to appear rotated by an angle θ around its center $(0.5,0.5)$, we have to compute new texture coordinates (u_1,v_1) using a 2D rotation formula:

$$(u_1,v_1) = \begin{array}{l} (\ cos(-\theta)*(u_0 - 0.5) + sin(-\theta)*(v_0 - 0.5) + 0.5 \\ - sin(-\theta)*(u_0 - 0.5) + cos(-\theta)*(v_0 - 0.5) + 0.5\ ) \end{array}$$

As the transformation is applied on texture coordinates, we have to use an angle of $-\theta$ to rotate the texture of an angle θ (see Figure 7).

If we want the texture to appear scaled by a factor of s from its center, we have to compute new texture coordinates (u_2,v_2) using a 2D scaling formula:

$$(u_2,v_2) = (\frac{(u_1 - 0.5)}{s} + 0.5, \frac{(v_1 - 0.5)}{s} + 0.5)$$

We have to scale texture coordinates by a factor of $\frac{1}{s}$ to scale the texture by a factor of s.

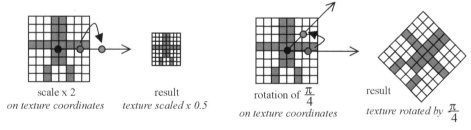

| scale x 2 | result | rotation of $\frac{\pi}{4}$ | result |
| on texture coordinates | texture scaled x 0.5 | on texture coordinates | texture rotated by $\frac{\pi}{4}$ |

Figure 7: Scaling texture coordinates

Applying this method to the tile of a sprite in the reference texture is straightforward: We can easily express the texture coordinates in the tile space. Indeed, given (u,v) coordinates in the reference texture, the corresponding coordinates in tile space are[4]:

$$(tu,tv) = (frac(u * T),frac(v * T))$$

---

4   Where *frac* extracts the fractional part of a floating-point number

The corresponding tile index is:

$$(si,sj) = (floor(u * T),floor(v * T))$$

From (tu,tv), we can go back to reference texture space by computing:

$$(u,v) = (\frac{(si+tu)}{T}, \frac{(sj+tv)}{T})$$

But wait! What will ensure that we are not going out of the sprite tile? Nothing! So we have to check whether we are going out of the tile; this is done by testing whether the coordinates still lie in [0,1]x[0,1] after transformation. This is important because as multiple sprites may be stored in the reference texture, neighboring sprites may become visible if we shrink a sprite beyond a certain threshold (even with the empty tiles; see Figure 8).

There are some constraints on the scaling that we can apply: If we enlarge a sprite too much, it may be clipped by the border of the offset map cells. However, we can shrink the sprite as much as we want. In order to allow arbitrary rotations, the shape of a sprite must also be contained in a circle centered at the tile center.

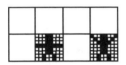

Figure 8: Reference texture

One sprite with scaling of 0.5 (2.0 in texture space). Only empty tiles are displayed.

If we shrink the sprite too much, other sprites become visible (left). If the hardware allows it (see the "Implementation" section), we can check that the texture coordinates are still in the sprite tile. If not, we display the background color (right).

Limitations

Overlapping Sprites

As each sprite requires four cells of the offset map, multiple grids should be used in order to allow the sprites to overlap. This could be done in multiple passes or in one pass, depending on the hardware that you are working with (see the Drops of Water effect implementation).

Precision

The limited precision of per-pixel arithmetic operations can result in positioning problems; an artifact can appear on the sprite at tile borders. This issue is mainly solved by carefully creating the positioning texture: All arithmetic operations are done with respect to 8 or 16 bits of precision. However, some artifacts may still be visible when the viewpoint is very close to the texture. On recent graphics boards, the introduction of floating-point textures and 32-bit precision solves this problem.

Filtering

- *Mipmapping* — As we are packing sprites in the same texture, we have to prevent the use of the latest mipmapping levels. Indeed, there is a level for which each pixel corresponds to the average color of one tile of the reference texture. All coarser levels are not correct, as they are computed by using pixels from multiple tiles.

- *Far viewpoint* — If the viewpoint is far from the surface, aliasing occurs on the offset map: Multiple cells of the offset map are projected onto one pixel of the screen. To solve this problem, we have to compute a color version of the offset map, where each pixel is the average color of the pixels displayed in the offset map cell. When far from the surface, this texture should be used instead of the texture sprites.

Implementation

Software Positioning

Software positioning of sprites is done by the PutSprite function. Its parameters are a sprite index, a texture coordinate, a rotation angle, and a scaling factor. The PutSprite function computes the indices of the four cells of the offset map that need to be updated in order to position the sprite. It also computes the relative coordinates of the sprites in these cells. Then it calls RefTexIJ2OffsetMapIJ, which updates each cell in order to display the sprite tile with the correct translation. Note that we pack the transformation data (i.e., rotation angle and scaling factor) in the blue and alpha channel of the offset map.

```
void PutSprite(int si,int sj,
               double u,double v,
               double angle,double scale)
{
    double ugrid,vgrid;
    double du,dv;
    int    gi,gj;

    // ensure u and v are both > 0.0 (because of modulo operations)
    // texture are cyclic with a period of 1.0:
    // adding an integer to texture coordinates
    // does not change the final result
    if (u < 0.0)
        u=1.0+(u-(int)u);

    if (v < 0.0)
        v=1.0+(v-(int)v);
    // compute pos in offset map
    ugrid=(u*m_dwOffsetMapRes);
    vgrid=(v*m_dwOffsetMapRes);
    // compute offset map cell index
    gi=(int)ugrid;
```

```
        gj=(int)vgrid;
        // compute texture coordinates relative to the cell
        du=ugrid-gi;
        dv=vgrid-gj;
        // cell i,j
        RefTexIJ2OffsetMapIJ(si,sj,
            gi,gj,
            du,dv,
            angle,scale);
        // cell i+1,j
        RefTexIJ2OffsetMapIJ(si,sj,
            gi+1,gj,
            du-1.0,dv,
            angle,scale);
        // cell i,j+1
        RefTexIJ2OffsetMapIJ(si,sj,
            gi,gj+1,
            du,dv-1.0,
            angle,scale);
        // cell i+1,j+1
        RefTexIJ2OffsetMapIJ(si,sj,
            gi+1,gj+1,
            du-1.0,dv-1.0,
            angle,scale);
        // update offset map in video memory
        UpdateOffsetMap();
}


void RefTexIJ2OffsetMapIJ(int si,int sj,
                          int gi,int gj,
                          double delta_u,double delta_v,
                          double angle,double scale)
{
    int     ti,tj;
    double  du,dv;
    int     _1_T,idu,idv;

    // ensure gi,gj are in grid bounds
    gi %= m_dwOffsetMapRes;
    gj %= m_dwOffsetMapRes;
    // compute what tile would be here if we were not using an offset map
    ti=gi % m_dwRefTexNbTiles;
    tj=gj % m_dwRefTexNbTiles;
    // compute offset to apply in this cell
    du=(si-ti) - delta_u;
    dv=(sj-tj) - delta_v;
    // encoding du,dv as 8-bit integers (low precision !)
    _1_T=128 / m_dwRefTexNbTiles;
    idu=(int)(du*_1_T);
    idv=(int)(dv*_1_T);
    // write to grid
```

```
    m_OffsetMap[(gi+gj*m_dwOffsetMapRes)*4  ]=(BYTE)idu;
    m_OffsetMap[(gi+gj*m_dwOffsetMapRes)*4+1]=(BYTE)idv;
    // transformation data in blue and alpha channel of offset map
    m_OffsetMap[(gi+gj*m_dwOffsetMapRes)*4+2]=(BYTE)(angle*256.0/360.0);
    m_OffsetMap[(gi+gj*m_dwOffsetMapRes)*4+3]=(BYTE)(255.0*scale);
}
```

GeForce 3/4 (and higher) *ps 1.3* (no rotation, no scaling)

With ps 1.3, the implementation relies on the texbem instruction to add the translation encoded in the offset map to the texture coordinates of the reference texture.

```
ps.1.3

tex     t0
texbem  t1, t0
mov     r0, t1
```

Radeon 8500 (and higher) *ps 1.4* (no rotation, no scaling)

The implementation is straightforward; we simply read the offset map and add the offset to the texture coordinates.

```
ps.1.4

texcrd r0.xyz, t1     // read texture coordinates
texld r1,     t0      // read offset map

add r1.xyz, r0, r1_bx2 // add offset to tex coords

phase

texld r0, r1.xyz      // read reference texture
```

GeForce FX / Radeon 9700 *HLSL/ps 2.0*

The implementation includes rotation and scaling of sprites. The transformation of texture coordinates is done by the transformedLookup function. The Cg code would be almost the same.

```
half4 transformedLookup(uniform sampler2D tex,
                half2 ctex,
                half angle,half scale)
{
    half4 c;

    // transform coordinates from reference texture space to tile space
    half2 gcoords=ctex*RefTexNbTiles;
    half2 uv0=frac(gcoords);          // tile space
    half2 isprite=floor(gcoords);     // sprite index (si,sj)

    // apply rotation
    half si,cs;
```

```
    sincos(-angle*6.28,si,cs);

    uv0=uv0-0.5;
    half2 uv1=half2( uv0.x*cs + uv0.y*si,
                     -uv0.x*si + uv0.y*cs);
    uv1=uv1+0.5;

    // apply scaling
    uv1=uv1-0.5;
    half2 uv2=uv1/scale;
    uv2=uv2+0.5;

    // are coordinates still in sprite tile?
    if (   uv2.x > 1.0 || uv2.x < 0.0
        || uv2.y > 1.0 || uv2.y < 0.0)
        c=bkgColor;
    else
        c=tex2D(tex,(uv2+isprite)/RefTexNbTiles);
    return c;
}

float4 ps20TSprite(VS_OUTPUT In) : COLOR
{
    float4 color;

    // read offset map
    float4 mapdata=tex2D(SOff0,In.Tex);
    // unpack offset
    float2 offset=2.0*mapdata.rg-1.0;
    // apply offset
    float2 uv0=offset+In.Grid;
    // apply transformation
    float angle=mapdata.b;
    float scale=mapdata.a;
        color=transformedLookup(STex0,uv0,angle,scale);
        return (color);
}
```

Implementation Notes

With ps 2.0/ps 2.x, it is possible to get rid of the empty tiles in the reference texture by testing if the texture coordinates are outside of the sprite tile. If the texture coordinates are outside, we use the background color. As there was no
conditional statement before ps 2.0, we had to use empty tiles.

Extensions

Several extensions of this method are possible, such as random positioning of
sprites according to a spatial probability distribution or aperiodic tiling. Please
refer to the paper [2] for more information on extensions of this method.

The Drops of Water Effect

The Drops of Water effect involves the following techniques:

- Texture sprites for the positioning of drops
- Magnification effect for the rendering of drops
- Phong illumination model for the rendering of surfaces

The Phong illumination model will not be described here. Please refer to the article "Fragment-level Phong Illumination" in Section II by Emil Persson.

Drops Motion

The animation of drops is obtained by computing a direction and speed for each drop. At each time step, we update the position of each drop using its direction vector multiplied by its speed. The direction is basically a straight line going from top to bottom with some random angle perturbation. The speed depends on the size of the drop and is also randomly perturbed. If we want drops to fall along a complex surface, we must also take curvature into account.

Wet Surface

The best way to render the appearance of a wet surface is to begin by looking at a real wet surface. Let's drop some water on a table (the computer keyboard is not a good example — avoid it). What happens? Basically, you can see that the surface becomes darker and shinier. In terms of the Phong illumination model, this implies that the diffuse coefficient of the surface decreases while the specular coefficient increases.

To keep track of wet areas, drops are rendered in a texture as white spots. This texture is called the *wet areas texture*. At each time step, the drops are rendered at their new position on top of the previous time step wet areas texture. To obtain a drying effect, we simply darken the previous time step texture. This results in a white trace following the path of each drop. The more time passes, the darker the trace becomes.

The wet areas texture is then used to modify the diffuse and specular coefficients of the final surface. If there is a white pixel in the wet areas texture, a low diffuse coefficient and a high specular coefficient are used. The darker the pixel, the higher the diffuse coefficient and the lower the specular coefficient.

Now we have animated drops that leave a wet trace on the surface!

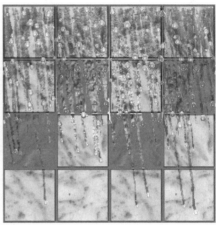

Figure 9: The wet area's texture...

Figure 10: ...and the corresponding final result (See Color Plate 8.)

Magnification Effect

Looking carefully at a real drop of water, we can see that it behaves like a small magnifying glass. This is due to the refraction of light rays passing from air to water [4]. Even if it were possible to compute the exact refraction of rays hitting the drop surface [5], it would be costly.

There is a much simpler way to render such an effect (which has absolutely no physical correctness!). The idea is to compute an offset to be added to the texture coordinates of the underlying texture at each pixel. This offset is computed in order to render the behavior of a magnifying glass: It depends both on the surface shape and the viewpoint position.

The offset formula is:

$$offset = -\left(mag_{coeff} \frac{(texcoords - center)}{height(texcoords)} \right) - view_{vector} \cdot view_{coeff}$$

offset, *texcoords*, *center*, and *view*$_{vector}$ are 2D vectors, and *height(texcoords)* returns the height of the drop at *texcoords*. It is a scalar value. *mag*$_{coeff}$ and *view*$_{coeff}$ are also scalar values. Increasing *mag*$_{coeff}$ results in an increased magnification effect. Increasing *view*$_{coeff}$ results in more dependency between the viewpoint and the aspect of the drop. The demo application allows interactively changing these parameters.

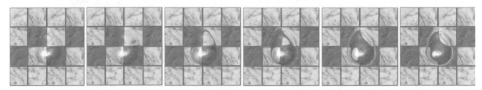

Figure 11:
$mag_{coeff} = 0.00$ $mag_{coeff} = 0.15$ $mag_{coeff} = 0.30$ $mag_{coeff} = 0.45$ $mag_{coeff} = 0.60$ $mag_{coeff} = 0.75$

Combining All

Each drop is encoded as a sprite. The final effect uses multiple layers of texture sprites in order to allow the overlapping of drops. The program detects overlapping after updating the position of drops and tries to put overlapping drops in different texture layers. It also merges close drops into bigger drops. The rendering algorithm for multiple layers of sprites proceeds as follows: First it renders the background surface, and then it renders each layer of sprites.

```
Render object with background texture
For I=1 to number of sprite layers
   If there are some sprites in the layer I
      Render object using texture sprites shader for layer I
```

For each layer of texture sprites, only pixels that effectively correspond to a sprite are rendered. All other pixels are discarded. The drop of water effect begins by rendering the wet areas texture and then renders the final object. The complete algorithm is as follows:

```
Animate drops

Set render target to wet areas texture
Render wet areas texture with a darkening factor
For each layer of drops,
   If there are some drops in the layer
      Render drops as white spots

Set render target to screen
Render surface with per-pixel Phong model
For each layer of drops,
   If there are some drops in the layer
      Render drops with magnification effect and Phong model
```

Note that if the program only uses one or two layers of sprites, all the previous operations can be done in one fragment program (i.e., in one pass). The choice of multipass versus all-in-one pass depends on the complexity of the geometry; if there is a lot of geometry, a more complex pixel shader should be used, as the rendering of the geometry will take a long time. If the geometry is simple, we can use multipass rendering, as the geometry can be rendered very quickly. Nevertheless, to determine which approach is the best in a particular case, it is best to test both approaches. Indeed, rendering bottlenecks are difficult to identify on modern hardware, and testing is often better than assuming.

The Drops of Water effect is written using Cg. It runs on hardware with ps 2.x support. It cannot run on ps 2.0 because of the program length limitation (64 instructions on ps 2.0). It is, however, possible to simplify the code in order to make it shorter. There are three Cg fragment programs; the first program renders the drops as white spots for the wet areas textures, the second program renders the underlying surface with the Phong model, and the third program renders a layer of drops of water. The textures used by the programs are:

OffsetMap	Texture sprites offset map for the current layer
DropNrms	Reference texture encoding drop normals in RGB channels and drop height in alpha channel
ColorMap	Texture of the underlying surface
NrmsMap	Normal map of the underlying surface
WetAreas	Wet areas texture

The first Cg program (renders a layer of drops in the wet areas texture):

```
PixelOut main(DowV2F IN,
            uniform sampler2D OffsetMap   : texunit0,
            uniform sampler2D DropNrms    : texunit1)
{
    half3 color;
    half2 coords;
    half4 offset;
    half4 drop;


    // =====================================
    // texture sprites
    // -> look in offset map
    offset=h4tex2D(OffsetMap,IN.TCoords0.xy);
    offset.xy=(offset.xy-0.5)*2.0;
    coords.xy=(offset.xy+IN.TCoords1.xy);
    drop=transformedLookup(DropNrms,coords,offset.z,offset.w);
    // -> if not in a drop, discard fragment
    if (drop.w < 0.7)
        discard;
    // -> else output white color
    PixelOut OUT;
    OUT.COL = half4(half3(1.0,1.0,1.0),1.0);
    return OUT;
}
```

The second Cg program (renders the underlying surface):

```
PixelOut main(DowV2F IN,
            uniform sampler2D ColorMap   : texunit2,
            uniform sampler2D NrmsMap    : texunit3,
            uniform sampler2D WetAreas   : texunit4)
{
    half3 color;

    // ====================
    // floor lighting
    // -> compute per-pixel Light and View vector
    half3 nL=normalize(IN.L);
    half3 nV=normalize(IN.V);
    half3 H=(nV+nL)*0.5;
    // -> wet areas texture is used to control diffuse and specular
    //    coefficients
    half  wetfloor =h1tex2D(WetAreas,IN.TCoords0.xy);
```

```
half  diffatten=0.45+0.55*(1.0-wetfloor);
// -> read surface normal
half3 fnrm      =h3tex2D(NrmsMap,IN.TCoords0.xy)*2.0-1.0;
// -> compute diffuse and specular terms
half  fspec     =pow(dot(fnrm,H),50.0)*wetfloor;
half  fdiff     =diffatten*dot(fnrm,nL);
// -> final color
color=h3tex2D(ColorMap,IN.TCoords0.xy)*fdiff+fspec;

PixelOut OUT;
OUT.COL = half4(color,1.0h);
return OUT;
}
```

The third Cg program (renders a layer of drops):

```
PixelOut main(DowV2F IN,
          uniform sampler2D OffsetMap    : texunit0,
          uniform sampler2D DropNrms     : texunit1,
          uniform sampler2D ColorMap     : texunit2,
          uniform half MagCoeff,
          uniform half ViewCoeff)
{
    half3 color;
    half2 coords;
    half4 offset;
    half4 drop;

    // =====================================
    // texture sprites
    // -> look in offset map
    offset=h4tex2D(OffsetMap,IN.TCoords0.xy);
    offset.xy=(offset.xy-0.5)*2.0;
    coords=(offset.xy+IN.TCoords1.xy);
    coords=frac(coords);
    drop=transformedLookup(DropNrms,coords,offset.z,offset.w);
    // -> if not in a drop, discard fragment
    if (drop.w < 0.1)
        discard;

    // ====================
    // drop lighting
    // -> compute per-pixel Light and View vector
    half3 nL=normalize(IN.L);
    half3 nV=normalize(IN.V);
    half3 H=(nV+nL)*0.5;
    // -> magnification effect
    half2 decal=-(MagCoeff*(coords-0.75)/drop.w)-nV.xy*ViewCoeff;

    // -> unpack drop normal
    half3 nrm=(drop.xyz*2.0-1.0);
    // -> specular + diffuse
    half spec=pow(dot(nrm,H),20.0)*0.75;
```

```
half diff=(0.6+0.5*dot(nrm,nL));
// -> color
color=h3tex2D(ColorMap,IN.TCoords0.xy+decal.xy)*diff+spec;
// -> alpha for antialiasing of drop edges
half alpha=min((drop.w-0.1)/0.2,1.0);

PixelOut OUT;
OUT.COL = half4(color,alpha);
return OUT;
}
```

The Companion CD

There are two demos on the companion CD. The first program (tsprite) is written with DirectX/HLSL and illustrates the texture sprites technique with various hardware implementations. The second program (dow) is written with DirectX/Cg and demonstrates the Drops of Water effect. Both programs have parameters that can be interactively changed. Use the menus or press F1 for help.

Conclusion

The Drops of Water effect is a complex shader that involves many different techniques. It is an illustration of how much textures can improve the appearance of a surface and how they can be used to achieve complex animated effects. I hope that you had fun playing with these little drops and that you will find hundreds of different applications for the texture sprites technique.

Acknowledgments

Thanks to Przemek Prusinkiewicz, Julia Taylor-Hell, and Samuel Hornus for carefully proofreading this article.

References

[1] *3D Procedural texturing* in nVidia Cg Effect Browser — Cg Toolkit.

[2] Lefebvre, Sylvain and Fabrice Neyret, "Pattern Based Procedural Textures," Proceedings of the ACM SIGGRAPH 2003 Symposium on Interactive 3D Graphics, http://www-imagis.imag.fr/Membres/Sylvain.Lefebvre/pattern.

[3] Ebert, David S., F. Kenton Musgrave, Darwyn Peachey, Ken Perlin (Editor), and Steven Worley, *Texturing & Modeling: A Procedural Approach*, Academic Press, 2003.

[4] Glassner, Andrew S. (Editor), *An Introduction to Ray Tracing*, Academic Press, 1989.

[5] *Eye Raytrace* in nVidia Cg Effect Browser — Cg Toolkit.

Advanced Water Effects

Kurt Pelzer
Piranha Bytes

Introduction

A water simulation as realistic as possible and as widely usable as possible is desired for many targeted applications, such as a basic component of the game play, as an idyllic ambient element, or simply as a delimitation of game worlds. The first ShaderX book [Engel 2002] had several articles about this topic from different viewpoints using version 1.x shaders. Additionally, some tech demos and benchmark tools have presented impressive water effects.

In order to achieve a further increase in visual quality, we need the following features, among others:

- An exact mixing of the visible reflection and semitransparent underwater scene with respect to the involved materials at the boundaries (specifically single boundaries of less dense to more dense materials — for example, air-to-water) and the different angles of incidence between the line of vision and the tangent planes of the rippled water surface. Each wave and ripple has to be visible by a correct Fresnel reflection.

- The water surface must be animated as realistically as possible — that is, all ripples move in a common direction (but the smaller ones with a lower speed) and smoothly change their look at run time without visible repetitions at higher viewpoints.

- Depending on the distance from the water surface, the lighting of the visible underwater objects must be changed to make different water depth recognizable by the simulated absorption of light. This absorption should be adjustable for each color channel.

- The complete water effect must fade out at the water's edge to hide the coarseness of the game world's polygonal construction, and this fading should be done automatically to handle a changing water level or world geometry at run time.

Based on the new extended shaders as well as the increased performance of DirectX 9-compliant video cards, you can build a top-quality and fast water effect that includes the above features. This article presents an implementation using vertex and pixel shader version 2.0 instructions (it is possible to build shaders with reduced effects based on version 1.x instructions, but the goal of this article is to introduce the complete effects). The composition of the complete water simulation is presented first; all components are explained more precisely in later sections. Additionally, a demo application with included source code is available on the companion CD. Screen shots of the demo are shown in Color Plates 9 and 10.

Overview

Before we discuss each component of the advanced water effects, it makes sense to display the general idea of the complete water simulation.

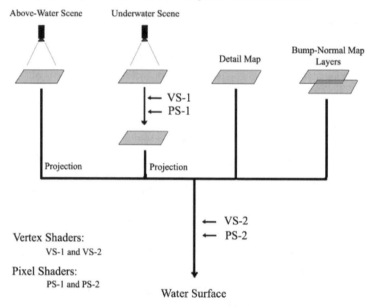

Figure 1: Overview of water simulation

Figure 1 and the following outline should help you find your path through this article:

Preparation of the Underwater Scene
    → Rendering the Underwater Scene (First Render Pass)
    → Modifications Dependent on Water Depth (Second Render Pass)
    → Projection of the Final Underwater Scene Texture
Preparation of the Above-Water Scene
    → Rendering the Reflection Map
    → The Detail Map
Faking Waves and Ripples
    → Animated Surface Bumping
    → Per-Pixel Fresnel Reflection
The Complete Shader Programs
    → The Final Vertex Shader
    → The Final Pixel Shader

Preparation of the Underwater Scene

We have to run two render passes to generate a realistic underwater scene view. The first pass simply fills a render-target texture with the scene (see the following section). Depending on the water depth, a second render pass modifies this texture to receive a more realistic absorption of the light and make different water depths recognizable (see the section "Modifications Dependent on Water Depth (Second Render Pass)"). Later on when the water plane is rendered, we have to project the final texture to the water surface (see the section "Projection of the Final Underwater Scene Texture"). Figure 2 displays the whole process.

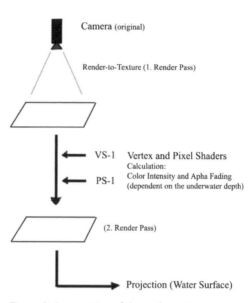

Figure 2: Preparation of the underwater scene

Rendering the Underwater Scene (First Render Pass)

We want to simulate a close-to-reality view into the water. The seabed and objects like fish or plants should be distortable by faked bumps (see the section "Animated Surface Bumping"). So, we have to render the underwater scene view each frame again into a render-target texture. For this job, we use the original camera. A clip plane cuts off the invisible part of the scene above the water surface (see Figure 3).

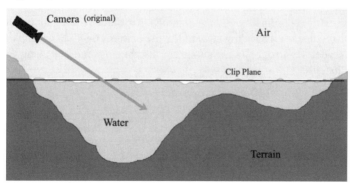

Figure 3: Original camera and clip plane

Modifications Dependent on Water Depth (Second Render Pass)

With a second render pass, this render target texture (containing the underwater scene view) will be modified so that afterward the alpha channel holds the blending for the water's edge and the color channels contain a darkened color (depending on the current water depth). This darkening is to make different water depths recognizable and simulate water pollution. To compute the intensity for each color channel, we use a reduction formula: $\exp(-d * \lambda)$. You may know this type of formula from the law of radioactive decay. The parameter d is the current depth of water, and the λ (may be three different values for red, green, and blue) will cause a water dye (see Figure 4).

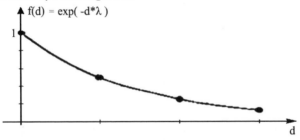

Figure 4: Reduction formula $\exp(-d * \lambda)$

Since in the pixel shader the exponential function with basis 2 is available, our three λ are the reciprocals of the half-life values for each color component. This is the depth underneath the waterline where the red, green, and blue components of the light are reduced to half of their brightness. So, our three λ are very simple: $\lambda_{red} = 1/\text{Half-Life-Of-Red}$, $\lambda_{green} = 1/\text{Half-Life-Of-Green}$, and $\lambda_{blue} = 1/\text{Half-Life-Of-Blue}$. If we select a greater value for λ_{blue}, its half-life is going to be smaller. That means the blue component quickly disappears from the water color, giving all underwater objects a dimmed blue color and yellow-dyed appearance. Our reduction formula requires knowing the depth (underwater, not z) of the current pixel being processed. To do this, we pass the vertex position to the pixel shader PS-1 as texture coordinates. This guarantees that the vertex position will be interpolated linearly, providing us with the underwater depth of each pixel. So, the vertex shader VS-1 is very simple (and can also be implemented using version 1.x instructions):

```
// VERTEX SHADER (for DX9 hardware and better)    VS-1
// FUNCTION:  Modifies underwater scene texture
//
// INPUT:
// v0           = position        (3 floats)
// c0 - c3      = world/view/proj matrix

// version instruction
vs_2_0
```

```
// declare registers
dcl_position   v0


// transform position into projection space
dp4     oPos.x,   v0, c0      // c0 = first row of transposed world/view/proj-matrix.
dp4     oPos.y,   v0, c1      // c1 = second row of transposed world/view/proj-matrix.
dp4     oPos.z,   v0, c2      // c2 = third row of transposed world/view/proj-matrix.
dp4     oPos.w,   v0, c3      // c3 = forth row of transposed world/view/proj-matrix.


// transfer position to pixel shader
mov     oT0,      v0          // We pass the vertex position to the pixel shader as tex coord.
```

This is the associated pixel shader PS-1:

```
// PIXEL SHADER (for DX9 hardware and better)    PS-1
// FUNCTION: Modifies underwater scene texture
//
// INPUT:
// t0        = object position (in world space)
// c0        = cam-point in object-space
// c1        = water height in y component, fading scale in alpha component
// c2        = λ's for absorption of light (λ(Red), λ(Green), λ(Blue))


// version instruction
ps_2_0


// define the constants
def     c3,     0.00f, 1.00f, 0.00f, 0.00f


// declare the used resources
dcl     t0


// calculate the alpha value for water's edge fading
mov      r1,     c3            // Calculate the underwater depth
mad      r1,     -t0, r1, c1   // (distance: water plane ↔ object),
mul_sat  r0.a,   c1.a, r1.g    // scale this value and clamp the result to [0,1].
rsq      r0.a,   r0.a          // We want to see a smooth fading, so computing the
rcp_sat  r0.a,   r0.a          // square root will be fine.


// calculate the underwater absorption of light
mul      r2.rgb, c2, r1.g      // Calculate d * λ for each color.
exp_sat  r0.r,   -r2.r         // exp( -d * λ ) for red color.
exp_sat  r0.g,   -r2.g         // exp( -d * λ ) for green color.
exp_sat  r0.b,   -r2.b         // exp( -d * λ ) for blue color.


// output color
mov      oC0,    r0            // Output: The final color intensities and the fading alpha.
```

The result of this second render pass must be multiplied by the current content in the underwater scene texture. Therefore, the alpha blending needs the following parameters:

D3DRS_SRCBLEND = D3DBLEND_DESTCOLOR;
D3DRS_DESTBLEND = D3DBLEND_ZERO;

Projection of the Final Underwater Scene Texture

To project the final underwater scene texture on the water surface, the vertex shader VS-2 must receive the transposed version of the following matrix:

ProjectionMatrix = OrigCam.ViewMatrix * OrigCam.ProjectionMatrix * TrafoMatrix

OrigCam.ViewMatrix*OrigCam.ProjectionMatrix transforms the world into projection space, where coordinates range from –1 to +1 (see Figure 5).

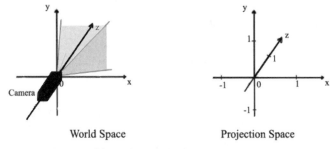

World Space   Projection Space

Figure 5: From world space to projection space

To map these coordinates from the projection space where (x, y) belongs to the range $[-1,+1]$ to the texture space where (x, y) belongs to the range $[0,1]$, we have to multiply a special TrafoMatrix. This transformation matrix causes the transition of the projection space to the texture space by scaling and translating the vertex positions of all objects.

$$
TrafoMatrix = \begin{matrix} 0.5 & 0 & 0 & 0 \\ 0 & -0.5 & 0 & 0 \\ 0 & 0 & 0 & 0 \\ 0.5 & 0.5 & 1 & 1 \end{matrix}
$$

A sign change in the y component is necessary for correct alignment because from the texture's point of view, the scene seems to be inverted (top↔down, the v components of texture coordinates use an inverted y direction — see Figure 6).

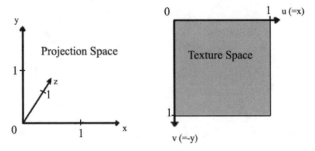

Figure 6: Inverted y (= v) direction for texture coordinates

The vertex shader VS-2 (used to build the water surface) computes the dot products of the water's vertex positions and the rows of this projection matrix. The resulting values are the new texture coordinates for the underwater scene texture and will be sent to the pixel shader PS-2:

```
// r0 contains the translated object position
dp4     r9.x,   r0, c8      // c8 = first row of transposed refraction-projection-matrix
dp4     r9.y,   r0, c9      // c9 = second row of transposed refraction-projection-matrix
dp4     r9.zw,  r0, c10     // c10 = third row of transposed refraction-projection-matrix
mov     oT2,    r9          // output: underwater scene tex coords (send to pixel shader)
```

Finally, in the pixel shader these texture coordinates will be bumped like those of the reflection map before sampling the texture, but with a lowered strength and contrarotated direction (see the section "Animated Surface Bumping").

Preparation of the Above-Water Scene

The above-water scene contains two different areas: objects that can be seen in the reflection and floating details on the water surface.

Rendering the Reflection Map

To simulate a close-to-reality reflection, we have to render the above-water scene view (maybe with a reduced object LOD) each frame again into a render-target texture. For this job, we need the original camera mirrored at the water surface. The invisible part of the scene under the water surface will be cut off by a clip plane to prevent obstructions of vision for this new camera (see Figure 7).

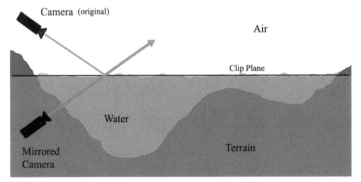

Figure 7: Mirrored camera and clip plane

Mirroring the original camera at the water plane is done by a simple modification of the view matrix. It works like mirroring the world about the water surface:

$$MirrorCam.ViewMatrix = MirrorTrafoMatrix * OrigCam.ViewMatrix$$

Starting with a vertex $v = (x, y, z)$ that is to be reflected, we translate the scene in the y direction by the negative water-level $v = (x, y–wl, z)$. So the mirror plane will become the xz plane. Subsequently, reflection about the translated plane is done by changing the sign of the y component of the input vertex v = (x, –(y–wl), z). Finally, the mirror plane will be shifted back to its old place again: v = (x, –(y–wl)+wl, z) = (x, –y+2*wl, z). The previous transformations can be put in the following matrix form:

$$MirrorTrafoMatrix = \begin{matrix} 1 & 0 & 0 & 0 \\ 0 & -1 & 0 & 0 \\ 0 & 0 & 1 & 0 \\ 0 & 2*WaterLevel & 0 & 1 \end{matrix}$$

To project this reflection map (rendered with the mirrored camera) on the water surface, the vertex shader VS-2 must receive the transposed version of the following matrix:

$ProjectionMatrix = MirrorCam.ViewMatrix * OrigCam.ProjectionMatrix * TrafoMatrix$

MirrorCam.ViewMatrix*OrigCam.ProjectionMatrix transforms the world into projection space. Just to map these coordinates from the projection space to the texture space, we have to multiply a special TrafoMatrix. This transformation matrix equals the one we used for projecting the underwater scene texture (see the section "Projection of the Final Underwater Scene Texture"). As done for the underwater scene map, the vertex shader VS-2 computes the dot products of the water's vertex positions and the rows of the projection matrix. The resulting values are the new texture coordinates for the reflection map and are sent to the pixel shader PS-2:

```
// r0 contains the water's vertex position
dp4    r9.x,    r0, c4    // c4 = first row of transposed reflection-projection-matrix
dp4    r9.y,    r0, c5    // c5 = second row of transposed reflection-projection-matrix
dp4    r9.zw,   r0, c6    // c6 = third row of transposed reflection-projection-matrix
mov    oT1,     r9        // output: reflection tex coords (send to the pixel shader)
```

Finally, in the pixel shader these texture coordinates will be distorted by animated bump-normals before sampling the texture (see the section "Animated Surface Bumping").

The Detail Map

To provide the water surface with additional details (like algae or oil), we add a separate texture that has an alpha channel to indicate sections of different transparency. This detail map must be able to be tiled seamlessly without showing visible artifacts. Sections without these details should be completely transparent, and objects like algae should get a semitransparent alpha value. The map will be translated each frame like the bump-normal maps (see the section "Animated Surface Bumping"), but this translation scales down to run at a lower speed. Thus, the realistic impression results in the water and the objects floating on it moving more slowly than the waves. Like the reflection and underwater scene maps, this detail texture will be distorted in the pixel shader PS-2 (but the bump-normal gets a different scaling factor for this job):

```
// r5 contains the bump (see section: Animated Surface Bumping)
mul    r0.rgb,   r5, c10.b    // c10.b = scaling factor to reduce the bumping
```

```
add     r0.rgb,  r0, t3     // t3 contains the original tex coords for the detail map
texld   r3,      r0, s3     // load filtered detail texel from tex sampler 3
```

This reinforces the impression of a close-to-reality animation of the water surface (see the following section). Blending with the remaining part of the water effect will happen later on in the pixel shader by calculating a linear interpolation:

```
lrp_sat r8.rgb,  r3.a, r3, r7  // r7 contains the blended reflection and underwater scene
```

Faking Waves and Ripples

Now we have to add realistic waves and ripples to the water surface. We make use of the interferences between multiple bump map layers and introduce an exact per-pixel Fresnel reflection to make each surface bump visible.

Animated Surface Bumping

The water surface animation is done with simulated waves and ripples that must smoothly change their shape at run time without visible repetitions at higher viewpoints (no visible tiles). As a basic resource, we only need to have one bump-normal map that can be tiled seamlessly without visible artifacts. This map must be used at least once again in a second layer to overlap the first one. We want to mix multiple bump-map layers to use interference effects between them. Each layer has to be scaled with a different factor and has its own time-stamp controlled translation (see Figure 8).

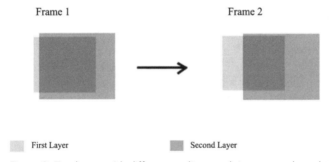

Frame 1   Frame 2

First Layer   Second Layer

Figure 8: Two layers with different scalings and time-stamp-based translation

For example, dealing with the first layer is done in the vertex shader VS-2, like this:

```
mov     r1,      c13.x    // c13.x = current time-stamp
mul     r2,      r1, c14  // c14 = translation for the first layer coords
frc     r2.xy,   r2       // only use the fractional component
mul     r3,      v8, c15  // v8 = original bump map coords, c15 = scaling factor for
                          // the first layer coords
add     oT0.xy,  r2, r3   // calc the final tex coords for first bump layer
```

The other layers must be scaled and translated in the same way (but with different parameters). The content mixing of the overlapping layers (with different weighting factors for each one) is done afterward in the pixel shader PS-2. For example, two bump-normal maps in four layers can be blended this way:

```
texld   r0,     t0, s0      // load first normal layer - first bump maps
texld   r4,     t4, s0      // load second normal layer - first bump map
texld   r5,     t5, s4      // load third normal layer - second bump map
texld   r6,     t6, s4      // load forth normal layer - second bump map
mul     r6.rgb, r6, c3      // c3 = scaling factor for forth normal
mad     r5.rgb, r5, c2, r6  // c2 = scaling factor for third normal
mad     r4.rgb, r4, c1, r5  // c1 = scaling factor for second normal
mad     r5.rgb, r0, c0, r4  // c0 = scaling factor for first normal
add     r5.rgb, r5, c4      // c4 = (-0.5f*(c0+..+c3)) for color-to-vector trafo
```

Each ripple and its strength can be detected by bumping the reflection, underwater scene, and detail maps. Also the change of the reflection and refraction shares in the final blending help to make out the ripples and waves (see the following section). Additionally, the contrarotated and different scaled bumping of the reflection and underwater scene maps increases the visual quality. The refraction at the air-water boundaries reduces the bump effect for the underwater scene map; therefore, the scaling factor for the refraction bumps should have a lesser absolute value (see Figure 9).

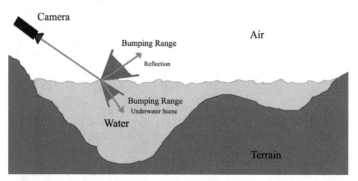

Figure 9: Reduced bumping range for the underwater scene map

Bumping the reflection and underwater scene maps is done in the pixel shader PS-2 this way:

```
// r5 = mixed bump vector, c12 and c13 = scaling factors for reflection and refraction bumps
mad     r7,     r5, c12, t1  // add scaled bump to reflection tex coords
mad     r8,     r5, c13, t2  // add scaled bump to refraction tex coords
texldp  r1,     r7, s1       // load filtered reflection texel
texldp  r2,     r8, s2       // load filtered refraction texel
```

Per-Pixel Fresnel Reflection

The Fresnel term gives a description of how much light is reflected at the boundaries of two materials. The rest of the light finds its refracted way into the second semitransparent material. We get the strongest reflection (total reflection) as long as the angle of incidence of the light ray (just as the ray of view) is greater than a "critical" angle (Snell's Law). When the light ray is orthogonal to the surface, there is only a dim reflection (see Figure 10).

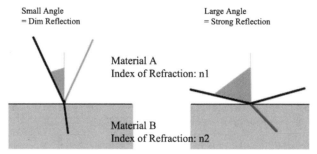

Figure 10: Different Fresnel reflections

A good approximation of the correct Fresnel term is this formula:

(1) $R(\alpha) = R(0) + (1 - R(0)) * (1 - \cos(\alpha))^5$
with $R(0) = (n1 - n2)^2 / (n1 + n2)^2$
(n1 and n2 are the indices of refraction for the involved materials.)

You may also use a much simpler approximation: $R(\alpha) = 1 - \cos(\alpha)$. But this formula doesn't take the indices of refraction into account and has a stronger divergence from the original graph. This divergence produces an unnaturally strong reflection (see Figure 11). That is why we prefer the better approximation (1). Although it's a more complex formula with higher run-time costs, we use it for our calculations.

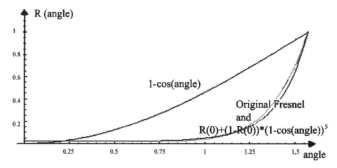

Figure 11: Original Fresnel for air-to-water and two approximations

The indices of refraction for air and water are these:

n1 = 1.000293 (air)   n2 = 1.333333 (water at 20°C / 68°F)

So we get the following constants for the Fresnel approximation at the air-to-water boundaries:

R(0) = 0.02037f   1 – R(0) = 0.97963f

The Fresnel reflection based on (1) is done in the pixel shader PS-2, like this:

```
// -r6 contains the normalized cam-to-surface vector and r5 is the surface normal
dp3_sat r7.a,   -r6, r5              // calculate the angle alpha
add     r8.a,   c10.a, -r7.a        // c10.a = 1.0f
mul     r6.a,   r8.a, r8.a          // squared
mul     r6.a,   r6.a, r6.a          // quadric
mul     r6.a,   r6.a, r8.a          // quintic
mad     r6.a,   c10.g, r6.a, c10.r  // c10.g = 1-R(0) and c10.r = R(0)
```

The cam-to-surface vector will be precalculated by the vertex shader VS-2 to send it (packed as color output) to the pixel shader PS-2:

```
add     r10,   r0, -c12            // r0 = position of current water vertex, c12 = cam-
                                   // point in object-space
nrm     r8,    r10                 // normalize the cam-to-surface vector (each component
                                   // must fit into [-1,1])
mad     oD0.xyz,r8, c22.z, c22.z   // c22.z = 0.5f
```

In the pixel shader, our vector must be unpacked again before running the Fresnel calculation. Also, a renormalization of the vector is necessary because a color interpolation may have taken place (Gouraud shading):

```
// v0 contains the pre-calculated cam-to-surface vector as color
add     r7.rgb,   v0, c5           // c5 = ( -0.5f, -0.5f, -0.5f, 0.0f )
nrm     r6.rgb,   r7               // normalize the cam-to-surface vector
```

The Fresnel code in the pixel shader receives the normal of the rippled water surface by normalization of the previously calculated bump vector and exchanging the y and z components afterward (see the section "Animated Surface Bumping"):

```
nrm     r6.rgb, r5                 // normalize bump vector
mov     r5.r,   r6.r               // keep the x component
dp3     r5.g,   r6, c14            // c14 = ( 0.0f, 0.0f, 1.0f, 0.0f )
dp3     r5.b,   r6, c15            // c15 = ( 0.0f, 1.0f, 0.0f, 0.0f )
```

The "lying bump vector" is set upright by this coordinate exchange and takes its correct place as a normal in the tangent space of the bumped water surface (see Figure 12).

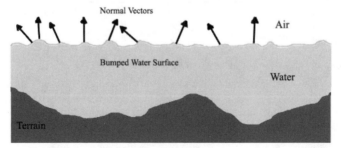

Figure 12: Normal vectors of the bumped water surface

Of course, the bump-normal maps must be prepared for this operation. We simply use a "bumped" height map and convert it into a bump-normal map using a method introduced by the Direct3D extensions (D3DX) utility library: the D3DXComputeNormalMap function. After calculating $R(\alpha)$, we are going to mix the underwater scene and the reflection by simply using a linear interpolation:

```
// r5.a contains the R(α) value
lrp_sat   r7.rgb,   r5.a, r1, r2     // r1 und r2 are the reflection and underwater
                                     // scene texels
```

Now we can see all reflections on the water with different strengths, depending on the ripples and waves. The detailed information in [Wloka 2002] should be useful for those of you who need indices of refraction for other materials or want to gain a better knowledge of this topic (approximating the Fresnel reflection).

The Complete Shader Programs

In this section, the final vertex and pixel shader programs (VS-2 and PS-2) are presented using shader instructions from version 2.0. They must be activated when rendering the water plane. Based on the calculated alpha value, the color result must be blended to the frame buffer's current content. So, the source and destination blending factors are:

> D3DRS_SRCBLEND   = D3DBLEND_SRCALPHA;
> D3DRS_DESTBLEND = D3DBLEND_INVSRCALPHA;

That will make the effect fade out at the water's edge (see Figure 13).

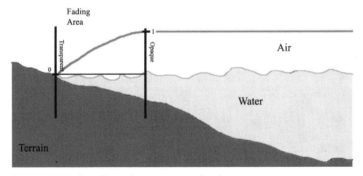

Figure 13: Fading dependent on water depth

The Final Vertex Shader

```
// VERTEX SHADER (for DX9 hardware and better)    VS-2
// FUNCTION:  Water effect
//
// INPUT:
// v0          = position              (3 floats)
// v1          = normal                (3 floats)
// v8          = tex coord stage 0     (2 floats – bump map)
// v9          = tex coord stage 1     (3 floats - reflection)
// v10         = tex coord stage 2     (3 floats - underwater scene)
```

Advanced Water Effects

```
// v11         = tex coord stage 3      (2 floats - surface details)
// c0 - c3     = world/view/proj matrix
// c4 - c7     = reflection texture trafo matrix
// c8 - c11    = underwater scene texture trafo matrix
// c12         = cam-point in object-space & water height
// c13         = time
// c14         = first bump-normal map coords translation
// c15         = first bump-normal map coords scalar
// c16         = second bump-normal map coords translation
// c17         = second bump-normal map coords scalar
// c18         = third bump-normal map coords translation
// c19         = third bump-normal map coords scalar
// c20         = fourth bump-normal map coords translation
// c21         = fourth bump-normal map coords scalar
// c22         = 0.5f in z component


// version instruction
vs_2_0


// define the constants
def           c22,   1.0f, 1.0f, 0.5f, 1.0f



// declare registers
dcl_position    v0
dcl_normal      v1
dcl_texcoord0   v8
dcl_texcoord1   v9
dcl_texcoord2   v10
dcl_texcoord3   v11


// transform position into projection space
mov     r0,     v0            // We are able to change the water level at run time.
add     r0.y,   r0.y, c12.w   // So, we have to add the current height difference
                              // to original water y coord.
dp4     oPos.x, r0, c0        // This lifted plane has to be transformed by the
                              // current world/view/proj matrix.
dp4     oPos.y, r0, c1        // (ditto)
dp4     oPos.z, r0, c2        // (ditto)
dp4     oPos.w, r0, c3        // (ditto)


// calc projective tex coords
dp4     r9.x,   r0, c4        // Based on lifted water position we calculate tex coords
dp4     r9.y,   r0, c5        // for the reflection map
dp4     r9.zw,  r0, c6        // (ditto)
mov     oT1,    r9            // and hand them over to the pixel shader.
dp4     r9.x,   r0, c8        // Based on lifted water position we calculate tex coords
dp4     r9.y,   r0, c9        // for the underwater scene map
dp4     r9.zw,  r0, c10       // (ditto)
mov     oT2,    r9            // and hand them over to the pixel shader.
mov     oT3.xy, v11           // Tex coords for detail map are passed to pixel shader.
```

```
// calc the distorted bump-normal map coords
mov    r1,    c13.x      // Based on the current time stamp we calculate some scaled
                         // and translated
mul    r2,    r1, c14    // coordinates for the bump-normal map layers.
frc    r2.xy, r2         // (ditto)
mul    r3,    v8, c15    // (ditto)
add    oT0.xy, r2, r3    // Output: Tex coords for the first bump-normal map layer.
mul    r2,    r1, c16    // (ditto)
frc    r2.xy, r2         // (ditto)
mul    r3,    v8, c17    // (ditto)
add    oT4.xy, r2, r3    // Output: Tex coords for the second bump-normal map layer.
mul    r2,    r1, c18    // (ditto)
frc    r2.xy, r2         // (ditto)
mul    r3,    v8, c19    // (ditto)
add    oT5.xy, r2, r3    // Output: Tex coords for the third bump-normal map layer.
mul    r2,    r1, c20    // (ditto)
frc    r2.xy, r2         // (ditto)
mul    r3,    v8, c21    // (ditto)
add    oT6.xy, r2, r3    // Output: Tex coords for the forth bump-normal map layer.


// compute the cam-to-water vector
add    r10,   r0, -c12   // Based on lifted water plane we calculate normalized current
nrm    r8,    r10        // cam-to-water vector.


// Prepare for per-pixel normalization
mad    oD0.xyz, r8, c22.z, c22.z  // This vector (packed in a color) has to be passed
                                  // to the pixel shader.
```

The Final Pixel Shader

```
// PIXEL SHADER (for DX9 hardware and better)    PS-2
// FUNCTION:  Water effect
//
// INPUT:
// v0      = cam-to-water vector in cam-space
// t0      = tex coords for first bump-normal map layer
// t1      = tex coords for reflection texture
// t2      = tex coords for underwater scene texture
// t3      = tex coords for surface detail texture
// t4      = tex coords for second bump-normal map layer
// t5      = tex coords for third bump-normal map layer
// t6      = tex coords for fourth bump-normal map layer
// s0      = first bump-normal map
// s1      = reflection texture
// s2      = underwater scene texture
// s3      = surface detail texture
// s4      = second bump-normal map
// c0      = scale first bump-normal map layer (z component must be 2.f)
// c1      = scale second bump-normal map layer (z component must be 2.f)
// c2      = scale third bump-normal map layer (z component must be 2.f)
// c3      = scale fourth bump-normal map layer (z component must be 2.f)
// c4      = weigthed shift for color-to-vector trafo (-0.5f*(c0+..+c3))
```

```
// c5       = shift for color-to-vector trafo
// c10      = r(0) (air&water), 1-r(0) for Fresnel, detail bump scaling, const 1
// c11      = shift bumped reflection map
// c12      = scale bumps in reflection map
// c13      = scale bumps in refraction map
// c14 + c15 = change y and z components of bump normal


// version instruction
ps_2_0


// define the constants
def     c5,  -0.5f, -0.5f, -0.5f, 0.0f
def     c10, 0.0204f, 0.9796f, 0.3f, 1.0f
def     c14, 0.0f, 0.0f, 1.0f, 0.0f
def     c15, 0.0f, 1.0f, 0.0f, 0.0f


// declare the used resources
dcl     v0
dcl     t0
dcl     t1
dcl     t2
dcl     t3
dcl     t4
dcl     t5
dcl     t6
dcl_2d  s0
dcl_2d  s1
dcl_2d  s2
dcl_2d  s3
dcl_2d  s4


// load the bump-normal map layers
texld   r0,  t0, s0  // Load content of first bump-normal layer (using first b-n map)
texld   r4,  t4, s0  // Load content of second bump-normal layer (using first b-n map)
texld   r5,  t5, s4  // Load content of third bump-normal layer (using second b-n map)
texld   r6,  t6, s4  // Load content of fourth bump-normal layer (using second b-n map)


// scale and add the content of the different bump-normal layers
mul     r6.rgb,  r6, c3      // All four sampled bump-normal colors have to be mixed
mad     r5.rgb,  r5, c2, r6  // (ditto)
mad     r4.rgb,  r4, c1, r5  // (ditto)
mad     r5.rgb,  r0, c0, r4  // (ditto)
add     r5.rgb,  r5, c4      // and unpacked (color-to-vector-trafo) to be usable as
                             // current bump vector.


// shift the bumped reflection map
add     r7,  r5, c11         // Shift the bump vector to prevent reflection artifacts
                             // at the water's edge.


// scale bumps in reflection and refraction map
mad     r7,  r7, c12, t1     // Use a scaled bump vector to modify the coords of
                             // the reflection map.
```

```
mad      r8,   r5, c13, t2        // Use a scaled bump vector to modify the coords of the
                                   // underwater scene map.

// load the bumped refraction and underwater scene
texldp   r1,   r7, s1             // Load reflection texel (using modified tex coords).
texldp   r2,   r8, s2             // Load underwater scene texel (using modified tex coords).

// exchange y and z components of bump-normal (from now on this vector can be used as
// normal vector)
nrm      r6.rgb,   r5             // Normalize the calculated bump-normal vector.
mov      r5.r,     r6.r           // Keep the x component of this vector.
dp3      r5.g,     r6, c14        // Exchange the y and z component of this vector.
dp3      r5.b,     r6, c15        // (ditto)

// load the surface detail (also bumped)
mul      r0.rgb,   r5, c10.b      // Bump the tex coords for surface details
add      r0.rgb,   r0, t3         // (ditto)
texld    r3,       r0, s3         // and load the surface detail texel.

// renormalize cam-to-water vector in v0
add      r7.rgb,   v0, c5         // Unpack cam-to-water vector (passed by vertex shader).
nrm      r6.rgb,   r7             // Renormalize this vector.

// dot cam-to-water vector with the mixed normal vector
dp3_sat  r7.a,    -r6, r5         // Calculate the cosine of the angle between both vectors.

// calculate the Fresnel term (air-to-water)
add      r8.a,    c10.a, -r7.a    // Use this cosine to calculate the Fresnel approximation.
mul      r6.a,    r8.a, r8.a      // (ditto)
mul      r6.a,    r6.a, r6.a      // (ditto)
mul      r6.a,    r6.a, r8.a      // (ditto)
mad      r6.a,    c10.g, r6.a, c10.r  // (ditto)

// blend underwater scene and reflection map
// use the alpha of the underwater scene map to reduce Fresnel reflection at water's edge
mul      r6.a,    r6.a, r2.a      // Modulate strength of Fresnel reflection with
                                  // underwater alpha.
lrp_sat  r7.rgb, r6.a, r1, r2     // Blend both maps (underwater scene and reflection).

// blend in the surface details
mov      r8.a,    r2.a            // (Yep, this line can be cancelled if we use
lrp_sat  r8.rgb, r3.a, r3, r7     // r2.rgb as target for lrp_sat result in this line
mov      oC0,     r8              // and move the complete r2 register to oC0)
```

Further Improvements

Of course, the top quality water simulation explained in this article has several areas that could stand further improvements, including these four:

■   The absorption of light calculated in the second render pass of the underwater scene (see the section "Modifications Dependent on Water Depth") should not only be based on the current distance between water surface and underwater object; the underwater part of the cam-to-object view line should also be taken into account. In fact, the light passes the area between water surface and object two times before it arrives at the camera (see Figure 14). This way, we receive a high absorption of light also for lower water levels if the camera looks with a flat angle of incidence.

■ A correct refraction of the line of sight is not simulated at the moment (see Figure 15). The angle of refraction β has to be calculated this way:

$$\beta = \arcsin(\ \sin(\alpha) * c_2 / c_1\ )$$

...with α = angle of incidence, c_1 = 1.000293 (refraction index of air), and c_2 = 1.333333 (refraction index of water).

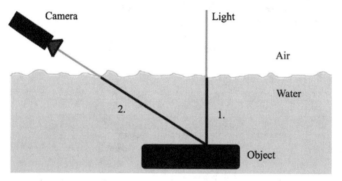

Figure 14: The light passes the area between water surface and object two times.

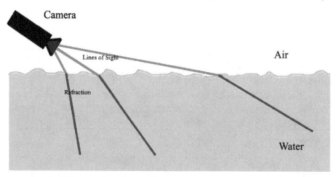

Figure 15: Refraction of the line of sight

■ Additional specular reflections will create highlights on the water surface and increase the visual quality. The water articles in the first ShaderX book [Engel 2002] present an easy way to add them.

■ This article is intended as an introduction to the presented advanced water effects. To increase the practical usability, we should implement the complete effect using a high-level shader language (like DX9-HLSL or Cg). This will raise the level of abstraction and decouple the programs from specific hardware.

There are many starting points to develop further improvements for the visual quality.

Conclusion

Using multiple render passes (reflection map 1, underwater scene 1+1, water surface 1), we created a close-to-reality water effect, including the desired features listed at the beginning. Especially in view of the per-pixel Fresnel reflection for each ripple, the water surface has a good three-dimensional look. Additionally, the contrarotated and different scaled bumping of the reflection and underwater scene maps increases the simulation's quality. Without decreasing quality, we are able to change the world geometry or the water level due to the dynamic darkening of the underwater scene map and also the supported alpha-fading at the water's edge. On the companion CD, you can find a demo application and complete source code presenting an executable implementation of the discussed water simulation.

References

[Engel 2002] Engel, Wolfgang F., ed., *Direct3D ShaderX: Vertex and Pixel Shader Tips and Tricks*, Wordware Publishing, 2002.

[Wloka 2002] Wloka, M., "Fresnel Reflection," nVidia Technical Report, 2002, http://developer.nvidia.com/docs/IO/3035/ATT/FresnelReflection.pdf.

Efficient Evaluation of Irradiance Environment Maps

Peter-Pike J. Sloan
Microsoft Corporation

Introduction

Irradiance environment maps [3] are an effective technique to render diffuse objects in arbitrary lighting environments. They are more efficient to compute and use fewer resources than diffuse cube maps [1]. In [3], a method is presented that uses spherical harmonics to efficiently represent an irradiance environment map. Based on the surface normal, two formulas for evaluation are presented. One is tailored for matrix/vector operations using the standard matrix form of a quadratic equation, and the other more direct technique is specified for "systems not optimized for matrix and vector operations." This article presents a more efficient mapping of the second formula; with the current vertex shader instruction set, it uses seven constant registers and 11 instructions versus 12 constant registers and 15 instructions using the quadratic form.

One significant benefit to dealing with lights using irradiance environment maps or diffuse cube maps is that the cost of evaluating the representation is independent of the number of lights. This is because the lighting environment is represented as a whole, and the integration is precomputed for all possible normals instead of evaluated on the fly for each light. Using spherical harmonics to represent irradiance environment maps is much more efficient than diffuse cube maps and can make other techniques built around them (like [1]) more efficient. Greger et al. [2] precomputes a regular volume of irradiance cube maps in a scene. Diffuse objects can be efficiently moved around inside the scene by interpolating between the different cube maps. Using spherical harmonics would just amount to interpolating the spherical harmonic coefficients instead. One limitation of these techniques is that they are only truly accurate for convex objects. If shadows or other global effects are to be modeled, other techniques, like precomputed radiance transfer (PRT) [4], need to be used.

Background

This article focuses on how to light a diffuse object with a distant spherical lighting environment, ignoring shadows and other global effects. This is done by computing the radiance (light) leaving a point on the object, which requires an

evaluation of the reflection integral: $R_p(\vec{v}) = \dfrac{\rho_d}{\pi} \int_s L(s) H_N(s) ds$ where ρ_d is the

diffuse reflectance (commonly referred to as the albedo) of the surface and is in the range [0,1]; the division by π guarantees energy conservation[1]. This integral represents the irradiance[2], where $L(s)$ is a spherical function representing the lighting environment and $H_N(s)$ is the cosine term (dot product of the surface normal at the given point and a unit direction clamped to zero if it is negative). The domain of integration is over the sphere of all incoming directions denoted by the variable s. It is possible to precompute this integral for every possible normal, since it is just a convolution of $H_N(s)$ against $L(s)$ for all possible normal directions. This results in a spherical function that can be evaluated to determine reflected radiance.

In image processing, when convolving large kernels, it is more efficient to use the fourier transform to project the image and the kernel into frequency-space, evaluate the convolution (which amounts to multiplication in frequency-space), and then inverse transform the image back into the spatial domain. The cosine kernel is a very large one, covering half the sphere. Ramamoorthi and Hanrahan [3] observed that the projection of $H_N(s)$ into the "frequency-space" of the sphere (using spherical harmonics, which is described in the next section) results in almost all of the energy existing in the first nine coefficients. This means that an accurate representation of the convolved spherical function representing exit radiance for any normal direction can be expressed using just nine numbers per color channel instead of a full diffuse cube map.

Spherical Harmonics for Rendering

Spherical harmonics are the natural basis functions to use on the sphere. This article only briefly describes them; for a more complete description, look at the references in [3] and [4]. The mathematical form of the complex spherical harmonics is as follows:

$$Y_l^m(\theta, \phi) = K_l^m e^{im\phi} P_l^{|m|}(\cos\theta); l \in N, -1 \le m \le l$$

...where the parameterization of the unit sphere is:

$$s = (x, y, z) = (\sin(\theta)\cos(\phi), \sin(\theta)\sin(\phi), \cos(\theta)) \tag{1}$$

---

1 The net energy leaving a point is never greater than the net energy impinging on it.

2 Irradiance is the integral of the lighting environment impinging on a point. For a diffuse object, the irradiance should be multiplied by the albedo of the surface divided by π to compute the light leaving the surface — this is commonly referred to as radiance.

The P_l^m are the associated Legendre polynomials, and K_l^m are the normalization constants.

$$K_l^m = \sqrt{\frac{(2l+1)(l-|m|)!}{4\pi(l+|m|)!}}$$

When representing lighting, the complex form is not interesting, so the real form of the spherical harmonics can be used:

$$y_l^m = \begin{cases} \sqrt{2}\operatorname{Re}(Y_l^m) & m > 0 \\ \sqrt{2}\operatorname{Im}(Y_l^m) & m < 0 \\ Y_l^0 & m = 0 \end{cases} \qquad (2)$$

The spherical harmonics can also be expressed as polynomials in 3D, where evaluation is restricted to the surface of the unit sphere. These polynomials can be computed by factoring equation (2) using the trigonometric forms for x, y, and z in equation (1) and trigonometric identities. The index l represents the band index and corresponds to the degree of the polynomial (analogous to frequency). A complete lth degree basis contains $(l+1)^2$ coefficients and can represent all polynomials through degree l. For simplicity, this article sometimes uses a form that represents each basis function with a single index y_i, where $i=l(l+1)+m+1$. The spherical harmonics are an orthonormal basis; this means that $\int y_i(s)y_j(s)ds = 1$ if $(i = j)$ and 0 if $(i! = j)$. One byproduct of the above definition is that the basis functions can be defined with any sign convention. Since sign conventions vary, care has to be taken when mixing between definitions of the basis functions found in different references. This is particularly true when using projection coefficients or code that is found on the web.

Since the spherical harmonics form an orthonormal basis, projecting a function into them is straightforward. Here is the formula for evaluating the projected function:

$$\tilde{f}(s) \approx \sum l_l^m y_l^m(s)$$

…where l_l^m are the projection coefficients of the function f into the spherical harmonic basis (i.e., a linear combination of the spherical harmonics with these coefficients results in an optimal approximation of the function). They can be computed by integrating the function against the basis functions over the sphere:

$$l_l^m = \int f(s) y_l^m(s) ds$$

If the function is band limited, a finite number of bands are required to exactly reconstruct the function. If the sequence is truncated before the band limit, the approximation is optimal in a least squares sense (this is the same with the fourier transform). This projection can be done using code from the web page of the author of [3] or by using the spherical harmonic projection functions in the latest version of the DirectX SDK.

The convolution formula for spherical harmonics is very simple. Given a circularly symmetric function h [3] oriented in z expressed in spherical harmonics, the convolution[4] of another function f (projection coefficients l_l^m) with h (projection coefficients h_l^m) is just:

$$c_l^m = \sqrt{\frac{4\pi}{2l+1}} h_l^0 l_l^m$$

...where c_l^m are the projection coefficients of the convolved function. All circularly symmetric functions oriented with z only have one non-zero basis function in each band[5] — namely the one where m is equal to zero.

Evaluating the spherical harmonics scaled by the convolved coefficients in a given direction results in the same value that one would get if one computed an integral of the product of h oriented in the chosen direction with f over the sphere. If h is a cosine lobe clamped to zero in the lower hemisphere, f is a lighting environment, and the direction is a surface normal, then this integral is exactly the irradiance evaluated at the corresponding point. The cosine lobe has most of its energy in the first nine coefficients, so the higher frequency terms of the lighting environment have a minimal contribution; this is the fundamental observation in [3].

Here are the explicit representations of the first nine spherical harmonics in polynomial form:

$$y_0^0 = \frac{1}{2\sqrt{\pi}}$$

$$(y_1^1; y_1^{-1}; y_1^0) = \frac{\sqrt{3}}{2\sqrt{\pi}}(-x; -y; z)$$

$$(y_2^{-2}; y_2^1; y_2^{-1}) = \frac{\sqrt{15}}{2\sqrt{\pi}}(xy; -xz; -yz)$$

$$y_2^0 = \frac{\sqrt{5}}{4\sqrt{\pi}}(3z^2 - 1)$$

$$y_2^2 = \frac{\sqrt{15}}{4\sqrt{\pi}}(x^2 - y^2)$$

In the shader in the next section, there are seven constant registers that have to be computed whenever the lighting environment changes. Given the projection of the lighting environment into spherical harmonics resulting in coefficients R_l^m, G_l^m, B_l^m for the red, green, and blue channel of the lighting environment, respectively, they are defined as follows:

---

3 A circularly symmetric function on the sphere is one that only has variation in one direction — i.e., if you align the direction of variation with the z axis, the function is constant along lines of constant latitude, and the function varies in θ but not ϕ using the spherical parameterization defined above.

4 A non-circularly symmetric function convolved with a spherical function would not result in a spherical function. This is because circularly symmetric functions can be aligned with a point on the sphere without any extra parameters (because of the single direction of variation).

5 When oriented in z there is no variation in the variable ϕ, and the basis function where $m \neq 0$ integrates to zero for any function that has this symmetry.

C/R	cAr	cAg	cAb	cBr	cBg	cBb	cC
x	$-c_1 R_1^1$	$-c_1 G_1^1$	$-c_1 B_1^1$	$-c_2 R_2^{-2}$	$-c_2 G_2^{-2}$	$-c_2 B_2^{-2}$	$c_4 R_2^2$
y	$-c_1 R_1^{-1}$	$-c_1 G_1^{-1}$	$-c_1 B_1^{-1}$	$-c_2 R_2^{-1}$	$-c_2 G_2^{-1}$	$-c_2 B_2^{-1}$	$c_4 G_2^2$
z	$-c_1 R_1^0$	$-c_1 G_1^0$	$-c_1 B_1^0$	$3c_3 R_2^0$	$3c_3 G_2^0$	$3c_3 B_2^0$	$c_4 B_2^2$
w	$-c_0 R_0^0 - c_3 R_2^0$	$-c_0 G_0^0 - c_3 G_2^0$	$-c_0 B_0^0 - c_3 B_2^0$	$-c_2 R_2^1$	$-c_2 G_2^1$	$-c_2 B_2^1$	x

...where:

$$c_0 = n_0; c_1 = h_1 n_1; c_2 = h_2 n_2; c_3 = h_2 n_4; h_1 = \frac{2}{3}; h_2 = \frac{1}{4};$$

$$n_0 = \frac{1}{2\sqrt{\pi}}; n_1 = \frac{\sqrt{3}}{2\sqrt{\pi}}; n_2 = \frac{\sqrt{15}}{2\sqrt{\pi}}; n_3 = \frac{\sqrt{5}}{4\sqrt{\pi}}; n_4 = \frac{\sqrt{15}}{4\sqrt{\pi}}$$

The h_i are the convolution coefficients divided by π (irradiance is turned into exit radiance), and the n_i are the normalization coefficients of the basis functions. The x in cC can be any value, since it is not used by the shader.

In [3] transforming the surface normals by the inverse of the lights' rotation relative to the model is proposed. While that is necessary for deformable objects, for rigid objects it is more efficient to rotate the lighting coefficients directly before loading them into the shaders — this saves three instructions. If materials are stored per vertex, the following shader would need one extra instruction that multiplies the lighting times the diffuse reflectance of the surface.

Shader

```
vs_1_1
dcl_position v0
dcl_normal v1

m4x4 oPos, v0, c0
mov r0, v1          ; read port limits on inputs
; compute 1st 4 basis functions — linear + constant
; v1 is the normal with a homogenous 1
; c* are precomputed constants

dp4 r1.r, r0, cAr   ; r channel from 1st 4 basis functions
dp4 r1.g, r0, cAg   ; g channel from 1st 4 basis functions
dp4 r1.b, r0, cAb   ; b channel from 1st 4 basis functions

; compute polynomials for next 4 basis functions

mul r2, r0.xyzz, r0.yzzx ; r1 is xy/yz/z^2/xz

; add contributions — store in r2

dp4 r3.r, r2, cBr
dp4 r3.g, r2, cBg
```

```
dp4 r3.b, r2, cBb

; compute the final basis function x^2-y^2

mul r0.xy, r0.xy, r0.xy   ; x^2 y^2 - other slots are free
add r0.x, r0.x, -r0.y     ; x^2-y^2,

mad r1.rgb, cC.rgb, r0.x, r3.rgb
add r0, r1.rgb, r2.rgb    ; r0 is now rgb lighting
```

Acknowledgments

Thanks to Dan Baker for carefully proofreading this article. Wolfgang Engel, Tom Forsyth, and Willem de Boer provided useful feedback on early versions as well.

References

[1] Brennan, C., "Diffuse Cube Mapping," *Direct3D ShaderX: Vertex and Pixel Shader Tips and Tricks*, Wolfgang Engel, ed., Wordware Publishing, 2002, pp. 287-289.

[2] Greger, G., P. Shirley, P. Hubbard, and D. Greenberg, "The Irradiance Volume," *IEEE Computer Graphics and Applications*, 6(11):1986, pp. 21-29.

[3] Ramamoorthi, R. and P. Hanrahan, "An Efficient Representation for Irradiance Environment Maps," *Computer Graphics*, SIGGRAPH 2001, pp. 497-500.

[4] Sloan, P., J. Kautz, and J. Snyder, "Precomputed Radiance Transfer for Real-Time Rendering in Dynamic, Low-Frequency Lighting Environments," *Computer Graphics*, SIGGRAPH 2002, pp. 527-536.

Practical Precomputed Radiance Transfer

Peter-Pike J. Sloan
Microsoft Corporation

Abstract

Precomputed radiance transfer (PRT) is a technique that enables rigid objects to be illuminated in low-frequency lighting environments with global effects like soft shadows and interreflections in real time. It achieves these results by running a lengthy preprocess that computes how light is transferred from a source environment to exit radiance at a point. This article discusses the technique in general and focuses on a practical example using the recently introduced compressed [7] form in a vertex shader.

Introduction

Generating accurate depictions of complex scenes in interesting lighting environments is one of the primary goals in computer graphics. The general solution to this problem requires the solution of an integral equation that is difficult to solve, even in non-interactive settings [1]. In interactive graphics, shortcuts are generally taken by making simplifying assumptions of several properties of the scene; the materials are generally assumed to be simple. The lighting environment is either approximated with a small number of point and directional lights or environment maps and transport complexity (i.e., how the light bounces around the scene — interreflections, caustics, and shadows are examples) are only modeled in a limited way. For example, shadows are computed for dynamic point lights but not for environment maps.

There is a lot of interesting previous work that has trade-offs different from those made with PRT. *Polynomial texture maps* [3] allow interactive rendering of diffuse objects with textures that capture local interreflections and scattering, but they are limited to point light sources. There are several papers that deal with prefiltering environment maps — most notably in [4], diffuse objects can be interactively rendered in arbitrary environments by projecting the lighting environment into spherical harmonics, and the prefiltering is done via convolution in the frequency domain. This technique is flexible and allows for dynamic geometry, but no transport complexity is modeled; it is technically only accurate for convex objects. In [5], a method is presented that can interactively render a wider range of materials but still does not handle other forms of transport complexity.

Extensions to precomputed radiance transfer is currently an active research area; while this work focuses on practical concerns and shaders for the most efficient formulation (diffuse objects), it has been successfully applied to more general reflectance models [2], integrated with ideas from bidirectional texture functions and texture synthesis [8], and compressed to handle higher frequency lighting and extended to handle subsurface scattering [7]. The primary limitations are relatively low-frequency lighting environments and, more importantly, while the objects are assumed to be rigid, they are not allowed to deform.

General Background on Precomputed Radiance Transfer

For a diffuse object illuminated in distant lighting environment L, the reflected radiance at a point P on the surface is:

$$R_p(\vec{v}) = \frac{\rho_d}{\pi} \int_s L(s) V_p(s) H_N(s) ds \qquad (1)$$

…where V_p represents visibility, a binary function that is 1 in a given direction if a ray in that direction originating at the point can "see" the light source and 0 otherwise. H_N represents the projected area (or cosine term), and the integration is over the hemisphere about the point's normal. The diffuse reflectance (or albedo) of the surface is ρ_d and is generally an RGB color, where each value is between zero and one. The division by π maps irradiance (the integral) into exit radiance (what we see) and guarantees energy conservation (i.e., the amount of energy reflected is never greater than the amount of energy arriving at a point).

With a point or directional light, the lighting environment is effectively a delta function, which turns the integral into a simple function evaluation — the cosine of the angle between the light and the normal if the direction is not in shadow or just zero if it is. Since the object is diffuse, the reflected radiance is the same in all directions, and the integral does not depend on the view direction. The key idea behind precomputed radiance transfer is to approximate the lighting environment using a set of basis functions over the sphere:

$$L(\vec{s}) \approx \sum_i l_i B_i(\vec{s})$$

…where the Bs are a set of basis functions and the ls are the coefficients corresponding to the optimal (in a least squares sense) projection of the lighting environment into the basis functions; that is, they minimize:

$$\int (L(\vec{s}) - \sum_i l_i B_i(\vec{s}))^2 ds \qquad (2)$$

If the basis functions are orthogonal, this just amounts to integrating the lighting environment against the basis functions, while in general it is necessary to integrate against the duals of the basis functions.

Now substitute the approximation of the lighting environment into (1):

$$R_p(\vec{v}) \approx \frac{\rho_d}{\pi} \int_s \left(\sum_i l_i B_i(\vec{s}) \right) V_p(\vec{s}) H_N(\vec{s}) ds \qquad (3)$$

Recall two concepts from basic calculus: the integral of a sum equals the sum of the integrals, and constants can be pulled outside of integrals[1]. This allows us to reformulate (3), as follows:

$$R_p(\vec{v}) \approx \rho_d \sum_i l_i \int_s \frac{1}{\pi} B_i(\vec{s}) V_p(\vec{s}) H_N(\vec{s}) ds \qquad (4)$$

The important thing to note about the above equation is that the integral only depends on the choice of basis functions, not on the value of the particular lighting environment or the albedo of the surface. This means that if you precompute the integral for each basis function at every point on the object, you are left with the following expression for reflected radiance:

$$R_p(\vec{v}) \approx \rho_d \sum_i l_i t_{pi}$$

A dot product between the global lighting coefficients and the spatially varying (through the index p) transfer vector scaled by the albedo is all that is required. If the lighting and transfer are represented as vectors (L and T, respectively), this equation becomes:

$$R_p(\vec{v}) \approx \rho_d (T \bullet L) \qquad (5)$$

Compression

As the number of basis functions grows, these transfer vectors become larger and the data size can become unwieldy. A compression technique was recently proposed [7] that can significantly reduce both the compute and storage requirements of the technique. The vertices (or texels) in a mesh are split into discrete clusters, and each cluster is approximated with a mean and an optimal linear basis. Mathematically:

$$T_p \approx M_k + \sum_j w_{pj} P_{kj}$$

...where T_p is the transfer vector at a point, M_k is the mean for cluster k, the P_{kj} represents the local linear basis for the cluster, and the w_{pj} represents the coordinates of T_p subtracted from the mean in the given basis. The important thing to note is that k and w_{pj} vary at every sample (vertex or texel), while M_k and P_{kj} are constant for a given cluster.

If this approximation for the transfer vector is now inserted into equation (5), the following equation results:

$$R_p(\vec{v}) \approx \rho_d \left(\left(M_k + \sum_j w_{pj} P_{kj} \right) \bullet L \right)$$

---

1   This is because integration is a linear operator, that is I(f+g) = I(f)+I(g) and I(s*f) = s*I(f) where f and g represent functions, s represents a scalar, and I represents integration.

Again, exploiting a linear operator (the dot product), the terms can be redistributed into the final form:

$$R_p(\vec{v}) \approx \rho_d \left((M_k \bullet L) + \sum_j w_{pj} (P_{kj} \bullet L) \right) \tag{6}$$

An important thing to note is that the dot products in the above equation only depend on per-cluster information, so they can be performed once per frame and stored as constants in the shader. This also makes the evaluation of reflected radiance independent of the dimensionality of the lighting basis. Given K clusters and N local basis vectors, K*(N+1)*3 coefficients have to be computed for each frame (the 3 is for colored lights) and stored as constants.

Choice of Basis Functions

While any basis functions that approximate the sphere can be used, much of the previous work has focused on using the real spherical harmonics. In this article we just touch on the basic formulation and some useful properties. More thorough descriptions can be found in the references in [6]. The mathematical form of the complex spherical harmonics is as follows:

$$Y_l^m(\theta, \phi) = K_l^m e^{im\phi} P_l^{|m|}(\cos \theta); l \in \mathbf{N}, -1 \leq m \leq l$$

...where the parameterization of the sphere is:

$$s = (x, y, z) = (\sin(\theta)\cos(\phi), \sin(\theta)\sin(\phi), \cos(\theta)) \tag{7}$$

The P_l^m are the associated Legendre polynomials, and the K_l^m are the normalization constants.

$$K_l^m = \sqrt{\frac{(2l+1)(l-|m|)!}{4\pi(l+|m|)!}}$$

The real form of the spherical harmonics is:

$$y_l^m = \begin{cases} 2\mathrm{Re}(Y_l^m) & m > 0 \\ 2\mathrm{Im}(Y_l^m) & m < 0 \\ Y_l^0 & m = 0 \end{cases} \tag{8}$$

The spherical harmonics can also be expressed as polynomials in 3D where evaluation is restricted to the surface of the unit sphere. These polynomials can be computed by factoring equation (8) using the trigonometric forms for x, y, and z in equation (7) and trigonometric identities; [4] has examples through the quadratics. The index l represents the band index and corresponds to the degree of the polynomial; a complete lth degree basis contains $(l+1)^2$ coefficients and can represent all polynomials through degree l. For simplicity, we sometimes use a form that represents each basis function with a single index y_i, where $i = l(l+1) + m + 1$. The spherical harmonics are what is known as an orthonormal basis; this means that $\int y_i(s) y_j(s) ds = \delta_{ij} = 1 \, if \, (i = j) \, and \, 0 \, if \, (i! = j)$.

One byproduct of the above definition is that the basis functions can be defined with any sign convention. Care has to be made when mixing between definitions of the basis functions found in different references, particularly when using projection coefficients or code that is found on the web. Generating the least squares optimal projection coefficients that minimize equation (2) is simple for any orthogonal basis:

$$l_i = \int y_i(s)f(s)ds$$

One other important property of spherical harmonics is that they are rotationally invariant. This is analogous to the translation invariance in the fourier transform and can be mathematically expressed as follows: $R(proj(f(s))) = proj(f(R(s)))$, where R is a rotation matrix and *proj* represents a projection into spherical harmonics. This means that the shape of the projection is stable under rotations, so there will not be any temporal artifacts as the light or object is rotated. Rotations can be computed in various ways, but all forms ultimately are a linear combination of the projection coefficients (i.e., the rotated coefficients can be computed by a matrix multiplication); for low orders, symbolic integration can be used to compute the entries in these rotation matrices, which happen to be polynomials of the coefficients of R. See [2] and [6] for a more thorough description and other references.

Setting up the Shaders

Before PRT can be used, several things have to occur. Any lights in the scene have to be represented using spherical harmonics and combined into a single spherical function (just add them together, possibly rotating them independently), the spherical function representing the lights has to be transformed into object space (i.e., the basis functions have to be oriented in the same way they were during the precomputation), and if compression is used, the per-cluster dot products have to be performed.

The latest DirectX SDK update has several functions for mapping lights into spherical harmonic coefficients and rotating them using any pure rotation matrix. In particular, directional/cone/spot lights can be evaluated, and cube maps can be directly projected. After the lights have been evaluated in world space, they need to be rotated into object space (using the transpose of the rigid rotation mapping the object from object space to world space) or, alternatively, always evaluated directly in object space (i.e., one rotation applied directly to coefficients or the "lighting" functions evaluated with direction vectors mapped into object space).

If compression is used, the shader constants need to be evaluated (the per-cluster dot products from equation (6)) before being uploaded.

The uncompressed form requires a transfer vector to be stored at every texel or vertex, while the compressed form requires a mapping into the start of the corresponding sample's clusters' constants (in the constant table) and coefficients in the clusters' linear subspace (generally much fewer than the number of basis functions used to represent the lighting environment). If more clusters are used than can be represented in the constant table of the graphics card, a multi-pass technique described in [7] must be employed instead.

Compressed Shader

The following shader is written in HLSL and parameterized by a single variable NPCA representing the number of PCA basis vectors stored in each cluster. This has to be passed in to the compiler or set with a #define at the top of the shader. The HLSL code assumes that NPCA is a multiple of 4. If NPCA is zero, the technique is pure vector quantization (this is an inferior compression technique and should not be used in general). BLENDWEIGHT0 has to index into the start of the cluster for each vertex. The per-cluster data (from equation (6)) is stored to minimize the number of constant registers. The mean is first stored as an RGB color, and then all of the dot products of the PCA vectors with the R lighting coefficients are stored, followed by G and B. Constraining NPCA to be a multiple of 4 allows this more efficient packing scheme that reduces the number of constant registers and the number of assembly instructions that are required. If a single color is stored for each basis vector (effectively wasting all of the alpha channels), NPCA+1 constant vectors are needed for each cluster, while this scheme requires (NPCA/4)*3 + 1 registers per cluster — wasting only one slot (the alpha channel of the dot product with the per-cluster mean).

```
// inputs stored per vertex
struct VS_INPUT
{
    float4      vPosition           : POSITION;
    int         vClusterInfo        : BLENDWEIGHT0;
#if (NPCA>0)
    float4      vPCAWts[(NPCA+3)/4] : BLENDWEIGHT1;
#endif
};

// outputs - position and color
struct VS_OUTPUT_DIFF
{
    float4      vPosition           : POSITION;
    float4      vDiff               : COLOR;
};

// all of the constant registers are mapped
// if vs1.1 is used have to use the appropriate #
// This assumes that the first 4 constants contain
// the complete transformation matrix to NDC space.

float4 c[255] : register(vs_2_0, c0);

VS_OUTPUT_DIFF DiffShader(const VS_INPUT v)
{
    VS_OUTPUT_DIFF o;
```

Practical Precomputed Radiance Transfer

```
    // 1st four constants are the transformation matrix

    matrix mXform;
    mXform[0] = c[0];
    mXform[1] = c[1];
    mXform[2] = c[2];
    mXform[3] = c[3];

    o.vPosition = mul(mXform,v.vPosition); // xform point

    int iIndexBase = v.vClusterInfo.x;

    float4 vRes = c[iIndexBase];              // cluster mean color
#if (NPCA > 0)
    float  PCACoefs[NPCA] = (float[NPCA])v.vPCAWts;

    // accumulate R/G/B each in a 4 vector

    float4 vRed   = 0;
    float4 vGreen = 0;
    float4 vBlue  = 0;

    // compute the sum from equation 6
    // do R/G/B in parallel, 4 coefficients at a time

    for(int i=0;i<NPCA/4;i++) {
        vRed += v.vPCAWts[i]*c[iIndexBase+i+1];
        vGreen += v.vPCAWts[i]*c[iIndexBase+i+1+(NPCA/4)];
        vBlue += v.vPCAWts[i]*c[iIndexBase+i+1+(NPCA/4)*2];
    }

    float3 vTmp;

    // sum across the accumulation register for each color channel
    // adding it to the mean color

    vTmp.r = dot(vRed,1);
    vTmp.g = dot(vGreen,1);
    vTmp.b = dot(vBlue,1);

    vRes.rgb += vTmp.rgb;
#endif

    o.vDiff = vRes;

    return o;
}
```

Acknowledgments

This article is based on research results generated in collaboration with several individuals — in particular John Snyder, Jan Kautz, and Jesse Hall. Jason Sandlin and Ben Luna have been extremely helpful discussing these ideas. Wolfgang Engel provided valuable feedback and encouragement while I wrote this article.

References

[1] Kajiya, J., "The Rendering Equation," SIGGRAPH 1986, pp. 143-150.

[2] Kautz, J., P. Sloan, and J. Snyder, "Fast, Arbitrary BRDF Shading for Low-Frequency Lighting Using Spherical Harmonics," 12th Eurographics Workshop on Rendering, pp. 301-308.

[3] Malzbender, T., D. Gelb, and H. Wolters, "Polynomial Texture Maps," SIGGRAPH 2001, pp. 519-528.

[4] Ramamoorthi, R. and P. Hanrahan, "An Efficient Representation for Irradiance Environment Maps," SIGGRAPH 2001, pp. 497-500.

[5] Ramamoorthi, R. and P. Hanrahan, "Frequency Space Environment Map Rendering," SIGGRAPH 2003, pp. 517-526.

[6] Sloan, P., J. Kautz, and J. Snyder, "Precomputed Radiance Transfer for Real-Time Rendering in Dynamic, Low-Frequency Lighting Environments," SIGGRAPH 2002, pp. 527-536.

[7] Sloan, P., J. Hall, J. Hart, and J. Snyder, "Clustered Principal Component for Precomputed Radiance Transfer," SIGGRAPH 2003, pp. 382-391.

[8] Sloan, P., X. Liu, H. Shum, and J. Snyder, "Bi-Scale, Low-Frequency Radiance Self-Transfer," SIGGRAPH 2003, pp. 370-375.

Advanced Sky Dome Rendering

Marco Spoerl and Kurt Pelzer

Krauss-Maffei Wegmann   Piranha Bytes

Introduction

With the current interest of both hobbyist and professional game programmers in landscape rendering and the shift from indoor to outdoor environments in game design, one aspect has become very important: the sky. Traditional approaches for rendering skies only used texture-mapped domes. This is acceptable for indoor environments, since the player only sees a glimpse of it. Such sky domes can be implemented both easily and efficiently. But their major drawback is a lack of flexibility, which makes it difficult to render dynamic effects like changes with the time of day.

This article describes a better solution and illustrates the implementation of a basic vertex color sky dome that:

- Computes the correct position of both the sun and the moon, depending on time of day
- Changes its color depending on the position of the sun
- Renders a projection of the sun at its correct position
- Renders a projection of the moon at its correct position, including the moon's current phase using per-pixel lighting

Position of Sun and Moon

[SchlyterA] and [SchlyterB] give excellent instruction for computing the positions of sky objects from their orbital elements. Although the algorithms presented there are significantly simplified, they still work well for real-time computer graphics.

Using the equations in [SchlyterA], it's simple to compute the position of the sun. The orbital elements used are longitude of perihelion (w), mean distance (a) measured in astronomical units (AU), eccentricity (e), and mean anomaly (M). Most of those and the obliquity of the ecliptic (oblecl) depend on the current time. From these, all other elements needed to determine the position of the sun are computed: mean longitude (L), eccentric anomaly (E), rectangular coordinates (x, y), distance (r) measured in astronomical units, true anomaly (v), and longitude (lon). Finally, the ecliptic rectangular coordinates are calculated and stored as the sun's current position.

In addition to the basic orbital elements mentioned above, the moon needs the longitude of the ascending node (N) and inclination (i). Everything else is computed similar to the sun with the exception of the longitude (lon) and the new parameter latitude (lat), which are computed using the ecliptic rectangular coordinates and the fact that all distances are not measured in astronomical units but Earth radii. After that, the longitude, latitude, and distance are corrected using the perturbations of the moon, and the resulting final coordinates are stored as the current position. The computation of the moon's position is completed with two important values, elongation and the resulting phase angle, needed later to display the moon's phase.

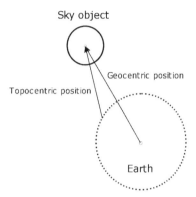

Figure 1: Difference between geocentric and topocentric coordinates

The computed positions, as illustrated in Figure 1, are geocentric (i.e., the viewer is located at the center of the Earth). Although this affects the results for the moon (but not for the sun, as it's too far away), the position is not shifted to topocentric coordinates for the sake of clarity. Still another correction has to be made to both results regarding the geocentric position: the influence of the Earth's rotation. Without it, one "day" would last one year — the time needed for the Earth to circle the sun or, from a geocentric point of view, for the sun to circle the Earth. To simulate the effect, the sky object's position vector is simply transformed by a matrix built from a rotation around the z-axis by an angle relative to the time of day. Of course, any other axis of rotation could be chosen to simulate a lower course instead of the current one, which always leads through the zenith.

Rendering the Dome

The dome itself is a simple sphere created at run time. Only the position and normal of each vertex are stored. Texture coordinates and vertex color are computed in the vertex shader. One characteristic of the dome is its transformation. The viewer is always in the center of the sky sphere (i.e., the sky dome moves as the viewer moves). To take this into account, the translational part of the view matrix is set to zero before building the transformation matrix for the vertex program.

As the dome has to be huge to cover the whole world while moving around with the viewer, another modification has to be made. When transforming the vertex position to clip space inside the vertex shader, the z- and w-coordinates are made equal (that is, after the division of the x-, y-, and z-coordinates by the w-component z becomes 1, making the vertex lie on the far clipping plane).

```
; v0  = position
; c0 - c4 = proj matrix * view matrix

vs_1_1

dcl_position v0

; transform position
dp4 oPos.x, v0, c0
dp4 oPos.y, v0, c1
dp4 oPos.zw, v0, c3 ; simply force z to 1.0f by making it equal to w
```

NOTE   Throughout this article, the world matrix is ignored, as it's always the identity matrix.

Determination of the sky color is roughly oriented to [Nishita], which defines equations to compute the color using single and multiple scattering. Compared to the equations presented in that paper, this article uses a slightly different, much simplified formula to calculate the final vertex color.

$$C_V(\theta) = (K_r F_r(\theta) + K_m F_m(\theta))SC_S$$

F_r and F_m are the phase functions for molecule and aerosol scattering, respectively. K_r and K_m are the colors of the molecules and aerosols. S is a scaling factor relative to the vertex's y-coordinate, and C_s is the current color of the sun.

The shader starts with the calculation of the scaling value and an exponent needed later:

```
(...)
; v0 = position
; c16 = constants (-1000.0f*fInvR*fInvR, 3000.0f, 0.0f, 2.0f)

; calculate steps
mul r0.x, v0.y, v0.y
mad r0.xw, r0.x, c16.xxzz, c16.yyww
(...)
```

The angle needed to calculate molecule and aerosol scattering is computed using the sun normal and the current vertex normal. This is feasible, as the viewer is always standing at the dome's center.

```
; v1 = normal
; c12 = sun normal (sunN.x, sunN.y, sunN.z, 0.0f)
(...)
dcl_normal v1
(...)
"; calc angle normal - sunnormal
dp3 r0.y, v1, c12
(...)
```

Molecule scattering is performed using the equation:

$$F_r(\theta) = \frac{3}{4}(1+\theta^2) = \frac{3}{4} + \frac{3}{4}\theta^2$$

```
; c15 = constants (0.0f, 1.0f, 0.75f, 0.9f)
(...)
; calculate fr (molecule scattering)
lit r3.z, r0.yyww
mad r4.x, r3.z, c15.z, c15.z
(...)
```

Aerosol scattering is simply a scalar 1.75f or 0.75f, depending on the magnitude of the angle calculated earlier.

```
"; c15 = constants (0.0f, 1.0f, 0.75f, 0.9f)
(...)
; calculate fm (aerosol scattering)
max r6.x, r0.y, -r0.y
sge r6.x, r6.x, c15.y
add r5.x, r6.x, c15.z
(...)
```

Afterward, the final color is computed as follows:

```
; c11 = sun color (red, green, blue, 0.0f)
; c12 = sun normal (sunN.x, sunN.y, sunN.z, 0.0f)
; c13 = constants (KrRed, KrGreen, KrBlue, 0.0f)
; c14 = constants (KmRed, KmGreen, KmBlue, 0.0f)
(...)
; Calculate the color regarding to the scattering values
mul r7.xyz, c13, r4.x        ; multiply Fr by Kr color of the molecules
mad r9.xyz, c14, r5.x, r7    ; multiply Fm by Km color of the aerosols and add
mul r9.xyz, r9.xyz, r0.x     ; scale by steps
mul oD0.xyz, r9, c11         ; output vertex color scaled by the sun's current color
(...)
```

Rendering the Sun

Drawing the sun is actually quite simple. Every sky object has a camera associated with it. As seen in Figure 2, this camera is used as a texture projector located at the world origin and looks at the sun's current position.

Its projection and view matrix are concatenated with a special matrix needed to handle the transformation from projection space to texture space.

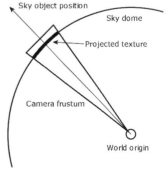

Figure 2: Basic texture projection setup

$$TexSpaceMatrix = \begin{pmatrix} 0.5f & 0.0f & 0.0f & 0.0f \\ 0.0f & -0.5f & 0.0f & 0.0f \\ 0.0f & 0.0f & 0.0f & 0.0f \\ 0.5f & 0.5f & 1.0f & 1.0f \end{pmatrix}$$

The transposed view-projection-texspace-matrix is passed into the vertex shader where the texture coordinates for the projected sun texture are computed based on the current vertex position.

```
; v0 = position
; c5 - c7 = view matrix * projection matrix * texspace matrix (sun projector)
; c15 = constants (0.0f, 1.0f, 0.75f, 0.9f)
(...)
dp4 oT0.x, v0, c5
dp4 oT0.y, v0, c6
dp4 r0.zw, v0, c7
sge r1.w, r0.w, c15.x
mul oT0.zw, r0, r1.w
(...)
```

The extra operations before storing the oT0.zw coordinates are needed to avoid a second projection behind the sky object's camera.

The pixel shader is a simple fixed-function-style ADDSMOOTH to blend the sun texture (as seen in Figure 3) indexed via the texture coordinates with the calculated sky color passed in via v0.

Figure 3: The sun texture

```
; v0 = calculated sky color
; t0 = sun texture
ps_1_1
tex t0 ; fetch sun texture
(...)
mad_sat r0, t0, 1 - v0, v0
(...)
```

Rendering the Moon and Its Phase

Displaying the moon is basically the same as drawing the sun. Again, a transposed view-projection-texspace-matrix is passed in to the vertex shader to compute the texture coordinates.

```
; v0 = position
; c8 - c10 = view matrix * projection matrix * texspace matrix (moon projector)
; c15 = constants (0.0f, 1.0f, 0.75f, 0.9f)
```

```
(...)
dp4 r2.x, v0, c8
dp4 r2.y, v0, c9
dp4 r0.zw, v0, c10
sge r1.w, r0.w, c15.x
mul r2.zw, r0, r1.w
mov oT1, r2
mov oT2, r2
```

If rendered like this (just with the texture, as seen in Figure 4), the moon will always appear full because its predominant feature — the moon's phase — is missing. To solve this, per-pixel lighting using a spherically based normal map is necessary. There's only one problem; as the moon itself is not a real object, how do you compute the tangent space matrix needed for per-pixel lighting? Simple answer: You don't. An imaginary viewer on Earth mostly sees the same side of the moon (i.e., the moon "object" can be thought of as a simple textured quad always facing the viewer). The imaginary sun rotates around that object (remember that geocentric coordinates are used — that is, both sun and moon are circling the Earth) with the light vector being perpendicular to the front of the quad at full moon and perpendicular to the back at new moon. So the light vector used is simply a vector (0.0f, 0.0f, –1.0f) rotated around the quad's local y-axis by the moon's phase angle computed earlier. Figure 5 shows the solution.

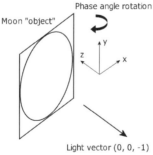

Figure 4: The moon texture

Figure 5: Setup for lighting the moon

Figure 6: The moon normal map

With this composition, the tangent space matrix would be the identity matrix and is omitted altogether. Bearing that in mind, the transformation of the light vector inside the vertex program is easy.

```
; c17 = lightvec sun->moon (light.x, light.y, light.z, 0.5f)
(...)
mov r0, c17
mad oD1.xyz, -r0.xyz, c17.w, c17.w
(...)
```

The pixel shader uses the normal map, as seen in Figure 6, and the light vector passed with oD1 or v1, respectively, to "light" the moon texture. The resulting value is multiplied by an external factor and added to the current color. This factor is relative to the sun's current normalized y-position and is used to "disguise" the moon during the day.

```
; c0 = scaling factor for the moon color
; v1 = transformed light vector for the moon phase
ps_1_1
(...)
tex  t1 ; fetch moon texture
tex  t2 ; fetch moon normal map
(...)
dp3 r1, t2_bx2, v1_bx2 ; calculate angle light vector / moon normal
mul_sat r1, t1, r1 ; light moon texture
mad_sat r0, r1, c0, r0 ; multiply by scaling factor and add to current color
(...)
```

Putting It All Together

These are the final shaders:

```
;************************************************************************

; Vertex Shader
; Author: Marco Spoerl
; Function: Sky dome

; v0 = position    (3 floats)
; v1 = normal (3 floats)
; c0 - c4 = proj matrix * view matrix
; c5 - c7 = view matrix * proj matrix * texspace matrix (sun projector)
; c8 - c10 = view matrix * proj matrix * texspace matrix (moon projector)
; c11 = sun color (red, green, blue, 0.0f)
; c12 = sun normal (sunN.x, sunN.y, sunN.z, 0.0f)
; c13 = constants (KrRed, KrGreen, KrBlue, 0.0f)
; c14 = constants (KmRed, KmGreen, KmBlue, 0.0f)
; c15 = constants (0.0f, 1.0f, 0.75f, 0.9f)
; c16 = constants (-1000.0f*fInvR*fInvR, 3000.0f, 0.0f, 2.0f)
; c17 = lightvec sun->moon    (light.x, light.y, light.z, 0.5f)


;************************************************************************

vs_1_1

dcl_position v0
dcl_normal v1

; transform position

dp4 oPos.x, v0, c0
dp4 oPos.y, v0, c1
dp4 oPos.zw, v0, c3  ; simply force z to 1.0f by making it equal to w
; calculate steps
```

```
mul r0.x, v0.y, v0.y
mad r0.xw, r0.x, c16.xxzz, c16.yyww

; calc angle normal - sunnormal

dp3 r0.y, v1, c12

; calculate fr (molecule scattering)

lit r3.z, r0.yyww
mad r4.x, r3.z, c15.z, c15.z

; calculate fm (aerosol scattering)

max r6.x, r0.y, -r0.y
sge r6.x, r6.x, c15.y
add r5.x, r6.x, c15.z

; Calculate the color regarding to the scattering values
; Kr color of the molecules

mul r7.xyz, c13, r4.x

; Km color of the aerosols

mad r9.xyz, c14, r5.x, r7

; scale by steps

mul r9.xyz, r9.xyz, r0.x

; output color scaled by current sun color

mul oD0.xyz, r9, c11

; output transformed light vector for the moon phase

mov r0, c17
mad oD1.xyz, -r0.xyz, c17.w, c17.w

; output projected texcoord0 (sun)

dp4 oT0.x, v0, c5
dp4 oT0.y, v0, c6
dp4 r0.zw, v0, c7
sge r1.w, r0.w, c15.x
mul oT0.zw, r0, r1.w

; output projected texcoord1/2 (moon/moonnormals)

dp4 r2.x, v0, c8
```

```
dp4 r2.y, v0, c9
dp4 r0.zw, v0, c10
sge r1.w, r0.w, c15.x
mul r2.zw, r0, r1.w
mov oT1, r2
mov oT2, r2
;**************************************************************************

; Pixel Shader
; Author: Marco Spoerl
; Function: Sky dome

; c0 = scaling factor for the moon color

; v0 = calculated vertex color
; v1 = transformed light vector for the moon phase

; t0 = sun texture
; t1 = moon texture
; t2 = moon normal map

;**************************************************************************

ps_1_1

; Fetch textures

tex  t0  ; sun
tex  t1  ; moon
tex  t2  ; moon normals

; ADDSMOOTH vertex color and sun

mad_sat r0, t0, 1 - v0, v0

; Calculate moon color

dp3 r1, t2_bx2, v1_bx2
mul_sat r1, t1, r1

; ADD current color and scaled moon color

mad_sat r0, r1, c0, r0
```

Where to Go from Here

There are a number of improvements that can be made to these shaders. Among them are the following:

- Currently, no stars are displayed. They can be implemented using a static cube map made from photographs of the night sky. A better approach is the run-time creation of a map using the positional data from the public Bright Star Catalogue (BSC) or displaying them as points using the information from the BSC. Furthermore, the star map must be rotated by the time of day to simulate the Earth's rotation.

- In addition to the position of the sky objects, [SchlyterA] gives equations to compute the apparent diameter. The resulting value can be used to change the projected size of the object.

- The texture for the moon and the sun can be generated at run time using real 3D objects. A solar and lunar eclipse would be possible.

- Other sky objects can be simulated (e.g., planets, asteroids, and comets).

- The topocentric position can be used instead of the geocentric one. Note that when using topocentric coordinates, the positions of the stars have to change depending on the position of the viewer. The night sky in the northern hemisphere, for example, is different from that in the southern side.

- A better night sky model can be applied simulating the influence of the moonlight, the stars, and phenomena like zodiacal light or airglow. [Jensen] has some great ideas on that.

- Fog and haze are missing. The method outlined in [Hoffman] can be useful as an expansion or substitution.

- Clouds are missing, a topic that could fill many books. They can be implemented using simple noise textures or with approaches described in [Harris] or [Miyazaki], for example. With clouds, effects like rainfall, snowfall, and maybe even rainbows or lightning can be simulated.

Conclusion

This article showed a basic approach for implementing a simple, non-static sky dome. Although incomplete and not very accurate, it is a good starting point for further research into the topic of outdoor rendering. The complete source code and a sample application can be found on this book's companion CD. In addition, Color Plates 9 and 10 show screen shots of the sky along with the advanced water effects discussed earlier in the book.

Acknowledgments

Thanks to Max Dennis Luesebrink and Matthias Wloka for their work on the very early version of the sky dome and its vertex shader.

References

[Harris] Harris, Mark J. and Anselmo Lastra, "Real-Time Cloud Rendering," Eurographics 2001 Proceedings, Vol. 20, no. 3, pp. 76-84.

[Hoffman] Hoffman, Naty and Arcot J. Preetham, "Rendering Outdoor Light Scattering in Real Time," Proceedings of the 2002 Game Developers Conference.

[Jensen] Jensen, Henrik Wann, Fredo Durand, Michael M. Stark, Simon Premoze, Julie Dorsey, and Peter Shirley, "A Physically-Based Night Sky Model," SIGGRAPH 2001, Computer Graphics Proceedings, Annual Conference Series, pp. 399-408.

[Miyazaki] Miyazaki, R., S. Yoshida ,Y. Dobashi, and T. Nishita, "A Method for Modeling Clouds based on Atmospheric Fluid Dynamics," Pacific Graphics 2001, pp. 363-372.

[Nishita] Nishita, Tomoyuki, Yoshinori Dobashi, Kazufumi Kaneda, and Hideo Yamashita, "Display Method of the Sky Color Taking into Account Multiple Scattering," SIGGRAPH 1996, Computer Graphics Proceedings, Annual Conference Series, pp. 379-386.

[SchlyterA] Schlyter, Paul, "How to compute planetary positions," available online at http://hem.passagen.se/pausch/comp/ppcomp.html.

[SchlyterB] Schlyter, Paul, "Computing planetary positions — a tutorial with worked examples," available online at http://stjarnhimlen.se/comp/tutorial.html.

Deferred Shading with Multiple Render Targets

Nicolas Thibieroz
PowerVR Technologies

Introduction

Traditional rendering algorithms submit geometry and immediately apply shading effects to the rasterized primitives. Complex shading effects often require multiple render passes to produce the final pixel color with the geometry submitted every pass. Deferred shading (aka quad shading) is an alternative rendering technique that submits the scene geometry only once, storing per-pixel attributes into local video memory to be used in the subsequent rendering passes. In these later passes, screen-aligned quads are rendered, and the per-pixel attributes contained in the buffer are retrieved at a 1:1 mapping ratio so that each pixel is shaded individually. The following figure illustrates the principle of deferred shading.

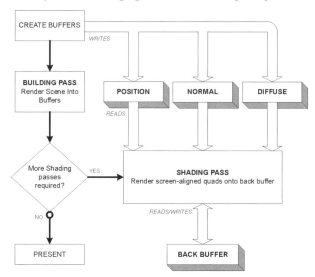

Figure 1: Deferred shading flow diagram with arbitrary examples of stored data (position, normal, and color)

Deferred shading has a number of advantages over traditional rendering. Firstly, only a single geometry pass is required, even if shadow algorithms are used. By

251

virtually eliminating multiple geometry passes, the saved vertex throughput can be used to dramatically increase the polygon budget of the single geometry pass, improving the scene's realism without compromising the performance of the shading passes (as they are not dependent on underlying geometry).

Secondly, all shading calculations are performed *per-pixel*, as each pixel has a unique set of properties. For shading effects that simulate lighting, this is preferable to using interpolated vertex shader outputs. This subtle difference can have a dramatic impact on the quality of the visual results.

Thirdly, deferred shading has the advantage of reducing pixel overdraw, as only the initial geometry pass may have an average overdraw value above 1. This is because all shading passes operate on pixels that are already visible; thus, no overdrawn pixel will ever be touched by the pixel shader during the shading passes.

These advantages make deferred shading an interesting alternative to traditional multi-pass rendering, though the accrued memory footprint and bandwidth requirements need careful consideration when implementing this technique. This article describes deferred shading in detail and gives practical implementation examples that show how deferred shading can be applied to current and future games using the DirectX 9 API and beyond.

Multiple Render Targets

Prior to DirectX 9, one could only output a maximum of 32 bits consisting of four color components to a render target in a single pass. However, deferred shading requires a greater number of components to accommodate the pixel attributes calculated during the initial pass. Multiple render targets (MRTs), a new feature of DirectX 9, allow up to four render targets to be written to in the same rendering pass, bringing the total number of output components to 16 and the maximum precision to 512 bits (although these can vary depending on the host 3D device). Without MRT support, outputting more than four components would require additional geometry passes.

These MRTs are used to store scene information during the geometry pass (or "building pass") and are then accessed as textures during the shading passes. Note that MRTs have the following limitations in the DirectX 9 API:

- They must be of identical size.
- They can only be of different bit depths if the D3DPMISCCAPS_MRTINDEPENDENT-BITDEPTHS cap is exported by the 3D device.
- Dithering, alpha testing, fogging, blending, or masking are only supported if the 3D device exposes the D3DPMISCCAPS_MRTPOSTPIXELSHADERBLENDING cap.
- They may not be antialiased.

Each MRT contains per-pixel information about the scene and therefore should be of the same size as the main render target (the back buffer). Because the back buffer's width and height are usually not a power of two, 3D devices not supporting the D3DPTEXTURECAPS_NONPOW2CONDITIONAL cap will need to create MRTs at the next power of two size above the main render target dimensions (e.g., for a 1280x1024 back buffer, the MRT's size will be 2048x1024). Although non-power of two MRTs have limitations, these do not directly affect the algorithm.

Multi-element textures (METs) are another feature, albeit less flexible, of DirectX 9 that closely resembles MRTs. METs are basically a set of textures *of the same format* packed together. This limitation and the fact that DirectX 9 exports a single MET format called D3DFMT_MULTI2_ARGB8 (two textures of 8888 format) make METs unsuitable for deferred shading.

Attribute Buffer

The attribute buffer is the name that we give to the scene data we are storing in our MRT textures during the building pass. The choice of stored data depends on the shading model. For instance, Gouraud-shaded directional (or parallel) lights only require each pixel's normal and material properties, whereas Phong-shaded point or spotlights require the pixel's position in addition to its normal and material properties.

The implementation detailed in this article assumes all lights required during the shading passes are based on the Phong model, and therefore the attribute buffer contains the following:

- Pixel position (X, Y, Z)
- Pixel normal vector (X, Y, Z)
- Pixel diffuse color (R, G, B)

Pixel Position

This is the world space position of the pixel. Note that it is also possible to store the position in a different coordinate system (eye space being the other logical alternative), providing all data stored and used in the pixel shader during the lighting passes is in the same space.

World space pixel positions can be calculated by transforming each vertex in the vertex shader by the world matrix for the associated model and outputting the result to a 3D texture coordinate. The iterated texture coordinates in the pixel shader define the world space position for this pixel.

A 16-bit per-channel float format is ideal to store the pixel's world position in order to accommodate a wide range of possible values with sufficient precision (i.e., D3DFMT_A16B16G16R16F). See Color Plate 11 for an illustration of position data.

Pixel Normal Vector

This is the world space normalized normal vector for the pixel. There are two options that we can choose when producing the world space normal vectors for storage in the property buffer: model space and tangent space.

Pixel Normals Defined in Model Space

The first and simplest option is to have the normals in bump maps already defined in *model space*. Model space normal maps are sometimes calculated with a software tool to generate a low-poly model with model space normal maps from a high-poly model. With normals defined in model space, a simple world matrix transformation in the pixel shader is all that is required to obtain world space normals. Although this solution is simple to implement in terms of calculations, it also requires more texture memory, since texture maps are usually unique for each model. Also, the artist may have the scene's normal data already defined in *tangent space*, so it might be more convenient from a design point of view to use these instead.

Pixel Normals Defined in Tangent Space

The second option is more complicated but operates from normals defined in *tangent space* (also called *texture space*). Tangent space is a coordinate system indicating the texture surface orientation at each vertex. Traditional per-pixel lighting usually involves transforming the light vector into tangent space so that a DOT3 operation can be performed with the tangent space normals contained in the bump map. See Equation (1).

$$\vec{V}_{TS} = \vec{V}_{MS} \times (TS) = \vec{V}_{MS} \times \begin{pmatrix} T_X & N_X & B_X \\ T_Y & N_Y & B_Y \\ T_Z & N_Z & B_Z \end{pmatrix} \tag{1}$$

With deferred shading, the *normals* need to be transformed from tangent space to world space. In the same way a vector is transformed from model space to tangent space using the tangent space matrix, a tangent space vector can be transformed to model space using the *inverse* of the tangent space matrix. Conveniently, the tangent space matrix is a pure rotation matrix, so its inverse is simply its transpose. See Equation (2).

$$\vec{V}_{TS} = \vec{V}_{TS} \times \begin{pmatrix} T_X & N_X & B_X \\ T_Y & N_Y & B_Y \\ T_Z & N_Z & B_Z \end{pmatrix}^T = \vec{V}_{TS} \times \begin{pmatrix} T_X & T_Y & T_Z \\ N_X & N_Y & N_Z \\ B_X & B_Y & B_Z \end{pmatrix} \tag{2}$$

Because we need the normal vectors in world space, we also need to transform them with the rotation part of the world matrix associated with the current model. The equation becomes:

$$\vec{V}_{WS} = \vec{V}_{TS} \times (TS)^T \times (W) \tag{3}$$

For static models, it is a good idea to have their local orientation match their orientation in world space so that only a simple transformation with the transpose of the tangent space matrix is necessary. This saves a few instructions compared to the dynamic object's case, which requires Equation (3) to be fully honored.

Because we need a set of transposed tangent space vectors at each *pixel*, the normal, binormal, and tangent vectors are passed to the pixel shader through a set of three 3D texture coordinates. The iterated vectors define our tangent space matrix for the current pixel. In theory, these vectors need renormalization before they can be used to transform the normal; however, in practice the difference in visual quality is negligible, provided the scene tessellation is high enough.

Precision and Storage

In both cases it can be desirable to renormalize the iterated normals for improved accuracy. Although linearly interpolated normals are usually close enough to unit vectors, the error margin accumulates when complex math operations are performed on these vectors (e.g., calculation of reflection vectors).

Although a float format could be used to store world space normal vectors in the attribute buffer, it is more economical and usually sufficiently accurate to use a 32-bit integer format instead (D3DFMT_A2W10V10U10, D3DFMT_A2B10G10R10, D3DFMT_Q8W8V8U8, D3DFMT_A8R8G8B8).

The deferred shading implementation described in this article uses tangent space normal maps. See Color Plate 12 for an illustration of normal data.

Pixel Diffuse Color

The pixel's diffuse color is stored in the property buffer. This color is extracted from the diffuse texture associated with the model. This color can be stored using a simple 32-bit texture format (D3DFMT_A8R8G8B8). Diffuse data is shown in Color Plate 13.

Building Pass

This section details how the attribute buffer is constructed and stored in MRTs. During the building pass, all the data relevant to the scene is calculated and stored in our MRTs. The pixel shader sends the relevant data into each of the three MRTs (i.e., pixel position, normal, and color).

Vertex Shader Code

The vertex shader code used for the building pass is fairly simple.

```
;-------------------------------------------------------------------
; Constants specified by the app
; c0-c3 = Global transformation matrix (World*View*Projection)
; c4-c7 = World transformation matrix
;
; Vertex components
; v0          = Vertex Position
; v1, v2, v3 = Inverse of tangent space vectors
; v4          = 2D texture coordinates (model coordinates)
;-------------------------------------------------------------------
vs_2_0

dcl_position v0          ; Vertex position
```

```
dcl_binormal v1        ; Transposed binormal
dcl_tangent  v2        ; Transposed tangent
dcl_normal   v3        ; Transposed normal
dcl_texcoord v4        ; Texture coordinates for diffuse and normal map

; Vertex transformation
m4x4 oPos, v0, c0      ; Transform vertices by WVP matrix

; Model texture coordinates
mov oT0.xy, v4.xy      ; Simply copy texture coordinates

; World space coordinates
m4x3 oT1.xyz, v0, c4   ; Transform vertices by world matrix (no w
                       ; needed)

; Inverse (transpose) of tangent space vectors
mov oT2.xyz, v1
mov oT3.xyz, v2
mov oT4.xyz, v3        ; Pass in transposed tangent space vectors
```

Pixel Shader Code

The pixel shader version used has to be able to output multiple color values. Therefore, pixel shader 2.0 or higher is required. The model texture coordinates are used to sample the pixel diffuse color and normal from their respective textures. The world space coordinates are directly stored into the position MRT. Finally, the transposed tangent space vectors are used to transform the sampled normal before storing it into the normal MRT.

```
;-------------------------------------------------------------------
; Constants specified by the app
; c0-c3 = World transformation matrix for model
;-------------------------------------------------------------------
ps_2_0

; Samplers
dcl_2d s0    ; Diffuse map
dcl_2d s1    ; Normal map

; Texture coordinates
dcl t0.xy    ; Texture coordinates for diffuse and normal map
dcl t1.xyz   ; World-space position
dcl t2.xyz   ; Binormal
dcl t3.xyz   ; Tangent
dcl t4.xyz   ; Normal (Transposed tangent space vectors)

; Constants
def c30, 1.0, 2.0, 0.0, 0.0
def c31, 0.2, 0.5, 1.0, 1.0

; Texture sampling
texld r2, t0, s1     ; r2 = Normal vector from normal map
```

```
texld r3, t0, s0    ; r3 = Color from diffuse map

; Store world-space coordinates into MRT#0
mov oC0, t1         ; Store pixel position in MRT#0

; Convert normal to signed vector
mad r2, r2, c30.g, -c30.r    ; r2 = 2*(r2 - 0.5)

; Transform normal vector from tangent space to model space
dp3 r4.x, r2, t2
dp3 r4.y, r2, t3
dp3 r4.z, r2, t4    ; r4.xyz = model space normal

; Transform model space normal vector to world space. Note that only
; the rotation part of the world matrix is needed.
; This step is not required for static models if their
; original model space orientation matches their orientation
; in world space. This would save 3 instructions.
m4x3 r1.xyz, r4, c0

; Convert normal vector to fixed point
; This is not required if the destination MRT is float or signed
mad r1, r1, c31.g, c31.g    ; r1 = 0.5*(r1 + 0.5)

; Store world-space normal into MRT#1
mov oC1, r1

; Store diffuse color into MRT#2
mov oC2, r3
```

We've already established that all models rendered with an identity rotation in their world matrix do not need to have their normals further transformed by this matrix. As shown above, skipping this step would save three pixel shader instructions. However, this implies using two different shaders, one for dynamic models and another for static ones. As these are usually not rendered in a defined order, the amount of swapping between the two pixel shaders could be excessive. Using extended pixel shader 2.0 (ps_2_x) or pixel shader 3.0, static flow control can be used to determine if transformation with the world matrix is needed.

Note that all texture filtering, such as trilinear or anisotropic, need only be performed in the building pass; the shading passes will directly access the already-filtered pixels from the MRT surfaces that we have rendered (using point sampling).

NOTE   It is possible to store extra components into the attribute buffer using some form of compression. For instance, bias and scale operations would allow two 16-bit integer components to be stored in a 32-bit component. Pixel shader instructions are required to pack and unpack the data, but it enables more elements to be stored in case there are not enough outputs available.

Shading Passes

Each shading pass needs only to send a screen-aligned quad so that the shading calculations affect the entire render surface. The quad's texture coordinates have to be set up so that all pixels in the quad reference our MRT data at a 1:1 mapping ratio. Direct3D's sampling rules stipulate that an offset is required in order to achieve a perfect texel-to-pixel mapping. Given the width (W) and height (H) of the back buffer, the vertices forming the full-screen quad need to be set up in the following way:

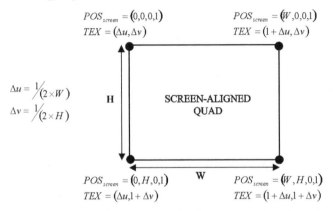

Figure 2: Setting up the vertex structure for a screen-aligned quad

POS_{screen} is the vertex position in screen space coordinates. TEX represents the 2D texture coordinates to use for this vertex.

NOTE The same 1:1 mapping ratio is achieved by offsetting screen space positions by –0.5 and setting texture coordinates to (0,0), (1, 0), (0, 1), and (1,1).

Because the contents of the MRTs already represent visible pixels, there is no need to enable depth buffering during the shading passes, saving valuable memory bandwidth.

Vertex Shader Code

No vertex processing is required, since screen space coordinates are directly sent to the pixel shader. To skip vertex processing, the vertex declaration must include the `D3DDECLUSAGE_POSITIONT` definition. In this case, only the transformed position and the texture coordinates are required, thus the vertex declaration is:

```
D3DVERTEXELEMENT9 declTPositionUV[] =
{
  { 0, 0, D3DDECLTYPE_FLOAT4, D3DDECLMETHOD_DEFAULT, D3DDECLUSAGE_POSITIONT, 0},
  { 0, 16, D3DDECLTYPE_FLOAT2, D3DDECLMETHOD_DEFAULT, D3DDECLUSAGE_TEXCOORD, 0},
```

```
D3DDECL_END()
};
```

Pixel Shader Code

The calculations to be performed during the shading passes obviously depend on the needs of the application. It is up to the programmer to decide what lighting or special effects can be applied with the data available in the attribute buffer. The actual shading algorithms are not affected by their transition to a deferred shading context.

The following pixel shader is based on Phong lighting and implements diffuse and specular shading with distance attenuation. Each active light's contribution is accumulated by additively blending a full-screen quad onto the frame buffer. A number of optimizations can be implemented in this shader, but for simplicity they are not shown here. For example, another lookup texture could be used to replace the 3-slot pow instruction or a simpler falloff model could be used, etc. A cube normalization map is used for vector normalization, although the nrm instruction is an alternative choice. The falloff texture is a simple lookup texture containing the light attenuation based on the pixel's distance from the light divided by its maximum range (texture clamping is used).

```
;-------------------------------------------------------------------
; Constants specified by the app
; c0 : light position in world space
; c8 : camera position in world space
; c22: c22.a = 1/(light max range), c22.rgb = 1.0f
;-------------------------------------------------------------------
ps_2_0

; Samplers
dcl_2d s0    ; MRT#0 = Pixel position in world space
dcl_2d s1    ; MRT#1 = Pixel normal vector
dcl_2d s2    ; MRT#2 = Pixel diffuse color
dcl_2d s3    ; Falloff texture
dcl_cube s4  ; Cube normalization texture map

; Texture coordinates
dcl t0.xy                  ; Quad screen-space texture coordinates

; Constants
def c20, 0.5, 2.0, -2.0, 1.0
def c21, 8.0, -0.75, 4.0, 0.0

; Retrieve property buffer data from MRT textures
texld r0, t0, s0           ; r0.xyz = Pixel world space position
texld r2, t0, s1           ; r2.xyz = Pixel normal vector
texld r3, t0, s2           ; r3.rgb = Pixel color

; Convert normal to signed vector
; This is not required if the normal vector was stored in a signed
```

```
; or float format
mad r2, r2, c20.y, -c20.w    ; r2 = 2*(r2 - 1)

; Calculate pixel-to-light vector
sub r1.xyz, c0, r0           ; r1 = Lpos - Vpos
mov r1.w, c20.w              ; Set r1.w to 1.0
nrm r4, r1                   ; Normalize vector (r4.w = 1.0/distance)

; Compute diffuse intensity
dp3 r5.w, r4, r2             ; r5.w = (N.L)

; FallOff
rcp r6, r4.w                ; r6 = 1/(1/distance) = distance
mul r6, r6, c22.a           ; Divide by light max range
texld r6, r6, s3            ; Sample falloff texture

; Compute halfway vector
sub r1.xyz, c8, r0          ; Compute view vector V (pixel to camera)

texld r1, r1, s4            ; Normalized vector with cube map
mad r1, r1, c20.y, -c20.w   ; Convert vector to signed format

add r1, r1, r4             ; Add view and light vector
texld r1, r1, s4           ; Normalize half angle vector with cube map
mad r1, r1, c20.y, -c20.w   ; Convert to signed format

; Compute specular intensity
dp3_sat r1.w, r1, r2        ; r1.w = sat(H.N)
pow r1.w, r1.w, c21.r       ; r1.w = (H.N)^8

; Set specular to 0 if pixel normal is not facing the light
cmp r1.w, r5.w, r1.w, c21.w ; r1.w = ( (N.L)>=0 ) ? (H.N)^8 : 0

; Output final color
mad r0, r3, r5.w, r1.w      ; Modulate diffuse color and diffuse
                            ; intensity and add specular
mul r0, r0, r6             ; Modulate with falloff
mov oC0, r0                ; Output final color
```

Advanced Shading Passes

The simple lighting pass shown above is only the beginning of what can be
achieved with deferred shading. Because shading passes are no longer geome-
try-dependent and only applied to visible geometry, their utilization is optimal.
This performance saving can be used to implement more complex shaders or
effects.

Better Lighting

A "real" specular calculation based on the camera reflection vector is straightforward to implement, since both the pixel and camera position are known. That is, instead of calculating $(\vec{H}.\vec{N})$, the light reflection vector around the normal (given by $\vec{R} = 2 \times (\vec{N}.\vec{L}) \times \vec{N} - \vec{L}$) can be calculated and used in a dot product operation with the view vector. The specular properties of each pixel could be stored in the attribute buffer (e.g., using the alpha of the diffuse texture in our implementation) and used as the power of the specular calculation.

Different types of light can be implemented, from directional and point lights to spotlights or custom-shaped lights (light volumes are discussed later in this article). More complex light attenuation models can be implemented using math instructions inside the pixel shader instead of a texture lookup. Light maps can be used for custom-shaped lights or when there is a need to restrict light contribution to a defined area. The demo on the CD offers some implementations of the effects mentioned above.

Extended Attribute Buffer

Providing memory storage and bandwidth are not limiting factors (see later in this article for a discussion about bandwidth considerations), the attribute buffer can be used to store additional data relevant to the scene properties, allowing more complex effects to be implemented later on in the shading passes.

In the example shown in this article, the material properties are simply approximated to a diffuse color issued from each model's diffuse map. Other properties, like specular maps, specular power maps, detail maps, tangent vectors for anisotropic lighting, a Fresnel term, BRDF data, etc., could be stored in the attribute buffer. There are potentially so many material properties to store that there might not be enough space to accommodate them. Various tricks can be used to effectively compress as much data as possible in a reasonably allocated MRT space, like storing material IDs, using volume textures, etc.

Shadows

Deferred shading is fully compatible with the rendering of shadows within the scene.

Let's consider stencil shadows (as used in the demo). In the traditional rendering case (e.g., Doom III-style rendering), each shadow-casting light requires the scene geometry to be submitted (on top of shadow volumes) so that only non-shadowed areas are affected by the lighting calculations. When a high number of lights are used, the number of geometry passes quickly becomes overwhelming. With deferred shading, only the shadow volumes and a full-screen quad per light are required:

Building pass
For each light:
    Clear stencil buffer, disable color writes

Render shadow volumes onto stencil buffer
Enable color writes, stencil test passes for non-shadowed areas
Light pass

Shadow maps are also compatible with deferred shading. Since the world space pixel position can be stored in the attribute buffer, the distance from the pixel to the current light can be calculated in the shading pass. It can then be compared to the depth value in the shadow map to determine if the pixel is in shadow or not. This technique is sometimes referred to as forward shadow mapping.

Higher Color Range

DirectX 9 does not allow blending into floating-point render targets. Because of this limitation, alpha blending cannot be used to accumulate high dynamic range lighting calculation results into a destination frame buffer in float format. With fixed-point render targets, color channels are automatically clamped to 1.0 during the blending process, and so if a higher color range is not needed, it is more economical and straightforward to blend all shading contributions into a fixed-point frame buffer. High color range effects, however, require an alternative solution.

The most obvious workaround to this limitation is to ignore the hardware blending capabilities and perform alpha blending on the pixel shader manually. The idea is to alternate between two floating-point render targets; one contains the current contents of all shading contributions prior to the current pass and is set as a texture input to the pixel shader, while the other is set as the destination render target and receives the new color values updated with the contributions of the current pass.

Translucency

In traditional rendering, alpha-blended polygons require a rendering pass of their own. With deferred shading, alpha polygons requiring shading (e.g., stained-glass objects) also need separate processing, although punch-through polygons (i.e., alpha-tested) can be sent with all other opaque triangles during the building pass. This is because the attribute buffer can only store properties for a single pixel; thus, any translucent pixels rendered on top of these would need to be stored elsewhere. Unless additive blending is used, real translucent pixels (using an order-dependent blending mode like SRCALPHA-INVSRCALPHA) need to be blended with the back buffer only *once* to avoid repeated contributions from themselves. Hence, all shading passes need to be performed on the translucent pixels *before* any blending with the background takes place. Another problem is overlapping translucency; any translucent pixel rendered on top of a previously rendered translucent pixel will need to take into account the new pixel color at this location (i.e., resulting from the previous blending). These two points are of paramount importance, since ignoring them can cause visual errors in the resulting render.

Unfortunately, there is no easy way to overcome these problems. For a real-time application relying on performance, the best idea is probably to avoid using translucent objects that require lighting (light-independent translucent objects like explosions, laser beams, smoke, etc., are unaffected because they typically do not need to be shaded). One could attempt to concatenate all shading passes in one large shader and gross-sort the translucent triangles from back to front using this shader. However, this might not be practical because of the sampler and instruction limits in the pixel shader. Furthermore, this might not be compatible with some shadowing techniques like stencil buffering. If lit translucent objects *are* a requirement of your scene and you are prepared to "go all the way," then a solution is *depth peeling* (i.e., shading each "layer" of translucency separately before blending it with the frame buffer). In practice the additional memory, performance, and complexity caused by depth peeling do not make it a very attractive solution to the translucency problem inherent in deferred shading.

Deferred Shading Optimizations

MRT Configuration and Bandwidth

Care must be taken when choosing the format and bit depth of the MRTs to use with deferred shading. With DirectX 9 support for IEEE float formats, one might be tempted to use four MRTs in the D3DFMT_A32B32G32R32F format for the added precision and robustness they bring. However, not only will the memory requirements be considerable (at a 1024x768 screen resolution, this corresponds to total of 48MB), but also the required memory bandwidth for each frame is likely to cause a performance bottleneck.

Let's examine in detail how much memory bandwidth deferred shading requires. We define the following variables and assume some practical values for them:

Variable Name	Description	Values	Justification
W, H	Render width, height	1024, 768	Typical rendering resolution
Z_{BPP}, BB_{BPP}	Depth/stencil buffer bit depth, back buffer bit depth	32 bpp, 32 bpp	Typical depth/back buffer bit depth
Overdraw	Average overdraw per pixel	3	Average overdraw
Sorting	Average number of pixels arranged in a back to front order. In the worst case where all pixels are ordered back to front this value equals Overdraw; in the best case it will be equal to 1: $1 \leq Sorting \leq Overdraw$.	1.5	We assume that half of overdrawn pixels are drawn back to front.
T_{BPP}	Average texture bit depth (e.g., if half of textures are 32bpp and other half is 16bpp, then $T_{BPP}=24$)	24 bpp	Mix of compressed, 32bpp and 32bpp+ textures

Variable Name	Description	Values	Justification
T_B, T_S	Average number of texture lookups in building pass/shading pass pixel shader	2, 4	Two texture lookup in building pass (e.g., diffuse and normal map), four in shading pass (e.g., light maps, cube normalization map, etc.)
n	Number of shading passes to perform	8	Average of eight full-screen shading passes
n_{MRT}	Number of MRT surfaces: $1 \leq n_{MRT} \leq 4$	-	Variable
MRT_{BPP}	MRT bit depth	-	Variable

Table 1: Description of variables used in bandwidth calculation

Assumptions

Because of different 3D acceleration implementations among graphic adapters, it can be difficult to model a universal bandwidth equation. However, by making a number of assumptions about the rendering environment, we can get close to an accurate result. Firstly, we assume the target 3D accelerator is an immediate mode renderer with some form of early Z support (i.e., the depth test is performed before the pixel shader — we can reasonably expect this optimization from all new DX9 accelerators). Secondly, we assume a texture sample needs only a single texel fetch, regardless of texture filtering. Finally, we ignore any form of cache effectiveness.

Let's see how much memory needs to be transferred across the bus for a single frame using deferred shading. We start by analyzing each feature requiring memory traffic during the building pass:

Depth/Stencil: $W \times H \times Z_{BPP} \times (Overdraw + Sorting)$

Back Buffer: 0 (the back buffer is not read nor written during the building pass)

Textures: $W \times H \times T_{BPP} \times T_B \times Sorting$

Geometry buffers (vertex and index buffers): $C_{Geometry}$ (constant value)

MRTs: $n_{MRT} \times W \times H \times MRT_{BPP} \times Sorting$

Adding these together, we get:

$$Memory_{OneFrame} = W \times H \times [Z_{BPP} \times (Overdraw + Sorting) + \tag{4}$$
$$T_{BPP} \times T_B \times Sorting + n_{MRT} \times MRT_{BPP} \times Sorting] + C_{Geometry}$$

Let's now examine how much memory needs to be transferred across the bus during the n shading passes.

Depth/Stencil: 0 (depth buffer disabled)

Back Buffer: $2_{(R/W)} \times W \times H \times BB_{BPP} \times n$

Textures: $W \times H \times T_S \times T_{BPP} \times n$

Geometry buffers: 0

MRTs: $n_{MRT} \times W \times H \times MRT_{BPP} \times n$

Adding these together we get:

$$Memory_{OneFrame} = W \times H \times n \times \lfloor 2_{(R/W)} \times BB_{BPP} + T_S \times T_{BPP} + n_{MRT} \times MRT_{BPP} \rfloor \quad (5)$$

By adding the amounts of external memory accesses to perform during the building and the n shading passes and multiplying by a desired frame rate of 60 fps, we obtain the following bandwidth formula:

$$Bandwidth_{60\,fps} = \left(W \times H \times \begin{bmatrix} MRT_{BPP} \times n_{MRT} \times (Sorting + n) \\ + Z_{BPP} \times (Overdraw + Sorting) \\ + T_{BPP} \times T_B \times Sorting \\ + n \times (2 \times BB_{BPP} + T_S \times T_{BPP}) \end{bmatrix} + C_{Geometry} \right) \times 60\,\text{Bytes} / \text{Sec} \quad (6)$$

Practical Example

Using our practical values, the bandwidth equation becomes:

$$Bandwidth_{60\,fps} = \left(1024 \times 768 \times \begin{bmatrix} MRT_{BPP} \times n_{MRT} \times (1.5 + 8) \\ + 8 \times (3 + 1.5) \\ + 3 \times 2 \times 1.5 \\ + 8 \times (2 \times 4 + 4 \times 3) \end{bmatrix} + 16.10^6 \right) \times 60\,\text{Bytes} / \text{Sec}$$

$$Bandwidth_{60\,fps} = 0.05 \times [MRT_{BPP} \times n_{MRT} \times 9.5 + 205] + 1\,\text{GBytes} / \text{Sec}$$

A gross approximation of the end result is:

$$Bandwidth_{60\,fps} = \frac{n_{MRT} \times MRT_{BPP}}{2} + 10\,\text{GBytes} / \text{Sec} \quad (7)$$

Here are some examples of bandwidth values for a defined number of MRTs and their bit depth for the selected variables:

	MRT_{BPP}=32 bpp	MRT_{BPP}=64 bpp	MRT_{BPP}=128 bpp
n_{MRT}=2	14 GBytes/Sec	18 GBytes/Sec	26 GBytes/Sec
n_{MRT}=3	16 GBytes/Sec	22 GBytes/Sec	34 GBytes/Sec
n_{MRT}=4	18 GBytes/Sec	26 GBytes/Sec	42 GBytes/Sec

Table 2: Bandwidth figures for various MRT configurations with selected variables

This table clearly shows the overwhelming bandwidth requirements when an unreasonable MRT configuration is chosen. Of course, other factors influence the bandwidth requirements (notably the number of shading passes to perform), but overall it is wiser to select the minimum possible number and bit depth for MRTs, which can accommodate the stored data.

Optimized MRT Configuration

The implementation described in this article stores position, normal, and diffuse color into MRTs, totaling $64+32+32=128$ bits of data. Providing the 3D device supports the D3DPMISCCAPS_MRTINDEPENDENTBITDEPTHS cap, this data can be rearranged in an optimized configuration so that memory bandwidth and footprint are reduced. Consider the following configuration of four MRTs:

- MRT#0: D3DFMT_G16R16F: Store X, Y position in Red and Green channels
- MRT#1: D3DFMT_R16F: Store Z position in Red channel
- MRT#2: D3DFMT_A8R8G8B8: Store diffuse color in RGB, normal Z in A
- MRT#3: D3DFMT_A8L8: Store normal X in A, Y in L

This equates to a total of 96 bits. Note that the 3D device has to support these formats as render targets for this configuration to be valid. The pixel shader code in the building and shading passes needs to be adjusted to write and read MRT data into their appropriate components.

Using 2D Shapes to Optimize Shading Passes

Sending full-screen-aligned quads for all shading passes results in all the screen pixels being processed by the pixel shader. Depending on the number of passes to perform, screen resolution, and shader complexity, this can lead to excessive and costly pixel processing. By knowing the boundaries at which a light or special effect ceases to contribute to the scene, only the screen pixels that are inside those limits need to be sent (e.g., for a point light, this would be a 2D-projected sphere whose radius is the maximum range of the light). Explosions, cone lights, etc., can also benefit from using 2D shapes during the shading passes.

Projected Volumes

Unless the screen coordinates to which an effect is to be applied are already known (HUD, part-screen filters, etc.), in most cases the 2D shapes to deal with will be projections of 3D volumes into screen coordinates. This is required so that world space units can be correctly transformed and mapped into screen space.

Let's consider a simple point light of maximum range, MaxRange. Instead of sending a full-screen quad during the shading pass, a sphere of radius MaxRange is transformed and rasterized. This results in only the pixels inside the sphere to be affected by the light and thus processed. Note that the pixel shader's falloff calculation must match the range used by the volume (i.e., pixels whose distance from the light source is greater than MaxRange have a falloff of zero); otherwise the difference in intensity between pixels inside and outside the sphere will be clearly visible.

Sending a volume will have the same visual result as sending a full-screen quad but without the overhead of processing out-of-bounds pixels. Color Plate 14 demonstrates this idea of processing only those pixels that are affected by the light.

Back Faces Only

Because the camera could be located *inside* the volume, it is important to render the *back faces* of the volume only. Providing the volume is closed, is convex, and does not intercept the far clip plane, this will ensure the projected shape is always visible on the screen (for non-convex light volumes, a convex bounding volume should be used). If the culling order was not reversed for those volumes, then the projected shapes would only be correct if the camera was outside the volumes. Rendering back faces only ensures the projected shape is correct regardless of the camera position. Note that turning back-face culling off completely is not a solution because some screen pixels end up being processed twice.

Because we are interested in the intersection of the light area with the visible pixels in the scene, a further optimization to this technique is to only render the back-facing pixels of a volume whenever the normal depth buffer visibility test fails. This can be achieved by simply inverting the Z test when rendering the volume (e.g., using D3DCMP_GREATER instead of D3DCMP_LESSEQUAL).

Mapping Volume Texture Coordinates to Screen Space

Calculating screen space texture coordinates for the 2D projection of a volume is more complicated than for an already-transformed full-screen quad. Given the homogenous clipping coordinates x_H, y_H, z_H, w_H and the back buffer dimensions Width and Height, the equation to retrieve screen-space texture coordinates u_S and v_S is given by:

$$u_S = \frac{1}{2} \times \left(\frac{x_H}{w_H} + 1 \right) + \frac{1}{2 \times Width}$$

$$v_S = \frac{1}{2} \times \left(1 - \frac{y_H}{w_H} \right) + \frac{1}{2 \times Height}$$

(8)

Although the vertex shader could pass homogenous clipping coordinates directly to the pixel shader, a sensible optimization is to precalculate the texture coordinates in the vertex shader so that the pixel shader need only perform the projective divide. Conveniently, the latter can be obtained during the sampling process by projected texture lookup. The equation becomes:

$$u_S = \frac{1}{w_H} \times \left(\frac{x_H}{2} + \frac{w_H}{2} + \frac{w_H}{2 \times Width} \right)$$

$$v_S = \frac{1}{w_H} \times \left(\frac{w_H}{2} + \frac{y_H}{2} + \frac{w_H}{2 \times Height} \right)$$

(9)

Vertex Shader Code

```
;-------------------------------------------------------------
; Constants specified by the app
; c0-c3 = Global transformation matrix (World*View*Projection)
; c9    = 1.0f/(2.0f*dwScreenWidth), 1.0f/(2.0f*dwScreenHeight)
```

```
;
; Vertex components
; v0    = Vertex Position
;----------------------------------------------------------------
vs_2_0

dcl_position v0                    ; Vertex position

def c8, 0.5, -0.5, 0.0, 0.0

; Vertex transformation
m4x4 r0, v0, c0                    ; Transform vertices by WVP matrix
mov oPos, r0                       ; Output position

; Compute texture coordinates
mul r0.xy, r0, c8                  ; x/2, -y/2
mad r0.xy, r0.w, c8.x, r0         ; x/2 + w/2, -y/2 + w/2
mad r0.xy, r0.w, c9, r0           ;  x/2 + w/2 + w/(2*Width),
                                   ;  -y/2 + w/2 + w/(2*Height)

mov oT0, r0                        ; Output texture coordinates
```

Pixel Shader Code

The iterated texture coordinates issued from the vertex shader are divided by w_H and used as texture coordinates to sample the MRT textures using a projected texture lookup.

```
ps_2_0

; Texture coordinates
dcl t0.xyzw                        ; iterated texture coordinates

; Samplers
dcl_2d s0                          ; MRT#0 = World space position
dcl_2d s1                          ; MRT#2 = World space normal vector
dcl_2d s2                          ; MRT#3 = Pixel Diffuse Color

; Projected texture lookup into MRT textures
texldp r0, t0, s0                  ; r0 = world space position
texldp r1, t0, s1                  ; r1 = world space normal
texldp r2, t0, s2                  ; r2 = Diffuse map color
```

NOTE   With pixel shader 3.0 support, the process of retrieving texture coordinates for a projected shape is simpler; the position register (which contains the x, y screen position of the pixel currently being processed) can be used with some scaling and biasing to perform this calculation directly.

Using shapes is better suited for smaller lights and special effects with limited range. For bright lights or global effects likely to affect the entire render, a full-screen quad is a better solution.

CD Demo

The demo on the companion CD shows a scene using deferred shading (see Color Plate 15). A total of nine lights are used — one point light affecting the entire screen ("full-screen" light), two point lights rendered using projected sphere shapes, and six cone lights rendered using projected cone shapes. A DX9-class 3D accelerator with vertex shader 2.0/pixel shader 2.0 and MRT support is required to run this demo.

The application can be controlled using menu options (press Alt to bring up the menu in full-screen mode). The latest version of the demo is available on the PowerVR Developer Relations web site at www.pvrdev.com.

Summary

This article described deferred shading and showed how to implement this technique using multiple render targets in DirectX 9. The two-phase process of the algorithm was detailed with shader code examples as supportive material. Some advanced deferred shading effects were proposed, and the robustness and overall simplicity of the technique should encourage graphics programmers to invent their own ideas for even better usage of this rendering algorithm. Finally, performance and memory footprint considerations were discussed, and optimizations were suggested to improve the effectiveness of the technique.

Meshuggah's Effects Explained

Carsten Wenzel

Crytek

Before We Start...

What exactly is Meshuggah? It's the name of my final year project at university and was released in March 2001 at http://meshuggah.4fo.de. It uses DirectX 8.1 class hardware to render a number of shader effects. All of them are of a different flavor and range from simple to fairly advanced. Meshuggah has two modes of operation. There's a demo mode where all effects run in a sequence and are synchronized to a music track. The other mode is the interactive browser mode, which allows you to view each effect individually and tweak all of its parameters. One of the main goals while developing those shader effects was eye candy. This means that the effects described herein are not pure vertex or pixel shader tricks. Rather, they combine various techniques with shader technology to produce something "visually stunning." Quite a few of them were heavily inspired by some great productions released by different demo scene groups during the last couple of years. Others are my take on research results published in various papers.

You are reading these words because Wolfgang Engel somehow came across Meshuggah's web site (around the time *Direct3D ShaderX* was hitting the shelves) and sent me an e-mail asking whether I'd like to contribute to the successor.

I hope the following pages offer some useful and interesting stuff to shader fanatics — Xbox and PC game developers alike. I'm sure there are still a handful of developers targeting DirectX 8.1. Before we delve into the details, please have a look at the demo on the companion CD to get an idea of what you can expect to find on the following pages. The demo comes with full source code for you to study and experiment with. It contains some changes made to the original version; specifically, these are minor fixes, speed-ups and cleanups in shader and demo code.

Infinite Zoom on the z Plane

The subject of the first effect is a zoom into an "infinitely" detailed picture placed on the z plane. Instead of starting to blur or get blocky, the picture constantly reveals new detail. Ideally, hand-drawn pictures are used to render the zoom sequence, as shown in *Contour* by The Black Lotus and *Spot* by Exceed (both downloadable at [1]). Due to the author's lack of artistic skills, we use fractals (e.g., the *Mandelbrot set*) instead of hand-drawn art. Don't confuse it with a typical fractal zoom though; we don't evaluate the Mandelbrot set for each frame that we render. It's a strictly image-based rendering effect.

The basic algorithm works as follows. Given is a sequence of bitmaps for a predefined zoom path, each bitmap refining a certain area of the previous one (see Figure 1).

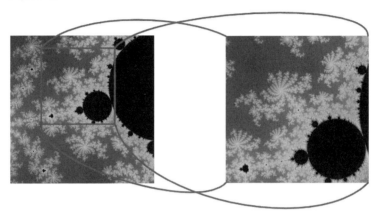

Figure 1: Two consecutive bitmaps of a zoom sequence

Some rules apply in order to maintain the illusion of a zoom.

■ As mentioned before, each bitmap has to reside strictly within the previous one.

■ Each bitmap should cover at least one quarter of the previous one. This way, new detail will always be available for the area we're zooming into, thus preventing blurry results.

■ The bitmap resolution should at least match the screen resolution. This avoids blurry parts in the corners of a rendered frame.

Achieving a zoom effect is now just a matter of drawing these bitmaps properly. The bitmap sequence needs to be laid out on the z plane. Position and size — width and height if it's not a square — of the first bitmap are set to some default values (e.g., (0, 0) and 1). For the following bitmaps, position and size result from their absolute location within the first bitmap and how much of its area they occupy (see Figure 2).[1]

---

1 As we zoom into the Mandelbrot set, we can also derive position and size values from the complex coordinates used to render the bitmap sequence.

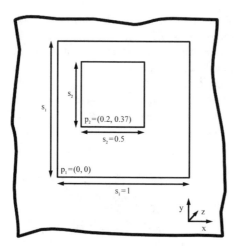

Figure 2: Possible layout of bitmaps for a zoom sequence

To render a frame of the zoom, we draw the sequence of bitmaps in ascending order with depth test and write being disabled. The position and size values for each bitmap are used to form a quad or rectangle, respectively. In fact, not all bitmaps need to be drawn. It is enough to begin with the bitmap having the highest index in the sequence and still filling the entire screen for the current zoom position of the camera.

The camera hovers over the z plane, looking straight down using a 90 degrees field of view. Its position is determined by evaluating a spline function based on the key points of the zoom path for a given time t. Each key point maps directly to a bitmap. It describes the position of the camera necessary to see the associated bitmap entirely at full resolution. For a 90 degrees field of view, the key point c_i for bitmap i placed at position p_i and having a size of s_i (or width w_i and height h_i) is as follows:

$$c_i.x = p_i.x + s_i \cdot 0.5 \qquad \text{or} \qquad c_i.x = p_i.x + w_i \cdot 0.5$$

$$c_i.y = p_i.y + s_i \cdot 0.5 \qquad \text{or} \qquad c_i.y = p_i.y + h_i \cdot 0.5$$

$$c_i.z = -(s_i \cdot 0.5) \qquad \text{or} \qquad c_i.z = -(\max(w_i, h_i) \cdot 0.5)$$

Applying those formulas to the two bitmaps in Figure 2 yields $c_1 = (0.5, 0.5, -0.5)$ and $c_2 = (0.45, 0.62, -0.25)$.

The shaders used for rendering the zoom are straightforward. The vertex shader transforms each quad/rectangle into clip space and feeds the vertex shader with texture coordinates. The pixel shader just fetches a color from a bitmap and stores it as the output color.

Meshuggah uses ten mipmapped textures with a resolution of 1024x1024 pixels to represent the sequence of bitmaps for a zoom. Each texture alone would take up 6MB if stored as a raw 32-bit ARGB texture. To save texture memory and bandwidth without compromising zoom depth, compressed textures are used. This way (using DXT1), we can cut down the required storage space to one-eighth of the original uncompressed textures. Obviously, all this isn't for free. Saving a texture in a compressed format will introduce artifacts that are more or less visible, depending on the texture's content. Also, compressed texture formats usually store colors at a lower depth (16 bits for the colors at either extreme of a compression block in DXT1), thus introducing color bleeding. In order to remedy this and improve texture quality, dithering should be performed when saving textures in a compressed format.

Anisotropic Lighting on Hair Strands

In this section, we generate hair strands that move around, bend under the force of gravity and inertia, and have anisotropic lighting applied to them. For some of you, it might be reminiscent of the hair effect in *Lapsus* by Maturefurk (also available for download at [1]).

Let's first talk about how physics are implemented in order to animate the hair. As mentioned above, the two forces used to animate the hair in this effect are gravity and inertia. Gravity is simply a constant vector for all hairs. Inertia is simulated by calculating the second derivative of a function describing each hair tip's current position.

What information is necessary to create hair strands? Well, assuming each hair starts at the origin and ends at some point on a unit sphere, we only need a unitized normal for the default hair direction (in case there is zero gravity and zero inertia). To get some variation, we also store the hair length as well as a 1D texture coordinate. The 1D texture coordinate will be used in conjunction with a 1D noise texture to model streaks running along the hair. Using randomized values to set up all components gives each hair an individual and more natural look.

It's time to generate the hairs. Each hair has a fixed number of joints for which a position needs to be calculated. We start at the origin and set the current hair direction to its default. For the rest of the joints, we sum up the current direction, the global gravity vector, and the hair's inertia vector to a new temporary direction vector. This temporary direction vector needs to be normalized. The position for each hair joint is then calculated by taking the position of the previous joint and adding the normalized temporary direction vector scaled by the hair length to it. The current hair direction is updated by setting it to the normalized temporary direction vector. This translates into the following code:

```
vCurPos = ( 0, 0, 0 );
vCurDir = vHairDir;

for( int i( 0 ); i < NUM_JOINTS; ++i )
{
    vTempDir = vCurDir + vGravity + vHairInertia;
    Normalize( vTempDir );
    vCurPos += vTempDir * fHairLength;
    vCurDir = vTempDir;
}
```

This is the generation of one hair. Bold arguments indicate hair and physics parameters.

We connect all adjacent joints by generating quads between them. In DirectX this can be done efficiently using triangle strips. Note that multiple hairs can be put into one big triangle strip by stitching them together to increase rendering performance. In order to generate a quad, we actually need two position vectors per joint. Otherwise, we would be generating lines — that is, triangles with an area of zero! By crossing the initial direction vector of each hair with the global gravity vector and normalizing the result, we get a vector that when shortened by some amount (depending on how thick the hair should be) can be added to each joint's position vector to get the second position vector that we need. At this point, we should also prepare a 1D texture coordinate for both position vectors so we can form vertices that can be sent to the vertex shader later. The 1D texture coordinate for the first position vector is simply the one specified for each hair; the 1D texture coordinate for the second position vector is the sum of the first one and an arbitrary value, which is constant for all hairs. The bigger this arbitrary constant value, the thinner the streaks.

Now that we have generated the geometry, we need to define an appropriate vertex and pixel shader to give the hair the proper look. Rendering the hair by applying normal Phong shading works, although the result looks rather plastic. Instead we take advantage of an anisotropic shading model to get the kind of lighting that we're after. [2] and [3] describe how this can be done in hardware using a 2D texture as a lookup table for diffuse and specular intensities. The following two formulas denote the diffuse and specular intensity for a given point P on a surface with L being the vector from P to the light source, N the surface normal in P, T the tangent vector in P, V the vector from P to the viewer, and R the reflected light vector in P.

Diffuse intensity: $\quad L \cdot N = \sqrt{1-(L \cdot T)^2}$

Specular intensity: $\quad V \cdot R = \sqrt{1-(L \cdot T)^2} \cdot \sqrt{1-(V \cdot T)^2} - (L \cdot T) \cdot (V \cdot T)$

As you can see from those formulas, the only two values we need for the texture lookup are $L \cdot T$ and $V \cdot T$. We pass the tangent vector for each joint of a hair (that is, the current hair direction) along with the position vector and the 1D texture coordinate to the vertex shader. Here we calculate L and V for each vertex and dot them with T to get the proper texture coordinates for a lookup in the anisotropic light map. Care must be taken to map $L \cdot T$ and $V \cdot T$ from [–1, 1] to [0, 1], since the result of a dot product for two normalized vectors is in [–1, 1] but the corresponding texture address range is [0, 1].

The following is a hair vertex shader:

```
#include "..\..\Effects\Hair\HairShaderConstants.h"


#define srcP    v0
#define srcT    v1
#define srcTex0 v2


#define V       r2
#define T       r0
```

```
#define L        r3

#define PWorld  r1

#define Temp     r10
#define Temp1    r11

vs.1.1

// def CV_CONSTANTS, 0.0, 0.5, 1.0, 2.0

// compute world space position
dp4 PWorld.x, srcP, c[ CV_WORLD_0 ]
dp4 PWorld.y, srcP, c[ CV_WORLD_1 ]
dp4 PWorld.z, srcP, c[ CV_WORLD_2 ]
dp4 PWorld.w, srcP, c[ CV_WORLD_3 ]

// vector from vertex position to eye
add V, c[ CV_VIEWERPOS ], -PWorld
dp3 V.w, V, V
rsq V.w, V.w
mul V, V, V.w

// transform tangent into world space
dp3 T.x, srcT, c[ CV_WORLDIT_0 ]
dp3 T.y, srcT, c[ CV_WORLDIT_1 ]
dp3 T.zw, srcT, c[ CV_WORLDIT_2 ]

// normalize tangent
dp3 T.w, T, T
rsq T.w, T.w
mul T, T, T.w

// vector from vertex position to light
add L, c[ CV_LIGHTPOS ], -PWorld
dp3 L.w, L, L
rsq L.w, L.w
mul L, L, L.w

// generate texture coordinates for anisotropic lighting
// and map from [-1, 1] to [0, 1]
dp3 Temp.x, V, T
dp3 Temp.y, L, T
mad oT0.xy, Temp.xy, c[ CV_CONSTANTS ].y, c[ CV_CONSTANTS ].y

// copy texture coordinate for 1D hair streaks texture
mov oT1.x, srcTex0.x

// transform vertex into clip space
dp4 oPos.x, srcP, c[ CV_WORLDVIEWPROJ_0 ]
dp4 oPos.y, srcP, c[ CV_WORLDVIEWPROJ_1 ]
dp4 oPos.z, srcP, c[ CV_WORLDVIEWPROJ_2 ]
```

```
dp4 oPos.w, srcP, c[ CV_WORLDVIEWPROJ_3 ]
```

The pixel shader finally computes the lighting. It fetches the diffuse and specular intensity from the anisotropic light map as well as the color of the streaks from the 1D noise texture. The colors and intensities are modulated and combined in the following way:

```
#include "..\..\Effects\Hair\HairShaderConstants.h"

ps.1.1
tex t0              // get texel from anisotropic texture
tex t1              // get texel from 1D hair streaks texture

// r1 = specular intensity * specular color
mul r1, c[ CP_SPECULAR_COLOR ], t0.a
// r1 *= hair streak
mul r1, r1, t1
// r0 = diffuse intensity * hair streak
mul r0, t0, t1
// r0 = r0 * diffuse color + specular term in r1
mad r0, r0, c[ CP_DIFFUSE_COLOR ], r1
```

Reflections and Refractions on Soft Objects

Soft objects are usually expressed implicitly by mathematical functions. In order to render them, it is therefore necessary to determine the polygonal representation of their so-called iso-surface first. This is where the marching cubes algorithm or one of its derivatives comes into play.[2] It allows us to determine the polygonal surface of a 3D density field for a given density threshold. The density data either comes from 3D volumetric data sets (e.g., taken from MRI scans) or is generated by evaluating density functions (e.g., those used to describe soft objects). Meshuggah's soft objects are a conglomeration of simple blobs. A blob can be defined as follows[3]:

$$\vec{p} = (p_x\ p_y\ p_z)^T$$
$$\vec{o} = (o_x\ o_y\ o_z)^T$$
$$F(\vec{p}) = \frac{1}{|\vec{p} - \vec{o}|^2}$$

F returns the density at a given point p for a blob originated at o. Given such a density function, we are able to calculate its partial derivative to obtain the normal N for a point p in our density field. Having correct normals is crucial when rendering the surface later on.

The following is a partial derivative of a density function $F(p)$ and its application to calculate a normal $N(p)$.

---

2 For an introduction to the marching cubes algorithm, refer to [4]. It also provides a C/C++ implementation.

3 Other formulas for modeling soft objects are presented in [5].

$$\nabla F(\vec{p}) = \left(\frac{\partial F(\vec{p})}{\partial x} \quad \frac{\partial F(\vec{p})}{\partial y} \quad \frac{\partial F(\vec{p})}{\partial z} \right)^T$$

$$\nabla F(\vec{p}) = 2 \frac{\left(\vec{o} - \vec{p} \right)}{\left| \vec{p} - \vec{o} \right|^4}$$

$$N(\vec{p}) = -\nabla F(\vec{p})$$

$$N(\vec{p}) = 2 \frac{\left(\vec{p} - \vec{o} \right)}{\left| \vec{p} - \vec{o} \right|^4}$$

$$N(\vec{p}) = 2 \frac{\left(p_x - o_x \quad p_y - o_y \quad p_z - o_z \right)^T}{\left[\left(p_x - o_x \right)^2 + \left(p_y - o_y \right)^2 + \left(p_z - o_z \right)^2 \right]^2}$$

For more complicated density functions, N can be approximated this way:

$$\delta = 10^{-\varepsilon}$$

$$\varepsilon \geq 1$$

$$N_{approx}(\vec{p}) = \frac{1}{\delta} \begin{pmatrix} F(\vec{p}) - F\left(\vec{p} + \left(\delta \quad 0 \quad 0 \right)^T \right) \\ F(\vec{p}) - F\left(\vec{p} + \left(o \quad \delta \quad 0 \right)^T \right) \\ F(\vec{p}) - F\left(\vec{p} + \left(o \quad 0 \quad \delta \right)^T \right) \end{pmatrix}$$

To build a complex soft object, the density functions of several individual blobs are summed up. The normal at a given point p in space is the sum of each blob's $N(p)$.

As mentioned earlier in the text, we use the marching cubes algorithm to find the polygonal surface of the soft object. However, the tessellation code in Meshuggah takes special care to avoid brute-force testing of all voxels of the 3D density field, which would result in a run-time complexity of $O(n^3)$. Since the soft object's surface usually cuts through just a small fraction of the total number of voxels, we track its surface to limit further processing to those only. For each blob we therefore trace a line from its center out (any direction will do) until we find a voxel that the soft object's surface cuts through. If it hasn't been tessellated yet, we compute the polygonal surface for it and then progress to all neighbors also cut by the surface until all interlinked voxels have been visited. Otherwise, the blob penetrates another one that has already been processed. An algorithm outline is given in [6]. Figure 3 illustrates the tessellation procedure on a slice of a 3D density field for a soft object consisting of five blobs.

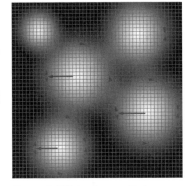

Figure 3: Efficiently tessellating a soft object. The arrows indicate surface tracking. The lines around the object indicate the soft object's surface for a given density threshold.

Now that the polygonal representation of the surface has been generated, we can focus on the shaders. The goal is to render the soft object like a liquid. To do this, a vertex shader has to calculate the reflected view vector and an approximately refracted view vector for each vertex. It also computes an approximation of the Fresnel term given in [7], which is used later in the pixel shader to combine two colors sampled from an environment map that corresponds to the reflected and refracted view direction.

The following is a reflection and refraction vertex shader:

```
#include "..\..\Effects\SoftObjects\SoftObjectsShaderConstants.h"

#define srcP    v0
#define srcN    v1

#define N       r0
#define V       r1

#define NShort  r9
#define Temp    r10
#define Temp1   r11

vs.1.1

// def CV_CONSTANTS, 0.0, 0.5, 1.0, 2.0

// normalize normal
dp3 N.w, srcN, srcN
rsq N.w, N.w
mul N, N.w, srcN

// vector from vertex to eye
add V, c[ CV_VIEWERPOS ], -srcP
dp3 V.w, V, V
rsq V.w, V.w
mul V, V, V.w

// calculate approximated Fresnel term F
// F = Fresnel_factor * ( 1 - V.N ) ^ 2
dp3 Temp, V, N
add Temp, c[ CV_CONSTANTS ].z, -Temp
mul Temp, Temp, Temp
mul oD0.xyz, Temp, c[ CV_FRENSEL_FACTOR ].x

// calculate reflection vector
// R = 2 * (E.N) * N - V
dp3 Temp, N, V
mul Temp1, Temp, c[ CV_CONSTANTS ].w
mul Temp1, Temp1, N
add oT0.xyz, Temp1, -V

// calculate refraction vector
```

```
// R' = 2 * (E.NShort) * N - V
mul NShort, N, c[ CV_REFRACT ]
dp3 Temp, NShort, V
mul Temp1, Temp, c[ CV_CONSTANTS ].w
mul Temp1, Temp1, NShort
add oT1.xyz, Temp1, -V

// transform vertex to clip space
dp4 oPos.x, srcP, c[ CV_WORLDVIEWPROJ_0 ]
dp4 oPos.y, srcP, c[ CV_WORLDVIEWPROJ_1 ]
dp4 oPos.z, srcP, c[ CV_WORLDVIEWPROJ_2 ]
dp4 oPos.w, srcP, c[ CV_WORLDVIEWPROJ_3 ]
```

Reflection and refraction pixel shader:

```
#include "..\..\Effects\SoftObjects\SoftObjectsShaderConstants.h"

ps.1.1

tex t0  // get reflected color
tex t1  // get refracted color

// blend between refracted color and reflected color
// using Fresnel term
lrp r0, v0, t0, t1
```

Volumetric Beams via Radial Blur

Volumetric beams as the result of a spherical object emitting light can be rendered quite convincingly using a radial blur. This technique doesn't suffer from artifacts usually found at silhouette edges when rendering shafts of light via multiple additively blended shells — that is, by extruding the object's mesh several times.

The beams effect in Meshuggah demonstrates the use of a radial blur by rendering a "seething" sun. To achieve this, two things need some further thought:

■ How to render the turbulent surface of a sun

■ How to efficiently implement a radial blur in 3D hardware

Let's begin with how to render the sun surface. It's basically a textured sphere. A great source for textures of that kind is [8], where you can find real sun pictures shot by SOHO — the Solar & Heliospheric Observatory project carried out by the European Space Agency (ESA) and the U.S. National Aeronautics and Space Administration (NASA). One of the sun pictures provided there was taken to create the texture in Figure 4 (on the following page).

In Figure 4 the alpha channel (left) is a filtered version of the color channel (right) at a higher scale. Photoshop's Glowing Edges filter was used to create it. Bright pixels indicate areas of high sun activity, which will eventually end up as long, intense beams. To make things more interesting, texture data from the alpha channel should be animated when rendering the sun surface to gain a complex motion. The following vertex and pixel shaders take care of this job. The following is a sun surface vertex shader:

```
#include "..\..\Effects\Beams\RenderSunShaderConstants.h"

#define srcP     v0
#define srcTex   v1

#define Temp     r0

vs.1.1

// apply texture scale factor
mul Temp, srcTex, c[ CV_TEXSCALE ]

// animate texture coordinates
add oT0.xy, Temp.xy, c[ CV_TEXOFFSET_0 ].xy
add oT1.xy, Temp.xy, c[ CV_TEXOFFSET_1 ].xy
add oT2.xy, Temp.xy, c[ CV_TEXOFFSET_2 ].xy
add oT3.xy, Temp.xy, c[ CV_TEXOFFSET_3 ].xy

// transform surface vertex into clip space
dp4 oPos.x, srcP, c[ CV_WORLDVIEWPROJ_0 ]
dp4 oPos.y, srcP, c[ CV_WORLDVIEWPROJ_1 ]
dp4 oPos.z, srcP, c[ CV_WORLDVIEWPROJ_2 ]
dp4 oPos.w, srcP, c[ CV_WORLDVIEWPROJ_3 ]
```

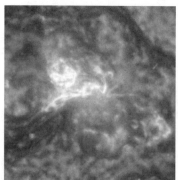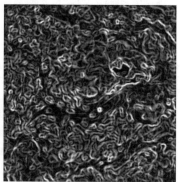

Figure 4: Sun surface texture

The vertex shader creates four unique texture coordinates by scaling and translating the original uv coordinates fed to it. These are used later in the pixel shader to create a complex motion of the sun's surface. The offset constants are updated per frame. Care must be taken when setting these values. Ideally, none of the texture coordinates move into the same direction at any time. Otherwise, the eye will be able to keep the animation of individual textures coordinates apart, thus destroying the illusion of a complex motion.

The following is a sun surface pixel shader:

```
#include "..\..\Effects\Beams\RenderSunShaderConstants.h"

ps.1.1

// get four samples from sun surface texture map
tex t0
tex t1
tex t2
tex t3

// calculate weighted sum of four alpha values
mul r0.a, t0.a, c[ CP_SURFACE_BLEND_VALUE ].a
mad r0.a, t1.a, c[ CP_SURFACE_BLEND_VALUE ].a, r0.a
mad r0.a, t2.a, c[ CP_SURFACE_BLEND_VALUE ].a, r0.a
mad r0.a, t3.a, c[ CP_SURFACE_BLEND_VALUE ].a, r0.a

// modulate weighted alpha value on
// surface color to compute final output
mul r0, t0, r0.a
```

The sun's surface is animated by sampling the surface texture four times and calculating the weighted sum of the alpha values — i.e., $0.25 \cdot (t0.a + t1.a + t2.a + t3.a)$. The result is then modulated on the color of the first sample to get the final output color (see Figure 5a).

Now that the sun's surface is rendered a radial blur has to be applied to it to get volumetric beams. But how do we implement a radial blur taking advantage of 3D hardware? One way is to transform the image from Cartesian coordinates (x, y) to polar coordinates (r, φ) and then do a horizontal blur (or vertical blur depending on which axis corresponds to r and φ after the transformation) and finally transform the result back to Cartesian coordinates. The problem with this approach is that the CPU needs frame buffer read access to do it, a big performance bottleneck on current 3D hardware. Fortunately, there is another way to do the very same thing, which is particularly well suited for hardware-accelerated rendering.

To accumulate a series of gradually zoomed-in versions of a source texture, we render it into a destination texture with alpha blending being enabled. The source texture contains the image to be used for the radial blur. In our case, it's the sun's surface that we just rendered in the previous step. The destination texture stores the result of the radial blur. Have a look at the following code snippet in which we render a radial blur:

```
Clear( pDstTexture );
SetRenderTarget( pDstTexture );

SetTexture( 0, pSrcTexture );

EnableAlphaBlending( true );
SetSourceBlend( ONE );
SetDestinationBlend( ONE );
```

```
EnableDepthTest( false );

for( int i( 0 ); i < NUM_RADIAL_BLUR_STEPS − 1; ++i )
{
    struct SScreenVertex2D
    {
        float x, y;
        float u, v;
    };

    float fW( (float) GetViewPort().GetWidth() );
    float fH( (float) GetViewPort().GetHeight() );
    float fUVOffset( i * 0.0075f );

    SScreenVertex2D pvQuad[ 4 ] =
    {
        { 0.0f, 0.0f,        fUVOffset,        fUVOffset },
        {   fW, 0.0f, 1.0f - fUVOffset,        fUVOffset },
        {   fW,   fH, 1.0f - fUVOffset, 1.0f - fUVOffset },
        { 0.0f,   fH,        fUVOffset, 1.0f - fUVOffset }
    }

    float fTextureFactor( (float) ( NUM_RADIAL_BLUR_STEPS - i ) /
                          (float) ( 8 * NUM_RADIAL_BLUR_STEPS ) );

    SetTextureStageState( 0, COLOROP, MODULATE );
    SetTextureStageState( 0, COLORARG1, TEXTURE );
    SetTextureStageState( 0, COLORARG2, fTextureFactor );

    DrawScreenQuad( pvQuad );
}
```

As you can see, the code draws a number of screen quads into the destination texture with depth testing being disabled. They all have the same size covering the entire viewport of the destination texture. The only difference is that with every new quad that gets drawn, we zoom into the source texture by moving the texture coordinates toward the source texture's center at (0.5, 0.5). Additively, blending the individual quads together results in a radial blur effect. Pixels with a high intensity in the source texture get smeared in radial fashion, thus creating beams. A texture factor is applied while rendering the quads in order to let beams fade out (see Figure 5b).

In a final step, the destination texture is stretched over the screen. To maintain a correct aspect ratio, the sun surface should have been rendered into the source texture using the aspect ratio of the screen, as opposed to using the one of the source texture itself. This ensures that the sun appears as a spherical and not elliptical object when finally making its way to the screen.

a.　　　　　　　　　　　　　　　　　　b.

Figure 5: Sun surface (a) and radial blur applied to it (b)

Simple, Faked Displacement Mapping

Due to the fast pace at which new generations of GPUs are developed, displacement mapping has become more and more a standard feature in hardware-accelerated rendering. Displacement maps, as opposed to bump maps, won't destroy the impression of surface detail once a certain part of an object that you're looking at has turned to such a degree that it shows its silhouette. With bump maps, this impression fades at the silhouette edges of an object because these bumps don't really exist physically; they have influence on lighting only. Displacement maps, however, alter geometry based on the height values stored in them, which affects both an object's silhouette and lighting. Another advantage of displacement mapping is that it can reduce memory bandwidth during rendering. A low-resolution mesh of an object with a displacement map applied can be used to render a highly detailed version of the same object. Since tessellation happens entirely on the GPU geometry, data transfer can be kept minimal. Nevertheless, bump maps have their place when rendering miniscule surface details, such as scratches, creases, pores, etc.

So how does it work in general? Take a triangle of an arbitrary mesh, for example. For each vertex there is a position, a normal, and a 2D texture coordinate for the displacement map. Upon sending the triangle to the GPU, it gets subdivided multiple times. Position, normal, and texture coordinates for each vertex inserted artificially due to subdivision are interpolated. Now every vertex position needs to be altered. Otherwise, we would end up having a lot of small triangles representing the original one. Therefore, for each vertex, the GPU determines the height value from the displacement map at the provided 2D texture coordinate and uses this value to displace the vertex position along the vertex normal. Likewise, vertex normals need to be perturbed, as the object's surface has changed.

At the time that Meshuggah was created, DirectX didn't support displacement mapping. That's why this section demonstrates a very simple approach to fake it with the help of the CPU.

To keep the workload of subdivision low, we limit ourselves to one quad that should be displacement mapped. This way, we can simply subdivide it in a grid-like fashion. There's no need to interpolate normals, and the position as well as texture coordinates can be derived directly from the grid position. Also, the displaced position of a vertex and its perturbed normal can be calculated directly from the associated height value and its neighbors in the displacement map. To get a high-quality displacement map effect, the quad needs to be subdivided quite a bit depending on the amount and size of detail provided in the displacement map. In Meshuggah, the displacement map has a size of 256x256 pixels. The quad is split into 255x255 tiny pieces that need to be rendered every frame. For each row of quads, a triangle strip is built and sent to the GPU.

The above technique should now be able to lift a 2D logo up into three dimensions. Environment and decal mapping enhance the visual detail after displacement mapping has been applied.

The vertex shader calculates the reflected view vector as well as the Fresnel term for each vertex. It's very similar to the soft object vertex shader. The pixel shader uses the reflected view vector to fetch a color from an environment map. It is multiplied by the material color of the logo. The result is combined with the material to blend in reflections. Since we want certain parts of the logo to appear darker, we create a copy of that color with half the intensity. The final output color is computed by taking the logo texture into account. Its RGB channels contain a decal value to blend between the two colors that we've just calculated. As a last step, we copy the value from the alpha channel of the logo texture to mask out all invisible logo parts.

The following is a pixel shader to render the displaced logo:

```
#include "..\..\Effects\DisplacementMap\DisplacementMapConstants.h"

ps.1.1

tex t0      // get texel from logo map (decal in rgb, mask in alpha)
tex t1      // get texel from environment map

// environment * material
mul r0, t1, c[ CP_MATERIALCOLOR ]

// blend between material color and environment * material color
// based on Fresnel term
lrp r0, v0, c[ CP_MATERIALCOLOR ], r0

// get the same color with half the intensity
mov_d2 r1, r0

// use logo decal value to blend between light and dark color and
// mask out parts of the logo that are invisible (co-issuing)
lrp r0.rgb, 1 - t0, r0, r1
+ mov r0.a, t0.a
```

Ocean Scene

The ocean scene is Meshuggah's most complex effect, both visually/computationally and in terms of shader usage. It's based on a statistical model to realistically animate ocean waves ([9] and [10]). In combination with shaders to calculate color of water and per-pixel bumpy reflections[4], it results in a highly believable rendering of an ocean. Making use of a high dynamic range Fresnel term allows better visualization of glossy spots on the ocean surface while still maintaining a high image contrast. The color of water is evaluated utilizing simplified equations from [11] to determine the view-dependent color of water. Contrast enhancement is based on an approach described in [12] to further improve the visual results when rendering ocean water.

First and foremost, a realistic model for simulating and animating ocean water is necessary to generate an appropriate mesh used for rendering. As mentioned above, [9] — in some greater detail — and [10] describe a statistical model based on observations of the real sea. In this model, a wave height field is decomposed into a set of sinus waves with different amplitudes and phases. While the model itself provides formulas to generate these amplitudes and phases, an inverse Fast Fourier Transformation (iFFT) converts them back into the spatial domain, thus creating a wave height field required for building the ocean mesh. It also allows calculating proper normals and displacement vectors for the height field. These are used for lighting calculations and forming choppy waves.

A big advantage of this particular model is that it produces an ocean height field that tiles perfectly. In Meshuggah, a 64x64 ocean height field is repeated four times, both horizontally and vertically, to form a 256x256 ocean mesh.

Ocean color computations performed in the shaders take several contributing factors into account to determine a final pixel color. First up, there is the color of water. As mentioned above, we can take the equations provided in [11] and simplify them by treating the water surface as a flat plane. The result is an equation only depending on the angle between the viewer v, a point p, and its normal n on the ocean surface. It returns greenish colors for angles of about 90 degrees (viewer looks over wave) and dark blue colors for angles near or equal to 0 degrees (viewer looks straight at wave). Another factor influencing the final color is a reflected skylight taken from an environment map. To further enhance details of the water, surface reflections will be per-pixel based, meaning that the viewer will be able to see little ripples on the water surface coming from a dynamically updated bump map.[5] In order to not overemphasize reflections, we calculate a Fresnel term for the air to water case (slightly different than the one used in previous sections), multiply it by the reflected skylight color, and add the result to the color of water. Otherwise, reflections would make the water look more like liquid metal. [10] proposed the following approximation of the Fresnel term for the air to water case. α denotes the angle between viewer v and surface normal n.

---

4 These represent low-scale ripples on the water surface.
5 The normals of the current ocean height field are used here.

$$Fresnel(\alpha) = \frac{1}{(1 + \cos(\alpha))^8}$$

The Fresnel term is a good candidate for performing contrast enhancement. It influences how much reflected skylight should be added to the color of water for a given pixel. By multiplying an exposure factor to the Fresnel term, we can increase the intensity in areas of the ocean surface where direct sunlight is reflected while leaving other areas relatively dark. Further details follow the listing of the ocean scene vertex shader:

```
#include "..\..\Effects\OceanScene\ShaderConstants.h"
#include "..\..\Effects\OceanScene\OceanShaderConstants.h"

#define srcP    v0
#define srcN    v1
#define srcTex  v2

#define P       r0
#define V       r1

#define S       r2
#define SxT     r3
#define T       r4

#define Temp    r10
#define Temp1   r11

vs.1.1

// def CV CONSTANTS, 0.0, 0.5, 1.0, 2.0

// scale and translate vertex
mul P, srcP, c[ CV_MESH_XYZ_SCALE ]
add P, P, c[ CV_MESH_XYZ_OFFSET ]

// apply curvature
add Temp, P, -c[ CV_VIEWERPOS ]
mul Temp, Temp, c[ CV_CONSTANTS ].zxz
dp3 Temp, Temp, Temp
mad P.y, -Temp.x, c[ CV_CURVATURE ].x, P.y

// generate S, T and SxT
dp3 SxT.w, srcN, srcN
rsq SxT.w, SxT.w
mul SxT, srcN, SxT.w

mov S, c[ CV_CONSTANTS ].zxx

mul T, S.zxyw, SxT.yzxw
mad T, S.yzxw, SxT.zxyw, -T

dp3 T.w, T, T
```

```
rsq T.w, T.w
mul T, T, T.w

mul S, SxT.zxyw, T.yzxw
mad S, SxT.yzxw, T.zxyw, -S

// set up transformation matrix for bump map normals
mov oT1.x, S.x
mov oT2.x, S.y
mov oT3.x, S.z

mov oT1.y, SxT.x
mov oT2.y, SxT.y
mov oT3.y, SxT.z

mov oT1.z, T.x
mov oT2.z, T.y
mov oT3.z, T.z

// set up view vector for per-pixel reflections
// put it into per-pixel reflection matrix
add oT1.w, c[ CV_VIEWERPOS ].x, -P.x
add oT2.w, c[ CV_VIEWERPOS ].y, -P.y
add oT3.w, c[ CV_VIEWERPOS ].z, -P.z

// set up texture uv for bump map
mul oT0.xy, srcTex.xy, c[ CV_BUMP_UV_SCALE ].xy

// calculate normalized view vector
add V, c[ CV_VIEWERPOS ], -P
dp3 V.w, V, V
rsq V.w, V.w
mul V, V, V.w

// set up lerp factor for ocean color
dp3 oD0.xyz, V, SxT

// calculate approximated Fresnel term F
//                        1
// F = -----------------------------------
//      ( 1 + V.N ) ^ FresnelApprox_PowFactor
dp3 Temp, V, SxT
add Temp, c[ CV_CONSTANTS ].z, Temp
mov Temp.y, c[ CV_FRESNELAPPROX_POWFACTOR ].x
lit Temp.z, Temp.xxyy
rcp Temp.z, Temp.z
mul Temp.z, Temp.z, c[ CV_DYNAMIC_RANGE ].x

// set up high dynamic range Fresnel term
expp Temp1.y, Temp.z
mov oD0.w, Temp1.y
```

```
add Temp.z, Temp.z, -Temp1.y
mul oD1.w, Temp.z, c[ CV_DYNAMIC_RANGE ].y

// transform vertex to clip space
dp4 oPos.x, P, c[ CV_WORLDVIEWPROJ_0 ]
dp4 oPos.y, P, c[ CV_WORLDVIEWPROJ_1 ]
dp4 oPos.z, P, c[ CV_WORLDVIEWPROJ_2 ]
dp4 oPos.w, P, c[ CV_WORLDVIEWPROJ_3 ]
```

The first step transforms a vertex of our generated ocean mesh into world space. Then a curvature factor is applied to the world space position. It alters the height (y) of each ocean vertex based on the squared x/z distance to the current view position.

Doing per-pixel reflections requires setting up a transformation matrix, which is used to transform normals fetched from a bump map into world space[6] so that the view vector is reflected correctly. Normals stored in the bump map are compatible to our (left-handed) world space coordinate system. That is, if the ocean surface is a flat (y) plane, the transformation matrix is set to identity. Since our ocean mesh is based on a height field, which in turn is based on a rectangular grid, generating the transformation matrix is easy. It's formed by three normalized vectors x, y, z (also called s, t, and sxt), which are copied into the consecutive output texture registers $oT1$-$oT3$. $oT0$ is reserved for the bump map's texture coordinates. The following is a matrix to transform bump map normals:

$$\vec{y} = normal\ of\ ocean\ mesh\ vertex$$
$$\vec{z} = (1\ \ 0\ \ 0)^T \times \vec{y}$$
$$\vec{x} = \vec{y} \times (0\ \ 0\ \ 1)^T$$
$$M = (\vec{x}\ \ \vec{y}\ \ \vec{z})^T$$

The view vector, which is also necessary for the reflection computations later in the pixel shader, is stored in the w components of $oT1$-$oT3$.

To calculate the color of water, we determine a lerp factor that is used in the pixel shader to blend between two colors. As you can see, it is a really stripped-down version of the original formulas given in [11]. For a given ocean mesh vertex, the lerp factor is just the cosine of the angle between viewer and vertex normal. A more complex color function encoded in an environment map, as in [10], was avoided since all available texture slots are already reserved for other purposes and a second render pass was omitted for performance reasons.

The next step determines the Fresnel term to be used for blending in reflected skylight in the pixel shader. As mentioned earlier, it serves as a high dynamic range value. In order to overcome DirectX 8.1 class hardware's limited range of color inputs and color math, we do the following steps. The Fresnel term is multiplied by a constant user-customizable exposure factor. Its range is limited to [0, 4], thus saving pixel shader instructions as we will see later. Since any value written to output color registers $oD0$ or $oD1$ gets clamped to [0, 1], we need to split up our Fresnel term. The fractional portion of it is extracted and copied to

---

6   It's the inverse orthonormal basis for the tangent space of each vertex.

oD0. The integer portion is divided by the maximum exposure factor and copied to *oD1*. This way, we avoid any clamping of color values. That's it for the vertex shader. Let's have a look at the ocean scene pixel shader to see how it does its work:

```
#include "..\..\Effects\OceanScene\ShaderConstants.h"
#include "..\..\Effects\OceanScene\OceanShaderConstants.h"


ps.1.1


tex         t0          // get normal from bump map
texm3x3pad  t1, t0      // transform normal.x into world space
texm3x3pad  t2, t0      // transform normal.y into world space
texm3x3vspec t3, t0     // transform normal.z into world space
                        // and get color for reflected view vector


// apply high dynamic range Fresnel term to env map
mul_x4 r0, t3, v1.a
mad    r0, t3, v0.a, r0


// calculate ocean color
lrp r1, v0, c[ CP_OCEAN_COLOR_DARK ], c[ CP_OCEAN_COLOR_LIGHT ]


// combine ocean and env color
add r0, r0, r1
```

The reflected skylight color is determined via transforming a normal from our bump map into world space using the interpolated per-pixel transformation matrix stored in *t1-t3* and then reflecting the view vector to look up a color in the corresponding skylight environment map.

To apply the high dynamic range Fresnel term, we first multiply the reflected skylight color from the environment map by *v1* (corresponds to *oD1*) and use the *_x4* instruction modifier to even out the division that was performed when splitting up the Fresnel term in the vertex shader. Then we multiply the reflected skylight color from the environment map by *v0* (corresponds to *oD0*) and add it to the previous result. This yields the desired *Fresnel · reflected skylight* color, which is added to the color of water.

Volumetric Light via Ray Casting

The second volumetric light effect in Meshuggah creates shafts of light via ray casting. These are shining through a bitmap (e.g., a logo) mapped onto a plane in 3D. Each ray starts traveling from the light's origin and runs along its given direction until it either hits the plane (that is, an opaque part of the bitmap) or its intensity has fallen below a certain threshold. To simplify things, we cast rays on the z plane. The following equation shows the intersection of a ray with the z plane.

$$r(t) = \vec{o} + t \cdot \vec{d}$$

$$\vec{n} = (0 \quad 0 \quad 1)^T$$

$$\vec{p} = (0 \quad 0 \quad 0)^T$$

$$n_x \cdot x + n_y \cdot y + n_z \cdot z = \vec{n} \cdot \vec{p}$$

$$z = 0$$

$$o_z + t \cdot d_z = 0$$

$$t_{Intersection} = \frac{-d_z}{o_z}$$

$$r(t_{Intersection}) = \vec{o} + t_{Intersection} \cdot \vec{d}$$

If a ray hits the plane and the intersection point is actually within the boundary of the bitmap mapped onto the plane, then the corresponding opacity value from the bitmap determines whether the ray should continue or stop traveling.

Rendering is split up into three parts:

1. For each ray, draw the part from the origin of the light to its intersection point with the z plane. At the intersection point, the ray's intensity is set to one over traveled ray length. Another distance-based attenuation function can be used as well.

2. Blend the bitmap mask onto the result of the last render step.

3. For each ray that didn't hit the bitmap, draw the part from its intersection point with the z plane to infinity.

To allow smooth changes between "ray hit" and "ray didn't hit" in step three, we store opacity values at eight bits instead of one bit. This way, we can gradually fade out a ray when it comes close to an opaque part of the bitmap. All rays are rendered using alpha blending with both source and destination blend factor set to one. Ray edges can be smoothed by applying a 1D gradient texture (black → white → black) perpendicular to the ray direction.

The shaders involved in this effect are rather simple. Texture coordinate and ray color (the intensity was already premodulated at ray setup) are copied by the vertex shader. The pixel shader modulates the interpolated ray color on the color fetched from the gradient texture.

Transition Effects

This final section deals with transition effects. It describes the technique used in Meshuggah to make things more interesting than a simple color fade. The basic idea is to have a per-pixel ramp function determine how much to blend between two corresponding pixels in a source and destination frame. To allow arbitrary transition patterns, we use a texture to store per-pixel threshold values (see Figure 6), which will later be accessed by a transition pixel shader to evaluate a ramp function. The transition effect is applied as some sort of post-processing step. Therefore, a screen space rectangle is rendered stretching the transition texture over the entire frame to feed the transition shader with a per-pixel threshold value.

All threshold values stored in the texture are in range [0, 1]. The darker a pixel in the transition texture, the longer it takes a pixel of the source frame to appear in the final image and vice versa. To control the transition's progress, we introduce a constant value $fTransTime$, $0 \le fTransTime \le 1$, which is set per frame. Setting $fTransTime$ to zero and gradually increasing it to one will smoothly blend between the destination and source frame. The following ramp function implements the specified behavior:

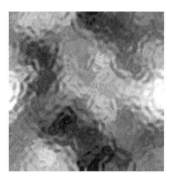

Figure 6: A texture containing threshold values for the transition pixel shader

$$f(fTransTime, fTransThreshold) = clamp_0^1(16 \cdot (fTransThreshold + 2 \cdot fTransTime - 1))$$

Obviously, this ramp function was chosen to be efficiently evaluated in a pixel shader. It directly translates to the following pixel shader code:

```
#include "TransitionShaderConstants.h"

ps.1.1

tex t0     // get threshold value

// set color of source frame and calculate
// first part of ramp function (co-issuing)
   mov    r0.rgb, c[ CP_TRANSITION_COLOR ]
+ add_x4 r0.a, t0, c[ CP_TRANSITION_TIME ]_bx2

// calculate final part of ramp function
mov_x4 r0.a, r0.a
```

It computes and stores the result of the ramp function in the alpha channel of the output color register. During alpha blending, this value is used to combine the source and destination frame accordingly. It should be noted that in this implementation, the source frame is just a constant color. But your app could also render the source frame into a texture and use that instead. The destination frame is stored in the frame buffer. Figure 7 shows the result of the transition shader applied to the ocean scene in Meshuggah.

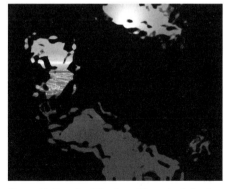

Figure 7: Result of the transition pixel shader for fTransTime = 0.5 using the texture shown in Figure 6

Wrapping It Up

In the last few sections, various real-time graphic effects that take advantage of DirectX 8.1-style vertex and pixel shaders were presented. The shaders primarily dealt with typical tasks found in computer graphics, such as animation, lighting, and texturing. Implementing the effects required developing different tricks to overcome some limitations of the DirectX 8.1 class hardware and enable hardware-friendly rendering. Porting the shaders to DirectX 9 vertex and pixel shader assembly or re-engineering them to HLSL or Cg should be fairly simple and might be interesting for further experiments.

References and Further Reading

[1] Resources for demo scene productions http://www.scene.org, http://www.pouet.net.

[2] Heidrich, Wolfgang and Hans Peter Seidel, "Anisotropic Reflections in OpenGL," http://www9.informatik.uni-erlangen.de/eng/research/rendering/anisotropic/.

[3] Kilgard, Mark J.,"Hardware Accelerated Anisotropic Lighting," http://developer.nvidia.com.

[4] Bourke, Paul, "Polygonising a Scalar Field," http://astronomy.swin.edu.au/pbourke/modelling/polygonise/.

[5] Bourke, Paul, "Implicit Surfaces," http://astronomy.swin.edu.au/pbourke/modelling/implicitsurf/.

[6] Jönsson, Andreas, "Fast Metaballs," http://www.angelcode.com/articles/metaballs/metaballs.asp.

[7] Watt, Alan and Mark Watt, *Advanced Animation and Rendering Techniques,* Addison Wesley, 1992.

[8] "The very latest SOHO images," http://sohowww.nascom.nasa.gov/data/realtime-images.html.

[9] Tessendorf, Jerry, "Simulating Ocean Water," http://home1.gte.net/tssndrf/index.html.

[10] Jensen, Lasse S. and Robert Goliáš, "Deep Water Animation and Rendering," http://www.swrendering.com/water, http://www.gamasutra.com/gdce/jensen/jensen_01.htm.

[11] Cohen, Jonathan, Chris Tchou, Tim Hawkins, and Paul Debevec, "Real-time High Dynamic Range Texture Mapping," http://www.ict.usc.edu/~jcohen/hdrtm.html.

[13] Nishita, Tomoyuki and Eihac hiro Nakamae, "Method of Displaying Optical Effects within Water using Accumulation Buffer," http://nis-lab.is.s.u-tokyo.ac.jp/~nis/pub_nis.html.

Layered Car Paint Shader

John Isidoro, Chris Oat, and Natalya Tatarchuk
Boston University   ATI Research   ATI Research

Figure 1: Two-tone, suspended microflake car paint rendered in real time using an HLSL pixel shader in DirectX 9

The application of paint to a car's body can be a complicated process. Expensive auto body paint is usually applied in layered stages and often includes dye layers, clear coat layers, and metallic flakes suspended in enamel. The result of these successive paint layers is a surface that exhibits complex light interactions, giving the car a smooth, glossy, and sparkly finish. The car model shown here uses a relatively low number of polygons but employs a high-precision normal map generated by an appearance-preserving simplification algorithm (visit http://www.ati.com/developer/ for more information on the ATI Normal Mapper tool). Due to the pixel shader operations performed across the smoothly changing surfaces (such as the hood of the car), a 16-bit per-channel normal map is necessary.

Normal Map Decompression

The first step in this pixel shader is normal decompression. Since the normals are stored in surface local coordinates (aka tangent space), we can assume that the z component of the normals is positive. Thus, we can store x and y in two channels of a 16-16 texture map and derive z in the pixel shader from $+\mathrm{sqrt}(1 - x^2 - y^2)$. This gives us much higher precision than a traditional 8-8-8-8 normal map (even 10 or 11 bits per channel is not enough for this particular shader) for the same memory footprint.

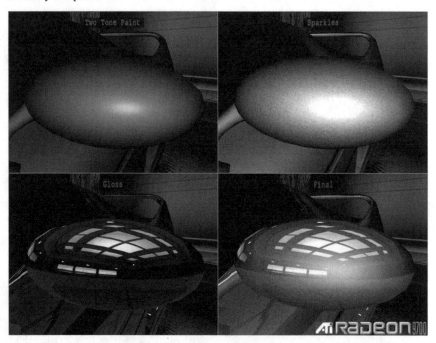

Figure 2: Two-tone, microflake, clear coat, and final lighting on side rearview mirror

Base Color

The normal decompression described above is performed on a surface normal map, which is generated from an appearance-preserving simplification process (N) and a high-frequency normalized vector noise map (N_n), which is repeated across the surface. These two normals are used to compute two perturbed normals that are used to simulate the two-toned nature of the paint as well as the microflake suspended in an inner coat of the paint.

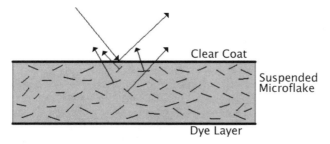

Figure 3: Metallic microflakes, suspended in clear enamel, are applied over a base paint coat (dye layer) and result in subsurface light scattering.

These normals, N_s and N_{ss}, are computed as follows:

$$N_s = \frac{aN_n + bN}{|aN_n + bN|} \text{ where } a < b$$

$$N_{ss} = \frac{cN_n + dN}{|cN_n + dN|} \text{ where } c = d$$

The coefficients a, b, c, and d above are constant input parameters to the pixel shader that determine the distributions of the perturbed normals. The magnitude of these perturbed normals determines the width of the region in which the microflake is readily visible. The two normals are dotted with the view vector and used as parameters in the following polynomial, which determines the color of the base coat and strength of the microflake term:

$$c_0(N_s \bullet V) + c1(N_s \bullet V)^2 + c2(N_s \bullet V)^4 + c3(N_{ss} \bullet V)^{16}$$

The first three terms of this polynomial perform the blend between the two tones of the paint. The fourth term adds an extra layer of sparkle for the microflake's contribution. Constants $c0$, $c1$, and $c2$ correspond to the base paint colors, while $c3$ corresponds to the microflake color.

Clear Coat Paint Layer

The final step in rendering the painted areas of the car is the inclusion of the clear coat through the addition of an environment map, as shown below.

One interesting aspect of the clear coat term is the decision to store the environment map in an RGBScale form to simulate high dynamic range in a low memory footprint. The alpha channel of the texture, shown on the right in Figure 4, represents one-sixteenth of the true range of the data, while the RGB, shown on the left, represents the normalized color. In the pixel shader, the alpha channel and RGB channels are multiplied together and multiplied by eight to reconstruct a cheap form of HDR reflectance. This is multiplied by a subtle Fresnel term before being added to the lighting terms described above.

Figure 4: The top face of the HDR cubic environment map with RGB channels on the left and the alpha channel on the right

The full HLSL pixel shader for the car paint and trim is shown here:

```
struct PsInput
{
    float2 Tex        : TEXCOORD0;
    float3 Tangent    : TEXCOORD1;
    float3 Binormal   : TEXCOORD2;
    float3 Normal     : TEXCOORD3;
    float3 View       : TEXCOORD4;
    float3 SparkleTex : TEXCOORD5;
};

float4 main(PsInput i) : COLOR
{
    // fetch from the incoming normal map:
    float3 vNormal = tex2D( normalMap, i.Tex );

    // Scale and bias fetched normal to move into [-1.0, 1.0] range:
    vNormal = 2.0f * vNormal - 1.0f;

    // Microflakes normal map is a high frequency normalized
    // vector noise map which is repeated across the surface.
    // Fetching the value from it for each pixel allows us to
    // compute perturbed normal for the surface to simulate
    // appearance of microflakes suspended in the coat of paint:
    float3 vFlakesNormal = tex2D(microflakeNMap, i.SparkleTex);

    // Don't forget to bias and scale to shift color into [-1.0, 1.0] range:
    vFlakesNormal = 2 * vFlakesNormal - 1.0;

    // This shader simulates two layers of microflakes suspended in
    // the coat of paint. To compute the surface normal for the first layer,
    // the following formula is used:
    //    Np1 = ( a * Np + b * N ) / || a * Np + b * N || where a < b
```

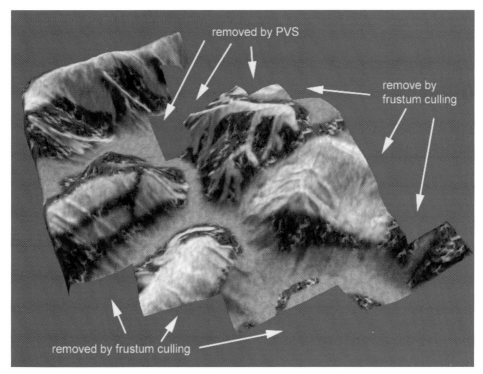

Color Plate 1. A PVS optimized scene (See page 26.)

Color Plate 2. Planet with cloud cover, noise texture, ocean, and per-pixel lighting (See page 38.)

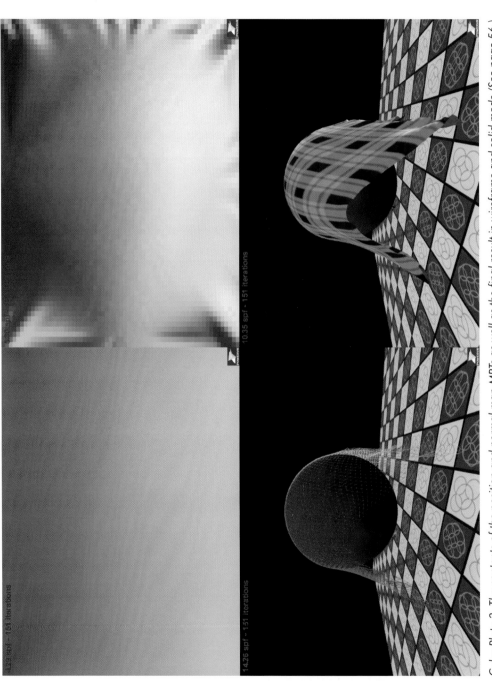

Color Plate 3. The contents of the position and normal map MRTs as well as the final result in wireframe and solid mode (See page 56.)

Color Plate 4. (left) Diffuse (dot3) sunlight plus radiosity hemisphere lookup. (right) With the addition of specular and Fresnel contributions, using a static cube map holding an image of typical surroundings. (See page 113.)

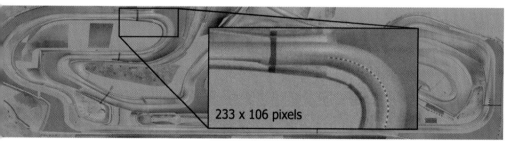

233 x 106 pixels

Color Plate 5. (left) The images in Figures 1, 4, and 5 in the "Hemisphere Lighting with Radiosity Maps" article were created along the zoomed-in section on this 2048x512 radiosity map. (See page 116.)

Color Plate 6. These images show the hemisphere lighting on its own, using a single DXT1 format radiosity map that encodes both shadow and ground color information. (See page 117.)

Color Plate 7. The complete lighting model, combining a base texture, radiosity hemisphere, Fresnel cube map, and dot3 sunlight. (See page 121.)

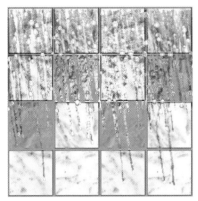

Color Plate 8. Rendering drop of water (See page 202.)

Color Plate 9. Screen shot from the water demo illustrating advanced water and sky dome effects (See pages 208 and 249.)

Color Plate 10. Screen shot from the water demo illustrating advanced water and sky dome effects (See pages 208 and 249.)

Color Plate 11. Position data (See page 253.)

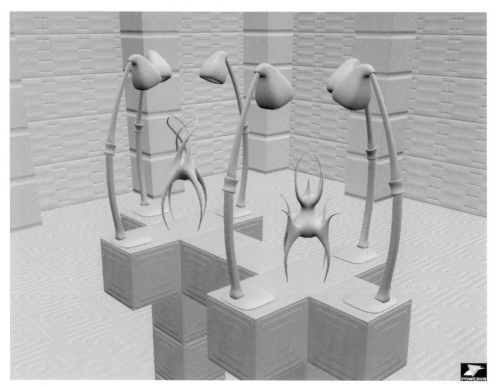

Color Plate 12. Normal data (See page 255.)

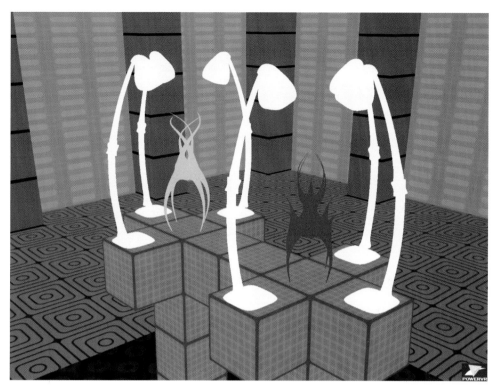

Color Plate 13. Diffuse data (See page 255.)

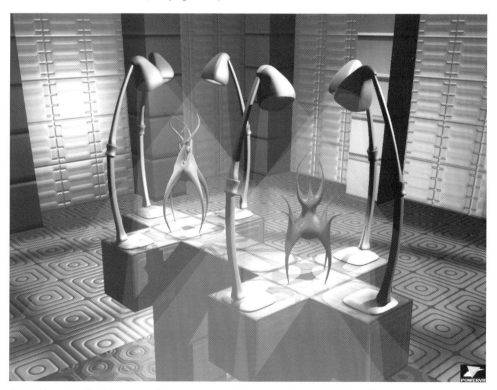

Color Plate 14. The blue cone shapes represent the areas where the lights affect the scene, i.e., the pixels on which the pixel shader will be executed. (See page 266.)

Color Plate 15. Final render using deferred shading from demo (See page 269.)

Color Plate 16. A screen shot from the Animusic demo shows motion blur via geometry and shading distortion. (See page 299.)

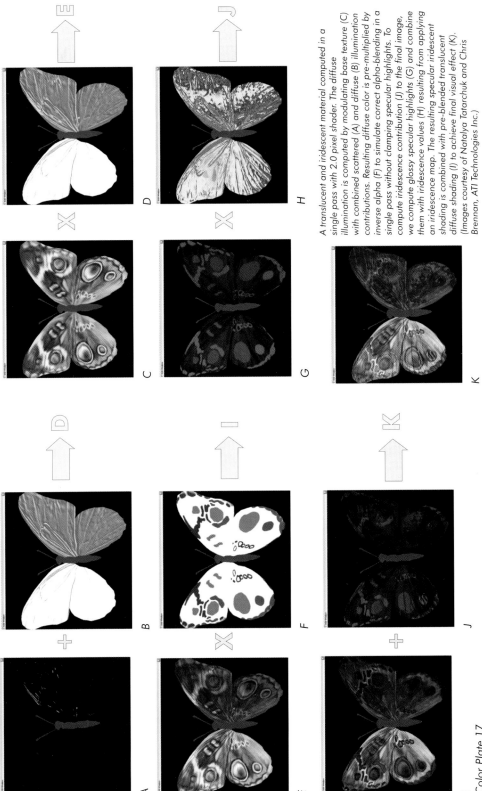

A translucent and iridescent material computed in a single pass with 2.0 pixel shader. The diffuse illumination is computed by modulating base texture (C) with combined scattered (A) and diffuse (B) illumination contributions. Resulting diffuse color is pre-multiplied by inverse alpha (F) to simulate correct alpha-blending in a single pass without clamping specular highlights. To compute iridescence contribution (J) to the final image, we compute glossy specular highlights (G) and combine them with iridescence values (H) resulting from applying an iridescence map. The resulting specular iridescent shading is combined with pre-blended translucent diffuse shading (I) to achieve final visual effect (K). (Images courtesy of Natalya Tatarchuk and Chris Brennan, ATI Technologies Inc.)

Color Plate 17

Color Plate 18. Stereoscopic rendering in hardware (See page 336.)

Color Plate 19. Result of a hand-drawn image as input in a 3D scene (See page 346.)

Color Plate 20. A real-time implementation of Paul Debevec's Rendering with Natural Light animation using the separable Gaussian filter. (See page 451.)

Figure 1 (See page 471.)

Figure 2 (See page 471.)

Figure 3 (See page 473.)

Figure 4 (See page 474.)

Figure 5 (See page 475.)

Figure 6 (See page 476.)

Color Plate 21

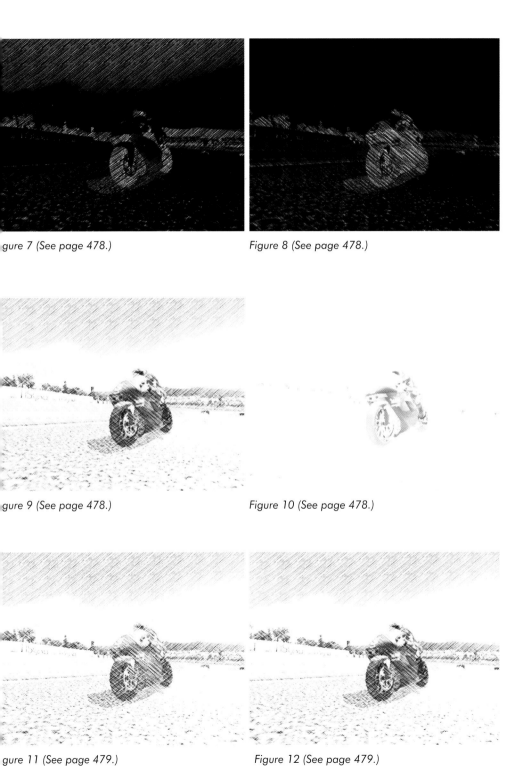

gure 7 (See page 478.)

Figure 8 (See page 478.)

gure 9 (See page 478.)

Figure 10 (See page 478.)

gure 11 (See page 479.)

Figure 12 (See page 479.)

olor Plate 22

Color Plate 23. The two ripple centers are colored magenta and fade as the ripple fades. These five images show, in left to right order, the ripples' dissipation after they have fully propagated. (See page 498.)

Color Plate 24. A 5x5 Kuwahara filter plus outlines based on the Sobel edge detection filter has been applied to the image for real-time posterization. (See page 505.)

Color Plate 25. A 7×7 Kuwahara filter plus outlines based on the Sobel edge detection filter has been applied to the image for real-time posterization. The 7×7 filter's advantage over the 5×5 filter is better posterization for about the same number of instructions. (See page 510.)

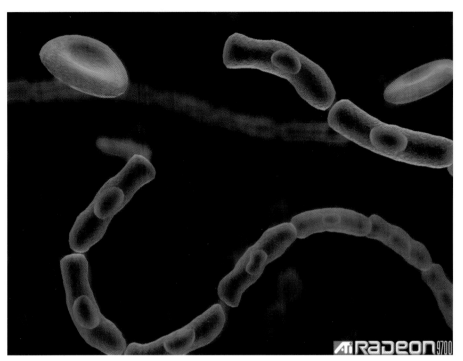

Example of real-time depth of field simulation using post-processing techniques described in the article "Real-Time Depth of Field Simulation." Courtesy of ATI Technologies, Inc. (See page 556.)

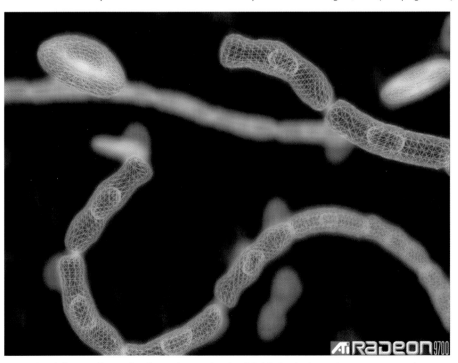

Example of the wireframe for the real-time depth of field simulation using post-processing techniques described in the article "Real-Time Depth of Field Simulation." Courtesy of ATI Technologies, Inc. (See page 556.)

Color Plate 26

Code: F. Brebion
Art: D. Cornibert

Screen shot taken from the soft shadows demo. This 6,000-triangle temple scene features six lights, two of which are casting spherical soft shadows, and runs at up to 35 fps on a Radeon 9700. The two lights are animated. (See page 578.)

Code: F. Brebion
Art: D. Cornibert

Another screen shot from the temple scene, with a different viewpoint. The white dot near the cattaur (a cross between a cat and a centaur) shows the main light's position. (See page 578.)

```
//
float3 vNp1 =
      microflakePerturbationA * vFlakesNormal + normalPerturbation * vNormal ;


// To compute the surface normal for the second layer of microflakes, which
// is shifted with respect to the first layer of microflakes, we use this formula:
//    Np2 = ( c * Np + d * N ) / || c * Np + d * N || where c == d
//
float3 vNp2 = microflakePerturbation * ( vFlakesNormal + vNormal ) ;


// The view vector (which is currently in world space) needs to be normalized.
// This vector is normalized in the pixel shader to ensure higher precision of
// the resulting view vector. For this highly detailed visual effect, normalizing
// the view vector in the vertex shader and simply interpolating it is insufficient
// and produces artifacts.
float3 vView =  normalize( View );


// Transform the surface normal into world space (in order to compute reflection
// vector to perform environment map lookup):
float3x3 mTangentToWorld = transpose( float3x3( Tangent, Binormal, Normal ) );
float3   vNormalWorld    = normalize( mul( mTangentToWorld, vNormal ));


// Compute reflection vector resulted from the clear coat of paint on the metallic
// surface:
float  fNdotV      = saturate(dot( vNormalWorld, vView));
float3 vReflection = 2 * vNormalWorld * fNdotV - vView;


// Here we just use a constant gloss value to bias reading from the environment
// map, however, in the real demo we use a gloss map which specifies which
// regions will have reflection slightly blurred.
float fEnvBias = glossLevel;


// Sample environment map using this reflection vector:
float4 envMap = texCUBEbias( showroomMap, float4( vReflection, fEnvBias ) );


// Premultiply by alpha:
envMap.rgb = envMap.rgb * envMap.a;


// Brighten the environment map sampling result:
envMap.rgb *= brightnessFactor;


// Compute modified Fresnel term for reflections from the first layer of
// microflakes. First transform perturbed surface normal for that layer into
// world space and then compute dot product of that normal with the view vector:
float3 vNp1World = normalize( mul( mTangentToWorld, vNp1) );
float  fFresnel1 = saturate( dot( vNp1World, vView ));


// Compute modified Fresnel term for reflections from the second layer of
// microflakes. Again, transform perturbed surface normal for that layer into
// world space and then compute dot product of that normal with the view vector:
float3 vNp2World = normalize( mul( mTangentToWorld, vNp2 ));
float  fFresnel2 = saturate( dot( vNp2World, vView ));
```

```
//
// Compute final paint color: combines all layers of paint as well as two layers
// of microflakes
//
float  fFresnel1Sq = fFresnel1 * fFresnel1;

float4 paintColor = fFresnel1   * paintColor0 +
                    fFresnel1Sq * paintColorMid +
                    fFresnel1Sq * fFresnel1Sq * paintColor2 +
                    pow( fFresnel2, 16 ) * flakeLayerColor;

// Combine result of environment map reflection with the paint color:
float  fEnvContribution = 1.0 - 0.5 * fNdotV;

float4 finalColor;
finalColor.a = 1.0;
finalColor.rgb = envMap * fEnvContribution + paintColor;

return finalColor;

}
```

Conclusion

This shader was developed using empirically gathered phenomenological illumination characteristics rather than actual physical material attributes. Many different car paint swatches were observed under various lighting conditions. This shader strives to reproduce the observed characteristics of those swatches. This article demonstrated a compelling simulation for the illumination of car paint using a real-time pixel shader.

Motion Blur Using Geometry and Shading Distortion

Natalya Tatarchuk, Chris Brennan, Alex Vlachos, and John Isidoro
ATI Research   ATI Research   ATI Research   Boston University

Introduction

When our demo team decided to implement a real-time version of the Animusic *Pipe Dream* animation shown in the SIGGRAPH 2001 Electronic Theater, we realized that we needed to create a fast, reliable technique for rendering a convincing motion blur effect for the many balls moving around the complicated music machine shown in Figure 1. Although enough approaches existed for simulating motion blur for computer-generated images, some of them weren't fast enough or accurate enough for our purposes. Rather than draw the moving balls several times at different points in space and time, as one might do with an accumulation buffer [Haeberli90], we chose to draw each ball once, distorting its appearance to make it appear as if it were in motion during the frame "exposure." This technique is an extension to the approach taken by [Wloka96].

Figure 1: A screen shot from the real-time Animusic Pipe Dream demo (See Color Plate 16 for another view of the demo.)

The motion blur effect on film appears due to finite camera shutter speeds. When the object moves too quickly compared to the shutter speed, the resulting image of that object seems to move along the film surface while the shutter is opened. The image on film appears smeared, depending on how fast the object was moving with respect to the observer. Motion blur is an important cue for realistic rendering of our world, and it becomes ever more significant as computer-generated imagery approaches the detailed look of cinematic art. Motion blur is very common in photography and motion pictures and can be used in different ways for specific artistic choices. Some artists use motion blur deliberately to delineate dynamic motion in photographs. Human beings perceive motion blur as natural, and thus it is expected for convincing computer-generated simulation.

Simulating Motion Blur Effect

For our purposes, let's consider the movement of objects in object space. There, motion blur is caused by the object moving through a finite amount of space during a short time step (equivalent to the exposure time due to an opened shutter). This allows us to use the distance that the object moved since the previous time step as an approximation for the instantaneous velocity value necessary to compute the blurring of the object. The previous work by Wloka and Zeleznik eliminates the obvious discrete renderings of the ball, which is inevitable in an accumulation buffer approach, while our technique also accounts for blurring of the object and computing a more accurate approximation to its contribution to the scene over time. To achieve the look we wanted, we used a vertex shader and a pixel shader to distort both the shape and shading of the balls.

Sample RenderMonkey Workspace

The RenderMonkey IDE, an environment for shader development, can be downloaded from http://www.ati.com/developer/sdk/radeonSDK/html/Tools/Render Monkey.html. Along with the application itself, it installs a series of workspaces, including one called *Motion Blur.rfx*. This workspace contains the effect that we are describing in this article. Feel free to modify any of the parameters to the shaders to explore their effects on the final visual result. Of course, you can also modify the actual shaders to understand the algorithms in greater depth.

Geometry Distortion

We distort the shape of the ball along the movement direction vector to simulate the stretching of the object as it moves quickly across the image plane with respect to the observer. Each individual ball is modeled as a "capsule" (two hemispheres with a connecting cylinder), which is aligned with the direction of motion. The vertex shader stretches the ball tangent to the direction of motion, as shown below. The vertices of the front half of the capsule (those whose normals have a positive dot product with the direction of motion) are pushed in the direction of motion, and the vertices of the back half of the capsule (those whose normals

have a negative dot product with the direction of motion) are pulled in the opposite direction. Naturally, the total amount of stretching is the amount of distance
the ball moved since the previous frame.

In Figure 2, we show how the ball's shape is distorted by the vertex shader in
the direction tangent to the path of motion at the time instant centered in the current finite shutter time.

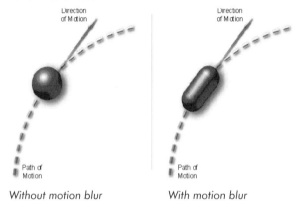

Without motion blur   With motion blur

Figure 2: Shape distortion

The capsule geometry is stretched in the vertex shader as a function of distance
traveled, d, measured in ball diameter units. Figure 3 shows a snapshot from the
demo showing a distorted ball moving quickly in the scene.

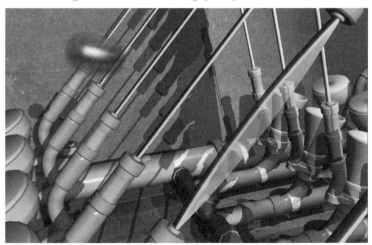

Figure 3: Geometry distortion for a quickly moving object

The vertex shader also computes a blurriness factor from $1 / (1 + d)$. The object
becomes more blurred as it moves faster past the observer; thus, it is very important to use relative speed rather than the actual movement of the ball in the
scene, since motion blur is relative to the observation point. The motion blur
amount is measured as a distance traveled relative to the camera's motion. If the

observer moves along with the same speed as the object, no motion blur is perceived. To determine the rate of fade-out for the object, we calculate how much visible area is covered as the ball moves (which is measured in ball widths). The fade-out rate is calculated in the range of [0..1] and interpolated across the polygons to be used in the pixel shader to determine how much to blur the shading of the balls.

Vertex Shader

Below you can see an example of the vertex shader that performs shape distortion. It is also used to compute diffuse illumination contribution from two run-time lights, which is propagated to the pixel shader.

```
float4x4 mBallOrientation;
float4x4 inv_view_matrix;
float4x4 view_proj_matrix;
float4x4 mWOMatrix;

float4 vColor;
float4 vExtensionDirection;
float4 vObjectCenter;
float4 vMotionDirection;
float4 vAmbientPos3;
float4 vAmbientPos1;
float4 vAmbientPos2;
float4 vAmbientColor1;
float4 mLight1Pos;
float4 mLight2Pos;
float4 vLight1Color;
float4 vLight2Color;
float4 vAmbientColor3;
float4 vAmbientColor2;

float fBallSize;
float fObjectScale;
float fSpeed;
float fZoom;

struct VS_OUTPUT
{
    float4 ProjPos : POSITION;
    float3 Diffuse : COLOR0;
    float4 Normal  : TEXCOORD0;
    float3 View    : TEXCOORD1;
    float3 Light1  : TEXCOORD2;
    float3 Light2  : TEXCOORD3;
    float3 Pos     : TEXCOORD4;
};

VS_OUTPUT main( float4 Pos: POSITION, float3 Normal: NORMAL)
{
```

```
VS_OUTPUT o = (VS_OUTPUT).5;


Pos = float4(Pos.xyz*fObjectScale, 1);
float4 vCameraPosition = mul(inv_view_matrix, float4(0,0,0,1));


// Calculate View Vector
float3 vView = normalize(vCameraPosition - mul(mWOMatrix, Pos));


// Calculate velocity relative to the eye
float3 vVelocity  = vMotionDirection * fSpeed;


// motion vector as seen by the eye
float3 vEyeMotion = vVelocity - vView * dot(vVelocity, vView);


// Speed as relative to the observer:
float  fEyeSpeed  = length(vEyeMotion);


// Calculate the area that the stretched ball will take on
// the screen — it is dependent on the instantaneous velocity
// of the moving object and its size:
float fBallCoverage = 1 + fEyeSpeed / fBallSize;


// Calculate the blurriness factor for later alpha blending of
// the ball — the faster it moves, the more "smeared" it will
// appear:
float fBlurriness = 1 - 1/fBallCoverage;


// Export blurriness factor the pixel shader:
o.Normal.w = fBlurriness;


// Translate object to object origin:
float4 vObjectPos = Pos - vObjectCenter;


// Extend the position to elongate the ball relative to the speed:
vObjectPos += fSpeed * vExtensionDirection * -sign(Normal.z);


// Re-orient the ball along its motion path:
float3 vOrientedPosition = mul((float3x3)mBallOrientation, vObjectPos);


// Rotate ball into correct orientation:
vOrientedPosition = mul(vOrientedPosition, (float3x3)mWOMatrix);


// Remove world matrix rotation
vOrientedPosition += vObjectCenter;


//
// Translate object back to where it started:
//


// Transform position into world space and output it:
float4 vWorldPos = mul(mWOMatrix, float4(vOrientedPosition, 1));
o.Pos = vWorldPos;
```

```
    o.ProjPos = mul(view_proj_matrix, float4(vWorldPos.xyz*fZoom, vWorldPos.w));

    //
    // Calculate Normal
    //

    // Rotate normal into correct orientation:
    float3 vWorldNormal = mul((float3x3)mBallOrientation, Normal);

    // Remove world matrix rotation of normal:
    vWorldNormal = mul(vWorldNormal, mWOMatrix);

    // Translate to world space:
    vWorldNormal = mul(mWOMatrix, vWorldNormal);

    o.Normal.xyz = vWorldNormal;

    //
    // Light vectors for specular lighting:
    //

    // Light vector 1:
    o.Light1 = normalize((float3)mLight1Pos - (float3)vWorldPos);

    // Light vector 2:
    o.Light2 = normalize((float3)mLight2Pos - (float3)vWorldPos);
    //
    // Compute diffuse illumination contribution:
    //
    o.Diffuse  = max(dot(vWorldNormal, normalize(vAmbientPos1 -
                        vWorldPos)), 0) * vAmbientColor1;
    o.Diffuse += max(dot(vWorldNormal, normalize(vAmbientPos2 -
                        vWorldPos)), 0) * vAmbientColor2;
    o.Diffuse += max(dot(vWorldNormal, normalize(vAmbientPos3 -
                        vWorldPos)), 0) * vAmbientColor3;
    o.Diffuse += max(dot(vWorldNormal, o.Light1), 0) * vLight1Color;
    o.Diffuse += max(dot(vWorldNormal, o.Light2), 0) * vLight2Color;
    o.Diffuse  = o.Diffuse * vColor;

    // More accurate view vector
    o.View = normalize(vCameraPosition - vWorldPos);

    return o;
}
```

Shading Distortion

In addition to merely stretching the capsule geometry along the tangent to the path of the ball's motion, the shading of the object is affected by the blurriness factor computed above. The most important visual cue for motion blur effect is the increasing transparent quality of the object as it moves quicker on the screen. This creates the impression that the object really is moving rapidly in the scene.

Figure 4 shows comparison rendering of two objects moving at different speeds — even just glancing at the two snapshots, we get the impression that the ball in the right picture is moving much faster than the ball in the left picture.

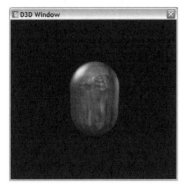 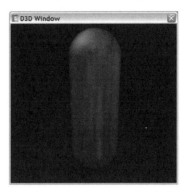

Slowly moving ball (speed = 0.6)   *Quickly moving ball (speed = 2.15)*

Figure 4: Velocity-dependent shading distortion

In our shader, blurring is achieved in multiple ways. There are a number of factors that contribute to the final ball color, including two specular highlights and an environment map, all of which are blurred as a function of the ball's motion during the frame. In the case of the two specular highlights on each ball, the specular exponent and its intensity are lowered as the ball goes faster, which effectively broadens the highlight on the surface of the ball. This serves to spread out the highlight and make it appear to be blurred in the direction of the ball's motion. In essence, the goal is to spread the energy radiating from the specular highlight among the pixels that the specular highlight would move across during a finite frame exposure time. In the case of the environment map, we use the texCUBEbias pixel shader instruction, which applies a per-pixel bias to selectively sample the smaller mip levels. This blurs the environment map term. The texCUBEbias intrinsic is used to perform biased texture sampling, where the bias can be computed per-pixel. This is done to induce some over-blurring of the texture as the ball moves faster through the image.

```
...

    // Apply environment map to the object, taking into account
    // speed-dependent blurring:
    float3 vCubeLookup = vReflection + i.Pos/fEnvMapRadius;

    float4 cReflection = texCUBEbias(tCubeEnv,
        float4(vCubeLookup, fBlur * fTextureBlur)) * vReflectionColor;

...
```

In the last few instructions of the pixel shader, the diffuse and specular components of illumination are combined. Because the specular contribution can be greater than one, we perform part of the frame buffer compositing operation (Src * SrcAlpha) in the pixel shader before the colors are clamped to the zero-to-one range. Each pixel is composited with the frame buffer with a src + srcAlpha * Dest blend. Doing the Src * SrcAlpha premultiplication in the pixel shader gives a more accurate result, since it happens prior to pixel shader output color saturation. See [Tatarchuk03] for a more detailed description of this blending approach as it is used for preserving specular highlights and color saturation for a translucent and iridescent surface.

Pixel Shader

Following is the complete pixel shader used for the effect described in this article. This is a DirectX HLSL pixel shader, which can be compiled to the ps_2_0 target.

```
float4 vReflectionColor;
float4 vLight1Color;
float4 vLight2Color;

float fBaseSpecularIntensity;
float fTextureBlur;
float fSpecularExpBlurScale;
float fSpecularExp;
float fSpecularDimScale;
float fEnvMapRadius;

sampler tCubeEnv;

struct PS_INPUT
{
    float3 Diffuse : COLOR0;
    float4 Normal  : TEXCOORD0;
    float3 View    : TEXCOORD1;
    float3 Light1  : TEXCOORD2;
    float3 Light2  : TEXCOORD3;
    float3 Pos     : TEXCOORD4;
};

float4 main(PS_INPUT i) : COLOR
{
    // Extract blurring factor from the normal vector interpolator:
    float fBlur = i.Normal.w;

    // Compute reflection vector:
    float3 vNormal     = normalize(i.Normal);
    float3 vReflection = normalize(2 * dot(i.View, vNormal) * vNormal - i.View);

    // Compute fade out rate for the moving ball taking into
    // account Fresnel effect:
    float fFirstBallWidthFade = saturate(2 * fBlur);
    float fRestBallWidthFade  = saturate(2 - 2 * fBlur);
    float fFresnel            = 1 - saturate(dot(vNormal, i.View));

    float fAlpha = fRestBallWidthFade * (1 - fFirstBallWidthFade * fFresnel);
```

```
// Environment map the object taking into account
// speed-dependent blurring:
float3 vCubeLookup = vReflection + i.Pos/fEnvMapRadius;

float4 cReflection = texCUBEbias(tCubeEnv,
    float4(vCubeLookup, fBlur * fTextureBlur)) * vReflectionColor;

// Compute smearing of specular highlights depending on the amount
// of motion blur:
float fBlurredSpecularExp = max(1, fSpecularExpBlurScale*fBlur + fSpecularExp);

float fSpecularIntensity = fBaseSpecularIntensity * (1 - (fBlur * fSpecularDimScale));

// Compute specular contribution for the first light:
float3 cSpecular1 = pow(saturate(dot(vReflection, i.Light1)),
    fBlurredSpecularExp) * fSpecularIntensity * vLight1Color;

// Compute specular contribution for the second light:
float3 cSpecular2 = pow(saturate(dot(vReflection, i.Light2)),
    fBlurredSpecularExp) * fSpecularIntensity * vLight2Color;

// Compute input diffuse contribution with both specular
// highlight areas and environment map term:
float3 cColor = cReflection + cSpecular1 + cSpecular2 + i.Diffuse;

// Determine the actual blending amount:
float alpha = fRestBallWidthFade *
    (1 - fFirstBallWidthFade * (1-saturate(dot(-vNormal, -i.View))));

// Pre-multiply by alpha and output color:
return float4(cColor*alpha, alpha);
}
```

Summary

In this article we described an efficient way to implement convincing motion blur effect by using speed-dependent shape distortion and alignment of objects along the path of movement combined with shading distortion to simulate accurate blurring of objects as they move quickly on the screen. Figure 5 shows the progression of a ball slowing down to collide with another object, a drum, and quickly moving away after the collision. On each of the pictures in that figure, we can see how the geometry and shading is changed to provide visual cues about the movement of the ball.

The ball is moving quickly toward the drum.

The ball is about to hit the drum.

The moment right after impact

The ball moving away after the collision

Figure 5: Motion blurring of moving ball

References

[Haeberli90] Haeberli, Paul E. and Kurt Akeley, "The accumulation buffer: Hardware support for high-quality rendering," SIGGRAPH 1990, pp. 309-318.

[Tatarchuk03] Tatarchuk, N. and C. Brennan, "Simulation of Iridescence and Translucency on Thin Surfaces," *ShaderX²: Shader Programming Tips & Tricks with DirectX 9*, Wolfgang Engel, ed., Wordware Publishing, 2004, pp. 309-318.

[Wloka96] Wloka, M. and R.C. Zeleznik, "Interactive Real-Time Motion Blur," *Visual Computer*, Springer Verlag, 1996.

Simulation of Iridescence and Translucency on Thin Surfaces

Natalya Tatarchuk and Chris Brennan

ATI Research   ATI Research

Introduction

This article focuses on simulating the visual effect of translucency and iridescence of thin surfaces such as butterfly wings. When creating a visual impression of a particular material, an important characteristic of that surface is the luminosity of the material. There are various ways that a surface can be luminous. These include sources with or without heat, from an outside source, and from the object itself (other than a mere reflection). Luminous objects that exhibit certain combinations of these characteristics can be described as translucent or iridescent, depending on the way that the surface "scatters" incoming light.

Translucency of a material is determined by the ability of that surface to allow light to pass through without full transparency. Translucent materials can only receive light and thus can be luminous only when lit from an outside source. Although there has been ample research in recent years of interactive simulation of fully translucent surfaces such as marble or wax [Jensen01], this article focuses on simulating translucency for thin surfaces. A good example of the visual effect of translucency of thin surfaces is if you were to take a piece of rice paper and hold it against a light source (for example, Chinese lanterns). You would see that the light makes the rice paper seem to glow from within, yet you cannot see the light source through the paper because the paper scatters incoming light.

Iridescence is an effect caused by the interference of light waves resulting from multiple reflections of light off of surfaces of varying thickness. This visual effect can be detected as a rainbow pattern on the surface of soap bubbles and gasoline spills and, in general, on surfaces covered with thin film diffracting different frequencies of incoming light in different directions. The surface of a soap bubble exhibits iridescence due to a layer of air, which varies in thickness, between the top and bottom surfaces of the bubble. The reflected colors vary along with the thickness of the surface. Mother-of-pearl, compact discs, and various gemstones share that quality. Perhaps most captivating of all, however, is the iridescence seen on the wings of many beautiful butterflies, such as blue pansy butterflies, *Junonia orithya*, or the malachite butterflies, *Siproeta stelenes*. These wings exhibit vivid colorful iridescence (see Figure 1 for examples), the color of which has been shown to be independent of the pigmentation of the wings and is

309

attributed to the microstructure of the scales located on and within butterfly wings.

Blue pansy butterfly, Junonia orithya

Malachite butterflies, Siproeta stelenes

Figure 1: Butterflies in nature

The effect described in this chapter simulates translucency and iridescent patterns of delicate butterfly wings. To generate iridescence, we have merged the approaches described in "Bubble Shader" [Isidoro02] and "Textures as Lookup Tables for Per-Pixel Lighting Computations" [Vlachos02].

Algorithm

Inputs

This effect uses a geometric model with a position, a normal, a set of texture coordinates, a tangent, and a binormal vector. All of these components are supplied to the vertex shader. At the pixel level, we combine gloss, opacity, and normal maps for a multi-layered final look. The gloss map is used to contribute to "satiny" highlights on the butterfly wings. The opacity map allows the wings to have variable transparency, and the normal map is used to give wings a bump-mapped look to allow for more surface thickness variations. The input texture coordinates are used to sample all texture maps.

Sample RenderMonkey Workspace

The RenderMonkey IDE, an environment for shader development, can be downloaded from http://www.ati.com/developer/sdk/radeonSDK/html/Tools/Render Monkey.html. Along with the application itself, the RenderMonkey installer installs a series of workspaces, including one called *Iridescent Butterfly.rfx*. This workspace contains the effect that we are describing in this article. Feel free to modify any of the parameters to the shaders to explore their effect on the final visual result. Of course, you can also modify the actual shaders to understand their algorithms in greater depth.

Vertex Shader

The vertex shader for this effect computes vectors that are used by the pixel shader to compute the illumination result. At the pixel level, the view vector and the light vector are used for calculating diffuse illumination and scattered illumination off of the surface of the wings, which contributes to the translucency effect. The halfway vector will be used for generation of glossy highlights on the wing's surface. In the vertex shader, however, these vectors are simply transformed to tangent space.

```
struct VS_OUTPUT
{
    float4 Pos   : POSITION;
    float2 Tex   : TEXCOORD0;
    float3 View  : TEXCOORD1;
    float3 Light : TEXCOORD2;
    float3 Half  : TEXCOORD3;
};


VS_OUTPUT main( float4 Pos      : POSITION,
                float4 Normal   : NORMAL0,
                float2 Tex      : TEXCOORD0,
                float3 Tangent  : TANGENT0,
                float3 Binormal : BINORMAL0 )
{
    VS_OUTPUT Out = (VS_OUTPUT) 0;

    // Output transformed vertex position:
    Out.Pos = mul( view_proj_matrix, Pos );

    // Propagate input texture coordinates:
    Out.Tex = Tex;

    // Compute the light vector (object space):
    float3 vLight = normalize( mul( inv_view_matrix, lightPos ) - Pos );

    // Define tangent space matrix:
    float3x3 mTangentSpace;
    mTangentSpace[0] = Tangent;
    mTangentSpace[1] = Binormal;
    mTangentSpace[2] = Normal;

    // Output light vector in tangent space:
    Out.Light = mul( mTangentSpace, vLight );

    // Compute the view vector (object space):
    float3 vView = normalize( view_position - Pos );

    // Output view vector in tangent space:
    Out.View = mul( mTangentSpace, vView );
```

```
// Compute the half angle vector (in tangent space):
Out.Half = mul( mTangentSpace, normalize( vView + vLight ) );

return Out;
}
```

Pixel Shader

The pixel shader computes the illumination value for a particular pixel on the surface of the butterfly wings, taking into account the light propagated through the surface of the wings due to the translucency effect and light emitted due to the iridescence of the wings.

First, we load the color value from a base texture map. For efficiency reasons, we have stored the opacity in the alpha channel of the base texture map. We also load a normal vector (in tangent space) from the precomputed normal map and a gloss value, which is used to modulate highlights on the surface of the wings. The scalar gloss map is stored in the alpha channel of the normal map. Combining three-channel texture maps with single-channel grayscale value maps allows us to load two values with a single texture fetch.

```
float3 vNormal, baseColor;
float  fGloss, fTransparency;

// Load normal and gloss map:
float4( vNormal, fGloss ) = tex2D( bump_glossMap, Tex );

// Load base and opacity map:
float4 (baseColor, fTransparency) = tex2D( base_opacityMap, Tex );
```

Don't forget to scale and bias the fetched normal map into the [–1.0, 1.0] range:

```
// Signed scale the normal:
vNormal = vNormal * 2 - 1;
```

Figure 2 displays the contents of the texture maps used for this effect:

Base texture map for wings texture

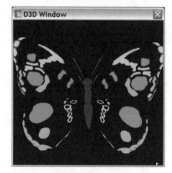

Opacity texture map

Normal map for bump mapping   Gloss map

Figure 2: Input texture maps

The texture address mode should be set to *CLAMP* in u and v for both of these texture maps. Also, they should be trilinearly filtered (MAGFILTER = *linear*, MINFILTER = *linear*, and MIPFILTER = *anisotropic*).

Translucency

Next we compute the translucency effect. The amount of light scattered through a thin surface is proportional to the incident angle of the light on the back side. So, similar to a Lambertian diffuse calculation, we dot the light vector but with the negative of the normal vector. We also use a prespecified translucency coefficient in addition to the fetched opacity value to control the amount of scattered light:

```
float3 scatteredIllumination = saturate(dot(-vNormal, Light)) *
                               fTransparency * translucencyCoeff;
```

As described above, the scattered light contribution is dependent on both the direction of incident light as well as the surface normal for the pixel location. This contribution to diffuse illumination of the wings' surface is what accounts for their subtle glow. Figure 3 illustrates the contribution of scattered reflected light on the surface of the wings. If you modify the pixel shader for this effect in the Render-Monkey workspace to output only the scattered light contribution, you will be able to investigate how this contribution changes as you rotate the model.

To simulate varying thickness of scales on the surface of butterfly wings as well as within them, we use a normal map to perturb the normal vectors. The usual diffuse illumination is computed with a simple dot product and a global ambient term:

```
float3 diffuseContribution = saturate(dot(vNormal,Light)) +
                             ambient;
```

Figure 3 shows the result of computing diffusely reflected light for the butterfly wings.

Scattered light contribution   *Diffuse term*

Figure 3: Diffuse illumination

In the next step we combine the base texture map with the diffuse term and the scattered reflected light contribution to compute a final value for diffuse surface illumination:

```
baseColor *= scatteredIllumination + diffuseContribution;
```

Figure 4 illustrates the results of this operation. Now we can see how scattered reflected light contributes to the translucency effect of the butterfly wings in the more illuminated portions of wings in the final picture in Figure 4.

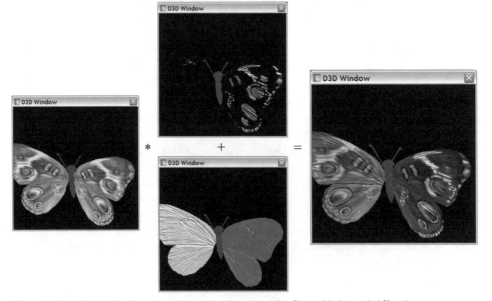

Figure 4: Combining the base texture map with scattered reflected light and diffusely reflected light

Since butterfly wings in nature have varying transparency, we had our artists paint in the appropriate opacity values. However, since the desired effect has transparent geometry, which also has specular highlights, we must take care when doing blending to properly achieve transparency. Typically, blending transparent materials is done during the blending stage of the rendering pipeline. However, if the object that you are rendering as transparent is a specular surface, blending should be done before actually applying specular highlights to the surface. A brute-force approach for this is to render two separate passes (the diffuse alpha-blended pass first) and adding specular highlights in the second pass. But to speed up our effect, we wanted to do it all in one pass. This requires some tricks with the way alpha blending is used. Since the specular pass is additive and the diffuse is blended, we want to pre-blend the diffuse color and add the specular color in the shader. Then, during the blending stage, the source color is not modified; it's simply added, since that portion of the blending equation is already taken care of in the shader code. The destination has the same blend as it normally would with the standard two-pass "brute-force" approach. If we look at the blending equation, the two-pass approach is expressed in the following form:

> *Pass 1:*   *diffuseIlluminationColor * α + destination * (1 – α)*
> *Pass 2:*   *specularColor + destination*

The single-pass approach can be expressed as follows:

> *Pass 1:*   *(diffuseIlluminationColor * α + specularColor) * 1 +*
> *destination * (1 – α)*

Here's the portion of the shader that premultiplies the diffuse illumination result with the alpha:

```
float fOpacity = 1 - fTransparency;

// Premultiply alpha blend to avoid clamping:
baseColor *= fOpacity;
```

Figure 5 illustrates the effect of this action on the diffuse illumination result.

Figure 5: Premultiplied alpha blending

Iridescence

One of the reasons why butterflies are so captivating in nature is the iridescence of their wings. To simulate iridescent patterns on the surface of our simulated butterfly wings, we use an approach similar to the technique described in the

"Bubble Shader" article in the original *Direct3D ShaderX* book [Isidoro02]. Irides-cence is a view-dependent effect, so we can use the view vector, which was com-puted in the vertex shader and interpolated across the polygon in tangent space. We also use scale and bias coefficients to scale and bias the index to make irides-cence change more quickly or slowly across the surface of the wings. You can explore the effects of these parameters by modifying the variables iridescence_ speed_scale and iridescence_speed_bias in the Iridescent Butterfly.rfx RenderMonkey workspace.

```
// Compute index into the iridescence gradient map,
// which consists of N·V coefficients
float fGradientIndex =
        dot( vNormal, View ) * iridescence_speed_scale +
        iridescence_speed_bias;

// Load the iridescence value from the gradient map based on the
// index we just computed above:
float4 iridescence = tex1D( gradientMap, fGradientIndex );
```

This effect uses a 1D gradient texture map (Figure 6) for computing color-shifted iridescence values. This texture should have trilinear filtering enabled and *MIRROR* texture address mode selected for both u and v coordinates.

Figure 6: Gradient texture map

Figure 7 illustrates the resulting iridescence value.

Figure 7: Iridescence of butterfly wings

To add satiny highlights to the surface of the wings, we use a gloss map generated by the artist. We compute the gloss value based on the result fetched from the gloss map and *N·V* for determining the placement of specular highlights. Finally, we add the gloss contribution to the previously computed diffuse illumination result to obtain the final result:

```
// Compute the final color using this equation:
// N*H * Gloss * Iridescence + Diffuse
float fGlossIndex = fGloss *
```

```
                    ( saturate( dot( vNormal, Half )) *
                    gloss_scale + gloss_bias );

baseColor += fGlossIndex * iridescence;
```

Figure 8 shows the final color for the butterfly wings.

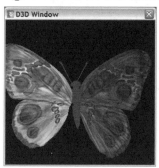

Figure 8: Assembled final color

To render the final effect correctly, we output the previously computed scalar fOpacity in the alpha channel of our result:

```
return float4( baseColor, fOpacity );
```

Because of the premultiplication mentioned earlier, this means that our alpha blend factors should be *ONE* for the SRCBLEND render state and *IVRSRCALPHA* for DESTBLEND.

Summary

In this chapter we presented a technique for simulating translucency and iridescence on thin surfaces, such as butterfly wings. Our technique combines scattered reflected light with diffusely reflected light and a color-shifted iridescence value for a visually interesting final result. You can see this effect in Color Plate 17 and in the *Chimp Demo* in the ATI Radeon 9800 demo suite on the ATI web site (see Figure 9): http://www.ati.com/developer/demos/r9800.html.

References

[Isidoro02] Isidoro, J. and D. Gosselin, "Bubble Shader," *Direct3D ShaderX: Vertex and Pixel Shader Tips and Tricks*, Wolfgang Engel, ed., Wordware Publishing, 2002, pp. 369-375.

[Jensen01] Jensen, H.W., S.R. Marschner, M. Levoy, and P. Hanrahan, "A Practical Model for Subsurface Light Transport," proceedings of SIGGRAPH 2001.

[Vlachos02] VlachosA., J. Isidoro, and C. Oat, "Textures as Lookup Tables for Per-Pixel Lighting Computations," *Game Programming Gems 3*, Charles River Media, 2002.

Simulation of Iridescence and Translucency on Thin Surfaces

Figure 9: Transluscent and iridescent shader-based effects are used to render the butterfly in the ATI Radeon 9800 Chimp Demo using hardware acceleration. (Image courtesy of ATI Technologies Inc.)

Floating-point Cube Maps

Arkadiusz Waliszewski

arsil@acm.org

Introduction

Floating-point computations are one of the most welcome features in DX9-compatible hardware. Floating-point surfaces add more precision and make many algorithms possible to implement. Unfortunately, the current hardware line implements them with many limitations. This article addresses issues related to the floating-point textures.

Floating-point Cube Maps

Cube maps are a very important texture paradigm in computer graphics. They allow texture lookups based on the direction of the three-dimensional vector. Unfortunately, not all hardware supports cube maps based on floating-point surfaces.

We can use 64-bit textures instead (16 bits per component) if we do not care about dynamic range and memory footprint. But what if hardware also does not support this format with cube maps or we need greater dynamic range?

The trick is to use a classic 32-bit RGBA texture to represent IEEE 32-bit floating-point values with limited precision. We pack floating-point values (RGB) into a single 32-bit texture, where RGB channels keep mantissas of the original floating-point values and the A channel keeps the common exponent. This format is known as Radiance RGBE format.

The common exponent keeps the greatest exponent from the RGB floating-point channels. Because of that, all mantissas must be normalized into a [0.5, 1] range and adjusted to the common exponent. This means loss of precision on channels, which keeps values significantly smaller than a channel with the greatest exponent. This loss of data is perfectly acceptable in many areas (e.g., in high dynamic range environmental mapping) because significantly smaller components would not be visible after conversion from high-dynamic range values to the visible range (8-bit back buffer).

The following example illustrates this idea:

Floating-point values:
R = 0.9, G = 0.01, and B = 0.1

are encoded into RGBE format as:
R = 230, G = 2, B = 25, and E (exponent) = 128

This is because 230/255 is about 0.9, 2/255 is 0.008, 25/255 is 0.098, and the common exponent is 2 to the power of 0 (because 128 in signed 8-bit representation is 0).

The second example shows a much greater dynamic range:

Floating-point values:
R= 355.0, G = 0.01, and B = 10.003

are encoded into RGBE format as:
R = 177, G = 0, B = 5, and exponent E = 137

This means the exponent is 2 to the power of 9 (512) and decoded values are:
R = 177/255 * 512 = 355.388
G = 0/255 * 512 = 0
B = 5/255 * 512 = 10.03

We lost all data from the green channel, but the value from the green channel is significantly smaller than from the red and blue channels, so its contribution to the final image is insignificant.

The following HLSL pixel shader code decodes the RGBE format into an RGB high dynamic range value (it assumes that the BaseMapSampler sampler is defined and holds cube map texture).

```
// samples cube map texture and decodes into a high dynamic range value
// fPos – direction vector (for lookup into the cube map texture)
float3 sampleCube(float3 fPos)
{
    float4 tmp = texCUBE(BaseMapSampler, fPos);
    return tmp.rgb * exp2(tmp.a * 255.0 – 128.0);
}
```

RGBE format covers about 76 orders of magnitude with 1 percent relative accuracy. It is perfectly acceptable in areas where the alpha channel is not needed, and loss of data in some circumstances is acceptable. This solution requires all mantissas to be positive. Negative values are uncommon but can be handled with additional code and the loss of one mantissa's bit.

Cube Map Filtering

Although some hardware supports floating-point cube maps, there is no hardware that supports floating-point surface with filtering better than point sampling. Sometimes such a limitation is not important, but usually aliasing artifacts related to the point sampling are unacceptable.

The solution to this problem is to write our own filtering routine in a pixel shader. We limit our discussion to bilinear filtering and cube maps.

First, we must understand how bilinear filtering works. Consider one-dimensional texture. Graphics hardware converts a texture's coordinate from the floating-point value (range [0, 1]) to the "texel space" (range [0, width of the 1D texture]). For point sampling, a filtered value comes from one texel, which is closest to the converted texture coordinate. For bilinear sampling, hardware fetches two texels that lie closest to the converted coordinate (the converted coordinate is usually between two texels). Then the hardware computes the contribution of each texel based on the distance from the coordinate value in "texel space" and lerps these two texels to produce the final pixel.

Filtering in action:
Texture coordinate in "texel space" is 1.35.

Point filtering:
Filtering will return texel 1.

Bilinear filtering:
Filtering will return
(texel 1) * (1 - 0.35) + (texel 2) * (0.35)

Figure 1: Filtering

This approach is directly applicable to the two- and three-dimensional textures. In the case of cube maps, this is not always true. This is because of the cube map face selection step, which usually precedes the filtering phase. It means that on some hardware, cube map bilinear (or above) filtering is done "per cube face," and some artifacts are noticeable on the boundaries of the faces (you will notice it if you know what to search for).

We take another approach. We completely eliminate the face selection phase from the pixel shader. We treat cube map texture coordinates like regular 3D texture coordinates, and we use these coordinates to fetch eight texels from the cube map and lerp them to produce the final pixel. Although this approach is not 100 percent mathematically correct, it usually produces images better filtered than built-in hardware filtering and simplifies pixel shader code.

We can summarize this by writing some pseudocode of the algorithm:

■ Multiply each component of the texture coordinate by the size of the texture (in pixels) to get the coordinate in "texel space."

■ For each component, compute two closest integer values (e.g., 123.4 value gives 123 and 124).

■ Compute contribution of each integer part by using the fractional part of the component (e.g., 123.4 gives us integer 123 with contribution $1 - 0.4 = 0.6$ and 124 with contribution 0.4).

■ From these integer values, construct eight possible texture coordinates and fetch eight texels (first divide these coordinates by the texture size to get coordinates in the 0-1 range).

■ Compute the final pixel value using contributions and fetched texels (the exact formula is in the following shader code).

The following HLSL shader code demonstrates this technique:

```
float4 hlsl_filtered_cube_shader(float3 uvw : TEXCOORD0) : COLOR
{
    // should be defined outside the shader
    float3 textureSize = float3(32, 32, 32);
    float3 textureSizeDiv = float3(0.03125, 0.03125, 0.03125);

    float3 halfPixel   = float3(0.5, 0.5, 0.5);
    float3 oneConst    = float3(1.0, 1.0, 1.0);

    // multiply coordinates by the texture size
    float3 texPos = uvw * textureSize;

    // compute first integer coordinates
    float3 texPos0 = floor(texPos + halfPixel);

    // compute second integer coordinates
    float3 texPos1 = texPos0 + oneConst;

    // perform division on integer coordinates
    texPos0 = texPos0 * textureSizeDiv;
    texPos1 = texPos1 * textureSizeDiv;

    // compute contributions for each coordinate
    float3 blend = frac(texPos + halfPixel);

    // construct 8 new coordinates
    float3 texPos000 = texPos0;
    float3 texPos001 = float3(texPos0.x, texPos0.y, texPos1.z);
    float3 texPos010 = float3(texPos0.x, texPos1.y, texPos0.z);
    float3 texPos011 = float3(texPos0.x, texPos1.y, texPos1.z);
    float3 texPos100 = float3(texPos1.x, texPos0.y, texPos0.z);
    float3 texPos101 = float3(texPos1.x, texPos0.y, texPos1.z);
    float3 texPos110 = float3(texPos1.x, texPos1.y, texPos0.z);
    float3 texPos111 = texPos1;

    // sample cube map (using function defined earlier)
    float3 C000 = sampleCube(texPos000);
    float3 C001 = sampleCube(texPos001);
    float3 C010 = sampleCube(texPos010);
    float3 C011 = sampleCube(texPos011);
    float3 C100 = sampleCube(texPos100);
    float3 C101 = sampleCube(texPos101);
    float3 C110 = sampleCube(texPos110);
    float3 C111 = sampleCube(texPos111);

    // compute final pixel value by lerping everything
    float3 C = lerp(
        lerp(lerp(C000, C010, blend.y),
            lerp(C100, C110, blend.y),
            blend.x),
```

```
        lerp( lerp(C001, C011, blend.y),
            lerp(C101, C111, blend.y),
            blend.x),
        blend.z);

    return float4(C.r, C.g, C.b, 1.0f);
}
```

Conclusion

This article showed how to overcome the lack of floating-point cube maps and floating-point surface filtering. By combining the two techniques presented here, we can use high dynamic range cube maps on hardware that does not support them natively.

Demo

A simple demo application on the CD shows the presented techniques in action. The left part of Figure 2 shows the classic teapot rendered with a pixel shader that implements the described algorithms, whereas the right part is rendered with a standard 32-bit cube map. Corresponding source code also shows how to simply convert floating-point values into an RGBE format.

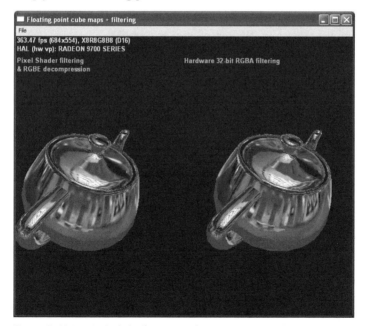

Figure 2: Using a pixel shader vs. a cube map

Stereoscopic Rendering in Hardware Using Shaders

Thomas Rued
Digital Arts

Introduction

Even though we push more polygons than ever before, use modern rendering hardware, and the resolution and bit depth continues to get better and better, we still end up letting our projection matrix project our 3D space into a 2D image that is presented on the screen. This works fine for many applications, but since we are striving for more photorealistic images and illusions of the real world as we see it, it is only natural to expand this 2D imaging into a full 3D stereoscopic image.

Volumetric visualization of medical data is only one area where the perception of depth can be critical. Games and virtual reality applications can also use the third axis as a cool gimmick for the users. Earlier, this was only done by using expensive VR equipment, shutter-glasses, and the like.

The anaglyph (red/green) method (invented by Wilhelm Rollmann in 1853) is an easy and cheap way to get started with stereoscopy. Early on, it could be implemented in software, but with the advent of rendering hardware the pixel processing power increased; in the beginning it was limited to whatever capabilities the rendering hardware had.

With the appearance of programmable graphics hardware, the stereoscopic possibilities opened up even more. Now it is possible to use more than just traditional anaglyph encoding. New innovative ways of rendering stereo can be developed and implemented directly through the use of shaders.

Stereoscopic Rendering Overview

Stereoscopic rendering can be done in many ways, depending on the needs, equipment, and requirements of the final picture.

Active and Passive Stereo

When using special glasses that actually take part in the encoding of the stereoscopic image, it's called active stereo. Typical systems using active stereo are shutterglass systems. When the glasses don't do anything other than decode the image, it is called passive stereo. Passive stereo is the area that we are going to explore in this article, since this is the technique we can implement and use through pixel shaders on modern 3D rendering hardware.

Generic Stereoscopy

To do stereoscopic rendering in a generic way, we need to expand our normal geometric pipeline a bit. First, we work with two cameras instead of one (left/right eye). Second, we need to do a final compositing of the left and right images to create the final stereoscopic image presented on the screen.

The compositing itself requires temporary storage of image data in a render target and good control of the viewport and FOV. We go through the setup and use of these primitives.

Even though there are a handful of different ways to actually compose the stereo image, they all share the same virtual camera setup. This is the best way to have a good stereo image. Consequently, we use a fair amount of space on a detailed description on that aspect.

We also look at stereoscopic artifacts and what we can do about it. Finally, we go through three different shaders doing stereoscopic compositing.

Stereoscopic Camera Setup

Before rendering anything, we have to set up our camera(s) in the correct way. Failing to do this results in an incorrect stereo image. This results in perception of depth anomalies and an incorrect visualization of the geometry in the scene.

Basic Scene

For our demonstration purposes, we assume a simple scene consisting of an object and a camera. For stereoscopic rendering, we need two cameras. But for this part, we assume a single camera setup, since the double scene rendering due to an extra camera pass is trivial.

Figure 1: Our basic test scene with an object and a camera

Viewport and Aspect Ratio

Since we are using render targets for our intermediate results and our final compositing is done using shaders, we need to use textures for render targets. Like all textures, we have to select power of 2 sized textures. This isn't exactly what we want for 800x600 display modes, etc., but with a little help from our projection matrix, field of view, and aspect ratio, we can render to the full target that when scaled to the screen looks correct.

Figure 2: Basic scene rendered to a quadratic render target texture with respect to the aspect ratio of the final destination

Figure 3: Render target rendered on final destination. Now the aspect ratio of the image is correct, but scaling artifacts may occur.

First we set the virtual camera viewports to the actual render target size (512x 512, for example). Then we set up the projection matrix to render the scene as if it was actually rendered to our destination viewport size (1024x768, for example). This is accomplished by specifying a horizontal and vertical FOV that corresponds to the aspect ratio of the 1024x768 viewport.

If we choose to set a horizontal FOV, we have to calculate the vertical FOV by using the formula below:

Vertical FOV (radians) = 2 * tan–1(1/aspect * tan(horizontal FOV/2))

For example: for a 1024x768 viewport, the traditional 4:3 aspect will be 1.333333. Setting the horizontal FOV to 60 degrees (1.047 radians) results in a vertical FOV as follows:

Vertical FOV (radians) = 2 * tan–1(0.75 * tan(1.047/2))

Doing this makes use of the total allocated texture size and still gets a correct aspect on the final image when it is used on the original destination viewport. However, if a texture with a different size than the actual viewport is used, the final image will contain scaling artifacts. In practice, these artifacts can be limited by using traditional texture filtering.

If you need a full 1:1 mapping between render target pixels and screen pixels, you have to make a render target texture with at least the size of the destination viewport and then only use a subpart of this texture. By doing this you will not need to set up a special projection matrix. You can render directly to the render target, using the same viewport and projection matrix as you would use for non-render target rendering. Just remember that later on you need to use special texture coordinates to obtain the rendered part of the render target. Also, you will not make use of the total amount of allocated render target memory.

Figure 4: Basic scene rendered to an oversized quadratic render target, resulting in waste of expensive memory

Figure 5: Render target rendered on the final destination. Only the original subpart of the quadratic render target has been retrieved.

Camera Optics

Even though the camera FOV in computer graphics typically is expressed in terms of degrees and/or radians, it is often practical to express it in mm. In that way, we get closer to the real photographic world, but we also get values that we can reuse later in the *basis* calculation (see below). The FOV is translated from mm to radians below:

Horizontal FOV (radians) = 2 * tan–1(36 / (2 * mm))

The vertical FOV can be calculated by using the formula above.

Depth Buffer

Setting up render targets for scene rendering requires the attachment of a depth buffer. We need two render targets but can reuse the depth buffer between render sessions:

Clear left render target and common depth buffer
Render scene to left render target
Clear right render target and common depth buffer
Render scene to right render target

In this way, we reuse the depth buffer memory. You must make sure that you do not use a multipass render back end, as that presumes a certain state of the depth buffer between passes.

Parallax, Exo-, Endo-, and Meso-Stereo

In general, the amount of stereo can be expressed as the parallax in the picture. The zero parallax is located at the screen plane with the positive parallax inside the screen and the negative outside. When all the objects in a scene are in front of the screen plane, having only negative parallax, it is called exo-stereo, and when all the objects in a scene are behind the screen plane, having only positive parallax, it is called endo-stereo. Normally, the scene is composed in a way where both a negative and positive parallax is present, resulting in meso-stereo.

We can calculate a correct parallax difference for the scene by using:

$$\Delta = A / n$$

where:

Δ = parallax difference

A = the distance between the eyes equal to 65 mm (international standard value)

n = the scale factor between the physical width of the filmstrip and the width of the screen

Figure 6: Visualization of the parallax in a stereoscopic scene. Notice that the object outside the screen plane has a lighter shadow to the right and the object inside the screen plane to the left. The object located at the screen plane doesn't have any parallax (zero parallax).

We started by setting the camera's horizontal FOV and aspect ratio with respect to the render target size and frame buffer destination viewport size. Then we found the needed parallax for the scene. Now it's time to set up the relationship between the two cameras — the relationship between "the two eyes," so to speak.

Basis

First, let me point out that the basic way you set up two virtual cameras for any kind of stereoscopic rendering is in a parallel way. Some systems wrongly make use of converging cameras, which doesn't result in a correct stereo simulation. The only way to set the cameras up (both virtual and real cameras) is to let their aiming lines be parallel.

Figure 7: Converging cameras. This is the incorrect way to set up the camera's aiming lines.

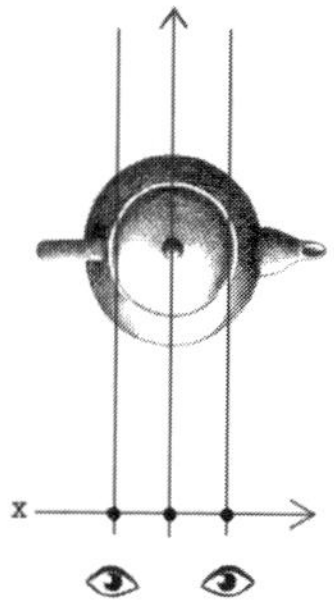

Figure 8: Parallel cameras. This is the correct way to initially set up the camera's aiming lines.

That said, the distance between the camera's aiming lines is denoted as the *basis*. To define a good basis is the "holy grail" of getting good stereo perception.

Calculating the basis can be done in different ways, depending on the scene rendered and the available amount of data.

Optimal Depth

When rendering a big scene, it's difficult to accurately define where the far point is. In that case, we calculate the basis in the following way:

$$b = \Delta * ((N / f) - 1)$$

where:

b = Basis
Δ = Parallax difference in final picture
N = Near point
f = Focal length

Maximum Depth

If the far distance is known (which is the case for a simple model viewer and the like), we can estimate the near and far point exactly and calculate the basis:

$$b = (\Delta * F * N) / (f * (F - N))$$

where:

F = Far point

Notice that the near and far points aren't necessarily the same as the near and far z clip planes of the projection matrix.

Here is an example: We have a simple scene with a known far point distance, so we use the latter basis formula:

A = 65 mm

n = 1500 mm / 36 mm = 42, normal PC screen and filmstrip

Δ = 65 mm / 42 = 1.56 mm

F = 900 mm

N = 300 mm

f = 35 mm, typical wide-angle lens

b = (1.56mm * 900mm * 300mm) / (35mm * (900mm–300mm))

b = 20 mm

Depending on our scene, we have to scale this from millimeters into world units.

Basis Factor

Often, the basis is calculated through the use of a basis factor (bf). We can calculate the basis factor based on the optimal depth formula above and deduce the formula below:

bf = N/b

where:

bf = basis factor

The basis factor is used to recalculate the basis in situations where the scene setup is the same and only the camera translation and rotation has changed. In these situations, the near point changes a lot, and we can benefit from recalculating the basis the following way:

b = N/bf

where:

bf = basis factor found from the initial scene setup

Giantism and Lilliputism

It should be noted that if the camera basis is smaller than the distance between the eyes (retinal disparity), the result is called *giantism*. If the basis is bigger than the distance between the eyes, it is called *lilliputism*. These artifacts can be useful in situations where the amount of stereo isn't good enough. If we are simulating a large terrain, it's difficult to get good stereo from objects far away. In this case, we can use a larger basis resulting in artificial depth on the distant objects (lilliputism – *model effect*). The opposite scenario could also be the case if we had a game concentrated on nano-technology and we needed to visualize small objects. In this case, we can get a good stereo effect by using a smaller basis (giantism).

Now that our basis is set up correctly, let's talk about how these two virtual cameras are used within a dynamic scene with frequent camera transformation updates.

Camera Transformation

Since it is important that the two virtual cameras maintain their basis within the lifetime of the application, we must guarantee that the transformations made to the cameras don't break this individual relationship. So, instead of using a traditional lookat function directly on the left and right camera, you should use a dummy matrix.

If our scene graph contains a forward kinematics/attachment system, it's easy to make a dummy actor and attach the two cameras to this actor, which is the one controlled and moved around by the user. If that isn't the case, we need to use a matrix stack or multiply the dummy element and camera matrices. In either case, we have to set the initial transformation for the virtual cameras.

Initial Transformation

This is a fairly simple step. By initializing the virtual camera's transformation matrix to the identity matrix and only offsetting them in x direction by the basis, we can multiply them with the camera dummy's transformation matrix and maintain the correct basis even after the camera is translated and rotated arbitrarily.

A common mistake is to offset the cameras with a +/– basis, resulting in a distance between the cameras of 2*basis. This can be fixed by offsetting with +/– basis/2.

1	0	0	+/– Basis/2
0	1	0	Y
0	0	1	Z
0	0	0	1

The illustrations below show the setup. Here the cameras are initially positioned attached to a dummy — or at least transformed by a dummy matrix. Then the "stereo-camera" can be moved around freely.

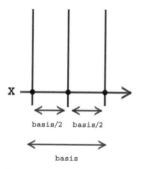

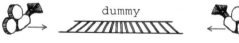

Figure 10: The cameras are attached to a dummy or manipulated by a matrix stack.

Figure 9: Initial x offset of the cameras to set up the parallel aiming lines with the basis distance

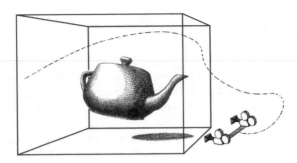

Figure 11: The dummy object can be moved freely around the scene. Traditional matrix math guarantees that the parallel aiming lines and the basis are maintained.

Stereo Window

When looking at a stereo image that has a correct basis setup, we will typically have some objects in the scene behind the screen plane and some objects in front of the screen plane.

For static images or prerendered movies, we have a good chance of controlling how and where this is happening, but for real-time graphics, we can't guarantee what the user is doing and the user will consequently get into situations where the stereo perception will break down (diplopia).

The problem arises when an object located outside of the screen is suddenly clipped by the screen's border. This doesn't happen in the real world. Neither will an object that is located farther away block an object located nearer in a real-world situation. In these situations, the brain receives conflicting depth information and the stereoscopic effect is destroyed.

One trick is to use blurry borders (StereoWindowSuppress), since this will blur out the artifact for the brain and make it more believable. However, this doesn't look good on ordinary scenes, but for a sniper rifle or submarine periscope, this could be a good solution.

A general solution though is to move the conflicting object behind the stereo window, resulting in a more positive parallax. In practice, this means that we push our scene into the screen until the objects clipped by the border are behind the border, resulting in correct stereo perception by the brain.

Figure 12: An object located in front of the stereo window but clipped by the border of the screen. This results in bad stereo perception.

Figure 13: The object is moved behind the stereo window, resulting in a correct perception of depth.

Image Offset

Traditionally, offsetting the "left" and "right" images in the horizontal direction does this. The "left" is moved in one horizontal direction, and the "right" is moved in the other. Consequently, this results in missing pixels at the left and right borders. Since we are working in a virtual world, we do not always have to do things the traditional way, so why not do the offsetting at the matrix projection level?

Matrix Offset

By offsetting at the matrix projection level, we do exactly the same thing as the image offsetting, but since we are doing it at matrix level, we do not get the artifacts of missing pixels. To do this, we need to look at the projection matrix:

??	0	+/– stereo window offset	0
0	??	??	0
0	0	??	??
0	0	1	0

Notice that even though we pushed the rendered scene into the screen in this situation to fix a stereo artifact, we could also use the same technique to move things out of the screen, making them fly over the keyboard. Just make sure that the screen borders don't clip the objects, since that ruins the stereo effect, as stated earlier. Also make sure that a hyper-/hypo-stereo artifact doesn't appear.

Stereo Window — Basis Relationship

Since both the basis and stereo window are manipulating the parallax of the final stereoscopic image, it should be noted that these two depend on each other. Sometimes we have to readjust the basis when the stereo window is set and vice versa. Unfortunately, the relationship in many ways depends on the given scene, so a general rule can't be set forth. It is a subjective evaluation by a person used to looking at stereoscopic images. Advanced formulas can be used, but in the end it still depends on the scene's content. So, for this article we do not go into depth on that aspect.

Compositing

When rendering a scene in stereo, we need to render the scene twice, one for each eye. Two virtual cameras (left and right eye) render the scene from its point of view, resulting in a slight difference, which is used by our brain to calculate the depth. This is exactly the same case when we look at the real world through our eyes.

We cannot render the scene directly to the frame buffer, since we have to post-process the two rendered scenes into a final stereoscopic image. We therefore store the intermediate result in a separate render target for later use, one for each eye.

Render Targets

In DirectX, render targets are either handled as a surface (IDirect3DSurface9) or as a texture (IDirect3DTexture9). Since we need the render target to be able to be used as a texture later on, we do not use the CreateRenderTarget(...) method, since it creates a surface (IDirect3DSurface9). Instead, we use the traditional CreateTexture(...) method. We have to create a new texture by using the D3DUSAGE_RENDERTARGET flag, and we have to allocate it in the default memory pool by using the D3DPOOL_DEFAULT. The memory is updated per frame and is therefore too expensive for the texture manager to update. On the backside, this means that we have to check if the target is lost and restore/recreate it if this is the case.

For the final image presentation, a screen-sized quad is used, which renders the scene by using the two render targets as texture inputs and using a pixel shader to do the actual mixing of the pictures.

Vertex Format

The quad's vertex format can be constructed in different ways, depending on what kind of information we need. One common part though is the transformed position of the position.

```
struct Vertex
{
    float x,y,z,w;
    .
    .
    .
};
```

After this declaration, we continue on and allocate a vertex buffer containing the four corners of the screen (0,0,1024,768). Remember to set the w value to 1.

```
LPDIRECT3DVERTEXBUFFER9 vb;
CreateVertexBuffer(4*sizeof(Vertex),0,D3DFVF_XYZRHW | ..., D3DPOOL_MANAGED, &vb, NULL);
```

Rendering

Later on in the rendering pipeline, we do the actual rendering by setting the pipeline up in the following way:

Set the current stream: SetStreamSource(0, vb, 0, sizeof(Vertex));
In this case we do not use any vertex shader: SetVertexShader(NULL);
Set the vertex format used in the creation: SetFVF(D3DFVF_XYZRHW | ...);
Set the stereoscopic pixel shader: SetPixelShader(...);
Set left render target: SetTexture(0,...);
Set right render target: SetTexture(1,...);
Draw the quad: DrawPrimitive(D3DPT_TRIANGLESTRIP,0,2);

Pixel Shader Implementation

Doing stereoscopic rendering using pixel shaders doesn't include shutter glasses, polarized glasses, and similar devices, since these solutions require a special hardware setup. We only make use of the 3D hardware, the monitor, and some special glasses.

We look into three different methods: the traditional anaglyph, an enhanced anaglyph (ColorCode 3-D), and finally the ChromaDepth system.

Traditional Anaglyph

Anaglyph is widely known from the '50s as the special "red/green" glasses that people use in cinemas to get an extra illusion of realism. The system is quite simple and only requires some cheap cardboard viewers with a red filter covering the left eye and a green filter covering the right. The system gives good perception of depth but lacks the reproduction of color. Later the system was expanded to be a red/cyan solution, in which colors were better preserved since no color information was discarded. A red/cyan pixel shader can be found in the following code.

```
ps.1.1  // GeForce 3 class hardware support
def c0, 1.0f, 0.0f, 0.0f, 0.0f   // R separation mask (for left).
def c1, 0.0f, 1.0f, 1.0f, 0.0f   // GB separation mask (for right).

tex t0            // Declaration of left.
tex t1            // Declaration of right.

// Left
mul r1, t0, c0    // Remove GB channels.

// Right
mad r0, t1,c1, r1    // Add GB to R.
```

The shader starts off by removing the GB channels from the left RGB input. This is done by multiplying R*1, G*0, and B*0; the result is saved in r1. The second step multiplies the right RGB input: R*0, G*1, and B*1 and adds the saved result from r1. Finally, it outputs the result to r0. In short, the shader takes the R from the left and the GB from the right and forms a new RGB value that is output.

Colors

Even though the creation of the red/cyan anaglyph system was a great improvement to the red/green and red/blue system, it didn't make it all the way. The problem is that the red/cyan filters separate both color and depth, and the eye-brain system can only manage to recombine the depth information — not the colors. This has resulted in a quite good stereo effect but very limited and distorted colors, plus a very possible stereoscopic sheen.

ColorCode 3-D

In 1997 a Danish scientist found that instead of splitting both color and depth between the eyes, it would be easier for the brain to use one eye for color and one for depth. The result was ColorCode 3-D. In many ways the ColorCode 3-D system is similar to the traditional anaglyph system. The big difference is the way the picture is stereo encoded and later decoded by the glasses and the brain. At first, it seems like the ColorCode 3-D system hurts the eyes more than the traditional anaglyph system, but after a few seconds the brain adapts to this system and you experience stereo in full color.

Ghosting

Both shutter glasses, polarized glasses, and anaglyph-based systems lack a 100 percent perfect separation of the left and right image. Consequently, this results in a "ghosting" effect, where some of the left image can be seen by the right eye and vice versa. The ColorCode 3-D system has greatly reduced this problem by using a finalizing step in its encoding of pixels. By implementing a special ghost-removing algorithm, special color correction steps, etc., the final result gets rid of most of the ghosting and other color artifacts.

Since the appearance of programmable hardware, the ColorCode 3-D encoding and color correction/ghost removal steps have been possible to implement using pixel shader 1.1 and above. It must be implemented as a two-step solution on ps < 1.4 and can be implemented as a single-step solution on ps >= 1.4 by using the *phase* instruction. The system is protected by patent and license, so I can't show the full pixel shader here, but a pseudocode version of pixel shader 1.4 can be found in the following code. Additionally, a screen shot of the output is shown in Color Plate 18.

```
ps.1.4 // // ATI Radeon 8500 class hardware support

def c0, 1.0f, 1.0f, 0.0f, 0.0f   // RG separation mask (for left).
def c1, 0.0f, 0.0f, 1.0f, 0.0f   // B separation mask (for right).
def c2, ...                      // Weights for right blue channel.
def c3, 1.0f, 1.0f, 1.0f, 0.0f   // Mask for collapsing weighted RGB values into B.

texld r0,t0        // Declaration of left.
texld r1,t1        // Declaration of right.

// Left - calculate color
mul r3, r0, c0        // Remove B channel, and store in r3

// Right - Calculate depth
mul r0, r1, c2        // Compose new B value as a weighted RGB value
dp3 r0, r0, c3        // Collapse RGB values into a grayscale
mad r0, r0, c1, r3    // Separate B and add to existing RG result in r3
```

```
phase

texld r2,r0              // Dependent lookup in a volume texture using rgb as uvw
mov r0,r2                // Result of full color-converted ColorCode encoding
```

The shader starts by removing all blue from the left RGB. A balanced grayscale is then made from the right RGB values, which are added as the blue channel. Lastly, the result is stored in r0. In ps<1.4, we would have to handle the final color conversion in different ways, but with pixel shader 1.4 and above we can do a simple dependent read from a volume texture containing the correction. Originally, this was a full 256x256x256 volume, but testing has shown that good results can be attained by using only a 32x32x32 texture and linear filtering/interpolation of colors.

ChromaDepth

As a special artistic stereoscopic phenomenon, the ChromaDepth should be mentioned. Forget for a moment all that we have been running through — of stereo settings, basis, etc. — and imagine that we just render our scene to the graphics card the traditional way. By doing this, we actually have a 3D picture of our scene already (color and depth buffer). By visualizing the depth buffer, we actually get a stereoscopic view of our scene. No colors can be reproduced, since the colors are used to reproduce the depth, but for special gaming situations and/or artistic setup, the ChromaDepth should be considered a viable solution. The technology uses the fact that red has a different bandwidth than blue, and by using some ChromaDepth viewers from ChromaTek, we are able to experience red as close and blue as far. A ChromaDepth shader can be found in the following code:

```
vs.2.0 // ATI Radeon 9700, nVidia GeForceFX class hardware support

dcl_position v0

def c4, 300.0f, 800.0f, 0.0f, 0.0f // Near plane & far plane

m4x4 r0, v0, c0          // Transform position to screen space
mov oPos, r0             // Output position

sub r0.z, r0.z, c4.x     // Get distance from near plane
sub r0.y, c4.y, c4.x     // Get distance from near to far plane
rcp r0.w, r0.y           // Calculate 1/w
mul r0.z, r0.z, r0.w     // Scale z by 1/w
mov oT0.xy, r0.zw        // Output texture coord
ps_2_0                   // ATI Radeon 9700, nVidia GeForceFX class hardware support

dcl_t0.xy                // Texture coord contains scaled z(0..1)
dcl_2d s0

add r1, t0.x, c0.x       // Add stereo window offset to scaled z
texld r1, r1, s0         // Use scaled z as texture coord
mov oC0,r1               // Output color
```

The ChromaDepth encoding is split into two shaders. The vertex shader retrieves the z, scales it to fit within a [0..1] range value, and outputs it as a texture coordinate. Once that is done, the pixel shader only needs to take the z (located in t0.x), adjust the calculated texture coordinates (to simulate the stereo window), and do a lookup into a 1D texture. The texel retrieved is then output.

Stereo Comparison

Looking at the different results from the three types of encoding shaders, it's clear that they all give a feeling of depth but are very different at the same time.

Anaglyph

The traditional anaglyph is easy to implement, and it is widely used. Consequently, a lot of viewers are already out there, resulting in a lot of potential users. It also gives good quality stereo. On the downside, it is lacking in the reproduction of color.

ColorCode 3-D

ColorCode 3-D takes care of the color problem. It's a bit more difficult to use for the very first time, but after a few seconds, the picture is clearly much better. The stereo quality is even comparable with the much more expensive shutter glass systems because the ColorCode 3-D system uses a post-processing step where the picture is finalized and the stereo artifacts removed. On the downside, ColorCode 3-D isn't that widely used, and it is protected by a patent, so you have to contact ColorCode 3-D Ltd. for more information on the full hardware-accelerated ColorCode 3-D implementation.

ChromaDepth

ChromaDepth is the only system using clear separation filters. This results in both good stereo and clean colors. Unfortunately, the whole system's depth encoding is based on the visible spectrum of colors to reproduce stereo. So, for generic use, the system isn't very usable. Also, it should be noted that since the system uses clear filters, the separation isn't that good, resulting in a lot of ghosting. However, if we need to create artistic stereo that from the start has been designed for ChromaDepth, the system is good. Finally, we have shown that a ChromaDepth shader can be implemented as a visualization of the depth buffer, resulting in minimal rendering overhead (the scene needs to be rendered only once), so it is clearly the fastest method of doing stereo if colors aren't needed.

Conclusion

It has been proven scientifically that stereo images improve visual perception by as much as 400 percent. Stereo is a direction on the road to a more realistic simulation of reality. Therefore, stereo must be considered an option on the same level as more geometry, better light calculations, smoother shadows, more detailed textures, etc.

Viewing Ortho-, Hypo-, and Hyper-stereo

It should be noted that when a given scene is viewed from the same initial position as it was first recorded, it is called ortho-stereo. The normal goal for stereoscopic rendering is to achieve the highest possible reproduction of the initial scene. However, if the scene is viewed from a closer distance, it results in less stereo (hypo-stereo), and if the distance is larger, there is more stereo (hyper-stereo). These general rules should be kept in mind when presenting stereoscopic images on bigger screens for audiences, etc.

Future Implementation

Even though these general stereoscopic setup rules hold for both current and future stereoscopic systems that make use of virtual camera setups, there are still issues to consider. Traditionally, game development has included a lot of tricks and hacks to make it all work in real time. One of these hacks is to make use of imposters for complex imaging. Particles, flares, beams, trees, grass, etc., all make use of some kind of "quad-based" system. This works fine for traditional non-stereo 3D applications, but if translated into a stereo system directly, these illusions are suddenly noticeable by the viewer. A flat quad-based flare appears flat and consequently destroys the illusion of a glowing ball of fire.

The solution is to use even more advanced shaders, where depth is considered and a kind of fake depth image is made, resulting in a correct visual appearance when viewed in stereo. Depth sprites might be one of the steps in the right direction, but research must be done in this area.

Acknowledgments

Svend B. Sørensen, ColorCode 3-D Ltd., www.colorcode3d.com.

Tammy Barnett and William K. Chiles, American Paper Optics, www.chromatek.com.

Niels Husted Kjær, Medical Insight, www.medical-insight.com.

Mark Rudings, Titoonic, www.titoonic.com.

Illustrations: Kristina Gordon, Dotrix, www.dotrix.dk.

Modeling: Thomas Suurland, www.suurland.com.

Hatching, Stroke Styles, and Pointillism

Kevin Buchin and Maike Walther

http://page.inf.fu-berlin.de/~buchin/npr/

Introduction

Hatching is a common technique used in non-photorealistic rendering (NPR). For hatching, a series of strokes are combined into textures. These compositions of strokes can convey the surface form through stroke orientation, the surface material through stroke arrangement and style, and the effect of light on the surface through stroke density.

Up until now, an important issue of real-time hatching techniques has been how to employ the limited programmability of the graphics hardware currently available. Pixel programmability has now reached a state where we can shift the focus to adding more flexibility to the hatching scheme and combining hatching with other techniques for creating new effects.

We present a hatching scheme and some extensions to it, namely changing the stroke style interactively and hatching with specular highlights. Then we show how we integrate hand drawings into a scene, taking into account the effect of lighting. Finally, we show how to choose a color for each stroke — depending on the background color — that can be used for a pointillistic style.

Approaches to Hatching

For hatching, strokes have to be chosen from a collection of possible strokes to convey some tonal value. A possible approach to this problem is to think of each stroke having a priority and choose strokes according to their priority (i.e., using only the most important strokes for light tonal values and adding less important strokes in areas of darker tonal values). Such collections of strokes are called *prioritized stroke textures* [Winkenbach94] and can be seen as the basis for current hatching schemes.

For real-time hatching, stroke textures for some specific tonal values and different mipmap levels can be precomputed and blended at run time according to the given tonal value [Praun01]. To maintain a constant stroke width in screen space, the mipmap levels contain strokes of the same texel width. Thus, higher mipmap levels contain fewer strokes than lower mipmap levels for representing the same tonal value. This technique can be implemented using pixel shaders, as presented in the first ShaderX book [Card02].

Prioritized stroke textures can also be implemented using a *thresholding scheme* (i.e., encoding intensity thresholds and information on resulting color values in a texture). For instance, this information can be differences in tone [Webb02]. While strokes fade in gradually when blending stroke textures for given tonal values, using a thresholding scheme lets strokes appear more suddenly.

There is more to hatching than the actual rendering. In particular, texture-based hatching only works well with an appropriate texture parameterization. An overview of the complete hatching process is given in [Domine01]. Here we focus on the shader used for hatching.

Our Thresholding Scheme

Our approach is to encode a stroke by its color and intensity threshold. Figure 1 shows a sample stroke texture with grayscale values (a) and corresponding intensity thresholds (b). An advantage of this approach is that we don't need to decide how the stroke color is combined with the background color (for instance, adding, overlaying, modulating, or replacing the background color) when creating the textures.

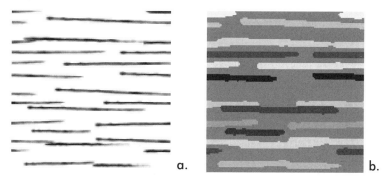

Figure 1: (a) A texture containing the stroke colors as grayscale values, (b) a texture containing the corresponding intensity thresholds

The stroke colors can be stored in the RGB channels of a texture and the corresponding intensity thresholds in the alpha-channel of the same texture. To be able to distinguish the color values and intensity thresholds of the different strokes in one texture, the texture may not contain overlapping strokes. For drawing overlapping strokes, we use several textures (for instance, two for horizontal strokes and two for vertical strokes). Instead of actually using several textures, we can reuse one stroke texture by translating and/or rotating the original texture coordinates. To keep the pixel shader simple, we do this in the vertex shader by adding several texture coordinates to the output Out and — for two horizontal and two vertical stroke textures — the following lines:

```
Out.Tex0 = Tex0;
Out.Tex1 = Tex0 + offset1.xy;
Out.Tex2 = Tex0.yx + offset1.zw;
Out.Tex3 = Tex0.yx + offset2.xy;
```

To each stroke texture we assign an intensity interval *[start, end]* and map the threshold *t* in the alpha channel to this interval by *start + t/(end-start)*. After computing a desired intensity, we can modulate the background color with the stroke color using the following lines of code:

```
float4 stroke = tex2D(stroke_sampler, Tex0);
color *= (intensity < start + stroke.a/q) ? stroke.rgb : 1.0;
```

...with *q = end-start*. In the pixel shader, we compute an intensity using a lighting model and, again in the case of two horizontal and two vertical applications of one stroke texture, add the following lines:

```
float3 color = background_color.rgb;
float4 stroke = tex2D(stroke_sampler, Tex0);

color *= (intensity < 0.75 + stroke.a/4) ? stroke.rgb : 1.0;
stroke = tex2D(stroke_sampler, Tex1);
color *= (intensity < 0.5 + stroke.a/4) ? stroke.rgb : 1.0;
stroke = tex2D(stroke_sampler, Tex2);
color *= (intensity < 0.25 + stroke.a/4) ? stroke.rgb : 1.0;
stroke = tex2D(stroke_sampler, Tex3);
color *= (intensity < stroke.a/4) ? stroke.rgb : 1.0;

return float4(color.r, color.g, color.b, background_color.a);
```

A teapot rendered with this technique is shown in Figure 2.

Figure 2: A teapot hatched using our thresholding scheme

Varying the Line Style

We can extend the above technique to allow variation of the hatching strokes at run time. For this, we do not encode strokes directly into a stroke texture but instead encode lookups into single-stroke textures. We call these textures *stroke-lookup textures.*

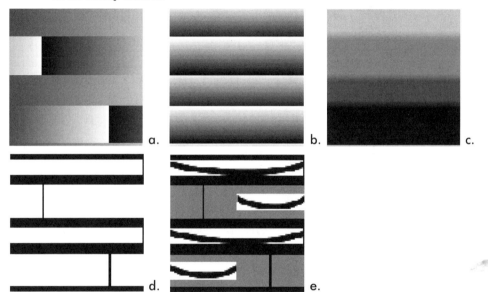

a.　b.　c.

d.　e.

Figure 3: (a) – (d) show the RGBA channels of a stroke-lookup texture and (e) is an illustration of a lookup. (a) shows the R channel that contains the lookup in s, (b) the G channel that contains the lookup in t, (c) the B channel that contains the threshold, and (d) the A channel that is used as a stencil.

A simple example of a stroke-lookup texture is shown in Figure 3. The channels R and G store the lookups in t and s, channel B stores the threshold, and alpha is used as a stencil to prevent incorrect interpolation. For achieving a roughly uniform screen width of the strokes — as in hand-drawn hatchings — we use mipmap levels with strokes of the same texel size. Standard generation of mipmap levels would halve the texel width of a stroke in each level, thus strokes farther away from the viewer would be thinner than those close to the viewer. For correct interpolation between these mipmap levels, we extend the stroke-lookup coordinates from [0,1] to [–0.5,1.5]. For this we scale the texture coordinates appropriately, as illustrated in Figure 4.

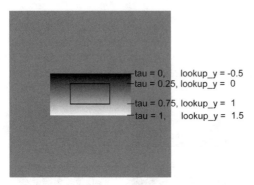

Figure 4: Illustration of the texture coordinates tau and scaled stroke-lookup coordinates lookup_x and lookup_y

The above calculations have to be adapted in the following way:

```
float4 lookup = tex2D(stroke_lookup_sampler, Tex0);
lookup.xy = (lookup.xy - 0.25)*2;
bool stroke_flag = (intensity < interv.x + interv.y*lookup.b) && (lookup.a > 0.99);
color *= stroke_flag ? tex2D(single_stroke_sampler, lookup.xy) : 1.0;
```

For different strokes, we use lookups into several different single-stroke textures. For this, we use an additional texture with indices for single-stroke textures. Alternatively, we could encode the indices into the stenciling channel. To keep the pixel shader simple, we assume that we have done the lighting computation in the vertex shader. The simple pixel shader, using lookups into two different single-stroke textures — a short and a long stroke — could look like this:

```
float4 getStrokeColor(float2 texCoord, float shiftedIntensity) {
    float4 lookup = tex2D(stroke_lookup_sampler, texCoord);
    lookup.xy = (lookup.xy - 0.25)*2;
    float stroke = tex2D(index, texCoord);
    float4 stroke_color =  (stroke < 0.5) ?
    tex2D(short_stroke, lookup.xy) : tex2D(long_stroke, lookup.xy);
    bool stroke_flag = (lookup.w > 0.99) && (shiftedIntensity < lookup.z/4.0);
    stroke_color = stroke_flag ? stroke_color : 1.0;
    return stroke_color;
}

float4 main(
    float2 Tex0  : TEXCOORD0,
    float2 Tex1  : TEXCOORD1,
    float2 Tex2  : TEXCOORD2,
    float2 Tex3  : TEXCOORD3,
    float2 Tex4  : TEXCOORD4,
    float4 Diff  : COLOR0 ) : COLOR
{
    float4 color = 1.0;
    color *= getStrokeColor(Tex0, Diff.x - 0.75);
    color *= getStrokeColor(Tex0, Diff.x - 0.75);
    color *= getStrokeColor(Tex1, Diff.x - 0.5);
```

```
    color *= getStrokeColor(Tex2, Diff.x - 0.25);
    color *= getStrokeColor(Tex3, Diff.x - 0.0);
    return color;
}
```

Figure 5 shows the use of different stroke styles in combination with specular highlights.

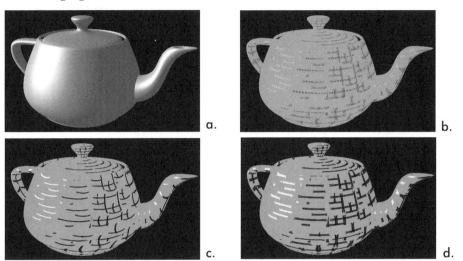

Figure 5: (a) A shaded teapot and (b) – (d) the same teapot hatched with specular highlights and different stroke styles

Hatching with Specular Highlights

So far, we have used strokes only to darken a rendition where the desired intensity is below a certain threshold. But we can also draw light strokes — assuming the background is not white. We use this for drawing specular highlights. To draw light strokes, we just need to check whether the intensity is above a given threshold. We can use the same stroke textures as for dark strokes — and possibly combine dark and light strokes — by taking one minus the previous threshold to maintain the stroke priorities. This effect is illustrated in Figure 5.

Lighting Hand-drawn Illustrations

Hatching can be used for lighting a hand-drawn illustration and integrating it into a 3D scene. We use billboards for placing the illustration in the scene. For the lighting computation, we need to provide normals for the illustration. We do this by roughly approximating our hand drawing by simple primitives and rendering these with a pixel shader outputting the color-encoded (normalized) normal vectors or with a normalization cube map. Using the normals, we choose which strokes to draw according to the light. Figure 6 (a) shows a hand-drawn image that we approximated with the shape in (b) and placed in a scene in (c).

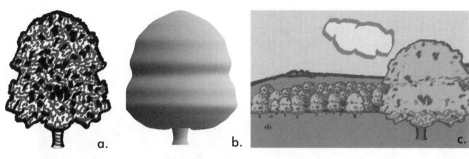

Figure 6: (a) A hand-drawn image as input, (b) approximation of the shape, (c) resulting image in a 3D scene (See Color Plate 19.)

Stroke Colors and Pointillism

The last effect chose the stroke color according to the background color. The resulting strokes were unicolored simply because the background color of one stroke did not change. In the case of varying background or base color for a stroke, we would still like to draw unicolored strokes — as is typical for stroke-based illustrations, such as mosaics, oil paintings, and many others. We can do this by encoding offsets into the strokes, which are used for reading the base color so that all points of a stroke read the same color. Figure 7 shows the R channel of such a stroke. The brush uses values from black (0) to white (1). This value has to be scaled by the maximal relative brush width and height `offset_scale.xy` in the pixel shader. If brushes of different sizes are used simultaneously, smaller brushes should use values from a smaller interval. The code for modifying the texture coordinate used to determine the base color could look like this:

```
float2 offset = (tex2D(offset_sampler, Tex.xy*scale).xy - 0.5) * offset_scale.xy / scale;
float2 newTex = Tex + offset;
```

Used on its own, this technique can create a pointillistic style. Figure 8 shows some examples.

Conclusion

Pixel shaders offer great possibilities for implementing stroke-based rendering techniques. As examples of this we have shown a hatching scheme and several effects extending this scheme. We hope that these examples may serve as an inspiration for the many more effects that are possible.

Figure 7: R channel of the texture with the brush used in Figure 8 and the relative maximal brush width `offset_scale.x`.

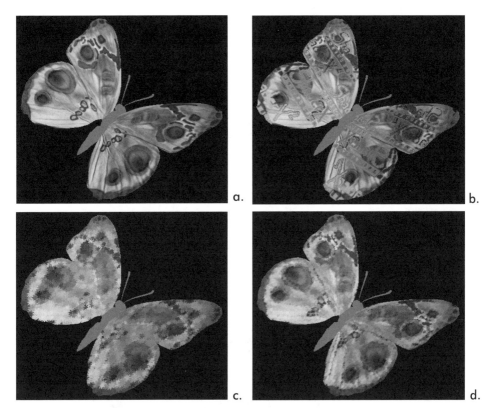

Figure 8: The RenderMonkey Iridescent Butterfly rendered (a) without the effect, (b) using a brush in form of the word "ShaderX²," (c) and (d) using the brush shown in Figure 7 with different values for scale.

References

[Card02] Card, Drew and Jason Mitchell, "Non-Photorealistic Rendering with Pixel and Vertex Shaders," *Direct3D ShaderX: Vertex and Pixel Shader Tips and Tricks*, Wolfgang Engel, ed., Wordware Publishing, 2002, pp. 319-333.

[Domine01] Dominé, Sébastien, Ashu Rege, and Cem Cebenoyan, "Real-Time Hatching (Tribulations in)," GDC, 2001.

[Praun01] Praun, Emil, Hugues Hoppe, Matthew Webb, and Adam Finkelstein, "Real-Time Hatching," proceedings of SIGGRAPH 2001, pp. 581-586.

[Webb02] Webb, Matthew, Emil Praun, Adam Finkelstein, and Hugues Hoppe, "Fine Tone Control in Hardware Hatching," proceedings of NPAR 2002, pp. 53-ff.

[Winkenbach94] Winkenbach, Georges and David H. Salesin, "Computer-Generated Pen-and-Ink Illustration," proceedings of SIGGRAPH 1994, pp. 91-100.

Layered Fog

Guillaume Werle

Montecristo Games

Overview

Vertical or layered fog can drastically change the mood and realism level of the scenes produced by your rendering engine. It is also probably one of the easiest effects that you can implement using shaders. If you're learning shaders and want quick, good-looking results, this article is for you.

Figure 1: Volumetric fog in action

As shown in Figure 1, the basic idea is to use the height from some plane instead of the depth or distance from the viewpoint as the density factor. The technique described in this article computes the height on a per-vertex basis and uses the texture coordinate interpolator to get per-pixel precision. This way, the faces don't have to be split at the fog's boundaries.

Integrating Fog in Your Engine

The key to success when designing a shader-driven engine is modularity. To increase efficiency and reduce the number of shaders needed, the rendering should be split into independent passes.

Since it uses alpha blending, fog needs to be computed and rendered in the final stage of the rendering pipeline. D3D's blending render states need to be set in the following way to mix the fog with the frame buffer content:

```
SetRenderState(D3DRS_ALPHABLENDENABLE, TRUE);
SetRenderState(D3DRS_SRCBLEND, D3DBLEND_SRCALPHA);
SetRenderState(D3DRS_DESTBLEND, D3DBLEND_INVSRCALPHA);
```

Depth precision issues (also known as Z-fighting) may appear when using multiple passes for rendering. A little bit of tweaking of your projection matrix should eliminate these artifacts. Additional information on this topic can be found on Tom Forsyth's web page at http://tomsdxfaq.blogspot.com/2002_07_01_tomsdxfaq_archive.html#79344425.

Density Formula

Since the density of the fog is based on its height, we want to have maximum opacity at the low boundary of our fog range (*FogLowRange*) and no fog at all when our height is equal or above the high boundary (*FogHighRange*).

Using this very simple formula, we get a coefficient representing this value.

$$VertexDelta = (FogHighRange-VertexHeight)$$

$$FogDelta = (FogHighRange-FogLowRange)$$

$$VertexDensity = \frac{VertexDelta}{FogDelta}$$

Implementation

Since we can't divide in a vertex shader, we have to multiply *VertexDelta* by the reciprocal of *FogDelta (InvFogDelta)*.

$$InvFogDelta = \frac{1.0}{FogHighRange - FogLowRange}$$

$$VertexDensity = (FogHighRange-VertexHeight)*InvFogDelta$$

Now, let's take a look at the vertex shader implementation:

```
vs.1.1

// constants 0 1 2 3 = world * view * projection matrix
m4x4 oPos, v0, c0        // vertex in screenspace output
```

```
mov oT0, v7              // copy diffuse texture coordinates

// constants 4 5 6 7 = world matrix
dp4 r0, v0, c5           // vertex y position in world space

// constant 8 = (FogHighRange, InvFogDelta, 0.0f , 1.0f)
sub r0, c8.xxxx, r0      // (high - y)
mul oT1, r0, c8.yyyy     // output = (high - y) * InvFogDelta
```

The density value might exceed the range [0.0 → 1.0], but this isn't an issue. The density value will be interpreted in the pixel shader using the texcoord instuction. This opcode interprets texture coordinates as RGBA values and will clamp them.

The final pixel density also depends on the camera height. *CameraDensity* can be computed using the same formula as the vertex density. This value should be computed only one time per frame and then passed to the pixel shader using a constant register. This value will need to be clamped in the range [0.0 → 1.0].

The diffuse texture might use alpha blending for transparency, so we also need to take this into account.

If we summarize the above, we end up with this formula:

FogPixel.a = saturate(VertexDensity+CameraDensity)*FogColor.a*Diffuse.a
FogPixel.rgb = FogColor.rgb

Here is the pixel shader implementation:

```
ps.1.1

tex    t0              // diffuse texture
texcoord   t1          // vd = vertex density
                       // t1 = (vd, vd, vd, 1.0f)

// c2 = red mask (1.0f , 0.0f, 0.0f, 0.0f)
dp3   r0, t1, c2       // copy the red component everywhere
                       // r0 = (vd, vd, vd, vd)

// cd = camera density
// c1 = (cd, cd, cd, cd)
add_sat r0, r0, c1     // VertexDensity + CameraDensity

// c0 = fog color
mul    r0, r0, c0      // c0.a = fog density
mul    r0, r0, t0      // diffuse texture opacity

mov    r0.rgb, c0      // output
                       // r0.rgb  = fog color
                       // r0.a= fog density
```

NOTE   The DirectX documentation states that the alpha value of a pixel fetched with the texcoord instruction should be 1.0, but I haven't seen any piece of hardware that follows this rule. You usually get the .w value passed by the vertex shader.

Final Words

I implemented this shader for a demo scene application called Raw Confession. The demo can be found on the companion CD or downloaded from my web page: http://cocoon.planet-d.net/raw/!Raw_Beta.zip.

Special thanks to Jeff Kiel from nVidia for proofreading this article.

Dense Matrix Algebra on the GPU

Ádám Moravánszky

NovodeX AG

Introduction

Perhaps the most important innovation of the latest generation of programmable graphics processors (GPUs) is their capability to work with floating-point color data. Previous generations of GPUs have worked with up to a byte of integer data per color channel. Developers working on graphics engines with advanced lighting effects often complained about banding artifacts, even in true-color video modes, because multiplicative effects quickly made the round-off error caused by the limited precision noticeable. The advent of GPUs that represent each color channel with a 32-bit floating-point value has thus been widely celebrated in the real-time graphics community.

More importantly, while 8-bit color channel precision is often adequate, the dynamic range is quite limited. Floating-point color buffers make it possible to work with brightness values well beyond the maximum value that can be represented in the final image. Though the dynamic range of output device stays the same, intermediate values during a computation are no longer clamped to this range. This way, a much more realistic simulation of lighting is possible, resulting in vibrant images.

The topic of this article is made possible by the emergence of floating-point color support as well, but we will not be dealing with either of the often-cited advantages of floating-point buffers described above. In fact, we will not be rendering images in the conventional sense at all. Instead, we look at the GPU as a powerful vector coprocessor to the CPU. We use it to solve two common problems in scientific computing: solving systems of linear equations and linear complementarity problems. Both of these problems come up in dynamics simulation, which is a field drawing increasing interest from the game developer community.

By implementing these algorithms on the GPU, we hope to achieve a performance gain or at least free up CPU resources, which can then be better spent running algorithms that are not vectorizable. Because the GPU usually has its hands full rendering graphics in a computer game, and because GPUs with floating-point color support are anything but widespread, the results of this article are initially primarily of theoretical interest for the game community. However, if we can show convincing performance figures that make such application of GPUs desirable, we may soon find these applications becoming practical and widespread. If GPU performance continues to grow at its present rate, we may eventually see researchers and engineers abandoning expensive supercomputers for clusters of GPU-equipped PCs.

Previous Work

The fundamental concept of linear algebra is the matrix. Matrices are used in simulation in order to describe a linear relationship in a concise way. A significant amount of research has gone into working with large dense matrices. BLAS (Basic Linear Algebra Subprograms) [2, 7] has emerged as the standard interface to linear algebra libraries. Freely available implementations of BLAS include ATLAS (Automatically Tuned Linear Algebra Software) [9], a linear algebra library that includes Intel SSE2 and AMD 3DNow optimized matrix multiply kernels. These fast kernels, combined with ATLAS' cache-friendly memory access pattern achieved by special ordering of the input data, make it one of the fastest dense matrix libraries available on the PC platform. In [6], Larsen and McAllister first investigated using GPUs for linear algebra. At the time of its publication, floating-point pixel processing was not yet available, so their results were not practical for real-world problems. The papers [1, 5], made available after this article was initially submitted, tackle the representation of sparse matrices on the GPU.

While ATLAS provides a selection of higher-level linear algebra operations, such as solving linear systems, the code of ATLAS is a high-performance matrix multiply kernel, which is then leveraged by the high-level operations. We follow the same principle in our GPU matrix library: We implement a few basic matrix operations using shaders, including matrix multiply, and then use these as building blocks to solve the higher level problems. While we have not written a full GPU BLAS implementation due to time constraints, we show how to implement all the basic components necessary for this goal.

Implementation

Our implementation consists of a matrix class that carries out all the core arithmetic operations. It interfaces with the GPU using the DirectX 9 Graphics SDK. The user interface is a script interpreter that parses matrix operation instructions out of a text stream, manages matrix variable names, reads and writes matrix variable data to file, and passes operations for execution to the matrix class. We discuss the matrix class below, as well as two examples of its use.

Matrix Textures

If the GPU is to perform large matrix multiplication for us, the first thing we need to do is represent the matrix data in a format that is accessible by the GPU. GPUs can in principle work on two basic types of data: geometry and texture maps. Textured geometry is preferable because of the more compact representation when compared with highly tessellated geometry with vertex colors. Also, unlike geometry, textures can be output by the GPU in the form of render target surfaces. If we store a matrix as a texture and then perform a matrix operation, such as matrix addition by rendering two textures with additive blending into a third render target surface, the storage format of the resulting matrix can be identical to the input format. This is a desirable property because this way we can immediately reuse the resulting texture as an input to another operation without having to perform format conversion.

We would like our library to work with matrices of real numbers because this domain is the most generally useful for simulation problems, especially dynamics simulation. Integers would be too restrictive, while complex numbers are usually not required. Note that the system we present could be extended to handle complex numbers should this be the case. Real numbers are most efficiently approximated on computers using floating-point numbers of various precisions. Unfortunately, GPUs still only support single-precision floating-point, and future support for double or higher precision is unlikely, as this sort of precision is not thought to be needed for graphics applications. Nonetheless, single-precision floating-point is adequate for many applications.

Storage Format

There are several ways in which the elements of a matrix can be mapped to the pixels of a texture image. Perhaps the most obvious approach would be to take a luminance (one channel per pixel) image and fill it with the matrix data using a direct mapping of elements to pixels in either row or column major format. The disadvantage is, of course, that GPUs are optimized to process RGBA pixels and thus have four-way SIMD for executing pixel shaders. A luminance texture would only use a quarter of the available bandwidth.

Instead, we pack four adjacent matrix elements into a single pixel's RGBA channels. The simplest possibilities are to either pack rows or columns of four. While this packing does make square matrices into 4:1 aspect rectangular textures, it makes the writing of the pixel shaders for multiplication quite straightforward. Other schemes, such as packing 2x2 rectangular submatrices into each pixel, complicates the pixel shaders for doing matrix multiplication and offers no clear advantage. It is interesting to note that CPU linear algebra packages like ATLAS primarily get their speed boost by storing the matrices in a convoluted but very cache-friendly way. Data locality is an important key to performance. Unfortunately, in contrast to CPU programming, we have only a relatively high-level control of the GPU. In particular, the order in which pixels get processed is an undocumented implementation detail. Usually, the GPU automatically stores textures in a swizzled form to improve cache coherence. It may be interesting to investigate if more exotic storage formats can boost performance, but one would have to do quite a bit of experimentation, without necessarily being able to generalize the results to different GPUs.

The final question regarding data storage is whether there is any difference between packing rows or columns of four into a pixel. One important difference comes up when we consider doing vector operations. It is important that pixels be created along the length of a vector, instead of across. In the latter case, a vector would only fill one color channel and leave three empty. In this implementation, we arbitrarily decided to go with storing CPU matrices in row major format and working with column vectors. Thus, we put 4×1 sub-column vectors into each pixel. The width of a texture that corresponds to an n×m matrix is thus m, while the height is $\left\lceil \dfrac{n}{4} \right\rceil$.

To create a matrix texture from some source data, we create an appropriately sized render target surface using the D3DFMT_A32B32G32R32F floating-point pixel format. We don't need any mipmapping; in fact, we render with point sampling to prevent texture filtering from falsifying our computations.

Creating a render target texture is technically only necessary if we want the matrix to serve as a destination for matrix operations; in our application, we choose not to keep track of this distinction and treat all matrices equally for the sake of simplicity.

Unfortunately in DirectX 9, it is not possible to lock render target surfaces, so we need to create an identically formatted temporary texture in the SYSTEMMEM pool. This texture's surface is then locked, and the matrix data is read into it. Finally we use the DirectX method UpdateTexture() to copy the temporary texture into our render target texture.

Reading back from the matrix texture happens in the same way. This time the method GetRenderTargetData() is used to copy from the matrix texture to the temporary texture.

Matrix Operations

After reading in the data, we are ready to perform some matrix operations. We start by implementing three basic operations — matrix assignment, addition, and multiplication. Later we will add some others as required by our higher level algorithms. Note that some operations are not strictly necessary and could be expressed using others. For example, assignment could be emulated by adding a zero matrix to the source matrix. Still, writing special-case code when optimizations are possible is a good idea.

Assignment

Matrix assignment is the most elementary operation, so we cover it first to introduce some details in our code:

```
void Matrix::copy(Matrix & other)   {
```

Note that while the reference rasterizer works fine with the render target surface being the same as one of the source textures, this case is not officially supported by Direct3D and should be avoided. In the case of assignment, it is obviously a null operation to assign a matrix to itself, so we can early out in this case.

```
if (this == &other)     return;
```

If the destination texture is not the same size as the source texture, it needs to be resized. We resize a texture by releasing it and creating a new one of the correct size.

```
resize(other.getNRows(), other.getNCols());
```

If one of the dimensions of the matrix is 0, there is nothing to do:

```
if (nRows * nCols == 0)      return;
```

Next, we set the destination texture as the render target, begin the scene, assign vertex and pixel shaders, and assign the source texture to the 0th sampler. For this simple operation, we do not really need shader support and could do the same operation with the fixed-function pipeline and texture combiners. On the other hand, any hardware that supports floating-point pixel formats will most likely have shader support as well, so we might as well use them. We omit DirectX error handling in the cited code for clarity.

```
d3dDevice->SetRenderTarget(0,mathSurface);
d3dDevice->BeginScene();
d3dDevice->SetVertexShader( vertexShaders[VS_SINGLE_TEX_QUAD] );
d3dDevice->SetPixelShader( pixelShaders[PS_COPY] );
d3dDevice->SetTexture(0,other.mathTexture);
```

Next, we render a single quadrilateral polygon that exactly covers the destination texture by using a triangle fan with four vertices. This is what our vertex buffer contains:

```
MathVertex quad[4]=  {
    // x        y
    { -1.0f, -1.0f},
    { +1.0f, -1.0f},
    { +1.0f, +1.0f},
    { -1.0f, +1.0f}};
```

We have 2D clip space coordinates for each vertex. Because we won't be rendering 3D shapes, and because texture coordinates can be trivially generated in the vertex shader from this basic data, it is all we need. We place this data into a managed pool vertex buffer and do not worry about it anymore. It is used for all the matrix operations except multiplication.

The actual rendering code looks like this:

```
d3dDevice->SetStreamSource( 0, quadVertexBuffer, 0, sizeof(MathVertex));
float TexcoordBiasW = (1.0f/cols2TextureWidth(nCols))  * 0.5f;
float TexcoordBiasH = (1.0f/rows2TextureHeight(nRows)) * 0.5f;
float consts[4 * 2] = {
    0.5, -0.5, 0.5, 1,
    0.5+ TexcoordBiasW, 0.5 + TexcoordBiasH, 0, 0 };
d3dDevice->SetVertexShaderConstantF(0, consts, 2);
d3dDevice->DrawPrimitive( D3DPT_TRIANGLEFAN, 0, 2 );
d3dDevice->EndScene();
}
```

The function of the texture coordinate bias values that get passed to the vertex shader is to line up the destination pixels with the source texel centers by shifting the texture coordinates by half a texel. If we were to omit this, at each pixel the texture would be sampled halfway between texels, making it effectively random which of the four neighboring texels the point sampling would pick.

cols2TextureWidth() and rows2TextureHeight() simply map matrix dimensions to texture dimensions using the formula mentioned previously:

```
inline unsigned roundUpDivide(unsigned a, unsigned b) { return (a + b-1) / b; }
inline unsigned rows2TextureHeight(unsigned rows) { return roundUpDivide(rows,4); }
inline unsigned cols2TextureWidth (unsigned cols) { return cols; }
```

The vertex shader we use, SINGLE_TEX_QUAD, is shown below:

```
// c0 = [  0.5, -0.5, 0.5, 1]
// c1 = [  0.5+ TexcoordBiasW,  0.5 + TexcoordBiasH, 0 , 0]
vs_1_1
dcl_position v0
mov oPos, v0
mov oPos.zw, c0.zw
mov r0, c1
mad oT0.xy, v0.xy, c0.xy, r0.xy
```

We basically emit the vertices that we put in the vertex buffer in clip space after assigning some constant values to the z and w coordinates. The texture coordinates are computed from the vertex position in a single instruction, which involves the flipping of the vertical axis and the application of the bias constants described above.

Finally, the pixel shader is shown below. It serves to simply copy the input texture to the destination surface:

```
//PS_COPY  out = tex0
ps_2_0
dcl_2d s0
dcl t0
texld r0, t0, s0
mov oC0, r0
```

We have tried using HLSL to produce these shaders, and several of them were prototyped that way, but the DirectX shader compiler failed to produce efficient code for the more involved matrix multiply cases, so we decided to stay with hand-coded assembly for this project. The use of pixel shader 2.0 or greater is necessary in the case of this simple shader not because of any special instructions or even the number of instructions, but because lower pixel shader versions automatically clamp their final result to [0,1]. We would like to use the entire floating-point range.

Addition

Addition is very similar to assignment. Because we have the limitation that the destination texture may not be the same as either of the source textures, we need to code both a general add and an accumulate (+=) operation. We only cover the binary version here because the accumulate version is the same as the above assignment with additive blending with the existing render target turned on.

```
void Matrix::add(Matrix & a, Matrix & b)    {
if (a.nRows != b.nRows || a.nCols != b.nCols)
    throw "matrix dimensions don't agree";


if     (this == &a)  {   add(b);return; }
else if (this == &b)  {   add(a);return; }


resize(a.nRows, a.nCols);


if (a.nRows * a.nCols == 0)  return;


d3dDevice->SetRenderTarget(0,mathSurface);
d3dDevice->BeginScene();
d3dDevice->SetVertexShader( vertexShaders[VS_SINGLE_TEX_QUAD] );
d3dDevice->SetPixelShader( pixelShaders[PS_ADD] );
d3dDevice->SetTexture(0,a.mathTexture);
d3dDevice->SetTexture(1,b.mathTexture);
d3dDevice->SetStreamSource( 0, quadVertexBuffer, 0, sizeof(MathVertex) );


float TexcoordBiasW = (1.0f/cols2TextureWidth(nCols))  * 0.5f;
float TexcoordBiasH = (1.0f/rows2TextureHeight(nRows)) * 0.5f;


float consts[4 * 2] = {
    0.5, -0.5, 0.5, 1,
    0.5+ TexcoordBiasW,  0.5 + TexcoordBiasH, 0, 0 };


d3dDevice->SetVertexShaderConstantF(0, consts, 2);
d3dDevice->DrawPrimitive( D3DPT_TRIANGLEFAN, 0, 2 );
d3dDevice->EndScene();
}
```

There are only a few places where the above differs from the assignment code. First, we need to check if the dimensions of the two source textures match; otherwise, the addition operation is mathematically undefined. We also check if one of the source operands is the same as the destination and call the special-case accumulate code in this case. The second texture is also assigned to the second texture sampler. We use the same vertex shader as before.

The pixel shader is a different one but not much more complicated; it simply performs additive blending of the two source textures:

```
//PS_ADD  out = tex0 + tex1
ps_2_0
dcl_2d s0
```

```
dcl_2d s1
dcl t0
texld r0, t0, s0
texld r1, t0, s1
add r0, r0, r1
mov oC0, r0
```

Multiplication

Writing a general matrix multiply is a bit more challenging because unlike addition, it doesn't reduce to mere image blending. Figure 1 shows the schematic for our matrix multiply procedure.

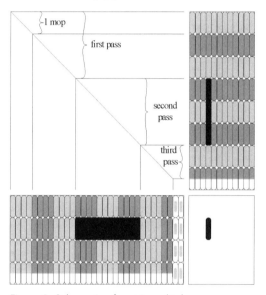

Figure 1: Schematic of matrix multiply

The texture corresponding to the left operand matrix A is shown on the left side. The texture of the right-side operand matrix B is at the top right. C, the result matrix, is shown at the bottom right. C = A B should hold after the operation completes.

By the definition of matrix multiplication, the number of columns in A has to equal the number of rows in B. We call this range of q numbers the *inner dimension*. Finally, the number of rows in A is equal to the number of rows in C, and the number of columns in B is equal to the number of columns in C. We call these the *outer dimensions*.

In our Figure 1 example, matrix A is 14×30 and matrix B is 30×12. The 4×1 submatrices stored by the textures in a single pixel are shown as ovals. Because the matrices' heights are not exactly divisible by four, the last two elements of the last row of pixels are unused, indicated by their white color. Note that the texture representing A is only 30 pixels wide. The last two columns of white ovals with gray markings represent samples read in by the pixel shader outside of the [0,1] texture coordinate range; these virtual texels need to read as zero. They are necessary so our pixel shader can always work with blocks of four texels, even if the input matrix sizes are not exact multiples of four.

As any pixel shader, the matrix multiply code has to emit a single (partially computed) pixel from the pixel shader. Each pixel stores four values, each of which is a dot product between a row vector of A and a column vector of B. Both of these vectors have q elements, where q is 30 in our example. Thus, at each pixel, we need to perform four of these dot products, which is the same as a 4×q matrix-vector multiplication. Because q may be quite large, our GPU may not be able to sample all the $1\frac{1}{4}q$ texels necessary in one pass due to pixel shader instruction count limits. Thus, we need to decompose this operation into a set of smaller operations depending on our instruction count limits.

Our atomic pixel shader operation is a 4×4 matrix-vector multiplication, where the 4×4 matrix is fetched from A and the 4×1 vector from B. We refer to this atomic multiply as a *MOP* for "matrix operation." We need to perform $\left\lceil \frac{q}{4} \right\rceil$ of these MOPs per pixel and accumulate the results in order to obtain the final result for an output pixel. We pack as many of these MOPs into our pixel shader as possible.

In our example, we assume a hypothetical pixel shader that can perform no more than three of these MOPs in a single pass. In general, we define the macro numMOpsPerFragment as the number of MOPs that can fit into a pixel shader. For ps 2.0, we managed to fit six of them.

If the hypothetical example shader can do three MOPs per pass, and we need a total of $\left\lceil \frac{30}{4} \right\rceil = 8$ MOPs for the final result, we need to perform $\left\lceil \frac{8}{3} \right\rceil = 3$ additive passes, as indicated in the figure. Ps 2.0 would only need two passes.

As an example, we have highlighted a pixel in the destination texture. The pixel shader that emits this pixel as part of the second additive pass samples the darkened 15 texels from A and B.

Of course, the outer dimensions we don't have to worry about; they are taken care of by the inherent parallel processing of the GPU in the form of adjacent pixels, just like in the assignment and addition shaders. Now that we have covered the theory, we present the implementation:

```
void Matrix::multiply(Matrix & a, Matrix & b)  {
```

As usual, we need to check if we're trying to render a texture onto itself. Here we do not have a backup plan, so we simply report an error:

```
if (this == &a || this == &b)
    throw "can't operate inplace -- not supported by D3D.";
```

If the matrix dimensions do not agree, matrix multiplication is undefined:

```
if (a.nCols != b.nRows)
    throw "matrix dimensions don't agree";

resize(a.nRows, b.nCols);
if (nRows * nCols == 0)        return;
```

First, we compute a few constants depending on the input sizes and the number of instructions permitted in the pixel shader. We render numQuads quads aligned with the destination surface, with additive shading. We compute numQuads with the formulas given above.

```
const unsigned numQuads = roundUpDivide(rows2TextureHeight(b.nRows),numMOpsPerFragment);
```

Like we did for assignment and addition, we compute texture coordinate bias values to ensure that texels are sampled at their centers. Here we have two input textures, so we need to do this twice:

```
const float TexcoordBiasW = (1.0f/cols2TextureWidth(nCols))  * 0.5f;
const float TexcoordBiasH = (1.0f/rows2TextureHeight(nRows)) * 0.5f;

const float TexcoordBiasAW = (1.0f/cols2TextureWidth(a.nCols))  * 0.5f;
const float TexcoordBiasBH = (1.0f/rows2TextureHeight(b.nRows)) * 0.5f;
```

A single pixel shader performs several MOPs. We supply it with texture coordinates for the first five samples corresponding to the first MOP but only provide texture coordinate increments relative to the first five, which can be used by the pixel shader to compute the texture coordinates of the subsequent samples. tcMOpIncrementBH is the height of a texel in B, which is the amount the pixel shader has to seek down in the texture to get to the pixel used for the next MOP.

```
const float tcPixelBH = 2 * TexcoordBiasBH;
const float tcMOpIncrementBH = tcPixelBH;
```

The second increment we need is that of the texture coordinates between the additive passes. These will be used by the vertex shader, as we will not pass explicit texture coordinates to minimize the size of our vertex buffer.

```
const float tcPassIncrementBH = numMOpsPerFragment * tcPixelBH;
```

The same constants are also computed for the other input texture:

```
const float tcPixelAW = 2 * TexcoordBiasAW;
const float tcMOpIncrementAW = 4 * tcPixelAW;
const float tcPassIncrementAW = numMOpsPerFragment * tcMOpIncrementAW;
```

The meaning of the vertex and pixel shader constants will become clear when we look at the shaders:

```
float vconsts[] = {
    0.5 + TexcoordBiasW,  0.5 + TexcoordBiasH, 0 + TexcoordBiasBH, 0,
    0 + TexcoordBiasAW, tcPixelAW + TexcoordBiasAW,
    2 * tcPixelAW +  TexcoordBiasAW, 3 * tcPixelAW + TexcoordBiasAW,
    tcPassIncrementBH, tcPassIncrementAW, 0, 0
    };
float pconsts[] = {
    1 * tcMOpIncrementAW, 0, 0,0,    //2 mops
    0, 1 * tcMOpIncrementBH, 0,0,
    2 * tcMOpIncrementAW, 0, 0,0,    //3 mops
    0, 2 * tcMOpIncrementBH, 0,0,
    3 * tcMOpIncrementAW, 0, 0,0,    //4 mops
```

```
   0, 3 * tcMOpIncrementBH, 0,0,
   4 * tcMOpIncrementAW, 0, 0,0,    //5 mops
   0, 4 * tcMOpIncrementBH, 0,0,
   5 * tcMOpIncrementAW, 0, 0,0,    //6 mops
   0, 5 * tcMOpIncrementBH, 0,0,
   };


d3dDevice->SetRenderTarget(0,mathSurface);
d3dDevice->BeginScene();
d3dDevice->SetVertexDeclaration( vertexDeclaration2 );
d3dDevice->SetVertexShader( vertexShaders[VS_MULT_1] );
d3dDevice->SetPixelShader( pixelShaders[PS_MULT_0] );
d3dDevice->SetTexture(0,a.mathTexture);
d3dDevice->SetTexture(1,b.mathTexture);
d3dDevice->SetStreamSource( 0, quadsVertexBuffer, 0,TINYVERTEX_SIZE );
d3dDevice->SetVertexShaderConstantF(1, vconsts, 3);
d3dDevice->SetPixelShaderConstantF(0, pconsts, 2 * numMOpsPerFragment);
```

The vertex buffer contains a triangle list in the following format:

```
/* x  y   quadIndex
{ -1, -1,   0 },
{ +1, -1,   0 },
{ +1, +1,   0 },

{ -1, -1,   0 },
{ +1, +1,   0 },
{ -1, +1,   0 },

{ -1, -1,   1 },
{ +1, -1,   1 },
{ +1, +1,   1 },

{ -1, -1,   1 },
{ +1, +1,   1 },
{ -1, +1,   1 },

....

{ -1, -1,  99 },
{ +1, -1,  99 },
{ +1, +1,  99 },

{ -1, -1,  99 },
{ +1, +1,  99 },
{ -1, +1,  99 },
*/
```

The first two numbers are the 2D clip space coordinates of the vertex, as before.
We have also added a value that is the index of the quad that the vertex belongs to
in the sequence. The vertex shader uses this index value for texture coordinate
generation. Because the data is so simple, we pack each vertex into a 32-bit word
and use the D3DDECLTYPE_UBYTE4 data type. As the bytes are unsigned, we add two

to the coordinates, storing –1 as 0 and 1 as 2. Finally, we render two numQuads of these triangles:

```
d3dDevice->DrawPrimitive( D3DPT_TRIANGLELIST, 0, 2 );

if (numQuads > 1)
    {
    d3dDevice->SetRenderState( D3DRS_ALPHABLENDENABLE,   TRUE );
    d3dDevice->DrawPrimitive( D3DPT_TRIANGLELIST, 6, 2 *  (numQuads - 1));
    d3dDevice->SetRenderState( D3DRS_ALPHABLENDENABLE,   FALSE );
    }
d3dDevice->EndScene();
}
```

On to the shaders. The vertex shader's job is to "decompress" the very frugal quantity of data from the vertex buffer and generate decent texture coordinates. Note how we have submitted all our rendering passes after the first in a single DrawPrimitive() call, so there is no room to perform any state changes between quads. The vertex shader has to use the quad index from the vertex buffer to tell which pass is being performed.

```
vs_1_1
dcl_position v0
def c0, 0.5, -0.5, 0.5, 1
def c4, -1, -1, 0, 0
```

Because we have encoded the input vertex coordinates as unsigned bytes, we map them to signed values by subtracting one.

```
add r3.xy, v0.xy, c4.xy  //map from [0,2] to [-1, 1]
mov oPos.xy, r3.xy    //emit pos
mov oPos.zw, c0.zw
```

We start the texture coordinate generation by taking the vertex coordinate as the starting point and inverting the vertical axis; this is the same as in the previous shaders.

```
mov r0.xy, c1.xy     //transform viewport axes to tex uv axes
mad r0.xy, r3.xy, c0.xy, r0.xy
```

Next, we need to compute the U texture coordinates for texture A and the V texture coordinates for texture B. These depend on which pass we are in; the pass index is stored in v0.w. This is multiplied by tcPassIncrementAW and tcPassIncrementBH, respectively, which are constants computed above, and stored in c3.

```
mul r1, v0.w, c3.zzxz //can't 'mad' as it would reference 2 consts in 1 instr
add r1, r1, c1
mul r2, v0.w, c3.yyyy
add r2, r2, c2
```

Finally, we emit the five texture coordinates needed for the first MOP of the pixel shader. The V coordinates of texture A and the U coordinate of texture B are simply stretched along with the quad to map linearly over the entire destination surface. Even though it would be trivial to compute the four texture coordinates of A in the pixel shader itself, we choose to do as much of this work as possible in the vertex shader. This way, we avoid bumping up against the very restrictive pixel shader instruction count limits, particularly the dependent texture sampling limits.

```
mov oT0.x, r2.x
mov oT1.x, r2.y
mov oT2.x, r2.z
mov oT3.x, r2.w

mov oT0.y,  r0.y
mov oT1.y,  r0.y
mov oT2.y,  r0.y
mov oT3.y,  r0.y

mov oT4.x, r0.x
mov oT4.y, r1.z
```

All the matrix element arithmetic is done in the pixel shader. We have made the pixel shader generic in the sense that it is made up of as many MOPs as it is possible to execute at once on the target architecture, which is six in ps 2.0. When new hardware becomes available that supports newer pixel shader versions, getting a performance boost should only be a matter of duplicating some additional MOP blocks in the shader and incrementing the ps version declaration. Our ps 2.0 implementation uses 30 texld instructions of the maximum 32 and is thus very close to optimal.

Inputs to the pixel shader are the registers t0...t3, the texture coordinates of four horizontally adjacent pixels in A, t4, the texture coordinate for texture B, and a large set of constants; c0.x holds the texture coordinate increment needed to move four pixels to the left in A, while c1.y has the increment needed to move one pixel down in B. c2 and c3 are two times c0 and c1, respectively. c4 and c5 are the same values times three and so on. Because we have many constant registers available and few instruction slots, it is good to precompute these values.

```
ps_2_0
dcl t0.xyzw
dcl t1.xyzw
dcl t2.xyzw
dcl t3.xyzw
dcl t4.xyzw
dcl_2d s0
dcl_2d s1
```

To perform the first MOP, we fetch the needed data:

```
texld r0, t0, s0
texld r1, t1, s0
texld r2, t2, s0
texld r3, t3, s0
texld r4, t4, s1
```

...and execute the 4×1 matrix vector multiply. The result is held in r5.

```
mul r5, r4.xxxx, r0
mad r5, r4.yyyy, r1, r5
mad r5, r4.zzzz, r2, r5
mad r5, r4.wwww, r3, r5
```

If we had defined numMOpsPerFragment as 1 above, we would just write r5 to oC0 and be done. However, we have not yet exhausted the capacities of the pixel shader, so we keep going:

```
#if numMOpsPerFragment >= 2
```

The texture coordinates are adjusted to correspond to the next set of inputs:

```
add r6, t0, c0
add r7, t1, c0
add r8, t2, c0
add r9, t3, c0
add r10, t4, c1
```

Then we sample the textures as before. Note, however, that we now use registers r6 through r10 instead of r0 through r4. This is because ps 2.0 does not allow us to sample a texture into any one register more than four times, so the destination registers have to be rotated.

```
texld r6, r6, s0
texld r7, r7, s0
texld r8, r8, s0
texld r9, r9, s0
texld r10, r10, s1
```

We accumulate the result of the second matrix-vector product with the first:

```
mad r5, r10.xxxx, r6, r5
mad r5, r10.yyyy, r7, r5
mad r5, r10.zzzz, r8, r5
mad r5, r10.wwww, r9, r5
#endif
```

MOps three to six are identical save for the register rotation we mentioned:

```
#if numMOpsPerFragment >= 3
add r0, t0, c2
add r1, t1, c2
add r2, t2, c2
add r3, t3, c2
add r4, t4, c3

texld r0, r0, s0
texld r1, r1, s0
texld r2, r2, s0
texld r3, r3, s0
texld r4, r4, s1
```

```
        mad r5, r4.xxxx, r0, r5
        mad r5, r4.yyyy, r1, r5
        mad r5, r4.zzzz, r2, r5
        mad r5, r4.wwww, r3, r5
#endif
#if numMOpsPerFragment >= 4
        add r6, t0, c4
        add r7, t1, c4
        add r8, t2, c4
        add r9, t3, c4
        add r10, t4, c5

        texld r6, r6, s0
        texld r7, r7, s0
        texld r8, r8, s0
        texld r9, r9, s0
        texld r10, r10, s1

        mad r5, r10.xxxx, r6, r5
        mad r5, r10.yyyy, r7, r5
        mad r5, r10.zzzz, r8, r5
        mad r5, r10.wwww, r9, r5
#endif
#if numMOpsPerFragment >= 5
        add r0, t0, c6
        add r1, t1, c6
        add r2, t2, c6
        add r3, t3, c6
        add r4, t4, c7

        texld r0, r0, s0
        texld r1, r1, s0
        texld r2, r2, s0
        texld r3, r3, s0
        texld r4, r4, s1

        mad r5, r4.xxxx, r0, r5
        mad r5, r4.yyyy, r1, r5
        mad r5, r4.zzzz, r2, r5
        mad r5, r4.wwww, r3, r5
#endif
#if numMOpsPerFragment >= 6
        add r6, t0, c8
        add r7, t1, c8
        add r8, t2, c8
        add r9, t3, c8
        add r10, t4, c9

        texld r6, r6, s0
        texld r7, r7, s0
        texld r8, r8, s0
        texld r9, r9, s0
```

```
        texld r10, r10, s1

        mad r5, r10.xxxx, r6, r5
        mad r5, r10.yyyy, r7, r5
        mad r5, r10.zzzz, r8, r5
        mad r5, r10.wwww, r9, r5
#endif
mov oC0, r5
```

There are a few additional details to be mentioned. Because a pixel shader operates on 4×(4 numMOpsPerFragment) submatrices, only input matrices with dimensions that are multiples of 4 numMOpsPerFragment are handled trivially. Other matrix sizes perform extra work because the pixel shading involving the last column-block of A and last row-block of B read in zeros and perform redundant computations. We even have to do work to ensure that, indeed, zeros get read in and not undefined values. First, we set the texture coordinate mapping mode to the black border color. Unfortunately, not all GPUs support this feature. To support these GPUs, we either need to change the way we store the matrices in the surfaces so that the edge texels are not used, set the edge pixels to black, and use clamp mode, or restrict ourselves to matrices with row and column counts that are multiples of 4 numMOpsPerFragment. Finally, the pixel shader does a lot of redundant work processing input matrices with the inner dimension significantly smaller than 4 numMOpsPerFragment. Of course, such small matrices are best processed on the CPU anyway to avoid the overhead of creating and reading back textures.

Transposed Multiplication

In practice, we rarely need to compute the transpose of a matrix as such but often need to multiply the transpose of a matrix with another matrix. We implement a transposed multiply operation to be able to do this. The operation we now describe implements $C := A^T B$, where A, B, and C are still defined as in the last section. The operation $C := A B^T$ is also useful, but its implementation would be very similar to this one, so we will omit it. As we see later, this operation ends up to be more costly than the plain multiply. For this reason, it may be worth it to implement a simple transpose operation $C := A^T$ as well, even though this operation can be inefficiently emulated using this code with B = 1. Such an operation would be a clear win if a sequence of multiplications were needed with a certain transposed matrix and perhaps even in general.

A trivial CPU implementation of the transposed multiply code would simply exchange the row and column indexing of A, but this is not so easy on the GPU because we have packed several matrix elements into a single pixel, so the transpose has to happen on two levels: The atomic 4×4 matrix pixel shader operation has to be transposed, and the ordering of these submatrices also needs to be reversed. An indication of this added complexity is that this time we only managed to fit four transposed MOPs into our ps 2.0 pixel shader, as opposed to six for the plain multiply. Because this new constant is different from the previous, we define it as numMTOpsPerFragment.

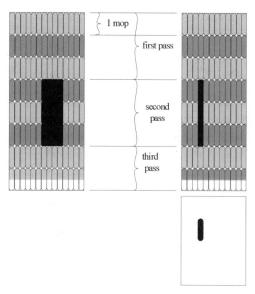

Figure 2: Schematic for transposed matrix multiply

A diagram to explain this algorithm is provided in Figure 2. This is exactly the same problem as given in Figure 1, with the matrix A now provided in a transposed form. To compute C as before, we transpose A while we perform the multiply. The matrix B and C are unchanged. The darkened regions again show the texels sampled to compute the contribution of the second pass to the black output pixel. Note that in matrix A, the region consists of three vertically stacked MOPs, each of which has four texels in a horizontal row. Our pixel shader will now be stepping four times to the left before resetting the horizontal offset and taking a step downward. The pixel shader has to move the starting texture coordinate of A downward between passes.

The C++ code for the operation is quite similar to the plain-vanilla multiply:

```
void Matrix::multiplyAT(Matrix & a, Matrix & b) {
if (this == &a || this == &b)
    throw "can't operate inplace -- not supported by D3D.";
if (a.nRows != b.nRows)
    throw "matrix dimensions don't agree";
resize(a.nCols, b.nCols);
if (nRows * nCols == 0)        return;

const unsigned numQuads = roundUpDivide(rows2TextureHeight(b.nRows),numMTOpsPerFragment);

const float TexcoordBiasW = (1.0f/cols2TextureWidth(nCols))  * 0.5f;
const float TexcoordBiasH = (1.0f/rows2TextureHeight(nRows)) * 0.5f;

const float TexcoordBiasAW = (1.0f/cols2TextureWidth(a.nCols))  * 0.5f;
const float TexcoordBiasABH = (1.0f/rows2TextureHeight(a.nRows)) * 0.5f;
```

We compute bias values as usual above, and the offsets for texture B are also unchanged below:

```
const float tcPixelBH = 2 * TexcoordBiasABH;
const float tcMOpIncrementBH = tcPixelBH;
const float tcPassIncrementBH = numMTOpsPerFragment * tcPixelBH;
```

The offsets for matrix A are now in both the horizontal and vertical directions:

```
const float tcPixelAW = 2 * TexcoordBiasAW;
const float tcPixelAH = 2 * TexcoordBiasABH;
const float tcMOpIncrementAH = tcPixelAH;
const float tcPassIncrementAH = numMTOpsPerFragment * tcMOpIncrementAH;
```

There is an additional issue in the transposed multiply that did not show up before. Previously, it was always proper for the vertex shader to simply linearly map vertex coordinates from the range [1,–1] to the texture coordinate range [0,1] to define the U or V texture coordinates of an input texture. Now, however, the U dimension of texture A is mapped vertically and the V dimension horizontally. If A is not square, and there are unused components in the bottom row of the destination texture because its height is not a multiple of four, the mapping has to be adjusted. We map the vertex range [1,–1] to [0, quotient], where quotient is computed below. In effect, we virtually round up the texture size to the nearest multiple of four. The rest of the code should be familiar.

```
const unsigned awidth = cols2TextureWidth(a.nCols);
unsigned modW = awidth % 4;
if (modW != 0) modW = 4 - modW;
const float quotient = (awidth + modW)/(float)awidth;
const float halfQuot = quotient * 0.5f;

float vconsts[] = {
    0.5, - halfQuot, 0.5, 1,
    0.5+ TexcoordBiasW,  0.5 + TexcoordBiasH, 0 + TexcoordBiasABH, 0,
    0   + TexcoordBiasABH, 0, 0, 0,
    0, q + TexcoordBiasAW, 0, 0,
    tcPassIncrementBH, tcPassIncrementAH, 0, 0
    };

float pconsts[] = {
    tcPixelAW, 0, 0,0,
    0, 1 * tcMOpIncrementBH, 0,0,
    0, 1 * tcPixelAH, 0,0,
    0, 2 * tcMOpIncrementBH, 0,0,
    0, 2 * tcPixelAH, 0,0,
    0, 3 * tcMOpIncrementBH, 0,0,
    0, 3 * tcPixelAH, 0,0,
    0, 4 * tcMOpIncrementBH, 0,0,
    0, 4 * tcPixelAH, 0,0,
    0, 5 * tcMOpIncrementBH, 0,0,
    0, 5 * tcPixelAH, 0,0,
    };

d3dDevice->SetRenderTarget(0,mathSurface);
d3dDevice->BeginScene();
```

```
d3dDevice->SetVertexDeclaration( vertexDeclaration2 );
d3dDevice->SetVertexShader( vertexShaders[VS_MULT_T] );
d3dDevice->SetPixelShader( pixelShaders[PS_MULT_T] );
d3dDevice->SetTexture(0,a.mathTexture);
d3dDevice->SetTexture(1,b.mathTexture);
d3dDevice->SetStreamSource( 0, quadsVertexBuffer, 0, TINYVERTEX_SIZE );
d3dDevice->SetVertexShaderConstantF(0, vconsts, 5);
d3dDevice->SetPixelShaderConstantF(0, pconsts, 1 + 2 * (numMTOpsPerFragment - 1) );
d3dDevice->DrawPrimitive( D3DPT_TRIANGLELIST, 0, 2 );
if (numQuads > 1)
    {
    d3dDevice->SetRenderState( D3DRS_ALPHABLENDENABLE,   TRUE );
    d3dDevice->DrawPrimitive( D3DPT_TRIANGLELIST, 6, 2 * (numQuads - 1) );
    d3dDevice->SetRenderState( D3DRS_ALPHABLENDENABLE,   FALSE );
    }
d3dDevice->EndScene();
}
```

The vertex shader code first extracts and emits the vertex position, as the straight multiply did:

```
vs_1_1
dcl_position v0
def c5, -1, -1, 0, 0
add r3.xy, v0.xy, c5.xy
mov oPos.xy, r3.xy
mov oPos.zw, c0.zw
```

The vertex to texture coordinate mapping is now done twice because, as discussed above, texture A's texture coordinate range is no longer always [0,1], while B's still is. These four instructions could be optimized into fewer instructions, but the vertex shader is no bottleneck here.

```
mov r0.xy, c1.xy
mad r0.xy, r3.xy, c0.xy, r0.xy

mov r1.xy, c3.xy
mad r1.xy, r3.xy, c0.xy, r1.xy
```

The code to add offsets to the texture coordinates is the same as in the plain multiply, except it works along different dimensions for A:

```
mul r3, v0.w, c4.zzxz
add r3, r3, c1
mul r2, v0.w, c4.yyyy
add r2, r2, c2
```

Note that unlike before, we only emit two texture coordinates. We were not able to optimize the pixel shader in this case by precomputing more texture coordinates here.

```
mov oT0.x, r1.y
mov oT0.y, r2.x
mov oT1.x, r0.x
```

```
mov oT1.y, r3.z
```

Below is the last shader presented in this article. Notice that after we fetch the first sample from A, we keep nudging the texture coordinates to the right to fetch the next three samples. The last texld samples the 4-vector from B.

```
ps_2_0
dcl t0.xyzw
dcl t1.xyzw
dcl_2d s0
dcl_2d s1
texld r0, t0, s0
add   r4, t0, c0
texld r1, r4, s0
add   r4, r4, c0
texld r2, r4, s0
add   r4, r4, c0
texld r3, r4, s0

texld r4, t1, s1
```

The transposed multiply can be accomplished with four dp4s, and the result goes to r5:

```
dp4 r5.x, r4, r0
dp4 r5.y, r4, r1
dp4 r5.z, r4, r2
dp4 r5.w, r4, r3
#if numMTOpsPerFragment >= 2
```

To execute the next MOP, we push the original t0 downward in A by adding c2 and then again sampling four consecutive pixels. We rotate the sampling destination registers so we avoid getting a fourth-order dependent read error in the shader compiler as long as possible.

```
add   r0, t0, c2
texld r6, r0, s0
add   r0, r0, c0
texld r7, r0, s0
add   r0, r0, c0
texld r8, r0, s0
add   r0, r0, c0
texld r9, r0, s0

add r1, t1, c1
texld r10, r1, s1

dp4 r6.x, r10, r6
dp4 r6.y, r10, r7
dp4 r6.z, r10, r8
dp4 r6.w, r10, r9
add r5, r5, r6
#endif
#if numMTOpsPerFragment >= 3
```

The third and fourth blocks simply continue to follow this pattern.

```
        add    r4, t0, c4
        texld r0, r4, s0
        add    r4, r4, c0
        texld r1, r4, s0
        add    r4, r4, c0
        texld r2, r4, s0
        add    r4, r4, c0
        texld r3, r4, s0

        add    r4, t1, c3
        texld r4, r4, s1

        dp4 r6.x, r4, r0
        dp4 r6.y, r4, r1
        dp4 r6.z, r4, r2
        dp4 r6.w, r4, r3
        add r5, r5, r6
#endif
#if numMTOpsPerFragment >= 4
        add    r0, t0, c6
        texld r6, r0, s0
        add    r0, r0, c0
        texld r7, r0, s0
        add    r0, r0, c0
        texld r8, r0, s0
        add    r0, r0, c0
        texld r9, r0, s0

        add r1, t1, c5
        texld r10, r1, s1

        dp4 r6.x, r10, r6
        dp4 r6.y, r10, r7
        dp4 r6.z, r10, r8
        dp4 r6.w, r10, r9
        add r5, r5, r6
#endif
```

Unfortunately, the above conditional block is the last one that compiles with ps 2.0 because the first texld of the next block produces a fourth-order texop error. This hand-coded assembly code still manages to pack much more math into the pixel shader than the HLSL compiler managed.

```
#if numMTOpsPerFragment >= 5
        add    r7, t0, c8
        texld r0, r7, s0
        add    r7, r7, c0
        texld r1, r7, s0
        add    r7, r7, c0
        texld r2, r7, s0
        add    r7, r7, c0
```

```
texld r3, r7, s0

add r4, t1, c7
texld r4, r4, s1

dp4 r6.x, r4, r0
dp4 r6.y, r4, r1
dp4 r6.z, r4, r2
dp4 r6.w, r4, r3
add r5, r5, r6
#endif
mov oC0, r5
```

Other Operations

From the operations described above, we create more by writing different variations and writing macro operations that build on them. We briefly summarize them here:

```
float Matrix ::dot(Matrix & vec);                //this *= vec'
```

This is only defined if both operands are vectors. The dot product of two vectors a and b equals $a^T b$, so we can reuse the transposed multiply operation. This results in a temporary 1×1 texture whose red component we read out and return.

```
float Matrix::normSquared();
```

Only defined for a vector a, this simply calls a.dot(a).

```
void Matrix::multiply(float c);                  //this *= c
```

Multiplication by a constant is implemented with a simple shader that does a multiplicative blend between the destination and a c-colored quad.

```
void Matrix::add(Matrix & b);                    //this += b
```

Unary accumulate is the copy() operation with additive blending with the render target turned on.

```
void Matrix::max(Matrix & a, float ref);         //this = max(a, ref)
```

This operation is also similar to copy() but also employs the max pixel shader opcode to compute the maximum of the corresponding matrix elements.

```
void Matrix::mad(Matrix & b, float c);                       //this += b * c.
void Matrix::mad(Matrix & a,Matrix & b,float c);            //this = a + b * c
void Matrix::mad(Matrix & a, Matrix & b);                   //this += a .* b
void Matrix::madad(Matrix & a, Matrix & b, Matrix & c, Matrix & d);
//this = a + (b + c) .* d
```

Finally, all the different flavors of the mad (multiply add) operation are a combination of the add and constant multiply shaders. We use .* to denote array multiplication. We also implemented some initialization operations. To create a zero matrix, we simply clear the texture to black. Identity matrices and other special matrices are best implemented by writing the appropriate data with the CPU. This is also how matrices are saved and loaded from file.

Applications

In this section we describe two high-level algorithms that use the operations we described above. None of them reads back intermediate results (other than scalars) from the CPU, so all the real work still happens on the GPU as a sequence of render-to-texture operations. It would be possible to optimize both of them by writing special-purpose *macro* shaders that combine several basic matrix operations to reduce the number of render-to-texture operations. We have done this to a small degree by implementing the multiply-add operations, but in general we would like to keep our operations small in number and reusable.

Both of the discussed methods are iterative. Iterative methods, in contrast to pivoting methods, are typically simple and perform a small number of matrix operations to converge to the desired result, rather than doing a number of scalar operations that are often difficult to vectorize.

Conjugate Gradients

The conjugate gradients algorithm was developed at the ETH Zurich in 1952 [4]. It is the most common iterative algorithm used to solve a system of linear equations of the form $Ax = b$, where the matrix A and the vector b are given and the vector x is to be found. Although this algorithm has been extended to handle more general classes of matrices, we only deal with the simplest version that requires A to be symmetric positive definite.

Our implementation of the algorithm does not have any DirectX or shader code of its own. Instead, it uses the methods of the matrix class we created. The three operand matrices are given:

```
Matrix & A = ...;
Matrix & x = ...;
Matrix & b = ...;

unsigned n = b.getNRows();
```

If the algorithm is used in a physics simulation context, it is often desirable to warm-start it with the solution of the problem in the previous simulation time step, with the hope that the solution of the current time step is nearby. If the size of the input vector x is compatible with the size of A, we assume that the user wants to warm-start with x; otherwise, we start with a first guess of zero:

```
if (x.getNRows() != n || x.getNCols() != 1)
    x.zeros(n, 1);
```

The algorithm uses three temporary vectors:

```
Matrix p, r, s;
```

```
p.copy(b);
r.copy(b);
float rr = r.normSquared();
s.multiply(A,p);
float t = p.dot(s);
float alpha = rr / t;
x.mad(p, alpha);
float rrnew = rr;
```

The conjugate gradients algorithm is proven to converge to the exact solution within n steps[1], though we could get an approximate solution with fewer iterations.

```
unsigned iter = n;

for (unsigned k = 2; k<=iter; k++)
    {
    r.mad(s, -alpha);
    rr = rrnew;
    rrnew = r.normSquared();
    float beta = rrnew / rr;
    p.mad(r, p, beta);
    s.multiply(A,p);
    t = p.dot(s);
    alpha = rrnew / t;
    x.mad(p, alpha);
    }
```

The most expensive operation in the algorithm is the matrix-vector multiply M*p above. All other operations are vector operations. This makes the algorithm relatively "lightweight" and less suitable for demonstrating the number-crunching abilities of the GPU. On the other hand, a much more expensive algorithm would be less practical, and therefore this example is a good real-world test of the GPU's applicability to real-world linear algebra applications.

Linear Complementarity Problem

The linear complementarity problem, while not as widely known as the problem of linear equation systems, is very useful for solving a wide variety of problems, including the dynamics of resting contact. Linear complementarity problems are a special kind of nonlinear programming problem, which in turn is a problem of constrained optimization. The LCP problem can be stated as:

$$x \geq 0$$
$$Ax + b \geq 0$$
$$x^T (Ax + b) = 0$$

1　This is only strictly true if we were using exact arithmetic. For a discussion of the convergence properties of conjugate gradients using floating-point arithmetic, see [3].

As before, A and b are given, and x is to be found. We use the projected Jacobi method [8] for solving the problem, which is perhaps the simplest way to do so, though not necessarily the one with the best convergence properties. The projected Jacobi algorithm can be stated succinctly as the recursion:

$$x_{i+1} = \max(x_i + D(Ax_i + b), \bar{0})$$

Where D is defined as:

$$D = \omega \operatorname{diagonal}(A)^{-1}$$

ω is a constant that steers convergence. Clever implementations of the algorithm tune this value, while the solver runs to speed up convergence; we just use a fixed value. This algorithm again requires A to be symmetric positive definite.

As before, we first receive the matrices we are to operate on. Note that because d is a constant, it is also expected to be provided as an input. This time, the number of iterations is also a mandatory input because with this algorithm, there is no guaranteed convergence for a certain number of iterations. In the code below we store the diagonal elements of the diagonal matrix D in a column vector d.

```
Matrix & x = ...;
Matrix & A = ...;
Matrix & d = ...;
Matrix & b = ...;
unsigned iter = ...;

unsigned n = b.getNRows();

Matrix w, t;
```

Here we again warm-start the algorithm with the initial value of x if it exists; otherwise, we start at zero:

```
if (x.getNRows() != n || x.getNCols() != 1)
    {
    x.zeros(n, 1);
    w.zeros(n, 1);
    }
else
    w.multiply(A, x);

t.madad(x, b, w, d);
x.max(t, 0);

for (unsigned k = 1; k<iter; k++)
    {
    w.multiply(A, x);
    t.madad(x, b, w, d);
    x.max(t, 0);
    }
```

The above loop implements the iteration presented above. Here too the most expensive operation is a matrix vector multiply.

Results

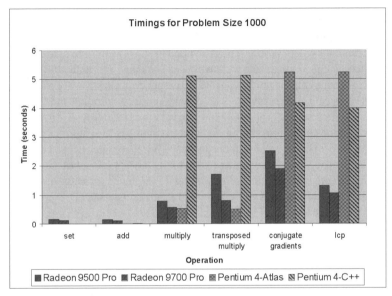

Figure 3: GPU vs. CPU performance for various operations involving a 1000×1000 matrix

Figure 3 summarizes the running times for the matrix copy, add, multiply, transposed multiply, conjugate gradients, and projected Jacobi algorithms. We have profiled four configurations: Our GPU implementation was run on a Radeon 9500 Pro that was plugged into a PC with an AMD Athlon 800 Mhz processor and 256 MB of RAM and a Radeon 9700 Pro in a P4 2.4 GHz, with 256 MB RAM. The two CPU configurations were a simple C implementation by the author and a program using the ATLAS library. Both of the CPU configurations were timed on a 1.6 GHz Intel Pentium 4 processor-equipped PC with 256 MB RAM. We used a version of ATLAS optimized for Pentium 4 CPUs with 8 KB L1 cache and 256 KB L2 cache; these specifications correspond to our test system. Note that while ATLAS gains a sizeable performance boost from this cache-size specific optimization, it means that the library has to be reconfigured for each target platform; this is somewhat impractical for interactive entertainment software that is to be distributed to end users. In comparison, a DirectX 9 program, which only indirectly interfaces with hardware and thus exploits the video card's manufacturer-specific driver optimizations, is more flexible.

All GPU timings represent the time elapsed between the call of the appropriate matrix class method and completion of the readback of the result matrix from video to system memory. Retrieving results to system memory is a significant portion of the time needed for copy and addition but are negligible for the other operations. The C implementation is an order of magnitude slower than either the ATLAS or the GPU implementation, which fall in the same performance class. The GPU transposed multiply is slower than the straight multiply because it needs more rendering passes. The CPU implementations' speeds are the same for straight and transposed multiply because here the difference boils down to a change in matrix indexing and computation order that does not even need to influence cache coherence.

The projected Jacobi algorithm for LCPs runs faster than conjugate gradients for a given problem size because the number of render-to-texture operations in the loop is much lower, and we never read back any intermediate values from the GPU — not even scalars. Conjugate gradients read back a scalar value in normSquared() — this is the result of a dot product operation and is retrieved from the 1×1 render target texture used in this case. Because it is only a single value, it does not stress the limited texture memory to system memory bandwidth of PCs, but it still hurts performance because it forces the CPU and GPU to work together in lockstep instead of working asynchronously. One could further optimize conjugate gradients by merging its sequence of vector operations into a single operation by writing a custom "macro" pixel shader. This is left as an exercise for the reader.

Because LCP and conjugate gradients consist of a sequence of vector-vector and matrix-vector operations, ATLAS is unable to leverage its optimized matrix-matrix kernel and instead adds significant overhead, losing out to the inlined C version. For these two algorithms, data caching is less of a bottleneck because there are fewer numbers to work with. Instead, raw floating-point performance is dominant, catapulting the Radeons into the lead.

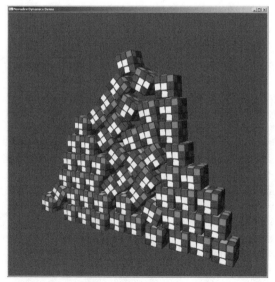

Figure 4: Collapsing wall of 60 cubes

Figure 4 shows a practical application: a wall of 60 cubes collapsing. The simulation is performed by the projected Jacobi code. The simulation uses $\omega = -0.1$ and does 2n iterations, where n is the size of the input matrix. If the problem is expressed as a single dense matrix (with an initial size of 400×400), the simulation runs at two seconds per frame. If the problem is dynamically decomposed into small sub-problems, real-time performance is achieved. Of course, more advanced LCP algorithms (which are less suitable for GPU implementation) can achieve even better results because of eventually lower storage overhead (sparse matrix) and much faster convergence.

Conclusion

In [6], Larsen and McAllister have benchmarked matrix multiplies on GeForce3 GPUs and found that the GPU, working with byte values, achieves similar performance to the CPU using single-precision floating-point, effectively operating on four times as much data. They were pessimistic about the prospect of a fourfold increase in GPU performance, even if GPUs were to integrate floating-point processing capabilities. Our results above indicate that this has indeed happened only two years later.

We have observed that the Radeon GPUs have outperformed optimized CPU code running on a mid-range PC when executing two important algorithms. Moreover, the performance penalty due to moving data to the GPU and back to main memory can be negligible compared to the overall cost of the computation when the problem size is sufficient. As a result, this additional source of computing power should not be ignored. Instead, algorithms must be found that can exploit the specific strengths of the GPU. Approaches that split the work between CPU and GPU and thus achieve maximum parallelism will make it possible to run simulations of previously untractable scales on low-cost PCs.

Acknowledgments

Thanks to Wolfgang Engel, Tom Forsyth, and ATI and nVidia developer relations for help with different aspects of this project and to Erwin Coumans, Mark Harris, Stephane Redon, and Jan Paul van Waveren for valuable suggestions.

References

[1] Bolz, Jeff, Ian Farmer, Eitan Grinspun, and Peter Schröder, "Sparse Matrix Solvers on the GPU: Conjugate Gradients and Multigrid," to appear in the proceedings of SIGGRAPH 2003.

[2] Dongarra, J.J., J. Du Croz, S. Hammarling, and R.J. Hanson, "An extended set of FORTRAN Basic Linear Algebra Subprograms," ACM Trans. Math. Soft., 14 (1988), pp. 1-17.

[3] Facius, Axel, "Iterative Solution of Linear Systems with Improved Arithmetic and Result Verification," Ph.D. thesis, Universität Karlsruhe, July 2000.

[4] Hestenes, M. and E. Stiefel, "Methods of conjugate gradients for solving linear systems," J. Research Nat. Bur. Standards 49, 1952.

[5] Krüger, Jens and Rüdiger Westermann, "Linear Algebra Operators for GPU Implementation of Numerical Algorithms," to appear in the proceedings of SIGGRAPH 2003.

[6] Larsen, E.S. and D. McAllister, "Fast Matrix Multiplies using Graphics Hardware," SuperComputing 2001 Conference, Denver, CO, November 2001.

[7] Lawson, C.L., R.J. Hanson, D. Kincaid, and F.T. Krogh, "Basic Linear Algebra Subprograms for FORTRAN usage," ACM Trans. Math. Soft., 5 (1979), pp. 308-323.

[8] Murty, K.G., *Linear Complementarity, Linear and Nonlinear Programming*, Helderman-Verlag, 1988.

[9] Whaley, R.C. and J. Dongarra, "Automatically Tuned Linear Algebra Software," SuperComputing 1998 Conference, Orlando, FL, November 1998.

Section III

Software Shaders and Shader Programming Tips

Software Vertex Shader Processing

Dean P. Macri

Intel Corporation

Introduction

Recent advances in processor performance coupled with the programmability available in the vertex shader models provided in Microsoft DirectX gives developers considerable freedom to write customized and specialized techniques for real-time graphics and gaming. DirectX 9 introduced the vs.2.0, vs.2.x, and vs.3.0 shader models that provide static and dynamic branching capabilities, looping, conditional execution, predication, and more flexible addressing and computational ability. Rather than waiting for a proliferation of graphics cards that support these features in hardware, developers can begin using these features today with software vertex processing. In addition, highly optimized vector processing for non-graphics data can be done using the software vertex processing pipeline.

This article explores optimization guidelines for writing shaders that use the software vertex processing pipeline. While that is the main goal, the techniques described here should also apply to vertex shaders written for graphics hardware. First I talk about why you'd want to use software vertex processing and I describe some non-graphics algorithms and techniques that can benefit from software vertex processing. Then I describe some of the processor features that give the pipeline significant performance capability and discuss some of the design characteristics of the Intel implementation of the software vertex processing pipeline. Next, I walk through the specific optimization guidelines, why they have an impact, and how to get the highest performance out of your shaders. Finally, I wrap up with a description of the included sample program and shaders.

Throughout this article, I refer to the Intel-optimized portion of the DirectX runtime as a *compiler* because it recompiles shader bytecode to IA-32 instruction sequences. Any reference to the word "compiler" is with that context in mind. If you're eager to just begin optimizing your vertex shaders and aren't really interested in the motivation or background material, feel free to skip ahead to the "Optimization Guidelines" section.

Why Software Vertex Processing?

Once you've looked at the vertex shader models provided by DirectX, several reasons for doing software vertex processing quickly come to mind:

- Support for graphics hardware that doesn't have vertex shaders
- Use of higher shader versions than is supported by available hardware
- Writing shaders with more instructions than the limits of hardware shaders

After some additional thought, other, less obvious reasons that might be envisioned for doing software vertex processing include:

- Doing work other than pixel processing on the output of the vertex shader
- Doing non-graphics type work using the familiar, vector-oriented shader model
- Ensuring predictable performance and compatibility across end-user systems

While each of these is relatively self explanatory, I want to focus on the first two items of the second list and discuss in more detail why you might want to do these things.

With all the flexibility that the programmable aspects of the DirectX pipeline provides, there are still some situations in which you want to short-circuit the pipeline and do your own work on the intermediate results. One example would be using the vertex shader portion of the pipeline for transforming bounding volumes for occlusion or collision detection tests. You don't want to send those transformed volumes through the pixel processing pipeline; you just want to do tests on them to determine whether or not *other* data should be sent through the graphics pipeline. In this case, developers have often chosen to implement their own transformation code to do the work, and often, the optimization level of that code is minimal. Using the ProcessVertices() method of the IDirect3DDevice9 interface, developers can write a small vertex shader that does the transformation and writes the results out to a system memory vertex buffer. That buffer can then be examined for doing the occlusion or collision tests. The end result is that fast Streaming SIMD Extensions (SSE) optimized code will be used on the transformations, resulting in a net performance gain with a minimal amount of development.

Another possibility would be using a vertex shader to update positions and velocities for a large particle system using numerical integration. The software vertex processing pipeline could quickly go through a large number of particles, again using the ProcessVertices() method of the IDirect3DDevice9 interface. After processing, additional work for preparing a graphical display of the data could be done.

These two examples should provide some reasonable motivation for why software vertex processing is useful. The next section describes how the high performance is achieved using the features of recent processors.

Processor Features and Performance Advances

With the introduction of the Intel Pentium 4 processor with hyper-threading technology, Intel has brought multi-processing to consumer PCs. Combined with the
SSE introduced in the Pentium III processor and the Streaming SIMD Extensions
2 (SSE2) introduced in the Pentium 4 processor, there's now support of SIMD
operations on 128-bit data in the form of single- and double-precision floating-point numbers as well as integer values from bytes to double-quadwords with
all sizes in between, as seen in Figure 1. The software implementation of the vertex processing pipeline described in the next section takes advantage of all these
features. To set the context for better understanding of that information, I briefly
describe some of these features here. Considerably more in-depth information on
the Pentium 4 processor and its features can be found at http://www.intel.com/
products/desktop/processors/pentium4/.

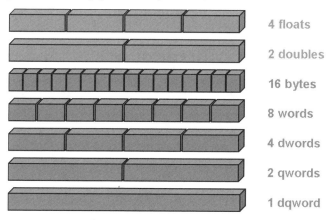

Figure 1: SSE and SSE2 data types

Streaming SIMD Extensions (SSE)

If you've been optimizing assembly routines or happen to have browsed through
the instruction set manuals for Intel's latest processors, you're well aware that
the vertex shader instructions don't map one-to-one to the IA-32 instruction set.
However, the SSE and SSE2 instructions are a fairly close fit. Using these
instruction set extensions, engineers at Intel have created a compiler that takes
already-compiled vertex shader bytecode and converts it to optimal SSE and
SSE2 instruction sequences.

The nature of the SSE and SSE2 instruction sets is most appropriate for
operating on data in pairs of registers rather than within a single register. Some
instructions in the vertex shader specifications, like dp3 and dp4, combine the values within a given register and produce a single result. If the vertex shader
instructions were mapped as directly as possible to SSE and SSE2 instructions,

then "horizontal" operations like dp3 and dp4 would eliminate three-quarters of the computation bandwidth provided. In an attempt to fully utilize the compute bandwidth provided for maximum performance, incoming data is transformed such that one 128-bit SSE/SSE2 register (also known as an XMM register) contains a single component (.x, .y, .z, or .w) of four vertices. So completely representing a four-component register from a vertex shader would require four XMM registers but would contain information for four vertices. Similarly, vertex shader constant registers are replicated (and stored in memory initially) so that a single constant register would also consume four XMM registers. Figure 2 shows an example of a single shader register transformed into four XMM registers.

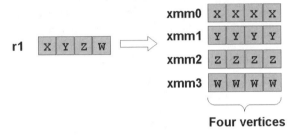

Figure 2: Transforming data from AOS to SOA

The data at the left of Figure 2 is known as array-of-structures (AOS) data because it could be represented by a C/C++ data structure with one element of the structure for each component of the vector. For multiple vectors, you'd have an array of the structures, hence the name. The data at the right of Figure 2 is known as structure-of-arrays (SOA) data because you could have a C/C++ structure with four arrays, one for the x components, one for the y components, etc.

Hyper-Threading Technology

The latest addition to the Pentium 4 processor family is support for symmetric multithreading with what's known as hyper-threading technology (HT technology). HT technology adds a second "logical" processor to the package of a Pentium 4 processor. The operating system can schedule processes and threads on the second processor, and behind the scenes the processor schedules operations from each of the logical processors onto the shared execution resources of the processor core. The processor caches and most internal data structures are shared between the logical processors, with only a few essential components being duplicated, as seen in Figure 3. Because typical IA-32 code sequences have branches or memory loads that stall the processor temporarily, each of the logical processors can make progress and combined can often achieve an additional 15 to 20 percent speedup over the same code running on a similar processor with only one logical processor active.

With HT technology reaching consumer desktop PCs, Intel engineers working on the shader compiler took the opportunity to create multiple threads of vertex shader processing code when sufficiently large batches of vertices are being processed. The exact number of vertices that produce the additional thread is determined at run time based on several factors. It's worth noting that if your application is doing software vertex processing and running on a multiprocessor system or a system with HT technology, one or more additional threads of execution may be created to boost performance.

With that sampling of background information, we now have sufficient information to look closely at the guidelines that we can use when writing software vertex shaders. The next section does just that.

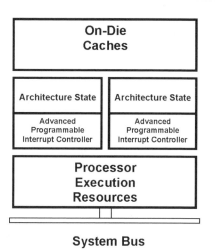

Figure 3: Intel Pentium 4 processor with HT technology diagram

Optimization Guidelines

The optimization guidelines listed here can help improve the performance of vertex shaders running in software. Following the list is a detailed description of each of the guidelines with some examples of how to apply them and why they impact performance.

- Use the highest shader version provided by the API.
- Use the macros.
- Define heavily used constants.
- Write directly to output registers.
- Use source swizzle and destination masks.
- Minimize dependency chains.
- Minimize temp register usage between basic blocks.
- Use rep instruction if aL isn't needed in a loop.
- Avoid address register usage or reorder vertices based on expected values.
- Try to eliminate unnecessary conditionals.
- Use predicates for a few instructions when masking won't work.
- Use the break instructions to early-exit from loops.
- Use conditionals to early-exit from rarely used code.
- Try to arrange conditional data based on expected behavior.
- Profile!

Use the Highest Shader Version Provided by the API

DirectX 9 introduced three new vertex shader models: vs.2.0, vs.2.x, and vs.3.0. For the software pipeline, the 2.x and 3.0 models also have vs.2.sw and vs.3.sw versions that eliminate the constraints on the number of instructions available as well as extend the register and label limits. By using the highest shader version available (vs.3.0 or vs.3.sw if limits are a concern), you can take advantage of all the features provided by that shader model to get the best performance possible. The Mandelbrot sample shader provided on the companion CD illustrates the performance advantage of having instructions like break_ge available to early-exit from loops. Using it yielded a 2.5x speedup in some cases over the vs.2.0 version.

Use the Macros

The shader models in DirectX 9 include several *macro* instructions — some new and some carried over from previous shader versions. Some examples are the matrix multiplication instructions (M4X4, M3X4, etc.) and cross-product (CRS) instructions. Using them helps the compiler make smarter decisions about which registers need to be temporarily saved to memory and which can be discarded after use. As a general guideline, if an operation can be done with a single shader instruction or a combination of other shader instructions, use the single instruction version. The following code sequence illustrates an example:

Before	After
dp4 r0.x, v0, c2	
dp4 r0.y, v0, c3	m4x4 r0, v0, c2
dp4 r0.z, v0, c4	
dp4 r0.w, v0, c4	
mul r2, v1.yzxw, v2.zxyw	crs r2, v1, v2
mad r2, –v2.yzxw, v1.zxyw, r2	

Define Heavily Used Constants

When you use the def, defi, and defb instructions to define constants in a shader, the compiler can examine the specific values and produce code that is more optimal than if the constants were defined through the DirectX APIs outside of the shader. As an example, if you use the def instruction to define a four-wide constant of all zeros (0.0f) or all ones (1.0f), the compiler can make smart decisions when that constant is used. Assuming these are in constants C0 and C1, respectively, if the compiler encounters an addition of C0 to another register, it won't have to generate any code because adding zero to a value won't change the value. Similarly, if a value is multiplied by C1, the compiler again wouldn't have to generate any code. Any constants that will be the same, regardless of how the shader is used, should be defined directly in the shader itself using the def, defi, and defb instructions.

Write Directly to Output Registers

As described previously, the small number of SIMD registers and the reformatting of the input data to work on four vertices at a time mean that the shader compiler must generate code to save temporary results to memory whenever they're generated but not immediately used. For this reason, if a result being generated is ultimately to be copied to an output register, modify the shader code to write directly to that output register rather than to a temporary register that eventually gets copied.

Use Source Swizzle and Destination Masks

Like the previous guideline, the limited number of SIMD registers available means that if results are calculated that aren't used, one or more SIMD registers are wasted and unnecessary instructions for spilling data to memory and then restoring it have to be generated. If you need fewer than all four components of a source register or you only need a subset of the results generated by an instruction, make certain to specify source swizzle and destination write masks to inform the compiler of that. In the following example, the mov on the left only uses one component of r0 and only writes one component of oPos. The code on the right shows how to improve this to minimize register usage. Note that the mov instruction doesn't change.

Before	After
dp3 r0, v0, r1	dp3 r0.x, v0.xyz, v1.xyz
add r0, r0, v1	add r0.x, r0.x, v1.x
mov oPos.x, r0.x	mov oPos.x, r0.x

Minimize Dependency Chains

When writing shader assembly, you're often faced with a situation of one instruction operating on the results generated by a previous instruction. A given sequence of instructions in which the input of each instruction is dependent on the output of previous instructions is called a *dependency chain*. When implementing your algorithms in shaders, try to make dependency chains as short as possible or eliminate them altogether. Also, try to keep the instructions of a dependency chain clustered closely together rather than spread throughout the shader. Doing so gives the compiler more flexibility in scheduling instructions and register usage so that long latency instructions can be overlapped with shorter latency instructions and less spilling of registers to memory needs to be done.

Minimize Temp Register Usage between Basic Blocks

A basic block is a piece of code that has no branching (in the form of if statements, call statements, and loop or rep constructs). The original vs.1.0 and vs.1.1 shader models consisted entirely of one basic block because no branching of any kind existed. In the vs.2.0 and higher shader models, however, multiple basic blocks can exist in a given shader. To assist the compiler in its optimizations, it's recommended that temporary registers are not reused between basic blocks. Otherwise, the compiler will have to generate code to save and restore the temp register from memory.

Use rep Instruction if aL Isn't Needed in a Loop

Two types of looping were introduced in the vs.2.0 shader model: rep and loop. The rep instruction enables a sequence of instructions to be repeated for a number of iterations based on an integer constant. The loop instruction works similarly, but it provides the aL register used as a loop counter for indexing into the constant pool. For loops where you don't need to access the constant registers based on the loop counter, use the rep instruction because the compiler generates less code for it.

Avoid Address Register Usage or Reorder Vertices Based on Expected Values

A common theme with the optimizations described here is that anything that hurts the performance due to the SOA arrangement of data should be eliminated or avoided. Another example in this area is the use of the address register, a0. The address register is used to index into the constant registers, and because it can be computed dynamically within the shader, it can have different values for different vertices. If you can accomplish a task without the use of the address register, do so — even if it means a few extra instructions in your shader.

Figure 4 shows the effect of using the address register when the values for the four vertices in the address register are not all the same. As you can see from the diagram, the compiler must produce code that extracts each of the four components (based on the four values in the address register x component) from the various constant values and then combine them together to produce the final result (r5.x). The overhead of doing this is approximately 20 clocks. If all four values of the address register across four vertices were the same, a single instruction would suffice. Therefore, if possible, reorder your vertices based on the expected values in the address register.

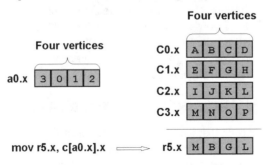

Figure 4: Address register usage effect on SOA data

Try to Eliminate Unnecessary Conditionals

Similar to the problem associated with address register usage, conditionals that vary from one vertex to the next can severely impact performance of software vertex shaders. When a conditional is encountered, the compiler must generate code to compute the outcome of the conditional for all four vertices and then execute both paths (for an if/else statement) and mask and combine the results. Because of this, it's best to avoid conditionals if at all possible.

One way to avoid conditionals is to use numerical masking. The sge and slt instructions compute a 1.0 or 0.0 result for each component of the destination register based on pair-wise comparisons between the source registers. By doing both comparisons, two multiplies, and an add, you can produce results that are commonly implemented with an if/else sequence. For example:

Before	After
if_lt r0.x, r1.x	slt r8, r0.x, r1.x
add r2, r2, r3	sge r9, r0.x, r1.x
else	mul r8, r8, r3 ; "if" portion
add r2, r2, r4	mul r9, r9, r4 ; "else" portion
endif	add r8, r8, r9 ; combined results
	add r2, r2, r8

Granted, this adds several instructions to the flow and is less easy to understand, but the performance gain can be significant because no branches are generated.

Use Predicates for a Few Instructions when Masking Won't Work

In cases where you have a small number of instructions in the if and else parts of a loop but where masking as described in the previous guideline won't work (or at least not as easily), you can use predicates to achieve the same results. Here's an example, similar to the previous one, that uses predicates to avoid branching:

Before	After
if_lt r0.x, r1.x	setp_lt p0. r0.x, r1.x
mul r2, r1.x, c8	(p0) mul r2, r1.x, c8
add r2, r2, r0.x	(p0) add r2, r2, r0.x
else	
mul r2, r0.x, c9	(!p0) mul r2, r0.x, c9
add r2, r2, r1.x	(!p0) add r2, r2, r1.x
endif	

The benefit of using predication is that the code is still fairly readable and the compiler can generate code that is still branch free to obtain the highest performance possible.

Use the Break Instructions to Early-exit from Loops

The old saying "the fastest code is the code that isn't executed" means that if you can avoid doing some computation, do so. With the break_xx instructions provided in the vs.2.x and vs.3.0 shader models, you can check for conditions being met and exit out of a loop that won't be doing any useful computation for the remainder of its iterations. The Mandelbrot sample included on the companion CD illustrates this quite nicely. As mentioned in the first tip, the speedup that resulted was very significant.

Use Conditionals to Early-exit from Rarely Used Code

Use of any of the transcendental instructions (log, exp, pow) in vertex shader code causes the compiler to generate a call to an optimized routine. However, the performance impact can be significant if a large number of these are used. In some cases, it's possible to do a dynamic branch based on comparison of values and avoid having to do the expensive computation. One example is when generating specular highlights in lighting code; by checking to see if the highlight color is black or if the specular power is very low, you can branch over the specular lighting calculation and avoid the call to the pow function. Whenever possible, use conditionals and branches (not masking or predication) to avoid expensive operations like log, exp, and pow.

Try to Arrange Conditional Data Based on Expected Behavior

When you do have to use conditionals with branching, if possible you can help the compiler achieve better performance by rearranging your data based on expected true/false behavior of the conditionals. A rudimentary example is a conditional that did something different based on whether a face was front facing or back facing. If you make sure to group your vertices based on spatial locality of the faces, you get better clustering of vertices that are all on front-facing triangles and vertices that are all on back-facing triangles. The processor's branch prediction is more accurate in these cases and the performance of your shader is higher.

Profile!

The best way to get great performance out of any piece of code, whether C++, assembly, or, in this case, vertex shader code, is to profile repeatedly with optimization in between. Other than watching frame rates as you make tweaks to the shader assembly, there hasn't been much that you could do to profile your vertex shaders, since the tools available are rather minimal. Now, Intel VTune Performance Analyzer 7.0 has a feature that makes profiling and optimizing software vertex shaders extremely simple. A trial version is available at http://www.intel.com/software/products/vtune/vpa/eval.htm. To get a trial license, visit http://www.intel.com/software/products/distributors/shader_x.htm.

If you write a test case that uses software vertex processing to process a batch of triangles and it does so in a repeatable way, when you profile the application using VTune Analyzer 7.0, you'll see a large spike in the module SWShaders.exe.jit where SWShaders will be replaced with the name of your application (see Figure 5).

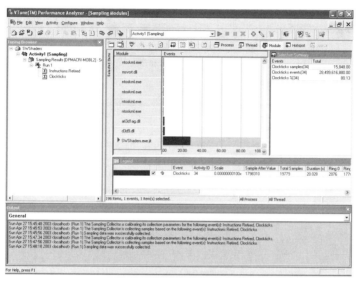

Figure 5: VTune Analyzer 7.0

Double-clicking on this module will list a few routines that are arbitrarily named, based on the order in which your vertex shaders and declarations were declared. If you have multiple vertex shaders, you'll see multiple routines, but with just one vertex shader, you should see a routine that handles the vertex declaration mapping and another that implements the vertex shader itself (see Figure 6).

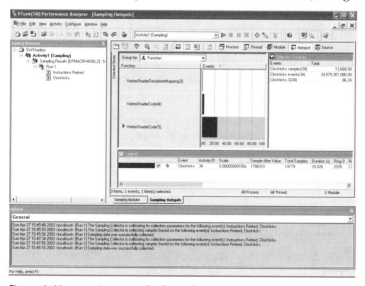

Figure 6: Hotspots in vertex shader code

Double-clicking on the vertex shader module brings up a listing of the vertex shader code with clockticks indicating which instructions consumed the most CPU time, as seen in Figure 7. In this example, we can see that the dp3 instruction contributed to the biggest portion of time in this shader.

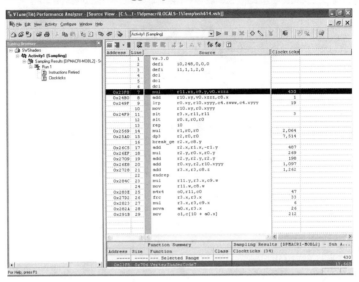

Figure 7: Vertex shader profile

One thing to be aware of when using the VTune Analyzer to profile software vertex shaders is that sampling must be *enabled* when the vertex shader declarations and shaders are created. Two common scenarios that would prevent this and leave you scratching your head trying to figure out why the biggest spike is in a module called Other32 are:

■ Using a start delay that causes the VTune Analyzer to miss the creation of the shaders. Start delays are often used to give your application time to launch and load data so you don't end up profiling all the startup operations.

■ Using the VTPause() and VTResume() APIs to only enable profiling of a specific portion of your application.

If you find that your sampling is primarily showing up in a module called Other32 (which you can't drill down into), then one of these situations is probably arising. The best recommended fix is to use the VTPause() and VTResume() APIs and make sure that you've enabled sampling around any creation of vertex shaders and declarations.

Sample Shader

The sample program on the companion CD, built on the DirectX 9 framework, can be used to see the relative performance of two shaders. The program uses a vertex shader to calculate values of the Mandelbrot set. In doing so, it illustrates how

Figure 8: Mandelbrot sample shader

the features available in later shader models can significantly improve the performance of software shaders in some cases. Figure 8 shows a screen capture from the sample shader.

It's interesting to note that as you zoom in on the Mandelbrot set using the dialog controls in the sample, it's possible to get to regions that are very *noisy* in terms of values staying close to the set and values escaping from the set. In those situations, the branching (in the form of a break instruction) in the optimized version can actually cause the performance to degrade. This is one reason why it's very important to profile your shader across as broad a sampling of uses as possible. Of course, if your shader doesn't have any branching, then the performance will be independent of the workload.

Conclusion

The software vertex processing support in DirectX 9 provides excellent performance to begin shipping game titles that incorporate vertex shading for doing both graphics and non-graphics-related computation. It provides a flexible and straightforward way to produce vectorized code that can take full advantage of the instruction sets and technology features of the latest processors to reach consumers. The guidelines presented here can help you ensure that your shaders will perform optimally, free the processor to do other game-related calculations, and enable your titles to stand out from the crowd.

Acknowledgments

I'd like to acknowledge a few individuals who made this article possible. First and foremost is Ronen Zohar at Intel. Ronen has worked closely with Microsoft in optimizing the Intel implementation of the processor-specific graphics pipeline in DirectX. Ronen also assembled the list of guidelines described in this article and wrote the original version of the Mandelbrot shader. Additional thanks go to Will Damon and Kim Pallister at Intel who provided source material, feedback, and suggestions that helped improve this article.

x86 Shaders–ps_2_0 Shaders in Software

Nicolas Capens

sw-shader.sourceforge.net

Introduction

Programmable graphics existed long before hardware acceleration. Unfortunately, the processors used back then were too slow for performing even the simplest shading tasks in real time. Nevertheless, software shaders are still more flexible than hardware-accelerated shaders. In this article we investigate the possibility of real-time software shading with modern processors like the Pentium III and 4. First, we see a few reasons why software rendering is still useful. Then we try to find out what makes the straightforward emulation so slow and what can be done about it. After that we discuss how to implement an efficient software renderer and DirectX pixel shader emulator. Finally, we solve a few practical problems encountered in the rendering pipeline.

x86 Shaders

If we could make software shaders reasonably efficient, they would have a good chance of surviving the battle against hardware-accelerated shaders because they have their own benefits. Although hardware-accelerated shader support is becoming more common for the professional industry and competitive gamers, it is not an obvious feature for low-budget, portable, or office computers. But even in these cases where top performance is not a requirement, the unlimited programmability of software shaders brings interesting new possibilities. Other benefits are getting exactly the same result on pretty much all systems without unsolvable driver issues or hardware limitations. It frees us from the complexity of handling graphics card capabilities, so we can focus on the actual application. Software rendering can also work together with hardware rendering to combine their advantages and implement the features not supported by the hardware as a fallback. Pentium III-compatible processors are much more widespread than graphics acceleration hardware with pixel shader support. Also remember that people who don't regularly play games commonly spend more money on a processor than on a good graphics card. Schools and universities mostly use computers without 3D graphics cards but often require 3D animations and simulations. Because software rendering has no limitations, it can be ahead of hardware to develop new technologies.

Current DirectX 9 support for pixel shaders is only useful as a reference because it takes several seconds per frame, even at low resolutions. There are a few reasons why the current shader emulation implementation is this slow. Writing an efficient software renderer for one specific task isn't very hard with the help of assembly optimizations, but as soon as we need multiple shaders, it is too much work to write different code for them and optimize everything manually. So we need to make it more generic by using lots of control statements to select different operations. On modern processors with deep pipelines, these control statements drastically reduce performance. If the processor cannot predict the result of a comparison correctly, it starts executing code from a wrong branch before it realizes this error. In this case, it has to stall for many cycles and has to start filling the pipelines again. Even when the comparisons are perfectly predictable, it still takes at least a compare and a jump per shader instruction and per render state. Also, an important performance bottleneck of modern processors is the memory throughput for the code, so it is necessary to make the inner loop small by avoiding redundant instructions — not to mention the cache incoherency we create by jumping.

So what we need is a way to eliminate these control statements. This can be done by selecting only those blocks of code that perform the wanted operation. This is just like conditional compilation, only at run time. In other words, instead of writing optimized routines manually, we need to generate them automatically. We can immediately make a parallel with hardware-accelerated shaders here, since these are also compiled at run time. Compilation of DirectX shaders is quite complex and generates much slower code than manually written assembly code, so what we need for maximum performance is a run-time assembler for our main processor's x86 assembly language. Instead of writing our shaders in the DirectX shader assembly language, we now write x86 shaders.

Let's see if this is feasible. Although 3D graphics cards have tremendous parallel processing power, the main processor is still clocked almost ten times higher. A quick calculation shows us that on a Pentium 4 running at 2.4 GHz, we could have 100 clock cycles available per pixel for a resolution of 800x600 and a target FPS of 50. So to get the most out of it, we need to use instructions that perform complex tasks in little time. The MMX and SSE instruction sets are especially very interesting for software rendering. The MMX instruction set is specialized in doing operations on four 16-bit integers in parallel, which is ideal for high-precision color operations. The SSE instructions operate on four single-precision floating-point numbers in parallel, so this is ideal for processing vertex components. Not only can the programmable shaders be run-time assembled, but also the fixed-function pipeline can be optimized this way. Some pixel shader instructions also depend on the current render state. With hardware, this isn't a problem, since one tiny transistor can decide what part of the silicon has to be used for the current operation. Here the compare will also be evaluated for all pixels, but this takes a negligible amount of time. In software, we again need conditional compilation. This way, only exactly those instructions needed for the current render state are assembled. We don't even need the transistor that the hardware needed. Instead of hard-wired logic, we now have soft-wired logic!

SoftWire is also the name of the assembler that we use throughout this article. Unlike many overcomplicated commercial assemblers that are aimed at generating executables and libraries from many source files, SoftWire is specialized at generating functions that can be called at run time. It is written in C++ and available as an open-source project under the LGPL license [1]. The object-oriented interface was designed especially with simplicity for run-time code generation in mind. We specify a file to assemble, along with the external data and conditional parameters, and it returns the corresponding block of machine code that can be called directly.

Let's try an easy example of an x86 shader assembled with SoftWire to get started. We subtract 1 from all color components, so we get a fade-to-black effect. Of course, this can also be done with graphics cards without shader support, but this example is only for illustrating the very basics. Suppose we already have the rest of our rendering pipeline and we want our inner pixel loop to be run-time assembled as a function. This isn't optimal yet, but the x86 code could look like this:

```
p0001h:                          // Label to reference static data
    DW 0001h                     // Used for subtracting 1 from every
    DW 0001h                     // 16-bit color component
    DW 0001h
    DW 0001h

Fade:
    mov        esi, [displayPointer]
    punpcklbw  mm0, [esi]        // Load pixel 32-bit -> 64-bit
    psubusw    mm0, [p0001h]     // Subtraction with saturation
    packuswb   mm0, mm0          // Pack pixel 64-bit -> 32-bit
    movd       [esi], mm0        // Write pixel

    emms
    ret
```

Let's store this in a Fade.asm file. Now all we need to do is tell SoftWire where the displayPointer external variable is stored by passing its address, and then we can assemble this code. The basic interface of the SoftWire::Assembler class looks like this:

```
Assembler(const char *fileName);

const void *callable(const char *entryPoint = 0);

static void defineExternal(void *pointer, const char *name);
static void defineSymbol(int value, const char *name);
```

To define the displayPointer external variable, we need to use the define-External method, like this:

```
defineExternal(&displayPointer, "displayPointer");
```

There is a handy macro to make it a little easier to do this:

```
ASM_EXPORT(displayPointer);
```

Because the `defineExternal` method is static, this works even when no `Assembler` has been constructed yet. Now that we have defined the externals, we are ready to assemble the file:

```
Assembler x86("Fade.asm");          // Construct an assembler called x86
```

At this point, the file has been translated to machine code, but it is not loaded into a block of memory, so it is not yet ready to be called. To link and load the code, we need to do the following:

```
void (*x86Shader)() = (void(*)())x86.callable("Fade");
```

We can now call `x86Shader()` in our inner pixel loop, and it will start executing from the `Fade` label. Pretty boring stuff for now, so let's start playing with the conditional compilation a bit. Fading to black can be useful, but fading to white is often used too. To do this, we only need a few extra lines:

```
Fade:
        mov       esi, [displayPointer]
        punpcklbw mm0, [esi]                // Load pixel 32-bit -> 64-bit
#if fadeBlack
        psubuswmm0, [p0001h]                // Subtraction with saturation
#else
        padduswmm0, [p0001h]                // Addition with saturation
#endif
        packuswb  mm0, mm0                  // Pack pixel 64-bit -> 32-bit
        movd      [esi], mm0                // Write pixel
```

Depending on the value of `fadeBlack`, this code now fades the screen to black or white. All we have to do is tell the assembler the value of `fadeBlack`, and we can assemble the file again. This is done with the `defineSymbol` method:

```
defineSymbol(fadeState(), "fadeBlack");
```

or a handy macro:

```
bool fadeBlack = fadeState();
ASM_DEFINE(fadeBlack);
```

That's it! These are the most important features that SoftWire is capable of for using x86 shaders. It all seems limited, but that's only because we've used the simplest example. The complete x86 instruction set is supported with all 32-bit addressing modes, and the conditional compilation can be made arbitrarily complex. Also, C++ functions can be called from within the assembly code — again by exporting it. It is also possible to jump to or call internal labels. For more information, please refer to the SoftWire documentation [1].

But why use SoftWire if we could just use inline x86 assembly and let our C++ compiler do the rest? SoftWire has one important extra advantage over inline assembly — namely the conditional compilation. Suppose the fixed-function vertex pipeline has more than 1000 different combinations of states and we would like to be able to do them all in software. Without using soft-wiring technology, we would have to write 1000 files and wait until they are all compiled before we can test them. But even if this could be done with things like macros and templates and we could put them in one huge library, it would still not be very useful. If we wanted to add just one extra feature, our library would have to double in size and it would take twice as long to compile. So this problem grows exponentially, and using a run-time assembler is the only option left as soon as we need more than a few render states.

Assembling takes time though. SoftWire was not designed for fast compilation. In practice, the average x86 shader takes almost a millisecond. If we had to assemble every shader for every frame and for every render state, it would disturb the rendering smoothness. Therefore, it is important that we use some sort of caching system to minimize the number of shaders being reassembled. In the future, SoftWire might feature a system for fast relinking when only a few constants are changed. This is possible because many of the instructions being assembled remain the same.

In many situations, we also need a rasterizer optimized for only one purpose. While conditional compilation allows supporting any render state, it doesn't give us optimal results, especially for simple operations. For example, deferred rendering techniques draw the scene in a first pass only to the depth buffer to have visibility information. In this case, a hand-optimized rasterizer could be faster because we can use all registers for just one task and even process a few pixels in parallel. Another example is the rasterization of small polygons. For geometry with a high polygon count, a scanline that is only one or two pixels long occurs a lot. These scanlines don't need the complex setup of longer scanlines, and a few approximations can be used that don't degrade quality. Affine texture mapping and per-polygon mipmapping are some examples of approximations that can significantly boost performance. This can be implemented together with the caching technique. When we need a certain rasterizer for the first time, we first check if any of the specialized rasterizers support the current render mode. If this fails, we use the general rasterizer. This doesn't mean that the specialized rasterizers can't use conditional compilation. For example, the specialized depth buffer rasterizer could use conditional compilation for the different depth compare modes. If a rasterizer is needed again, we first search if there's a compatible rasterizer in the cache. Since we search for rasterizers in the order of most specialized to most general, we know that the first compatible rasterizer that we find will also be the most efficient.

x86 shaders probably sound great in theory, but what about the results? Well, SoftWire was designed especially for a software-only renderer. It is still a work in progress, but it's already reaching 20 FPS in 640x480x32 display mode on a Celeron running at 1200 MHz for Quake III [2] scenes with all features turned on. This includes bilinear filtering, exact mipmapping, lightmapping, per-pixel perspective correction, dynamic lighting, fog, and more. On a Pentium 4 running at 2400 MHz, we get 22 FPS. This is a disappointingly low improvement over the Celeron and is caused by the Pentium 4's much higher latency for SIMD instructions. On a Pentium III running at 450 MHz, we get 9 FPS, which shows that the

Celeron suffers a bit from its smaller cache and slower front side bus. We can conclude that performance can be considered real time for a 1 GHz Pentium III or a 2 GHz Pentium 4. Note that Quake III was not designed for software rendering, so with some specific optimizations aimed at preventing overdraw, it could be much faster. For more recent information and screen shots, please visit the SoftWire web site [1].

A great advantage of SoftWire over hardware-accelerated shaders is that we have access to the complete x86 instruction set and all memory! We can make our shader code as long and as complex as we like, we can do operations that are not available in current hardware shader languages, and we have full control over memory. Want to implement your own filtering method? Need an extra memory buffer for storing certain parameters? Want to render voxels instead of polygons? Want to do ray tracing or call a recursive function for photon mapping? This is all no problem when using SoftWire. It is also open source, so adding specific features is easy. The conditional compilation can also help make the code processor independent. When SSE support is not detected, we can fall back to regular FPU instructions or use AMD's 3DNow! instructions. Note however that MMX uses the same registers, and a slow emms instruction is needed when switching from MMX to FPU mode. For AMD processors, a faster femms instruction can be used, but 3DNow! uses the same FPU registers once again. Because of this and because SSE operates on four instead of two floating-point numbers, it is far superior. Luckily, the newest generation of AMD's Athlon processors also supports SSE. The SSE instruction set also has some important instructions that complement the MMX integer instructions, so it is a must for efficient rendering on an x86 processor.

But there are also disadvantages when using x86 shaders. We cannot expect to reach the same performance as dedicated hardware. Although it has a higher clock frequency, the main processor's power lies primarily in its versatility, not raw number crunching. The conditional compilation also has a disadvantage over writing everything manually; it is hard to do instruction scheduling, since we cannot know in advance which instructions will be assembled. But this slight performance loss is nothing compared to the flexibility that it brings. For people who are not familiar with x86 code and especially the SIMD instruction sets, SoftWire might not seem very interesting. Why not immediately compile the DirectX shader instructions to x86 assembly? Although we see how to do this later, there are two main reasons why using x86 assembly is ideal when aiming for maximum performance. First of all, to use software shaders, we also need a fixed-function geometry pipeline and scan converter. To make these efficient, they need to be written using x86 assembly anyway. Secondly, even if we already had these and we would still like to write the shaders with the DirectX shader languages, we can never generate code as optimal as manually written code. So it is best to just regard it as another shader assembly language. But never fear — SoftWire can be used for much more than pure x86 shaders.

This brings us to another powerful feature supported by SoftWire that we haven't touched yet. SoftWire supports a form of macros that is ideal for abstracting the x86 code into more powerful "instructions" like with DirectX shaders. They are much like the C++ inline functions, and they use a similar syntax:

```
inline mad(dest, src0, src1, src2)
{
    movq    dest, src0
    psrlw   dest, 1
    pmullw  dest, src1
    psrlw   dest, 7
    paddw   dest, src2
}
```

...which can be invoked like this:

```
mad    mm0, mm1, mm2, mm3
```

Assuming the MMX registers hold the data in signed 8.8 fixed-point format, this "instruction" is compatible with the ps 1.3 mad instruction. It is even possible to use the ps 1.3 register names with some macros. The r0 and r1 registers can be mapped onto mm0 and mm1, t0 to t3 can be mapped onto mm2 to mm5, and the read-only registers can be held in memory. This leaves mm6 and mm7 available for temporary results in the macros. This way, ps 1.3 can be implemented efficiently with a very similar syntax.

ps_2_0 Shaders

So what about the more advanced pixel shaders from DirectX 9 like ps 2.0? These shaders use floating-point numbers everywhere, so MMX is of little use for the pixel operations. Unfortunately, SSE instructions are also at least twice as slow as MMX instructions, so it is less suited for real time. On the other hand, MMX needed many shift instructions for fixed-point arithmetic, which can now be eliminated. We now also have all MMX registers available for things like texture filtering. But the number of registers is still a limiting factor. The ps 2.0 standard specifies no less than 12 temporary registers, which is more than what SSE offers. So we can't simply map DirectX 9 registers onto x86 registers like we could with ps 1.3. These extra problems make it too slow for games on the current generation of processors. But with soft-wiring techniques and SIMD instructions, it is still much faster than the reference rasterizer. For things like CAD, the frame rate only has to be interactive and the viewport is usually smaller than the screen resolution.

Let's first focus on how to actually compile ps 2.0 shaders into x86 assembly. Because we need to use SSE and MMX, we need a convenient way to generate many different instructions. As a first attempt, we could create a string with the instruction and its operands and let SoftWire assemble this. This is hopelessly cumbersome. We would need to write many functions to generate code for just a few instructions. Also note that this is a huge detour because we first select an instruction and its operands, write that to a string, let SoftWire parse this string, and check its syntax and semantics; only then can we generate the machine code.

Luckily there's a shortcut called run-time intrinsics. In SoftWire, run-time intrinsics are a list of member functions of the Assembler with the same names as the x86 instructions, which generate the corresponding machine code at run time and put it into the assembler's internal buffer. So we can simply construct a new Assembler instance without specifying a file in the constructor, and we can start generating code by writing the assembly instructions as intrinsics. Besides being very easy to use, they are also safer than assembling from a file because the syntax is checked almost completely at compile time. Also, because it is still written in C++, things like passing pointers to external data and conditional compilation become trivial.

To become familiar with the use of run-time intrinsics, let's write something more useful than the fade code. Suppose we want to compute the dot product of two 3D vectors r0 and r1 and store the result in r2. Also suppose that we have a class SwShader derived publicly from SoftWire::Assembler:

```
void SwShader::encodeDP3()
{
    movaps(xmm0, xmmword_ptr [r0]);
    movaps(xmm1, xmmword_ptr [r1]);

    mulps(xmm0, xmm1);
    movhlps(xmm1, xmm0);
    addss(xmm1, xmm0);
    shufps(xmm0, xmm0, 0x01);
    addss(xmm0, xmm1);

    movss(dword_ptr [r2], xmm0);
}
```

This clearly shows that the C++ intrinsics syntax closely resembles the usual assembly syntax, so it is easy to convert existing code. In the above example, we used fixed source and destination "registers" stored in memory. Of course, we can just as easily parse the instruction and its operands from a ps 2.0 shader file and encode the instruction with the according registers.

For the parsing job, many tools for generating a parser from a grammar are available. Popular scanner and parser generators like Flex and Bison are slightly too sophisticated and do not produce C++ code. A simple parser generator more suited for this simple task is CppCC by Alec Panovici [3]. It produces understandable C++ code, and it's very easy to derive the SwShader class used above from the parser class. This allows parsing the file and directly storing the data in a list of ps 2.0 intermediate code instructions in the SwShader class.

Notice that in the example only two SSE registers are used, and three memory operations are needed. A much better situation would be to use all available registers to eliminate most of the loading and storing, but as we discussed before, we can't directly map ps 2.0 registers to SSE registers. The best compromise is to map as many ps 2.0 registers as possible to SSE registers and keep the rest in memory. This is known as virtual register allocation. Optimal register allocation cannot be solved in polynomial time, so a few heuristics are available. The most straightforward method is to just assign SSE registers to the most frequently used ps 2.0 registers. Unfortunately, this means that when we use any other ps 2.0 register, an SSE register needs to be freed by writing it back to memory. This is called spilling and adds lots of extra instructions with slow memory accesses. Most compilers use a graph coloring heuristic. Although near-optimal for the amount of spill code needed, it is also quite complex to compute. The most popular solution for run-time compilation is linear-scan register allocation [4]. It is also quite straightforward, marking when registers need to be allocated and when they are free for other variables to avoid much of the spill code. When a spill is necessary, a simple heuristic decides which register is needed the least. It is very fast and does not produce too much spill code.

Let's see how we can integrate linear-scan register allocation into SoftWire's run-time intrinsics. Since it's all written in C++, we can write a function xmmreg, which takes a ps 2.0 register as an argument and returns the SSE register to where it is mapped. This can then be used as the argument for the run-time intrinsic. If the ps 2.0 register is not already mapped to an SSE register, the xmmreg function adds spilling code if necessary. Similarly, we can write a function r_m128, which returns either a register or memory reference. This needs some illustration. Suppose the destination ps 2.0 register is stored in dst, the source registers in src0 and src1, and tmp0 and tmp1 are temporary registers; then the code would look like this:

```
void SwShader::encodeDP3(Operand &dst, Operand &src0, Operand &src1)
{
    movaps(xmmreg(tmp0), r_m128(src0));
    mulps(xmmreg(tmp0), r_m128(src1));

    movhlps(xmmreg(tmp1), xmmreg(tmp0));
    addss(xmmreg(tmp1), r_m32(tmp0));
    shufps(xmmreg(tmp0), r_m128(tmp0), 0x01);
    addss(xmmreg(tmp0), r_m32(tmp1));

    movss(xmmreg(dst), r_m32(tmp0));
}
```

We have solved two problems now: We've made the source and destination registers variable, and if there are enough SSE registers available, we've eliminated many memory operations. But it's still not optimal. The first instruction is only needed for preserving the source register. If the destination register is equal to one of the source registers, we can eliminate some instructions. Here we can use run-time conditional compilation again. Thanks to run-time intrinsics, this can simply be written in C++. Let's try this for the abs instruction:

```
void SwShader::encodeABS()
{
    if(dst != src0)
    {
        movaps(xmmreg(dst), xmmreg(src0));
    }

    typedef __declspec(align(16)) float float4[4];
```

```
    static float4 = {0x7FFFFFFF, 0x7FFFFFFF, 0x7FFFFFFF, 0x7FFFFFFF};

    andps(xmmreg(dst), signMask);
}
```

Another important optimization is not to copy data from a register to itself. This can be done by overloading the mov* instructions and detecting when the operands are equal. The list of optimizations that can be done is almost endless, and with run-time intrinsics, they can be implemented in a convenient manner.

Note that when a render state changes, we need to reassemble the shader because it can modify the behavior of texture lookup instructions and the like. Luckily, we don't need to parse the file again; only the code generation has to be redone. Since run-time intrinsics work directly with the SoftWire code, this takes little time. As we discussed before, caching techniques can further eliminate unnecessary work.

For a proof of concept for compiling ps 2.0 shaders to x86 assembly using SoftWire and CppCC, take a look at the swShader project [5]. This work in progress shows the details of how to implement the above techniques. Preliminary tests on the Celeron 1200 show that a pixel fill rate of five million pixels per second can be reached for a long shader of 40 arithmetic instructions translated to 150 SSE instructions. Compared to hardware-accelerated pixel shaders, this is very little, but it is certainly a lot better than the reference rasterizer. At modest resolutions, this is sufficient for interactive rendering.

Rendering Pipeline Operations

This article is complemented with the efficient solutions to a few practical problems when implementing a software renderer. An efficient implementation of shader emulation using soft-wiring and SIMD instructions isn't worth anything if the rest is inefficient or inaccurate. Since we already discussed the operations at pixel level, let's build it up all the way to the primitive level, which is the input of the renderer. Keep in mind that with software rendering, we are not limited in the way we implement something, but the following methods have proven their usefulness in practice.

Closest to the pixels are the frame buffer, the depth buffer, and the textures. The most limiting factor here is the memory bandwidth. Take for example the Pentium 4 with 400 MHz front side bus, which has a theoretical memory bandwidth limit of 3.2 GB/s. Suppose we render at a resolution of 800x600 with a 32-bit frame buffer and depth buffer. Per frame we might want to clear the frame buffer, clear the depth buffer, and then refill them both with the new frame. With an average overdraw of two and the double amount of depth buffer tests, this results in 15MB per frame. This seems small, but when we target 30 FPS, this takes one-seventh of the time for one frame, and that's even without all the other memory accesses, like for texturing and fetching code. That's millions of clock cycles where the processor can hardly do any useful arithmetic instructions.

We can't overcome this bandwidth limit, so it's important to minimize the number of memory accesses. In most situations, it is possible to eliminate clearing the frame buffer, since the whole scene is redrawn and fills the frame buffer. Reducing overdraw can be done efficiently when rendering from front to back and using one bit per pixel to indicate if it's already been filled. Unfortunately, sorting the polygons is not easy, so using a depth buffer is often the only option. Clearing the depth buffer can be eliminated by using positive depth values in even frames and negative values with the inverted depth compare mode in odd frames. With soft-wiring, we can change the compare mode instantly. So by sacrificing the sign bit of the depth buffer values, we can clear it at almost no cost. Texture memory access is something completely different. Because the addresses are not successive, the data is often not ready in the cache and the CPU has to read them from the RAM. Not only does the memory bus have a maximum throughput, the memory itself also requires time before the data is available. With an access time of 6 ns, this requires roughly a dozen clock cycles waiting for a few bytes and a lot more for actually finishing the move instruction. For this reason, the SSE instruction set also features prefetch instructions. They load the requested data into the cache without blocking other operations. When they are used a couple of instructions before the data are used, no memory stall will occur because the data will be available in the cache.

When a triangle is rasterized, it is broken up into horizontal lines of pixels called scanlines. The scanline setup is responsible for providing the input to the pixel shader. This is the ideal phase to convert some parameters from floating-point format to fixed-point integer format, since these are faster to interpolate and it is quite slow to do conversions per pixel. For colors with integer components, it is important to use saturated interpolation to avoid artifacts at the edges. Run-time conditional compilation can be used to interpolate only those parameters needed by the pixel shader. More specifically for DirectX shaders, the dcl instructions determine what texture coordinates need to be interpolated.

The triangle setup stage is a lot more advanced. First of all, it is responsible for determining where each scanline starts and ends (called scan-conversion). An excellent reference for this is the "Perspective Texture Mapping" article by Chris Hecker [6]. Calculating gradients for interpolants like the depth value and texture coordinates is another important task of the triangle setup. A common pitfall is to compute them per scanline. This is not necessary, since the slope of a triangle is equal everywhere. Another problem is precision. Let's take, for example, the horizontal slope of the z-value: $\Delta z/\Delta x$. Most implementations compute Δz at the longest scanline and divide that by its length. This 2D method brings many problems with sub-pixel accuracy, and it also doesn't work well with thin polygons. A much more robust 3D solution is to use the plane equation:

$$Ax + By + Cz + Dw = 0$$

Now we want to know $\Delta z/\Delta x$, which is equal to $\partial z/\partial x$, since it is constant. This can be computed by differentiating:

$$A\partial x + B\partial y + C\partial z + D\partial w = 0$$

Keeping y and w constant, we get:

$$\frac{\partial z}{\partial x} = -\frac{A}{C}$$

For the gradient in the y direction, we get $-B/C$. Starting from the plane equation, we get all our other gradients in a similar way. We just need to substitute z with the parameter for which we want to compute the gradients and recalculate the plane equation with the cross product for this new parameter. A nice property is that C is independent of the coordinate for which we calculate the gradients, so it only has to be computed once for all gradients. This is because C is twice the area of the triangle, which is of course constant. We can even compute $-1/C$ at once to multiply it with the different A and B values to avoid many divisions. D is never needed, so only A and B have to be computed for every interpolant. With SSE, this takes just a few clock cycles when computing four gradients in parallel.

This method of computing gradients is also an argument to only render triangles. We could be tempted to render polygons with more than three vertices, but this brings many problems. To compute the plane equation, we can use only three vertices, so the other vertices would need to be on the plane to be able to use the same gradient. This is easy to visualize for the z component. If not all vertices lie in the same plane, the polygon is not flat, and so the z gradients can't be constant. To avoid precision artifacts and to keep things simple, it is advisable to only rasterize triangles. With n-gons, we always need a loop, while with triangles, we avoid the loop setup and the stalls caused by mispredicted jumps.

Mipmapping requires computing the compression of the texture with respect to screen coordinates. In general, the relationship between screen coordinates and homogeneous texture coordinates is given by:

$$u' = \frac{\partial u'}{\partial x} x + \frac{\partial u'}{\partial y} y + u_0'$$

$$v' = \frac{\partial v'}{\partial x} x + \frac{\partial v'}{\partial y} y + v_0'$$

…where we use an apostrophe to denote that these texture coordinates are homogeneous and u_0' and v_0' are the coordinates at the origin of the screen ($x = 0$, $y = 0$). So the texture compression in the affine x direction is the length of the vector ($\partial u/\partial x$, $\partial v/\partial x$):

$$m_x = \sqrt{\left(\frac{\partial u}{\partial x}\right)^2 + \left(\frac{\partial v}{\partial x}\right)^2}$$

To get the affine texture coordinates u and v, we need to divide the homogeneous coordinates by w:

$$m_x = \sqrt{\left(\frac{\partial \left(\frac{u'}{w}\right)}{\partial x}\right)^2 + \left(\frac{\partial \left(\frac{v'}{w}\right)}{\partial x}\right)^2}$$

Even though there are fast SSE instructions for computing the square root and we already have $1/w$ for perspective correct texture mapping, it's not that simple. The gradients of the affine texture coordinates are not constants like the gradients of the homogeneous texture coordinates. So we have to try to find out how it changes as a function of the screen coordinates. First we use the quotient rule for derivatives:

$$= \sqrt{\left(\frac{\frac{\partial u'}{\partial x}w - \frac{\partial w}{\partial x}u'}{w^2}\right)^2 + \left(\frac{\frac{\partial v'}{\partial x}w - \frac{\partial w}{\partial x}v'}{w^2}\right)^2}$$

$$= \frac{1}{w^2}\sqrt{\left(\frac{\partial u'}{\partial x}w - \frac{\partial w}{\partial x}u'\right)^2 + \left(\frac{\partial v'}{\partial x}w - \frac{\partial w}{\partial x}v'\right)^2}$$

We now have a function where all gradients are constant and can be computed with the plane equation method. We now investigate how this compression value changes when we step from one pixel to the next in the hope that we can simplify the formula. So let's write u', v', and w as a function of x and y and substitute that into the formula. To simplify notation, we remove the apostrophe for homogeneous coordinates:

$$u = \frac{\partial u}{\partial x}x + \frac{\partial u}{\partial y}y + u_0$$

$$v = \frac{\partial v}{\partial x}x + \frac{\partial v}{\partial y}y + v_0$$

$$w = \frac{\partial w}{\partial x}x + \frac{\partial w}{\partial y}y + w_0$$

$$\Rightarrow$$

$$m_x = \frac{1}{w^2}\sqrt{\left(\frac{\partial u}{\partial x}\left(\frac{\partial w}{\partial y}y + w_0\right) - \frac{\partial w}{\partial x}\left(\frac{\partial u}{\partial y}y + u_0\right)\right)^2 + \left(\frac{\partial v}{\partial x}\left(\frac{\partial w}{\partial y}y + w_0\right) - \frac{\partial w}{\partial x}\left(\frac{\partial v}{\partial y}y + v_0\right)\right)^2}$$

Suddenly we lose the dependency in x under the square root. So although this formula looks horrible, only the w in the front changes when we step along the scanline. In other words, we only need to compute the square root for every scanline; but there's more. The u_0, v_0, and w_0 are constants, and we can collect them into other constants. If we give these new constants a logical name, we can also make this long formula look a little nicer:

$$C_u = \frac{\partial u}{\partial x}\frac{\partial w}{\partial y} - \frac{\partial w}{\partial x}\frac{\partial u}{\partial y}$$

$$C_v = \frac{\partial v}{\partial x}\frac{\partial w}{\partial y} - \frac{\partial w}{\partial x}\frac{\partial v}{\partial y}$$

$$U_x = \frac{\partial u}{\partial x}w_0 - \frac{\partial w}{\partial x}u_0$$

$$V_x = \frac{\partial v}{\partial x}w_0 - \frac{\partial w}{\partial x}v_0$$

$$m_x = \frac{1}{w^2}\sqrt{\left(C_u y + U_x\right)^2 + \left(C_v y + V_x\right)^2}$$

For the compression in the y direction, m_y, we have a similar formula but now with constants U_y and V_y. The biggest compression factor determines which mipmap level we have to use:

$$m = \max\left(m_x, m_y\right)$$

We could evaluate the maximum at every pixel, but this is not necessary. We can approximate this by computing m only at the vertices and using interpolation in between. This is also what is done by many hardware implementations, since the difference is hardly noticeable. By multiplying m by w^2 at the vertices and multiplying twice by $1/w$ at every pixel, this becomes simple linear interpolation. We already need $1/w$ for perspective texture mapping, so this adds no extra cost. Computing the maximum at the vertices saves us from needing to interpolate both compression factors. The gradients for m can again be computed using the method with the plane equation. The last thing that needs to be done per pixel is taking the $\log_2$ of m because mipmap dimensions are progressively divided by two. This can be implemented efficiently by either using the exponent of the floating-point representation or converting to integer and using the bsr instruction to find the index of the highest bit. It can be handy to index the mipmaps starting from 0 for $2^{16} \times 2^{16}$ texture size to 15 for 1×1 texture size. For non-square textures, the biggest dimension determines the index to avoid over-blurring.

One last trick that can be used in the triangle setup is the method used to sort the vertices from top to bottom. Normally, sorting involves copying the elements to a temporary location and swapping values. For vertices with many components, this can cost a considerable amount of time. Fortunately, this is not necessary, since we can just sort their references. This trick can be used for any sorting problem, but it is often forgotten.

Before triangles can be rasterized, they need to be clipped, projected, and then scaled into the viewport. It is very important to do this in homogeneous space to have z-values independent of the w coordinate, which is needed for perspective correction. We could use a clipping volume like the one used in DirectX, but there is a more efficient choice. If we use $[0, 1] \times [0, 1] \times [0, 1]$ as a clipping volume, the distances from a vertex to the left, bottom, and front clipping planes are equal to the x, y and z coordinate, respectively:

$$0 \le x \le 1$$
$$0 \le y \le 1$$
$$0 \le z \le 1$$
$$\Updownarrow$$
$$0 \le X \le W$$
$$0 \le Y \le W$$
$$0 \le Z \le W$$
$$\Updownarrow$$
$$0 \le X \wedge 0 \le W - X$$
$$0 \le X \wedge 0 \le W - Y$$
$$0 \le Z \wedge 0 \le W - Y$$

In this notation, lowercase letters are screen coordinates, while capital letters are clip space coordinates. As we can see, only three subtractions are needed. For the comparisons, it is advisable to use the sign bit of the floating-point format instead of using the compare instructions because this is faster and also works with SSE so we can stay in MMX mode. This can be useful for interpolating color values efficiently when an edge is clipped. To interpolate only those values needed by the rasterizer, we can once more use run-time conditional compilation.

In this article we focused primarily on pixel shading instead of vertex T&L because the latter can be performed efficiently by DirectX. However, if we want to develop an API-independent renderer, soft wiring can also make a big difference in performance for vertex processing. Implementing a vertex shader compiler is similar to the pixel shader. There's just one important difference, which allows another big optimization. With pixel shaders, we have to work per-pixel, but with vertex shaders, we can work per-component. For example, when transforming a vertex in a straightforward manner, we need a lot of shuffle instructions to do the dot products. All internal data movement is wasted time, so we'd like to eliminate that. We can do this by noting that the x, y, z, and w coordinates can be computed independently. So transforming all vertices separately or first transforming all x components, then all y components, etc., gives no difference in the operations being performed. However, when working per-component instead of per-vertex, we do not need any shuffle instructions because four x coordinates from different vertices in an SSE register are independent. So what we do is store a structure-of-arrays for the components instead of storing an array-of-structures for the vertices. The components are then processed in groups of four in a tight loop. To implement this, it is useful to first write the SSE code using only the single-scalar instructions and then replacing them all with packed-scalar instructions to do exactly the same operation on four components at a time.

As mentioned before, manual scheduling of instructions is not possible. However, we could develop an automatic optimizer. First, a peephole optimizer can be used and then a scheduler. Scheduling can considerably improve performance, since a Pentium III and 4 cannot execute dependent instructions or instructions that use the same execution unit in parallel. Unfortunately, optimal scheduling cannot be done in polynomial time. There exist some heuristics, but they need to know many parameters for each instruction. This includes the throughput, the latency, and the execution units that it uses. Since there are so many instructions and variants, this is hard to implement. The Pentium III and 4 are superscalar, pipelined processors with out-of-order execution, which basically means that we can't predict when a certain instruction is executed. Instructions are also composed of one or more micro-instructions, but this micro-code is a well-kept secret. It is stored in a ROM that is model specific, making it almost impossible to have accurate parameters for the heuristical scheduler.

A much easier approach is to treat the processor as a theoretical black box. A block of code goes in, and we can only see the results. We don't even care how it works internally. Practically, this means that we just measure the execution time of the code and see what happens if we change the instruction order. We use a brute-force approach by doing many tests, and we keep the code that had the smallest execution time. By constructing a graph of instruction dependencies, every permutation of the instructions that preserves dependencies can be tested. This can quickly become billions of possibilities, but with a good heuristic, a near-optimal solution can be found in linear time. However, this method is not that easy to implement in a renderer because an accurate performance measurement is needed. A benchmark with only one small triangle could execute in less than a millisecond, but this is not always consistent because of interrupts, task switches, and other stalls. So the test has to be repeated long enough to have a reliable average. We often also need more than one shader, so we can't let the user wait hours before we start rendering at around 20 percent higher performance. One solution is to run the scheduler in the background in another thread. By temporarily setting the thread priority higher, we can try to avoid the task switches. The longer the user runs the application, the more the shaders get optimized. This also means that when the user closes the application, the optimal scheduling is lost. It is also useless to use 20 percent of processor time for scheduling if we only expect, at most, a 20 percent performance increase from it. Another solution is to compile them in advance and put them in a library, but then we lose flexibility. The system that has been used for scheduling can also differ significantly from the user's system, which influences the optimal instruction order. The last solution is to give the user the option to run a long benchmark to schedule the shaders for the current settings and keeping the results.

The brute-force scheduling method isn't very practical for graphics shaders, but there are still other options. One method that certainly deserves attention is peephole scheduling. Looking at only a few instructions at a time, we can reduce dependencies between them and empirically schedule the execution unit usage. This method is very fast, since it doesn't need to measure the performance of the altered code, and it is scalable. On the other hand, changes that appear to be beneficial at first can work adversely in practice because of the badly predictable behavior of processors with out-of-order execution. So in the end, we just have to accept that we can't do a perfect job here.

Conclusion

We conclude this article by summarizing the results. Software rendering shows new potential thanks to the speed of modern SIMD processors, the optimization via soft wiring, and the ultimate programmability of x86 shaders. For applications where reliability and a wide market are more important than the race for performance, it is an interesting alternative. It's also very discussable that games need a great deal of eye candy and more frames per second than can be perceived to have good gameplay. Let's not forget web multimedia, where we can't assume that everyone has hardware acceleration that supports the wanted features but where soft-wiring can get the best performance out of any type of CPU. It is also useful for scripting engines, JIT-compilers, and optimization in general. Run-time intrinsics are very easy to use, so it takes little time to convert existing assembly code to intrinsics. Application areas like real-time sound and video processing also benefit a lot from it, as it is less common to have hardware support for these tasks. In these cases, it also might be worth it to spend a few minutes trying to get a near-optimal instruction order. So let's break free from our dependability on hardware support and do things that have never been tried before!

References

[1] Capens, Nicolas, SoftWire Run-Time Assembler Library, http://softwire.sourceforge.net.

[2] id Software, Quake III, http://www.idsoftware.com.

[3] Panovici, The C++ Compiler Compiler, http://cppcc.sourceforge.net.

[4] Poletto, Massimiliano and Vivek Sarkar, "Linear-scan register allocation," *ACM Transactions on Programming Languages and Systems*, Volume 21, Issue 5 (Sept. 1999), pp. 895-913, http://www-124.ibm.com/developerworks/oss/jikesrvm/info/pubs.shtml#toplas99.

[5] Capens, Nicolas, SoftWire Shader Emulator, http://sw-shader.sourceforge.net.

[6] Hecker, Chris, "Perspective Texture Mapping," April/May 1995, http://www.d6.com/users/checker/misctech.htm.

SoftD3D: A Software-only Implementation of Microsoft's Direct3D API

Oliver Weichhold

In this article I describe the process of making SoftD3D and some of the challenges that had to be overcome along the long road to completion.

Some time ago, our company decided to shift part of its focus toward the upcoming generation of embedded devices like the Compaq IPAQ. There was a variety of products in the pipeline — among them an application that required real-time 3D graphics. After a great deal of internal discussion and brainstorming, the team opted against the acquisition or in-house development of a proprietary 3D engine. Instead, I was assigned to develop a piece of software that would allow everyone involved to continue to work on the new platform with a well-known technology. That technology was Direct3D 8.

Fortunately, at the time I was carrying out the initial planning stage for the project, a subset of the DirectX 8 API was already available for our target platform (Compaq IPAQ). Unfortunately, due to the lack of built-in 3D hardware, Direct3D was present but not operational on this platform. I recalled that the IDirect3D8 interface featured a member called `RegisterSoftwareDevice`, which according to the documentation could be used to plug in arbitrary (software) rasterizers. I reckoned that I just had to write a software rasterizer instead of reinventing the entire API.

Despite the fact that the `RegisterSoftwareDevice` member was not supported on the Win32 platform, I started my research and consumed every piece of publicly available documentation and software related to the task, ranging from the Windows DDK (device development kit) to actual graphics device driver source code. After a few days, I came to the conclusion that it wasn't meant to be; `RegisterSoftwareDevice` was either not supported at all or reserved for internal use by Microsoft. I had to do it the hard way.

At first I felt overwhelmed by the challenge of writing a compatible implementation of a technology that Microsoft had developed using significant manpower. True, I had a good deal of experience with all major Direct3D releases, but that experience was based on the standpoint of an application developer, not that of an API implementer or even a device driver developer.

After concluding my initial research about the inner workings of the Direct-3D pipeline, during which the diagrams by Rich Thomson proved to be extremely useful, I began to iron out the object hierarchy. Since DirectX is based on Microsoft's Component Object Model (COM) technology, decisions had to be made in regard to how the Direct3D COM interfaces would be exposed. Under normal circumstances, this process should be pretty straightforward, but when you are dealing with a real-time environment where every clock cycle counts, things can easily get a bit more complicated.

The goal was to produce a Dynamic Link Library (DLL) that would be binary compatible to Microsoft's own D3D8.DLL that implements the core of Direct3D version 8. That task was easily accomplished because D3D8.DLL exports only a single function relevant to application developers. The name of this function is Direct3DCreate8. The implementation of the Direct3DCreate8 function exported by SoftD3D.dll is shown below:

```
Direct3D8 * __stdcall Direct3DCreate8(UINT SDKVersion)
{
    CComObject<Direct3D8> *p;
    CComObject<Direct3D8>::CreateInstance(&p);
    if(p)
        p->AddRef();

    return p;
}
```

The next task involved creating a set of skeleton classes from the object model whose sole purpose for now was to expose the associated COM interfaces to get things running. The actual implementation of most interface members was left blank at that time. The skeleton for the class implementing the IDirect3DDevice8 interface is shown below:

```
class ATL_NO_VTABLE Device8 :
    public CComObjectRootEx<CComSingleThreadModel>,
    public IDirect3DDevice8
{
    BEGIN_COM_MAP(Device8)
        COM_INTERFACE_ENTRY_IID(IID_IDirect3DDevice8, IDirect3DDevice8)
    END_COM_MAP()

    protected:
    // IDirect3DDevice8
    STDMETHOD(TestCooperativeLevel)();
    STDMETHOD_(UINT, GetAvailableTextureMem)();

    ...
};
```

NOTE Some readers might notice that I'm using the ActiveX Template Library (ATL) and are wondering why I did this, considering the real-time nature of the project. The answer is that it is comfortable and has virtually no performance impact.

Section III — Software Shaders and Shader Programming Tips
SoftD3D: A Software-only Implementation of Microsoft's Direct3D API

415

Then it was time to implement the "adapters" that would be responsible for displaying the rendered images on screen. This task was especially tricky since I was planning on doing most of the work on Win32 to speed up the development process. As always, if you develop something on a host platform that is primarily targeted to another platform that is far inferior performance-wise, you have to be very careful not to make design decisions that don't work out on the target platform later on.

The plan was to employ DirectDraw 7 for frame buffer management on Windows. To make sure that I wouldn't hit a dead end when porting the project to the target hardware, I began evaluating and benchmarking various libraries dealing with frame buffer and off-screen surface management on PocketPCs. Luckily, it turned out that the approach taken by most of those libraries was close to optimal performance and even better — conceptually compatible with DirectDraw.

Having solved that problem, I wrote two adapters: one for Windows using DirectDraw and another for the Compaq IPAQ using the GapiDraw library.

```
class ATL_NO_VTABLE DDraw7Adapter :
    public CComObjectRootEx<CComSingleThreadModel>,
    public IAdapter
{
    BEGIN_COM_MAP(DDraw7Adapter)
        COM_INTERFACE_ENTRY_IID(__uuidof(IAdapter), IAdapter)
    END_COM_MAP()

    // IAdapter
    STDMETHOD_(UINT, GetModeCount)();
    STDMETHOD(EnumModes)(UINT Mode, D3DDISPLAYMODE* pMode);
    STDMETHOD(BeginScene)();
    STDMETHOD(EndScene)();
    STDMETHOD(Flip)();

    ...
};
```

Before even thinking about working on the actual rendering pipeline, another problem had to be solved: floating-point calculations. Unlike almost every modern personal computer, embedded devices such as PocketPCs are usually not equipped with special hardware that handles floating-point calculations. The IPAQ is no exception. Floating-point calculations are nonetheless possible on these devices, but they are slow — very slow. Even the fastest floating-point libraries for StrongARM processors (which power the IPAQ) are between ten and 100 times slower than integer calculations. This fact poses a huge problem to software that primarily deals with floating-point calculations. However, there is a solution called fixed-point math. For the reader unfamiliar with this concept, here is a quick rundown:

Fixed-point math is a simple way to speed up floating-point calculations by using integers to represent fractional numbers. Fixed-point formats are usually expressed using the xx.yy form, where xx describes the number of bits before the decimal point and yy the number of bits after the decimal point. In the case of 16.16 fixed-point, 65535.99998 is the largest possible number.

Because the actual calculations are performed using integer math, fixed-point runs at an acceptable speed, even on the low-end CPUs used in embedded devices. But there's a hook; by using fixed-point calculations, you sacrifice precision and range — things that easily render the performance gain irrelevant if not used correctly.

Regardless of the potential problems, I decided to add support for fixed-point math right from the start. Thanks to C++'s operator overloading, it was relatively easy to produce a fixed-point class that, if used in conjunction with custom type definitions, handles all floating-point calculation by changing a simple preprocessor symbol.

The next step involved writing all the resource management and setup code necessary to create and initialize the device, frame buffer, textures, depth buffer, and vertex and index buffers allocated by a client application. At that point, I was already using DirectX SDK samples for testing and everything worked quite well — at least with the SDK samples, as I soon found out.

Let's now move on to the implementation of the rendering pipeline.

Vertex Stream Splitting

The first thing that happens when any of the DrawPrimitive member functions of the IDirect3DDevice8 are called is the stream setup. This stage performs the separation of incoming vertex data for further processing. The term "incoming" refers to vertex streams specified using a previous call to SetStreamSource or the vertex data passed to any of the DrawPrimitiveUP functions.

```
class VertexStreamsInfo
{
    public:
    VertexStreamsInfo();
    virtual ~VertexStreamsInfo();

    // Attributes
    VertexStreamInfo m_Streams[VSTREAM_MAX];
    DWORD m_dwTexCoordCount;
    DWORD m_dwCombinedFVF;
    DWORD m_dwMaskAllocated;     // bitmask indicating streams that were allocated in the
                                 // vertex pipeline and should be freed after processing

    // Implementation
    HRESULT Init(StreamInfo *pSI, DWORD dwVertexShader);
    HRESULT Init(BYTE *pData, DWORD dwStride, DWORD dwVertexShader);
    HRESULT Init(StreamInfo *pSI, DWORD *pDeclaration);
};
```

The Init member is overloaded three times to facilitate the following cases:

■ Fixed-function pipeline

- Fixed-function pipeline using `DrawPrimitiveUP`
- Programmable pipeline

After the `Init` function returns, the incoming vertex stream(s) have been separated into 1-n stream information blocks stored in `m_Streams`, which will be passed further down the pipeline.

For example, an FVF (flexible vertex format) of D3DFVF_XYZ | D3DFVF_TEX2 is split into three distinct streams — one for the vertex position and one for each of the two texture coordinates.

Depending on whether we are dealing with transformed or untransformed vertices, the following section can be skipped.

Vertex Processing

During this stage, the incoming vertex streams are processed. This is done by concatenating one or more discrete implementations of the internal IVertexStreamProcessor interface.

```
interface IVertexStreamProcessor
{
    STDMETHOD(ProcessStreams)(VertexStreamsInfo *pVSI, DWORD dwStartVertex, DWORD
            dwNumVertices) PURE;
    STDMETHOD_(void, SetNext)(IVertexStreamProcessor *pNext) PURE;
};
```

Each vertex processor operates on all vertices between `StartVertex` and `NumVertices` using single or multiple input streams, producing 0-n output streams. The resulting set of vertex streams is then passed to the next processor in the chain (if present).

There are various reasons behind the decision to handle vertex data in a streaming manner, as opposed to processing them as needed:

- Best performance with indexed primitives
- The use of SIMD instructions (single instruction multiple data) like MMX, SSE, 3DNOW. These instructions are best suited for larger batches of data and may even cause heavy speed penalties when the processor has to switch often between modes (FPU <-> MMX).
- The memory layout of vertex buffers is optimized for processor cache friendliness and SIMD instructions

The following vertex processors are currently implemented:

- VSP_XFormWorldViewProjection — Applies world/view/projection transformation and produces XYZW output stream from incoming XYZ stream
- VSP_XFormWorldViewProjection_X86_SSE — Applies world/view/projection transformation and produces XYZW output stream from incoming XYZ stream; SSE optimized

- VSP_XFormWorldView — Applies world/view transformation and produces XYZW output stream from incoming XYZ stream
- VSP_VertexFog — Produces FOG output stream from incoming XYZW stream
- VSP_VertexFogRange — Produces FOG output stream from incoming XYZW stream — range-based fog
- VSP_TexGen_CameraSpace_Normal — Texture coordinate generation
- VSP_TexGen_CameraSpace_Position — Texture coordinate generation
- VSP_TexGen_CameraSpace_ReflectionVector — Texture coordinate generation
- VSP_TC_Transform — Texture coordinate transformation
- VSP_Lighting — Direct3D fixed-function pipeline conformant vertex lighting; produces DIFFUSE and SPECULAR output streams
- VSP_Lighting_X86_SSE — Direct3D fixed-function pipeline conformant vertex lighting — produces DIFFUSE and SPECULAR output streams; SSE optimized

The number and type of vertex processors that get concatenated to a processing chain solely depends on the current renderstate settings.

Rasterizer/Interpolator Setup

This stage consists of a large switch tree that picks the rasterizer that is best suited to handle the current renderstate settings. SoftD3D implements more than 40 distinct rasterizers and interpolators, which only differ by the number and quality of interpolated values. This might sound like a lot of work (and it is), but fortunately this high level of specialization can be accomplished by excessive use of C++ templates to combine simple fragments into more powerful ones. More on this later.

At this point, we enter the main triangle loop. This loop iterates over all triangles that are affected by the current DrawPrimitive call.

Backface Culling

Depending on the current value of the D3DRS_CULLMODE renderstate, triangles get backface culled. There are a number of possible approaches to backface culling. SoftD3D performs backface culling in object space because of the advantage of the possible rejection of triangles very early in the pipeline.

To do this, we first compute the viewer position in object space using the following pseudocode:

```
ViewerPosition.x = -Transform[D3DTS_VIEW].m[0][0] * Transform[D3DTS_VIEW].m[3][0] -
                    Transform[D3DTS_VIEW].m[0][1] * Transform[D3DTS_VIEW].m[3][1] -
                    Transform[D3DTS_VIEW].m[0][2] * Transform[D3DTS_VIEW].m[3][2];
```

```
ViewerPosition.y = -Transform[D3DTS_VIEW].m[1][0] * Transform[D3DTS_VIEW].m[3][0] -
                    Transform[D3DTS_VIEW].m[1][1] * Transform[D3DTS_VIEW].m[3][1] -
                    Transform[D3DTS_VIEW].m[1][2] * Transform[D3DTS_VIEW].m[3][2];

ViewerPosition.z = -Transform[D3DTS_VIEW].m[2][0] * Transform[D3DTS_VIEW].m[3][0] -
                    Transform[D3DTS_VIEW].m[2][1] * Transform[D3DTS_VIEW].m[3][1] -
                    Transform[D3DTS_VIEW].m[2][2] * Transform[D3DTS_VIEW].m[3][2];
```

After that, we calculate a vector from the object space viewer position to the triangle and take the dot product of this vector and the normal vector of the triangle. The resulting scalar is treated differently depending on whether D3DRS_CULLMODE = D3DCULL_CCW or D3DRS_CULLMODE = D3DCULL_CW.

Because this process is repeated for *every* triangle, optimized implementations for different processor architectures exist.

Vertex Assembly

At this point, almost all the data required by the rasterizer is available. The vertex processing stage has transformed the vertices using the world/view/projection matrices, lit the vertices, and applied texture transformations and fog. But the generated data has been stored in a stream layout, which is not exactly optimal for the rasterizer.

To avoid time-consuming pointer arithmetic at the rasterizer stage, the data from all streams is now reconciled into a single vertex structure. This is achieved by dereferencing the streams using pointer arithmetic. To speed up this process, optimized versions of the code for each Direct3D primitive type have been implemented.

```
class TLVertex
{
    public:
    Vector4 Position;
    Vector2D<int> ScreenPosition;       // Computed AFTER clipping
    TLColor Diffuse;                     // normalized for interpolation
    TLColor Specular;                    // normalized for interpolation
    _float Fog;
};

class TLVertexTex : public TLVertex
{
    public:
    TexCoord tc[MAX_TEX_COORD];
};
```

After all three vertices of the current triangle have been initialized, they are passed down to the next stage.

Clipping

During clipping, we test an individual triangle against the canonical view frustum in homogeneous clip space ($-w <= x <= w, -w <= y <= w, 0 <= z <= w$). This is controlled by D3DRS_CLIPPING. The actual implementation is described in various documents and beyond the scope of this article.

One aspect about the implementation worth mentioning is the use of vertex pointer arrays. To avoid excessive copying of vertex data and optimize data cache coherency, the clipping function gets passed an array of pointers to vertices (computed in the last section). Whenever a vertex passes the clipping test, only the pointer to the vertex is copied to the input array for the next clipping stage.

Once all vertices of the current primitive have passed the clipping stage, the function determines if there are sufficient vertices to render the primitive. If this test fails, the primitive is skipped.

Homogeneous Divide and Viewport Mapping

We are now entering the final step before the rasterizer is going to render the primitive.

With view frustum clipping completed, each group of vertex coordinates is projected by computing x/w, y/w, and z/w. The resulting values are multiplied and offset by the parameters that control the size of the viewport into which the primitives are to be drawn (D3DVIEWPORT8 structure). The resulting screen coordinates are then converted to integer values for further use by the rasterizer.

This process may sound trivial, but surprisingly, it turned out to be a major performance bottleneck during my tests. Why? Look at this code snippet:

```
v.ScreenPosition.x = v.Position.x;
v.ScreenPosition.y = v.Position.y;
```

Looks simple, doesn't it? The problem with this code is the conversion of floating-point numbers to integer numbers. The Visual C++ compiler for Win32 performs this conversion using a function call that is, of course, rather slow. To speed this up, I chose to manually perform the conversion using an inline function:

```
__forceinline int FastFloat2Int(float fFloat)
{
    static DWORD nTemp;
    _asm
    {
        fld fFloat
        fistp nTemp
        mov eax, nTemp
    }
}
```

Before you can use this function, you have to configure the rounding mode of the floating-point unit. This code does the trick:

```
__forceinline void FastFloat2Int_SetFloor()
{
    _asm
    {
        fnstcw wFastFloatTemp
        mov ax, wFastFloatTemp
        and ax, ~(3 << 10)
        or ax, 1 << 10                  // set _RC_DOWN
        mov wFastFloatTemp, ax
        fldcw wFastFloatTemp
    }
}
```

Initializing the FPU rounding mode once and repetitively calling FastFloat2Int turned out to be more than ten times faster than the compiler-generated code.

After the integer conversion of screen coordinates has been completed, one last check is performed on the screen coordinates against the viewport dimensions. This is because it is perfectly legal to pass in pretransformed vertices to DrawPrimitive, effectively bypassing the stages covered in the "Vertex Processing" and "Vertex Assembly" sections. Unfortunately, some applications (can you say "Unreal Engine") provide coordinates that lie slightly out of the viewport area, causing visual artifacts. 3D hardware accelerators simply alleviate this problem through guard band clipping.

Triangle Setup

NOTE   Although Direct3D supports other primitive types besides triangles, for simplicity, we focus solely on triangles for the remainder of the article.

In order to render a triangle to the render target (usually the screen), a triangle has to be broken up into scanlines, which are then rendered one at a time. This process is called *scan conversion*. There is a variety of different solutions for performing scanline conversion and interpolation. SoftD3D uses a derivate of Chris Hecker's excellent solution described in [1].

During triangle setup, a number of so-called "gradients" is calculated. These gradients are used to interpolate values from the triangle's vertices across the visible surface of the triangle. The type and number of the computed gradients is affected by several renderstates, including D3DRS_ZENABLE, D3DRS_ALPHABLEND-ENABLE, D3DRS_SHADEMODE, D3DRS_LIGHTING, D3DRS_SPECULARENABLE, D3DRS_FOG-ENABLE, and all texture mapping-related renderstates.

For example, let's assume that we want to render a single triangle that is lit by a light source. Let's also assume that D3DRS_LIGHTING is true, D3DRS_SPEC-ULARENABLE is false, and D3DRS_ZENABLE is false. A possible vertex structure would consist of just the vertex position and a normal vector. During vertex lighting (performed in the "Vertex Processing" section), a new component is computed for each vertex: the diffuse color. In this case, the rasterizer needs to interpolate xs, ys, z, and diffuse along the edges of the triangle and across each scanline.

SoftD3D implements interpolators for:

- x and y coordinates in screen space
- w for depth buffering
- Diffuse color (not perspective correct)
- Specular color (not perspective correct)
- Fog color (not perspective correct)
- One to eight texture coordinates (perspective correct)

Obviously, there's quite a large number of possible combinations. Computing all gradients regardless of the renderstate settings is not an option because doing so wastes a huge amount of processor time. What we need is a set of interpolators that only work on values that are really going to be used for rendering. One could write customized code for each possible case, but not only would this be a cumbersome process but also very prone to human errors. Once again, C++ templates come to our rescue.

If we could split up the problem into smaller parts and let the compiler combine those fragments into a working unit without suffering a performance impact, we'd be set. This is exactly how SoftD3D implements its set of more than 40 distinct rasterizers. Take a look at the following class declaration:

```
template<class TFramebuffer, class TVertex, class TEdge, class TGradient, class TDerived>
class Rasterizer : public IRasterizer
{
...
};
```

The Rasterizer class acts as a template-based abstract base class for all rasterizers, importing its entire functionality from the template arguments specified by derived classes.

The class declaration below shows a discrete rasterizer that is responsible for rendering Gouraud-shaded triangles not using a depth buffer. The RTriGouraud rasterizer really consists of just the declaration. No additional code or data had to be added.

```
class RTriGouraud : public Rasterizer<TFramebuffer, TLVertex, RasterEdgeGouraud_
      Diffuse, RasterGradientsGouraud_Diffuse<RasterGradientsdXY>, RTriGouraud>
{
};
```

Now take a look at this one:

```
template<class TFramebuffer>
class RTriGouraudZ : public Rasterizer<TFramebuffer, TLVertex,
      RasterEdgeZ<RasterEdgeGouraud_Diffuse>,
      RasterGradientsGouraud_Diffuse<RasterGradientsZ>, RTriGouraudZ>
{
};
```

As you might have guessed, this rasterizer also renders Gouraud-shaded triangles, but this version includes support for interpolating depth values (1/w).

Let's summarize this stage again. During triangle setup, we compute a set of constants called gradients that allow us to interpolate arbitrary values across the surface of the triangle for further processing.

Scanline Rendering

When the rendering process gets down to the scanline level, things start getting interesting — and complicated. The scanline level is the place where the most time is spent during rendering, and performance can be gained but more often is lost. This is the place where every processor cycle matters. Speed is the name of the game.

There are three main techniques for implementing the scanline loop:

A single complex loop	Multiple simple loops	Dynamic compilation

Pixel p;
 	
for(i = Left;i<=Right;i++)
{
    if(Feature1)
        DoSomething(&p);
 	
    if(Feature2)
        DoSomethingElse(&p);
 	
    DisplayPixel(p);
}
	PixelArray pa[Width];
	
	if(Feature1)
	{
	    for(i = Left;i<=Right;i++)
	        DoSomething(pa[i]);
	}
	
	if(Feature2)
	{
	    for(i = Left;i<=Right;i++)
	        DoSomethingElse(pa[i]);
	}
		This advanced technique works by compiling small assembly fragments into complex subroutines at run time.
		
		The previous article by my colleague Nicolas Capens is dedicated to this topic.

At present, SoftD3D uses the multiple simple loops technique. The disadvantages of this approach:

■ Multiple loops instead of a single one, thus more branch instructions

■ An increased number of memory accesses

The advantages:

■ Elimination of many branch instructions from the inner loop, which are very costly on processors with long pipelines like the Intel Pentium 4

■ Possibility to write (SIMD) optimized code for every stage of the pipeline

■ Very hot data caches, most likely L1. (OK, this is not really an advantage, but it at least softens up the performance impact caused by the increased number of memory accesses.)

When the scanline loop is entered, all color values have been already converted to a 32-bit RGBA format that will be used until the final output stage is reached.

Texture Blending Cascade

Very early on in the pipeline (during the step described in the "Rasterizer/Interpolator Setup" section) checks are made that determine whether the rasterizer will have to deal with textures or fog. If any of these conditions is true, then a suitable texture cascade is assembled for later use.

The heart of the system is an interface called ITSSProcessor.

```
interface ITSSProcessor
{
    STDMETHOD_(void, SetNext)(ITSSProcessor *pNext) PURE;
    STDMETHOD_(ITSSProcessor *, GetNext)() PURE;
    STDMETHOD_(BOOL, IsStatic)() PURE;


    virtual void __fastcall Process(Device8 *pD3DD, int Width, BOOL bUsePMask) PURE;
    virtual void __fastcall ProcessBounds(Device8 *pD3DD, int Width, BOOL bUsePMask) PURE;
};
```

Classes that implement this interface are called TSSProcessors and act as a hybrid between the interpolator and processor that handles an entire scanline.

Similar to the vertex processing chain explained in the "Vertex Processing" section, TSSProcessors are concatenated to a chain that, once it is done processing, has completed the entire Direct3D texture cascade plus fog blending.

The process of assembling the texture cascade represented one of the biggest challenges because it had to meet the following requirements:

■ Very fast

■ Perform texture usage tracking — detect and eliminate combinations of texture stage states and texture settings that will effectively result in no texture output, thus eliminating the very costly texel lookup phase

■ Perform data flow tracking — detect and eliminate cases where data is transported and/or processed in earlier texture stages only to be discarded later in the cascade

■ Produce accurate results

Because of the highly speed-sensitive nature of every piece of code executed in the context of a scanline, a large number of specialized TSSProcessors exist. TSSProcessors can be categorized into the following groups:

■ **Texel fetchers:** Fill a color channel with color and alpha data from a texture with or without bilinear filtering

■ **Color operators:** Carry out operations defined by the Direct3D D3DTOP enumeration

■ **Fog blenders**

Texel fetchers represent the most heavily optimized code in SoftD3D. Specialized implementations for virtually all combinations of processor architectures and texture formats exist.

Color operators have been heavily (MMX) optimized as well, although not to the same extent as texel fetchers.

Section III — Software Shaders and Shader Programming Tips
SoftD3D: A Software-only Implementation of Microsoft's Direct3D API

425

Alpha Testing

If D3DRS_ALPHATESTENABLE is true, then the alpha testing stage is fed with either the output of the final TSSProcessor in the texture blending cascade or the output of the scanline color interpolator.

The actual comparison is performed by one implementation of the IAlphaTester interface:

```
interface IAlphaTester
{
    virtual void SetRef(DWORD dwAlphaRef) PURE;
    virtual void Test(ScanLineContext *pSLC, int Width) PURE;
};
```

SoftD3D features IAlphaTester implementations for each member of the D3DRS_ALPHAFUNC enumeration.

Once a call to the Test() method is complete, a bit in the pixel mask contained in the ScanLineContext object is set for each pixel that didn't pass the alpha test, and the number of pixels that didn't pass the test is returned.

Z-Testing

If D3DRS_ZENABLE is true, then the Z-testing stage is fed with output of the 1/w interpolator.

```
interface IZTester
{
    virtual void SetBuffer(IDirect3DSurface8 *pSurface) PURE;
    virtual void SetStart(int x, int y) PURE;
    virtual void SkipX() PURE;

    virtual int Test(ScanLineContext *pSLC, int Width, BOOL bUsePMask, BOOL bUpdate) PURE;
};
```

The actual comparison is performed by one implementation of the IZTester interface, which works exactly like the aforementioned IAlphaTester interface.

Pixel Mask Check

Alpha testing and Z-testing is always performed as early as possible in the pipeline. According to the Direct3D specification, alpha testing is always performed before Z-testing.

Either testing method produces both a bitfield of masked (skipped) pixels and a pixel skip counter. If the value of the counter equals the width of the current scanline, this case is treated as an early out condition, and the entire scanline is skipped.

If no early out condition is met, all of the following operations must obey the state of the pixel mask produced by either or both testing stages.

426

Alpha Blending

If D3DRS_ALPHABLENDENABLE is true, alpha blending is performed on all non-masked pixels produced by the previous stages.

This is another area of the pipeline that posed a serious challenge. The first problem that I encountered had something to do with memory accesses. To explain the problem, we recall how color blending actually works:

If an application enables texture blending, Direct3D must then combine the color value of the processed polygon pixel with the pixel already stored in the frame buffer. Direct3D uses the following formula to determine the final color for each pixel in the primitive's image [2].

$$FinalColor = TexelColor \times SourceBlendFactor + PixelColor \times DestBlendFactor$$

Right, "Direct3D must then combine the color value of the processed polygon pixel with the pixel already stored in the frame buffer." The end of the quote is the important part.

We must read from the frame buffer! So what's the problem, you might ask. The problem is the frame buffer itself. When you allocate a frame buffer intended for displaying real-time graphics, you preferably allocate video memory on the graphics card. This way, you get the fastest performance if and only if you restrict yourself to writing to that chunk of memory because when a frame has been rendered and must be presented to the user, the video driver only has to change a memory address on the card in the best case or perform a fast video memory to video memory transfer in the worst case. That's great, but unfortunately, this is not the case with alpha blending because, as mentioned above, we have to read the frame buffer; reading from video memory is very slow because that memory area is not cached by the host CPU.

Initially I thought the performance advantage of a video memory frame buffer would outweigh the slow memory access during blending operations. This assumption indeed applies to simple test applications. But with real-world applications, the picture shifted into the opposite direction, which in the end forced me to abandon video memory frame buffers, bite the bullet, and suffer from system memory to video memory transfers for every frame.

Another problem was the huge number of possible blending operations resulting from:

■ The number of defined blend factors independently set for both source and destination (15)

■ The number of different frame buffer formats (2)

My solution was to write small code fragments that handle each of the aforementioned cases and glue those fragments together using macros: DECLARE_ALPHA-BLENDER(ONE, ZERO);

The device object tracks the various alpha blending-related render states at all times and provides a suitable alpha blending handler to the rasterizer on demand, which is cached as long as the affected render states remain unchanged.

Output to the Render Target

Finally, we have reached the last stage of the rendering pipeline.

As I've mentioned before, the entire pixel pipeline operates on 32-bit RGBA packed color values organized into streams. The result of all the previous rendering stages is a single output stream that represents an entire scanline.

The final task is to write this stream to the correct location within the render target surface, optionally performing a conversion of the RGBA32 value to the pixel format of the target surface.

The color conversion turned out to be another major bottleneck, but at least on the x86 platform the performance gained from employing MMX and SSE instructions for the color conversion was tremendous.

This concludes our trip down the graphics pipeline of SoftD3D.

Related Problems

Clearing the Depth Buffer

During one of my profiling sessions, I noticed a spike in VTune's function graph. It turned out to be the `Clear()` member of the ZBufferSurface32 class. Ironically, I only noticed how much time was actually spent in that function because of a bug in my test client that yielded no polygon output. Therefore, almost 99 percent of the processor time was spent clearing the depth buffer and blitting the off-screen render target surface into the video memory.

Today I know that clearing the Z buffer can be avoided with software rasterizers, but back then I spent a good amount of time optimizing the `Clear()` function. The result outperforms the initial `rep stosd` solution by 300 to 400 percent on an AMD Athlon CPU.

The secret behind this huge performance increase is the use of the new `movntq` instruction, which writes directly to a location in memory, bypassing the cache hierarchy.

Real-world Applications

When the feature set of SoftD3D grew beyond the scope of DirectX SDK samples, we began to test the library with real-world applications. This proved to be a very good decision. The first real-world test was done using Unreal Tournament. Of course, the game crashed.

A debugging session quickly unveiled several problems with SoftD3D's resource management. As those problems were ironed out, the game was still crashing. But this time, it was not because of a bug in SoftD3D but simply a result of the game not honoring some of the bits in the D3DCAPS8 structure — a problem more or less repeated by almost any application we tried for testing.

One application would simply refuse to initialize if certain caps bits were not available, although the application wouldn't even make use of those features, and another one insisted on creating textures using unsupported formats. This forced me to add some features that were initially excluded from SoftD3D's feature set and write several workarounds to overcome problems caused by applications making tricky assumptions about the availability of features and the internal format of some resources.

Yes, it was a lot of work, but the result was one giant leap toward a mature product.

The Future

The outlook of the future of SoftD3D begins with a quick glance back to the days when I was working on the pixel pipeline of the library.

I was just working on an SSE-optimized version of a texture filter object when it struck me: Wouldn't it be cool if we could generate this assembly code at run time instead of writing dozens of specialized routines? Coincidently, I was working on another Direct3D-related project at the same time, and nVidia's NVLink tool [3] was used for this project to generate D3D vertex shaders at run time.

NVLink works by taking a number of small pieces of vertex shader code called fragments and "sewing" them together at run time. The advantage is that one no longer has to write specialized shaders for each rendering state. DirectX 9 offers a very similar functionality through the ID3DXFragmentLinker interface [2]. Take a look at these vertex shader fragments:

```
#beginfragment f_load_r_diffusecolor_incoming_diffuse
mov r_diffusecolor, v2
#endfragment

#beginfragment f_write_diffuse_result
mov oD0, r_diffusecolor
#endfragment
```

The most obvious departure from ordinary vertex shader code is that hardware registers have been replaced by symbolic names. These symbols act as virtual registers and define an "interface" between fragments. For example, the virtual register r_diffusecolor is referenced by both the f_load_r_diffusecolor_incoming_diffuse and the f_write_diffuse_result fragments. The assembly code generated by NVLink for a shader program using both fragments would look like this:

```
mov r0, v2
mov oD0, r0
```

Because of NVLink's optimizing capabilities, the final output is this:

```
mov oD0, v2
```

The unnecessary use of a temporary register has been eliminated.

This concept inspired me to try a different solution for implementing SoftD3D's pipeline. However, my own solution differed in a number of aspects from NVLink. My first decision was to define the shader fragments as binary x86 assembly code blocks to avoid the difficult task of writing a parser. Because of this decision, the project was doomed! But read on.

The shader fragments were implemented as C++ inline assembly:

```
PXOAPI void PXO_LERP_DIFFUSE_MMX_X86()
{
    asm
    {
        movq mm0, QWORD PTR [ebx + PXOC_Diffuse]
        paddsw mm0, QWORD PTR [ebx + PXOC_DiffuseStep]
        movq QWORD PTR [ebx + PXOC_Diffuse], mm0
    }
}
```

The C++ compiler does all the dirty work and generates the data to embed the fragments into SoftD3D in binary form. In order to avoid the tracking of processor register usage by fragments, a bank of "virtual" registers was defined and all real processor registers declared as scratch registers.

At run time, SoftD3D generated a list of fragments depending on the current render states and the available processor features and linked them together into one big chunk of assembly code. It worked — somehow. The code was slower than the compiler-generated code! This was mainly because of the ever-increasing need to move certain data from processor registers to main memory in order to resolve register conflicts between fragments. Now I was paying the price for not writing a parser and thus losing the ability to easily track the use processor registers by the combined fragment program. I decided to discontinue this part of the project.

Looking back, I feel that my initial attempt at implementing a programmable software pipeline was merely half-baked, and its failure was actually a good thing because I've learned quite a lot from this failure, and most importantly it cleared the way for a better implementation. Ironically, the solution was there all the time, but I didn't realize it — until now.

I was trying to figure out why one of my shaders (for another project) didn't produce the expected results, and I suspected a compiler bug. So I dug down into the compiled shader token array. The token array is a simple collection of codes emitted by the vertex or pixel shader assembler. These codes instruct the driver on how to create the shader. The format of tokens within each shader code determines its uniqueness. A shader code token is a DWORD with a specific format. The driver (in this case, SoftD3D) reads the shader code's tokens to interpret the code.

Each individual shader code is formatted with a general token layout. The first token must be a version token. The version token provides the version number of the code and also determines whether the code is for a pixel or vertex shader. Shader content follows the version token and is composed of various instruction tokens, perhaps intermingled with comment tokens and white space. Depending on the precise operation that an instruction token specifies, destination and source parameter tokens can also be part of the shader content and follow an instruction token. For example, if the instruction token specifies an add operation, the driver determines that one destination and two source parameter tokens follow the instruction token. An end token completes the shader code.

- **Version token:** Describes the version number of the shader code and informs the driver whether the shader code is for a pixel or vertex shader
- **Instruction token:** Informs the driver of a specific operation to perform
- **Destination parameter token:** Describes properties of a destination register
- **Source parameter token:** Describes properties of a source register
- **Label token:** Used for certain operations (for example, D3DSIO_CALLNZ)
- **Comment token:** Describes the length of the comment that follows
- **End token:** Informs the driver of the end of the shader code

The video driver parses the token array and compiles it into a set of hardware-specific opcodes and register states. It should be possible to mimic that behavior by compiling the tokens into processor-specific assembly language at run time. Because compilation occurs at run time, processor-specific extensions could be used. It would all depend on the quality of the token compiler. The idea was born.

Before I got to work on the actual implementation, I wrote a series of tools to improve my understanding of the subject. The logical first step was a shader disassembler. Not only was I forced to understand the meaning of every single bit but the resulting source code still acts as an invaluable reference as well.

```
C:\SDASM.exe
vs_3_0
dcl_sample0 v3.x
dcl_position0 v0
dcl_normal0 v1
dcl_position0 o0
dcl_color0 o1
m4x4 o0, v0, c100
mov r2, c113
m4x3 r0.xyz, v0, c104
m3x3 r1.xyz, v1, c108
loop aL, i0
mov r5, c[aL + 8]
mov r6.x, c112.y
call 10
endloop
loop aL, i1
add r5, r0.xyzz, -c[aL + 9]
dp3 r7.x, r1.xyzz, -r5
if_gt r7.x, c112.x
dp3 r6.y, r5, c[aL + 8]
if_gt r6.y, c112.x
dp3 r6.z, r5, r5
rsq r6.z, r6.z
mul r5, r5, r6.z
mov r6.x, c112.y
```

Figure 2: Shader disassembler

After the disassembler was done, I felt that my understanding of the subject was still not proficient enough, and I began to work on its counterpart — a macro assembler. Should the requirement of compiling shader source code at run time ever arise, the technology would be there.

Now I won't go into the gory details, but I have to say that it was actually less complicated than expected thanks to a dream team called Flex & Yacc — well known in the UNIX world.

Armed with in-depth knowledge and lots of sample code, I went on with the implementation. I quickly realized that the integration of the shader framework into the existing pipeline of SoftD3D was not an easy task. Some architectural decisions still had to be made before real work could be done. The most important one was how to map the hardware register set exposed by vertex and pixel shaders in the correct way.

As mentioned before, the final implementation is supposed to compile the assembled shaders into processor-specific assembly code. This process is far from being a trivial issue, and implementing it with parts of the execution environment yet to be determined would be crazy. An interim implementation was necessary — an interpreter. This is exactly where SoftD3D stands now. It executes vertex shaders up to version 3.0 using an interpreter. Of course, the interpreter works slowly, but this is irrelevant because its sole purpose was laying the foundation for the final goal: the shader compiler — and this has been accomplished.

References

[1] Hecker, Chris, "Perspective Texture Mapping," *Game Developer* magazine, April/May '95, http://www.d6.com/users/checker/misctech.htm.

[2] Microsoft, *DirectX 9.0 Programmer's Reference*, 2002.

[3] NVLink, nVidia, http://developer.nvidia.com/view.asp?IO=nvlink_2_1.

Named Constants in Shader Development

Jeffrey Kiel
nVidia

If you're like me, you have been looking at the articles in this book saying things like, "Wow, look at that!" or "I didn't think you could do something that cool!" Inevitably, you decide that some shader does have the exact effect that will put your app over the top (with your own tweaks added, of course), so you start to delve deeper into the workings of the code. While doing this, you come across some code that looks like this:

```
ps.1.0
tex t0
dp3 r0, c0, t0
...
```

So, of course, you look just a few lines below this and see:

```
float c0[4] = {0.2125f, 0.7154f, 0.0721f, 1.0f}; // Convert RGB to Grayscale
pDevice->SetPixelShaderConstant(0, c0, 1);
```

Being the expert programmer that you are, you figure out that the data in the float array c0 is being placed into constant register 0, which corresponds to c0 in the shader code. You further deduce that it is taking the color value retrieved from the texture and modulating it by this constant to convert it into a grayscale value.

You continue this exercise on some more lines of shader code and quickly get overwhelmed trying to remember what the different constants actually mean, flipping back and forth between the shader definition and the setting of the constants, which you can only hope happen in close proximity. Finally, you tear the page out of the book and turn it over so you can look at them side by side. Frustrated, you get out your colored pens and begin to color code the constants in the shader with those in the code where they are set. Darn, why don't they make highlighters in all colors, like my crayons as a kid? ARGH! OK, OK, calm down. Maybe you aren't as hyped up on caffeine to let it get this far (yeah, right), but it can be difficult to make sense of other people's code that uses numeric identifiers for things like constants. You would probably fire the guy who wrote his C code like we used to write Pascal back in high school — with variable names like v1. There must be a better way.

Yes, there is. Though the implementation is simple (trivial, really), the usefulness is enormous. This article shows you an easy, useful way to incorporate named constants into your code that make development easier, help with bug finding, and even help with performance.

The Way Things Should Be

Here is the example from above with named constants:

```
ps.1.0
tex t0
dp3 r0, c[RGB TO GRAYSCALE], t0
...

float afRGBToGrayscale[4] = {0.2125f, 0.7154f, 0.0721f, 1.0f}; // Convert RGB to grayscale
pDevice->SetPixelShaderConstant(RGB_TO_GRAYSCALE, afRGBToGrayscale, 1);
```

This is obviously much more readable and maintainable.

How Did They Do That?

The real magic in this solution happens with a data structure to map the string names to enumerated values and some #define macros. First, let's look at how to make the constants file. Typically, you want to create one include file (that does not have any multiple include guards on it like #ifndef or #pragma) that contains all of your constants. Remember, this is a normal include file, so comments are just fine. In my example, all of the constants can only contain alphanumeric and underscore characters, but you can change the parser to take other characters into account. For example:

```
////////////////////////////
// shaderdefines.h
// This file defines all of the shader constants

// Vertex shader constants
DEFINECONSTANT(ONE, 1)
DEFINECONSTANT(TRANSPOSE WORLDVIEWPROJ MATRIX, 2)  // Transpose WORLDVIEWPROJ matrix

// Pixel shader constants
DEFINECONSTANT(RGB_TO_GRAYSCALE, 0)                // Convert RGB to grayscale
```

I placed some other examples to help you to see that any constant from any shader can be defined here.

In some other code (either an include file if you have multiple source files containing shaders or in the single shader source file), you need to define the enumeration that enables you to use these values as constants in your C code. This is how it is done:

```
#define DEFINECONSTANT(name, n) name = n,
enum SHADERCONSTANTS {
#include "shaderdefines.h"
};
```

```
#undef DEFINECONSTANT
```

As you can see, we define a macro that takes the first parameter as the name and the second parameter as the enumerated value. Understand that you can reuse elements in the enumeration, thereby having multiple names with the same numeric value.

Once the enumeration is defined, we need to create the data structure used when parsing the shader. This should probably be done in the same source file that contains the parser. This is a simple version of it:

```
typedef struct ShaderConstNameMap {
  char *pcName;
  int nID;
} ShaderConstNameMap;
```

As you can see, this simply provides a table to map from the ASCII name to the associated number. We populate this table with the following code:

```
#define DEFINECONSTANT(name, n) {#name, n},
ShaderConstNameMap G aSCNameMap[] = {
#include "shaderdefines.h"
};
#undef DEFINECONSTANT
```

We now have the enumeration and the mapping table defined; all that is left is creating the parser.

Parsing the Shader Values

I decided that efficiency was not that important for the parser, since it is a small part of the loading effort. Rather than spending a lot of time on a superefficient parser with lots of bells and whistles, I decided to make it simple and just add the capability of having integer offsets for the constants (i.e., c[RGB_TO_GRAY-SCALE + 2]). Here is the code for this simple parser:

```
#define elementsof(x) (sizeof(x)/sizeof(x[0]))

void ProcessConstants(char *pcOriginal, char *pcProcessed)
{
  char *pcWalker = pcOriginal, *pcTagWalker, *pcLengthWalker;
  char *pcOutWalker = pcProcessed;
  int ii, nTagLength, nTagCount = elementsof(G aSCNameMap);
  int nMultiplier = 1, nOffset = 0;
  bool bTagFound;
  char zTmp[8], zThisTag[80];

  while(*pcWalker != '\0') {
    bTagFound = false;

    if(*pcWalker == '[') {
      pcTagWalker = pcWalker + 1;
```

```
// Figure out how many chars to the next nonalphanum & non-underscore char
pcLengthWalker = pcTagWalker;
while(isalnum(*pcLengthWalker) || *pcLengthWalker == '_')
  pcLengthWalker++;


// Copy this tag into a temporary buffer
strncpy(zThisTag, pcTagWalker, pcLengthWalker - pcTagWalker);
zThisTag[pcLengthWalker - pcTagWalker] = '\0';


// Look for the tag in the table
for(ii = 0; ii < nTagCount; ii++) {
  nTagLength = strlen(G aSCNameMap[ii].pcName);

  if(!strcmp(G aSCNameMap[ii].pcName, zThisTag)) {
    // We have a match, check for additions and subtractions...
    pcTagWalker += nTagLength;       // Skip past the tag name

    while(*pcTagWalker != '\0' && *pcTagWalker != ']') {
      if(*pcTagWalker == '+') {
        // It is assumed to be addition, so skip it
        pcTagWalker++;
      }
      else if(*pcTagWalker == '-') {
        nMultiplier = -1;
        pcTagWalker++;
      }
      else if(*pcTagWalker == ' ') {
        // OK, skip it
        pcTagWalker++;
      }
      else if(isdigit(*pcTagWalker)) {
        nOffset = atoi(pcTagWalker);

        // Skip over all of the digits...
        while(isdigit(*pcTagWalker))
          pcTagWalker++;
      }
      else {
        // Probably should complain here...
        pcTagWalker++;
      }
    }

    // OK, now that we have the tag and the offset, replace this in the outgoing
    // string...
    if(*pcTagWalker == ']') {
      sprintf(zTmp, "%d", G aSCNameMap[ii].nID + (nMultiplier * nOffset));
      *pcOutWalker = '\0';            // Temporary so the strcat will work
      strcat(pcOutWalker, zTmp);
      pcOutWalker += strlen(zTmp);
      pcWalker = pcTagWalker + 1;     // Skips the close bracket we are on
```

```
          bTagFound = true;
          nOffset = 0;      // Reset to 0 in case it was used
          break;
        }
        else {
          // Probably should complain here...
        }
      }
    }
  }

  if(!bTagFound) {
    *pcOutWalker = *pcWalker;
    pcOutWalker++;
    pcWalker++;
  }
}

*pcOutWalker = '\0';
}
```

Wrap-up

Hopefully this provides a good basis for using named constants in your code. Another nice feature of using named constants is that you can rearrange the constants in your code to make uploading them more efficient. If you do some timing tests, you can see that the more you group the constants that change, the better performance you see when setting them. Also, you could use this same code to redefine the texture registers (t0/SetTexture()), temporary registers, etc. It might lead to shaders that are very large, but since you will probably compile them and ship a binary version, it might be worth the added readability during development time.

Section IV

Image Space

Advanced Image Processing with DirectX 9 Pixel Shaders

Jason L. Mitchell, Marwan Y. Ansari, and Evan Hart

ATI Research

Introduction

With the introduction of the ps_2_0 pixel shader model in DirectX 9, we were able to significantly expand our ability to use consumer graphics hardware to perform image processing operations. This is due to the longer program length, the ability to sample more times from the input image(s), and the addition of floating-point internal data representation. In *Direct3D ShaderX: Vertex and Pixel Shader Tips and Tricks*, we used the ps_1_4 pixel shader model in DirectX 8.1 to perform basic image processing techniques, such as simple *blurs*, *edge detection*, *transfer functions*, and *morphological operators* [Mitchell02]. In this chapter, we extend our image processing toolbox to include *color space conversion*, a better edge detection filter called the *Canny filter*, separable *Gaussian* and *median* filters, and a real-time implementation of the *Fast Fourier Transform*.

Review

As shown in our original image processing article in the *Direct3D ShaderX* book, post-processing of 3D frames is fundamental to producing a variety of interesting effects in game scenes. Image processing is performed on a GPU by using the source image as a texture and drawing a screen-aligned quadrilateral into the back buffer or another texture. A pixel shader is used to process the input image to produce the desired result in the render target.

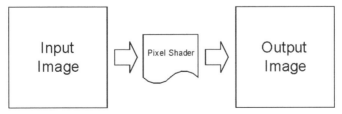

Figure 1: Using a pixel shader for image processing by rendering from one image to another

439

Image processing is especially powerful when the color of the destination pixel is the result of computations done on multiple pixels from the source image. In this case, we sample the source image multiple times and use the pixel shader to combine the data from the multiple samples (or *taps*) to produce a single output.

Color Space Conversion

Before we get into interesting multi-tap filters, we present a pair of shaders that can be used to convert between HSV and RGB color spaces. These shaders perform some relatively complex operations to convert between color spaces, even though they are only single-tap filters.

For those who may not be familiar with HSV space, it is a color space that is designed to be intuitive to artists who think of a color's tint, shade, and tone [Smith78]. Interpolation in this color space can be more aesthetically pleasing than interpolation in RGB space. Additionally, when comparing colors, it may be desirable to do so in HSV space. For example, in RGB space the color {100, 0, 0} is very different from the color {0, 0, 100}. However, their V components in HSV space are equal. Colors, represented by {*hue, saturation, value*} triples, are defined to lie within a hexagonal pyramid, as shown in Figure 2.

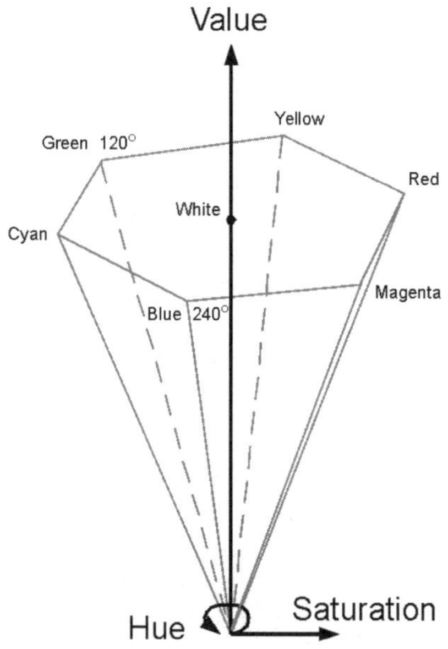

The *hue* of a color is represented by an angle between 0° and 360° around the central axis of the hexagonal cone. A color's *saturation* is the distance from the central (achromatic) axis, and its *value* is the distance along the axis. Both *saturation* and *value* are defined to be between 0 and 1.

Figure 2: HSV color space

We have translated the pseudocode RGB-to-HSV transformation from [Foley90] to the DirectX 9 High Level Shading Language (HLSL) and compiled it for the ps_2_0 target. If you are unfamiliar with HLSL, you can refer to the "Introduction to the DirectX 9 High Level Shading Language" article in *ShaderX²: Introductions & Tutorials with DirectX 9*. As described in [Smith78], you can see that the RGB_to_HSV() function in this shader first determines the minimum and maximum channels of the input RGB color. The max channel determines the *value* of the HSV color or how far along the achromatic central axis of the hexagonal cone the HSV color will be. The saturation is then computed as the difference between the max and min RGB channels divided by the max. Hue (the angle around the central achromatic axis) is then a function of the channel that had the max magnitude and thus determined the value.

```
float4 RGB_to_HSV (float4 color)
{
    float  r, g, b, delta;
    float  colorMax, colorMin;
    float  h=0, s=0, v=0;
    float4 hsv=0;

    r = color[0];
    g = color[1];
    b = color[2];

    colorMax = max (r,g);
    colorMax = max (colorMax,b);
    colorMin = min (r,g);
    colorMin = min (colorMin,b);
    v = colorMax;                  // this is value

    if (colorMax != 0)
    {
        s = (colorMax - colorMin) / colorMax;
    }

    if (s != 0) // if not achromatic
    {
        delta = colorMax - colorMin;
        if (r == colorMax)
        {
            h = (g-b)/delta;
        }
        else if (g == colorMax)
        {
            h = 2.0 + (b-r) / delta;
        }
        else // b is max
        {
            h = 4.0 + (r-g)/delta;
        }

        h *= 60;

        if( h < 0)
        {
            h +=360;
        }

        hsv[0] = h / 360.0;    // moving h to be between 0 and 1.
        hsv[1] = s;
        hsv[2] = v;
    }

    return hsv;
}
```

The HSV-to-RGB transformation, also translated from [Foley90], is shown below in HLSL.

```
float4 HSV_to_RGB (float4 hsv)
{
    float4 color=0;
    float  f,p,q,t;
    float  h,s,v;
    float  r=0,g=0,b=0;
    float  i;

    if (hsv[1] == 0)
    {
        if (hsv[2] != 0)
        {
            color = hsv[2];
        }
    }
    else
    {
        h = hsv.x * 360.0;
        s = hsv.y;
        v = hsv.z;

        if (h == 360.0)
        {
            h=0;
        }

        h /=60;
        i = floor (h);
        f = h-i;
        p = v * (1.0 - s);
        q = v * (1.0 - (s * f));
        t = v * (1.0 - (s * (1.0 -f)));

        if (i == 0)
        {
            r = v;
            g = t;
            b = p;
        }
        else if (i == 1)
        {
            r = q;
            g = v;
            b = p;
        }
        else if (i == 2)
        {
            r = p;
            g = v;
```

```
            b = t;
        }
        else if (i == 3)
        {
            r = p;
            g = q;
            b = v;
        }
        else if (i == 4)
        {
            r = t;
            g = p;
            b = v;
        }
        else if (i == 5)
        {
            r = v;
            g = p;
            b = q;
        }

        color.r = r;
        color.g = g;
        color.b = b;
    }

    return color;
}
```

Other Color Spaces

It is worth noting that RGB and HSV are not the only color spaces of interest in computer graphics. For example, the original paper [Smith78] that introduced HSV also introduced a color space called HSL (for *hue*, *saturation*, and *lightness*), where L is often the same as the Luminance (Y) channel used in the YIQ color space. If you are interested in learning more about color spaces, [Smith78] and [Foley90] both provide excellent discussions.

Now that we have introduced some reasonably advanced single-tap image operations for converting between color spaces, we can discuss a few multi-tap filters that perform some sophisticated image processing operations.

Advanced Edge Detection

In *Direct3D ShaderX*, we discussed the Roberts and Sobel edge detection filters [Mitchell02]. Here, we expand upon those filters and introduce an implementation of the Canny edge detection filter [Canny86].

Step-by-Step Approach

As outlined in [Jain95], the Canny edge detection filter can be implemented by performing the following operations:

1. Apply a Gaussian blur.
2. Compute the partial derivatives at each texel.
3. Compute the magnitude and direction of the line (tan⁻¹) at each point.
4. Sample the neighbors in the direction of the line and perform nonmaxima suppression.

Naturally, we implement this in a series of steps, each using a different shader to operate on the output from the preceding step. A Gaussian blur is the first shader that is run over the input image. This is done to eliminate any high frequency noise in the input image. Various filter kernel sizes can be used for this step.

The next step in the process is computation of the partial derivatives (P and Q) in the u and v directions, respectively:

Partial u Kernel

-1	1
-1	1

Partial v Kernel

-1	-1
1	1

Then the magnitude of the derivative is computed using the standard formula:

$$Magnitude = \sqrt{P^2 + Q^2}$$

Finally, the P and Q values are used to determine the direction of the edge at that texel using the standard equation:

$$\theta = \text{atan2}(Q, P)$$

Magnitude and θ are written out to an image so that the next shader can use them to complete the Canny filter operation. The edge direction, θ, is a signed quantity in the range of $-\pi$ to π and must be packed into the 0 to 1 range in order to prevent loss of data between rendering passes. In order to do this, we pack it by computing:

$$A = \text{abs}(\theta) / \pi$$

You've probably noticed that due to the absolute value, this function is not invertible, hence data is effectively lost. This does not present a problem for this particular application due to symmetries in the following step.

The final pass involves sampling the image to get the magnitude and the edge direction, θ, at the current location. The edge direction, θ, must now be unpacked into its proper range. Figure 3 shows a partitioning of all values of θ (in degrees) into four sectors.

The sectors are symmetric and map to the possible ways that a line can pass through a 3×3 set of pixels. In the previous step, we took the absolute value of θ and divided it by π to put it in the 0 to 1 range. Since we know that θ is already between 0 and 1 from the previous step, we are almost done. Since the partitioning is symmetric, it was an excellent way to reduce the number of comparisons needed to find the correct neighbors to sample. Normally, to complete the mapping, we would multiply A by 4 and be done. However, if you look closely at Figure 3 you can see that the sectors are centered around 0 and 180.

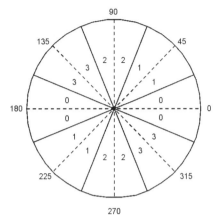

Figure 3: The 360 degrees of an angle partitioned into four sectors

In order to compensate for this, the proper equation is:

$$\text{Sector} = \text{floor}((A - \pi/16) * 4)$$

Next, we compute the neighboring texel coordinates by checking which sector this edge goes through. Now that the neighbors have been sampled, we compare the current texel's magnitude to the magnitudes of its neighbors. If its magnitude is greater than both of its neighbors, then it *is* the local maximum and the value is kept. If its magnitude is less than either of its neighbors, then this texel's value is set to zero. This process is known as *nonmaxima suppression*, and its goal is to thin the areas of change so that only the greatest local changes are retained. As a final step, we can threshold the image in order to reduce the number of false edges that might be picked up by this process. The threshold is often set by the user when he or she finds the right balance between true and false edges.

As you can see in Figure 4, the Canny filter produces one-pixel-wide edges unlike more basic filters such as a Sobel edge filter.

Figure 4: One-pixel-wide edges from the Canny filter

9 Tap Edge Detection Using 2 Sobel Operators

Figure 5: Gradient magnitudes from the Sobel filter (see [Mitchell02])

Implementation Details

This shader is implemented in the VideoShader application on the companion CD (see the section 4\04 folder) using HLSL and can be compiled for the ps_2_0 target or higher. In this implementation, the samples are taken from the eight neighbors adjacent to the center of the filter. Looking at the HLSL code, you can see an array of float two-tuples called `sampleOffsets[]`. This array defines a set of 2D offsets from the center tap, which are used to determine the locations from which to sample the input image. The locations of these samples relative to the center tap are shown in Figure 6.

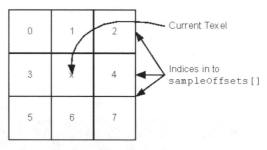

Figure 6: Locations of taps as defined in `sampleOffsets[]`

The four steps of the Canny edge detection filter described above have been collapsed into two rendering passes requiring the two shaders shown below. The first shader computes the gradients P and Q followed by the Magnitude and direction (θ). After packing θ into the 0 to 1 range, Magnitude and θ are written out to a temporary surface.

```
sampler InputImage;
float2 sampleOffsets[8] : register (c10);
```

```
struct PS_INPUT
{
    float2 texCoord:TEXCOORD0;
};

float4 main( PS_INPUT In ) : COLOR
{
    int i =0;
    float4 result;
    float  Magnitude, Theta;
    float  p=0,q=0;
    float  pKernel[4] = {-1, 1, -1, 1};
    float  qKernel[4] = {-1, -1, 1, 1};
    float2 texCoords[4];
    float3 texSamples[4];
    float  PI = 3.1415926535897932384626433832795;


    texCoords[0] = In.texCoord + sampleOffsets[1];
    texCoords[1] = In.texCoord + sampleOffsets[2];
    texCoords[2] = In.texCoord;
    texCoords[3] = In.texCoord + sampleOffsets[4];


    for(i=0; i <4; i++)
    {
        texSamples[i].xyz =  tex2D(InputImage, texCoords[i]);
        texSamples[i] = dot(texSamples[i], 0.33333333f);
        p += texSamples[i] * pKernel[i];
        q += texSamples[i] * qKernel[i];
    }

    p /= 2.0;
    q /= 2.0;

    Magnitude = sqrt((p*p) + (q*q));
    result = Magnitude;

    // Now we compute the direction of the
    // line to prep for Nonmaxima supression.
    //
    // Nonmaxima supression - If this texel isn't the Max,
    // make it 0 (hence, supress it)
    Theta = atan2(q,p); // result is -pi to pi

    result.a = (abs(Theta) / PI); // Now result is 0 to 1
                            // Just so it can be written out.
    return result;
}
```

In the second pass of the Canny edge detector, Magnitude and θ are read back from the temporary surface. The edge direction, θ, is classified into one of four sectors and the neighbors along the proper direction are sampled using dependent reads. The magnitudes of these neighbor samples along with a user-defined threshold are then used to determine whether this pixel is a local maximum or not, resulting in either 0 or 1 being output as the final result.

```
sampler InputImage;

float2 sampleOffsets[8]  : register (c10);
float4 UserInput         : register (c24);

struct PS_INPUT
{
    float2 texCoord:TEXCOORD0;
};

float4 main( PS_INPUT In ) : COLOR
{
    int i =0;
    float4 result;
    float  Magnitude, Theta;
    float2 texCoords[4];
    float4 texSamples[3];
    float  PI = 3.1415926535897932384626433832795;


    // Tap the current texel and figure out line direction
    texSamples[0] = tex2D( InputImage, In.texCoord);
    Magnitude = texSamples[0].r;

    // Sample two neighbors that lie in the direction of the line
    // Then find out if this_texel has a greater Magnitude.
    Theta = texSamples[0].a;


    // Must unpack theta. Prior pass made Theta range between 0 and 1
    // But we really want it to be either 0,1,2, or 4. See [Jain95]
    // for more details.
    Theta = (Theta - PI/16) * 4 ; // Now theta is between 0 and 4
    Theta = floor(Theta); // Now theta is an INT.

    if( Theta == 0)
    {
        texCoords[1] = In.texCoord + sampleOffsets[4];
        texCoords[2] = In.texCoord + sampleOffsets[3];
    }
    else if(Theta == 1)
    {
        texCoords[1] = In.texCoord + sampleOffsets[2];
        texCoords[2] = In.texCoord + sampleOffsets[5];
    }
    else if(Theta == 2)
    {
        texCoords[1] = In.texCoord + sampleOffsets[1];
```

```
        texCoords[2] = In.texCoord + sampleOffsets[6];
    }
    else //if(Theta == 3)
    {
        texCoords[1] = In.texCoord + sampleOffsets[0];
        texCoords[2] = In.texCoord + sampleOffsets[7];
    }


    // Take other two samples
    // Remember they are in the direction of the edge
    for(i=1; i <3; i++)
    {
        texSamples[i].xyz =  tex2D( InputImage, texCoords[i]);
    }


    // Now it's time for Nonmaxima supression.
    // Nonmaxima supression - If this texel isn't the Max,
    // make it 0 (hence, supress it)
    // This keeps the edges nice and thin.
    result = Magnitude;
    if( Magnitude < texSamples[1].x || Magnitude < texSamples[2].x )
    {
        result =0;
    }


    // Threshold the result.
    if(result.x < UserInput.z)
    {
        result =0;
    }
    else
    {
        result = 1;
    }


    return result;
}
```

You can see in Figure 4 that this produces one-pixel-wide edges, which may be more desirable for some applications. You may see some gaps in the detected edges, and in some cases, it may be useful to apply a dilation operation to fill in these gaps [Mitchell02].

Separable Techniques

Certain filtering operations have inherent symmetry, which allows us to implement them more efficiently in a separable manner. That is, we can perform these 2D image processing operations with a sequence of 1D operations and obtain equivalent results with less computation. Conversely, we can implement a large separable filter kernel with the same amount of computation as a small, non-separable filter. This is particularly important when attempting to apply "blooms" to final frames in high dynamic range space to simulate light scattering. In this final section of the chapter, we discuss three separable filtering operations: the Gaussian blur, a median filter approximation, and the Fast Fourier Transform.

Separable Gaussian

A very commonly used separable filter is the Gaussian filter, which can be used to perform blurring of 2D images. The 2D isotropic (i.e., circularly symmetric) Gaussian filter, $g2D(x, y)$, samples a circular neighborhood of pixels from the input image and computes their weighted average, according to the following equation:

$$g_{2D}(x, y) = \frac{1}{\sqrt{2\pi\sigma^2}} e^{-\frac{x^2+y^2}{2\sigma^2}}$$

...where σ is the standard deviation of the Gaussian and x and y are the coordinates of image samples relative to the center of the filter. The standard deviation, σ, determines the size of the filter.

This means that we sample a local area of texels from the input image and weight them according to the above equation. For example, for a Gaussian with $\sigma = 1$, we compute the following filter kernel (after normalization).

In theory, the Gaussian has infinite extent, but the contribution to the final result is insignificant for input texels outside of this 5×5 region.

An extremely important property of the Gaussian is that it is separable. That is, it can be rearranged in the following manner:

0.0037	0.0146	0.0256	0.0146	0.0037
0.0146	0.0586	0.0952	0.0586	0.0146
0.0256	0.0952	0.1502	0.0952	0.0256
0.0146	0.0586	0.0952	0.0586	0.0146
0.0037	0.0146	0.0256	0.0146	0.0037

$$g_{2D}(x, y) = \left(\frac{1}{\sqrt{2\pi}\sigma} e^{-\frac{x^2}{2\sigma^2}} \right) \bullet \left(\frac{1}{\sqrt{2\pi}\sigma} e^{-\frac{y^2}{2\sigma^2}} \right)$$

$$= g_{1D}(x) \bullet g_{1D}(y)$$

This means that we can implement a given Gaussian with a series of 1D filtering operations: one horizontal ($g_{1D}(x)$) and one vertical ($g_{1D}(y)$). This allows us to implement Gaussians with much larger kernels (larger σ) while performing the same amount of calculations that are required to implement a smaller non-separable filter kernel. This technique was used in our real-time implementation of Paul Debevec's *Rendering with Natural Light* animation as seen in Figure 7.

After rendering the scene in high dynamic range space, Debevec performed a number of large Gaussian blurs on his 2D rendered scene to obtain blooms on bright areas of the scene. In order to do this in real-time, we exploited the Gaussian's separability to perform the operation efficiently. In our case, we used $\sigma = 7$, which resulted in a 25×25 Gaussian.

Figure 7: Frame from real-time Rendering with Natural Light (See Color Plate 20.)

Due to the fact that we have only eight texture coordinate interpolators in the ps_2_0 pixel shader programming model, we must derive some of our texture coordinates in the pixel shader as deltas from the center tap location. To make the most efficient use of the hardware, we can perform as many reads from the input image as possible using non-dependent texture reads.

In our implementation, we divided our samples into three types: *inner taps*, *outer taps*, and the *center tap*. The center tap (**c**) and inner taps (**x**) shown in Figure 8 are performed using interpolated texture coordinates (and hence non-dependent texture reads).

o	o	o	x	x	x	c	x	x	x	o	o	o

Figure 8: Layout of 13 taps of separable Gaussian

The outer taps (**o**) shown in Figure 8 are sampled using texture coordinates computed in the pixel shader. That is, they are done with dependent reads. Note that the center tap (**c**) uses pick-nearest filtering and is aligned with the center of a specific texel in the input image. The other 12 taps all use bilinear filtering and are aligned so that they sample from two different texels in the input image. This Gaussian filter is implemented in HLSL in the following shader:

```
float4 hlsl_gaussian (float2 tapZero    : TEXCOORD0,
           float2 tap12      : TEXCOORD1,
           float2 tapMinus12 : TEXCOORD2,
           float2 tap34      : TEXCOORD3,
           float2 tapMinus34 : TEXCOORD4,
           float2 tap56      : TEXCOORD5,
           float2 tapMinus56 : TEXCOORD6 ) : COLOR
```

```
{
    float4 accum, Color[NUM_INNER_TAPS];
    Color[0] = tex2D(nearestImageSampler, tapZero);       // sample 0
    Color[1] = tex2D(linearImageSampler, tap12);          // samples 1, 2
    Color[2] = tex2D(linearImageSampler, tapMinus12);     // samples -1, -2
    Color[3] = tex2D(linearImageSampler, tap34);          // samples 3, 4
    Color[4] = tex2D(linearImageSampler, tapMinus34);     // samples -3, -4
    Color[5] = tex2D(linearImageSampler, tap56);          // samples 5, 6
    Color[6] = tex2D(linearImageSampler, tapMinus56);     // samples -5, -6

    accum  = Color[0] * gTexelWeight[0]; // Weighted sum of samples
    accum += Color[1] * gTexelWeight[1];
    accum += Color[2] * gTexelWeight[1];
    accum += Color[3] * gTexelWeight[2];
    accum += Color[4] * gTexelWeight[2];
    accum += Color[5] * gTexelWeight[3];
    accum += Color[6] * gTexelWeight[3];

    float2 outerTaps[NUM_OUTER_TAPS];
    outerTaps[0] = tapZero *  gTexel0ffset[0]; // coord for samp 7,   8
    outerTaps[1] = tapZero * -gTexel0ffset[0]; // coord for samp -7,  -8
    outerTaps[2] = tapZero *  gTexel0ffset[1]; // coord for samp 9,  10
    outerTaps[3] = tapZero * -gTexel0ffset[1]; // coord for samp -9, -10
    outerTaps[4] = tapZero *  gTexel0ffset[2]; // coord for samp 11, 12
    outerTaps[5] = tapZero * -gTexel0ffset[2]; // coord for samp -11,-12

    // Sample the outer taps
    for (int i=0; i<NUM_OUTER_TAPS; i++)
    {
        Color[i] = tex2D (linearImageSampler, outerTaps[i]);
    }

    accum += Color[0] * gTexelWeight[4]; // Accumulate outer taps
    accum += Color[1] * gTexelWeight[4];
    accum += Color[2] * gTexelWeight[5];
    accum += Color[3] * gTexelWeight[5];
    accum += Color[4] * gTexelWeight[6];
    accum += Color[5] * gTexelWeight[6];

    return accum;
}
```

Applying this shader twice in succession (with different input texture coordinates and the gTexel0ffset[] table), we compute a 25×25 Gaussian blur and achieve the bloom effect that we are looking for.

Separable Median Filter Approximation

Another important filter in image processing is the median filter, the output of which is the median of the set of input data sampled by the filter kernel. For those who may not recall, the median of a set of values is the middle value after sorting or ranking the data. For example, if you have the following set of numbers: {9, 3,

6, 1, 2, 2, 8}, you can sort them to get {1, 2, 2, 3, 6, 8, 9} and select the middle value 3. Hence, the median of these values is 3. In image processing, a median filter is commonly used to remove "salt and pepper noise" from images prior to performing other image processing operations. It is good for this kind of operation because it is not unduly influenced by outliers in the input data (i.e., the noise) the way that a mean would be. Additionally, the output of a median filter is guaranteed to be a value that actually appears in the input image data; a mean does not have this property.

As it turns out, an approximation to a 2D median filter can be implemented efficiently in a separable manner [Gennert 03]. Say we have sampled a 3×3 region of our input image and the data are ranked in the following order:

1	2	3
4	5	6
7	8	9

We can first take the median of the rows of the ranked data:

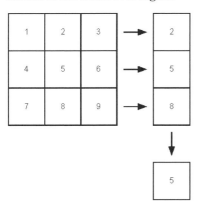

We can then take the median of these medians to get an approximation to the median of the whole 3×3 region:

From this, we obtain the data in the fifth-ranked image sample, which is the correct value. We say that this method is only an approximation to a true median filter because the true median will not be found if the ranked data is not so evenly distributed within the filter kernel. For example, if we have the following ranked data, we can get an incorrect median:

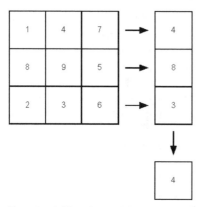

For a 3×3 filter kernel, however, the worst case that this separable median filter implementation will give you is the fourth or sixth rank instead of the fifth, which may be adequate for many applications.

We have implemented this separable approximation to a median filter with a two-pass rendering approach. The first pass finds the median of each 3×1 region of the image and outputs it to an intermediate buffer. The second pass performs the same operation on each 1×3 region of the intermediate buffer. The end result is equivalent to the separable median algorithm outlined above.

Median Filter HLSL Implementation

In our HLSL implementation of the separable median approximation, both passes will use the FindMedian() function, which takes three scalar inputs:

```
float FindMedian(float a, float b, float c)
{
    float median;

    if( a < b )
    {
        if( b < c)
        {
            median = b;
        }
        else
        {
            median = max(a,c);
        }
    }
    else
    {
        if( a < c)
        {
            median = a;
        }
        else
        {
```

```
            median = max(b,c);
        }
    }
    return median;
}
```

The first pass of the 3×3 median filter, shown below, takes three samples from the input image: the texel at the current location and the left and right neighbors. The median red, green, and blue values are found independently, and the result is written out to a temporary surface.

```
sampler InputImage;
float2 sampleOffsets[8];

struct PS_INPUT
{
    float2 texCoord:TEXCOORD0;
};

float4 main( PS_INPUT In ) : COLOR
{
    int i =0;
    float4 result;
    float2 texCoords[3];
    float3 texSamples[3];

    texCoords[0] = In.texCoord + sampleOffsets[3];
    texCoords[1] = In.texCoord;
    texCoords[2] = In.texCoord + sampleOffsets[4];

    // the left and right neighbors of this texel
    for(i=0; i <3; i++)
    {
        texSamples[i].xyz = tex2D( InputImage, texCoords[i]);
    }

    result.r = FindMedian(texSamples[0].r,texSamples[1].r,texSamples[2].r);
    result.g = FindMedian(texSamples[0].g,texSamples[1].g,texSamples[2].g);
    result.b = FindMedian(texSamples[0].b,texSamples[1].b,texSamples[2].b);
    result.a = 0;

    return result;
}
```

In the second pass of the 3×3 median filter, the texel at the current location and the top and bottom neighbors are sampled. The median red, green, and blue values are found independently, and the final result of the shader is computed.

```
sampler InputImage;
float2 sampleOffsets[8];
struct PS_INPUT
{
    float2 texCoord:TEXCOORD0;
```

```
};

float4 main( PS_INPUT In ) : COLOR
{
    int i =0;
    float4 result;
    float2 texCoords[3];
    float3 texSamples[3];

    texCoords[0] = In.texCoord + sampleOffsets[1];
    texCoords[1] = In.texCoord;
    texCoords[2] = In.texCoord + sampleOffsets[6];

    // the top and bottom neighbors of this texel
    for(i=0; i <3; i++)
    {
        texSamples[i].xyz = tex2D( InputImage, texCoords[i]);
    }

    result.r = FindMedian(texSamples[0].r,texSamples[1].r,texSamples[2].r);
    result.g = FindMedian(texSamples[0].g,texSamples[1].g,texSamples[2].g);
    result.b = FindMedian(texSamples[0].b,texSamples[1].b,texSamples[2].b);

    result.a = 0;

    return result;
}
```

Median Filter Results

To test the ability of this median filter approximation to remove salt and pepper noise, we have added noise to a test image and run the median filter over it twice to obtain the results shown in Figure 9.

(a) Original   (b) One median pass   (c) Two median passes

Figure 9: Median filter results

The original image (Figure 9a) has had some noise added to it. With only one pass of the median filter, much of the noise is removed (Figure 9b). Applying the median filter a second time eliminates the noise almost completely (Figure 9c).

Median-filtering the red, green, and blue channels of the image independently is a reasonably arbitrary decision that seems to work well for our data. You may find that another approach, such as converting to luminance and then determining the median luminance, works better for your data.

Fourier Transform

A very powerful concept in image processing is transformation of *spatial domain* images into the *frequency domain* via the Fourier Transform. All of the images that we have discussed so far have existed in the spatial domain. Using the Fourier Transform, we can transform them to the frequency domain, where the images are represented not by a 2D array of real-valued brightness values distributed spatially, but by a 2D array of complex coefficients that are used to weight a set of sine waves, which when added together would result in the source image. This set of sine waves is known as a Fourier series, named for its originator, Jean Baptiste Joseph Fourier. Fourier's assertion was that any periodic signal can be represented as the sum of a series of sine waves. This applies to any sort of signal, including images. The conversion from the spatial domain to the frequency domain is performed by a *Fourier Transform*. In the case of digital images consisting of discrete samples (pixels), we use a *Discrete Fourier Transform* (DFT). The equations for performing a DFT and its inverse on a two-dimensional image are shown below:

Fourier Transform

$$H(u,v) = \frac{1}{MN} \sum_{x=0}^{M-1} \sum_{y=0}^{N-1} h(x,y) e^{-i2\pi(ux/M+vy/N)}$$

Inverse Fourier Transform

$$h(x,y) = \sum_{x=0}^{M-1} \sum_{y=0}^{N-1} H(u,v) e^{i2\pi(ux/M+vy/N)}$$

...where $h(x,y)$ is the value of the pixel located at location (x,y), $H(u,v)$ is the value of the image in frequency space at location (u,v), M is the width of the image in pixels, and N is the height of the image in pixels.

For these equations, it is important to remember that these are complex numbers (i is the square root of -1). Additionally, from complex math:

$$e^{ix} = \cos(x) + i\sin(x) \text{ and } e^{-ix} = \cos(x) - i\sin(x)$$

GPU Implementation

A naïve implementation of these operations would be an extremely expensive processing step, $O(n^4)$ in big O notation. Fortunately, much research has gone into a class of algorithms known as *Fast Fourier Transforms* (FFTs). These algorithms refactor the transform equations above to reduce the complexity to $O(n * \log n)$. The initial algorithm described to accomplish this is referred to as "Decimation in Time" and was published in 1965 by Cooley and Tukey [Cooley65]. As it turns out, the decimation in time algorithm translates very naturally to multipass rendering on graphics hardware with floating-point pixel processing pipelines. Our multipass rendering technique is based on the code listed in [Crane96].

The FFT uses two primary optimizations to minimize its computational complexity. The first optimization that the FFT makes is to exploit the transform's separability and break the two-dimensional transform into several one-dimensional transforms. This is done by performing a one-dimensional FFT across the rows of the image followed by a one-dimensional FFT along the columns of the resulting image. This greatly reduces the growth in complexity of the operation as the image size grows. The next optimization uses the fact that a Fourier Transform of size N can be rewritten as the sum of two Fourier Transforms of size N/2, eliminating redundant computations. This portion of the optimization reduces the cost of the one-dimensional transforms from $O(n^2)$ to $O(n * \log n)$.

The first thing to note when using a GPU to implement an FFT based on the decimation in time algorithm is that, to maintain most of its efficiency improvements, the algorithm must be implemented in multiple passes by rendering to floating-point temporary buffers. If the spatial domain image is color (i.e., has multiple channels), these temporary buffers need to be set up as multiple render targets, since the frequency domain representation of the image uses complex numbers, thus doubling the number of channels on the output.

For a *width* × *height* image, the decimation in time FFT algorithm takes $\log_2(width) + \log_2(height) + 2$ rendering passes to complete. For example, a 512×512 image takes 20 rendering passes, which renders at approximately 30 frames per second on today's fastest graphics processors. Because each step of the computation is based solely on the previous step, we are able to conserve memory and ping-pong between two floating-point renderable textures to implement the following steps of the decimation in time algorithm:

1. Horizontal scramble using *scramble map* to do dependent texture reads from the original image
2. $\log_2 (width)$ butterfly passes
3. Vertical scramble using scramble map again
4. $\log_2 (height)$ butterfly passes

Let's describe each of these steps in detail.

Scramble

The decimation in time algorithm starts with a phase referred to as a *scramble*. This phase reorders the data such that:

data[i] :=: data[rev(i)]

…where rev(i) is the bit reverse of i.

In other words, the data member at location i is swapped with the data member at the location at the bit-reversed address of i. The bit reverse of a given value is its mirror image written out in binary. For example, the bit reverse of 0111 is 1110. Figure 10 shows an example of a scramble of a 16-element image.

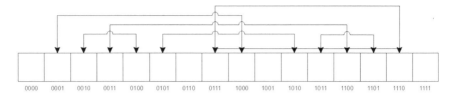

Figure 10: Simple scramble of 16×1 image

Values connected by arrows in Figure 10 are swapped during the scramble step. Obviously, symmetric values such as 0000, 0110, 1001, and 1111 are left in place. Since pixel shaders can't easily do such bit-twiddling of pixel addresses, the most effective way to perform the scramble step is via a dependent read from the input image using a specially authored *scramble map* stored in another texture to provide the bit-twiddled address from which to do the dependent read. The shader to perform such a dependent read for the horizontal scramble is shown below:

```
sampler  scramble    : register(s0);
sampler  sourceImage : register(s1);

struct PS_INPUT
{
    float1 scrambleLoc:TEXCOORD0;
    float2 imagePos:TEXCOORD1;
};

float4 main( PS_INPUT In ) : COLOR
{
    float2 fromPos;

    fromPos = In.imagePos;

    // scramble the x coordinate
    // fromPos.x gets assigned red channel of texture
    fromPos.x = tex1D(scramble, In.scrambleLoc);

    return tex2D(sourceImage, fromPos);
}
```

It is important to remember that the scramble map must contain enough bits to uniquely address each texel in the source image. Typically, this means the texture should be a 16-bit single channel texture, preferably an integer format such as D3DFMT_L16.

Butterflies

Once the image has been scrambled, a series of *butterfly* operations are applied to the image. In each butterfly pass, a pair of pixels is combined via a complex multiply and add. Due to the inability of graphics processors to write to random locations in memory, this operation must be done redundantly on both of the pixels in the pair, and therefore some of the ideal FFT efficiency gains are lost. The locations of the paired pixels are encoded in a butterfly map. The butterfly map is as wide as the source image and has one row for each butterfly step. The code for applying horizontal butterflies is shown below.

```
//all textures sampled nearest
sampler butterfly   : register(s0);
sampler sourceImage : register(s1);

struct PS_INPUT
{
    float2 srcLocation:TEXCOORD0;
};

//constant to tell which pass is being used
float pass;  // pass = passNumber / log2(width)

float4 main( PS_INPUT In ) : COLOR
{
    float2 sampleCoord;
    float4 butterflyVal;
    float2 a;
    float2 b;
    float2 w;
    float temp;

    sampleCoord.x = srcLocation.x;
    sampleCoord.y = pass;

    butterflyVal = tex2D( butterfly, sampleCoord);
    w = butterflyVal.ba;

    //sample location A
    sampleCoord.x = butterflyVal.y;
    sampleCoord.y = srcLocation.y;
    a = tex2D( sourceImage, sampleCoord).ra;

    //sample location B
    sampleCoord.x = abs(butterflyVal.x);
    sampleCoord.y = srcLocation.y;
    b = tex2D( sourceImage, sampleCoord).ra;

    //multiply w*b (complex numbers)
    temp = w.x*b.x - w.y*b.y;
    b.y = w.y*b.x + w.x*b.y;
    b.x = temp;

    //perform a + w*b or a - w*b
    a = a + ((butterflyVal.x < 0.0) ? -b : b);

    //make it a 4 component output for good measure
    return a.xxxy;
}
```

The shader performs an extremely simple operation to accomplish its goal. First, it fetches a texture to determine where on this line of the image to get two parameters a and b. This same texel contains a factor w that is combined with a and b to produce the final result. From these parameters, the algorithm can actually produce two of the results needed for the next pass (a' and b'), but since GPUs do not perform random writes to memory, the texture also includes a flag for which value to leave at this location. The following equation, a butterfly operation, shows the math used to convert a and b to a' and b'.

$$a' = a + wb$$
$$b' = a - wb$$

The shader only concerns itself with a single channel image and expects that the real component is fetched into the first component and the imaginary component is fetched into the fourth component. To handle more components, the shader does not need to change significantly, but it does need to use separate textures and multiple render targets to handle more than two channels simultaneously. The largest amount of magic is in the special butterfly texture. This texture contains the offsets of the a and b parameters to the function in its first two components and the real and imaginary parts of the w parameter in its last two components. Additionally, the second texture coordinate is given a sign to encode whether this execution of the shader should produce a' or b'. To ensure an accurate representation of all this with the ability to address a large texture, a 32-bit per-component floating-point texture is the safest choice.

After the scramble and butterfly passes are applied in the horizontal direction, the same operations are applied to the columns of the image to get the vertical FFT. The overall algorithm looks something like the following pseudocode:

```
// Horizontal scramble first
SetSurfaceAsTexture( surfaceA); //input image
SetRenderTarget( surfaceB);
LoadShader( HorizontalScramble);
SetTexture( ButterflyTexture[log2(width)]);
DrawQuad();

// Horizontal butterflies
LoadShader( HorizontalButterfly);
SetTexture( ButterflyTexture[log2(width)]);
for ( i = 0; i < log2( width); i++)
{
    SwapSurfacesAandB();
    SetShaderConstant( "pass", i/log2(width));
    DrawQuad();
}

// Vertical scramble
SwapSurfacesAandB();
LoadShader( VerticalScramble);
SetTexture( ButterflyTexture[log2(height)]);
DrawQuad();
```

```
// Vertical butterflies
LoadShader( VerticalButterfly);
SetTexture( ButterflyTexture[log2(height)]);
for ( i = 0; i < log2( height); i++)
{
    SwapSurfacesAandB();
    SetShaderConstant( "pass", i/log2(height));
    DrawQuad();
}
```

To transform back to the spatial domain, the same operations are performed on the data, except that as one final step the data has a scaling factor applied to bring it into the correct range.

Results

So, now that we know how to apply an FFT to an image using the graphics processor, what have we computed? What does this frequency domain representation look like, and what does it mean?

The output of the Fourier Transform consists not only of complex numbers but also typically spans a dynamic range far greater than what can be displayed directly in print or on a monitor. As a result, the log of the magnitude of the frequency is typically used when displaying the Fourier domain. The function used to visualize the Fourier domain in this article is given below:

$$f(x) = 0.1 * \log\left(1 + \sqrt{x.re^2 + x.i^2}\right)$$

Finally, the image is also shifted into what is referred to as normal form. This is done primarily as a way to simplify the interpretation of the data. The shift can be done on graphics hardware by setting the texture wrap mode to repeat and biasing the texture coordinates by (–0.5, –0.5). In this format, the lowest frequencies are all concentrated in the center of the frequency-domain image, and the frequencies are progressively higher, closer to the edges of the image.

Figure 11: Original image

Figure 12: Fourier Transform (raw)

Figure 13: Fourier Transform in normal form

Utilizing the FFT

Besides just providing an interesting way to look at and analyze images, the frequency space representation allows certain operations to be performed more efficiently than they could be in the spatial domain.

First, removing high frequencies that contribute to aliasing can be most easily performed in frequency space. The simplest implementation of this simply crops the image in frequency space to remove the higher frequencies. This is the application of what is called the ideal filter, but its results tend to be anything but ideal on an image of finite size. The ideal filter really has an infinite width in the spatial domain, so when the cropped image is transformed back to the spatial domain, sharp edges will *ring* with ghosts propagating in the image. Other filters have been designed to work around such issues. One well-known filter for this sort of purpose is the Butterworth filter.

Additionally, frequency space can be used to apply extremely large convolutions to an image. Convolutions in image space are equivalent to multiplication in the frequency domain. So instead of having a multiply and add for each element of a convolution mask at each pixel, as would be required in the spatial domain, the operation takes only a multiply per pixel in the frequency domain. This is most useful on large non-separable filters like the Laplacian of Gaussians (LoG), which produces a second order derivative that can be used to find contours in images. In Figure 14, a LoG filter has been applied to the reference image used throughout the section. To apply the filter in the frequency domain, the image and the filter must first both be transformed into the frequency domain with the Fourier Transform. The filter must also be centered and padded with zeros so that it is the same size as the image to which it is being applied. Once in the frequency domain, the filter and image — both of which contain complex numbers — must undergo a complex multiplication. The result is next run through the Inverse Fourier Transform. Finally, the image must be translated similar to the way in which the frequency space images are translated to get the correct image. This last step appears to be often unmentioned in discussions of this operation, but failure to do it can lead to a fruitless bug hunt.

Figure 14: 17×17 Laplacian of Gaussian operation

Conclusion

In this chapter, we've added some sophisticated tools to our image processing toolbox, including HSV↔RGB color space conversion, the Canny edge detection filter, and separable implementations of a Gaussian blur, a median filter, and the decimation in time formulation of the Fast Fourier Transform. We hope that these implementations, presented here in the industry standard DirectX 9 High Level Shading Language, are easy for you to drop into your own image processing applications. We also hope that they inspire you to create even more powerful image processing operations specific to your needs.

Sample Application

The image processing techniques presented in this chapter were developed using live and recorded video fed to Direct3D via the Microsoft Video Mixing Renderer (VMR). The sample app, VideoShader, demonstrates the use of Direct3D and the VMR, with the above filters and several others implemented using HLSL. Source for the sample application and all of the shaders is available on the companion CD as well as the ATI Developer Relations web site (www.ati.com/developer). The latest version of VideoShader is available at http://www2.ati.com/misc/demos/ATI-9700-VideoShader-Demo-v1.2.exe.

Acknowledgments

Thanks to John Isidoro of Boston University and ATI Research for the separable Gaussian filter implementation. Thanks to Michael Gennert of Worcester Polytechnic Institute and David Gosselin of ATI Research for discussions that resulted in the implementation of the separable median filter approximation.

References

[Canny86] Canny, John, "A Computational Approach to Edge Detection," IEEE PAMI 8(6) 679-698, November 1986.

[Cooley65] Cooley, J. W. and O. W. Tukey, "An Algorithm for the Machine Calculation of Complex Fourier Series," *Mathematics of Computation*, 19, 297-301, 1965.

[Crane96] Crane, Randy, *A Simplified Approach to Image Processing: Classical and Modern Techniques in C*, Prentice Hall, 1996.

[Foley90] James Foley, Andries van Dam, Steven K. Feiner, and John F. Hughes, *Computer Graphics: Principles and Practice*, Second Ed., Addison-Wesley, 1990.

[Gennert03] Gennert, Michael, personal communication, 2003.

[Jain95] Jain, Ramesh and Rangachar Kasturi, et al., *Machine Vision*, McGraw Hill, 1995.

[Mitchell02] Mitchell, Jason L., "Image Processing with 1.4 Pixel Shaders in Direct3D," *Direct3D ShaderX: Vertex and Pixel Shader Tips and Tricks*, Wolfgang Engel, ed., Wordware Publishing, 2002, pp. 258-269.

[Smith78] Smith, Alvy Ray, "Color Gamut Transform Pairs," SIGGRAPH '78, pp. 12-19.

Night Vision: Frame Buffer Post-processing with ps.1.1 Hardware

Guillaume Werle
Montecristo Games

Introduction

A few years ago, when hardware-accelerated rendering was starting to be a common feature in every game engine, players complained that all games were somehow looking quite the same.

Now that programmable hardware is available, the entire rendering process can be configured. This means that any game with a creative graphic programmer or a skilled technical artist can have its own graphic touch and look that is different from the others.

Frame buffer post-processing is one of the easiest ways to achieve a unique look. Many resources on these topics are available on the Internet nowadays, but most of them make use of ps.1.4 hardware. In this article I describe how to use texture-dependent reads on ps.1.1 class hardware to achieve the following effect (see Figures 1 and 2).

Figure 1: Scene from the Raw Confessions demo (models and textures by Christophe Romagnoli and Guillaume Nichols)

Figure 2: Scene from the Raw Confessions demo (models and textures by Christophe Romagnoli and Guillaume Nichols)

465

Description

Texture-dependent reads are definitely harder to use when targeting ps.1.1 hardware. The rendering process is split into several passes to take care of this issue.

Here's a quick description of the required steps to achieve this effect:

1. Render the scene in a texture.
2. Convert to grayscale while rendering in another render texture.
3. Use the luminance value of each pixel as an index into a gradient texture and render in the frame buffer.

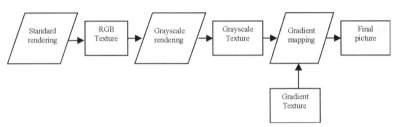

Technical Brief on Render Texture

Instead of rendering directly in the frame buffer, the rendering must be done in a texture. Create a texture with the same size, color format, and depth format as your frame buffer, and then use the ID3DXRenderToSurface interface provided with the D3DX library to map that the BeginScene() and the EndScene() calls.

NOTES

■ Render textures' dimensions don't need to be aligned on a power of two if the caps D3DPTEXTURECAPS_NONPOW2CONDITIONAL is set.

■ Don't use the D3DXCreateTexture() function to create your render texture; this function will round the dimensions to the nearest power of two, even if it's not needed.

Converting to Grayscale

The luminance value of a color can be computed using a dot product.

Luminance = Red * 0.3 + Green * 0.59 + Blue * 0.1

The following pixel shader applies this formula to output the luminance value in every color channel:

```
ps.1.1
tex t0            // rgb texture
// c0 = (0.3, 0.59, 0.1, 1.0)
dp3 r0, t0, c0    // r0 = t0.r * 0.3 + t0.g * 0.59 + t0.b * 0.1
```

Quad Rendering

Once the scene is stored in the texture, a quad is used for rendering into the frame buffer.

The Microsoft Direct3D texture sampling rules say that texels are fetched in the top-left corner. For example, when enabling bilinear filtering, if you sample a texel at the coordinates (0,0) and if the addressing mode is set to warp, the resulting color will be a mix of the four corners of the texture.

Knowing this, an offset of a half-texel size (0.5 / TextureSize) must be added to the texture coordinates.

Color Remapping

This is the last step of the effect. The pixel shader in charge of the color remapping uses the texreg2gb dest, src instruction. This opcode is able to interpret the green and blue color components of the source register — the grayscale texture — as texture coordinates to sample the destination register — the gradient texture.

The gradient texture is a simple 1D texture. Figure 3 shows the gradient used to produce Figures 1 and 2.

Figure 3: 1D gradient texture

This code snippet shows the whole pixel shader :

```
ps.1.1

// t0 grayscale texture
// t1 gradient

tex        t0         // grayscale texture
texreg2gb  t1, t0     // sample t1 at the coordinates (t0.g, t0.b)

mov r0, t1            // output
```

Enhancement

Those shaders leave a great deal of room for visual improvements and experimentation; for example, a blur filter can be applied while converting the picture to grayscale, and some extra textures can be blended with the gradient remapping results. Figures 1 and 2 use this technique to achieve the scanline screening effects.

Final Words

I implemented this shader for a demo scene application called Raw Confession. The demo can be found on the companion CD or downloaded from my web page: http://cocoon.planet-d.net/raw/!Raw_Beta.zip.

The corresponding RenderMonkey workspace can be found on the companion CD as well.

Special thanks to Bertrand Carre and David Levy for proofreading this article.

Non-Photorealistic Post-processing Filters in MotoGP 2

(or fun stuff to play with when you get bored of what you are supposed to be working on)

Shawn Hargreaves
Climax Brighton

Stylized rendering techniques are cool, and with programmable shader hardware, they can be easy to implement too. This article discusses how such effects can be applied as a post-process over the top of a conventional renderer. The goal is to have a minimal impact on the structure of an existing engine so that if you are already using 100 different shaders, adding a new stylized filter should only increase this to 101, rather than needing a modified version of every existing shader.

The idea is to render your scene as normal but to an off-screen texture instead of directly to the D3D back buffer. The resulting image is then copied across to the back buffer by drawing a single full-screen quad, using a pixel shader to modify the data en route. Because this filter is applied entirely as a 2D image space process, it requires no knowledge of the preceding renderer. In fact, these techniques can just as easily be used over the top of video playback as with the output of a real-time 3D engine.

Setting Up the Swap Chain

The first step in getting ready to apply a post-processing filter is setting up a swap chain that lets you hook in a custom pixel shader operation. A typical D3D swap chain looks something like this:

Depending on which D3DSWAPEFFECT you specified when creating the device, the Present() call might swap the two buffers or it might copy data from the back buffer to the front buffer, but either way there is no room for you to insert your own shader anywhere in this process.

To set up a post-processing filter, you need to create a texture with D3D-USAGE_RENDERTARGET and an associated depth buffer. You can then set EnableAutoDepthStencil to FALSE in the D3DPRESENT_PARAMETERS

469

structure, since you will not need a depth buffer while drawing to the D3D back buffer. This results in a triple-buffered swap chain:

The rendering process now looks like:

- BeginScene().
- Set your texture as the active render target.
- Draw the 3D scene.
- Restore the D3D back buffer as the render target, and set your texture surface as the active texture.
- Draw a full-screen quad to copy the image, applying pixel shader filtering effects.
- Draw 2D user interface elements such as menus and the heads-up display, which will not be affected by stylistic processing.
- Call D3D Present() and EndScene().

An incidental benefit of extending the swap chain in this way is that if you create your device with D3DSWAPEFFECT_COPY (so the D3D back buffer will persist from one frame to the next), you can turn on alpha blending during the filter operation to get a cheap full-screen motion blur, blending in some proportion of the previous frame along with the newly rendered image.

The main disadvantage is that texture render targets do not support multisampling, so you cannot use any of the clever antialiasing techniques found in modern GPUs.

What Size Render Target?

Display resolutions tend to have dimensions like 640x480, 1024x768, or 1280x1024, which are not powers of two. This is OK as long as the driver exposes the NONPOW2CONDITIONAL texture capability, but some hardware does not support this, and even on cards that do, pixel shader versions 1.0 to 1.3 do not allow dependent reads into such textures.

The solution is simple: Round up your render target size to the next larger power of two, which for a 640x480 display mode is 1024x512. While drawing the scene, set your viewport to only use the top-left 640x480 subset of this image, and when you come to copy it across to the D3D back buffer, modify your texture coordinates accordingly.

Beware of a common "gotcha" in the calculation of those texture coordinates. To preserve correct texture filtering during a full-screen image copy, a half-texel offset must be added. When copying the top-left portion of a 1024x512 render target onto a 640x480 back buffer, the correct texture coordinates are:

Top left:	$u = 0.5 / 1024$	$v = 0.5 / 512$
Bottom right:	$u = 640.5 / 1024$	$v = 480.5 / 512$

Color Conversions

OK, so we are all set up to feed the output of our main renderer through the pixel shader of our choosing. What do we want that shader to do?

The most obvious, and probably most widely useful, type of operation is to perform some kind of colorspace conversion. This could be as simple as a colored tint for a certain type of lens or a gamma curve adjustment to simulate different camera exposure settings. The image could be converted to monochrome or sepia tone, and by swapping or inverting color channels, night vision and infrared effects can easily be imitated.

The most flexible way of transforming colors is to use the RGB value sampled from the source image as coordinates for a dependent read into a volume texture. A full 256x256x256 lookup table would be prohibitively large (64MB if stored in a 32-bit format!), but thanks to bilinear filtering of the volume texture, a much smaller table can still give adequate results. Even a small volume texture is still much bigger than a pixel shader, though, and its effects cannot so easily be changed just by modifying a few constants. So wherever possible, I think it is better to do your work directly in the shader.

This is the saturation filter from MotoGP 2. The result of using this filter on Figure 1 is shown in Figure 2 (see Color Plate 21). It makes bright colors more intense and primary, while converting the more subtle tones to grayscale. This demonstrates several important principles of pixel shader color manipulation.

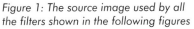

Figure 1: The source image used by all the filters shown in the following figures

Figure 2: Color saturation filter

```
ps.1.1

def c0, 1.0, 1.0, 1.0, 1.0
def c1, 0.3, 0.59, 0.11, 0.5
tex t0                        // sample the source image

1: mov_x4_sat r0.rgb, t0_bx2  // saturate
2: dp3_sat r1.rgba, r0, c0    // do we have any bright colors?
3: dp3 r1.rgb, t0, c1         // grayscale
4: lrp r0.rgb, r1.a, r0, r1   // interpolate between color and grayscale
5: + mov r0.a, t0.a           // output alpha
```

Instruction #1 (mov_x4_sat) calculates an intensified version of the input color. The _bx2 input modifier scales any values less than 0.5 down to zero, while the _x4 output modifier scales up the results, so anything greater than 0.625 will be saturated right up to maximum brightness. It is important to remember the _sat modifier when doing this sort of over-brightening operation because if you leave it out, calculations that overflow 1.0 will produce inconsistent results on different hardware. DirectX 8 cards will always clamp the value at 1.0 (as if the _sat modifier was present), but ps 1.4 or 2.0 hardware will not.

Instruction #3 calculates a monochrome version of the input color by dotting it with the constant [0.3, 0.59, 0.11]. It doesn't really matter what values you use for this, and [0.33, 0.33, 0.33] might seem more logical, but these values were chosen because the human eye is more sensitive to the luminance of the green channel and less sensitive to blue. These are the same scaling factors used by the standard YUV colorspace.

Instruction #4 chooses between the saturated or monochrome versions of the color, based on what instruction #2 wrote into r1.a. That summed all the saturated color channels to create a Boolean selector value, which contains 1 if the input color is bright enough to saturate upward or 0 if the input is dark enough for the _bx2 modifier to round it down to black. In C, this calculation would be:

color = (source brightness > 0.5) ? saturated color : monochrome color

The cnd pixel shader instruction seems ideal for such a task, but in fact it is almost always better to use lrp instead. A discrete test such as cnd tends to cause popping artifacts as the input data moves past its selection threshold, where a lrp can give a smooth transition over a range of values.

Displacement Effects

You can do color conversions by using the input color as source coordinates for a dependent texture read into a lookup table. But what if you reversed this and used another texture as the source for a dependent read into the image of your main scene? The shader is trivial:

```
ps.1.1

tex t0                      // sample the displacement texture
texm3x2pad t1, t0_bx2
texm3x2tex t2, t0_bx2       // sample the source image

mov r0, t2
```

But by the appropriate choice of a displacement texture, all sorts of interesting effects can be achieved — heat haze, explosion shock waves, refraction of light through patterned glass, or raindrops on a camera lens (or in this case, sticking with a non-photorealistic theme, the mosaic effect shown in Figure 3; see Color Plate 21).

Our goal is to cover the screen with a grid of hexagons, each filled with a solid color. Imagine what a 160x100 CGA mode might have looked like if IBM had used hexagonal pixels...

This can be done by tiling a hexagonal displacement texture over the screen. The values in this texture modify the location at which the main scene image is sampled. With the right displacement texture, all pixels inside a hexagon can be adjusted to sample exactly the same texel from the source image, turning the contents of that hexagon into a single flat color.

Figure 3: Hexagonal mosaic filter using dependent texture reads

The texture coordinates for stage 0 control how many times the displacement texture is tiled over the screen, while stages 1 and 2 hold a 3x2 transform matrix. If the hexagon pattern is tiled H times horizontally and V times vertically, your vertex shader outputs should be:

oPos	oT0	oT1	oT2
(0, 0)	*(0, 0)*	*(0.5 * (right – left) / H, 0, left)*	*(0, 0.5 * (bottom – top) / V, top)*
(1, 0)	*(H, 0)*	*(0.5 * (right – left) / H, 0, right)*	*(0, 0.5 * (bottom – top) / V, top)*
(1, 1)	*(H, V)*	*(0.5 * (right – left) / H, 0, right)*	*(0, 0.5 * (bottom – top) / V, bottom)*
(0, 1)	*(0, V)*	*(0.5 * (right – left) / H, 0, left)*	*(0, 0.5 * (bottom – top) / V, bottom)*

left, *right*, *top*, and *bottom* are the texture coordinates given in the "What Size Render Target" section.

The horizontal offset comes from the red channel of the displacement texture and the vertical offset from the green channel. The blue channel must contain solid color, as this will be multiplied with the last column of the oT1/oT2 matrix to give the base coordinates onto which the displacement is added.

The only remaining question is what to put in your displacement texture. If you are good with Photoshop, you could probably draw one using the gradient fill tools, but it is easier to generate it in code. My hexagon pattern was created by a render to texture using the function:

```
void draw_mosaic_hexagon()
{
    //          x    y    r    g    b
    draw_quad(Vtx(0.0, 0.0, 0.5, 0.5, 1.0),
              Vtx(0.5, 0.0, 1.0, 0.5, 1.0),
              Vtx(0.5, 0.5, 1.0, 1.0, 1.0),
              Vtx(0.0, 0.5, 0.5, 1.0, 1.0));

    draw_quad(Vtx(1.0, 1.0, 0.5, 0.5, 1.0),
              Vtx(0.5, 1.0, 0.0, 0.5, 1.0),
              Vtx(0.5, 0.5, 0.0, 0.0, 1.0),
              Vtx(1.0, 0.5, 0.5, 0.0, 1.0));

    draw_quad(Vtx(1.0, 0.0, 0.5, 0.5, 1.0),
```

```
          Vtx(0.5, 0.0, 0.0, 0.5, 1.0),
          Vtx(0.5, 0.5, 0.0, 1.0, 1.0),
          Vtx(1.0, 0.5, 0.5, 1.0, 1.0));

  draw_quad(Vtx(0.0, 1.0, 0.5, 0.5, 1.0),
            Vtx(0.5, 1.0, 1.0, 0.5, 1.0),
            Vtx(0.5, 0.5, 1.0, 0.0, 1.0),
            Vtx(0.0, 0.5, 0.5, 0.0, 1.0));

  draw_quad(Vtx(0.0, 0.333, 0.0, 0.333, 1.0),
            Vtx(1.0, 0.333, 1.0, 0.333, 1.0),
            Vtx(1.0, 0.667, 1.0, 0.667, 1.0),
            Vtx(0.0, 0.667, 0.0, 0.667, 1.0));

  draw_tri( Vtx(0.0, 0.333, 0.0, 0.333, 1.0),
            Vtx(1.0, 0.333, 1.0, 0.333, 1.0),
            Vtx(0.5, 0.167, 0.5, 0.167, 1.0));

  draw_tri( Vtx(0.0, 0.667, 0.0, 0.667, 1.0),
            Vtx(1.0, 0.667, 1.0, 0.667, 1.0),
            Vtx(0.5, 0.833, 0.5, 0.833, 1.0));
}
```

This displacement texture produces a hexagonal mosaic pattern.

Rendering more complex animating patterns into the displacement texture can produce a huge range of cubist or pointillistic style distortions; check out the Kaleidoscope filter in MotoGP 2 for some examples. Scaling or rotating the offset values in oT1 and oT2 also gives interesting results.

Cartoon Rendering

The main characteristics of a cartoon style are black lines around the edges of objects and the use of flat color where there would normally be textured detail or smooth lighting gradients. There are plenty of ways to achieve these effects, most of which have been described in detail elsewhere, but the technique presented here is unusual in that it requires minimal changes to an existing renderer and no artwork or mesh format alterations whatsoever.

The first step is to add black borders by running an edge detect filter over the image of our scene. This is done by setting the same texture three times on different stages with the texture coordinates slightly offset. The pixel shader compares the brightness of adjacent samples and, if the color gradient is steep enough, marks this as an edge pixel by turning it black. The following shader produced the image shown in Figure 4 (see Color Plate 21):

Figure 4: The cartoon shader starts by applying an edge detect filter.

```
ps.1.1

def c0, 0.3, 0.59, 0.11, 0

tex t0                      // sample the source image
tex t1                      // sample offset by (-1, -1)
tex t2                      // sample offset by (1, 1)

dp3 r0.rgba, t1, c0         // grayscale sample #1 in r0.a
dp3 r1.rgba, t2, c0         // grayscale sample #2 in r1.a

sub_x4 r0.a, r0, r1         // diagonal edge detect difference
mul_x4_sat r0.a, r0, r0     // square edge difference to get absolute value

mul r0.rgb, r0, 1-r0.a      // output color * edge detect
+ mov r0.a, t0.a            // output alpha
```

More accurate edge detection can be done by using a larger number of sample points or by including a depth buffer and looking for sudden changes in depth as well as color (see the references at the end of this article), but in this case we don't actually want that precise of a result! With the samples offset along a single diagonal line, the filter favors edges in one direction compared to the other, which gives a looser, more hand-drawn appearance.

Image-based edge detection can pick out borders that would be impossible to locate using a geometric approach, such as the lines around individual clouds in the sky texture.

Getting rid of unwanted texture detail is not as easy to do as a post-process, so for that we do need to change the main rendering engine. This is a trivial alteration, however, as you undoubtedly already have flat color versions of all your textures loaded into memory. Simply set D3DSAMP_MAXMIPLEVEL (or D3DTSS_MAXMIPLEVEL in DX8) to something greater than zero, and all that nasty high-resolution texture detail will go away, as shown in Figure 5 (see Color Plate 21).

While you are at it, if you have any alpha texture cutouts, such as trees, a few trivial changes can make their black borders thicker and more solid. You probably already have a good idea how to

Figure 5: Changing the mipmap settings to remove texture detail

do that, as chances are that you spent quite a while trying to get rid of those very same black borders at some point in the past. If you are using premultiplied alpha, disable it. If you are using alpha blending, turn it off and go back to simple alpha tests. If you have D3DRS_ALPHAREF set to something sensible, change it to 0 or 1 — instant black borders around everything you draw!

Unfortunately, this still isn't quite enough to give a plausible cartoon effect, so I'm going to have to break the "no new shaders" rule and change the lighting model. Smooth gradients from light to dark just don't look right in a cartoon world. The lighting should be quantized into only two or three discrete levels, with sudden transitions from light to shadow.

This is easy to do with a texture lookup. Discard everything but the most significant light source, and then in your vertex shader, output the light intensity as a texture coordinate:

```
#define LIGHT_DIR 1          // object space light direction vector

dp3 oT1.x, v1, c[LIGHT_DIR]   // dot vertex normal with the light direction
```

This light value is used to lookup into a 1D texture containing three discrete levels of brightness:

Figure 6 (see Color Plate 21) shows the final cartoon renderer, combining the edge detect filter, changes to the mipmap and alpha test settings, and three-level quantized lighting. It isn't quite a pure post-processing effect, but it still only required three new shaders: one pixel shader for the edge detection and two vertex shaders for the toon lighting (one for the bike, another for the animating rider).

Figure 6: The complete cartoon mode uses a discrete three-level lighting shader on bike and rider.

Pencil Sketch Effect

The most important characteristics of a pencil sketch can be summarized as:

- Drawing starts with an empty piece of white paper, which is then darkened down by the addition of pencil strokes.
- Both the intensity and direction of the strokes may be varied to convey shape and form, but stroke direction is mostly regular.
- Sketches are often entirely monochrome. Even when colored pencils are used, there will be a limited color palette.
- When animations are made from a series of sketches, they tend to be at extremely low framerates due to the amount of manual labor involved in drawing them.

The first step is obviously to create a texture holding a suitable pattern of pencil strokes. I used two images with slightly different stroke graphics aligned in opposite directions:

These are combined into a single texture, with the first stroke pattern in the red channel and the second in the blue channel. This combined stroke texture is tiled over the screen, set on texture stage 1, while the main scene image is set on stage 0. This is then processed through the shader:

```
ps.1.1

def c1, 1.0, 0.0, 0.0, 0.0
def c2, 0.0, 0.0, 1.0, 0.0

    tex t0                        // sample the source image
    tex t1                        // sample the stroke texture

1:  mul_x4_sat r0.rgb, t0, c0     // scale the frame buffer contents
2:  mul r0.rgb, 1-r0, 1-t1        // image * pencil stroke texture

3:  dp3_sat r1.rgba, r0, c1       // r1.a = red channel
4:  dp3_sat r1.rgb, r0, c2        // r1.rgb = blue channel

5:  mul r1.rgb, 1-r1, 1-r1.a      // combine, and convert -ve color back to +ve

6:  mov_x4_sat r0.rgb, t0         // overbrighten the frame buffer contents

7:  mul r0.rgb, r1_bx2, r0        // combine sketch with base texture

8:  mul_x2 r0.rgb, r0, v0         // tint
9:  + mov r0.a, v0.a
```

Instruction #1 scales the input color by a constant (c0), which is set by the application. This controls the sensitivity of the stroke detection — too high and there will be no strokes at all but too low and the strokes will be too dense. It needs to be adjusted according to the brightness of your scene: somewhere between 0.25 and 0.5 generally works well.

Instruction #2 combines the input color with the stroke texture in parallel for both the red and blue channels. It also inverts both colors by subtracting them from one. This is important because sketching operates in a subtractive color-space. Unlike a computer monitor, which adds light over a default black surface, a pencil artist is removing light from the white paper. It seems highly counterintuitive from my perspective as a graphics programmer, but the hatching in the blue sky area is actually triggered by the red color channel, while the hatching on the red bike comes from the blue channel! This is because there is no need for any hatching to add blue to the sky, all colors already being present in the default white background. On the contrary, the sky needs hatching in order to remove the unwanted red channel, which will leave only the desired shade of blue. We are drawing the absence of color rather than its presence, and this means we have to invert the input values to get correct results.

Instructions #3 and #4 separate out the red and blue color channels, creating Figure 7 and Figure 8, while instruction #5 combines them back together, producing Figure 9 (see Color Plate 22). Although this is purely a monochrome image, the input color is controlling the direction of the stroke texture. The blue sky and red bike are shaded in opposing directions, while dark areas such as the wheels combine both stroke directions to give a cross-hatch pattern.

Figure 7: Sketch strokes keyed off the inverse of the red color channel

Figure 8: Sketch strokes in the alternate direction keyed off the inverse blue

Figure 9: Both stroke directions combined together

Instruction #6 scales up the input color by a massive amount, producing Figure 10 (see Color Plate 22). Most of the image has been saturated to full white, with only a few areas of intensely primary color retaining their hue. When this is multiplied with the sketch pattern (instruction #7, producing Figure 11), it reintroduces a small amount of color to select parts of the image, while leaving the bulk of the hatching in monochrome.

Figure 10: Overbrightening the source image removes all but the most primary of colors.

The final step, in instruction #8, is to apply a colored tint. Figure 12 (see Color Plate 22) shows the final image with a sepia hue.

Figure 11: The stroke pattern from Figure 9 is multiplied with the color data from Figure 10.

Figure 12: The final sketch image is given a yellow tint.

This is all very well for a still image, but how is a pencil sketch to move? It looks silly if the pencil strokes stay in exactly the same place from one frame to the next, with only the image beneath them moving. But if we randomize the stroke texture in any way, the results will flicker horribly at anything approaching a decent refresh speed. Real sketched animations rarely run any faster than ten or 15 frames per second, but that is hardly desirable in the context of a 3D game engine!

My compromise was to run at full framerate, redrawing the input scene for each frame but to only move the stroke texture at periodic intervals. The low framerate movement of the pencil strokes can fool the eye into thinking that the scene is only being redrawn at a plausible pencil sketch type of rate, but it remains smooth and responsive enough for a player to interact with the underlying game.

References

Better edge detection methods:

Mitchell, Jason L., "Image Processing with 1.4 Pixel Shaders in Direct3D," *Direct3D ShaderX: Vertex and Pixel Shader Tips and Tricks*, Wolfgang Engel, ed., Wordware Publishing, 2002, pp. 258-269.

Mitchell, Jason, Chris Brennan, and Drew Card, "Real-Time Image-Space Outlining for Non-Photorealistic Rendering," SIGGRAPH 2002, http://www.ati.com/developer/SIGGRAPH02/NPROutlining_Mitchell.pdf.

Applying image post-processing techniques to video streams:

Ansari, Marwan, "Video Image Processing Using Shaders," ATI Research, http://www.ati.com/developer/gdc/GDC2003_VideoShader.pdf.

Doing "proper" sketch rendering with awareness of the underlying geometry, rather than as an image post-process. These techniques can give far more sophisticated results but are less easy to fit over the top of an existing renderer:

Buchin, Kevin and Maike Walther, "Hatching, Stroke Styles, and Pointillism," *ShaderX²: Shader Programming Tips & Tricks with DirectX 9*, Wolfgang Engel, ed., Wordware Publishing, Inc., 2004, pp. 340-347.

Praun, E., H. Hoppe, M. Webb, and A. Finkelstein, "Real-time hatching," SIGGRAPH 2001, http://research.microsoft.com/~hoppe/hatching.pdf.

The conventional approach to cartoon rendering, using geometry rather than image post-processing:

NVidia sample program, http://developer.nvidia.com/view.asp? IO=Toon_Shading

The cartoon and pencil sketch techniques presented in this article were developed for the Xbox game MotoGP by Climax and published by THQ. MotoGP 2 adds new filters such as saturate and mosaic and supports these effects in the PC version as well as on the Xbox.

Image Effects with DirectX 9 Pixel Shaders

Marwan Y. Ansari
ATI Research

Introduction

When most engineers think of pixel and vertex shaders, they instantly think of fully 3D scenes with animations and textures and the like. However, in the article "Image Processing with 1.4 Pixel Shaders in Direct3D" [Mitchell02] as well as the article "Advanced Image Processing Using DirectX 9 Shaders" in this book, it was shown that shaders can be used for far more than the hardware architects planned.

In "Advanced Image Processing Using DirectX 9 Shaders," shaders are used to perform image processing operations, such as Canny edge detection, $HSV \leftrightarrow RGB$ color conversions, and the Fast Fourier Transform. In this article, we deal more with the implementation of cool (well, at least we think so) image space special effects rather than the science of image processing.

This chapter discusses three classes of image effects:

- Transitions
- Distortions
- Posterization

All of the effects discussed in this chapter were developed using the VideoShader application supplied on the companion CD and found on the ATI developer relations web site. Furthermore, all of the effects you see here run in real time on live video (most at better than 30 frames per second on Radeon 9700 class hardware).

Some Review and Notes about This Article

The techniques in this article rely on some basic concepts when processing images. Firstly, all techniques discussed here are applied to images stored in textures. Though these algorithms were built to be applied to live video, they are not limited to that field. The incoming texture can be the result of a 3D rendered scene, live video, or any 2D image.

The vertex shader does little more than transform the vertex positions and normals. It does, however, pack both transformed and raw normal information into texture coordinates so that the pixel shader can use them.

The geometry used for these effects is a simple screen-aligned quad. When we render the screen-aligned quad, we put the image that we want to process on one of the texture samplers, typically sampler 0, and render. We term each rendering of the quad a *pass*. For 3D graphics engineers, this makes complete sense. However, in the area of image processing and image effects, rather than saying we rendered a single quad, we say we "processed the image" once or "went over the image" once. So in this article, though each pass does render a screen-aligned quad, it is referred to as a pass over the image.

The two implementations of the Kuwahara filter rely on multiple passes over the image while the other effects in this article are single pass. In some cases, the output of pass n is used as the input to pass $n+1$. In other cases, one pass outputs to a temporary buffer (a renderable texture), the next pass outputs to another temporary buffer (another renderable texture), and a third pass samples both of those buffers in order to get the final resultant image.

Some algorithms discussed in this article and in the "Advanced Image Processing Using DirectX 9 Shaders" article rely on constants that are loaded from the application. Some constants may not change over time, while some may change every frame. Below is a list of constants used in the effects discussed in this chapter:

- **sampleOffsets[8]:** Offsets for sampling the 3×3 area around the current texel. See Figure 1. Therefore, sampleOffsets[2] contains pixel width in the x component and pixel height in the y component. Pixel width and height are defined as 1/*image width* and 1/*image height*, respectively. sampleOffsets[6] contains 0 in the x component and negative pixel height in the y component. These values are added to the incoming texture coordinate inside the pixel shader to sample the eight nearest neighbors.

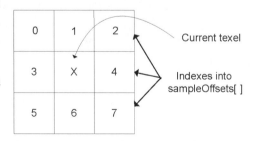

Figure 1: X represents the current texel surrounded by its eight nearest neighbors. The values in the neighboring texels (0...7) are what the indexes use to reference them in

- **viewMatrix**: View matrix. This is used in distortion effects.
- **UserInput.z**: Last X location the user clicked. This is used in thresholding images. The left edge is 0 and the right edge is 1.
- **UserPoint1.xy**: First location that the user clicked. Coordinates in the range [0,1]. Used in ripple shader.
- **UserPoint2.xy**: Second location that user clicked. Coordinates in the range [0,1]. Used in ripple shader.
- **Timers.w**: Time value oscillating between -1 and 1. This allows effects to use time to animate. The application updates this value on behalf of the shader. It takes about 15 seconds for the time value to cycle from 1 to -1 and back to 1.
- **Pt1Time.x**: Time value remaining for first click. It decreases from 1 to 0. This allows effects to run for a while and then stop without having the application swap out the shader. Used in the ripple shader.
- **Pt1Time.y**: Time value remaining for first click. It increases from 0 to 1. This allows effects to run for a while and then stop without having the application swap out the shader. Used in the ripple shader.
- **Pt2Time.x**: Same as Pt1Time.x but for the second ripple.
- **Pt2Time.y**: Same as Pt1Time.y but for the second ripple.

Finally, all of the shaders in this chapter are implemented using Microsoft's High Level Shading Language (HLSL) compiled for the ps.2.0 shader model under DirectX 9. For more information on HLSL, the ps.2.0 shader model, or DirectX 9, please see the Microsoft web site, the DirectX 9 SDK help files, or *Shader X²: Introductions & Tutorials with DirectX 9* [Mitchell04].

Transition Effects

Transition effects can be used when creating cut scenes in a game or when switching between multiple video streams. They are the simplest of image effects to perform because they tend to rely on spatial positioning inside the image more than the content of the pixels. In this section we discuss three transition effects: *left-right slide*, *spin and shrink away*, and *spice transitions* (created by Pixelan Software LLC).

Left-Right Slide

The left-right slide transition is fairly straightforward. It creates the appearance that one image is sliding in over the other. All the work is done in the pixel shader, and no constants other than time are needed.

Figure 2 shows snapshots of the progression of the left-right slide transition.

Figure 2: In the five snapshots above, you can see the image of the messy cubicle slide over the product logo until it is finally completely hidden.

The left-right slide algorithm:

```
For each texel (u,v)
    time = time * 1.1
    u' = u - time
    If(u' < 0 ||u' > 1)
        Sample first image using u,v
    Else
        Sample second image using u',v
    Return sample
```

The first step for this shader is to remap the time value to range from –1.1 to 1.1. We do this to give the effect a nice feel, as the image slides completely off the screen. If we were to leave the time value range at [–1,1] the image would immediately reverse its direction once it has completely slid off the screen. By changing the range to [–1.1, 1.1], we allow a fraction of a second to elapse after the image has slid off to one side and is completely removed from screen. Then, as time crosses into the (0,1) range, the image becomes visible again.

As you can see, the u coordinate is computed for each texel based on time. As time approaches –1.1, u' has a range across the image of [–1,0] or mostly all clipped. The same is true as time approaches 1.1 (when u' has a range of [1,2]). The image is only completely visible when *time = 0* and u' has a range of [0,1].

The net result is that the image appears to slide left and right without having to render a separate pass of geometry.

The left-right slide transition:

```
//-----------------------------------------------------//
// LRSlidingTransitionNoScale.hlsl
//
// Slide one image left and right over a second image.
//
// Marwan Y. Ansari - ATI Research, Inc. - 2003
//-----------------------------------------------------//
sampler inputImage;                  // incoming image
sampler productImage;                // transition image
float4 Timers;                       // for sliding animation
struct PS_INPUT
{
    float2 texCoord:TEXCOORD0;       // incoming tex coord.
};
float4 main( PS_INPUT In ) : COLOR
{
    // xPosition is fancy name of u coord (as in u,v)
```

```
// xPosition = [-1.1, 1.1]
float  xPosition = Timers.w * 1.1;
float2 newCoords;
float4 c = .5;


//==========================================//
// Calc new u Coord by subtracting off time. //
// (time range : [-1.1, 1.1])                //
//==========================================//
xPosition = In.texCoord.x - xPosition;

//if u coord is outside 0 to 1 range,
// background image is showing.
if((xPosition < 0) || (xPosition > 1))
{
    c = tex2D(productImage, In.texCoord);
}
else
{
    newCoords.y = In.texCoord.y;
    newCoords.x = xPosition;
    c = tex2D( inputImage, newCoords);
}

return c;
}
```

Left-Right Squeeze

In a similar vein, we can squeeze the two images to make the transition. Again, the only constant used is time. Instead of clipping the images against the left or right side of the window, we keep one image touching the left edge while the other is always touching the right edge. As time changes, the images squeeze and stretch in the window. Figure 3 shows snapshots of the progression of the left-right squeeze.

Figure 3: In the five snapshots above, you can see the image of the messy cube squeeze against the product image as time goes forward.

The left-right squeeze transition algorithm:

```
For each texel
    Length  = Scale and bias time to be between 0 and 1
    If( Length < u)
        u' = u scale
        Sample first image using u',v.
    Else
```

u' = u scaled based on length
Sample second image using u',v.
Return sample

This algorithm scales and biases time from –1 to 1 into the range of 0 to 1. Doing so allows us to use the new time value as the current location of the boundary between the two images. Bear in mind that time ranges from 0 to 1 independently of u'.

Then the algorithm goes on to compute u' based on the length of one of the images.

$$u' = \frac{u - length}{1 - length}$$ if the new time value is less than this texel's u value.

...or:

$$u' = \frac{u}{length}$$ if the new time value is greater than this texel's u value.

Here, $(u - length)$ is the distance between the texel and the left edge of the image and $(1 - length)$ is the total width of the image during this time. This division results in a value that ranges from [0,1].

The left-right squeeze transition:

```
//------------------------------------------------------------//
// LRSlidingTransition20.hlsl
//
// Left to right squeezing transition between two images.
// Compute the squeezing square's current position based on
// time...see if the current pixel is inside or outside that
// square and pick the right sample to display.
//
//
// Marwan Y. Ansari - ATI Research, Inc. - 2003
//------------------------------------------------------------//
sampler inputImage;                   // image to be processed
sampler productImage;                 // Background image
float4  Timers;                       // Time value
struct PS_INPUT
{
    float2 texCoord:TEXCOORD0;
};
float4 main( PS_INPUT In ) : COLOR
{
    float  length = Timers.w;         // length = [-1..1]
    float2 scaledCoords;
    float4 c = .5;


    //==================================================//
    // Get the length of the shrinking area based on the
    // time...this is done above.
    // Here we make length = [0..1]
```

```
//================================================//
length = (length * 0.5) + 0.5 ;

// find out where this point is in relation to the image;
if ( length < In.texCoord.x )
{
    //================================================//
    // y doesn't change
    // x =
    //
    //     1
    //    ---      *  ( texcoord.x - length.x)
    //    1-length
    //
    // Which will map the image into the right side of
    // the screen.
    //================================================//
    scaledCoords.y = In.texCoord.y;
    scaledCoords.x = (1.0 / ( 1.0 - length)) *
                     (In.texCoord - length);
    c = tex2D(productImage, scaledCoords);
}
else
{
    //================================================//
    // y doesn't change
    // x =
    //
    //     1
    //    ---      * texcoord.x
    //    length
    //
    // Which will map the image into the left side of the
    // screen.
    //================================================//
    scaledCoords.y = In.texCoord.y;
    scaledCoords.x = (1.0 / ( length)) * In.texCoord;
    scaledCoords.x = saturate(scaledCoords);
    c = tex2D( inputImage, scaledCoords);
}
return c;
}
```

Spin and Shrink Away

Another interesting transition effect can give the appearance of geometry without
actually sending any new vertices down the pipe. Below is the algorithm for a
transition that makes one image appear to spin and shrink away from the viewer.
This is quite simple to do by applying a transformation in the pixel shader. Again,
only one set of vertices are ever sent down. As seen in the shaders above, this
method relies on knowing where you are in the image (by way of u,v) and picking

an image to display. Figure 4 shows snapshots of the progression of the spin and shrink away transition.

Figure 4: In the five snapshots above, you can see the image of the messy cubicle rotate and shrink away until it is completely gone.

The spin and shrink transition algorithm:

```
For each texel (u,v)
    Length = time scaled and biased to be 0 to 1
    Get sine and cosine based on length
    Construct rotation matrix
    Rotate coordinates(u,v) about its center
    If(current u,v are inside the transformed coordinates)
        Compute u',v' based on time and rotation of u,v
        Sample first image using u',v'
    Else
        Sample second image using u,v
    Return sample
```

A 1D texture is used to compute the sine and cosine values used in the rotation matrixes. The texture filter naturally and linearly interpolates to compute values not present in the sine table. Since sine and cosine can be considered the same function one quarter out of phase, you can do the following:

sin = fetch into sin texture (length)

cos = fetch into sin texture (length + .25)

After constructing the rotation matrix, the coordinates must be translated to the origin before transformation. Rather than building this directly into the matrix through matrix concatenation, we simply subtract the 0.5 offset before the transformation. This saves operations, since it reduces matrix multiplies and does vector addition instead and centers the square at (0, 0) instead of at (0.5, 0.5).

Now the current coordinate, which may or may not be an element of the spinning shrinking square, has been translated to the center about the origin. All the points in the spinning shrinking square are bound between (lengthOver2, lengthOver2)… (–lengthOver2, –lengthOver2). Since all the coordinates are symmetric and are bound by lengthOver2, we can simplify the comparison by taking the absolute value of the coordinates. If the absolute value of either u' or v' is greater than lengthOver2, then this point is considered *outside* the rotating square. See Figure 5.

If the current texel is considered outside the spinning shrinking square, we can simply display the background image. If it is inside the square, we must recompute the texture coordinates based on rotation and the shrinking effect. This is done in two steps. First, compute the coordinates inside the square and then rotate those coordinates.

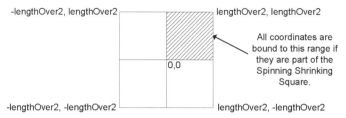

-lengthOver2, lengthOver2   lengthOver2, lengthOver2

0,0

All coordinates are
bound to this range if
they are part of the
Spinning Shrinking
Square.

-lengthOver2, -lengthOver2   lengthOver2, -lengthOver2

Figure 5: We can optimize the number of comparisons that we need to perform by using the absolute value of our coordinates. This limits their range to the shaded area above.

The square's edge (in texture space) that corresponds to 0, 0 will be at *offset* = *0.5 – lengthOver2*.

That is the offset from either the left edge or the bottom of the texture. Subtracting that value from our current *u,v* and dividing the entire amount by *length* scales the current *u,v* properly, based on its shrinking as time progresses.

$$u', v' = ((u, v) - (0.5 - lengthOver2)) * \frac{1}{length}$$

The resulting *u',v'* is measured relative to (or from) the top-left edges of the square (this is actually a translation of u,v axes from the top-left corner of the texture to the top-left corner of the square). Then, division by *length* results in *u,v* pairs that are in the range [0,1]: (0,0) at the top-left corner of the square, (1,1) at the bottom-right corner of the square. Thus, the texture is completely mapped onto the spinning shrinking square.

The coordinate *u',v'* is correctly placed inside the shrunken square and ready for the final step, which is a rotation about the center of the square. As we did before, subtract 0.5 from the coordinates, multiply by the rotation matrix built earlier, and add 0.5 to the result.

$$u', v' = (u, v) - 0.5$$
$$u', v' = mul((u', v'), rotationMatrix) + 0.5$$

The *u',v'* coordinates computed are now properly scaled down and rotated based on time. Now sample the image to be shrunk and spun away with the *u',v'* coordinates and return the sample.

The spin and shrink away transition:

```
//-------------------------------------------------------------//
// SpinTransition_2_20.hlsl
//
// Rotates image as it spins to and from the user.
// Compute the shrinking, spinning square's current position
// based on time...see if the current pixel is inside or
// outside that square and pick the right sample to display.
//
// Marwan Y. Ansari - ATI Research, Inc. - 2003
```

```
//-------------------------------------------------------------//
sampler inputImage;
sampler sinTexture;
sampler productImage;
float4  Timers;
struct PS_INPUT
{
    float2 texCoord:TEXCOORD0;
};

float4 main( PS_INPUT In ) : COLOR
{
    float    length = Timers.w;        // length = [-1..1]
    float    lengthOver2, sinValue, cosValue;
    float2   sinCoords = 0;
    float3x3 rotMat =0;                // initialize the matrix to 0
    float3   coords=0;
    float3   rotatedCoords;
    float4 c = .5;

    //================================//
    // Get the length of the shrinking square based
    // on the time...this is done above.  Here we make
    // length = [0..1]
    length = ((length * 0.5) + 0.5 ) ;

    lengthOver2 = length * 0.5;

    // Use length and length - .25  to sample sin and cos
    sinCoords.x = length;
    sinValue = tex2D( sinTexture, sinCoords);
    sinCoords.x = length - .25;
    cosValue = tex2D( sinTexture, sinCoords);

    // build rotation matrix
    rotMat[0][0] =  cosValue;
    rotMat[0][1] =  sinValue;
    rotMat[1][0] = -sinValue;
    rotMat[1][1] =  cosValue;
    rotMat[2][2] =  1.0;

    // Rotate the box around the screen center
    coords.xy = In.texCoord -.5 ;
    rotatedCoords = mul( coords, rotMat);

    // Now the coords have been x-lated and rotated about the
    // origin.  Test if its abs() goes past the lengthOver2.
    // This method simplifies the compare to a simple <=0 .
    // Since the point, which is an element of the spinning
    // shrinking square, has been x-lated to the origin, all the
    // points in the spinning shrinking square are inside of...
    // -lengthOver2,-lengthOver2... lengthOver2,lengthOver2
```

```
//
// Since all the coords are symmetric...and since they are
// bound by lengthOver2, we can simplify the comparison by
// taking the absolute value of the coords.
// If the abs value of either x or y is greater than lengthOver2,
// then this point is considered outside the rotating square.

rotatedCoords = abs(rotatedCoords);
if( lengthOver2 <= rotatedCoords.x ||
    lengthOver2 <= rotatedCoords.y )
{   // the current pixel is outside of the box.
    c = tex2D( productImage, In.texCoord);
}
else
{   // the current pixel is inside of the box.
    float3 scaledCoords = 0;

    //==================================================//
    // offset of edge of square = (1-length) /2  ... or
    //                            (0.5 - lengthOver2)
    // compute distance current pixel is IN from square's left
    // edge   (tex - (0.5 - lengthOver2))
    //
    // new tex is (dist from square edge)/(distance from image edge)
    //
    //
    //==================================================//
    //
    //                          1-d     1
    //              ( texcoord -  ---  ) * ---
    //                           2       d
    //
    //==================================================//
    scaledCoords.xy = (In.texCoord + (lengthOver2 - 0.5)) *
                      (1.0/length);

    // now xlate , rotate, xlate to get the new coords
    scaledCoords.xy -= 0.5;
    scaledCoords.xy = mul( scaledCoords, rotMat) + 0.5 ;
    c = tex2D( inputImage, scaledCoords);
}

return c;
}
```

Spice Transitions from Pixelan Software, LLC

Rather than animate the transition, sometimes it is best to simply dissolve from
one image into another based on either an algorithm or some map. Pixelan Software, LLC provides some interesting transition products that do exactly that.
Very cool effects can be achieved by using cleverly created transition maps, allowing the pixel shader to be very short. The algorithm uses two maps, one for the

transition effect and one to help blending. The transitions, called spices, can be used as plug-ins to a number of video editing tools. See the Pixelan web site for more details.

The spice transition algorithm:

```
For each texel
    Sample image1, image2, and transition map
    LUTcoord = transition map sample + time  // time = [-1, 1]
    Sample LUTblender based on LUTcoord
    Result = lerp between image1 and image2 based on LUTblender
    Return Result
```

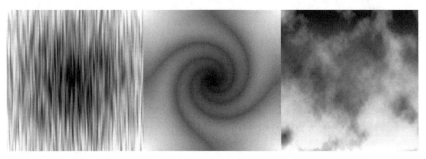

Figure 6: Three spice transition maps. As time increases, the light areas are the first to transition between the two images while the dark areas are the last. As time decreases, the light areas transition last and the dark areas transition first.

Figure 7: Lookup table (LUT) used for transitioning between two images. The gray area in the center keeps the edges from making hard noticeable transitions.

Figure 6 shows three transition maps. As time increases, the light areas are the first to transition between the images, while the dark areas are last. Figure 7 shows the lookup table (LUT) that is used to linearly interpolate (lerp) between the two images. The gray area in the middle ensures that the edge transitions are not too harsh.

What is particularly useful about this approach is that you can create many interesting effects by changing the transition maps. More transition maps are available on the CD in the VideoShader application (see Figure 8).

However, these are just a few possible transition effects. Just about any transition effect that is currently available today in the television or movie industry can be done inside of a pixel shader.

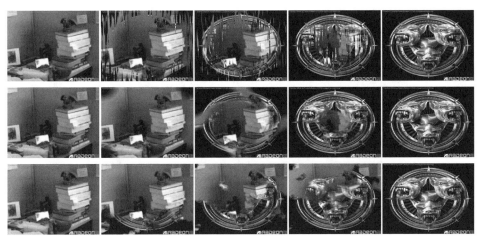

Figure 8: Spice transitions using the maps shown in Figure 6 over time.

A spice transition:

```
//---------------------------------------------------------------//
// ImageFade20.hlsl
//
// Performs a wipe transition between 2 images.
//
// Marwan Y. Ansari - ATI Research, Inc. - 2002
//---------------------------------------------------------------
sampler inputImage;
sampler ProductImage;
sampler WipeTransition;             // Transition map
sampler LUT;                        // Lookup table
float4  Timers;

struct PS_INPUT
{
    float2 texCoord0:TEXCOORD0;
};

float4 main( PS_INPUT In ) : COLOR
{
    float4 c = .5;
    float4 currFrameSample;
    float4 targetSample;
    float4 transitionSample;
    float4 lutSample;
    float2 lutCoord;
    float  timeScalar;

    currFrameSample  = tex2D( inputImage, In.texCoord0);
    targetSample     = tex2D( ProductImage, In.texCoord0);
    transitionSample = tex2D( WipeTransition, In.texCoord0);
```

```
timeScalar = Timers.w;

// .7 just slows the transition down.
// Saturate ensures that we clamp from 0 to 1.
lutCoord = saturate(transitionSample + .7* timeScalar);

lutSample = tex2D( LUT, lutCoord);

c = lerp(targetSample, currFrameSample, lutSample);

return c;
}
```

Distortion Effects

The effects discussed so far have dealt with blending between images for scene transitions. They were based on time and the spatial position of the current pixel shader coordinate or on the value of a transition map at a pixel location. Other techniques involve directly affecting the image by distorting it. Distorting the image is a common effect in gaming as well as in the movie industry.

Distortion effects executed fully in the pixel shader can be useful when the application does not want to or cannot create the extra geometry to perturb the image. This section shows how, in some cases, environment mapping could be used to fake geometry and even animation.

For example, the ripple effect discussed here uses no normal maps and no extra geometry to create the ripples. They are all generated inside the pixel shader based on a time value.

Fun House Mirror

The first distortion effect mimics the fun house mirror that you might see at a carnival. A fun house mirror is simply a mirror with a curve in it. When you look into it, instead of seeing a 1:1 reflection of yourself, you see a distorted image due to the curves in the material.

Rather than actually rendering the curvy geometry in real time, we use a normal map that was generated using ATI's Normal Mapper Tool (available for

Figure 9: Fun house mirror effects

download on the ATI developer web site).

The normal map used here is 16-bit per component and contains only the x and y components. The z component (assumed to be positive) can be derived from x and y using the following relation:

$$z = \sqrt{1 - \left(x^2 + y^2 \right)}$$

Computing this third component costs three instructions in a ps.2.0 shader. However, the savings of writing 32 bytes per normal map pixel vs. writing 64 bytes is significant. Conversely, with this approach we are able to store a 16-bit per component normal map in the same footprint as an 8-8-8-8 texture, gaining much-needed precision.

The fun house mirror algorithm:

```
For each texel
    Fetch normal from Normal map
    Compute third component (this step could be optional)
    Derive per-vertex eye vector using camera position
    Compute reflection vector
    Sample from cube map based on reflection vector
    Return Sample
```

As you can see, this is simple cube mapping, except that rather than using geometry to compute the surface normal, we use a normal map. This method is particularly effective when used with live video, as the interactivity is what makes the effect interesting.

Since we are dealing with a single image rather than a full 3D environment, we need to discuss how exactly we populate the cube map. Only one face of the cube map (the positive z face) is populated with the target image, while the rest of the image is initialized to blue.

Also, when we compute the normal in the shader, we add a "fudgeFactor" component. This has nothing to do with the actual algorithm. It is strictly to overcome an issue with the normal map used that caused the normals to point outside the positive z face. This is strictly an aesthetic issue, not an algorithmic one. fudgeFactor was found by trial and error until the final image was acceptable. The VideoShader application allows you to edit the shader files using any text editor and reload the new shader without having to restart the application. See the documentation in the VideoShader directory for more information.

A fun house shader using a cube map:

```
//----------------------------------------------------------------//
// FunHouseCubeShader.hlsl
//
// Renders the image with fun house mirror effect
// using a cube map.
//
// Marwan Y. Ansari - ATI Research, Inc. - 2002
//----------------------------------------------------------
sampler normalMap;
```

```
sampler cubeTexture;
float3x3 viewMatrix;               // World view matrix

struct PS_INPUT
{   float2 texCoord0:TEXCOORD0;
    float3 texCoord4:TEXCOORD4; //interpolated pos in obj space.
};
float4 main( PS_INPUT In ) : COLOR
{

    float4 fudgeFactor = {0, -0.00001, 0.21, 0.0};
    float4 c = .5;
    float2 normalCoord = In.texCoord0;
    float3 normal =0, reflection =0, xformedEye;

    normalCoord.y = 1.0 -normalCoord.y;//Texture is upside down
    normal = tex2D( normalMap, normalCoord);

    // the normals are coming in on two components,
    // we need to derive the third component k = sqrt( i^2 + j^2)
    normal.z = sqrt( 1.0f -((normal.x * normal.x) +
                            (normal.y * normal.y)));
    normal += fudgeFactor;

    //derive per-vertex eye vector using camera position
    //Use the (-untransformed position) as a camera in obj space
    //and x-form it to view space.  Resultant vector taken as
    //vector from camera to current position.
    xformedEye.xyz = mul( -In.texCoord4, viewMatrix);
    xformedEye.xyz = normalize(xformedEye);

    // Compute viewer's reflection vector
    reflection.xyz = dot(normal, xformedEye) * 2 * normal -
                     (dot(normal,normal) * xformedEye);

    // Flip the right and left so that it acts like a mirror.
    reflection.x = -reflection.x;

    // sample the cube map
    c = texCUBE( cubeTexture, reflection );
    return c;
}
```

Shower Door

3D graphics applications commonly combine environment mapping with bump
mapping to achieve a bumpy-shiny effect (EMBM). EMBM can also be used
to give the impression of looking through glass of varying thicknesses as in Figure 10.

For this effect, we first compute the eye vector and perturb it by a noise map
that is generated offline. Finally, we use the perturbed vector to sample into our

environment map. Since the effect is only applied to a single image, we perform a cube map lookup.

Figure 10: The shower door effect is created by using a noise texture to perturb the normals used in environment mapping.

Shower door effect algorithm:

```
For each texel
    Derive per-vertex eye vector using camera position
    Sample noise map
    Add noise sample to eye vector
    Compute reflection vector
    Sample from texture map based on reflection vector
    Return sample
```

The shower door effect:

```
//-------------------------------------------------------------//
// BumpVideo20.hlsl
//
// EMBM the video image.
//
// Marwan Y. Ansari - ATI Research, Inc. - 2003
//-------------------------------------------------------------
sampler inputImage;
sampler noiseMap;
float3x3 viewMatrix;

struct PS_INPUT
{
    float2 texCoord0:TEXCOORD0;
    float3 texCoord4:TEXCOORD4;      // vertex position
    float3 texCoord6:TEXCOORD6;      // normal
};

float4 main( PS_INPUT In ) : COLOR
{
```

```
float4 c          = 0.5;
float3 normal     = In.texCoord6;
float3 xformedEye = 0;
float3 reflection = 0;

//derive per-vertex eye vector using camera position
xformedEye.xyz = mul(-In.texCoord4, viewMatrix);
xformedEye.xyz = normalize(xformedEye);

// Multiply by .25 to decrease the effect of the normal map
normal.xyz += tex2D(noiseMap, In.texCoord0) * .25;

// Compute viewer's reflection vector
reflection.xyz = dot(normal, xformedEye) * 2 * normal -
                 (dot(normal,normal) * xformedEye);

// perform cube map lookup to just one face because
// I know there is only one face.
reflection.xy *= 1.0/ reflection.z;
reflection.xy  = (-.5*reflection) + .5;

// reflect about the X
reflection.x = 1-reflection.x;

c = tex2D(inputImage, reflection);
return c;
}
```

Ripple

Figure 11: The two ripple centers are colored magenta and fade as the ripple fades. These five images show, in left to right order, the ripples' dissipation after they have fully propagated. (See Color Plate 23.)

The above shaders show how environment mapping and bump mapping can be used to simulate geometric perturbations. With a little more effort, we can simulate more interesting effects, such as ripples. Figure 11 shows two ripples affecting an image over time. This is a common effect used in the film industry.

Though manipulating vertex information to simulate a ripple effect is commonplace in computer graphics, the interesting notion here is that all the computations are done in the pixel shader. No vertex information other than the normal is required with this method.

The overall ripple shader algorithm:

For each texel
    Compute the normal for ripple one at this point in time

```
Compute the normal for ripple two at this point in time
Combine ripples one and two with the vertex normal
Derive per-vertex eye vector using camera position
Compute reflection vector
Sample from map based on reflection vector
Return Sample
```

The algorithm for computing the ripple normal:

```
(Calling function passes in ripple center, time left on ripple, and
    current texel position)
Compute wave radius
Compute the vector from ripple center to current texel (direction vector)
If current texel is inside ripple
        Look up sine value of current pixel based on frequency
        Compute ripple effect as sine * height * decreasing time
        Result = Direction vector * ripple effect
        Return Result
```

The interesting piece of the algorithm is the function to compute the ripple's normal. In the ps 2.0 shader model, we can compute two ripples in a single pixel shader using the method described here. There are methods that allow for an arbitrary number of ripples, but they require writing to an extra buffer and are left as an exercise for the reader.

We first compute the ripple's radius based on the amount of time elapsed since the ripple was started. The radius of the ripple is its time multiplied by the ripple's speed. In this shader, speed is a constant. Then we compute the distance and direction vector from the ripple center to the current texel location.

Next, since we want the ripple to propagate out from a central point, we can test if the current texel has been affected by the ripple yet. This is easily done by comparing the distance (from the current texel to the ripple center) to the wave radius. If the distance is less than the wave radius, then this texel is part of the ripple.

Now that we know this texel is affected by the ripple, we need to compute exactly what effect the ripple will have. The ripple we use is based on a sine wave. Rather than computing the sine value inside the shader, it is more efficient to use a lookup sine table stored in a texture. Computing the texture coordinates for the sine texture is done by multiplying the ripple frequency by the distance from the ripple center. After the sine value is retrieved, it must be multiplied by the ripple height and its remaining time. Multiplying by the remaining time dampens the ripple to 0 as the ripple runs out. The only step remaining is multiplying the ripple effect by the direction vector (from the ripple center to the current texel). This constructs a normal that is pointed in the correct direction from the ripple center.

It should be noted that the ripple normals only have values in the x and y components, while the z component is zero. After combining the two ripple normals with the vertex normal, the z component of the combined normal is equal to the z component of the vertex normal.

After the combined normal is computed, the remaining steps are just environment mapping. For more information on environment mapping see *Real-Time Rendering* [Möller99].

The ripple shader:

```
//-----------------------------------------------------------//
// TwoRipple20.hlsl
//
// Creates 2 ripples in the image and propagates them out over
// time.
//
// Marwan Y. Ansari - ATI Research, Inc. - 2002
// Many thanks to Chris Brennan (ATI Research) for his help.
//-----------------------------------------------------------//

sampler  inputImage;
sampler  sinTexture;

float3x3 viewMatrix;
float4   UserPoint1;                // first click position
float4   UserPoint2;                // second click position
float4   Pt1Time;
float4   Pt2Time;

struct PS_INPUT
{
    float2 texCoord0:TEXCOORD0;     // current location
    float3 texCoord4:TEXCOORD4;     // position in obj space
    float3 texCoord6:TEXCOORD6;     // Normal
};

float3 ComputeRippleNormal(float2 CurrLocation,
                           float4 RippleCenter, float4 PtTime)
{
    float4 ptModulator;
    float3 ptDistance =0;
    float3 ptDirectionVector =0;
    float2 ptsSin =0;
    float2 sinCoords = 0;
    float3 ripple=0;
    float  distanceToCenter;
    float  freqTweak      = 4.0;
    float  waveSpeedTweak = 9.4;
    float  waveHeightTweak = .125;
    float  waveRadius;
    float  isInsideWave;

    ptModulator = PtTime * 0.5 ;  // time/2 to slow it a bit.
    // y ranges from 0 to 0.5
    waveRadius = ptModulator.y * waveSpeedTweak;

    ptDistance.xy     = (RippleCenter - CurrLocation);
    ptDirectionVector = normalize(ptDistance);

    // As time goes on... waveRadius increases
```

```
        // b/c waveAge increases.
        isInsideWave = waveRadius -
                                sqrt(dot(ptDistance,ptDistance));


        if(isInsideWave > 0)  // Allows the ripples to grow from RippleCenter.
        {                     // Otherwise, all pixels would be affected by
                              // the ripple at time 0.

            // mul -waveRadius by freq to get sin coord
            // make sinCoords.x negative so we start with a trough
            // instead of a crest.
            sinCoords.x = -isInsideWave * freqTweak;

            ptsSin = tex2D(sinTexture, sinCoords);  // Get sin value

            // Keep in mind that ptModulator.x ranges from -0.5 to .5
            // ...it decreases over time. mul by 1/8 just to tweak...
            // then dampen the ripple effect with time..
            ptsSin  *= waveHeightTweak * ptModulator.x;
            ripple = ptsSin.x * ptDirectionVector;
        }
        return ripple;
}


float4 main( PS_INPUT In ) : COLOR
{
    float4 c = .5;
    float3 xformedEye;
    float3 reflection =0;
    float3 combinedNormal;
    float3 ripple1=0, ripple2 =0;

    ripple1 = ComputeRippleNormal(In.texCoord0,
                                    UserPoint1,
                                    Pt1Time);
    ripple2 = ComputeRippleNormal(In.texCoord0,
                                    UserPoint2,
                                    Pt2Time);

    // build normal for environment mapping by adding ripples
    // vertex shader is sending texCoord6 in negated, we must
    // also negate it.
    combinedNormal   =  (ripple1 + ripple2) - In.texCoord6;

    //derive per-vertex eye vector using camera position
    xformedEye.xyz = mul(-In.texCoord4, viewMatrix);
    xformedEye.xyz = normalize(xformedEye);

    // Compute viewer's reflection vector
    reflection.xyz =dot(combinedNormal, xformedEye) *
                2 * combinedNormal -
                (dot(combinedNormal,combinedNormal) * xformedEye);
```

```
// perform cube map lookup to just one face because I
// know there is only one face.
reflection.xy *= 1.0/reflection.z;
reflection.xy = (-.5*reflection) + .5;

// sample the reflection map
c = tex2D(inputImage, reflection);

return c;
}
```

As you can see, it is easy to simulate geometric perturbations using environment mapping in the pixel shader. As long as the normal is computable procedurally, it can be stored in a texture or both.

Posterization

So far in this chapter we have discussed transition and distortion effects that are applied to images. With the growing popularity of non-photorealistic rendering (NPR) in real-time computer graphics, we have also looked into image-space NPR techniques. In this section, we discuss the use of a Kuwahara filter to generate an NPR look. We discuss two Kuwahara kernels (5×5 and 7×7). The 5×5 kernel is simpler to implement and only requires two passes. The 7×7 kernel is harder to implement and must be broken into four passes. As the kernel size increases, it becomes more complicated to apply.

Kuwahara (5×5 filter size)

The Kuwahara filter is a non-linear edge preserving smoothing operation [Young]. The filter is centered at the current texel and relies on sampling the neighboring texels to compute the new value for the current texel.

This filter operates on a given 5×5 region by breaking it into four sub-regions that overlap by a single pixel in the horizontal and vertical direction. Our implementations here are based on 5×5 and 7×7 square regions, as shown in Figure 12.

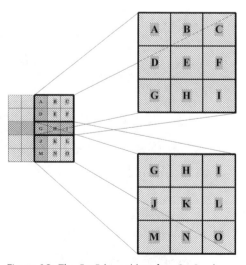

Figure 12: The 5×5 kernel has four 3×3 sub-regions. Here, two of those sub-regions have been broken out to emphasize the one-pixel-wide overlap.

The sub-region size is determined using the following method described in [Young]:

Given a square kernel of length k, sub-regions are of size j×j, where:

$$j = \frac{k+1}{2}$$

So given our 5×5 kernel, our sub-regions are:

$$j = \frac{5+1}{2} = 3$$

$$j \times j = 3 \times 3$$

Again, in this implementation, we use square kernels, but other sizes and shapes can be computed by applying this formula to the length and width.

For each sub-region, the mean color and sample variance (referred to in this article simply as variance) are computed. Once all four mean/variance pairs are computed, the variances are compared. The lowest variance is found and its matching mean is taken as the color for the current pixel. So, the color for the current texel is selected based on which of the four areas has the smallest change in color.

This effect requires two passes to implement. The first pass renders not into the frame buffer but rather into a renderable texture. The second pass uses the renderable texture from the first pass as its input.

The algorithm for a 5×5 Kuwahara kernel:

```
First pass
    For each texel
        Sample 3×3 region around this texel and find the mean.
        Compute the variance of this 3×3 region.
        Store the mean as rgb, store the variance in the alpha.
        Return the mean/variance as a texel. (Stores into
            renderable texture)

Second Pass (use first pass as input)
    For each texel
        Sample the 4 texels that are diagonal from this texel.
        Compare the texels' variances (alpha) finding the lowest.
        Return the mean associated with the lowest variance.
```

The first pass computes the mean color by sampling the current texel and its eight neighbors. The sampling is achieved by storing the pixel width (1/width) and pixel height (1/height) offsets into a set of constant registers (see the "Some Review and Some Notes about This Article" section earlier in this article). These offsets are individually added to this texel's location and then used as new texture coordinates.

After the nine samples are taken (one for each texel in the 3×3 sub-region), the texels are summed component-wise, and the total is divided by 9 (the number of samples). For example, if we had two pixels, $\{r_1, g_1, b_1\}$ and $\{r_2, b_2, g_2\}$, after summing component-wise, the result would be $\{r_1 + r_2, g_1 + g_2, b_1 + b_2\}$. The final result of the mean is:

$$\left\{ \left(\frac{r_1 + \ldots + r_9}{9} \right), \left(\frac{g_1 + \ldots + g_9}{9} \right), \left(\frac{b_1 + \ldots + b_9}{9} \right) \right\}$$

Computing the variance is just as straightforward. The variance is defined as:

$$v = \sigma^2 = \frac{1}{N} \sum_{i=1}^{N} \left(sample_i . r - mean . r \right)^2 + \left(sample_i . g - mean . g \right)^2 + \left(sample_i . b - mean . b \right)^2$$

…where v is the variance and σ^2 is the squared standard deviation [Weisstein].

As you can see, it is also possible to get the standard deviation this way by taking the square root of the variance and storing it. It should be noted, however, that there is the possibility of artifacts appearing due to the quantizing of the standard deviation (σ). Recall that σ's range is [0,1] and that σ^2 will logically be at the lower end of that scale. Since we store σ^2 into an 8-bit value, it is possible that it will be quantized to the same value as some other σ^2, even though the values are slightly different. There are two solutions to this issue. The first is to use higher precision render targets. The other is to take the square root of σ^2 inside the shader, since that operation can be done at floating-point precision. In our implementation, we did not need to find the standard deviation, so this issue is just something that you may want to keep in mind.

Once the mean and variance are computed, we store them in the output pixel with the mean replicated into the RGB components and the variance stored in alpha. The result is that this pass creates a mean/variance map, which is used by the next pass. Each texel in the mean/variance map contains the mean and variance of the corresponding 3×3 area in the original image.

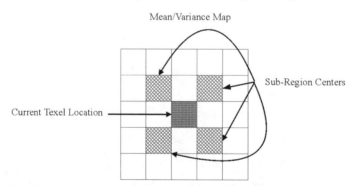

Figure 13: The centers for the four 3x3 sub-regions in a Kuwahara filter are diagonal from the current texel location in the mean/variance map.

In the second pass, we only need to compare the variances for the regions of the Kuwahara filter to find the lowest. To get the variances, we simply sample the four pixels of the mean/variance map that lie on a diagonal to the current pixel. If this texel is at u,v, then we want to sample the mean-variance map at:

> *u + (1/width), v + (1/height)*
> *u + (1/width), v − (1/height)*
> *u − (1/width), v + (1/height)*
> *u − (1/width), v − (1/height)*

See Figure 13. The texture-wrapping mode should be set to CLAMP in order to prevent edges from interfering with each other. After sampling these values, it is trivial to compare the variances and store the mean.

This technique is excellent for posterizing images. However, since the filters are so small (5×5 in this case), the effect is very tiny after just one iteration is applied. We found that in order to get interesting results, we need to run the 5×5 Kuwahara kernel a total of four times. That makes four filters at two passes per filter for a total of eight passes. This will vary, however, with image size.

Finally, after all the passes have been done, we can add a last touch to the image. In order to get a nice NPR effect, we need to add black outlines to the image to highlight the different color regions the way comic books or cartoons do.

An easy and effective way of doing this is to use an edge detection filter. In the article "Advanced Image Processing Using DirectX 9 Shaders," we discussed the Canny edge detection filter. We have found that although the Canny edge detection filter is impressive, its thin edges are not adequate for outlining. The Sobel edge detection filter gives rather thick edges, however, and is perfect for the kind of outlining we wanted to aesthetically complement the Kuwahara filter.

For a full discussion of the theory behind the Sobel edge detection filter, see [Jain95] or [Gonzalez92]. For a two-pass implementation of the filter, see [Mitchell02], or for a single-pass implementation, see the VideoShader application on the CD.

By modifying the Sobel edge detector to combine the resultant edges with the posterized scene, we can achieve our thick outlines. After the Sobel edge detector finds the edges, we subtract the result from one and threshold it based on user input. This way the user can select what he or she perceives as enough edges or outlines interactively.

See Figure 14 for the output of the 5×5 Kuwahara filter with Sobel outlines. The filter was run four times over the image with a fifth pass to add the outlines.

The following computes the mean and variance of a 3×3 area for the 5×5 Kuwahara filter:

Figure 14: A 5x5 Kuwahara filter plus outlines based on the Sobel edge detection filter has been applied to the image for real-time posterization. (See Color Plate 24.)

```
//-----------------------------------------------------------
// MeanVarianceGeneric.hlsl
//
// Get the mean and variance of the 3x3 area around this pixel.
```

```
//
// Marwan Y. Ansari - ATI Research, Inc. - 2002
//--------------------------------------------------------------
sampler inputImage;
float2 sampleOffsets[8];
struct PS_INPUT
{
    float2 texCoord:TEXCOORD0;
};
float4 main( PS_INPUT In ) : COLOR
{
    int i =0;
    float4 c = .5;
    float2 texCoords[9];
    float4 texSamples[9];
    float4 total = 0;;
    float4 mean;
    float  variance;

    // get the coords ready for sampling 3x3 region
    for(i =0; i < 8; i++)
    {
        texCoords[i] = In.texCoord + sampleOffsets[i];
    }
    texCoords[8]  =  In.texCoord;

    // sample the 3x3 and add up the total
    for(i=0; i <9; i++)
    {
        texSamples[i] =  tex2D(inputImage, texCoords[i]);
        total += texSamples[i];
    }
    // compute the mean.
    mean = total / 9.0;
    total =0;
    // Compute the (squared) variance
    for(i=0; i < 9 ; i++)
    {
        total += (texSamples[i]-mean)*(texSamples[i]-mean);
    }

    // we don't need the root...so don't bother...
    // but we need to add the r, g, and bs together.
    variance = dot(total,1.0/9.0);
    c.xyz = mean;              // store mean into rgb.
    c.a   = variance;          // store variance into alpha.
    return c;
}
```

This finds the lowest variance for a 5×5 filter:

```
//--------------------------------------------------------------
// MeanVarianceSelectionGeneric.hlsl
```

```
//
// Select the color based on the lowest variance.
//
// Marwan Y. Ansari - ATI Research, Inc. - 2002
//------------------------------------------------------------
sampler inputImage;
float2 sampleOffsets[8];
struct PS_INPUT
{
    float2 texCoord:TEXCOORD0;
};
float4 main( PS_INPUT In ) : COLOR
{
    float2 sampleCoords[4];
    float4 s0, s1, s2, s3;
    float4 lowestVariance, lowestVariance2;
    float  s0a,s1a,s2a,s3a,1a,12a;

    sampleCoords[0] = In.texCoord + sampleOffsets[0];//up left
    sampleCoords[1] = In.texCoord + sampleOffsets[2];//up right
    sampleCoords[2] = In.texCoord + sampleOffsets[5];//dn left
    sampleCoords[3] = In.texCoord + sampleOffsets[7];//dn right

    s0 = tex2D(inputImage, sampleCoords[0]);
    s1 = tex2D(inputImage, sampleCoords[1]);
    s2 = tex2D(inputImage, sampleCoords[2]);
    s3 = tex2D(inputImage, sampleCoords[3]);

    s0a = s0.a;    s1a = s1.a;
    s2a = s2.a;    s3a = s3.a;

    // Compare first 2 samples
    if( s0a < s1a )
    {
        lowestVariance = s0;
        1a = s0a;
    }
    else
    {
        lowestVariance = s1;
        1a = s1a;
    }

    // Compare second 2 samples
    if( s2a < s3a )
    {
        lowestVariance2 = s2;
        12a = s2a;
    }
    else
    {
        lowestVariance2 = s3;
```

```
    l2a = s3a;
}

// Compare the winners of the 2 previous compares.
if( l2a < la )
{
    lowestVariance = lowestVariance2;
}

return lowestVariance;
}
```

Kuwahara (7×7 filter size)

Next we discuss the implementation of a 7×7 Kuwahara filter, which, due to its large area, must be performed in four passes. Recall that a Kuwahara filter breaks an area into four sub-regions, as shown previously. Hence, a 7×7 filter breaks into four 4×4 regions.

■   The algorithm for 7×7 Kuwahara

```
First Pass - input is input image.
    Compute the mean for the 4x4 around this texel.
    Store result to a mean map.
Second Pass - input is input image and mean map.
    Compute the partial variance of the 4x4 sub-region by computing
        the variance of the 3x3 area around the current texel.
    Store to partial variance map
Third Pass - input is input image, mean map, and partial variance map
    Compute the partial variance of the 4x4 sub-region by computing
        the partial variance for the remaining L-shaped region.
    Combine both partial variances into a final variance.
    Store into a final mean/variance map.
Fourth Pass - input is mean/variance map.
    Sample the four 4x4 sub-region centers.
    Select the mean/variance pair with the lowest variance.
```

The first pass of our four-pass 7×7 Kuwahara filter is solely dedicated to computing the mean for each texel in the image. Inside the shader, this is done in two steps. The first step computes the offsets for the 3×3 area around the current texel and fetches the texture samples for them. Next, those nine samples are summed. The offsets for the remaining L-shaped region (see Figure 15) are then computed, and those seven texels are also sampled and added to the total. Finally, we divide the sum by 16 and store it to the mean map.

The next two passes of this effect are dedicated to computing the variance. Due to the high number of instructions needed to compute the variance across a 4×4 region, we must compute the variances in two passes (passes two and three of this effect).

The second pass computes the partial variance of the 4×4 sub-region by computing the variance of the 3×3 region surrounding the current texel. This is performed in the same way that the 5×5 Kuwahara was performed. Figure 15 shows where the 3×3 region is located inside the 4×4 sub-region. The partial variance is stored to a partial variance map and is used in the next pass.

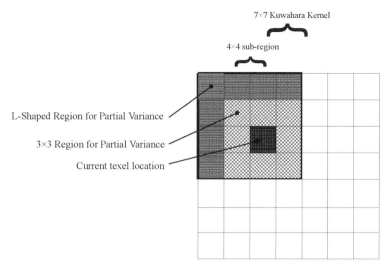

Figure 15: The variance for the 7×7 Kuwahara filter is implemented by calculating the variance of the 3×3 area and the L-shaped area in two separate passes. The 3×3 region's variance is computed first, and the L-shaped region is computed next. The "current texel location" is the location of the ouput texel for this 4×4 sub-region.

The third pass computes the partial variance for the remaining area of the 4×4 sub-region. The seven pixels that create the L-shaped region on one side of the 3×3 area surrounding the current texel (see Figure 16) are sampled. Their partial variance is then combined with the partial variance from the previous pass to compute the final variance for the 4×4 sub-region. As before, the mean is replicated across RGB and the variance is stored in alpha, creating a final mean/variance map for this 4×4 sub-region.

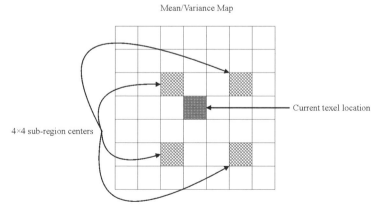

Figure 16: The mean, both partial variances, and the final mean/variance results are all stored in the same positions relative to the current texel location in each 4x4 sub-region.

The fourth and final pass of our 7×7 Kuwahara filter implementation happens exactly in the same way as the final pass of the 5×5 Kuwahara filter with the exception that the four texel samples are not direct diagonals of the current texel. Rather, they are located at:

$$u - (1/width), \quad v + (1/height) \qquad // \textit{up and to the left}$$
$$u + (2 * 1/width), \quad v + (1/height) \qquad // \textit{up and to the right}$$
$$u - (1/width), \quad v - (2 * 1/width) \qquad // \textit{down and to the left}$$
$$u + (2 * 1/width), \quad v - (2 * 1/width) \qquad // \textit{down and to the right}$$

The reason for this odd offsetting may not seem clear at first. Remember in the prior steps that the current texel has always been three rows over and three rows down from the top-left corner of the 4×4 sub-region. That texel holds the correct mean/variance for the 4×4 sub-region, and we must be careful to get our sample point from the correct location. Figure 16 shows the relative locations.

Now that the 7×7 Kuwahara has been applied, we can finalize the posterizing effect by adding one more pass to perform the Sobel outlines as discussed above. As you can see in Figure 17, we achieve a very nice posterizing effect on images using this method.

The benefit to using the 7×7 Kuwahara kernel over the 5×5 kernel is that you get better posterization with fewer passes. The 5×5 kernel required four passes of

Figure 17: A 7×7 Kuwahara filter plus outlines based on the Sobel edge detection filter has been applied to the image for real-time posterization. The 7×7 filter's advantage over the 5×5 filter is better posterization for about the same number of instructions. (See Color Plate 25.)

the entire filter (eight passes total) to achieve good results. The 7×7 kernel only requires two passes (eight passes total) to achieve a better result. They may require the same number of passes over the image, but the 7×7 requires fewer full kernel passes. By performing fewer kernel passes, the edge gradients are better maintained and you get nicer outlines while still posterizing based on larger sub-regions. So for the same number of passes and roughly the same amount of work, you can get better posterization using a larger kernel.

The following computes the mean of a 4×4 area for the 7×7 Kuwahara:

```
//-----------------------------------------------------------
// Mean4x4.hlsl
//
// Get the Mean of the 4x4 area around a pixel
//
// Marwan Y. Ansari - ATI Research, Inc. - 2002
```

```
//-------------------------------------------------------------
sampler inputImage;
float2 sampleOffsets[8];
struct PS_INPUT
{
    float2 texCoord:TEXCOORD0;
};
float4 main( PS_INPUT In ) : COLOR
{
    int i =0;
    float4 c = .5;
    float2 texCoords[9];
    float4 texSamples[9];
    float4 total = 0;;
    float4 mean;
    for(i =0; i < 8; i++)
    {
        texCoords[i] = In.texCoord + sampleOffsets[i];
    }
    texCoords[8]  = In.texCoord;

    for(i=0; i <9; i++)
    {
        texSamples[i] = tex2D(inputImage, texCoords[i]);
        total += texSamples[i];
    }


    // OK now get the mean for the remaining seven.
    //
    //          6 0 1 2
    //          4 * * *
    //          3 * X *      X= this texel
    //          5 * * *

    for(i =0; i < 3; i++)
    {   // creates top row
        texCoords[i] = texCoords[i] + sampleOffsets[1];
    }
    // creates side samples
    texCoords[3].x += sampleOffsets[3].x;
    texCoords[5].x += sampleOffsets[3].x;
    texCoords[4]    = texCoords[3] + sampleOffsets[0];
    texCoords[6]    = texCoords[4] + sampleOffsets[0];

    for(i=0; i <7; i++)
    {
        total += texSamples[i];
    }
    mean = total / 16.0;

    c.xyz = mean;
    c.a   = 0.0;
```

```
    return c;
}
```

A variance over a 3×3 area just for a 7×7 Kuwahara:

```
//----------------------------------------------------------
// Variance3x3.hlsl
//
// Get the partial variance of the 4x4 area by getting the 3x3
// area around this pixel.
//
// Marwan Y. Ansari - ATI Research, Inc. - 2002
//----------------------------------------------------------
sampler inputImage;
sampler meanMap;
float2 sampleOffsets[8];
struct PS_INPUT
{
    float2 texCoord:TEXCOORD0;
};
float4 main(PS_INPUT In) : COLOR
{
    int i =0;
    float4 c = .5;
    float2 texCoords[9];
    float4 texSamples[9];
    float4 total = 0;;
    float4 mean;
    float  variance;

    for(i =0; i < 8; i++)
    {
        texCoords[i] = In.texCoord + sampleOffsets[i];
    }
    texCoords[8]  = In.texCoord;

    for(i=0; i <9; i++)
    {
        texSamples[i] = tex2D(inputImage, texCoords[i]);
    }
    // Sample mean from the mean map
    mean = tex2D(meanMap,In.texCoord);
    total =0;
    for(i=0; i < 9 ; i++)
    {
        total += (texSamples[i]-mean)*(texSamples[i]-mean);
    }
    // Store the partial variance; we will pick this up in the next pass.
    c.xyz  = total;

    return c;
}
```

A variance over an L-shaped area for a 4×4 area for a 7×7 Kuwahara:

```
//-----------------------------------------------------------
// Variance_LShaped.hlsl
//
// Get the variance of the L-shaped region for a 4x4 area for a 7x7 Kuwahara.
//
// Marwan Y. Ansari - ATI Research, Inc. - 2002
//-----------------------------------------------------------
sampler inputImage;
sampler meanMap;
sampler variance3x3Map;
float2 sampleOffsets[8];
struct PS_INPUT
{
    float2 texCoord:TEXCOORD0;
};
float4 main(PS_INPUT In) : COLOR
{
    int i =0;
    float4 c = .5;
    float2 texCoords[7];
    float4 texSamples[7];
    float  variance, xOffset,yOffset;
    float4 total = 0;
    float4 v3x3, vLShaped, mean;

    xOffset = sampleOffsets[0].x *2;
    yOffset = sampleOffsets[0].y *2;

    // Compute sample offsets for the L-shape.
    //          0 1 2 3
    //          4 * * *
    //          5 * X *       X= this texel
    //          6 * * *

    texCoords[0].x = In.texCoord.x + xOffset;
    texCoords[0].y = In.texCoord.y + yOffset; // 0

    texCoords[1].x = In.texCoord.x + sampleOffsets[0].x;
    texCoords[1].y = In.texCoord.y + yOffset; // 1

    texCoords[2].x = In.texCoord.x ;
    texCoords[2].y = In.texCoord.y + yOffset; // 2

    texCoords[3].x = In.texCoord.x - sampleOffsets[0].x;;
    texCoords[3].y = In.texCoord.y + yOffset; // 3

    texCoords[4].x = In.texCoord.x + xOffset;
    texCoords[4].y = In.texCoord.y + sampleOffsets[0].y; // 4

    texCoords[5].x = In.texCoord.x + xOffset;
```

```
    texCoords[5].y = In.texCoord.y ; // 5

    texCoords[6].x = In.texCoord.x + xOffset;
    texCoords[6].y = In.texCoord.y - sampleOffsets[0].y; // 6

    // Sample the L-shape.
    for(i=0; i <7; i++)
    {
        texSamples[i] =  tex2D(inputImage, texCoords[i]);
    }
    // Sample mean map.
    mean = tex2D(meanMap,In.texCoord);
    total =0;

    //  Compute the the partial variance for the L-shape.
    for(i=0; i < 7 ; i++)
    {
        total += (texSamples[i]-mean)*(texSamples[i]-mean);
    }

    // Sample the partial result from a prior pass.
    v3x3 = tex2D(variance3x3Map, In.texCoord);

    total += v3x3;        // Sum the two partials and finalize variance.
    variance = dot(total, 1.0/16.0);

    c.xyz   = mean;       // store mean as rgb.
    c.a     = variance;   // store variance as alpha.

    return c;
}
```

A variance selection for a 7×7 area:

```
//----------------------------------------------------------
// MeanVarianceSelection7x7.hlsl
//
// Select the color based on the lowest variance.
//
// Marwan Y. Ansari - ATI Research, Inc. - 2002
//----------------------------------------------------------
sampler inputImage;
float2 sampleOffsets[8];
struct PS_INPUT
{
    float2 texCoord:TEXCOORD0;
};
float4 main(PS_INPUT In):COLOR
{
    int i =0;
    float2 sampleCoords[4];
    float4 s0, s1, s2, s3;
    float4 lowestVariance, lowestVariance2;
```

```
float s0a,s1a,s2a,s3a,la, l2a;

sampleCoords[0] = In.texCoord + sampleOffsets[0]; //up left

sampleCoords[1] = In.texCoord + sampleOffsets[2] + sampleOffsets[1]; //up right

sampleCoords[2] = In.texCoord + sampleOffsets[5] + sampleOffsets[6]; //dn left

sampleCoords[3] = In.texCoord + sampleOffsets[7] + sampleOffsets[7]; //dn right

s0 = tex2D(inputImage, sampleCoords[0]);
s1 = tex2D(inputImage, sampleCoords[1]);
s2 = tex2D(inputImage, sampleCoords[2]);
s3 = tex2D(inputImage, sampleCoords[3]);

s0a = s0.a;     s1a = s1.a;
s2a = s2.a;     s3a = s3.a;

// Compare first two samples
if( s0a < s1a )
{
    lowestVariance = s0;
    la = s0a;
}
else
{
    lowestVariance = s1;
    la = s1a;
}


// Compare second two samples
if( s2a < s3a )
{
    lowestVariance2 = s2;
    l2a = s2a;
}
else
{
    lowestVariance2 = s3;
    l2a = s3a;
}

// Compare the winners of the two previous compares.
if( l2a < la )
{
    lowestVariance = lowestVariance2;
}

return lowestVariance;
}
```

Using Sobel edge detection to create outlines:

```
//----------------------------------------------------------
// SobelOutlines.hlsl
//
// Compute edges using Sobel operators, and then recomposite the
// edges onto the image as outlines.
//
// Marwan Y. Ansari - ATI Research, Inc. - 2002
//----------------------------------------------------------
sampler inputImage;
float2 sampleOffsets[8];
float4 UserInput;
struct PS_INPUT
{
    float2 texCoord:TEXCOORD0;
};
float4 main(PS_INPUT In) : COLOR
{
    int i =0;
    float4 c = .5;
    float2 texCoords;
    float4 texSamples[8];
    float4 vertGradient;
    float4 horzGradient;

    for(i =0; i < 8; i++)
    {
        // add sample offsets
        texCoords = In.texCoord + sampleOffsets[i];
        // take sample
        texSamples[i] =  tex2D(inputImage, texCoords);
        //  convert to b&w
        texSamples[i] = dot(texSamples[i], .333333f);
    }
    // Vertical gradient
    vertGradient = -(texSamples[0] + texSamples[5] + 2*texSamples[3]);
    vertGradient += (texSamples[2] + texSamples[7] + 2*texSamples[4]);

    // Horizontal gradient
    horzGradient = -(texSamples[0] + texSamples[2] + 2*texSamples[1]);
    horzGradient += (texSamples[5] + texSamples[7] + 2*texSamples[6]);

    // we could approximate by adding the abs value...
    // but we have the horsepower
    c = 1- sqrt(horzGradient*horzGradient + vertGradient*vertGradient) ;

    // Threshold the edge value to keep only good edges.
    if(c.x < UserInput.z)
    {
        c = 0;
    }
```

```
// combine Sobel edge with current image.
c *= tex2D(inputImage, In.texCoord);
return c;
}
```

Combining Effects Using the VideoShader Application

The techniques presented in this chapter were developed using live and recorded video fed to Direct3D via the Microsoft Video Mixing Renderer (VMR). The sample app, VideoShader, demonstrates the use of Direct3D and the VMR, with the above filters and several others implemented using HLSL. Source for the sample application and all of the shaders is available on the companion CD as well as the ATI Developer Relations web site (www.ati.com/developer).

The effects that we have discussed in this chapter are excellent stand-alone effects. However, you may want to concatenate the effects to get a greater distortion or transition between distorted and undistorted images, etc.

The VideoShader application has a set of combined shader effects mapped to the F keys and the number keys. Adding effects is done when the application is running in windowed mode. By right-clicking on the left window pane, a menu appears with a list of shaders that you may insert. You can choose to insert your chosen effect before or after the shader that you right-clicked on.

Conclusion

This article discussed three classes of image effects that are possible with modern hardware: transitions, distortions, and posterizations. All can run in real time on today's DirectX 9 hardware and are relatively easy to implement. Since all of them run in image space, no extra geometry is needed to get some really cool results. We hope that this article has persuaded you to try out some of these effects in your own work.

Acknowledgments

Thanks to Jason Mitchell and Evan Hart for their help in writing this chapter. Thanks also to Chris Brennan, David Gosselin, and Chris Oat (all from ATI Research) who helped in various stages of getting the effects implemented for the VideoShader application.

Special thanks to Jason Mitchell for giving me the idea to implement the Kuwahara filter and to Larry Seiler of ATI Research for his ideas on optimizing the 5×5 Kuwahara filter.

Finally, many thanks to Muhammad Haggag at Ain Shams University, Egypt, for his help in proofreading this chapter.

References

ATI Developer web site, http://www.ati.com/devrel

Pixélan Software, LLC, http://www.pixelan.com

[Gonzalez92] Gonzalez, Rafael C. and Richard E. Woods, *Digital Image Processing*, Addison-Wesley, 1992.

[Jain95] Jain, Ramesh and Rngachar Kasturi, et al., *Machine Vision*, McGraw Hill, 1995.

[Mitchell02] Mitchell, Jason L., "Image Processing with 1.4 Pixel Shaders in Direct3D," *Direct3D ShaderX: Vertex and Pixel Shader Tips and Tricks*, Wolfgang Engel, ed., Wordware Publishing, 2002, pp. 258-269.

[Mitchell04] Mitchell, Jason L. and Craig Peeper, "Introduction to the DirectX High Level Shading Language," *Shader X²: Introduction & Tutorials with DirectX 9*, Wolfgang Engel, ed., Wordware Publishing, 2004, pp. 1-61.

[Möller99] Möller, Tomas and Eric Haines, *Real-Time Rendering*, A.K. Peters, Ltd., 1999.

[Weisstein] Weisstein, Eric, "Eric Weisstein's World of Mathematics," http://mathworld.wolfram.com/Variance.html.

[Young] Young, I.T., J.J. Gerbrands, and L.J. van Vliet, "Image Processing Fundamentals — Smoothing Operations," http://www.ph.tn.tudelft.nl/Courses/FIP/noframes/fip-Smoothin.html.

Using Pixel Shaders to Implement a Mosaic Effect Using Character Glyphs

Roger Descheneaux and Maurice Ribble
ATI Research

Introduction

A *mosaic* is a picture made by setting small pieces of glass or colored tiles onto a surface. Individually, the small pieces look nothing like the picture, but when assembled into an image and viewed from a distance, they form a cohesive whole that accurately represents the intent of the image.

The technique described here uses a post-processing pixel shader that takes a screen image and converts it into a mosaic. Rather than using glass or tiles to form the mosaic, we use window-aligned rectangles containing images of various intensities. While this technique is appropriate for use with any images, in our example we use character glyphs to represent the screen image as a sequence of letters and numbers. The difference in brightness between the various glyphs can be viewed as forming a monochromatic image. Here is an example of an image processed using this technique:

 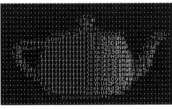

The teapot on the left is the original image, while the teapot on the right is the result of post-processing this image and converting it into character glyphs. This technique occurs entirely in hardware. It can be performed in a single-pass pixel shader, though in the following example we use several passes for the sake of simplicity.

Algorithm Overview

The original image is divided into a series of image-aligned blocks. Each block is the size of one glyph in the character set to be rendered. We compute the intensity of the color in this block by downsampling the image using a linear texture filter to compute the pixel averages. We then rescale the image to its original size, replacing the original pixel color with the average color for each pixel block.

We then use a pixel shader to replace each pixel in the original image with one pixel from the character set to be rendered. The pixel chosen is based on the intensity of the block in the downsampled image to which the pixel belongs and the offset of the pixel within the pixel block.

Sample Program

```
// Step 1: Draw the image to the back buffer.
glViewport (0, 0, width, height);
glDisable(GL_FRAGMENT_PROGRAM_ARB);
glDisable(GL_TEXTURE_2D);


glClear(GL_COLOR_BUFFER_BIT | GL_DEPTH_BUFFER_BIT);


glMatrixMode(GL_MODELVIEW);
glLoadIdentity();
glRotatef(angle, 1.0, 1.0, 1.0);

// Draw the base image first. We'll convert it later as a
// postprocessing step.
glEnable(GL_LIGHTING);
glEnable(GL_DEPTH_TEST);
glColor3f(1.0, 1.0, 0.0);
glutSolidTeapot(0.5);
glDisable(GL_LIGHTING);
glDisable(GL_DEPTH_TEST);
glFlush();

// Step 2: Downsample the image.
glActiveTextureARB(GL_TEXTURE0_ARB);
glEnable(GL_TEXTURE_2D);
glTexParameteri(GL_TEXTURE_2D, GL_TEXTURE_MAG_FILTER, GL_LINEAR);
glTexParameteri(GL_TEXTURE_2D, GL_TEXTURE_MIN_FILTER, GL_LINEAR);
glLoadIdentity();

// Step 2a: Copy the screen to a texture.
glCopyTexSubImage2D(GL_TEXTURE_2D, 0, 0, 0, 0, 0, texImageWidth, texImageHeight);

// Step 2b: Draw the image back to the screen at half its previous resolution.
glViewport (0, 0, texImageWidth / 2, texImageHeight / 2);
glBegin(GL_QUADS);
glTexCoord2f(0.0, 0.0);
```

```
glVertex2f(-1.0, -1.0);
glTexCoord2f(1.0, 0.0);
glVertex2f(1.0, -1.0);
glTexCoord2f(1.0, 1.0);
glVertex2f(1.0, 1.0);
glTexCoord2f(0.0, 1.0);
glVertex2f(-1.0, 1.0);
glEnd();

// Step 3.  Repeat the process to get it to 1/4 its original size.
glCopyTexSubImage2D(GL_TEXTURE_2D, 0, 0, 0, 0, 0, texImageWidth / 2, texImageHeight / 2);
glViewport (0, 0, texImageWidth / 4, texImageHeight / 4);
glBegin(GL_QUADS);
glTexCoord2f(0.0, 0.0);
glVertex2f(-1.0, -1.0);
glTexCoord2f(0.5, 0.0);
glVertex2f(1.0, -1.0);
glTexCoord2f(0.5, 0.5);
glVertex2f(1.0, 1.0);
glTexCoord2f(0.0, 0.5);
glVertex2f(-1.0, 1.0);
glEnd();

// Step 4:  Now 1/8th.
glCopyTexSubImage2D(GL_TEXTURE_2D, 0, 0, 0, 0, 0, texImageWidth / 4, texImageHeight / 4);
glViewport (0, 0, texImageWidth / 8, texImageHeight / 8);
glBegin(GL_QUADS);
glTexCoord2f(0.0, 0.0);
glVertex2f(-1.0, -1.0);
glTexCoord2f(0.25, 0.0);
glVertex2f(1.0, -1.0);
glTexCoord2f(0.25, 0.25);
glVertex2f(1.0, 1.0);
glTexCoord2f(0.0, 0.25);
glVertex2f(-1.0, 1.0);
glEnd();

// Now perform one more pass to scale the image.  We have to change
// the aspect ratio of the downsampled image to match the aspect
// ratio of the font, so each block of the character in the font
// matches the same color in the downsampled image.  The font is
// 8x10 pixels.  This means that we have to scale the Y direction
// of the rendering somewhat so that ten pixels in height correspond
// to one pixel in this final texture image.
glCopyTexSubImage2D(GL_TEXTURE_2D, 0, 0, 0, 0, 0, texImageWidth / 8, texImageHeight / 8);
glViewport (0, 0, texImageWidth / 8, texImageHeight / 8 / 1.25);
glBegin(GL_QUADS);
glTexCoord2f(0.0, 0.0);
glVertex2f(-1.0, -1.0);
glTexCoord2f(0.125, 0.0);
glVertex2f(1.0, -1.0);
glTexCoord2f(0.125, 0.125);
```

```
glVertex2f(1.0, 1.0);
glTexCoord2f(0.0, 0.125);
glVertex2f(-1.0, 1.0);
glEnd();

glTexParameteri(GL_TEXTURE_2D, GL_TEXTURE_MAG_FILTER, GL_NEAREST);
glTexParameteri(GL_TEXTURE_2D, GL_TEXTURE_MIN_FILTER, GL_NEAREST);
glCopyTexSubImage2D(GL_TEXTURE_2D, 0, 0, 0, 0, 0, texImageWidth / 8, texImageHeight / 8);
glViewport (0, 0, texImageWidth, texImageHeight);
glBegin(GL_QUADS);
glTexCoord2f(0.0, 0.0);
glVertex2f(-1.0, -1.0);
glTexCoord2f(0.125, 0.0);
glVertex2f(1.0, -1.0);
glTexCoord2f(0.125, 0.125 / 1.25);
glVertex2f(1.0, 1.0);
glTexCoord2f(0.0, 0.125 / 1.25);
glVertex2f(-1.0, 1.0);
glEnd();

// Copy the final downsampled image into our texture.
glCopyTexSubImage2D(GL_TEXTURE_2D, 0, 0, 0, 0, 0, texImageWidth, texImageHeight);

// These scaling factors are used to match texels in the
// downsampled image with pixels in the original screen image.
scaleW = 1.0 * width / texImageWidth;
scaleH = 1.0 * height / texImageHeight;

// Now activate the fragment program and re-render the scene using
// the original image as a texture source.
glTexParameteri(GL_TEXTURE_2D, GL_TEXTURE_MAG_FILTER, GL_NEAREST);
glTexParameteri(GL_TEXTURE_2D, GL_TEXTURE_MIN_FILTER, GL_NEAREST);

glEnable(GL_FRAGMENT_PROGRAM_ARB);
glViewport (0, 0, width, height);
glBegin(GL_QUADS);
glTexCoord2f(0.0, 0.0);
glMultiTexCoord2fARB(GL_TEXTURE1_ARB, 0.0, 0.0);
glVertex2f(-1.0, -1.0);
glTexCoord2f(scaleW, 0.0);
glMultiTexCoord2fARB(GL_TEXTURE1_ARB, 1.0 * width / 8.0, 0.0);
glVertex2f(1.0, -1.0);
glTexCoord2f(scaleW, scaleH);
glMultiTexCoord2fARB(GL_TEXTURE1_ARB, 1.0 * width / 8.0, 1.0 * height / 10.0);
glVertex2f(1.0, 1.0);
glTexCoord2f(0.0, scaleH);
glMultiTexCoord2fARB(GL_TEXTURE1_ARB, 0.0, 1.0 * height / 10.0);
glVertex2f(-1.0, 1.0);
glEnd();

// Display the final image.
glDisable(GL_FRAGMENT_PROGRAM_ARB);
```

```
glutSwapBuffers();

}
```

Explanation of the Sample Program

The first step of the process is to determine the average intensity of each character cell in the image. To do this, we downsample the image a number of times, which depends on the size of the font being used. In this example, we're using a font that is eight pixels wide by ten pixels high, so we downsample the image four times using a linear texture filter. This creates a texture in which each texel represents an 8x10 section of the original image containing the average intensity for that 8x10 section of the image. We then upsample the image using this average image as the source, creating a final texture that has a size equal to the original processed image but contains values in each 8x10 region that correspond to the average value of that 8x10 region on the original image.

Finally, we use that block image as the source texture of a final copy with the pixel shader enabled, which will replace each pixel with the corresponding pixel in an appropriate character.

When we render the font, we pass in two sets of texture coordinates. The first set of texture coordinates ranges from 0.0 to 1.0, encompassing the entire image. The second set of texture coordinates ranges from the width of the image/8, the font width, and the height of the image/10, the font height. Later we take the fractional part of this index, which will repeat every eight pixels in the x direction and every ten pixels in the y direction.

The code containing the font itself is not included here in the interest of saving space, but it consists of a single texture, which is 512 pixels wide and 16 pixels high. The image in the texture is a series of 8x10 characters arranged horizontally from left to right with the darkest characters in the leftmost part of the image and the brightest characters in the rightmost part of the image.

Sample Pixel Shader

```
!!ARBfp1.0
# Constants used by the program.
# This first constant is the scale factor to convert an RGB
# value to a black-and-white value.
PARAM  grayScale = {0.30, 0.59, 0.11, 1.0};
# This constant converts S, T coordinates in character space
# to coordinates in font string space. See below for details.
# The values here are 1/number_of_characters in the font
# and the ratio of the character height to the font height-
# in this case, 1/64 and 10/16.
PARAM charScale = {0.015625, 0.625, 0.0, 0.0};
# This constant is the number of characters in the glyph
# array. It is used in the operation that computes the
# beginning of a glyph in the s-direction.
```

```
PARAM numChars - {64.0, 0.0, 0.0, 0.0};
# This is the inverse of the constant above. It's used to
# convert the beginning of the character back into the
# glyph array space.
PARAM recipChars = program.local[2];
TEMP blockOffset;
TEMP sColor;
TEMP charOffset;
TEMP charCoords;
# Interpolants.
ATTRIB tc  = fragment.texcoord[0];
ATTRIB cc = fragment.texcoord[1];
OUTPUT oColor = result.color;
# Look up the pixel color for this character block.
TEX sColor, tc, texture[0], 2D;
# Compute its intensity
DP3 blockOffset, sColor, grayScale;
# Round it to the s-coordinate of the beginning of the
# nearest character to the computed intensity value.
MUL blockOffset, blockOffset, numChars;
FLR blockOffset, blockOffset;
MUL blockOffset, blockOffset, recipChars;
# Using the second set of texture coordinates, find the
# offset of this pixel within the character block. After
# this operation, both X and Y will be in the range 0-1,
# where 0 is the bottom left-most part of a character
# and 1 is the upper right-most part.
FRC charOffset, cc;
# Multiply this number in the 0-1 range by the fraction
# that represents a single pixel within the glyph array.
# In the x direction, this is 1/the number of characters in
# the font. In the y direction, it's the ratio of the font
# height to the height of the texture it's in.
# Add the result to the start of the glyph in the glyph
# array. The result is the coordinate of the texel with
# which this pixel should be replaced.
MAD charCoords, charOffset, charScale, blockOffset;
TEX oColor, charCoords, texture[1], 2D;
END;
```

The pixel shader has two parts. First, it determines the s-coordinate offset into the texture, which is the list of characters sorted from darkest to lightest. It does this by multiplying the intensity of the pixel by the number of characters in the font, taking the floor of that value and then dividing by the number of characters in the font, quantizing it so that the intensity value now falls on a coordinate that is the leftmost part of a character within the font texture.

The second part of the pixel shader adds the coordinates of the glyph within the glyph array to the start of the glyph array. It then performs a lookup into the glyph array and replaces the pixel on the screen with a texel from the glyph array.

Conclusion

The effect described above can be used to replace any block of an image with a rectangular glyph based on the intensity of that area of the image. Various improvements to the algorithm are possible. For example, the entire operation could be performed in a single pass by adding instructions to the pixel shader that compute the intensity value, rather than using the texture unit to downsample the image.

The effect above is also not limited to text glyphs. It can be used to render any image using a series of other images. For example, it could be used to draw a picture of a person with a mosaic of scenes from that person's life.

Neither is the effect limited to grayscale images. While grayscale is suitable for the rendering of character glyphs, lookups based on color are also possible — for example, using 3D textures, it would be possible to sort the image by the intensities of the different color components.

Acknowledgments

Thanks are due to Marwan Ansari for giving us the original idea for performing image processing using pixel shaders and for encouraging us to publish this work.

Mandelbrot Set Rendering

Emil Persson

http://esprit.campus.luth.se/~humus

Introduction

With the arrival of DirectX 9 level hardware, a whole new world of possibilities has opened up in graphics. One such possibility that the new floating-point pixel shaders have opened is the ability to evaluate advanced mathematical operations without significant precision loss or with limited range. The kind of applications that one tends to think of first where the capabilities of DirectX 9 shaders can be beneficial is often various lighting scenarios, atmospheric effects, animation, etc. These are all very interesting topics to dive deep into, but there's another dimension that these shaders open up that may not have crossed our minds the first time we learned about the new shaders. For the first time, we can utilize pixel shaders to visualize the wonderful world of fractals.

The Mandelbrot Fractal

Probably the most famous and well-known fractal is the Mandelbrot set. The Mandelbrot set basically consists of the complex number that after an infinite number of iterations of a simple formula is still within close range of the origin. While the higher math behind all this and all its implications is something that interests only a select few, the graphical art that you can produce with such a series is something that can amaze just about everyone.

How does one visualize the Mandelbrot set? Easy — you simply take a complex number, evaluate a function on this number, and get a new number. Then repeat this a sufficient number of times. The classical iteration looks like this:

$$Z_{i+1} = Z_i^2 + C$$

Here C is the original number and Z_i is the number that we are working with. We begin by setting Z_0 to C. Expanding this formula into real and imaginary parts of the complex number, we get these two formulas:

$$X_{i+1} = X_i^2 - Y_i^2 + C_x$$
$$Y_{i+1} = 2X_iY_i + C_y$$

The X is the real part, and Y is the imaginary part. Now we only need to do this math in a pixel shader. The first thing that we need to do is pass the constant C to the pixel shader. Where do we get C from, and what is it really? As we want to visualize the Mandelbrot set, we want to view every point in the XY plane that belongs to the Mandelbrot set, as these are clearly different from the pixel that doesn't belong to the set. This means that we are interested in those points in the XY plane that, after an infinite amount of iterations of the formulas above, is still close to the origin. So what we pass as C is basically the position of a point in the XY plane. We will define a subset of the plane (for instance, the rectangle (–2, –2) – (2, 2)) and draw this range as a quad covering the whole viewport. C is basically the position, and thus we will pass it as a texture coordinate, which will be interpolated over the surface. The Mandelbrot set definition declares that we need to loop the equations above an infinite number of times in order to decide whether a point is within the set or not. Obviously, this is impossible to do, so usually one just loops it a sufficient number of times and then decides if we are still close to the origin. If we are, then we assume that we are part of the Mandelbrot set, a fairly reasonable assumption.

An iteration of the formulas above can be done in three instructions. C is passed in texture coordinates t0, r0 contains our Z in its x and y components, and r2 is a temporary register. The implementation will look like this:

```
mad    r2.xy, r0.x, r0,   t0
mad    r1.x, -r0.y, r0.y, r2.x
mad    r1.y, r0.x, r0.y, r2.y
```

As you can see, the result ends up in another register, r1. This is because both the x and y components of the previous value are needed in the evaluation of the new value, so we can't overwrite any of them. So we write the results to r1 instead. In the next iteration, we can do the same thing again but with r0 and r1 reversed such that the next result ends up in r0 again. Then we only need to take these two iterations and cut and paste them until we reach the limit of the hardware. A Radeon 9700, for instance, accepts pixel shaders of at most 64 ALU instructions. This means that we can get, at most, 21 iterations, but probably fewer in reality because we probably prefer to do something cool with the end result before we write it to the frame buffer. In the code for this article, we end up with 19 iterations.

Visualizing It

We've done our 19 iterations — now what? Well, we need to transform it into something meaningful for the eye. There are billions of ways to do this, and which one we choose is arbitrary and can be based on our subjective preference. For all this to be meaningful though, we need to make the pixels that end up in the Mandelbrot set visually different from those that didn't. Traditionally, when one renders Mandelbrot sets on the CPU, people have used whatever number of loops it took until we ended up at a distance larger than two from the origin. This is then used to look up a color from a palette. Unfortunately, this kind of information is not available to us. As of publication, there's no support for data-based branching in the pixel shaders in any hardware available on the market, so we can't count loops. All the information that we have is the final position after all our iterations. This is sufficient, however, and we map this distance to a color. A large distance means that it's not in the Mandelbrot set, while a small distance means that it most likely is. To get some nice coloration, we use the distance as a texture coordinate and look up the color from a texture with a dependent texture read. This texture is one-dimensional and contains a color spectrum not too different looking from a rainbow, except that it softly fades to black to the right. The distance can be anywhere from zero to very high, so instead of just mapping it directly, we use a similar formula as when one maps high dynamic range images into the 0...1 interval with exposure control. We use the following formula:

$$R = 1 - 2^{-cd}$$

R is our resulting color, and d is our distance. Instead of bothering with taking the square root in order to find the distance, we just use the squared distance; mind you, this final step is no exact science — it is better classified as art. The constant c is just an arbitrary constant that says how far from the origin a point can be without mapping to our black edge of the texture. We select it purely on subjective grounds; I have found that something around 8 will suit us well. The final implementation is pretty straightforward:

```
def      c0, 0.0, 1.0, 8.0, 0.0
...

mov      r1.z, c0.x
dp3_sat r0, r1, r1
mul      r0.x, r0.x, c0.z

exp      r0.x, -r0.x
sub      r0, c0.y, r0.x

texld    r0, r0, s0

mov      oC0, r0
```

First we fill r1.z with a zero so we can use the dot product instruction without reading uninitialized components. You may wonder why we use a dp3_sat; shouldn't we use dp3? Well, we should. Unfortunately, in practice some implementations seem to have problems raising numbers to high negative numbers; this can create some noisy artifacts. However, as 2^{-8} is already a very small number, there is no visual difference if we clamp it. We should now have a nice colored Mandelbrot before our eyes.

Real-Time Depth of Field Simulation

Guennadi Riguer, Natalya Tatarchuk, and John Isidoro

ATI Technologies   ATI Research   Boston University

Introduction

Photorealistic rendering attempts to generate computer images with quality approaching that of real-life images. Quite often, computer-rendered images look almost photorealistic, but they are missing something subtle — something that makes them look synthetic or too perfect. Depth of field is one of those very important visual components of real photography that makes images look "real." In "real-world" photography or cinematography, the physical properties of the camera cause some parts of the scene to be blurred, while maintaining sharpness in other areas. While blurriness sometimes can be thought of as an imperfection and undesirable artifact that distorts original images and hides some of the scene details, it can also be used as a tool to provide valuable visual clues and guide a viewer's attention to important parts of the scene. Using depth of field effectively can improve photorealism and add an artistic touch to rendered images. Figure 1 shows a simple scene rendered with and without depth of field.

With depth of field   No depth of field

Figure 1: A scene rendered with and without depth of field

Recent developments in the field of programmable graphics hardware allow us to simulate complex visual effects such as depth of field in real time. This article presents two real-time implementations of the depth of field effect using DirectX 9 class hardware. The High Level Shading Language (HLSL) from Microsoft is used to simplify shader development.

529

Camera Models and Depth of Field

Computer images rendered with conventional methods look too sharp and lack the defects and artifacts of real cameras. Without these defects, it is hard to trick the eye into believing the images were captured by a real camera. Better camera models become even more important when computer-generated images have to be combined with ones produced by a real camera. The visual discrepancy mostly comes from the difference between physical cameras and the camera models normally used in computer graphics. Computer graphics generally implicitly use a pinhole camera model, while real cameras use lenses of finite dimensions.

Pinhole Camera Model

In the pinhole camera, light rays scattered from objects pass though an infinitely small pinhole lens. Only a single ray emanating from each point in the scene is allowed to pass though the pinhole. All rays going in other directions are ignored. Because only a single ray passes though the pinhole, only a single ray hits the imaging plane at any given point. This creates an image that is always in focus. Figure 2 illustrates the pinhole camera in action.

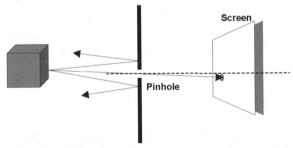

Figure 2: Pinhole camera

Thin Lens Camera Model

In the real world, all lenses have finite dimensions and let through rays coming from multiple different directions. As a result, parts of the scene are sharp only if they are located at or near a specific focal distance. For a lens with focal length f, a sharp image of a given object is produced at the imaging plane offset from the lens by v, when the object is at the distance u from the lens. This is described by a thin lens equation:

$$\frac{1}{u} + \frac{1}{v} = \frac{1}{f}$$

The distance from the image plane to the object in focus can be expressed as:

$$z_{\text{focus}} = u + v$$

Figure 3 demonstrates how the thin lens camera works.

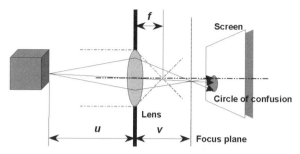

Figure 3: Thin lens camera

Multiple rays scattered from a given point on an object will pass through the lens, forming the cone of light. If the object is in focus, all rays will converge at a single point on the image plane. However, if a given point on an object in the scene is not near the focal distance, the cone of light rays will intersect the image plane in an area shaped like a conic section. Typically, the conic section is approximated by a circle called the *circle of confusion*.

The circle of confusion diameter b depends on the distance of the plane of focus and lens aperture setting a (also known as the *f*-stop). For a known focus distance and lens parameters, the size of the circle of confusion can be calculated as:

$$b = \left| \frac{D \cdot f \left(z_{focus} - z \right)}{z_{focus} \left(z - f \right)} \right|, \text{ where } D \text{ is a lens diameter}$$

$$D = \frac{f}{a}$$

Any circle of confusion greater than the smallest point a human eye can resolve contributes to the blurriness of the image that we see as depth of field.

Overview of Depth of Field Techniques

A number of techniques can be used to simulate depth of field in rendered scenes. One technique used in offline rendering employs distributed ray tracing. For each image point, multiple rays are shot through the lens. Coming from a single point of the image plane, these rays focus on the single point of the object if it is at the focal point. If the object is not in focus, the rays get scattered into the environment, which contributes to blurring. Because the rays accurately sample the surrounding environment, this method produces the most realistic depth of field effect, lacking many artifacts produced by other methods. The quality, however, comes at a cost, and this technique is unacceptable for real-time rendering.

Another method involves the accumulation buffer. The accumulation buffer integrates images from multiple render passes. Each of the images is rendered from a slightly different position and direction within the virtual lens aperture. While less complex than ray tracing, this method is also quite expensive because images have to be rendered many times to achieve good visual results.

A cheaper and more reasonable alternative for real-time implementation is the post-processing method. Usually, this method involves two-pass rendering. On the first pass, the scene is rendered with some additional information, such as depth. On the second pass, some filter is run on the result of the first pass to blur the image. This article presents two variations of this general post-processing approach. Each version has some strengths and weaknesses and can produce high-quality photorealistic depth of field effects on DirectX 9 graphics hardware.

Depth of Field Implementation via Simulation of Circle of Confusion

The first implementation that we present is an extension to the post-processing method proposed by Potmesil and Chakravarty in [Potmesil83]. On the first pass, we render the scene, outputting the color as well as the information necessary to blur the image. On the second pass, we filter the image from the first pass with a variable-sized filter kernel to simulate the circle of confusion. A blurriness factor computed on the first pass controls the size of the filter kernel used in the second pass. Special measures are taken to eliminate the leaking of color of objects in focus onto backgrounds that have been blurred.

Pass One: Scene Rendering

First, the whole scene is rendered by outputting depth and *blurriness factor*, which is used to describe how much each pixel should be blurred, in addition to the resulting scene rendering color. This can be accomplished by rendering the scene to multiple buffers at one time. DirectX 9 has a useful feature called Multiple Render Targets (MRT) that allows simultaneous shader output into the multiple renderable buffers. Using this feature gives us the ability to output all of the data channels (scene color, depth, and blurriness factor) in our first pass. One of the MRT restrictions on some hardware is the requirement for all render surfaces to have the same bit depth while allowing use of different surface formats. Guided by this requirement, we can pick the D3DFMT_A8R8G8B8 format for the scene color output and the two-channel texture format D3DFMT_G16R16 format for the depth and blurriness factor. As shown in Figure 4, both formats are 32 bits per pixel and provide us with enough space for the necessary information at the desired precision.

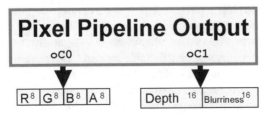

Figure 4: Pixel shader output for a scene rendering pass

Scene Rendering Vertex Shader

The vertex shader for the scene rendering pass is just a regular vertex shader with one little addition: It outputs scene depth in the camera space. This depth value is later used in the pixel shader to compute blurriness factor.

An example of a simple scene vertex shader is shown below:

```
///////////////////////////////////////////////////////////////

float3 lightPos;    // light position in model space
float4 mtrlAmbient;
float4 mtrlDiffuse;
matrix matWorldViewProj;
matrix matWorldView;

///////////////////////////////////////////////////////////////

struct VS_INPUT
{
    float4 vPos:      POSITION;
    float3 vNorm:     NORMAL;
    float2 vTexCoord: TEXCOORD0;
};

struct VS_OUTPUT
{
    float4 vPos:      POSITION;
    float4 vColor:    COLOR0;
    float  fDepth:    TEXCOORD0;
    float2 vTexCoord: TEXCOORD1;
};

///////////////////////////////////////////////////////////////

VS_OUTPUT scene_shader_vs(VS_INPUT v)
{
    VS_OUTPUT o = (VS_OUTPUT)0;
    float4 vPosWV;
    float3 vNorm;
    float3 vLightDir;

    // Transform position
    o.vPos = mul(v.vPos, matWorldViewProj);

    // Position in camera space
    vPosWV = mul(v.vPos, matWorldView);

    // Output depth in camera space
    o.fDepth = vPosWV.z;

    // Compute diffuse lighting
    vLightDir = normalize(lightPos - v.vPos);
```

```
vNorm    = normalize(v.vNorm);
o.vColor = dot(vNorm, vLightDir) * mtrlDiffuse + mtrlAmbient;

// Output texture coordinates
o.vTexCoord = v.vTexCoord;

return o;
}
```

Scene Rendering Pixel Shader

The pixel shader of the scene rendering pass needs to compute the blurriness factor and output it along with the scene depth and color. To abstract from the different display sizes and resolutions, the blurriness is defined to lie in the [0..1] range. A value of zero means the pixel is perfectly sharp, while a value of one corresponds to the pixel of the maximal circle of confusion size. The reason behind using the [0..1] range is twofold. First, the blurriness is not expressed in terms of pixels and can scale with resolution during the post-processing step. Second, the values can be directly used as sample weights when eliminating "bleeding" artifacts.

For each pixel of a scene, this shader computes the circle of confusion size based on the formula provided in the preceding discussion of the thin lens model. Later in the process, the size of the circle of confusion is scaled by the factor corresponding to the size of the circle in pixels for a given resolution and display size. As a last step, the blurriness value is divided by a maximal desired circle of confusion size in pixels (variable maxCoC) and clamped to the [0..1] range. Sometimes it might be necessary to limit the circle of confusion size (through the variable maxCoC) to reasonable values (i.e., ten pixels) to avoid sampling artifacts caused by an insufficient number of filter taps.

An example of a scene pixel shader that can be compiled to the ps 2.0 shader model is shown below:

```
/////////////////////////////////////////////////////////////////////

float focalLen;
float Dlens;
float Zfocus;
float maxCoC;
float scale;
sampler TexSampler;
float sceneRange;

/////////////////////////////////////////////////////////////////////

struct PS_INPUT
{
    float4 vColor:    COLOR0;
    float  fDepth:    TEXCOORD0;
    float2 vTexCoord: TEXCOORD1;
};
```

```
struct PS_OUTPUT
{
    float4 vColor: COLOR0;
    float4 vDoF:   COLOR1;
};

//////////////////////////////////////////////////////////////////

PS_OUTPUT scene_shader_ps(PS_INPUT v)
{
    PS_OUTPUT o = (PS_OUTPUT)0;

    // Output color
    o.vColor = v.vColor * tex2D(TexSampler, v.vTexCoord);

    // Compute blur factor based on the CoC size scaled and
    // normalized to the [0..1] range
    float pixCoC = abs(Dlens * focalLen * (Zfocus - v.fDepth) /
            (Zfocus * (v.fDepth - focalLen)));
    float blur = saturate(pixCoC * scale / maxCoC);

    // Depth/blurriness value scaled to the [0..1] range
    o.vDoF = float4(v.fDepth / sceneRange, blur, 0, 0);

    return o;
}
```

Pass Two: Post-processing

During the post-processing pass, the results of the previous rendering are processed, and the color image is blurred based on the blurriness factor computed in
the first pass. Blurring is performed using a variable-sized filter representing the
circle of confusion. To perform image filtering, a simple screen-aligned quadrilateral is drawn, textured with the results of the first pass. Figure 5 shows the
quad's texture coordinates and screen positions for a render target of W×H
dimensions. The quad corner positions are shifted by –0.5 pixels to properly align
texels to pixels.

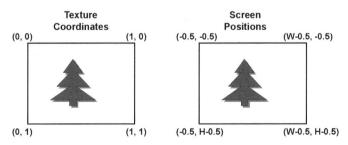

Figure 5: Texture coordinates and vertex positions for screen space quad

This vertex shader is designed for a vs 1.1 compilation target.

```
////////////////////////////////////////////////////////////////

float4 viewportScale;
float4 viewportBias;

////////////////////////////////////////////////////////////////

struct VS_INPUT
{
    float4 vPos:      POSITION;
    float2 vTexCoord: TEXCOORD;
};

struct VS_OUTPUT
{
    float4 vPos:      POSITION;
    float2 vTexCoord: TEXCOORD0;
};

////////////////////////////////////////////////////////////////

VS_OUTPUT dof_filter _vs(VS_INPUT v)
{
    VS_OUTPUT o = (VS_OUTPUT)0;

    // Scale and bias viewport
    o.vPos = v.vPos * viewportScale + viewportBias;

    // Pass through the texture coordinates
    o. vTexCoord = v.vTexCoord;

    return o;
}
```

Post-processing Pixel Shader

The filter kernel in the post-processing step has 13 samples — a center sample and 12 outer samples, as shown in Figure 6. The number of samples was dictated by practical reasons of real-time implementation and represents the maximum number of samples that can be processed by a 2.0 pixel shader in a single pass.

The center tap is aligned with the pixel being filtered, while the outer taps are sampled from nearby pixels. The filter uses stochastic sampling, and the outer samples are aligned in the filter according to a Poisson disk distribution. Other sample patterns can be used to achieve specific artistic results, as presented later in the "Bokeh" section.

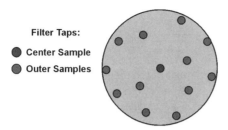

Filter Taps:

● Center Sample
● Outer Samples

Figure 6: Depth of field filter kernel

The filter size is computed per-pixel from the blurriness value of the center sample and the maximum allowable circle of confusion size. Figure 7 shows the relationship between blurriness and filter kernel size.

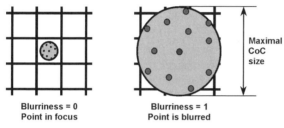

Blurriness = 0
Point in focus

Blurriness = 1
Point is blurred

Figure 7: Relationship between blurriness and filter size

The post-processing pixel shader computes filter sample positions based on 2D offsets stored in the filterTaps array and the size of the circle of confusion. The 2D offsets are locations of taps for the filter of one pixel in diameter. The following code shows how these values can be initialized in the program, according to the render target resolution.

```
void SetupFilterKernel()
{
    // Scale tap offsets based on render target size
    FLOAT dx = 0.5f / (FLOAT)dwRTWidth;
    FLOAT dy = 0.5f / (FLOAT)dwRTHeight;

    D3DXVECTOR4 v[12];
    v[0]  = D3DXVECTOR4(-0.326212f * dx, -0.40581f * dy, 0.0f, 0.0f);
    v[1]  = D3DXVECTOR4(-0.840144f * dx, -0.07358f * dy, 0.0f, 0.0f);
    v[2]  = D3DXVECTOR4(-0.695914f * dx, 0.457137f * dy, 0.0f, 0.0f);
    v[3]  = D3DXVECTOR4(-0.203345f * dx, 0.620716f * dy, 0.0f, 0.0f);
    v[4]  = D3DXVECTOR4(0.96234f * dx, -0.194983f * dy, 0.0f, 0.0f);
    v[5]  = D3DXVECTOR4(0.473434f * dx, -0.480026f * dy, 0.0f, 0.0f);
    v[6]  = D3DXVECTOR4(0.519456f * dx, 0.767022f * dy, 0.0f, 0.0f);
    v[7]  = D3DXVECTOR4(0.185461f * dx, -0.893124f * dy, 0.0f, 0.0f);
    v[8]  = D3DXVECTOR4(0.507431f * dx, 0.064425f * dy, 0.0f, 0.0f);
    v[9]  = D3DXVECTOR4(0.89642f * dx, 0.412458f * dy, 0.0f, 0.0f);
    v[10] = D3DXVECTOR4(-0.32194f * dx, -0.932615f * dy, 0.0f, 0.0f);
    v[11] = D3DXVECTOR4(-0.791559f * dx, -0.59771f * dy, 0.0f, 0.0f);
```

```
// Set array of offsets
pEffect->SetVectorArray("filterTaps", v, 12);
}
```

Once sample positions are computed, the filter averages color from its samples to derive the blurred color. When the blurriness value is close to zero, all samples come from the same pixel and no blurring happens. As the blurriness factor increases, the filter will start sampling from more and more neighboring pixels, thus increasingly blurring the image. All images are sampled with D3DTEXF_LINEAR filtering. Using linear filtering is not very accurate on the edges of objects where depth might abruptly change; however, it produces better overall quality images in practice.

One of the problems commonly associated with all post-filtering methods is leaking of color from sharp objects onto the blurry backgrounds. This results in faint halos around sharp objects, as can be seen on the left side of Figure 8. The color leaking happens because the filter for the blurry background will sample color from the sharp object in the vicinity due to the large filter size. To solve this problem, we will discard the outer samples that can contribute to leaking according to the following criteria: If the outer sample is in focus and it is in front of the blurry center sample, it should not contribute to the blurred color. This can introduce a minor popping effect when objects go in or out of focus. To combat sample popping, the outer sample blurriness factor is used as a sample weight to fade out its contribution gradually. The right side of Figure 8 shows a portion of a scene fragment with color leaking eliminated.

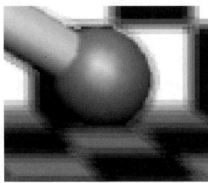 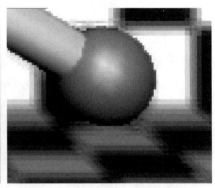

Leaking of sharp objects   *Sharp objects without color leaking*

Figure 8: Elimination of color leaking

Below, we show a depth of field pixel shader that implements the concepts discussed above. This shader can be compiled to the 2.0 pixel shader model.

```
//////////////////////////////////////////////////////////////////

#define NUM_DOF_TAPS 12

float maxCoC;
float2 filterTaps[NUM_DOF_TAPS];
```

//

```
struct PS_INPUT
{
    float2 vTexCoord: TEXCOORD;
};
```

//

```
float4 dof_filter_ps(PS_INPUT v) : COLOR
{
    // Start with center sample color
    float4 colorSum = tex2D(SceneColorSampler, v.vTexCoord);
    float totalContribution = 1.0f;
    // Depth and blurriness values for center sample
    float2 centerDepthBlur = tex2D(DepthBlurSampler, v.vTexCoord);

    // Compute CoC size based on blurriness
    float sizeCoC = centerDepthBlur.y * maxCoC;

    // Run through all filter taps
    for (int i = 0; i < NUM_DOF_TAPS; i++)
    {
        // Compute sample coordinates
        float2 tapCoord = v.vTexCoord + filterTaps[i] * sizeCoC;

        // Fetch filter tap sample
        float4 tapColor = tex2D(SceneColorSampler, tapCoord);
        float2 tapDepthBlur = tex2D(DepthBlurSampler, tapCoord);

        // Compute tap contribution based on depth and blurriness
        float tapContribution =
            (tapDepthBlur.x > centerDepthBlur.x) ?
            1.0f : tapDepthBlur.y;

        // Accumulate color and sample contribution
        colorSum += tapColor * tapContribution;
        totalContribution += tapContribution;
    }

    // Normalize color sum
    float4 finalColor = colorSum / totalContribution;
    return finalColor;
}
```

Now that we have discussed our implementation, which models the circle of confusion with a variable-sized stochastic filter kernel, we can describe an implementation that is based on a separable Gaussian filter.

Depth of Field Rendering by Blurring with Separable Gaussian Filter

This separable Gaussian filter approach differs from the previous approach of simulating depth of field in two ways. First, it does not utilize multiple render targets for outputting depth information. Second, to simulate the blurring that occurs in depth of field, we apply a Gaussian filter during the post-processing stage instead of simulating the circle of confusion of a physical camera lens.

Implementation Overview

In this method, we first render the scene at full resolution to an offscreen buffer, outputting depth information for each pixel to the alpha channel of that buffer. We then downsample this fully rendered scene into an image one-fourth the size (half in x and half in y) of the original. Next, we perform blurring of the downsampled scene in two passes by running the image through two passes of a separable Gaussian filter — first along the x axis and then along the y axis. On the final pass, we blend between the original full resolution rendering of our scene and the blurred post-processed image based on the distance of each pixel from the specified focal plane stored in the downsampled image. The intermediate filtering results are stored in 16-bit per-channel integer format (D3DFMT_A16B16G16R16) for extra precision. Let's discuss this method in more detail, going step by step through the different rendering passes and shaders used.

Pass One: Scene Rendering

During the scene rendering pass, we render the scene to the full resolution offscreen buffer, computing color information and a depth falloff value for each pixel. The depth falloff value will determine how much each pixel will be blurred during the subsequent post-processing stage. The distance from the focal plane is output to the alpha channel of the offscreen buffer.

Scene Rendering Vertex Shader

We compute the depth falloff value and the distance from the focal plane in the vertex shader. First, we determine the distance of each vertex from the focal plane in view space. We output scaled to the [0..1] range distance from the focal plane into the texture coordinate interpolator. This is illustrated in the following vertex shader, compiled to vertex shader target vs 1.1:

```
/////////////////////////////////////////////////////////////////

float3 lightPos;    // light position in model space
float4 mtrlAmbient;
float4 mtrlDiffuse;
matrix matWorldViewProj;
matrix matWorldView;
```

```
float fFocalDistance;
float fFocalRange;

//////////////////////////////////////////////////////////////////

struct VS_INPUT
{
    float4 vPos:      POSITION;
    float3 vNorm:     NORMAL;
    float2 vTexCoord: TEXCOORD0;
};

struct VS_OUTPUT
{
    float4 vPos:      POSITION;
    float4 vColor:    COLOR0;
    float  fBlur:     TEXCOORD0;
    float2 vTexCoord: TEXCOORD1;
};

//////////////////////////////////////////////////////////////////

VS_OUTPUT scene_shader_vs(VS_INPUT v)
{
    VS_OUTPUT o = (VS_OUTPUT)0;
    float4 vPosWV;
    float3 vNorm;
    float3 vLightDir;

    // Transform position
    o.vPos = mul(v.vPos, matWorldViewProj);

    // Position in camera space
    vPosWV = mul(v.vPos, matWorldView);

    // Normalized distance to focal plane in camera space,
    // used as a measure of blurriness for depth of field
    o.fBlur = saturate(abs(vPosWV.z - fFocalDistance) / fFocalRange);

    // Compute diffuse lighting
    vLightDir = normalize(lightPos - v.vPos);
    vNorm     = normalize(v.vNorm);
    o.vColor  = dot(vNorm, vLightDir) * mtrlDiffuse + mtrlAmbient;

    // Output texture coordinates
    o.vTexCoord = v.vTexCoord;

    return o;
}
```

Scene Rendering Pixel Shader

In the pixel shader, we render our scene as desired. The alpha channel receives the blurriness value expressed as the distance from the focal plane. This pixel shader is designed to be compiled into a ps 2.0 target.

```
///////////////////////////////////////////////////////////

sampler TexSampler;

///////////////////////////////////////////////////////////

struct PS_INPUT
{
    float4 vColor:    COLOR0;
    float  fBlur:     TEXCOORD0;
    float2 vTexCoord: TEXCOORD1;
};


///////////////////////////////////////////////////////////

float4 scene_shader_ps(PS_INPUT v) : COLOR
{
    float3 vColor;

    // Output color
    vColor = v.vColor * tex2D(TexSampler, v.vTexCoord);

    // Output blurriness in alpha
    return float4(vColor, v.fBlur);
}
```

Pass Two: Downsampling

To downsample the full resolution image, we simply render a quad one-fourth the size of the original image while sampling from the original image and outputting it to the smaller offscreen buffer. The alpha channel of the downsampled image receives a blurriness value computed as the scaled distance from the focus plane for each pixel. This information will be used during post-processing to control the amount of blurring applied to the downsampled image as well as to blend between a blurred image of the scene and the original rendering to simulate the effect of depth of field.

Downsampling Vertex Shader

In this simple vertex shader, we transform the vertices into clip space and propagate incoming texture coordinates to the pixel shader. Note that at this point, the incoming model must be a screen-aligned quad of dimensions one-fourth the size of the original image.

```
///////////////////////////////////////////////////////////////

matrix matWorldViewProj;

///////////////////////////////////////////////////////////////

struct VS_OUTPUT
{
    float4 vPos: POSITION;
    float2 vTex: TEXCOORD0;
};

///////////////////////////////////////////////////////////////

VS_OUTPUT main(float4 Pos: POSITION, float2 Tex: TEXCOORD0)
{
    VS_OUTPUT o = (VS_OUTPUT)0;

    // Output transformed vertex position:
    o.vPos = mul(matWorldViewProj, Pos);
    // Propagate texture coordinate to the pixel shader
    o.vTex = Tex;

    return o;
}
```

Downsampling Pixel Shader

In the pixel shader for the downsampling pass, we sample the original scene rendering using texture coordinates from the smaller screen-aligned quad and store the results in an offscreen render target. This pixel shader can be compiled to ps 1.4 or above.

```
///////////////////////////////////////////////////////////////

sampler renderTexture;

///////////////////////////////////////////////////////////////

float4 main(float2 Tex: TEXCOORD0) : COLOR
{
// Downsample rendered scene:
return tex2D(renderTexture, Tex);
}
```

Post-processing for Simulation of Depth of Field

One of the most frequently used filters for performing smoothing of an image is the Gaussian filter (see Figure 9). Typically, the filter is applied in the following way:

$$F = \frac{\sum_{i=1}^{n}\sum_{j=1}^{n} P_{ij}C_{ij}}{S}$$

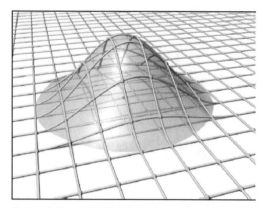

...where F is the filtered value of the target pixel, P is a pixel in the 2D grid, C is a coefficient in the 2D Gaussian matrix, n is the vertical/horizontal dimensions of the matrix, and S is the sum of all values in the Gaussian matrix.

Once a suitable kernel has been calculated, Gaussian smoothing can be performed

Figure 9: Gaussian filter kernel

using standard convolution methods. The convolution can in fact be performed fairly quickly since the equation for the 2D isotropic Gaussian is separable into x and y components. Thus, the 2D convolution can be performed by first convolving with a 1D Gaussian in the x direction and then convolving with another 1D Gaussian in the y direction. This allows us to apply a larger size filter to the input image in two successive passes of 1D filters. We perform this operation by rendering into a temporary buffer and sampling a line (or a column, for y axis filtering) of texels in each of the passes.

The size of the downsampled buffer determines the size of texels used for controlling sampling points for the Gaussian filter taps. This can be precomputed as a constant to the shader ahead of time. The following is an example of how the filter tap offset can be computed.

```
void SetupFilterKernel()
{
    // Scale tap offsets based on render target size
    FLOAT dx = 1.0f / (FLOAT)dwRTWidth;
    FLOAT dy = 1.0f / (FLOAT)dwRTHeight;

    D3DXVECTOR4 v[7];

    v[0]  = D3DXVECTOR4(0.0f, 0.0f, 0.0f, 0.0f);
    v[1]  = D3DXVECTOR4(1.3366f * dx, 0.0f, 0.0f, 0.0f);
    v[2]  = D3DXVECTOR4(3.4295f * dx, 0.0f, 0.0f, 0.0f);
    v[3]  = D3DXVECTOR4(5.4264f * dx, 0.0f, 0.0f, 0.0f);
    v[4]  = D3DXVECTOR4(7.4359f * dx, 0.0f, 0.0f, 0.0f);
    v[5]  = D3DXVECTOR4(9.4436f * dx, 0.0f, 0.0f, 0.0f);
    v[6]  = D3DXVECTOR4(11.4401f * dx, 0.0f, 0.0f, 0.0f);

    // Set array of horizontal offsets for X-pass
    m_pEffect->SetVectorArray("horzTapOffs", v, 7);

    v[0]  = D3DXVECTOR4(0.0f, 0.0f, 0.0f, 0.0f);
    v[1]  = D3DXVECTOR4(0.0f, 1.3366f * dy, 0.0f, 0.0f);
```

```
v[2] = D3DXVECTOR4(0.0f, 3.4295f * dy, 0.0f, 0.0f);
v[3] = D3DXVECTOR4(0.0f, 5.4264f * dy, 0.0f, 0.0f);
v[4] = D3DXVECTOR4(0.0f, 7.4359f * dy, 0.0f, 0.0f);
v[5] = D3DXVECTOR4(0.0f, 9.4436f * dy, 0.0f, 0.0f);
v[6] = D3DXVECTOR4(0.0f, 11.4401f * dy, 0.0f, 0.0f);

// Set array of vertical offsets for Y-pass
m_pEffect->SetVectorArray("vertTapOffs", v, 7);
}
```

Pass Three: Separable Gaussian Filtering in X Axis

First, we perform Gaussian filter blurring along the x axis of the downsampled image. For each pixel in the downsampled image, we sample n texture samples dynamically along the x axis in the following manner:

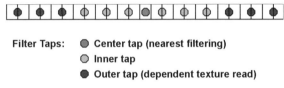

Filter Taps:	◐ Center tap (nearest filtering)
	○ Inner tap
	● Outer tap (dependent texture read)

Figure 10: Samples for applying 1D Gaussian filter

The center sample and the inner taps of the filter are done with interpolated texture coordinates, which are computed in the vertex shader. To compute the offsets for the first seven samples, we use input texture coordinates and the precomputed tap offsets based on the image resolution.

In the pixel shader, we sample the image for the center tap and the first six inner taps, using nearest filtering for the center sample and bilinear sampling for the inner samples.

The pixel shader code derives the texture coordinates for the outer samples based on precomputed deltas from the location of the center sample. The outer samples are fetched via dependent reads, as texture coordinates are derived in the pixel shader itself.

All samples are weighted based on the predefined weight thresholds and blurriness values and added together. This results in a weighted sum of 25 texels from the source image, which is large enough to allow us to create a convincing blurring effect for simulating depth of field without violating the maximum number of instructions for the 2.0 pixel shader.

Note that the output of this pass is directed to a separate offscreen buffer. At this point we have used three separate offscreen render targets: one to output results of the full scene rendering, one to output results of the downsampling pass, and one to output the results of Gaussian blurring.

Vertex Shader for X Axis of Separable Gaussian Filter

This vertex shader is designed for a vs 1.1 compilation target.

```
//////////////////////////////////////////////////////////////////

float4 viewportScale;
float4 viewportBias;
// Offsets 0-3 used by vertex shader, 4-6 by pixel shader
float2 horzTapOffs[7];

//////////////////////////////////////////////////////////////////

struct VS_INPUT
{
    float4 vPos:     POSITION;
    float2 vTexCoord: TEXCOORD;
};

struct VS_OUTPUT_TEX7
{
    float4 vPos:     POSITION;
    float2 vTap0:    TEXCOORD0;
    float2 vTap1:    TEXCOORD1;
    float2 vTap2:    TEXCOORD2;
    float2 vTap3:    TEXCOORD3;
    float2 vTap1Neg: TEXCOORD4;
    float2 vTap2Neg: TEXCOORD5;
    float2 vTap3Neg: TEXCOORD6;
};

//////////////////////////////////////////////////////////////////

VS_OUTPUT_TEX7 filter_gaussian_x_vs(VS_INPUT v)
{
    VS_OUTPUT_TEX7 o = (VS_OUTPUT_TEX7)0;

    // Scale and bias viewport
    o.vPos = v.vPos * viewportScale + viewportBias;

    // Compute tap coordinates
    o.vTap0 = v.vTexCoord;
    o.vTap1 = v.vTexCoord + horzTapOffs[1];
    o.vTap2 = v.vTexCoord + horzTapOffs[2];
    o.vTap3 = v.vTexCoord + horzTapOffs[3];
    o.vTap1Neg = v.vTexCoord - horzTapOffs[1];
    o.vTap2Neg = v.vTexCoord - horzTapOffs[2];
    o.vTap3Neg = v.vTexCoord - horzTapOffs[3];

    return o;
}
```

Pixel Shader for X Axis of Separable Gaussian Filter

This pixel shader is fine-tuned to compile for a ps 2.0 compilation target.

```
///////////////////////////////////////////////////////////////////

// Thresholds for computing sample weights
float4 vThresh0 = {0.1, 0.3, 0.5, -0.01};
float4 vThresh1 = {0.6, 0.7, 0.8, 0.9};

sampler renderTexture;
// Offsets 0-3 used by vertex shader, 4-6 by pixel shader
float2 horzTapOffs[7];

///////////////////////////////////////////////////////////////////

struct PS_INPUT_TEX7
{
    float2 vTap0:    TEXCOORD0;
    float2 vTap1:    TEXCOORD1;
    float2 vTap2:    TEXCOORD2;
    float2 vTap3:    TEXCOORD3;
    float2 vTap1Neg: TEXCOORD4;
    float2 vTap2Neg: TEXCOORD5;
    float2 vTap3Neg: TEXCOORD6;
};

///////////////////////////////////////////////////////////////////

float4 filter_gaussian_x_ps(PS_INPUT_TEX7 v) : COLOR
{
    // Samples
    float4 s0, s1, s2, s3, s4, s5, s6;
    float4 vWeights4;
    float3 vWeights3;
    // Acumulated color and weights
    float3 vColorSum;
    float  fWeightSum;

    // Sample taps with coordinates from VS
    s0 = tex2D(renderTexture, v.vTap0);
    s1 = tex2D(renderTexture, v.vTap1);
    s2 = tex2D(renderTexture, v.vTap2);
    s3 = tex2D(renderTexture, v.vTap3);
    s4 = tex2D(renderTexture, v.vTap1Neg);
    s5 = tex2D(renderTexture, v.vTap2Neg);
    s6 = tex2D(renderTexture, v.vTap3Neg);

    // Compute weights for first 4 samples (including center tap)
    // by thresholding blurriness (in sample alpha)
    vWeights4.x = saturate(s1.a - vThresh0.x);
    vWeights4.y = saturate(s2.a - vThresh0.y);
```

```
vWeights4.z = saturate(s3.a - vThresh0.x);
vWeights4.w = saturate(s0.a - vThresh0.w);

// Accumulate weighted samples
vColorSum = s0 * vWeights4.x + s1 * vWeights4.y +
    s2 * vWeights4.z + s3 * vWeights4.w;

// Sum weights using DOT
fWeightSum = dot(vWeights4, 1);

// Compute weights for three remaining samples
vWeights3.x = saturate(s4.a - vThresh0.x);
vWeights3.y = saturate(s5.a - vThresh0.y);
vWeights3.z = saturate(s6.a - vThresh0.z);

// Accumulate weighted samples
vColorSum += s4 * vWeights3.x + s4 * vWeights3.y +
    s6 * vWeights3.z;

// Sum weights using DOT
fWeightSum += dot(vWeights3, 1);

// Compute tex coords for other taps
float2 vTap4    = v.vTap0 + horzTapOffs[4];
float2 vTap5    = v.vTap0 + horzTapOffs[5];
float2 vTap6    = v.vTap0 + horzTapOffs[6];
float2 vTap4Neg = v.vTap0 - horzTapOffs[4];
float2 vTap5Neg = v.vTap0 - horzTapOffs[5];
float2 vTap6Neg = v.vTap0 - horzTapOffs[6];

// Sample the taps
s0 = tex2D(renderTexture, vTap4);
s1 = tex2D(renderTexture, vTap5);
s2 = tex2D(renderTexture, vTap6);
s3 = tex2D(renderTexture, vTap4Neg);
s4 = tex2D(renderTexture, vTap5Neg);
s5 = tex2D(renderTexture, vTap6Neg);

// Compute weights for three samples
vWeights3.x = saturate(s0.a - vThresh1.x);
vWeights3.y = saturate(s1.a - vThresh1.y);
vWeights3.z = saturate(s2.a - vThresh1.z);

// Accumulate weighted samples
vColorSum += s0 * vWeights3.x + s1 * vWeights3.y +
    s2 * vWeights3.z;

// Sum weights using DOT
fWeightSum += dot(vWeights3, 1);

// Compute weights for 3 samples
vWeights3.x = saturate(s3.a - vThresh1.x);
```

```
    vWeights3.y = saturate(s4.a - vThresh1.y);
    vWeights3.z = saturate(s5.a - vThresh1.z);

    // Accumulate weighted samples
    vColorSum += s3 * vWeights3.x + s4 * vWeights3.y +
        s5 * vWeights3.z;

    // Sum weights using DOT
    fWeightSum += dot(vWeights3, 1);

    // Divide weighted sum of samples by sum of all weights
    vColorSum /= fWeightSum;

    // Color and weights sum output scaled (by 1/256)
    // to fit values in 16 bit 0 to 1 range
    return float4(vColorSum, fWeightSum) * 0.00390625;
}
```

Pass Four: Separable Gaussian Filtering in Y Axis

In the next pass, we perform a similar operation but with blurring along the y axis. The input to this pass is the image that we just blurred along the x axis. The output of this pass is directed to an offscreen render target (blurredXYTexture), which is going to be used during final image compositing.

Vertex Shader for Y Axis of Separable Gaussian Filter

In the vertex shader we again compute the first set of texture sample offsets to be used in the pixel shader for sampling the pre-blurred image. This vertex shader uses exactly the same approach as the vertex shader in the previous pass but with different offset values. This particular vertex shader is designed for a vs 1.1 compilation target.

```
//////////////////////////////////////////////////////////////////

float4 viewportScale;
float4 viewportBias;
// Offsets 0-3 used by vertex shader, 4-6 by pixel shader
float2 vertTapOffs[7];

//////////////////////////////////////////////////////////////////

struct VS_INPUT
{
    float4 vPos:     POSITION;
    float2 vTexCoord: TEXCOORD;
};

struct VS_OUTPUT_TEX7
{
    float4 vPos:     POSITION;
    float2 vTap0:    TEXCOORD0;
```

```
    float2 vTap1:    TEXCOORD1;
    float2 vTap2:    TEXCOORD2;
    float2 vTap3:    TEXCOORD3;
    float2 vTap1Neg: TEXCOORD4;
    float2 vTap2Neg: TEXCOORD5;
    float2 vTap3Neg: TEXCOORD6;
};

//////////////////////////////////////////////////////////////

VS_OUTPUT_TEX7 filter_gaussian_y_vs(VS_INPUT v)
{
    VS_OUTPUT_TEX7 o = (VS_OUTPUT_TEX7)0;

    // Scale and bias viewport
    o.vPos = v.vPos * viewportScale + viewportBias;

    // Compute tap coordinates
    o.vTap0    = v.vTexCoord;
    o.vTap1    = v.vTexCoord + vertTapOffs[1];
    o.vTap2    = v.vTexCoord + vertTapOffs[2];
    o.vTap3    = v.vTexCoord + vertTapOffs[3];
    o.vTap1Neg = v.vTexCoord - vertTapOffs[1];
    o.vTap2Neg = v.vTexCoord - vertTapOffs[2];
    o.vTap3Neg = v.vTexCoord - vertTapOffs[3];

    return o;
}
```

Pixel Shader for Y Axis of Separable Gaussian Filter

Similar to processing the image in the previous pass, we again sample the first
seven samples along the y axis using interpolated texture offsets and combine
these samples using appropriate kernel weights. Then we compute the next six
offset coordinates and sample the image using dependent texture reads. Finally,
we combine all weighted samples and output the value into an offscreen buffer.
This pixel shader is compiled to a ps 2.0 target.

```
//////////////////////////////////////////////////////////////

float4 vWeights0 = {0.080, 0.075, 0.070, 0.100};
float4 vWeights1 = {0.065, 0.060, 0.055, 0.050};

sampler blurredXTexture;
// Offsets 0-3 used by vertex shader, 4-6 by pixel shader
float2 vertTapOffs[7];

//////////////////////////////////////////////////////////////

struct PS_INPUT_TEX7
{
    float2 vTap0:    TEXCOORD0;
```

```
        float2 vTap1:    TEXCOORD1;
        float2 vTap2:    TEXCOORD2;
        float2 vTap3:    TEXCOORD3;
        float2 vTap1Neg: TEXCOORD4;
        float2 vTap2Neg: TEXCOORD5;
        float2 vTap3Neg: TEXCOORD6;
};


/////////////////////////////////////////////////////////////////


float4 filter_gaussian_y_ps(PS_INPUT_TEX7 v) : COLOR
{
    // Samples
    float4 s0, s1, s2, s3, s4, s5, s6;
    // Accumulated color and weights
    float4 vColorWeightSum;

    // Sample taps with coordinates from VS
    s0 = tex2D(blurredXTexture, v.vTap0);
    s1 = tex2D(blurredXTexture, v.vTap1);
    s2 = tex2D(blurredXTexture, v.vTap2);
    s3 = tex2D(blurredXTexture, v.vTap3);
    s4 = tex2D(blurredXTexture, v.vTap1Neg);
    s5 = tex2D(blurredXTexture, v.vTap2Neg);
    s6 = tex2D(blurredXTexture, v.vTap3Neg);

    // Modulate sampled color values by the weights stored
    // in the alpha channel of each sample
    s0.rgb = s0.rgb * s0.a;
    s1.rgb = s1.rgb * s1.a;
    s2.rgb = s2.rgb * s2.a;
    s3.rgb = s3.rgb * s3.a;
    s4.rgb = s4.rgb * s4.a;
    s5.rgb = s5.rgb * s5.a;
    s6.rgb = s6.rgb * s6.a;

    // Aggregate all samples weighting them with predefined
    // kernel weights, weight sum in alpha
    vColorWeightSum = s0 * vWeights0.w +
        (s1 + s4) * vWeights0.x +
        (s2 + s5) * vWeights0.y +
        (s3 + s6) * vWeights0.z;

    // Compute tex coords for other taps
    float2 vTap4    = v.vTap0 + vertTapOffs[4];
    float2 vTap5    = v.vTap0 + vertTapOffs[5];
    float2 vTap6    = v.vTap0 + vertTapOffs[6];
    float2 vTap4Neg = v.vTap0 - vertTapOffs[4];
    float2 vTap5Neg = v.vTap0 - vertTapOffs[5];
    float2 vTap6Neg = v.vTap0 - vertTapOffs[6];

    // Sample the taps
```

```
s0 = tex2D(blurredXTexture, vTap4);
s1 = tex2D(blurredXTexture, vTap5);
s2 = tex2D(blurredXTexture, vTap6);
s3 = tex2D(blurredXTexture, vTap4Neg);
s4 = tex2D(blurredXTexture, vTap5Neg);
s5 = tex2D(blurredXTexture, vTap6Neg);

// Modulate sampled color values by the weights stored
// in the alpha channel of each sample
s0.rgb = s0.rgb * s0.a;
s1.rgb = s1.rgb * s1.a;
s2.rgb = s2.rgb * s2.a;
s3.rgb = s3.rgb * s3.a;
s4.rgb = s4.rgb * s4.a;
s5.rgb = s5.rgb * s5.a;

// Aggregate all samples weighting them with predefined
// kernel weights, weight sum in alpha
vColorWeightSum += (s1 + s3) * vWeights1.x +
    (s1 + s4) * vWeights1.y +
    (s2 + s5) * vWeights1.z;

// Average combined sample for all samples in the kernel
vColorWeightSum.rgb /= vColorWeightSum.a;

// Account for scale factor applied in previous pass
// (blur along the X axis) to output values
// in 16 bit 0 to 1 range
    return vColorWeightSum * 256.0;
}
```

Figure 11 shows the result of applying the 25×25 separable Gaussian to the downsampled image:

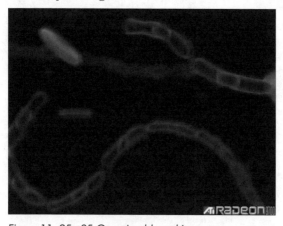

Figure 11: 25×25 Gaussian blurred image

Pass Five: Compositing the Final Output

In the final pass, we create a composite image of the actual scene rendering with the Gaussian blurred image using the distance from the focal plane information that is stored in the alpha channel of the original image. The two offscreen render targets are used to sample that information (in our example, renderTexture is used to sample from full-scene rendering pass results, and blurredXYTexture contains results of applying Gaussian filtering to the downsampled image). All textures are sampled using interpolated texture coordinates.

Vertex Shader for Final Composite Pass

In this vertex shader, we simply transform the vertices and propagate the texture coordinate to the pixel shader. The vertex shader is designed to compile to vs 1.1 target.

```
/////////////////////////////////////////////////////////////////

float4 viewportScale;
float4 viewportBias;

/////////////////////////////////////////////////////////////////

struct VS_INPUT
{
    float4 vPos: POSITION;
    float2 vTex: TEXCOORD;
};

struct VS_OUTPUT
{
    float4 vPos: POSITION;
    float2 vTex: TEXCOORD0;
};

/////////////////////////////////////////////////////////////////

VS_OUTPUT final_pass_vs(VS_INPUT v)
{
    VS_OUTPUT o = (VS_OUTPUT)0;

    // Scale and bias viewport
    o.vPos = v.vPos * viewportScale + viewportBias;

    // Propagate texture coordinate to the pixel shader
    o.vTex = v.vTex;

    return o;
}
```

Pixel Shader for Final Composite Pass

In this pixel shader, we actually do the compositing of the final image. In the pixel shader we retrieve the depth falloff distance stored in the downsampled image's alpha channel. This focal plane distance is used as a blending weight to blend between the post-processed Gaussian-blurred blurred image and the original full resolution scene rendering. This pixel shader is designed to compile to a ps 1.4 target or above.

```
/////////////////////////////////////////////////////////////////

sampler blurredXYTexture;
sampler renderTexture;

/////////////////////////////////////////////////////////////////

float4 final_pass_ps(float2 Tex: TEXCOORD0) : COLOR
{
    // Sample Gaussian-blurred image
    float4 vBlurred = tex2D(blurredXYTexture, Tex);

    // Sample full-resolution scene rendering result
    float4 vFullres = tex2D(renderTexture, Tex);

    // Interpolate between original full-resolution and
    // blurred images based on blurriness
    float3 vColor = lerp(vFullres, vBlurred, vFullres.a);

    return float4(vColor, 1.0);
}
```

Figure 12 shows the result of the final compositing stage.

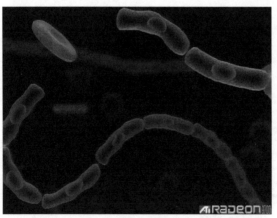

The images for Figures 11 and 12 are taken from a screen saver from the ATI Radeon 9700 demo suite, which you can download from http://www.ati.com/developer/screen-savers.html.

Figure 12: Final composite image for depth of field effect

Bokeh

Different lenses with the same apertures and focal distances produce slightly different out-of-focus images. In photography, the "quality" of an out-of-focus or blurred image is described by the Japanese term "bokeh." While this term is mostly familiar to photographers, it is relatively new to computer graphics professionals.

The perfect lens should have no spherical aberration and should focus incoming rays in a perfect cone of light behind the lens. In such a camera, if the image is not in focus, each blurred point is represented by a uniformly illuminated circle of confusion. All real lenses have some degree of spherical aberration, and always have non-uniform distribution of light in the light cone and thus in the circle of confusion. The lens' diaphragm and number of shutter blades can also have some effect on the shape of the circle of confusion. "Bokeh," which is a Japanese phoneticization of the French word *bouquet*, describes this phenomenon and is a subjective factor, meaning that there is no objective way to measure people's reaction to this phenomenon. What might be considered "bad" bokeh under certain circumstances can be desirable for some artistic effects and vice versa.

To simulate different lens bokehs, one can use filters with different distributions and weightings of filter taps. Figure 13 demonstrates part of the same scene processed with blur filters of the same size but with different filter taps distributions and weightings.

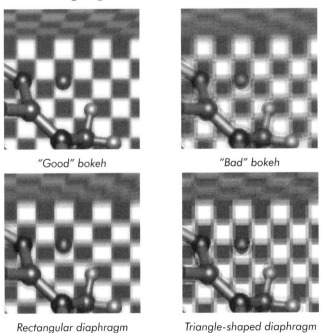

"Good" bokeh   "Bad" bokeh

Rectangular diaphragm   Triangle-shaped diaphragm

Figure 13: Real-time lens bokeh

Summary

This article presented two different real-time implementations of a depth of field effect using a DirectX 9 class programmable graphics hardware. Simulating depth of field is very important for creating convincing visual representations of our world on the computer screen. It can also be used in artistic ways to generate more cinematic-looking visual effects. See Color Plate 26 for examples of the techniques discussed in this article.

References

[Potmesil83] Potmesil, Michael and Indranil Chakravarty, "Modeling motion blur in computer-generated images," SIGGRAPH Proceedings of the 10th Annual Conference on Computer Graphics and Interactive Techniques, 1983.

Section V

Shadows

K3.com

Soft Shadows

Flavien Brebion

VRcontext

Presentation

In recent years, dynamic real-time shadowing has slowly replaced in the programmer's heart (if not in the implementation) the old, fake static techniques used for ages in games and other applications, but although this has improved the quality and realism of scenes, it is still far from being perfect. One of these techniques, commonly referred to as *shadow volumes* or *stencil shadows*, has a very plastic look because of its hard, sharp edges. In this article I propose a technique to fake real-time soft shadows that is an extension of the shadow volumes algorithm. By no means do I claim it is perfect or physically correct, but it gives decent results at interactive frame rates on DirectX 8 ps_1_4/DirectX 9-generation hardware.

Standard Shadowing Algorithms

There are a number of algorithms currently used for shadowing.

Per-vertex Shadowing

APIs such as DirectX or OpenGL implement their lighting equation per-vertex, but this does not handle shadowing. To handle shadows, one idea is to precalculate all the light contributions per-vertex and store it into a single color that is used later as a modulation factor. Although very fast, this technique requires the scene to be heavily tesselated, and the calculations are too slow to be done in real time. Consequently, the lights or occluders cannot move.

Lightmapping

Another popular technique is called *lightmapping*. This was used in the Quake and Unreal engines and derivatives a few years ago (and still are, to some extent). This is basically an extension of the per-vertex lighting to store the light's contributions per texel instead of per vertex. The lighting is also precalculated but embedded into small resolution textures called lightmaps. These lightmaps are modulated with the textures later on, giving a pretty realistic look and feel to the scene. Although they no longer rely on heavy tesselation, they require a lot of texture memory and still cannot be used for dynamic lights. It is still possible to generate many lightmaps per light (for example, to light/unlight a room), but this technique is inherently static.

Shadow Mapping

Shadow maps are more and more often used for real-time dynamic shadowing. Their concept is extremely simple: A depth buffer is rendered from the light's point of view, and the Z values are compared with the depth buffer normally computed from the viewer's point of view by projecting the light's buffer onto the scene. This effectively means that for a given pixel, the comparison result tells if the pixel is visible from the light or not. Unfortunately, shadow maps suffer from a number of problems like aliasing (due to the limited resolution or bits precision of the light's depth buffer) and Z-fighting (due to the projection of the light's depth buffer onto the scene's geometry) and require a hardware Z-comparison test. Last but not least, omni-directional lights are hard to support since an omni-light's point of view is a 360° sphere. It is still possible to use a cube map instead, but that means a *six-times* performance cost penalty. On the other hand, shadow maps do not generate any additional geometry or excessive fillrate needs.

Projected Shadows

The idea behind projected shadows is to generate an object's shadow into a shadow texture and to project it from the light's point of view to blend it over the scene. To avoid wasting one pass to project the shadow on the scene, it is possible to locate the subset of the scene where the shadow is lying. However, self-shadowing and omni-lights are not easily supported.

Stencil Shadows

With the addition of hardware-accelerated stencil buffers to consumer video cards, the technique known as *shadow volumes* has become more and more widely used. Lightmapping was static and needed the light maps to be precomputed; stencil shadows, on the other hand, are fully dynamic: The light or the scene's objects can move in real time with no restrictions. Shadow volumes generally use the stencil buffer to simulate a simple form of ray-casting (although it is also possible to use the color or alpha buffer to simulate the stencil buffer) to count, for each ray passing through a pixel of the screen, the number of times it intersects the shadow volumes, the definition of a shadow volume being a half-space formed by a light and an occluding triangle.

Shadow volumes (also commonly called *stencil shadows*) are not easy to implement. They suffer from many problems, two of which are the viewer-inside-volume problem and the heavy fillrate. The first problem appears as soon as the viewer enters the shadow volume; in that case, the intersection counter simulated by the stencil is messed up, and some shadowed areas appear lit while some lit areas appear shadowed. It is possible to fix that by capping the shadow volume to the near clipping plane, but it is not convenient due to the high CPU workload. Another possibility is to cast a ray from the viewer to the light and determine if it hits an occluder; however, the test is only valid for the single pixel that is located at the center of the screen, and artifacts can still occur when half the screen is inside the shadow volume while the other half is outside. Bill Bilodeau and Mike Songy [1] and John Carmack [2] (who arrived at the same approach independently) were the first to propose a modification of the basic shadow volumes algorithm by pushing the problem away to the far clipping plane instead. It is then possible to either limit the shadow volume length (in the case of attenuated lights) or tweak the projection matrix to push the far plane to infinity, which completely solves the problem since there is no longer any possible intersection.

The second problem with stencil shadows is that they generate a lot of new polygons to display; not only do new vertices have to be generated and transformed, but the polygons also have to be rasterized. Even if we disable color rendering and Z-buffering, since we just need to increase/decrease the stencil values, it still has a heavy cost. One solution, which is based on the fact that given two adjacent triangles in a mesh, their respective shadow volume contributions in the stencil buffer cancel each other, is to calculate the silhouette of the whole mesh on the CPU and generate a single, huge shadow volume for it, effectively decreasing the number of polygons to be displayed. This greatly improves the performance, but new vertices still have to be generated (by extruding the silhouette edges) and transformed. Fortunately, with the advent of vertex shaders, this step can be completely off-loaded to the GPU processor. For further details about the stencil shadows algorithm and its problems and solutions, please see "The Theory of Stencil Shadow Volumes" in *ShaderX²: Introductions & Tutorials with DirectX 9*.

Brotman and Balder [3] implemented real-time soft shadows in 1984 by jittering multiple shadow volumes; Instead of rendering one shadow volume for the light in black, they render n shadow volumes from n lights, all randomly displaced around the original light's center, and sum up their contributions. Unfortunately, this is not very practical since more than ten samples generally have to be used to obtain good results (Cass Everitt and Mark J. Kilgard [4] from nVidia have implemented it with a cluster of 12 lights), which means an effective fillrate cost increase of a factor of ten on an algorithm that is already fillrate intensive.

Overview of the Soft Shadows Algorithm

The real-time models previously described generally work for point lights, spotlights (projected shadows, shadow maps), or for perfect point, omnidirectionnal lights (shadow volumes, shadow maps). As a result, none of them effectively simulate the effect of a non-perfect light source (that is, a *volumetric light source*). In reality, no light is a point; even the sun in the sky has a visible radius causing *penumbras*. Perfect point lights generate *sharp/hard* shadows, but if we want to enhance the realism and quality of real-time computer-rendered scenes, we need a way to fake the *soft shadows* caused by volumetric lights. Figure 1 shows an example of a volumetric light as seen from the viewpoints A, B, and C. If you cast an infinite amount of rays from the light to the point, some of them might hit an occluder, while some of them might reach the point. When 100% of the light reaches the point, we say the point is completely visible from the light (point A).

When 0% of the light reaches the point, we say the point is completely shadowed by the light (point C). We define the penumbra as the set of points that receive more than 0% of the light rays but less than 100%; that is, all the points that are partially visible from the light (point B). Although this model is not perfectly accurate, it provides a good basis to start developing our soft shadows technique.

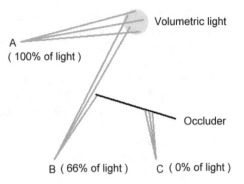

Figure 1: A volumetric light causing soft shadows. Point A receives 100% of the light (fully lit); point B receives around 60% of the light (partially lit) and is in the light's penumbra; point C receives no light at all (it is completely hidden by the occluder) and is in the occluder's shadow.

The idea behind the soft shadows algorithm is simple and works as an extension of the shadow volumes algorithm. We render the shadowed areas from screen-space to a texture, which we call the *shadow map* (not to be confused with the shadowing technique of the same name described in the "Shadow Mapping" section); pixels can basically take two values: 0 if the pixel is lit or 1 if it is shadowed. As the shadow volume algorithm works with a perfect point light source, no other values at that time are possible. Now, if we had a way to generate the penumbra area in that texture, we could just apply a blurring filter of the pixels of the penumbra near the *inner contour* to obtain a nice, smooth transition between completely shadowed pixels (0% of light received, texel value of 1) and completely lit pixels (100% of light received, texel value of 0). This is obviously not a physically accurate solution but would greatly help to enhance the visual quality of the scene and lessen that "plastic" look.

In reality, there are many types of volumetric lights. For the sake of simplicity, we are going to simulate a single, simple type of volumetric light: the spherical light, which is defined as a center point and an emission radius. As the shadow volumes algorithm does not work with spherical lights but with point lights, we need a way to locate the penumbra of a spherical light by using shadow volumes only. It's a tough task, but not impossible. Figure 2 shows a possible solution; a shadow volume is generated from a standard point light, located at the position of the spherical light. This volume defines the inner contour of the penumbra, which we call the *inner volume*. This process is using a vertex shader to optimize the shadow volumes calculation and is described in the "Standard Shadowing Algorithms" section. After that, a second volume is generated from a *jittered* point light. Jittering is the action of moving the position of the point light source by a small vector for each vertex of the scene. This jittering process is described in the "Outer Volume by Jittering the Point Light Source" section. Figure 3 shows a simple point light compared to a spherical light and a jittered point light. This new volume is called the *outer volume* and defines the outer contour of the penumbra.

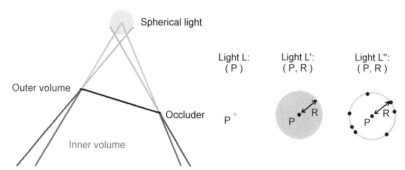

Figure 2: Inner and outer volumes for an area light

Figure 3: A point light source L (left) is defined as a position P. A sphere light source L' (middle) is defined as a position and a radius. A jittered light source L" (right) is a point light source whose center is displaced (jittered) by a vector of length R around P.

The inner and outer volumes are next rendered to the shadow map, each in one color component channel. For instance, the inner volume is stored in the red component, while the outer volume is stored in the green component. Other components (blue and alpha) are simply ignored. The blurring process uses this shadow map both as input and output recursively and needs to know which pixels are in the penumbra and which are not (hence the decomposition of the inner and outer areas into different channels). There is more on this in the section "Blurring the Penumbra."

After this blurring step, we can use a pixel shader to modulate the scene with a lightmap, obtained from the shadow map. This quite straightforward step is described in the section "Using the Shadow Map," followed by miscellaneous considerations in the section "Other Considerations."

Penumbra Generation

The first step to our algorithm is to determine the inner and outer volumes forming the penumbra. The inner volume is generated by using the shadow volumes algorithm with a point light located at the same position as the considered spherical light. Let's first see an overview of the shadow volumes algorithm and how it could be implemented in hardware by using vertex shaders. This vertex shader is later modified for the outer volume to support a jittering coefficient, which indicates how far the light has to be displaced.

Inner Volume Using Hardware Stencil Shadows

To generate a shadow volume for a simple point light, we use the Z-fail technique. The silhouette is first generated on the CPU by looking at which faces are visible from the point light's position and which are not. For each triangle, the plane equation is used to determine if the light is on the positive side (*front-facing triangle*) or the negative one (*back-facing triangle*). The algorithm looks like this:

```
For each triangle T,
    Let a, b, c and d be the coefficients of the plane equation for T;
    the normal N of the plane is then (a, b, c)
    Let L be the light's position vector,
    Triangle is front-facing if (N dot L) + d > 0
End For
```

Silhouette edges are then computed by looking at which edges are shared between two triangles that are not both on the same side in respect to the light's position:

```
For each triangle T,
    For each triangle T' that is adjacent to T,
        Let E be the edge defined by T and T',
        E is a silhouette edge when T is front-facing the light and T' is back-facing,
        OR when T is back-facing and T' is front-facing.
    End For
End For
```

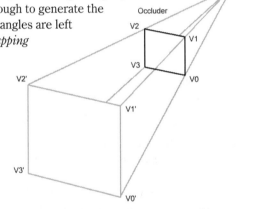

This information (silhouette edges, front-facing triangles, and back-facing triangles) are enough to generate the shadow volumes. Front-facing triangles are left untouched; they form the *near capping* of the volume. Back-facing triangles are *extruded away* from the light; they form the *far capping*. Finally, a quadrilateral is generated from a silhouette edge and its extruded equivalent. These form the sides of the volume. This process is shown in Figure 4 for a simple occluder quadrilateral.

Figure 4: The shadow volume generated from an occluder O is formed by the near capping (V0, V1, V2, V3), the far capping (V0', V1', V2', V3'), and the four sides (V0, V0', V1', V1; V1, V1', V2', V2; V2, V2', V3', V3; V3, V3', V0', V0).

To perform these operations in a vertex shader, we cannot generate any new vertices. The idea is to do the *extrusion* (which is the process of moving a vertex from the near capping to the far capping) in the vertex shader by associating an *extrusion weight* to each vertex and duplicating the vertex buffer; the original vertex buffer contains all the vertices with a weight of 0, and the duplicated buffer contains *the same vertices* but with a weight of 1 to indicate that they have to be extruded away from the light. The light position itself is passed as a shader constant. Since the shadow volume is not lit or textured, all we need for our vertex format is a triplet for the position and a single coefficient. We then append these two buffers together, as shown in Figure 5.

	Vertex 0	Vertex 1	Vertex 2	Vertex 3	Vertex 0'	Vertex 1'	Vertex 2'	Vertex 3'
Position	XYZ_0	XYZ_1	XYZ_2	XYZ_3	XYZ_0	XYZ_1	XYZ_2	XYZ_3
Extrusion weight	0	0	0	0	1	1	1	1

Figure 5: Simple vertex buffer format for shadow volume extrusion in a vertex shader

As a result, we end up with a vertex buffer of size *2N* (*N* being the original vertex buffer size for the whole mesh) that is completely static. Note that it is possible to use different streams to avoid the vertex buffer duplication if memory is a concern. But how do we form the shadow volume now, since it is different for every frame? One solution is to use a dynamic index buffer. We build the shadow volumes by referencing the vertices with an extrusion weight of 0 (for near capping) or by referencing the vertices with an extrusion weight of 1 (for far capping). So, for example, the side V0, V0', V1', V1 of the shadow volume shown in Figure 4 is formed by appending the indices *0, 4, 1, 1, 4, 5* (assuming we are working with triangle lists) to the index buffer. The following algorithm shows how to build the indices for shadow volumes:

```
Reset dynamic index array I for shadow volumes of mesh.
For each triangle T of the mesh,
    Let N be the number of vertices in the mesh (the vertex buffer has a length of
        2N vertices),
    Let V0, V1, and V2 be the mesh indices of the vertices of the triangle T,
    If T is back-facing the light,
        /// one triangle for the far capping
        Append the indices (V0 + N), (V1 + N) and (V2 + N) to I
    Else
        /// one triangle for the near capping
        Append the indices V0, V1 and V2 to I,

        /// now form the shadow volume sides from the silhouette edges
        If edge defined by V0-V1 is a silhouette edge,
            Append the indices V0, V1, (V0 + N), (V1 + N) to I
        Else if edge defined by V1-V2 is a silhouette edge,
            Append the indices V1, V2, (V1 + N), (V2 + N) to I,
        Else if edge defined by V2-V0 is a silhouette edge,
            Append the indices V2, V0, (V2 + N), (V0 + N) to I
        End If
    End If
End For
```

So now that we have generated the shadow volume vertices (statically) and indices (dynamically, or semi-statically, if the light does not move every frame), we still need to perform the extrusion in a vertex shader. This is not very hard; the vertex shader just translates the vertex away from the light by a distance that is dependent on the extrusion weight. The extrusion distance is a constant equal to the light attenuation radius; that is, the radius is the distance at which the light is no longer contributing anything to the scene. The different steps performed by the vertex shader are described in Figure 6.

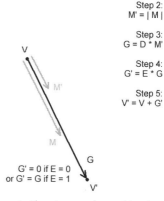

Step 1:
M = V - L

Step 2:
M' = | M |

Step 3:
G = D * M'

Step 4:
G' = E * G

Step 5:
V' = V + G'

G' = 0 if E = 0
or G' = G if E = 1

Figure 6: The steps performed by the vertex shader for shadow volumes extrusion. L is light's position (constant), D is radius (constant), V is incoming vertex's position, and E is vertex's extrusion weight (generally 0 or 1).

The following is the vertex shader's code for these steps:

```
vs.1.1

; Constants used the shader:
; c1.x: light radius
; c4-c7: world-view-projection matrix
; c20: light position in object space

dcl_position0 v0
dcl_blendweight0 v3

; step 1: calculate M
sub r8, v0, c20

; step 2: normalize M, result is M'
dp3 r8.w, r8, r8
rsq r8.w, r8.w
mul r8.xyz, r8.xyz, r8.w

; step 3: G = D * M'
mul r8, r8, c1.x

; step 4: G' = E * G
mul r8, r8, v3.x

; step 5: V' = V + G'
add r8, r8, v0

; r8.w is no longer correct, fix it
mov r8.w, v0.w

; transform vertex:
m4x4 oPos, r8, c4
```

Rendering the shadow volume is not very hard, and you can easily find a lot of information on that topic. The stencil buffer is first cleared to a constant (to avoid wrapping issues, assuming we have eight stencil bits, we use the reference value 128). Texture-mapping, Gouraud shading, and Z-buffer writes are all disabled, but we keep the Z-buffer test. We also disable writing to the color buffer, since we are only interested in the stencil values. We set up the stencil test to always pass and the stencil operation to increment on pixels that fail on the Z-buffer test. Back-face culling is enabled for clockwise triangles. Then, the shadow volumes are rendered using the extrusion vertex shader. Once this is done, we reverse the back-face culling order to counterclockwise and the stencil operation to decrement on the failed Z-buffer test, and we render the shadow volumes again. Note that rendering the shadow volumes can be collapsed to a single pass using the two-sided stencil test and operations if the hardware supports it.

Outer Volume by Jittering the Point Light Source

The outer volume is a bit different from the inner volume. To generate the inner volume, we have been using the shadow volumes algorithm without any slight modification. The outer volume, however, requires us to jitter the point light source (that is, for each vertex in the scene, to move the light source in order to simulate a volumetric light). We call the jittering vector the vector used to translate the light source per vertex. It has a direction and a length. We can use the radius of the spherical light as the length, but what about its direction? If we choose a constant direction, the penumbra does not exactly match the inner shadow, depending on where the occluder is compared to the light position. Another idea is to move the light toward the object center, but depending on the shape of the object, the same problem appears. Now let's consider the problem from another angle: The outer volume looks very similar to the inner volume as it would be generated from a "bigger" object, as demonstrated in Figure 7. Maybe we can inflate the object to generate the outer volume from a point light source. Let's see what happens when we try to do that.

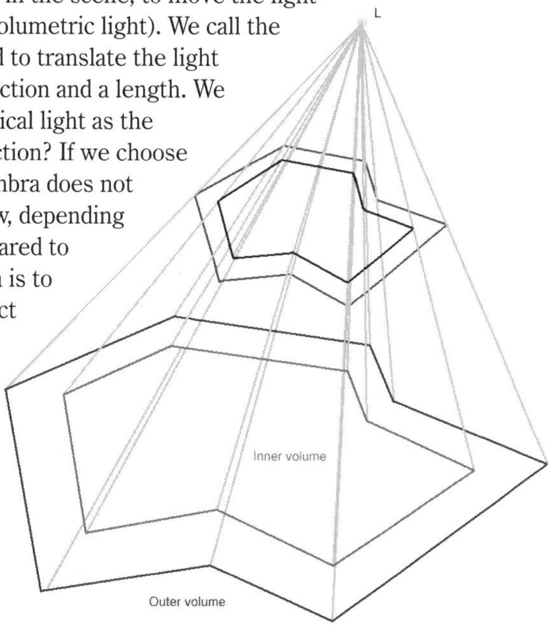

Figure 7: By using a simple point light L, we can generate an inner volume from an occluder object and an outer volume from the inflated object. The penumbra is defined by the outer area excluding the inner one.

The first problem is to generate the inflated object. Parker, Shirley, and Smits [5], who found a similar problem in their own technique, proposed using a transformation that is natural to the object (such as, for a sphere, a bigger sphere). Unfortunately, they do not propose a solution for an arbitrary mesh, as there is no information about its nature. One idea is to average all the normals for all the vertices of the object (independent of the angle between the faces or other conditions) and expand all the vertices in the direction pointed out by the normals, as demonstrated for a cube in Figure 8 (as shown on the following page).

The real problem with that approach is when you start to consider the situation in which an inflated face intersects another face, as demonstrated in Figure 9. In that case, *shadowing artifacts* appear.

These situations should be prevented. One idea is to use CSG operations to remove the vertices that lie inside the object's mesh and then clean up the mesh to keep it two-manifold (as required by the Z-fail stencil algorithm). It is also possible to ignore the problem if it is rare due to the nature of the object or if the inflation distance is pretty small compared to the object's size (in which case the artifacts are small or unnoticeable).

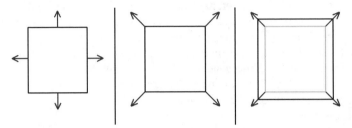

Figure 8: Side view of a simple cube with its face normals (left), same cube with averaged normals (middle), and inflated cube along the normals (right)

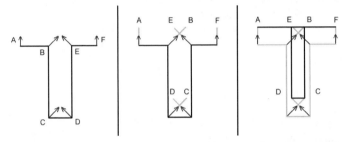

Figure 9: Problems with the inflating algorithm when face intersection occurs while inflating the mesh. Here we have the original object (left) with its inflation vectors (middle) and the object after inflation (right).

If we try to use this inflated object with the stencil shadows algorithm from a point light source, the generated outer volume is incorrect. First of all, the same depth values from the Z-buffer cannot be reused for the inner and outer volumes; shadow volumes require the Z-test to be enabled, but the vertices from the inflated object differ from the vertices of the normal object. Since the inner volume uses the normal object and the outer volume uses the inflated object, their vertices don't match. As a result, we have to reset the Z-buffer by rendering the scene once again between the inner and outer volume passes. It gets even worse if you start to consider multiple lights because this means you have to reset the Z-buffer not one time for the whole scene but two times per light.

Assuming we can live with this performance drop induced by not using the same vertices to render the inner and outer volumes, we still have another problem. Indeed, as the vertices don't match, the penumbra near the occluder doesn't match either, which is not correct, as seen in Figure 10. Compare with Figure 2, which is what we actually want.

So what choices do we have left? Remember that when we were speaking of jittering the light, we needed a direction and a length. We proposed to use the emission radius of the spherical light as the length, but we were unsure about the direction, as a constant vector wouldn't work. But what would happen if we used the direction of the inflation vector as our jittering direction? Figures 11 and 12 show that by actually using the inverse direction of the inflation vector, we can create an outer volume that has all the wanted properties. The vector N is the inflation vector for the vertex V. When extruding that vertex V away from the light, instead of using the center of the light P, we use jitter P by N'. N' is found by normalizing the inflation vector, negating it, and then multipying it by R (the radius of the spherical light).

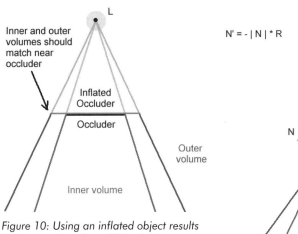

Figure 10: Using an inflated object results in a near-correct but still invalid outer volume near the original occluder vertices.

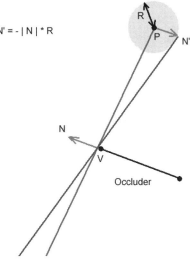

$$N' = -|N| * R$$

Figure 11: Using the inflation vector N at the vertex V to jitter the light's position P by a vector N'

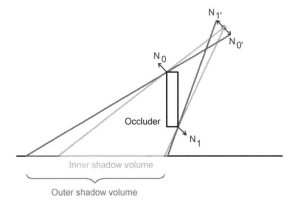

Figure 12: Side view of the jittering process for two vertices of a box occluder

This jittering operation is different for every vertex of the considered occluder(s), since the inflation vector N is different for every vertex V.

To implement that on top of our current shadow volume vertex shader, we only need one more piece of information: the normalized inflation vector N. Consequently, the vertex format for shadow volume vertices has to be updated (see Figure 13).

	Vertex 0	Vertex 1	Vertex 2	Vertex 3	Vertex 0'	Vertex 1'	Vertex 2'	Vertex 3'
Position	XYZ_0	XYZ_1	XYZ_2	XYZ_3	XYZ_0	XYZ_1	XYZ_2	XYZ_3
Extrusion weight	0	0	0	0	1	1	1	1
Inflation vector	$NxNyNz_0$	$NxNyNz_1$	$NxNyNz_2$	$NxNyNz_3$	$NxNyNz_0$	$NxNyNz_1$	$NxNyNz_2$	$NxNyNz_3$

Figure 13: Extended vertex buffer format to jitter the light while doing shadow volume extrusions

The vertex shader only needs minor additions:

```
; constants:
; c3.x contains the jittering distance
; c20 contains the light position P

; declare the inflation vector
dcl_normal0 v4

; jitter light position in r1
mul r1, v4, c3.x
sub r1, c20, r1
```

The jittering distance is equal to the radius of the spherical light if we are in the outer volume generation pass or to 0 for the inner volume pass. That way, we can use *the same shader* for both inner and outer volume passes. The complete shadow volume extrusion vertex shader code becomes:

```
vs.1.1

; Constants used in the shader:
; c1.x: light attenuation radius
; c3.x: light emission radius (radius of spherical light)
; c4-c7: world-view-projection matrix
; c20: light position in object space

dcl_position0 v0
dcl_blendweight0 v3
dcl_normal0 v4

; jitter the light
mul r1, v4, c3.x
sub r1, c20, r1

; step 1: calculate M
sub r8, v0, r1

; step 2: normalize M, result is M'
dp3 r8.w, r8, r8
rsq r8.w, r8.w
mul r8.xyz, r8.xyz, r8.w
```

```
; step 3: G = D * M'
mul r8, r8, c1.x

; step 4: G' = E * G
mul r8, r8, v3.x

; step 5: V' = V + G'
add r8, r8, v0

; r8.w is no longer correct, fix it
mov r8.w, v0.w

; transform vertex:
m4x4 oPos, r8, c4
```

Blurring the Penumbra

The initialization step of the blurring algorithm starts by rendering the inner volume to the red component of the shadow map and the outer volume to the green component of the shadow map. As the result of the shadow volumes algorithm can be seen as a boolean (inside shadow or outside shadow), we encode it as a color component with a value of 0 when the pixel is outside the shadow or a value of 1 (or 255) when the pixel is inside the shadow. Since there are two volumes (inner and outer), there are four possible combinations. One of them is actually not possible (full red, no green), since the outer shadow completely covers the inner shadow. Three combinations remain, as seen in Figure 14.

- No red, no green: both outside inner and outer shadows; pixel receives 100% of the light
- No red, full green: inside outer shadow but outside inner shadow; in penumbra
- Full red, full green: inside inner shadow; pixel receives 0% of the light

Blue and alpha components have no particular significance and are ignored.

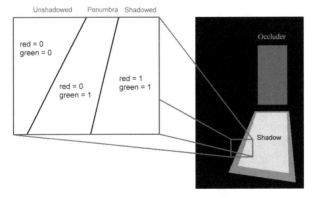

Figure 14: Contents of the color buffer of the shadow map after a typical penumbra generation

To render the shadow map, we enable render-to-texture, clear the background color to black, and initialize the depth and stencil buffers. First, we render the inner volume as described in the "Inner Volume Using Hardware Stencil Shadows" section by using a point light source with the shadow volumes algorithm. The result of this pass is restricted to the stencil buffer, so the next thing to do is output it to the red component of the shadow map. To do that, we just apply a simple red quadrilateral covering the viewport with the stencil test enabled. The same process is done for the green component with the outer volume; the stencil buffer is cleared again (but not the Z-buffer since the vertices haven't changed since the previous pass), the outer volume is rendered to the stencil buffer as described in the "Outer Volume by Jittering the Point Light Sources" section, and then a green quadrilateral is rendered with the stencil test enabled. At that point, the contents of the shadow map should be similar to what is seen in Figure 14. Here is a summary of the whole algorithm:

```
Enable render-to-texture for a NxN texels shadow map,
Clear color buffer to black, clear Z-buffer and stencil,
Render scene to the Z-buffer to prepare stencil shadows,
Render inner shadow volumes to the stencil buffer,
Enable stencil test, enable color mask (write to red only),
Display a red full-screen quadrilateral for pixels in inner shadow,
Clear stencil again,
Render outer shadow volumes by jittering the light with the inflation vectors,
Enable stencil test, enable color mask (write to green only),
Display a green full-screen quadrilateral for pixels in outer shadow,
Clean up states
```

The last step is to blur the pixels near the inner contour of the penumbra. The idea here is to apply a blur filter to the *red* component of the shadow map but allow reads or writes to texels that have full green values only (that is, texels inside the penumbra or the inner shadow). This should result in a nice, soft blur of the shadow around the penumbra without messing up the texels that are not shadowed. *It is important to note that the blur is only applied to the red component; the green component is left unchanged.*

First of all, let's see how blurring can be implemented in hardware without any read or write restriction. Blurring a texture works for a given texel by sampling neighboring texels of this texture and averaging their color value (see Figure 15). Since it is not possible to sample the same texture many times on the same texture unit sampler (except with dependent texture reads, but you don't want to do that for obvious performance reasons), what we actually do is bind the same texture to different texture unit samplers. Then it is all a matter of offsetting the texture coordinates by a small value for each sampler.

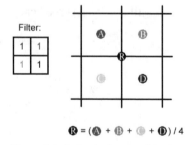

$$R = (A + B + C + D) / 4$$

Figure 15: A simple four-tap blurring filter. The black dot R represents the center texel; the A, B, C, and D dots represent four possible neighboring texels. They all have a weight of 1, hence the resulting texel is the average of its neighbors.

No vertex shader is needed, since the offsets can be precomputed directly. In Figure 16 a three-tap filter is used to show the texture coordinate offsets; a texture A is bound on unit 0 with an offset of (U + 0.025, V – 0.1); a texture B is bound on unit 1 with an offset of (U – 0.1, V + 0.025); a texture C is bound on unit 2 with an offset of (U + 0.1, V + 0.1). The following pixel shader code shows how to sample four textures and average them.

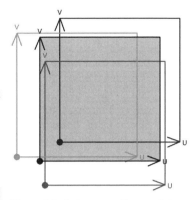

Figure 16: A three-tap filter and the texture offsets. The gray square represents the UV-space of the filtered texture output. The three input textures UV-space are all offset compared to the gray one.

```
ps_1_4

; weight for each sample
def c0, 0.25, 0.25, 0.25, 0.25

; simple 4-tap blur : sample 4 times
texld r0, t0
texld r1, t1
texld r2, t2
texld r3, t3

; weight r0
mul r0, r0, c0

; weight r1, sum up into r0
mad r0, r1, c0, r0

; weight r2, sum up into r0
mad r0, r2, c0, r0

; weight r3, sum up into r0
mad r0, r3, c0, r0

; now in r0 we've got 0.25 * t0 + 0.25 * t1 + 0.25 * t2 + 0.25 * t3
; which is the same as (t0 + t1 + t2 + t3) / 4
```

For our soft shadow algorithm, we use a custom blur filter using six taps (hence using six texture units). The taps are more or less arranged in a circle, as seen in Figure 17.

Now that we've seen how to implement a simple blur, we need to include the read and write restrictions so that we only blur texels near the penumbra. First, let's say that we are sampling a texel that is outside the outer shadow; its contribution should be ignored. One way is to

$$R = (R + A + B + C + D + E) / 6$$

Figure 17: The simple six-tap blur filter that we use for smoothing up our shadow map

keep track of the weights and only perform a blur between the texels that are
inside the outer shadow. For example, say that in Figure 17, only the R, A, and B
taps are inside the outer shadow; then we'd sum up the R, A, and B taps' contributions each with a weight of 1/3 only. Unfortunately, this is not practical, since
you'd have to use an additional counter register to keep track of the total weight
and divide the final result by it. Instead, it is possible to keep a constant weight of
1/6 by replacing the taps to ignore by the center tap's contribution, which is
always valid. Thus, in our example we'd sum up the A and B taps' contributions
once and the R tap's contribution four times (one normally, plus C, D, and E
ignored), always using a weight of 1/6. Here is the algorithm:

```
result = 0
For each tap in [R, A, B, C, D, E] do
If tap is inside outer shadow,
     result = result + current tap's contribution / 6
else
          result = result + R tap's contribution / 6
     End If
End Foreach
```

Note that testing whether a tap is inside the outer shadow basically means sampling the tap and testing if the green component is 1. The write restriction is no
more complex. We only want to blur the red channel of texels that are inside the
outer shadow, and we have an easy way to do that — by multiplying the computed
result by the green component of the center tap. Thus, if the center tap is outside
the outer shadow, the result is 0, independent of the neighboring texels' contribution. Otherwise, the contributions are not modified:

```
result = result * [If R tap is in outer shadow then 1 else 0]
```

The whole algorithm becomes:

```
If R tap is in outer shadow,
result = 0
For each tap in [R, A, B, C, D, E] do
     If tap is inside outer shadow,
               result = result + current tap's contribution / 6
          else
               result = result + R tap's contribution / 6
     End If
End Foreach
Else
     Result = 0
End If
Output.red = Result
Output.green = R tap's green component
```

To implement this algorithm with pixel shader 1.4, we need a way to do the "tap is
in outer shadow" test. The green component of a texel of the shadow map determines if that texel is inside (values of 1) or outside (values of 0) the outer shadow,
so with the cnd instruction we can perform the test and conditionally move the
considered tap's contribution or the black tap's contribution. We also need to
weight and accumulate (with a mad instruction) the contributions into a register
used as the result, which means we need to use at least 12 instructions — six for

the conditional moves plus six for the accumulations. This exceeds the maximum instruction count for a ps_1_4 phase, so we would have to use two phases. Fortunately, it is possible to accumulate the result into an alpha component and collapse the instructions to form pairs, as a color operation followed by an alpha operation counts as a single instruction in the ps_1_4 model. With this trick, it is possible to only use a unique phase with six texture samples. The following is the code for that pixel shader:

```
; Pixel shader version 1.4
ps_1_4

; weight constant for each incoming texture's contribution
def c0, 0.1666, 0.1666, 0.1666, 0.1666

; sample the 6 textures. t0 is at the center of the pixel;
; all other textures are sampled with an offset.
texld r0, t0
texld r1, t1
texld r2, t2
texld r3, t3
texld r4, t4
texld r5, t5

; stores in r1.r either r0.r or r1.r, depending on the
; value of r1.g. This is a conditional mov. In the meantime,
; we'll weight the contribution of r0.r in the alpha
; component of r0 and add it to the result.
cnd r1.r, r1.g, r1.r, r0.r
+mul r0.a, r0.r, c0.z

; basically does the same for r2 and the contribution of
; r1.r. As you notice, there's a 1-instruction "delay"
; between calculating the contribution of a texture and
; weighting and adding it to the final result.
cnd r2.r, r2.g, r2.r, r0.r
+mad r0.a, r1.r, c0.z, r0.a

; same here, but for r3's contribution and weighting r2.
cnd r3.r, r3.g, r3.r, r0.r
+mad r0.a, r2.r, c0.z, r0.a

; same here, but for r4's contribution and weighting r3.
cnd r4.r, r4.g, r4.r, r0.r
+mad r0.a, r3.r, c0.z, r0.a

; same here, but for r5's contribution and weighting r4.
cnd r5.r, r5.g, r5.r, r0.r
+mad r0.a, r4.r, c0.z, r0.a

; we need a final weighting due to the 1-instruction "delay."
; this is done here, by weighting r5 and adding it up to
; the final result, r0.
```

```
mad r0.r, r5.r, c0.z, r0.a

; this final one is masking the result depending on the
; value of r0.g; do not forget that the green component is
; always either 0 or 1. We basically only allow writing
; when the center pixel is from the penumbra or the inner
; shadow:
mul r0.r, r0.r, r0.g

; that's it! note that r0.g hasn't been modified at all
; by the shader; in summary, all the red components of the
; offset textures have been blurred by an average filter
; and the green component untouched (blurring doesn't affect
; the penumbra/shadowed areas)
```

To get a nice blur, this process has to be repeated a certain number of times (I found three or four to give pretty good results, but it is a performance trade-off). As it is not possible to render to the shadow map with the same shadow map input, a double (or more) buffer scheme has to be used, as seen in Figure 18.

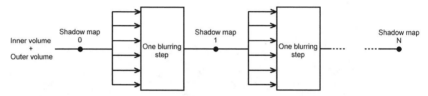

Figure 18: The complete blurring process pipeline

Using the Shadow Map

After the last blurring step, the shadow map's red component contains values in the [0, – 1] range that correspond to the intensity of light received by the pixel. To use the shadow map, we only need to project the shadow map onto the scene using a standard screen-space projection; that is, we directly use the screen-space coordinates of a vertex as input for the texture coordinates. We can implement any custom lighting equation in a pixel shader and modulate the light's contribution by the red component of the shadow map.

As you are completely free to use any lighting equation, the soft shadows method can be used for per-vertex lighting or per-pixel lighting with bump mapping or specular lighting (or anything else). Multiple lights can be collapsed into one pass; for example, if we use per-vertex lighting and six texture units, we can use one texture for the diffuse map and five shadow maps for five soft-shadowed lights and sum up the contributions of each light in a pixel shader. The following are the vertex and pixel shaders to perform the projection and access the shadow map:

```
vs.1.1
; constants :
; c0.y : 0.5
; c4-c7 : world-view-projection matrix
```

```
dcl_position0 v0
dcl_texcoord0 v2


; screen-space coordinates of vertex:
m4x4 r10, v0, c4


; generate texture coordinates for projection:
mov r6, r10
mov r6.z, r6.w


; r6.x = (x/z) * 0.5 + 0.5 = (x * 0.5 + 0.5 * z) / z
mul r6.x, r6.x, c0.y
mad r6.x, r6.z, c0.y, r6.x


; r6.y = 1 – (y/z) * 0.5 + 0.5 = (1 * z – y * 0.5 + 0.5 * z) / z
mul r6.y, r6.y, c0.y
mad r6.y, r6.z, c0.y, -r6.y


; outputs :
mov oPos, r10
mov oT0, v2
mov oT1, r6



ps_1_4


; sample t0 (diffuse map) and t1 (shadow map)
texld r0, t0
texld r1, t1_dw.xyw


; r1.r is the light contribution. Use 1-r1.r because values in the shadow map range
; from 0 (lit) to 1 (shadowed), and we want the contrary.
mul r0, r0, 1-r1.r
```

Other Considerations

The Z-fail shadow volume algorithm requires the scene meshes to be two-manifold and form closed volumes. For a given edge, there must be two — no less and no more — adjacent triangles. It is possible to tweak the geometry to handle non-closed meshes, but it is not obvious. This is something to keep in mind when trying to implement the CSG simplifications for intersecting faces when inflating objects, as after the CSG operation, the meshes have to remain two-manifold.

It is recommended that you keep a 1:1 ratio between the screen resolution and the shadow map size when possible, although you can decrease the shadow map size to increase performances. It is important to note that when using shadow maps smaller than the screen resolution, the shadow information can "melt" together and you can see "halos" appear around objects. This can be seen around the cat's legs and the temple columns in the demo on the companion CD. This is generally not too bad until you reach 1:4 ratios, like using a 256x256 shadow map for a 1024x768 screen. Aliasing also becomes visible when you start moving; shadows near the occluders, which should be sharp, are quickly blurred. On the other hand, there is a four times fillrate and pixel shading rate difference when reducing by two the size of a shadow map, so it is a trade-off.

One idea to save fillrate or pixel shading rate is to keep the stencil test enabled when blurring the shadow map. Unfortunately, this requires clearing the color buffer of the shadow map to black anyway (since this area is not written due to the stencil test), so in the end, there is no performance improvement.

To improve the blurring filter, it is possible to enable bilinear filtering on the shadow map inputs. However, this causes the green channel to be filtered too, which leads to a natural blur after a few blurring steps. To avoid that, as the green channel has to be preserved, filtering always has to be disabled for the center tap.

You might have to play with the shadow map offsets to ensure that the incoming and outgoing pixel positions do match on screen in order to avoid the shadow map being shifted by a few pixels after each blurring step.

Results

A demo is available on the companion CD. It requires DirectX 9 with a vertex shader 1.1 and pixel shader 1.4 compatible video card and at least six texture units (Radeon 8500 and up, GeForce fx and up). It shows a 6,000-triangle temple scene with six lights, two of which are casting real-time soft shadows. It runs at around 10 to 15 frames per second on a Radeon 8500 with a 512x512 shadow map and a four-step blur process. On a Radeon 9700, performance increases up to 30 frames per second. The stencil shadows algorithm could be optimized, and no culling of any sort is being done. Art is courtesy of Daniel Cornibert (danielcornibert@ hotmail.com). Figures 19 and 20 show some scenes from the demo.

Figure 19: Screen shot taken from the soft shadows demo. This 6,000-triangle temple scene features six lights, two of which are casting spherical soft shadows, and runs at up to 35 fps on a Radeon 9700. The two lights are animated. (See Color Plate 27.)

Code: F. Brebion
Art: D. Cornibert

Figure 20: Another screen shot from the temple scene, with a different viewpoint. The white dot near the cattaur (a cross between a cat and a centaur) shows the main light's position. (See Color Plate 27.)

References

[1] Bilodeau, Bill and Mike Songy, "Real Time Shadows," Creativity 1999, Creative Labs Inc. Sponsored game developer conferences, Los Angeles, California, and Surrey, England, May 1999.

[2] Carmack, John, unpublished correspondence, 2000.

[3] Brotman, Lynne and Norman Badler, "Generating Soft Shadows with a Depth Buffer Algorithm," *IEEE Computer Graphics and Applications*, October 1984, pp. 5-12.

[4] Everitt, Cass and Mark J. Kilgard, "Practical and Robust Stenciled Shadow Volumes for Hardware-Accelerated Rendering," March 2002.

[5] Parker, S., P. Shirley, and B. Smits, "Single Sample Soft Shadows," Tech. Rep. UUCS-98-019, Computer Science Department, University of Utah, October 1998.

Robust Object ID Shadows

Sim Dietrich

nVidia

Shadows are still an active area of research in real-time graphics. The two most popular approaches are shadow volumes and depth-based shadows, often called shadow maps.

Currently in wide use by newer graphics engines, shadow volumes can cost huge amounts of fillrate and cannot be cached from frame to frame. Also, shadow volumes are a vertex geometry-based approach, so any geometry created from texel or pixel manipulation, such as alpha testing, won't work with them.

Depth-Based Shadows

Texture or z-buffer-based approaches such as depth-based shadows handle all geometry types equally. In addition, they are view independent, so they can be cached to save fillrate. However, that very view independence causes various forms of aliasing artifacts [Stamminger02].

Projected shadow techniques rely on rendering the light's view of the scene into a texture or z-buffer, referred to here as the *light view texture*. This texture is then projected back onto the scene for each camera-visible pixel, and the depth from the light of each pixel is compared to the depth stored in the shadow map.

If the depth stored in the light view texture is closer to the light than the depth computed for the pixel under question, that pixel is deemed shadowed.

One form of aliasing that arises when using shadow maps is that of depth aliasing. The depth function in the light view texture is discontinuous because there is only a single depth value for each texel. If the view texture is magnified from the scene camera's point of view, the depth value calculated for the pixel will differ from the value looked up in the texture. This is due to resampling the depth function at two different frequencies.

This form of aliasing can be reduced by applying a bias to the depth calculation by adjusting the light's depth function either at the shadow creation or shadow testing phase to ensure there is some minimum distance between a shadow caster and receiver. The magnitude of this bias dictates the size of the smallest distance that can be supported between shadow caster and receiver.

However, since the polygon may be at an arbitrary slope with respect to the light, a scalar bias is not sufficient [Wang94]. Instead, z-based approaches can use the new DirectX 9 renderstate D3DRS_DEPTHBIAS, which allows for greater biases at greater polygon slopes.

In the diagram at right, the dotted line represents the true polygon depth, while the stair-step pattern represents the depth stored in the light view texture. Depending on exactly where the true polygon depth is sampled, it will appear in front of or behind the depth stored in the light view texture. A depth bias can effectively move either the stair-step line or the continuous line apart to try to avoid aliasing artifacts.

Figure 1: Depth aliasing

Texture-Based Depth Shadows

Not all graphics hardware supports true z-based shadows, which allow use of a z-buffer as a texture, so shader authors must rely on manipulating textures instead in order to encode depth [Dietrich01]. Because the polygonal depth bias is applied post-pixel shader, this renders the depth bias useless for texture-based shadow approaches. Scalar biases can still be used, but different scenes will require varying biases, making this shadow technique less general.

One way around this challenging depth aliasing problem is to avoid using depth entirely. Instead of storing depth in the light view texture, object IDs can be stored [Hourcade85].

Each object that can cast or receive shadows is assigned a unique object ID and rendered to the light view texture. Next, the object ID texture is projected back onto the scene, and each rendered object tests whether its object ID matches the projected object ID. If so, then that part of the object is nearest to the light and is not shadowed. If not, that must mean there is some other object at least partially blocking the light from this pixel.

By getting rid of the depth term, the depth aliasing problems go away completely. Object ID shadows do not require a depth bias at all.

There are a few remaining problems, however — how to assign object IDs and accounting for projection aliasing. One approach for assigning object IDs is to assign them per object or character, but that prevents the object or character from casting shadows onto itself. In order to achieve self-shadowing, another approach is to assign IDs per animation bone or model segment [Vlachos01]. An extension of this approach would assign a separate object ID for every triangle in the scene, including world geometry. Any of these approaches can work, but all share a common problem with object ID-based shadows — projection aliasing.

Let's say that we have a simple scene with a flat floor and a vertical wall that meet at a corner. Let's further assume that these two sections get assigned different object IDs, and the light is shining directly at the floor/wall junction (see Figure 2).

In this case, a naïve object ID shadowing algorithm would produce self-shadowing errors along the boundary between the wall and floor.

This happens due to the fact that we start with a line rasterized at some resolution and orientation on the screen. During the shadow testing pixel shader, the point at the center of each pixel is projected back to the light view texture, and point sampling takes place to look up an object ID along another line in texture space of a differing resolution and orientation. These two lines in screen space and texture space will always *almost* line up, but rarely will they line up perfectly.

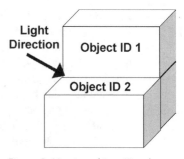

Figure 2: Varying object IDs along object boundaries

Since rasterization snaps to the nearest pixel center, any aliasing error can only be up to half a pixel wide. So, if we sample a 2x2 pixel area, thereby band-limiting the signal so that a single-pixel object ID difference is ignored, we can safely eliminate this form of aliasing.

This can be accomplished by sampling a 2x2 area in the light view texture and only applying shadowing in the case when *all four* samples agree that the pixel is in shadow [Dietrich01].

An easy way to achieve this for simple scenes is to restrict oneself to sorted 8-bit object IDs and use bilinear filtering [Vlachos01]. However, for scenes any more complex, 8 bits won't be enough for the more than 256 objects.

The following is a shader that can handle 2^{28} different object IDs on ps.1.1 hardware using DirectX 8.1 or higher. The large number of object IDs is important in cases where the shadowing technique will be used for both characters and world geometry. Two-hundred sixty million is enough IDs that any size level can be handled without having to sort or intelligently assign IDs. Simply avoiding duplicate IDs for various geometry pieces is enough.

One pass is required to pass down the object ID (typically stored in each vertex for API call efficiency) into the light view texture.

Pass 1: To Light View Texture

```
ps.1.1

// Just output the Object ID, stored across 7 bits each of
// R, G, B, & A from diffuse iterator

mov r0, v0
```

Two passes are required to test each object for shadowing, but the results are guaranteed not to suffer from projection or depth aliasing.

Both passes use the same pixel and vertex shader to sample two of the object IDs in the 2x2 texel region. The results of each pass are written to Dest Alpha as 1 for Lit and 0 for Shadowed.

That way, no matter if one or both achieve a result of Lit, the final result will be marked as Lit, preventing self-shadowing artifacts on object ID boundaries.

Following the second shadow test, the lighting can be additively blended into the scene, based on Dest alpha:

DestColor = SrcColor * DestAlpha + DestColor

Passes 2 and 3: To Back Buffer

```
ps.1.1

tex t0      // fetch id0
tex t1      // fetch id1

            // grab 1st ID & compare
sub_x4 r0, v0, t0           // diff0 * 8
add_x4 r0, r0, r0           // diff0 * 64

dp3_x4_sat t0.rgb, r0, r0   // square diff0, sum * 64
+
mul_x4_sat r0.a, r0.a, r0.a // sum * 64

            // grab 2nd ID & compare
sub_x4 r1, v0, t1           // diff0 * 8
add_x4 r1, r1, r1           // diff1 * 64
dp3_x4_sat t1.rgb, r1, r1   // square diffs, sum * 64
+
mul_x4_sat t1.a, r1.a, r1.a

add_x4_sat t1.rgb, t1, t1.a // sum * 64 * 4 = 256
+
add_x4_sat r0.a, r0.a, t0.b // sum * 64 * 4 = 256

add_sat r0, 1-r0.a, 1-t1    // reverse & add results of
                            // both id checks

// r0 now contains 1 for lit, 0 for shadowed
```

The main concept behind the shader is to perform two ID checks in parallel. Because the object IDs are not sorted by depth from the light but simply assigned at preprocess time, the difference between two IDs may be positive, negative, or zero.

The repeated _x4 scaling is used to try to force a possibly small difference in IDs, like 2 / 255, to be scaled all the way to –1, 0, or 1.

The dp3-based squaring is used as an absolute value, making negative differences count as positive differences. This is important so that during the summing up of the R, G, B, and A channels, negative differences don't cancel out positive ones.

In order to make this shader work, the object IDs must be allocated so that none of the R, G, B, or A channels differ by only an LSB. This basically means allocating IDs in twos on a per-channel basis.

Allocating IDs by twos for each color channel ensures that the minimum difference in any non-zero subtraction result is two. This allows us to shave off another "scale up by 2" instruction, which would have forced this to a three-pass approach.

Undersampling

This set of shaders completely solves the projection aliasing problem, but one problem still remains, which is inherent in all object ID shadowing methods: undersampling.

If a triangle in the scene projects to a very thin or small area in the light's view texture, such that it doesn't cross a pixel center and thus fails to be rasterized at all, the entire triangle will appear in shadow because some other nearby object ID is found in the light view texture instead during the shadow testing phase.

One can reduce this problem by not giving every triangle in a finely tessellated mesh its own object ID. Smaller triangles will undersample more often. Increasing the resolution of the light view texture decreases the occurrence of undersampling artifacts.

Undersampling is most common on silhouette edges with respect to the light and can be hidden to some degree by adjusting the lighting equation from N dot L to something like (N dot L)^2, which causes lighting on silhouettes to fade out more quickly.

Undersampling also occurs with depth-based shadows but is less serious because a depth bias can correct it to some degree.

Mipmapped Object IDs

One idea to work around object ID undersampling is to utilize mipmapping to select the object IDs.

Rather than store object IDs in the vertices of each triangle or mesh section, one can store them in a texture. Point sampling should be used to fetch the appropriate ID. The mipmaps for the object ID texture are constructed so that when sections that share the same object ID start to become thin or small and are at risk for undersampling, neighboring object ID sections are merged together. This allows a gradual lessening of shadow detail in a more controlled manner.

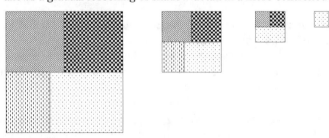

Figure 3: Mipmapped object IDs

The largest mipmap level contains areas of varying object ID. Each triangle in the shadow casting or receiving mesh has texture coordinates referencing one of these areas of constant object ID. The texture coordinates must be created such that they don't reference a neighboring object ID section.

The next smaller object ID mipmap is simply a smaller version of the first, whereas the next two mipmap levels show how the object ID sections are merged so that the smaller sections are sub-sumed into the larger sections. Eventually there is only a single object ID remaining, at which point the mesh will not self-shadow.

These mipmaps cannot be used in the traditional manner, however, because while they work fine from the light's point of view, when creating the light view texture one would have to write a complicated ps.2.0+ pixel shader in order to reproduce the mipmap selection from the light's point of view during the shadow testing phase.

One could instead simply choose a mipmap level for an entire mesh or mesh section. Unfortunately, that reduces batch sizes because it would require switching the LOD bias and mipmap clamping state in between each object draw call.

Object ID LOD

Rather than using mipmapping to solve the problem, one can simply use the concept of geometric LOD. When constructing discrete geometric LODs, one must generate object IDs to store in each vertex of every triangle of the mesh. The LOD algorithm used to reduce geometry will automatically simplify the mesh, and the object ID-creation algorithm is run on the resulting lower-polygon mesh.

This is still not a great solution for many applications, however. One reason is that not all geometry in the level may have LODs generated for it, such as the world geometry.

Another reason is that neither the mipmap nor LOD approach completely solves the problem of undersampling; rather, each approach reduces the frequency of errors.

Combining Object and Geometric LOD

Another approach to reducing object ID aliasing is to have a two-dimensional LOD table. One axis would represent distance from the shadowing light, and the other axis would represent distance from the scene camera. The camera distance axis would choose a mesh of a certain level of geometric complexity. The light distance axis would select a texture map that corresponds to a lower number of unique object IDs for the mesh.

Object ID Allocation for Convex Regions

Yet another approach that helps reduce undersampling problems is to identify convex areas or volumes of a mesh and make the entire convex section share the same object ID. This works because a convex mesh cannot shadow itself.

A simple version of this approach allocates object IDs via plane equations. Since two coplanar triangles can never shadow each other, no matter if they are adjacent or disjoint, one can give all coplanar triangles the same object ID. This is very effective in reducing object ID aliasing with world geometry because an entire floor or wall can share the same object ID, no matter how finely tessellated. Actually, each of the four walls and floor of a rectangular room could share the same ID, since they form a convex region, but this may be a hard case to detect in practice if not using a BSP for world geometry.

Summary

For a large class of applications that aren't tessellated enough for undersampling to cause significant problems, object ID shadows remain a viable alternative to depth-based approaches, given an efficient and robust method of achieving them, such as those presented above.

References

[Dietrich01] Dietrich, D. Sim, "Practical Priority Buffer Shadows," *Game Programming Gems 2*, Charles River Media, 2001, pp. 481-487.

[Hourcade85] Hourcade, J.C and A. Nicolas, "Algorithms for Antialiased Cast Shadows," *Computers and Graphics*, vol. 9, no. 3, 1985, pp. 259-265.

[Stamminger02] Stamminger, Mark and George Drettakis, "Perspective Shadow Maps," http://www-sop.inria.fr/reves/publications/data/2002/SD02/PerspectiveShadowMaps.pdf.

[Vlachos01] Vlachos, Alex, David Gosselin, and Jason Michtell, "Self-Shadowing Characters," *Game Programming Gems 2*, Charles River Media, 2001, pp. 421-423.

[Wang94] Wang, Y. and S. Molnar, "Second-Depth Shadow Mapping," http://www.cs.unc.edu/~molnar/Papers/Shadow.ps.

Reverse Extruded Shadow Volumes

Renaldas Zioma

Introduction

This article suggests a solution for dealing with shadowing artifacts that uses stenciled shadow volumes and allows proper self-shadowing while using occluder geometry, which is separate from the visible geometry. Occluder geometry can be simplified, improved for shadow volume extrusion in vertex shader, and real-time animated. This solution is derived and adopted for the stenciled shadow volumes from the work of Yulan Wang and Steven Molnar on shadow mapping [1].

The reverse extruded shadow volumes technique relies on a correct illumination model to hide shadowing artifacts. Breaking the illumination model, for example, when using a darkening approach (when light is subtracted in shadowed areas) [2], may produce artifacts on the polygons facing away from the light source and requires special treatment. The simple case of a darkening approach with one light source is discussed later.

Why Separate Occluder and Visible Geometry?

There are many scenarios when it's useful to have a separate geometry for shadow volume construction. You may have to add extra triangles along sharp edges and possibly extra vertices at the same position but with different normals, since normals in a visible mesh are used for lighting calculations and shadow volume extrusion needs face normals instead [3]. Maybe you have to remove unnecessary triangles to reduce occluder mesh complexity. Or you may go even further and reduce the number of bone influences per vertex in the animated occluder to gain some more speed (if the shadowing algorithm is not already fillrate bound).

Problems and Solutions

Separate occluder geometry is very useful for improving visual quality of the shadow or gaining some performance increase; however, when applied with the conventional shadow volume extrusion algorithm, it suffers from unacceptable lighting artifacts — harsh shadows appear on the lighted side of the visible geometry. This is caused by occluder geometry protruding from the visible geometry or ambiguities in depth values (z-fighting).

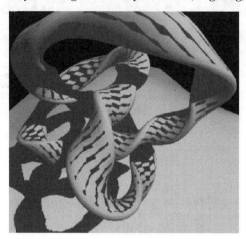

Figure 1: Shadowing artifacts on the lighted side of the visible geometry [8]

There are a number of ad hoc solutions that can be used to reduce such shadowing artifacts; however, as we see later, they are not very robust.

■ **Fit occluder mesh within the visible mesh [3]**

This solution works only for static geometry. In the case of dynamically modified geometry, even if all vertices of the occluder mesh are kept inside the visible mesh, there is no way to ensure that the occluder mesh isn't protruding.

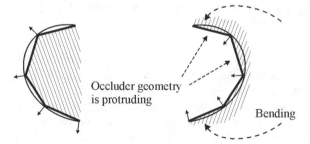

Figure 2: "Fitted within" mesh before and after bending

■ **Inset vertices of the occluder mesh along their normals**

This reduces protruding of the occluder mesh during the animations — but at the expense of smaller shadows. It also requires careful hand-tuning for each animation. However, there is another bad thing about this solution: It may break depending on the distance between the viewer and geometry, since depth buffer isn't linear (post-perspective divide means non-linear distribution) and the vertices are inset constantly (actual bias in depth buffer units will vary over the frustum) [4].

■ **Add bias to polygons of visible mesh in post-perspective space**

To add an offset to polygons in post-perspective space, the ZBIAS state in DirectX 8 (Tom Forsyth suggests near and far plane shifting as a better solution to ZBIAS [5], however) and the DEPTHBIAS and SLOPESCALE-DEPTHBIAS states in DirectX 9 are available. While this solution overcomes the non-linear distribution problem, it doesn't solve the problems listed earlier. Also, it introduces even more hand-tuning — a trade-off between eliminating shadowing artifacts and shadows that are too far away to be realistic.

The algorithm becomes more and more complex. It requires more hand-tuned parameters or introduces new restrictions. This encourages attacking the problem from another perspective and searching for more robust solutions.

Let's leave stenciled shadow volumes for a bit and look at another shadowing solution — shadow maps (light's depth buffers). The cleverness of shadow mapping is that the depth buffer generated by rendering a scene from the light is a precomputed light visibility test over the light's view volume. The visibility test is of the form:

$$p_z <= shadow\_map(p_x, p_y),$$

…where p is a point in the light's clip space [6].

Importantly, both shadowing solutions use volumes: stenciled shadow volume solution in the form of extruded geometry and shadow mapping solution in the form of a depth buffer. Both solutions use these volumes to partition space into two regions for a particular light: a shadowed region and unshadowed region.

Naturally, while implementing the shadow mapping technique, one may notice similar shadowing artifacts and similar ways to solve this problem. The shadow mapping algorithm, introduced by Lance Williams [7], requires a polygon offset to avoid self-shadowing artifacts. Usually, this is done by adding a small bias amount to the shadow map projection matrix in DirectX 8 [6] or using the DEPTHBIAS and SLOPESCALEDEPTHBIAS states, introduced in DirectX 9, while rendering occluder geometry. However, these solutions have similar disadvantages as earlier discussed for ad hoc solutions for stenciled shadow volumes.

Yulan Wang and Steven Molnar pointed out the non-robustness of these solutions and introduced another technique for shadow mapping to reduce the need for a polygon offset [1]. Their technique works by rendering only back faces into the shadow map, relying on the observation that back-face z-values and

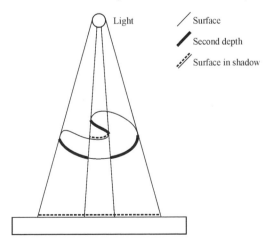

Figure 3: Polygons facing away from the light are casting shadows.

front-face z-values are likely far enough apart to not falsely self-shadow [6]. This allows transferring the artifacts from the front faces to the back faces. Artifacts on the back faces do not matter because they are already known to be in shadow and can be hidden by the illumination model.

If this technique works for shadow mapping, when the right parameters for correct illumination and suitable back-face and front-face z-values are chosen, it might work just as well for stenciled shadow volumes.

Bringing Shadow Mapping Wisdom to Shadow Volumes

The conventional shadow volume extrusion algorithm treats polygons facing the light source as light occluders (shadow casters). Polygons that are facing away from the light source are projected to infinity in order to form a shadow volume.

Once again, notice the similarity to the conventional shadow map technique when the front faces are used to fill the depth buffer, forming the "front" of the shadow volume, which in turn is extending to infinity.

Here is the conventional shadow volume extrusion algorithm (L is a light's direction, N is a normal of the occluder polygon):

- If L.N < 0, project vertex to infinity (or just far enough) along the normal.
- Leave other vertices unchanged.

Now let's try to apply Wang and Molnar's wisdom to stenciled shadow volumes. Instead of using polygons facing the light source as shadow casters, we could just use the polygons facing away from the light source instead; in other words, we need to reverse the conventional shadow volume extrusion technique.

Here is the reverse shadow volume extrusion algorithm:

- If L.N > 0, project vertex to infinity (or just far enough) along the normal.
- Leave other vertices unchanged.

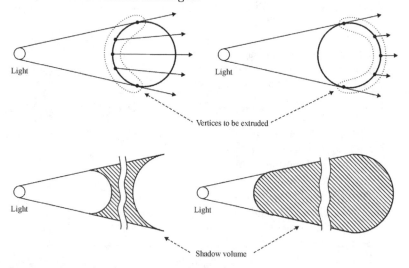

Figure 4: Reversed and conventional shadow volume extrusion

What does this technique do? It's the same as Wang and Molnar described it for shadow mapping — it doesn't reduce the shadowing ambiguities but transfers them from polygons that face the light source to polygons that are facing away from the light source. Since these polygons are always in shadow by definition, the illumination model will hide these artifacts automatically.

Figure 5: Shadowing artifacts on the lighted side, without light, and hidden by the light

Implementation of Reverse Shadow Volume Extrusion

The following code illustrates the reverse shadow volume extrusion algorithm implemented as a vertex shader. The first part of the vertex shader calculates the direction to the light and then normalizes it.

```
#define POSITION          v0.xyz
#define NORMAL            v3.xyz
#define WORLD_VIEW_PROJ   c0
#define LIGHT             c4.xyz      // light position in object space
#define EXTRUDE           c5.x        // extrusion offset
#define LN_THRESHOLD      c5.y

vertexshader vs =
#ifndef DX9
decl {
    stream 0;
    float v0[3];                      // position
    float v3[3];                      // normal
}
#endif
asm {
    vs.1.1

#ifdef DX9
    dcl_position  POSITION
    dcl_normal NORMAL
#endif
    add r0.xyz, LIGHT, -POSITION      // r0: L

    dp3 r0.w, r0.xyz, r0.xyz          // r0.w: |L|^2
    rsq r0.w, r0.w                    // r0.w: 1/|L|
    mul r0.xyz, r0.xyz, r0.www        // r0.xyz: normalize( L )
```

The following part of the shader calculates the dot product between the occluder normal and the direction to the light in order to decide if the occluder polygon is facing the light or not. If the dot product is greater than or equal to the threshold (the threshold usually equals 0), the polygon is considered as facing the light and should be projected away from the light. The result of the sge instruction, which equals 1 if the polygon is facing the light and 0 otherwise, is used as a mask for the projection distance.

Also, please note that the new vertex shader differs from the conventional shadow volume extrusion vertex shader only in one instruction. Instead of the slt instruction, it uses the sge instruction.

```
dp3  r0.w, r0.xyz, NORMAL        // r0.w: L . N
sge  r0.w, r0.w, LN_THRESHOLD    // r0.w: 1.0f if frontface!
                                 // r0.w: 0.0f if backface


mul  r0.w, r0.w, EXTRUDE         // r0.w: extrusion coefficient
```

The final part of the shader makes the actual extrusion of the vertex by adding projection distance to the vertex position. The work of the shader is finished with the transform of the vertex position to the projection space by the world-view-projection matrix.

```
mad  r0.xyz, -r0.xyz, r0.www, POSITION    // r0.xyz: extruded vertex
mov  r0.w, v0.w


m4x4  oPos, r0, WORLD_VIEW_PROJ            // vertex to projection space
};
```

Shadows via Darkening

If the shadowing approach when light is subtracted in shadowed areas is used, the reverse shadow volume extrusion technique may produce artifacts on the polygons that are facing away from the light.

This happens because such an approach is actually breaking the illumination model, and the reverse shadow volume technique relies on the right lighting calculations to hide the artifacts. The light may be subtracted from the polygons that were not in light, resulting in regions that are darker than the ambient term. In order to fix this problem for the single light source, the ambient term must be added to the frame buffer only after the darkening pass.

Analysis

The reverse shadow volume extrusion technique has the following strengths:

- The reverse shadow volume extrusion technique provides an easy way to use separate occluder and visible geometry for stencil shadows.

- The reverse shadow volume extrusion technique allows proper self-shadowing using stencil shadows.

- It's more robust than ad-hoc solutions for conventional shadow volume extrusion and does not introduce fragile algorithms and hand-tuned parameters.

- It's easy to migrate from conventional shadow volume extrusion to the reverse — the magic is done only in one instruction.

The reverse shadow volume extrusion technique has the following weaknesses:

- A closed mesh is required for shadow generation. Actually, if the vertex shader has already been used for shadow volume extrusion, it requires a closed mesh in any case. If the occluder mesh isn't closed, then the pre-processing step must generate a closed mesh. Notice that visible mesh can not be closed, since it is not involved in shadow volume extrusion at all.

- A correct illumination model is required. Since shadowing approach via darkening is breaking the illumination model, special treatment is needed when such an approach is used to avoid the artifacts on the polygons facing away from the light.

- The occluder geometry must be sufficiently sized — back faces should not protrude or z-fight with the front faces.

Summary

The reverse shadow volume extrusion technique introduces an easy way to use separate occluder and visible geometry and allows proper self-shadowing with the stenciled shadow volumes approach.

References

[1] Wang, Yulan and Steven Molnar, "Second-Depth Shadow Mapping," UNC-CS Technical Report TR94-019, 1994.

[2] Dietrich, Sim, "Shadow Techniques," GDC 2001.

[3] Everitt, Cass and Mark J. Kigard, "Optimized Stencil Shadow Volumes," GDC 2003.

[4] Kilgard, Mark J., "Shadow Mapping with Today's OpenGL Hardware," CEDEC 2001.

[5] Forsyth, Tom, "Why ZBIAS is not a good thing," http://tomsdxfaq.blogspot.com/.

[6] Everitt, Cass, Ashu Rege, and Cem Cebenoyan, "Hardware Shadow Mapping," http://developer.nvidia.com/docs/IO/1830/ATT/shadow_mapping.pdf.

[7] Williams, Lance, "Casting Curved Shadows on Curved Surfaces," *Computer Graphics*, SIGGRAPH '78 proceedings, pp. 270-274.

[8] Pranckevicius, Aras, "Reverse extruded shadow volumes," http://www.gim.ktu.lt/nesnausk/nearaz/texts/revext.html.

Section VI

3D Engine and Tools Design

595

Shader Abstraction

Tom Forsyth

Mucky Foot Productions

The Problems

There are many problems that crop up when writing any sort of graphics engine, whether aimed just at the PC platform or at multiple platforms, including consoles. The big one is almost always scalability, specifically the scalability of the shaders used for rendering the scene. Even when aiming at a single console platform, scalability is still important for allowing maximum detail in foreground areas while not spending time rendering this detail in the background, where it is not visible. When developing for multiple platforms or a sensible range of PC hardware, scalability becomes extremely important.

Various conventional solutions exist, none of them ideal. A brief list of the possible cases and their traditional solutions follows:

Multiple PC cards — TSS, PS1.1, PS1.3, PS1.4; FFP, VS1.1; P/VS 2.0, P/VS3.0[1]

- Use the lowest common denominator. Ugly.
- Fix a high "minimum spec." Reduces your possible market.
- Two or three versions of the low-level engine. Large coder, artist, and QA time.

Multiple platforms — PC, XB, PS2, GC

- Multiple and completely separate engines. Lots of coder time. Artists author multiple versions.
- Shared API layer. Essentially the lowest-common-denominator solution again.

Scalability within scenes according to distance

- Mesh Level of Detail (VIPM, static LoD) can help but only geometry, not fillrate.
- Fade stuff out (litter, incidental objects, texture layers) — looks rather strange.

---

1   TSS is TextureStateState, a reference to the SetTextureStageState call used to set up this style of pixel blending. FFP is the fixed-function pipeline — the transform and light part of Direct3D that was replaced by vertex shaders. PS is pixel shader. VS is vertex shader. P/VS is both pixel and vertex shader.

A Single Solution?

The solution proposed in this article is to abstract shaders. In many ways, this is just a combination of some of the above ideas, but it is much more thorough than the solutions above and affects the design of the entire engine. The abstraction of shaders means that the models (and therefore the artists that authored those models) specify a description of an ideal shader, but then in code the shader is allowed to degrade gracefully in quality according to both platform and distance from the camera.

This concept is not new. Features like detail textures have been optional extras for some time in many games, enabled only on higher-end systems, but they essentially work from the lowest common denominator upward by attempting to artificially add detail. This gives a much poorer quality result than working the other way — allowing artists to author high and scale down.

With the advent of some very complex shader models such as anisotropic BRDFs[2], self-shadowing bump maps, and displacement mapping, the gap between the lowest acceptable quality of shaders and the highest possible grows even wider. Adding a few noise functions over the top of a texture map fails to impress people any more, and the alternative is to discard the lower-end systems, which make up a large proportion of the market.

There is a small speed cost associated with this flexibility. However, the extra cost of this abstraction is matched by the considerable advantages — and the run-time speed difference is small, and in many cases the abstraction allows other optimizations to be applied that more than counteract the slight overhead.

Essentially, the idea is for the artists to design objects with the highest superset of features available. They model and describe objects with as much shader detail as they have time and resources for, without worrying too much about which target platforms can render the data they produce or how much of the scene will be rendered with all that data. Naturally, some judgment is required to balance time spent producing super-detailed shader information against the likely benefit, but the artists are not tied rigidly to the target platform(s) in the usual way.

For simplicity, I usually refer to the different types of PC cards as different platforms. The only difference between the two cases is that on the PC, the choice of "platform" is not known until game installation or start of day, while on the console it can be determined at compile time. However, the methods used do not add any performance penalty for this relatively late decision and the only slowdown is at load time, but even then it is small compared to the time taken to retrieve mesh and texture data from the hard drive.

---

2 Bidirectional Reflectance Distribution Functions

The Material

The core concept in this abstraction is the Material[3]. Frequently implemented as a C++ class, this is a black box that wraps up all the rendering details from the rest of the engine. Mesh data, textures, lighting, position, orientation, animation, and so on are fed into the Material and out come pixels on the screen. This data can be fed in when exporting from the various content creation stages and intermediate formats stored on the hard drive, CD, or DVD, or it can be fed in at run time for dynamic objects such as sprites, HUD, font draws, particle systems, and so on. Either way, there are a few well-defined input formats that are shared by all Materials, but the details of rendering and the internal data stored on the hard drive, CD, or DVD are all private to the specific Material.

The shared input interface allows a single mesh with complex shader data to be fed to a wide range of Materials with different rendering styles, and the Material deals with the details of efficient rendering at a certain quality and speed level. Because all the intermediate information (such as vertex buffers, shaders, texture formats, and content) is private to the Material, each Material can be individually optimized for particular situations and platforms without worrying about breaking any other parts of the code. In this way, the huge complexity of a multi-format highly scalable rendering system are kept manageable by reducing as many interdependencies as possible.

Materials are generally both subclassed (using virtual C++ classes) and instanced. A subclass is used when there is a different style of rendering — a different number of passes, different types of inputs (e.g., lighting info, shadow buffers, environment maps), and so on. A different instance is used when the code is the same but the details are different — for example, different render states or pixel or vertex shaders. Essentially, any time there is an "if" in the rendering function that tests data determined at start of day, it is probably time to use a different class rather than an instance.

A Simple Static Material

To help make a few of these ideas concrete, here is a very simple implementation of a static Material class. A static Material is used for meshes that do not have their mesh data changed by the CPU at run time — positions, texture coordinates, vertex coloring, and so on are purely determined at export time. However, this does include cases where data is generated by the GPU — animation, changing lighting conditions, environment mapping, and so on. This covers most meshes that are output from a 3D art package. The opposite is a dynamic class, such as a particle system or a font draw — these will be addressed later[4]. To keep it simple, this engine does not yet have any textures or animation:

---

3   To make it clear when I am talking about the code construct, I capitalize the M when talking about it, as opposed to a "material," which is usually used as a way of referring to the properties of a particular surface. The concepts overlap but are not always identical.

```
class Material
{
private:
    MaterialDescriptor desc;
    Material ( const MaterialDescriptor &md );
    virtual ~Material();
public:
    static Material *FindOrCreate ( const MaterialDescriptor &md );
    virtual void *Export ( size_t &SizeOfDataInBytes,
        const FatVertex *pVertices,
        const u32 *pIndices,
        int iNumVerts, int iNumTris ) = 0;
    virtual void Render ( const void *pExportedData,
        const Matrix43 &orientation ) = 0;
};

// And some derived classes would be:
class MaterialUnlit : Material;
class MaterialLit : Material;
class MaterialLitShiny : Material;
```

Note that Material is a base class and cannot be created directly. It can only be used as a template and interface for the other Materials derived from this class that implement specific rendering methods. However, the Material class is the interface that the rest of the engine uses; it does not (except in very specific circumstances) need to know about any of the derived Material classes. The following sections describe each part of this class.

MaterialDescriptor

MaterialDescriptor is a relatively large inefficient structure with various combinations of flags and enums that specifies the properties of a certain Material. The flags say things like "this material has a diffuse texture," "this material is shiny," "this material has vertex colors in the mesh data," and so on. This structure is used to uniquely identify a Material, and no two Materials will have the same MaterialDescriptor, even if they are different derived classes.

Material::FindOrCreate()

To ensure that no two Materials will have the same descriptor, the engine is not allowed to create Materials itself. What the engine does when it needs a new Material is create the appropriate descriptor and pass this to the Material::FindOrCreate() function. This will either return an existing Material or create a new one; it keeps an internal list of all existing Materials. This function is a simple version of a "class factory," where all the classes it can create are derived from Material, but the actual type (MaterialUnlit, MaterialLit, MaterialShiny) is determined by the descriptor that is fed in. Although searching through the list of

---

4   Note that on some platforms, the distinction is a little more precise; see "Dynamic Materials" later for more.

existing Materials and trying to match up the MaterialDescriptor is relatively slow (it can be sped up by hashing the descriptor as a quick test), this is only done when new objects and new materials are created, which is usually only at start of day or appropriate intervals, such as loading new levels. In practice, it is not a speed problem.

Material::Export()

The Export function is called by the developer when converting data from the format output by art packages into data to be written to the distribution media (CD, DVD, archive, WAD file, etc.). For each mesh that is placed in the game, a MaterialDescriptor is created that describes its rendering properties, FindOrCreate is used to find the specific Material that will do the rendering, and then the mesh data is sent to the Export() method of this Material.

The input vertex format — FatVertex — is shared across all Materials and frequently contains space for all the possible required data (such as tangent vectors, multiple texture coordinate sets, vertex colors, and so on), even if most Materials do not use or require this data. Similarly, the index data is in a standard format. Indexed triangle lists with 32-bit indices are very common because they are simple for content packages and load/save routines to use, but again the format is up to the application. Whether the target platform prefers indexed or non-indexed data, lists, strips, fans, or quads does not affect the input to Export — any expanding, reordering, splitting, etc. is handled internally by the Material::Export() call, since only it knows the rendering specifics.

The Export function takes all the mesh data (and texture data, which has been omitted for simplicity for now) and processes it into a hardware-friendly form that it can easily use at run time. This usually involves stripping or reordering the triangles for efficiency, reindexing them if needed, removing all the data in the FatVertex that is either not needed or cannot be used (for example, tangent-space data for a Material that cannot render bump maps), compressing the data for the target platform, and so on. The final processed data is packed into a single continuous chunk of bytes in whatever format the Material requires and passed back as the result of Material::Export(). The size of the data is written to SizeOf-DataInBytes. Of course, any sort of data-packaging method may be used — STL vectors of bytes and so on are also handy.

It is then the mesh's responsibility to write this data to the distribution media in a place where it can load it again later. The mesh will also write out the MaterialDescriptor that it used to find the Material.

Note that the same mesh data (FatVertices and indices) may be fed to almost any Material's Export() method. If data is provided that is not used by the Material's rendering style, it is either ignored or incorporated in some sensible manner to try to approximate the desired effect. For example, feeding a shininess map to a Material that only renders using vertex specular will probably make it look at the map, take the average shininess value, and use that as its overall shininess. Alternatively, if the Material uses a per-vertex shininess value, it may sample the shininess map at each of the mesh vertices. If there are two possible ways to process the data from input format to rendering format, the mesh can choose which to use by sending a standard set of flags to the Export() function.

If data is missing that the Material would normally require, it must be able to cope and generate default "NULL" data. For example, if a Material renders with a diffuse texture but is passed mesh data with no texture, it needs to generate a small pure white texture to use so that the same visual effect is seen on-screen. This is inefficient and should normally be flagged as a bad thing; ideally the mesh should have selected a different Material by specifying in the MaterialDescriptor that it did not have a diffuse texture. However, this should not be a fatal error, and the code should be able to cope and use sensible defaults. These cases do happen because, as can be seen later, Material::FindOrCreate() does not necessarily return the Material that was asked for.

Material::Render()

When the mesh is loaded while the game is running (for example, when loading a level that the mesh is in), it loads the MaterialDescriptor that it saves, calls Material::FindOrCreate(), and stores the Material* it gets back. It can then throw the bulky MaterialDescriptor away, since it doesn't need it any more — it has a pointer to the Material singleton instead. The mesh also loads the big chunk of data returned by Export(). It still doesn't know what is in this data, but it *does* know that if it passes the data to Material::Render() along with its current orientation, the mesh will appear on the screen.

The Render() call knows what format the data is in because this is the same Material class that created the data during the Export() call, so it can use the data directly to render the mesh on-screen in the most efficient way possible.

Scalability

Each Material instance has exactly one rendering style with one quality level on one target platform. A Material that renders on a PS2 will not render on an Xbox, and vice versa, although there may be two Materials that render using the same techniques and produce the same pixel output. Making the target platform (again, counting different classes of PC cards as different platforms) part of the MaterialDescriptor allows the export phase to be explicit about which targets it is exporting to. It can create two otherwise identical Materials, one for each platform, and call Material::Export() on both with the same mesh data. They can then do completely different things to transform the data into native formats for the target hardware, such as stripping, batching, and data format conversion.

Note that although the export phase can call Material::Export() on Materials that are destined for PS2 and Xbox, it cannot normally call the Material::Render() method on these Materials because that will only work on the target platform itself. One possible exception is that on a PC compile, these Materials may render some sort of emulation of the target hardware. This allows artists to preview how their data will look on various platforms without needing a full export cycle each time or needing a console development station at every desk. However, in the case of consoles, it is extremely hard to get the outputs looking identical, since one is on a high-resolution monitor and one is usually outputting to a television.

Each Material knows how to downgrade itself in quality, with the assumption that this method will be quicker to render. If one of the targets is the PC, Materials will also know how to downgrade themselves to require less sophisticated hardware — for example, to use a lower pixel or vertex shader version number, or to drop back to the TextureStageState pipe or the fixed-function texture and lighting pipeline. These are exposed by the methods Material::FindQuicker() and Material::FindSimpler() that both either return a different Material (via an internal call to FindOrCreate) or return NULL if there is no quicker or simpler way to render the data.

At export time, a mesh will call Material::FindOrCreate() with its desired MaterialDescription. This will find the highest-quality Material available, which should render the mesh with all its data on-screen. The mesh calls Export() and saves the data produced. It then keeps calling FindQuicker() and/or FindSimpler() and exporting more data each step of the way for each of the Materials until one or both return NULL for the quicker/simpler versions of the Material.

At run time, the same process is carried out to load the different versions of the mesh but this time calling Import() on each Material. FindOrCreate() finds the highest-detail Material, the mesh calls Import() on that, and then goes down the chain of Materials returned by successive FindQuicker() calls, importing each in turn.

Note that on the PC target there is no need to call FindSimpler() at run time. The initial FindOrCreate() call will have returned a Material that is valid for the current hardware capabilities. Once the highest-detail Material is returned, it guarantees that any FindQuicker() results will also be valid on the same platform. A FindQuicker() call should never return a Material that uses more hardware resources than the current Material. In some cases, especially when dealing with the legacy DX7 TextureStageState and fixed-function pipeline interfaces, this can get fairly tricky; in practice, what usually ends up happening is that there is a generic, single-texture LoD chain of Materials, a generic dual-texture chain, and also several chains specifically targeted at certain common chipsets. If the chipset detected is not one of those specifically supported, then the generic single- or dual-texture chain is used as appropriate. In theory there are various capability bits that can be checked for bits of functionality, but because of driver bugs, in practice it is safest to simply identify the card directly. If identification fails, use a generic "safe" feature set that seems to work on all known cards. Achieving good DX7 compatibility is a huge topic and outside the scope of this article, but using this Material system keeps the implementation relatively simple and easy to modify.

In some cases, the fact that each Material performs its own export call can produce duplicate data. For example, a Material that handles three vertex lights can degrade to a Material that only handles one vertex light, and the mesh data stored by each is usually the same — it is only the vertex shader that changes. To avoid this, when Material::Export() is called, it exports the data to a memory buffer rather than a file and compares the contents against all other previously exported mesh buffers. If it finds a match, it uses the existing file rather than duplicating the data. Using a suitable hash function such as a CRC keeps this comparison fast. The export is performed multiple times, but the extra time taken is not usually much, and this method removes any dependencies between the different Export() calls for different Materials — all it checks is whether their final output data is identical or not. This keeps maintenance problems to a minimum and maintains flexibility.

A further quality improvement is if each Material not only knows which other Material is a version of itself that is quicker to render but also knows how to smoothly downgrade itself visually to match that Material. For example, a Material that renders a diffuse and detail texture will fade the detail texture to nothing, and it then visually matches the simpler Material without a detail texture. This is done by adding an argument to the Material::Render() method that controls the Level of Detail (LoD). A value of 1.0 renders the Material with full detail. An LoD value of 0.0 renders the Material with reduced detail, making it visually identical to calling Material::FindQuicker()->Render() with an LoD version of 1.0. This allows the mesh to gradually degrade the current Material that it is using until it can then swap to using the quicker Material but avoiding any sudden pop. These sudden pops attract the eye of the player and are very distracting, whereas a smooth change is far harder to notice.

For continuous worlds that do not have any discrete boundaries, such as landscapes, each mesh (where a "mesh" is a section of landscape) cannot be given a single LoD value; otherwise, seams will appear between parts of the landscape. In this case, the LoD value will be calculated by the Material independently at each vertex. However, the calling program can still calculate the highest possible LoD for each mesh and call the appropriate Material for that LoD. This does complicate the system, but in practice continuous landscape engines are highly specialized anyway — these Materials are likely to always be used through a different set of interfaces designed specifically for landscape rendering.

In some cases, there may be Materials that do not do a transition themselves but link to a Material that can. This allows rendering to usually use Materials that do not transition (and therefore may execute faster), but when going from one to the other, it goes via a Material that can transition but executes slightly slower. The idea is that few things in the scene are using the transitional Materials at any one time, so performance is retained but without the visually objectionable popping of a sudden change. In practice, this is rarely necessary, as most effects (detail maps, bump maps) can be faded out with little speed impact.

Data-Hiding and Maintenance

Because almost all Material classes, whatever their descriptor, can be fed the same mesh data at export time and use the same external interfaces, it is easy to keep them isolated from each other. This means that the most common rendering cases can be separated out into their own separate Material and minutely optimized without breaking all the other Materials. All the less-common shader effects or combinations can be done by far more general Materials that may handle a lot of the cases by rendering more complex shaders and inserting dummy black or white colors or textures or constant factors of 0 or 1. Additionally, quite late in the project more Materials can be added that optimize the commonly used cases without changing any other Materials. This allows optimization to be done right up to the last moment without the fear of having broken some obscure combination of shader features, since that combination will still use well-tested general-purpose Materials.

This idea of starting with general cases that work everywhere (although perhaps not optimally) and specializing as the project goes on and the common requirements are better understood is a powerful one. It allows the engine to support a huge range of features without committing programmer time to optimizing every possible combination of supported features and without producing exponentially uglier code as the number of special cases increases.

Implementation Details

In practice, life is a little more complex. In addition to a Material::Export() method, there is usually a Material::Import() method that actually takes the large chunk of data. This method will create things like D3D vertex and index buffers, fill them with the data from the large chunk of data, then store the buffer pointers in a smaller chunk of data, which it will then hand back to the mesh. The large chunk of data can now be freed. It is this smaller chunk of data that the mesh passes to the Material::Render() method.

Along with the Material::Import() method, there is a Material::DeleteImportedData() method that is used to clean up the mesh data (for example, when loading a different level where this mesh is not used). This takes this same chunk of data as passed to Material::Render(), releases the vertex and index buffers, and frees the remaining memory.

Material::Export() also takes a number of miscellaneous mesh properties, such as overall shininess, overall diffuse color, bump map bumpiness factor, etc. These are frequently passed in either as an array of floats or Vec4s — the array is always a standard size, and data is in a standard offset within that array — or as a structure or class[5]. Again, this data is of a standard format across all Materials and can be passed to any Material::Export() call, and it will be interpreted correctly. The values that are used by the Material will also be stored in the big chunk of data that Material::Export() returns.

When created, Materials will bolt together and compile any shaders or render state blocks that they need. In our engine, this step has been separated out into a "validation" stage — the theory being that you can hang onto a shader and use Material::Validate (create shaders) and Material::Invalidate (free shaders) at will. This just lets us do some more memory management without worrying about reference counting and other annoying bookkeeping, but it is purely a style thing.

---

5   Although a structure or class is more sophisticated and makes for more readable code, in practice we use an array of Vec4s, since it can be indexed with a number rather than a name.

Dynamic Materials

A dynamic Material is essentially the same as a static Material except that its mesh data changes at run time. These are used for rendering items such as heads-up displays, scores, text fonts, particle systems, diagrammatic items like arrows and aiming reticles, incidental effects such as tracer trails, and decal effects such as bullet holes and footprints.

It is worth noting that the difference between static and dynamic Materials is fairly subtle on platforms such as the GameCube and PCs without hardware transform and lighting or animation capability. In these cases, the CPU performs the role of a GPU vertex unit and changes mesh data at run time. The distinction is whether the data is generated by relatively higher-level shared code (either cross-platform or cross-Material), as in the case of font and particle drawing, or if the routines are low level and specific to the Material, which is the case for animation and lighting. Essentially, a dynamic Material exposes its mesh format outside the Material, while a static Material does not.

To allow this, these meshes have a second Material::Render() method that takes pointers to various mesh structures — vertices and indices and so on. This interface can simply take the same arguments as the Material::Export() call, but using a wide format such as a FatVertex is usually inefficient. The usual way to deal with this is to have part of the MaterialDescriptor define the input data format. For static Materials, this entry is left as "none," but for dynamic Materials, this is explicitly and precisely defined.

Some Materials may have a common input format that can be driven by the same code on all target platforms, with a small bit of run-time manipulation to get it into a format usable by the hardware. A common example is the status display — it usually consists of a small number of elements with simple render techniques and is identical across all platforms. To keep code simple, a common format can be used, meaning that code written on one platform automatically works on the others.

Other cases may have very target-specific formats and be used only in code used on that platform; a common example is the particle system code, which although dynamic needs to be very fast. The common code for particle systems is usually at quite a high level to take advantage of hardware and CPU quirks, and the actual use of the Material::Render() method is buried deep in platform-specific code.

Textures

So far, the discussion of Materials has avoided textures in detail. One way to integrate them is to treat them like any other mesh data. They are fed in some standard form (for example, a linear 32-bit ARGB array) to Material::Export(), and the export code manipulates and combines the data to produce a given number of hardware textures in various formats. For example, a diffuse texture and an opacity texture (a grayscale map where white=opaque and black=transparent) would be fed in, and in most cases the Material would combine them into a single ARGB texture with the opacity map in the alpha channel. This texture then gets put into the big chunk of data returned by Material::Export(), and at run time the actual textures are created.

In practice this is not sensible. A lot of source textures are shared between many different meshes (for example, tarmac road textures, brickwork, tree and bush leaves, and so on), and this naïve export method removes the ability to share the hardware versions of the textures because each Material is by design isolated from other Materials. Removing the sharing uses a lot of memory and slows everything down.

One way to do this is to keep the texture export process separate from Materials. So if the artist uses the same image in two places, the same hardware texture is used, and both Material renderers must be able to use that hardware texture.

For simple Materials, this can work. But for more complex shaders, it is useless. A good example is with bump mapping. Typically, artists will provide a diffuse (unlit) texture and a grayscale heightfield bump map. There are three different styles of rendering.

The simplest is no bump map. The bump map is prelit at export time from some "standard" lighting direction (usually above the object), and this lighting is combined with the unlit diffuse texture to produce a single prelit diffuse texture.

The next method is emboss bump mapping. In the most common implementation, the bump map height is put in the alpha channel of a texture, and the unlit diffuse texture is placed in the RGB channels.

The third method is normal-map bump mapping. In this, the bump map heightfield is processed to find the gradients of the heightfield, and those are used to produce a normal map — a map of vectors where the XYZ of each normal is held in the RGB channels of a texture. The unlit diffuse texture is put into a second texture's RGB channels. The alpha channels of both maps are unused.

These three methods all require the source textures to be processed in some way, and two of them require that the two source images be combined so that, for example, using the same bump map with a different diffuse texture would require a different hardware texture.

To solve these conflicting requirements — wanting the Material to decide how to process its textures and yet letting textures be shared between otherwise unrelated Materials — Mucky Foot uses a class called a TextureSource. This class only exists in the exporter side of things, not on the target platforms, and each TextureSource describes a hardware texture. It does this not by storing pixels directly but by storing the processing steps that a Material has applied to a number of source images (TGAs, JPGs, etc.) to obtain the final hardware texture. All TextureSources share a common base class:

```
class TextureSource
{
private:
    TextureSource();
    virtual ~TextureSource();
```

```
public:
    virtual const Image *GenerateImage ( void ) = 0;
    virtual String GenerateName ( void ) = 0;
};
```

Some TextureSources directly describe images stored on disk:

```
class TextureSourceTGA : public TextureSource
{
public:
    TextureSourceTGA ( String sFilename );
};
```

Others describe an image in terms of an operation on other images:

```
class TextureSourceNormalMap : public TextureSource
{
private:
    TextureSource *ptsSource;
public:
    TextureSourceNormalMap ( TextureSource *ptsSource );
};


class TextureSourceAlphaColourCombine : public TextureSource
{
private:
    TextureSource *ptsAlphaSource, *ptsColourSource;
public:
    TextureSourceAlphaColourCombine (TextureSource *ptsAlphaSource,
                                     TextureSource *ptsColourSource );
};
```

These classes are created like so:

```
TextureSource *ptsBumpmap = new TextureSourceTGA ( "bumpy.tga" );
TextureSource *ptsDiffuse = new TextureSourceTGA ( "colours.tga" );
TextureSource *ptsNormal = new TextureSourceNormalMap ( ptsBumpmap );
TextureSource *ptsEmboss = new TextureSourceAlphaColourCombine (ptsBumpmap, ptsDiffuse );
```

TextureSources may be chained together indefinitely, sometimes producing chains like this:

```
TextureSource *ptsNormal = new TextureSourceNormalMap (
        new TextureSourceChangeContrast ( 2.0f,
        new TextureSourceInvert (
        new TextureSourceToGrayscale (
        new TextureSourceTGA ( "brick.tga" ) ) ) ) );
```

The TextureSource::GenerateImage() method returns an image (which is just a raw 32-bit ARGB linear format with a width and height) that is the actual result of the TextureSource. This image is cached so that GenerateImage can be called multiple times without redoing all the image generation work, which is why the result is a const Image*. For the TextureSourceTGA class, GenerateImage simply loads the TGA off disk and writes the data into its cached Image. For the

TextureSourceNormalMap class, GenerateImage() first calls ptsSource->GenerateImage() and processes the returned Image as a heightfield to create its own Image — a normal map. Similarly, TextureSourceAlphaColourCombine calls ptsAlphaSource->GenerateImage() and ptsColourSource->GenerateImage(), takes the alpha channel from the first and the color channels from the second, and combines them into its own ARGB Image, which it returns.

So using these, the Material::Export() call is passed in a set of TextureSources — almost always just TextureSourceTGA classes referring to raw texture artwork used on the mesh. The Material then processes these as it wants by creating new TextureSources, using the passed-in TextureSources as arguments to the constructors. These new processed TextureSources are then returned in a list by Material::Export() to tell the mesh what texture data the Material::Render() call is going to require. The exact number of TextureSources returned is up to the Material::Export() call, and the order they are returned in must match the order in which they are passed to the Material::Render() call.

Each of the TextureSources returned by Material::Export() then gets the GenerateImage() method called on them, and the resulting Image is processed into a hardware texture format and exported to the final target platform. As with the large contiguous chunk of data returned by Material::Export(), the main engine code does not know or care what data is inside those TextureSources.

Except in one respect. The main engine would like to know if that same data is used by any other meshes, so it can generate and load only one texture and pass it to all the meshes that need it. The way we do this is by calling TextureSource::GenerateName(), which returns a text string that describes the chain of TextureSource calls, usually something like "NormMap(Contrast(2.0,Invert(Grey (TGA("brick.tga"))))))." The strings for every exported texture in the world are kept; if two strings match, the outputs must be the same, and only one texture is created. Another way to do this would be to hash the contents and formats of hardware textures and compare the hashes. If the hashes match, a closer check is made on the individual texels; if they match, then the two can be merged into a single texture. This involves a lot more data checking and is slower but more aggressive. For example, "NormMap(Contrast(2.0,Grey(Invert(TGA("brick. tga")))))" describes exactly the same data, but it is a different string. It may be worth doing this aggressive check every now and again.

Note that this addresses the same problem as multiple Materials producing identical mesh data, but from the other end. The reasons for this are pragmatic — there is a lot more reuse of texture data than there is of mesh data; the operations performed on texture data are more tightly defined and shared by many Materials; and the time taken to produce texture images is far longer than for mesh data, so an early duplication check is far more important.

So two calls have changed now that textures have been added.

```
virtual void *Material::Export ( size_t &SizeOfDataInBytes,
        std::list<TextureSource*> &lptsOutputTextures,
        TextureSource *ptsInputTextures[],
        const FatVertex *pVertices,
        const u32 *pIndices,
```

```
         int iNumVerts, int iNumTris ) = 0;
virtual void Material::Render ( const void *pExportedData,
         Texture *ptexTextures[],
         const Matrix43 &orientation ) = 0;
```

Note that the array ptsInputTextures[] is always a fixed size, and the indexes are defined using a global enum or similar so that, for example, ptsInputTextures[0] is always the diffuse texture (if any exists), while ptsInputTextures[5] is always the bump map texture (if any exists).

However, the same is not true of ptexTextures[]; this array has the same number of elements as the returned list lptsOutputTextures, and the two have a one-to-one correlation (each TextureSource gets GenerateImage() called to get its Image, which is then turned into a platform-specific hardware Texture). Note that the Material::Render() call does not need to know how large ptexTextures[] is — it already knows because of the sort of Material it is.

Animation

When rendering an animated mesh, the animated skeleton is passed as yet another argument to the Material::Render() call in a standard form, and the Material deals with all the details of rendering with that set of bones. Similar processing can be performed by Material::Export() on the skeleton of the mesh, but it is usually not necessary and simplifies the code if there is a single shared format for skeleton and animation data.

Whether a mesh is animated or not is also a flag in the MaterialDescriptor, since animated meshes require a different sort of vertex processing and lighting pipeline to non-animated meshes.

Lighting

Lighting for a mesh must usually be generated at run time (with the exception of radiosity-style lightmaps). This causes problems because as the mesh moves around or the environment changes with gameplay, different numbers and types of lighting (spot, directional, etc.) will affect the mesh. One solution is for each Material to always use a fixed number of lights of each type. For example, a certain Material will always use two directional lights —no more and no less. This is acceptable for some situations, but if there are infrequent cases where more lights would give a better result, it would be useful to spend a small amount of time to do this. In the case where there is only one light affecting an object, it is a waste of performance to always use two (and set the second light to black, for example).

One solution is for each mesh to create an array of Materials that are all the same, except each is capable of doing a different number of lights and/or combination of lights. However, this rapidly produces a huge number of combinations (e.g., up to four lights of three types requires an array of 256 materials[6]). Although many of these may reference the same material, a pointer to the material and the chunk of data it requires has added 4 KB to every mesh and a potentially massive amount of exported mesh data. The other disadvantage is that the mesh has no knowledge of whether certain combinations are easy to reduce to simpler cases because it does not know anything about the specific platform capabilities.

A good example case is when using a relatively complex function, such as Spherical Harmonics[7] (SH), to perform vertex lighting but standard dot3 to do per-pixel lighting. This case assumes all lights are directional for ease of illustration. Typically only zero, one, or two lights shining on an object will have dot3 lighting (usually the brightest), and the others will be done using SH.

For a mesh without a bump map or on a platform with no bump map support, there is no per-pixel lighting at all, so all lights are encoded in the SH lighting, and the same Material can be used for any number of lights.

If the mesh has a bump map, it will use a different Material. On DX7-class hardware, the Material will want to apply the single brightest light as a bump-mapped light and encode the rest into SH. So there are two cases — no lights (or only ambient lights) and one or more lights.

On DX8-class hardware with pixel shaders, it is cheap and effective to bump map two lights. So now there are three cases — zero, one, or two bump-mapped lights. Additionally, there may be a threshold where turning off the second bump-mapped light gives a speed increase at very little loss of quality, and this threshold will be controlled by some combination of light brightness and mesh Level of Detail. The point is that this judgment is very specific to the rendering method used.

The mesh itself doesn't really want to have to deal with this sort of complexity every frame to decide which Material to use. It may end up doing a lot of work, only to have the particular Material not use the results at all (in the above case of hardware with no bump map support). The solution we found was to allow the Material itself to look at the lighting context and make judgment calls internally. This may mean switching vertex or pixel processing pipelines according to the number and type of lights, but that fits within what Materials are allowed to do. The mesh sets up the lighting system with pertinent instance-specific information, such as its position, size, and current animation state, and then it is the Material that asks how many and what sort of lights are affecting the mesh. It then uses that information to decide which shaders to use, puts the light data into the correct shader constants, and renders the mesh.

Another advantage is that optimizing lighting selection code in a single Material affects all meshes that use that Material; there is no need to change mesh code in multiple places to take advantage of this. This means the routines used can be extremely specific to that single Material. This is important if it is a frequently used Material — hand-tuning that one case may give useful speed or quality increases. Again, these improvements can be made late in the project, and

---

6   Counting a disabled light as a fourth "type," and without wasting CPU effort for each mesh at run time to reorder the incident lights, this requires 4*4*4 = 256 combinations.

7   SH lighting is roughly equivalent to sampling a low-res cubic environment map but done in the vertex shader and using cunning math rather than textures. Many more details can be found by Googling for "Spherical Harmonic Irradiance," but the important point here is that it captures the environment lighting well, and is the same cost no matter how many lights are in that environment.

since the changes are localized, the chance of adding unnoticed bugs in obscure cases is reduced.

Batching and Sorting

It has always been the case that some type of sorting of draw order is beneficial. The obvious example is sorting all alpha-blended objects, so they are drawn after all opaque objects, and then drawing them from back to front. Also helpful is sorting opaque objects by texture and/or shader. As shaders (both pixel and vertex) become larger, the benefit from this sorting grows. Also helpful is to sort opaque objects in a very rough front-to-back order, since this allows the Z-buffer to reject as many pixels as possible without shading them or writing them to the frame buffer.

Another sorting order is needed when using various forms of shadow buffer or reflection rendering. To reduce the amount of video memory needed, the usual method is to use only one or two render target textures, render the required information (shadow or reflection) to them, then render all the materials that use these, and repeat with the next shadow or reflection until the scene is complete. This requires the rendering to be sorted by which render target it uses. On lower-end hardware or in the distance, this type of rendering cannot be done, and a generic prerendered environment map or "blob shadow" texture will be used instead. No special sorting is required here; indeed, this type of sorting can slow down the rendering unnecessarily.

These examples illustrate that the criteria for sorting the drawing order of objects is yet again determined directly by the Material and not by the object itself. The way to do this is to change the relevant Material::Render() method so that it just wraps up the inputs to the call (textures, orientation, etc.) into a convenient data structure and adds it to a list. At the end of this phase, the lists are sorted according to the requirements of the Material(s) and replayed in order — this time actually rendering the data to the screen. Although this storage and traversal of lists takes CPU cycles and memory bandwidth, it is usually a savings overall because the expensive states of the graphics pipeline (texture, shader, etc.) are changed less often than when drawn in an arbitrary order.

Where this batching and sorting turns out not to be a savings in practice, it is easy to leave those Material::Render() methods doing actual immediate rendering. This is usually only true for a few special cases, such as rendering fonts and particle systems, both of which are typically batched well at a higher level.

Conclusion

Abstracting shaders and referencing them by desired rendering style rather than by actual rendering style allows excellent scalability for multiple platforms and multiple PC graphics cards without authoring multiple versions of artwork or sacrificing quality on the high end or speed and compatibility on the low end.

Using encapsulation or data hiding allows the implementation of individual Materials to be hidden from the rest of the engine and from each other, increasing code robustness and adaptability and allowing programmers to focus their optimization efforts on only the most common cases.

While the changes to a traditional game engine are major, once made, the system is robust, understandable, and flexible, again using the principles of data hiding and letting each Material decide what its inputs are going to be and what rendering schemes it will use, rather than forcing everything into the same system.

Post-Process Fun with Effects Buffers

Tom Forsyth
Mucky Foot Productions

Previous Work

Hardware is now becoming powerful enough that framebuffer post-processing effects can supplement pure polygon rendering. These effects treat the world not as geometric shapes but as an image to manipulate.

The most common current example is depth of field blur. Examples include samples from many graphics card manufacturers and the "Depth Of Field" DirectX 9 sample[1] and in games such as Splinter Cell[2] and others. The framebuffer is successively blurred to another surface[3], then parts of that blurred version are blended back onto the framebuffer to simulate parts that are out of focus.

Another common example is heat haze or distortion, as in Jak and Daxter[4] or Metroid Prime[5]. Here, rendered objects do not directly change the color of the framebuffer; they move pixels in the framebuffer around — either by only a few pixels to cause a heat-haze effect or by large amounts of the screen to give a "raindrops on glass" effect.

Overview

The idea behind this article is to generalize many of these effects into a unified framework where multiple effects can be added, tried out, and combined at run time without replicating shared code and keeping optimal speed and memory use when only a few of the effects are visible.

Multiple back buffers are created, all of which are texture render targets. The "main" buffer is the size of the screen and has the standard RGB scene rendered to it. The other buffers are called *effects buffers*. Various objects and particle systems render to them instead of (or in addition to) rendering to the main buffer.

---

1   DepthOfField sample demo, DirectX9 SDK, available from http://msdn.microsoft.com/directx

2   Tom Clancy's Splinter Cell by Ubisoft — full of frame post-processing features, notably the Xbox version (http://www.splintercell.com/)

3   In practice many implementations blur the image inside the pixel shader and use the result immediately, rather than rendering the blurred version to a separate surface, but the principle is the same.

4   Jak and Daxter by Naughty Dog (http://www.naughtydog.com/)

5   Metroid Prime by Retro Studios (http://www.metroidprime.com/)

Once the main scene and the effects buffers are rendered, they are all combined together using various texture-processing passes and rendered to the real back buffer, which is then presented. The values in the effects buffers are not usually colors, but they determine how much of a particular effect is done to the main buffer. For example, a high value in the "blur" effects buffer makes the main buffer very blurry at that pixel, while a low value leaves it sharp and unfiltered.

The Z-buffer is shared between all buffers. Usually, to make sure effects are occluded properly, the main buffer scene is rendered with standard Z-buffer settings, and then the effects buffers are rendered to with Z-tests turned on but Z-writes turned off. This ensures that the effects are properly occluded by solid objects so that effects such as a heat-haze hidden behind a solid wall do not affect the wall itself. Not writing to the Z-buffer means that effects do not sort perfectly between themselves, but in practice most effects renders use additive blending, which is commutative, or the incorrect sorting is hard to see, or the objects can be rendered in back-to-front order to fix the problem.

Rendering Structure

Traditional rendering engines go through each object in the list of objects in the world and compare them against the viewing frustum. If they are visible, they are rendered immediately.

This system is rather different because the effects buffers must be rendered after the main buffer so that they respect the Z-buffer information, and preferably all the objects for a single effect should be rendered together to reduce the number of render target and state changes.

To do this, each effect has a list of objects (meshes, particle systems, etc.) that produce or influence that effect. The lists are cleared at the start of each frame. The order of operations then becomes:

- Search the list of objects in the world for those visible.
- For each visible object, for each effect it uses, add it to that effect's list.
- Optionally sort each effect's list.
- For each effect, change to its rendering buffer and render all the objects in its list.
- Finally, combine all rendering buffers together to make the final image.

Of course, some sort of hierarchy or volume-query device is used for efficiency instead of checking every object in the world against the frustum. Many engines already have a lot of this structure in place for other reasons, but the use of effects buffers makes it even more integral to the rendering process.

Note that each object can contribute to multiple effects channels. For example, a flame particle system is partially rendered to the main buffer as visible flames but also rendered to both the blur and distortion buffers to get the heat-haze effect. For this reason, when an object adds itself to an effect's list, it uses some form of ID or a unique callback address, so when it is later called for rendering, it knows which effect style to render.

Dynamic Allocation

Conceptually, each effect has an independent buffer to which it renders. This buffer may be anywhere from one to four channels in size. For example, a single-channel effect, such as blur, could be allocated a render target with an A8 or L8 format. However, in practice all render targets are 32-bit ARGB buffers, and the four channels are shared out dynamically between any effects passes that are currently active (active means that there is something on-screen that produces this effect).

Allocating dynamically allows the minimum number of render targets to be used so that if no objects of a particular effect type are in the visible frustum, no rendering is performed for them and the number of buffers used can be reduced. This does complicate the writing of shaders to some extent, but the advantage is that multiple effects may be scattered around the environment at whim (or even subject to the player's actions — moving objects about and so on) with near-optimal rendering speed at all times.

To partially simplify matters, effects that require more than a single channel are always allocated the same color channels — usually RG, RGB, or ARGB, according to their design. These are allocated first. After this initial phase, any single-channel effects are allocated from the remaining free channels of the render targets. It is usually relatively simple to allow single-channel effects to change channels at run time using write masks and swizzling. Where exceptions exist, they can be restricted to certain channels during allocation, though it may lead to inefficient use of memory. Because there are typically many more single-channel effects than multi-channel effects, this order of allocation works well.

As mentioned, render targets could be allocated one-per-effect of the correct size. However, support for these buffer types is more limited, especially as render targets. Since the target is frequently PS 1.1-style hardware, the number of independent texture reads for the final combining pass is limited and has an effect on speed. Using only two texture reads instead of three or four, even if the number of bytes read is the same, usually has speed benefits from better texture cache use and allowing more parallelism. In addition, the SetRenderTarget call in DirectX is notoriously slow on some graphics cards (though slowly improving over time), and reducing the number of these calls is a big speed boost. Changing the write mask (D3DRS_COLORWRITEENABLE) is usually much faster than changing the render target.

One case where the allocation scheme needs to be modified slightly is feedback effects in channels. If the channel is not cleared between frames, dynamic allocation needs to be modified so that the same channel and target are used each time. This is easily done in code, though it can lead to inefficient allocation in some cases. If the feedback has a maximum number of frames that it will persist for before fading away, the channel can be turned off that many frames after the last object that is using that effect has moved out of the frustum.

Alpha-blended Objects

Traditionally, all solid objects need to be rendered first in rough front-to-back order. Then all alpha-blended objects must be rendered in back-to-front order, usually without writing to the Z-buffer. This partitioning into two phases is sometimes ugly and hacked together. The effect-buffer rendering scheme introduces the concept of multiple passes and channels as a first-class feature, which means it can be used to do this partitioning with a lot more elegance.

The two passes (opaque and alpha-blended) are made into separate "effects," but both allocated the same RGB channel to render to. Since the opaque pass is always rendered before all other effects passes and nearly all effects passes will use alpha-blending and not write to the Z-buffer, this handles the alpha-blended parts of the scene automatically. Additionally, since all objects are added to their respective effect buffer in a list before any are rendered, it is simple to insert a sorting phase on each effect's list. This can sort strictly back-to-front for the alpha-blended pass and other effects passes that require strict sorting and in whatever order is optimal for the opaque part — sorted by shader and texture, then rough front-to-back order, and so on.

Note that many objects render in both passes. The opaque parts of the object are rendered in the first pass using a high alpha-test value and alpha-blending disabled and the translucent parts rendered in the second pass using a low alpha-test value and alpha-blending enabled. This also reduces the need to self-sort complex self-intersecting objects, such as trees and bushes, which can normally be very costly in CPU cycles.

Different Sizes of Effects Buffers

One possible option is to use an effects buffer smaller than the standard back buffer in order to save fillrate and memory use. For many effects, this reduced resolution is sufficient; effects such as distortion and blur work perfectly well when halved in resolution in each direction, and in some cases the softer edges may be a desired effect. However, this does mean the effects buffer cannot simply share the existing Z-buffer. Two possibilities exist, depending on platform capabilities or application requirements.

First, the main buffer is rendered to a full-sized buffer to set up the Z-buffer. Then a shrink-blit is done from the Z-buffer to the smaller-sized Z-buffer used by the effect rendering. This shrink does not necessarily have to filter correctly (or at all), so frequently the hardware can be spoofed into performing this shrink-blit by pretending the contents are simply pixel or texel data and disabling filtering. This smaller Z-buffer is then used when rendering effects to reject pixels hidden by solid parts of the scene. Although this shrink-blit is not reliably or efficiently possible on PC cards, this method works well on most consoles.

Alternatively, the effect buffers can ignore the standard Z-buffer but set aside one of the channels where any rendering always writes depth into (8 bits is usually sufficient for this purpose). When doing the post-process pass to combine the main buffer and the effects buffers, this 8-bit channel is used to reject effect texels further away than the main buffer's Z value. For example, under DirectX this would be done using the texm3x2depth (PS 1.3) or texdepth (PS 1.4) instructions or by writing to the oDepth register (PS 2.0+). However, this has the problem that only one depth value can be stored, so a distant effect (behind a solid object) that is covered by a close effect (in front of the solid object) will still be rendered. These artifacts may be few or subtle enough to be acceptable for the reduction in fillrate.

Multiple Render Targets

DX9 exposes the concept of multiple render targets. Up to four render targets can be written to by a single draw call. This potentially removes the need to render objects multiple times, once for each effect. However, the savings are only useful in some situations.

First, most objects are only rendered to one of the buffers. Very few render the same triangles to multiple buffers, and where they do (for example, the displacement and blur values are frequently used together), it is easy to ensure that these channels are placed in the same buffer (RG and alpha channels in this case) and both rendered at once.

Using MRTs is also dogged by implementation problems. First, all render targets must be updated; the "texkill" instruction affects them all or none of them. The channel write masks are always respected, but if two effects need to use pixel-by-pixel kills on different pixels, they cannot be rendered in the same pass. Second, alpha-blending with MRTs is not well supported by hardware, which makes many effects impossible because most require additive blending. PS 3.0 requires that alpha-blending work on all render target formats and when using MRT, but in PS 2.0, this capability is modified by caps bits and is often missing.

On the other hand, some hardware prefers that four texture targets are bound as different outputs, and then the color write masks are used to completely turn some of those targets off for different renders. The alternative is multiple SetRenderTarget calls, which can be slow, especially if the Z-buffer needs to be shared between all the renders. At the time of publication, there is little or no hardware to test on to compare relative speeds of the various techniques, but it is worth noting the possibilities for the future.

Auto-gen Mipmapping

Many graphics cards can automatically calculate mipmaps of render target textures with very little speed impact. This is much easier than generating mipmap levels manually by successive render target changes and shrinking. Although this is all that most drivers are actually doing internally for auto-gen mipmapping, they can take advantage of any hardware quirks and the reduced API call overhead. In some cases, there is specialized hardware that performs the mipmapping operation, making it virtually free.

Because of this, it is worth looking at using this facility when performing blur processing. While simply using the lower mipmap levels raw can produce obvious and objectionable bilinear filtering artifacts, combining them with samples from larger mipmap levels can remove these artifacts while using fewer passes and/or samples than the more conventional single-layer filter kernels.

Specific Effects

A few common examples are given here as an illustration, and most are shown in action in the demo. However, the number of effects is huge, particularly odd game-specific ones such as magical, supernatural, or alien.

Saturation and Desaturation

One effect channel can control the amount of saturation a pixel receives. Complete desaturation is otherwise known as converting to grayscale, and it is easy to create in a pixel shader by doing a dot-product between the main buffer color and a "grayscale vector," which is usually something like (0.299, 0.587, 0.114)[6]. When the result of the dot-product is replicated to the RGB channels, this represents the fully unsaturated color. Simply interpolating between this and the main buffer color allows gradual desaturation of the color. It is the interpolation factor used that is stored in the effect buffer. Interpolating *away* from this grayscale produces a more saturated color with more vibrant colors. Note that in PS 1.x, the interpolant of the "lerp" instruction can be clamped to the range [0-1] before use[7]. Therefore, if interpolations outside this range are used, it is better to explicitly use a subtract instruction followed by a multiply-add to do the interpolation.

Any linear color transformation can be performed using the same technique — again, both toward and away from the post-transform result as desired. This can be used to perform "film grading" of images, and using an effect buffer to control it allows selected areas to be graded differently. For example, the lighting on a character's face may be accentuated, while the lighting on the background is muted to concentrate attention. Desaturation can portray illness or death without having to directly change the rendering style or the textures used. There are obvious applications for magical effects using particle systems that "suck the life" out of the surroundings. Subtle effects like these were used extensively in the *Lord of the Rings: The Fellowship of the Ring*[8].

Blur and Depth of Field

As a single channel effect, this holds a value going from 0 (no blur) to 1 (a heavy blur). Two classes of the effect can render into this buffer.

---

6   This vector is the Y vector of the RGB to the YIQ conversion matrix. Depending on whether you are working in gamma-corrected or linear space, these values may change slightly.

7   Not in all implementations, but in some common ones, so it is worth noting this restriction

8   *Lord of the Rings: The Fellowship of the Ring* — Special Extended DVD Edition, the section titled "Digital Grading"

The first is three-dimensional objects that cause blurring of the image beyond them. Heat haze above hot surfaces and flames produces blur (as well as the separate distortion effect), and these are usually rendered using particle systems that add values into this buffer. Frosted or dirty glass can also render additively into this buffer to blur objects behind them; these are rendered as objects that are the shape of the glass itself.

The second class is the depth-of-field simulation of a camera lens. A particular distance from the camera is chosen as the current focal length, and objects in front of or behind this depth will be blurred the further that they are from the depth. One way to do this is to render the entire opaque scene a second time, writing values corresponding to depth information into this buffer. This is done in many sample applications. The problem is that rendering the scene a second time is expensive in geometry throughput. One way around this is to ensure that this channel is the alpha channel of the main buffer and render both depth and color together. However, this clashes with the fake HDR rendering effect, which would also like to do this, and in many cases, there is a much simpler method available.

Depth is already rendered to the Z-buffer, and it is useful to be able to use this information. Some consoles can read the Z-buffer directly as pixel information, and with cunning scaling or lookup tables, this can be transformed into a depth-blur value. Alternatively, a simple method that works well is to wait until the Z-buffer is set up by the opaque pass and then render fullscreen planes at various distances using Z-testing. Because the depth of field blur is usually fairly subtle, having only eight or 16 different values (and therefore eight or 16 different planes) is enough. For objects further than the depth of focus, planes are rendered using additive blending at successively closer distances and lower blur values using a less-than Z-test but no Z-writes. Each pass sets a bit in the stencil buffer, and pixels are only rendered where the stencil buffer is clear. Using the stencil buffer ensures that each pixel is only shaded once and by the furthest "blur plane" that is still in front of the solid object at that pixel.

Although this requires rendering many fullscreen planes, this does not usually consume huge amounts of fillrate, since more cards have very fast Z-buffer rejection and most of the pixels in these planes will be rejected.

To blur objects closer than the focal depth, the same trick is used but by rendering planes close to the camera, moving away to the focal plane, and using a greater-than Z-test. In this way, the objects closest to the camera have the earlier planes render to the effect buffer and are the most blurred.

The actual blurring can be done in a variety of ways. Some very intricate and high-quality methods are available; see some of the graphics card manufacturer demos for examples on various bits of hardware. However, a common one that works on a wide variety of hardware is to apply a blur filter to the main buffer and then for each pixel blend between the blurred version and the unblurred main buffer according to the value in this buffer.

Fake High Dynamic Range Rendering

Any really shiny or inherently bright objects render a low-contrast version of themselves to this single-channel effect to approximate the "extra brightness" that they have. This extra brightness cannot be seen directly in the framebuffer because of the limited range of an integer framebuffer, but the extra is rendered into this channel.

In the back buffer composition pass, the main buffer is scaled by this effects channel, then blurred, and then added back onto the main buffer. Dark and normal-brightness objects write 0 to this channel, so they will be dark in this blurred version. Bright objects write positive values, and these will be blurred and added back. This simulates the "bloom" that over-bright images produce in both camera lenses and the human eye, and this bloom is very effective at conveying the "extra brightness" that the limited gamut of the monitor and framebuffer cannot directly convey.

For inherently bright objects such as the sun or light sources like fires or lamp bulbs, the value written to the effects buffer is a fixed value, depending on the object's brightness. For very shiny objects, their environment map is rendered as both RGB values and this extra brightness. Shiny objects simply modulate the extra brightness channel by their shininess and write it to the effects channel. This allows sunlight to bloom off shiny objects, such as chrome or car paint.

Note that the main buffer must be modulated by the extra brightness *before* being blurred; a bright object will produce a light bloom that covers a dark area. This is different from the depth of field effect, which usually needs to *avoid* this effect to look good. Additionally, the size of the blur filter for depth of field is usually much smaller than for this bloom effect. Therefore, the two blur passes cannot usually be combined into one.

As well as a general glow effect, the filter used can be all sorts of odd shapes, notably "star" filters, which blur the image in only a few discrete directions. This filter was used to extreme effect in Wreckless[9].

Because so many objects can write to this effect buffer in common scenes (notably anything even slightly shiny), it is common to put this buffer in the alpha channel of the main buffer and combine rendering of the two into a single pass. This can be tricky if the destination alpha channel is used for other rendering effects, but if these effects are used purely for opaque multi-pass texturing tricks, it is still possible, as long as the last pass always writes the extra brightness value to the channel.

Distortion

This effect displaces pixels from the main buffer to the screen with the X and Y screen offsets stored in two channels. This can be used for a heat-haze shimmer effect with particle systems, as seen in Jak and Daxter, or with larger distortions to produce water-droplet-on-glass effects, as seen in Metroid Prime, or with glass objects to simulate refraction of light through them.

---

9   Wreckless, also called DOUBLE S.T.E.A.L. Masaki Kawase's GDC2003 talk on this is available at http://www.daionet.gr.jp/~masa/.

The two effect channels store vertical and horizontal offset data, and in the final combiner, they are usually used as inputs to the "texbem" pixel shader instruction to look up offset data into the main buffer.

There are two problems here. First, texbem in PS 1.1 takes signed values (where 0x00 represents a value of 0.0), rather than the more usual offset values (where 0x80 represents a value of 0.0). Fortunately, PS 1.2 and above allow the _bx2 modifier on texbem that converts offset data to signed data before use, as when it is used with the dot3 instruction.

The other related problem is that when rendering data to the effect buffer, ideally an object should be able to use a blend that either decreases or increases the offset values as necessary so that accumulating offsets would work as expected, especially for multiple heat-haze particle systems. Some sort of additive blend would be ideal, but since the data is offset, a standard additive blend can only ever increase the data, never decrease it. By changing the D3DRS_BLEND-OP operation from D3DBLENDOP_ADD to D3DBLENDOP_SUBTRACT, a render pass can subtract data, but this change cannot be performed every pixel. Ideally, an "add bias" blend would be used, where buffer=buffer+texture–0.5, much like the D3DTOP_ADDSIGNED operation in the TextureStageState pipeline or the pixel-shader equivalent of using the _bias modifier on one of the arguments, but no such alpha-blend exists.

A simple solution that can work well in some cases is to blend between the two values using a SRCALPHA:INVSRCALPHA[10] blend rather than adding them. Although this is dependent on the rendering order of objects (unlike using proper addition) and is not at all correct (except in a few special cases), it can look convincingly good and has the advantage of not requiring multiple passes.

A more correct solution is to render twice — once using D3DBLEND-OP_ADD with a ONE:ONE blend, clamping negative texture values to zero, and once using D3DBLENDOP_REVSUBTRACT, inverting the texture and again clamping negative values to zero. This is the most flexible and accurate but requires two rendering passes of each object. It can also hit saturation problems. Within a single object or particle system, the positive offsets may balance the negative ones to give a net result of no change. However, if the initial value is 0.5 and all the positive offsets are rendered first to give an offset to +0.7, the result can saturate to 1.0, when in fact it should be 1.2. Then the negative ones are rendered and cause an offset of –0.7. Without saturation, this would give the initial value of 0.5, but because of saturation, the actual result is 0.3. This is usually not a very noticeable effect; when distortions of the image become large enough to saturate, they are typically so large that only a general idea of what they are doing is visually perceptible, and the errors caused by saturation are hidden.

Because many objects and special effects render to both the blur and distortion fields, such as heat-haze and frosted glass, these two channels are frequently dynamically assigned so that they are in the same render target and

---

10 I use the convention that an A:B blend means that D3DRS_SRCBLEND=D3DBLEND_A, D3DRS_DESTBLEND= D3DBLEND_B. This convention is now incomplete because it does not include the D3DRS_BLENDOP function, which was added in DX7, but it is nevertheless a useful shorthand, which many understand.

rendered to at the same time. In many cases, it may be worth combining them properly to make a single, three-channel effect. This means that depth of field rendering needs to know about the distortion channels and leave them alone, but this is an easy fix.

Edge Detection

For cartoon-style effects, performing edge detection on various bits of data can produce some very nice images. Edge detection can be performed purely on final framebuffer color information. However, the results are hard to predict in some cases and can pick up strange details and miss others. To be properly effective, edge detection needs to be performed on more user-defined data. The easiest way to provide this data is in a separate effects channel. These values are not necessarily linear values — all that matters is whether two are sufficiently different to produce an edge or similar enough not to. By simply assigning two polygons a "different enough" value, an edge is automatically produced. These values can come from textures, vertex colors, shading, or a combination of all three, which means that cartoon edges do not need to match geometry edges — a common problem with some techniques.

G-buffers

Geometry buffers are an interesting extension of having multiple output buffers. Instead of performing shading while rendering the geometry, the idea is to simply rasterise and Z-reject the raw geometric data and write that to a variety of buffers. Data such as depth (which along with screen position produces a world position), normal, material ID, and surface-local position (otherwise known as texture co-ordinates) are written to the G-buffers, and all texture compositing, lookups, and shading are performed once per screen pixel.

The advantage is that shading is performed once and only once on each screen pixel, allowing much more complex shaders (n) and larger depth complexity (m) but getting $O(n+m)$ cost rather than $O(nm)$ with traditional methods.

While a true G-buffer has many problems, such as dealing with translucency and large amounts of temporary storage, some of the concepts can be useful when designing special effects.

One example of this is the cartoon shader demo produced by ATI[11] that recorded material ID, depth, and normal and from those fields produced some impressive images.

Feedback

Sometimes feedback can be very useful in rendering special effects. It can produce interesting and complex patterns without requiring complex geometry or multiple rendering passes by using frame-to-frame image coherence. Examples

---

11 The "table with cheese and wine" demo from Real-Time 3D Scene Postprocessing presented at GDC 2003 — available from http://www.ati.com/developer/

include smoke, fire, fog, and others. In the game Blade2[12], we used a feedback effect on sprays of blood from sword or gunshot wounds. A simple low-cost particle system was used for the blood droplets, but they were rendered to an off-screen buffer. This buffer was not cleared each frame, just darkened, and while doing so, it was distorted by rendering it as a mesh to itself. The result was then blended over the framebuffer at the end of each frame. The visual effect was that the cheap particle system was given size and persistence and became more like a stream with volume than a group of particles. Producing the same effect purely with geometry every frame would have taken roughly ten times the fillrate and vertex processing.

The crucial thing is that only the blood should be used in feedback, whereas previous effects, such as motion blur, have performed feedback on the entire screen, which has limited application. Also note that the good thing about blood is that it is a single color. We only used a single channel (the destination alpha channel of the framebuffer, which was otherwise unused) for the intensity of the blood; when blending it back to the framebuffer, it was tinted red. At the same time, the intensity was oversaturated so that while the values in the effect buffer faded linearly to zero with time, the visual effect was not linear; it spent a while at full brightness followed by a fairly abrupt fade to nothing. This helped increase the apparent volume of the "stream" of blood. Very tasteful.

The Demo

The demo shows the use of a couple of these effects. The most important thing demonstrated is the dynamic allocation of channels in render targets, with each effect dynamically enabled/disabled according to toggles. In practice, these would be according to what objects are visible in the viewing frustum, and the intent is to minimize the average memory required for render targets and the average fillrate used to render the objects and combine the final image.

The demo also demonstrates the use of the callback system for rendering objects, the simple way that the previously special case of rendering alpha-blended objects last now fits easily into the more general framework, and the way that sorting each effect by different criteria is simple to add.

Conclusion

Many single effects have been previously demonstrated using secondary buffers or the alpha channel of an ARGB render target. A method has been shown for unifying the common features of many of these post-processing effects to apply them together in the same frame, use the minimum amount of run-time memory and fillrate to do so, and apply them selectively only to parts of the frame that require them.

---

12 Blade2 by Mucky Foot, published by Activision on PS2 and Xbox. The technique described here was only implemented on the Xbox version.

Shaders under Control (Codecreatures Engine)

Oliver Hoeller
Piranha Bytes

Introduction

Today, shaders can't be ignored by modern 3D engine design. There are new aspects in the design of a 3D engine that weren't considered in early engine architectures.

I would like to mention some points here beginning from the base architecture used in the Codecreatures engine (e.g., Codecreatures benchmark), which are important in complex environments.

The following aspects are described in this article:

- Multiple passes per object to map surface effects with several render passes

- Various shadow effects including scene rendering used for stencil shadows and dynamic reflections on surfaces (water, mirrors, shining structures)

- Seamless worlds with large ranges of visibility and expanded indoor areas, as well as the administration of resources like textures, materials, and meshes

Essential Base Architecture of a Modern 3D Engine

Here is a simplified structural overview of a modular 3D engine.

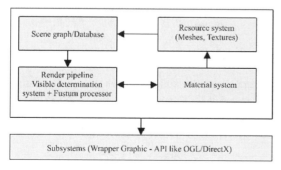

Figure 1: Modular engine architecture overview

The next sections describe all systems represented in Figure 1.

Subsystems

The lowest levels of all are the subsystems. They are thin wrappers for 3D APIs, such as OpenGL or DirectX. Primarily this wrapper serves to abstract different APIs.

Scene and Resource Management

This field is mostly underestimated. With complex scenes, it is accordingly important to have cache systems, organized as least recently used caches to handle data-intensive resources, for example.

Another underestimated topic is the enormous memory consumption of meshes. To gain flexibility in storage of meshes, they are put into streams, which don't match later with the desired hardware format. For this reason, it is meaningful that these hardware-abstracted meshes operate over an appropriate cache. If the engine uses non-visual relevant systems like collision (e.g., collision meshes), it can operate with the same cache systems.

Some aspects should be mentioned with the hardware-bound format of certain mesh data. The number of texture coordinate pairs in the flexible vertex format structure plays an important role. Also, "standard" deviating flexible vertex formats, which contain position, normals (diffuse, specular), and texture coordinate pairs, should be considered. Texture coordinate pairs are usually assigned to a specific texture type. For example:

Stage#0:   Diffusetexture
Stage#1:   Detailtexture
State#2-n: Lightmap per-pixel light, bump map, environmentmaps, etc.

The engine-specific interleaved vertex streams are converted from the resource system into the desired API (DirectX)-compliant vertex format before the render pipeline starts rendering the scene. In most cases, cache-friendly structures have a size of 32 or 64 bytes.

We use a directed acyclic (scene) graph to organize the scene content hierachically. Each object instances in the scene graph can be referenced using a unique value (such as a string name).

Visibility Determination System

In principle this system is composed of several stages that accomplish different optimizations in the view cone for the current camera. It is concerned with (object) culling, HSD (hidden surface determination), and HOD (hidden object determination), as well as an optimal representation of the still existing scene and its visible scene objects.

I don't want to introduce all of the stages here, but I refer to some important requirements that a modern render pipeline must accomplish. This system should be able to create arbitrary so-called frustum databases. These databases contain the excerpt of all optimizing stages of our render pipeline, thus all the objects that are still visible from the view cone (frustum) of used cameras.

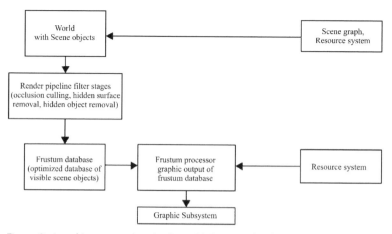

Figure 2: A multistage render pipeline with frustum databases

The distribution in databases that contain the optimized camera-adapted data stream are crucial for different things because new shader effects can often consist of multipass effects (see the section titled "Material System").

Frustum Processor

The function of the frustum processor (FP) is to reference existing data objects like meshes and/or textures through the resource system to convert these resources into an optimal format for hardware.

The optimized format for meshes is stored into one large vertex buffer or in various individual vertex buffers, depending on mesh type and size. Summarizing the adjusted materials and/or the choice of appropriate sort criteria (textures, shaders, z-depth, etc.) is important because these criteria concern how fast these objects can be rendered by hardware (bandwidth, texture state/shader state switches, occlusion culling).

Per-object Multipass Technique

A characteristic of the frustum processor is the multiple rendering of objects. How often an object must be rendered is determined by the specified material, which exports a function that returns an appropriate number of passes to render.

The render target used by the frustum processor can be changed transparently by the material system, which provides an available render target texture. The combination of textures, as well as their administration for mix and frame textures is completely directed by the material system.

Material System

With help from the material system, effects can be combined over arbitrary texture passes. It uses the ability of the frustum processor to utilize the object multipass technique. The frustum proccessor is informed about the number of necessary render passes.

The material system thereby supports the following steps, which can be blended accordingly:

- Illumination stage (lightmap, vertex/pixel light, dynamic shadows)
- Object stage (diffuse and detail texture, etc.)
- Environment stage (environment maps, etc.)

The material system needs this render-to-texture feature, called per-object multipass rendering, to map the object stage pass (mentioned above). For a case in which hardware can't mix the object material in one pass and it is not possible to blend this object in the frame buffer, this technique is used. The material system also contains surface or effect shaders, which are edited and used here. With support of the scene multipass technique (described in the following section), it is possible, for example, to implement in your game night-vision goggles or other "complete scene visual effects." Your material system can contain extra data and shaders to achieve this effect. A further interesting field is a material level of detail technique, which can be used in larger outdoor scenarios. To save rendering time, the material system can use different representations of shaders in a current material that is mapped onto a distant object.

Per-scene Multipass Technique

This technique, in contrast to the similar per-object multipass technique, enables rendering entire scenery to a texture surface.

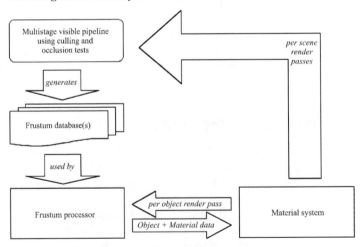

Figure 3: Workflow per scene/object render passes

This render-to-texture feature is set up in this situation to request current dynamic camera views of the scene (possible with certain criteria filtered and providing still existing objects with a special master material), which is then rendered to a texture and finally used as resource. This feature can be used with dynamic per-pixel illumination, during conversion of reflection and refraction effects (e.g., crystal sculptures, polished surfaces, or water), as well as real-time actualization of cube maps.

An appropriate frustum database that can be processed through the frustum processor must be created first. Infinite recursions must be prevented here. This can be made possible (e.g., over a frame-oriented reference counter or in a simple way) so that this problem is recognized by the material itself. It disables this feature, since it has activated the process.

Current Drawbacks

There are different problems to solve; some are mentioned here.

The frustum processor can have problems finding an optimal sorting for the scene objects, which must be drawn. We can also prepare precompiled optimizations like summarizing similar materials to reduce draw calls into the API to minimize render state changes. Unfortunately, there exists no reasonable universal solution that is sufficient for both indoor and outdoor scenarios.

These techniques described above that are used by per-object/scene multipass rendering have a serious restriction that concerns performance stalls and memory consumption. There is at present no way to render directly on compressed textures, so appropriate render target textures for those multipass techniques must be present in an uncompressed format.

Additional render target textures with different resolutions should possess their own depth buffer (for performance reasons). However, these depth buffers require additional memory on the graphic card; this type of texture resides on the graphic card and isn't paged out.

The intelligent administration of these textures is necessary because these resources otherwise need a lot of memory on the graphic card. These textures should (if they are used longer for effects that rarely or never change) be created during application starts (stored permanently in memory) or even compressed at run time. But compressing textures during run time can cause performance problems.

In addition, hardware stalls are possible if render target textures are needed too early. This means that if these targets are not filled by graphics hardware immediately but after utilization of hardware, all state changes are collected and executed. The difference between scene setup and drawing a scene can amount to three or four frames here. An early access (a Lock() function on a surface — e.g., for compression or similar immediate accesses, like SetTexture and a resulting draw call after scene setup) to this texture can cause unwanted stalls in graphics hardware.

Summary

Today's engine architecture designs differ substantially from earlier designs, which have reduced possibilities regarding geometry and pixel pipeline and were strongly dependent on the fixed-function system of graphics API.

The potential with DirectX 9 or appropriate OpenGL extensions makes it possible to intervene in geometry setup as well as the rasterizing pipeline. As described above, you have to consider many things in modern engine design to take advantage of the available API functions.

Outlook

The development concerning shaders and their flexibility and possibilities are at the beginning of development at the present time. Shader programs will become more extensive and more flexible in the future, the number of pixel pipelines will increase, and graphics hardware will be able to process more texture stages per pass.

The goal is to equip environments with better materials so that they work more realistically and/or correspond optimally to the conception of the designer. Improved HOD algorithms and refined shadow techniques would be conceivable.

Some basic features, however, should be implemented because they were so far neglected. These include:

- Rendering on compressed textures
- Status queries for rendering processes like render-to-texture (e.g., IsBusy, etc.)

Shader Integration in the Gamebryo Graphics Engine

Scott Sherman, Dan Amerson, Shaun Kime, and Tim Preston

www.gamebryo.com

Introduction

As can be seen from the results shown in many of the other articles in this book, well-written, creative pixel and vertex shaders can generate incredible visual impact. However, an often-overlooked aspect of shaders is their integration into a larger-scale graphics/rendering engine. As a provider of 3D graphics runtimes and tools, we at NDL have grappled with this issue directly. The framework, support code, and tools required to ensure that shaders can reach their full potential in a general game engine can be extensive. Every aspect of both game engine design and game development workflow comes into play, covering the gamut of shader integration with artist tools, loading of vertex and pixel shaders into the engine, shader asset management, and even shader parameter animation.

Above and beyond basic shader integration, today's game developers require the ability to customize their own shaders, requiring any shader-engine integration to be as flexible as it is complete. When designing the integration with NDL's Gamebryo (a very general, "genre-agnostic" engine), this flexibility requirement proved quite difficult to satisfy in a way that was both complete and easy to use.

This article discusses the approach that NDL took for integrating shaders in the latest release of our 3D graphics engine and toolkit, Gamebryo. We start out with a short history of shader support in our engine, discussing the original problems we anticipated and our attempt to solve them. A list of requirements determined as a result of our original system is presented, followed by in-depth coverage of the current system. The article concludes with a case study discussing the development of a sample application, Eturnum, which demonstrates the power of the new system.

The Past

The Initial Problem

When programmable shaders entered the development scene, much excitement and fanfare heralded the impressive graphics effects that were then possible on the new hardware. While many developers scrambled to take advantage of this

631

powerful new capability and improve the visual appeal of their games, initial acceptance of shaders in 3D games was nowhere near universal. Despite the best intentions of developers and hardware manufacturers alike, shaders did not have the immediate, intended effects on the look and feel of most games. Initially, this was often blamed on the lack of an installed base of shader-capable hardware. However, we felt (and later saw, through interactions with our customers) that there were other factors involved in this lack of shader usage.

The first stumbling block to shader integration is that in the most basic sense, shaders are just problem-specific, hardware-specific pieces of code. As an example, consider the case where a game is being developed with full shader support. To take advantage of the latest hardware, the team will need to write shaders to the most recent specifications.

However, legacy hardware will require support. The same shaders will have to be implemented for this older hardware, and a method for handling the effect without hardware shader support must also be developed. As you can see, the number of shader programs required can quickly add up. This situation is different than the case where customer hardware in general will have differing hardware capabilities, such as the number of textures per pass, available stages, and the like. Multitexturing capabilities, for example, can be handled far easier by having fixed-function effects fall back to multipass solutions on older hardware. When forming the passes for a fixed-function run, some simple capability checks and predefined blending rules allow for the same code to run on many hardware configurations. Pixel and vertex shaders, however, require a completely different version of the code to take full advantage of the hardware that the application is running on. Many developers were not ready to sacrifice the engines that they had developed in exchange for writing and optimizing hundreds of assembly programs to accomplish the same task. The feeling is similar to the time when developers had to write to graphic-card-specific APIs to get the results they wanted.

Another large inhibitor to widespread adoption is the integration of shaders with the art pipeline. Without a clean flexible framework supporting them, shaders essentially require the developer to hard-code data values placed into registers. This takes the creativity out of the hands in which it belongs: the artist's. This situation can lead to a large drain on your programmer productivity, as they will lose cycles while tweaking values in the shader code for the artist.

Finally, we believe that one reason for the lack of shader adoption is the set of available sample shaders. Oddly enough, the problem is not a lack of such sample shaders but rather the sheer number of different shader frameworks upon which these sample shaders are based. While this sounds contradictory, a large number of sample shaders were available everywhere from hobbyist web sites to the actual graphics card manufacturers, all implemented using completely different frameworks and assumptions. The available samples use DirectX effect files, the nVidia Effects Browser, ATI RenderMonkey, and even homebrew "editors" — most taking wildly different approaches to integrating shaders. No provider supplied a clear way to integrate their particular format into an actual game; their examples were very specific to the framework that they provided for viewing the effects.

The NetImmerse Solution

Gamebryo is a cross-platform 3D graphics engine and game toolkit that evolved from NDL's previous product, NetImmerse. The versatility of the engine is evident in the number of genres in which it has been utilized, including MMORPGs, role-playing, racing, and space combat.

Since Gamebryo originated from the NetImmerse engine, it is appropriate to give a short discussion on the shader system that NetImmerse contained, covering the problems and stumbling blocks that occurred with the system. The first version of shader integration, presented in NetImmerse 4.0, was known as the Configurable Texture Pipeline. It would have been more aptly named the Configurable *Rendering* Pipeline, as it allowed for developers to completely customize the rendering of objects with NetImmerse.

The original system functioned by supplying a class interface, the ConfigurableTextureData (CTD) class, through which the engine set up and executed the passes required for rendering an object. Most of the functions returned a code to the renderer allowing for sections of the pipeline to be skipped. For example, when the derived class would set a pixel shader on a pass, the function could return a value to the renderer, indicating it should not set the pixel shader. These return values provided complete customizability of the rendering pipeline. A derived class could simply skip a single step of the default rendering path all the way up to completely bypassing NetImmerse rendering an object at all.

While the system was quite powerful with respect to what could be accomplished with it, there were several problems with it. The base implementation of the class was the default rendering pipeline, which in hindsight was a mistake. The default pipeline of NetImmerse (and Gamebryo as well) is rather powerful, allowing for high-level representations of both dynamic and static effects to be applied to rendered objects and handled by the engine seamlessly. For example, multiple projected lights and shadows, fog and environment maps, and numerous other visual effects can be applied to an object. This system allowed a large amount of flexibility with respect to applying various effects to an object but added several member functions and variables that were not required to override the pipeline. This increased complexity ultimately led to confusion when developers were first starting out deriving their own custom implementations, and some did not have the time to invest in learning how to use the system effectively.

Another side effect of the base class being the default pipeline was that implementing simple shader programs (for example, a single-pass effect that utilized a vertex and pixel shader) required quite a bit of code to be written, proving to be more complex than necessary. A "simple" pipeline would require developers to implement six virtual functions that composed the rendering path. Since the default pipeline was so complex, it was difficult to leverage any of the base functionality of the class for simple operations. To accomplish relatively easy tasks, these functions typically had to be replaced completely in the derived CTD. This was a design oversight that, while providing a powerful interface to rendering, made their usage much more difficult and time consuming.

CTD usage was complicated further by the fact that the only way to access the functionality of the system was programmatically. There were no capabilities for streaming the classes to and from files, so assigning any CTD-derived class to an object required the application to do so "by hand" at run time. This omission prevented adding an easy way to integrate them into the art pipeline, which in turn hampered productivity, as the assets could only be viewed in the game itself or a modified viewer that contained the required derived classes.

With respect to supporting available formats, the system left that in the hands of the developer. Unfortunately, this typically would require that the derived class handle every aspect of rendering an object. In short, the system required far too much development for too little return.

Requirements of a Shader System

Once the CTD system was in the field, the issues listed above and others arose, which led to the compilation of a list of requirements for the next version of the system. The major issues that we felt should be addressed are presented here, with a brief description of each.

Ease of Use without Sacrificing Power or Flexibility

First and foremost, the system should be easy to use out of the box while still allowing more advanced users to implement any effect they can devise. It should take minimal time and, if possible, no source code compilation to apply a simple vertex and/or pixel shader program to a rendered object, but it should not "hand-cuff" developers by requiring they follow a strict implementation model. This will allow developers to utilize the system at a level at which they are both capable of and comfortable with.

Art Pipeline Integration

The system should allow shader support to be integrated directly into the art development pipeline. The system should also expose "editable" parameters to allow the artist to experiment to obtain the desired look. This is a key element of any shader system, as it keeps visually creative control in the hands of the artist and allows for asset viewers to display the object exactly as it appears in-game, reducing the model/export/view iterations.

Simple Access to Shader Collections

The system should provide a way for shader authors to easily distribute new and updated shaders to the rest of the development team. This will streamline the development process, allowing for quick integration of new shader assets. Shader collection support also aids in the integration of shader support in the art pipeline, as the art tools can work with a known interface.

Support Industry Standard Formats

The system should support as many viable shader file formats that are currently available as possible. This includes formats such as DirectX effect files, nVidia's CgFX files, and ATI RenderMonkey files. Doing so will allow the shader author to work in a format with which he is most comfortable. Supporting these formats also makes it easier to integrate samples gleaned from this book and other sources into a team's palette of shaders. The capability to leverage existing tools, such as RenderMonkey, is also gained with this approach.

Data-driven Support

The system should allow for rendering effects via a data-driven method. This means that it should be possible to integrate new shaders with no code compilation required. This aspect of the system could involve a script-based format that allows for text files to be written "describing" the effect. Another alternative would be to have an external shader editing application generate a binary file that contains the details of the rendering task.

A Unified Rendering Path

The system should have a well-defined interface for the way the renderer displays any geometric object. All objects, whether using a custom shader or the default pipeline, should be processed in the same manner by the renderer. There should not be two paths through the rendering pipeline; objects with a shader should follow the same pipeline as those without one. The interface must also supply sufficient low-level access such that the users can completely replace the default rendering pipeline by deriving from the interface class if they wish to. Providing the developer with a precise definition of what the renderer expects during each phase of displaying an object will allow for this. Finally, the interface should be as straightforward as possible, with a family of derived classes to increase the supplied functionality in logical increments. This will allow for developers to select their level of integration, easing the task of developing shaders while not restricting what can be accomplished.

The Gamebryo Shader System

With these requirements in mind, work began on the next implementation of shader integration in NDL's technology. The Gamebryo Shader System provides the classes and framework required to implement vertex and pixel shader support with all the power of the previous system, while providing alternative, more accessible methods for accomplishing the same tasks. The system is also fully integrated into the art pipeline, including support for custom coded shaders supplied by developers to be used with no tool modifications.

Within the context of Gamebryo, we use slightly different terminology than DirectX for shader-related components, so a short list of definitions may be helpful here.

- *shader*: An abstract representation of a complete rendering effect to apply to an object. A shader is a complete visual effect that is applied when rendering an object in the engine, including all passes and render states that are required to achieve said effect.

- *shader programs*: Vertex and pixel shaders in Gamebryo. This naming convention is intended to specify them with more relevance to their function/purpose. A *shader* can utilize numerous shader programs — one vertex and/or one pixel shader program per pass required to achieve the effect. In general, both pixel and vertex shaders are referred to as shader programs when they are not identified specifically as either a pixel or a vertex shader.

- *shader library*: A collection of shaders encapsulated in a DLL and/or static library package. The Xbox version of the shader system only supports static libraries, as DLLs are not available on the platform.

  Providing a DLL version is required for use in the art tools, so the system does not have to be recompiled to support new libraries. It can also refer to the interface functions defined for accessing the collection.

- *binary shader*: An interface to a completely data-driven implementation of a visual effect. This term can also refer to actual data representing a data-driven shader.

System Components

The Gamebryo Shader System contains several low-level classes that aid in the implementation and utilization of shaders in the pipeline. As any engine will contain a similar set of classes, we will not describe them in detail. The classes are straightforward, providing a direct representation of the hardware settings of the device when rendering. They cover render state and texture stage settings, pixel and vertex shaders, constant register mapping, and passes that make up a rendering effect, providing the building blocks used in the construction of the Gamebryo rendering pipeline.

Ease of Use without Sacrificing Power or Flexibility

The primary goal of the Gamebryo Shader System is to allow for developers to add shaders to their applications with minimal start-up time while still allowing for more advanced users to have complete control over the rendering pipeline if they desire. To allow developers to quickly prototype shaders, we supply a text-based format, the NDL Shader Format (NSF). We also support the use of existing "external" formats such as DirectX effect files, should shader authors opt for utilizing them in their development. CgFX and RenderMonkey support is also being added to provide developers with a wide selection of industry-supported shader formats. As shader authors generate more advanced effects that require capabilities beyond any of these formats, they can move to deriving their own shader interface classes from a number of supplied interfaces, ranging from a bare-bones interface class up to deriving from the default pipeline used by the engine. These derived classes may be grouped into a shader library for easy integration into both their application and the art pipeline.

Art Pipeline Integration

Why Integration Is Important

Art pipeline integration essentially requires shaders to be present in every step along the art pipeline. Integration does not mean writing shader code, although certainly some artists with a programming slant could do a good job of it. Art pipeline integration simply means exposing "editable" values to your artists and allowing them to preview the content in your engine throughout the pipeline. Any value that is not a required hard-coded shader constant is a great candidate to be an artist-adjustable value. For example, writing a toon shader usually involves an indirect texture lookup into a one-dimensional texture. This texture is a perfect candidate for an editable value. Often you'll be surprised with what an artist can accomplish when allowed to play with the parameters.

Artists using Gamebryo have the option to generate art content inside of either 3ds max or Maya, and our suite of plug-ins and tools converts the content into the Gamebryo format. Additionally, artists have the ability to view how their art will look inside the art package in a separate preview window. It is absolutely critical for the art pipeline integration to give instant feedback to the artist. This feedback is doubly necessary for shaders. Artists are used to seeing their options and playing around with them to achieve the visual result that they want. This is how most artists build a mental model of their art package. Often, nontraditional rendering effects require a fair bit of experimentation and tweaking to build a valid mental model. Rendering pipeline equations simply won't suffice. If the artist can tweak a few parameters and then preview what effect those changes had, he will feel more comfortable working with shaders and become productive with them significantly faster.

How We Integrated Shaders in the Art Pipeline

Adding additional, dynamic user interface items to any application can prove to be quite difficult. Unfortunately, this is precisely what was required for integration with the art package. Luckily, 3ds max and Maya both provide a simple mechanism for adding these items — "custom attributes" in Max and "extra attributes" in Maya. For the purposes of this discussion, we simply refer to both as custom attributes. In both art packages, custom attributes add additional data structures and optional user interface widgets that extend the normal meaning of objects. For instance, you could add a gradient ramp texture for a toon shader to a material. A custom attribute containing the texture and all of the GUI for editing that texture can be applied with a little bit of MEL or MAXScript. Furthermore, the underlying mechanisms for animation in the art package are automatically supported in the scripting language. Therefore, keyframe animation of values comes essentially "for free" with this approach. Supporting custom attributes and their keyframed values in the exporter is fairly straightforward.

Shaders and their descriptions are loaded at application startup by the Gamebryo plug-ins. All of the known shaders are available to the artist in Max's Gamebryo Shader or Maya's NiMultiShader. A drop-down list allows artists to select the shader that they wish to use. Descriptions of the overall shader, its attributes, supported pixel and vertex shader versions, and descriptions of each technique are available at the press of a button. Once the user applies the selected shader to the object, custom attributes are dynamically generated and applied to the current object. Artists can then edit these attributes just like any other attribute in the art package. For example, colors can be edited through the standard color picker. Textures can be edited through the standard user interface widgets. Animation of each shader attribute is as simple as animating anything else in Max or Maya.

See Figure 1 for an example of the shader parameter interface in 3D Studio MAX and Figure 2 for an example of the Maya interface.

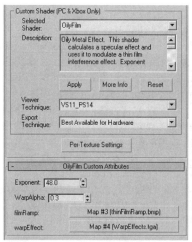

Figure 1: The 3D Studio MAX artist interface

This familiar user interface gets the artist up and running with shaders very quickly, but familiarity alone is not enough. We have found that shaders are often developed in a very iterative fashion. Programmers move effects from vertex

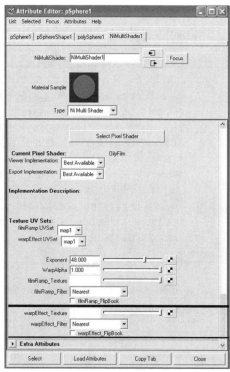

Figure 2: The Maya artist interface

code to pixel code, requiring different user interface widgets or artists asking programmers for more attributes to modify. Luckily, the custom attribute solution in both packages supports redefining custom attributes. As long as the attribute names don't change, their values, including all keyframes, can be transferred to the new definition. New attributes are filled in with their default values. These features are an incredible help to the artists in the development of a game. Without such features, artists would have to redo art assets any time the shader changed. We augment this process by auto-detecting whenever the shader changes by comparing its attribute definition in the Max or Maya file to the definition loaded at application startup. If the definitions are different, the user is notified and he can choose to upgrade his art assets or leave them as is.

Simple Access to Shader Collections

No matter how flexible or powerful a shader system is, if it does not supply an easy way to update the development team with new shaders, production can potentially be hindered during their integration into the application. To provide shader authors with a simple mechanism for supplying new and updated shaders to the rest of the development team, the Gamebryo Shader System takes a *shader library* approach. A shader library is an interface for accessing a collection of shaders via a static or dynamically linked library that contains the code for the shader(s).

To utilize the shader library system, the application simply registers a library with the system. When a call is made to attach a shader to an object, either by the file streaming system or the application itself, each registered library will be checked for the presence of the requested shader. If a library contains the shader, it will be retrieved and registered with the system using a reference counting system. A function in the shader class itself is then called to allow any special processing of the geometry that it may require, such as generating tangent space data if it is not already present in the geometric object. Applications may register as many libraries as they wish, allowing for shaders to be grouped into libraries by concepts such as level, unit type, spells, or any category that makes sense for the application.

For integration into the art tool chain, the shader library interface also contains a description mechanism. The supplied description contains a short description of the library itself as well as a description for each shader that it holds. The shader descriptions hold information on the various implementations of the shader, its requirements in terms of hardware and platform, and the attributes that it utilizes. These descriptions provide the means for exposing artist-editable shader parameters to the modeling tools, as well as comments to aid the artist by describing what a given shader does and what its parameters are used for.

Gamebryo ships with a shader library, NSBShaderLib, for recognizing and loading NDL Shader Binary (NSB) files. This format is a binary data representation of a visual effect to apply to a rendered object and is described in more detail later in this chapter. When registered with the system, the library will search a given directory, optionally recursing subfolders, identifying all NSB files contained within, and adding them to an internal list. When a particular shader is requested for attachment to a geometric object, the library will search this list. If the shader exists in the library but has not yet been loaded, the most appropriate implementation for the hardware is instantiated based on the capabilities of the system and the requested shader versions and returned.

Support Industry Standard Formats

To allow shader authors to work with the format that they are most comfortable with, the Gamebryo Shader System contains support for DirectX effect files, nVidia's CgFX files, and ATI's RenderMonkey files. Classes derived from our base shader interface were written to encapsulate the functionality required to utilize these formats. Some requirements for how they are authored were defined to ease the integration of these file types into the engine, such as identifying artist-editable values via annotations in DirectX effect files or using the grouping feature in ATI's RenderMonkey files to represent different implementations of the same effect. These should not hinder developers but do add an additional burden on those wishing to take full advantage of our system when using "external" formats.

By providing the support framework for a particular format in the form of a shader library, developers can easily integrate those shaders simply by registering the library with the shader system. This approach also allows NDL to handle integrating new formats without requiring the delivery of a full source code update to our customers. This adds significant expandability to the system, allowing for adding support for future updates and advances as simply as possible.

To give an example of the benefit of this type of shader library approach to external formats, just by deriving a shader class that implements the D3DXEffect interface and packaging it in a shader library, support for the DX9 FX file format was added with no code changes to the renderer. Other "industry standard" formats are each given their own shader library to handle accessing them. This will allow developers to select which formats, including their own custom ones, they wish to support in their applications simply by registering the corresponding library.

Data-driven Support

In an effort to simplify using the system and provide a rapid prototyping capability, Gamebryo shader integration was designed to provide data-driven support. When we speak of data-driven shaders, we mean allowing for a shader to be utilized with no source code compilation required. To accomplish this feature, data-driven shaders contain a list of passes which in turn contain render state and texture stage state settings, as well as the pixel and vertex shader programs and their corresponding constant register settings required to obtain the desired effect. One method that supplies this type of support is the previously mentioned binary shader format (NSB). NSB files are supported via a shader library, much like the DX9 effects support, and provide developers with the ability to quickly and easily add shaders to their game.

A key component for supplying data-driven shaders is a class that maps data values to shader constant registers.

Constant Register Mapping

To allow for mapping data values to shader constant registers, Gamebryo provides the constant mapping class. Two derived classes provide specific implementations for pixel shader and vertex shader constants. Each class consists of a map of entries representing the data and the register(s) to which it is mapped.

Support is included for several data source mappings to a given set of registers. A *constant* type maps a constant data value, such as the Taylor Series coefficients. A *predefined* type maps one of a set of Gamebryo-defined values. Each derived shader constant map class contains specific values for that usage type. For example, the vertex shader-specific class defines mappings for the World-ViewProjection transform and the diffuse material color. This data will be automatically updated and set on the device when the object is being rendered. A *per-object attribute* type maps a data value (or attribute) attached to the rendered object. This mapping allows for a single shader to achieve different visual results by having parameters differ for each object being rendered. The *global attribute*, similar to the per-object attribute, maps a data value from a global table of parameters. This mapping is helpful for setting values such as lighting parameters. Global attributes do require the application to update them as necessary. Finally, there is the *operator* type that allows the shader author to perform a mathematical operation on two other entries and map the result to the shader constant register(s). This mapping is useful for using the CPU to reduce shader instruction count and potentially the number of constant registers utilized. For example, transforming the light position to object space can be done once per object, as opposed to once per vertex, since the result is the same for all vertices in the mesh.

Entries include support for a number of data types, including Boolean values, vectors of one to four unsigned integers, vectors of one to four floats, 3x4 or 4x4 matrices, four floating-point component color values, and texture images.

Constant register mapping is a key feature of the engine, allowing for truly data-driven shaders. Creating a constant map greatly simplifies updating and setting shader constant register values for a pass. This automatic mapping of constant registers also eliminates one of the primary reasons most shader integration approaches require custom C++ code.

Binary Shaders and the NDL Shader Format

To facilitate a completely data-driven approach to implementing shaders, NDL developed a set of libraries that allow for text-based representations of shaders. Two libraries were created to support developers taking this approach to including shaders in their application.

The first library, NiBinaryShaderLib, implements a shader-derived class, NiBinaryShader, which has been extended to allow for directly setting groups of device states and pass configurations to implement a visual effect. This class removes the need for developers to write C++ code to implement shaders in the Gamebryo Shader System. By simply providing different data for the various class members, a wide range of effects can be achieved.

An abstract, platform-independent representation of this data is also supplied in this library via the class NSBShader. These shaders can be streamed to and from storage devices and written to NDL Shader Binary (NSB) files. Due to differences in enumeration values between Xbox, DX8, and DX9-based D3D implementations, a format that could be stored and subsequently used on all platforms was required, with the conversion code occurring at load time. The class also supports the concept of multiple implementations, which are different methods for achieving the same visual effect. This system is similar to Techniques in the DirectX effect file format. At load time, the system will search the implementations of an effect and return the most appropriate version, taking the system hardware and the requested versions into account to form the decision.

The second library that Gamebryo provides is a utility library, NSFParserLib, which parses NDL Shader Format files and generates the corresponding NSB files. The NDL Shader Format (NSF) is a text-based file format that allows developers to write shaders in a simple language and apply them to objects with no C++ code to write and no compilation required. Shader authors can define both global and per-object attributes, which in turn can be mapped to shader constant registers. All device settings can be defined in the file, including render states, texture stage settings, and pixel and vertex shader programs. The format is similar to the DirectX effect files, allowing multiple implementations of the same shader to provide legacy hardware support. The library operates by searching a given file directory, optionally recursing its subfolders, looking for NSF files. When found, the file will be parsed, and its corresponding NSB file will be written.

NOTE   The binary shader library was separated from the parser library to allow for developers to implement their own text-based formats without having to also develop an underlying binary representation.

The NSBShaderLib library used in conjunction with the NSFParserLib provides a complete system for rapid prototyping of shaders within applications or the tool chain. The application can simply run the NSFParser on all NSF files, generating the corresponding NSB files for all those found. Then by registering the NSBShaderLib, both existing NSB files and newly generated ones will be available for applying to rendered objects.

A Unified Rendering Path

A common path through the rendering pipeline is key to allowing shader developers to fully understand what is happening "under the hood" with their creations. A clean, consistent interface must exist that provides all the functionality required to allow not only the application of shader programs to rendered objects but also for the definition of a complete rendering pipeline through which the data will flow. The interface should be completely clear as to what the developer needs to implement in order to achieve the desired effect. As described previously, the original CTD system failed quite severely at this particular goal.

At the lowest level, the Gamebryo Shader System contains a class, NiShader, which is simply a name and implementation number for a shader. This interface is provided to minimize cross-platform compilation issues as well as keep the door open for future expansion to our other supported platforms. The heart of D3D-based shader integration in Gamebryo is an interface class derived from this, appropriately named NiD3DShaderInterface.

NiD3DShaderInterface

NiD3DShaderInterface defines how the engine renders geometric objects. It is the lowest level that a developer can derive from, giving them complete power to achieve what they wish to accomplish. This power also means the developer has complete responsibility for properly setting up the hardware for the rendering of the object. The concept is the same as the original CTD system design, with a bit more structure to the interface functions.

An Initialize function is called when a shader is created, allowing for any class-specific initialization required, such as registering shader programs and other one-time tasks. Pre- and post-process functions are called before and after any other processing of a rendered object is exposed to allow for any specialized setup and shutdown code required by the class. A function to update the pipeline is called once per rendered object to allow for the formation of passes based on higher-level static and dynamic effects. A derived class does not have to form the passes each time the object is rendered, but the approach is permitted.

For each pass on a rendered object, a call is made to configure the current pass on the hardware. A function for setting up the required transformations is also called. Typically, the calculation would be performed on the first pass and cached for subsequent passes. It is possible for an implementation to perform per-pass modifications to the results if needed. A call is then made to set optional shader programs and their corresponding constant registers. The final per-pass call is to prepare the geometry for rendering, which ensures that the geometry is packed in the format required for rendering. If the geometry has not been packed at this point, this function is expected to do so, as well as set the stream sources and indices.

Two additional functions exist in the interface: one to indicate to the shader that a new rendered object is being processed and another to indicate to the shader that the renderer is ready to begin the next pass.

These functions correspond to the steps that occur during the rendering of geometry in the Gamebryo engine. By defining this level of interaction, developers know exactly what is expected by the pipeline and can implement whatever effect they wish with minimal reworking of their ideas to fit within our framework. This interface replicates and extends the level of interaction that developers were permitted with the previous system, thus meeting one of our major design goals to provide the same power and flexibility of the original system.

The Shader Interface Extended

The system also provides additional classes to ease the integration of shaders in the engine. We opted to build these classes in a manner that supplies developers with increasing levels of functionality to aid in shader-based development. The default rendering pipeline is also implemented as a shader interface-based class.

NiD3DShader

NiD3DShader is derived from NiD3DShaderInterface, adding additional functionality and members to aid in the implementation of shader-based effects. It includes a definition of how to pack the geometry, an optional group of global render states that are set once for the entire effect (considered "global" states for the shader, such as setting the depth test to enabled), optional global shader constant register mappings for both vertex and pixel shader programs, and an array of pass instances that make up the complete rendering effect.

The NiD3DShader class provides an interface for implementing shader-based effects without requiring large amounts of code to be written. The derived class can simply fill in the members of the class with the appropriate settings and let the base implementation take care of the rendering details.

NiD3DDefaultShader

NiD3DDefaultShader implements the default rendering pipeline for the Gamebryo engine and is derived from the NiD3DShader class. It analyzes the platform-independent static and dynamic effects applied to the object and constructs the appropriate passes to achieve the complete effect. If a shader instance is not present on an object being rendered in Gamebryo, the default shader is used.

Deriving from the NiD3DDefaultShader class allows a developer to extend the pipeline that ships with Gamebryo in a number of ways. One could extend the existing pipeline to implement a new rendering technique that has not been incorporated into the engine yet. Another would be to alter the functionality provided (for example, the pipeline implements projected lights by modulating them, but a developer could derive from the class and implement projected lights as additive). One suggested usage is to implement "fast path" shaders, which remove sections of the construction step for effects that the developer will not be using. For example, if the game does not use projected lights, the part of the pipeline that analyzes and sets up projected lights could be removed, resulting in a faster path through the renderer while maintaining all the functionality with respect to other effects.

This three-tiered approach to the shader classes supplies a well-defined structure in which shaders can be developed. Depending on their needs, developers can opt for any of the interfaces that will provide them with their required level of access to the rendering pipeline. Figure 3 shows the options for deriving classes that the original CTD system presented to developers.

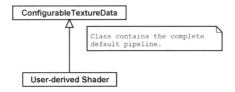

Figure 3: Class diagram for the NetImmerse shader system

As you can see from this diagram, developers had limited options for shader support; there is only one "entry point" for deriving their shader classes. Compound this with the fact that the interface was quite muddled with functionality for implementing the default pipeline, none of which was required for implementing shaders, and it is understandable why so many problems arose with its usage.

The Gamebryo system derivation options are displayed in Figure 4.

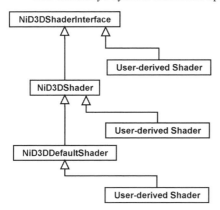

Figure 4: Class diagram for the Gamebryo shader system

The new system presents developers with far more options for what level they may derive from, from implementing shaders with no C++ code required to completely overriding the rendering of objects. The underlying interface to the rendering is much more clearly defined, laying out the functionality they are required to provide at each step. This makes the task of developing shaders far easier when using the Gamebryo engine.

Case Study: Eturnum

To understand the reasoning behind the design goals outlined in this chapter, it is helpful to consider a case study of a sample application. This section discusses different aspects and issues that arose in developing NDL's shader-driven demo for GDC 2003, Eturnum. We examine each of the six design goals and how Eturnum reinforced the applicability of those goals. Finally, we explore some of the lessons learned with Eturnum, paying particular attention to areas that still require improvement.

About Eturnum

The original idea for Eturnum was to showcase the Gamebryo Shader System by placing a highly detailed character in a realistic scene. In addition to showing high polygon throughput and performance, the demo renders almost every surface with a custom shader. These shaders implement a variety of fairly common pixel and vertex shader effects, such as dot3 bump mapping, palettized skinning, and thin film interference.

Design Goals

Since the final goal of Eturnum was to demonstrate the power of the Gamebryo Shader System, it makes sense to examine how the development of the demo reinforced the previously stated design goals.

Unified Rendering Path

Because all objects in Gamebryo take the same path through the renderer, we were able to leverage some utility out of the default, fixed-function pipeline in the development of Eturnum. Generally, neither art assets nor shader code exist at the beginning of a project. It is unsatisfactory to stall either aspect of development to wait for the other. Since the Gamebryo Shader System was designed with a unified rendering path in mind, it was possible to begin designing art assets for Eturnum that would later have shaders attached to them. Unifying the rendering path meant that no work would be lost when shaders were applied. All the parameters for materials, textures, etc. carried directly over from the default pipeline shader to the custom shaders written for Eturnum.

Data-driven Support

Shaders for Eturnum were developed using NSF files. As stated previously, NSF files contain information for a rendering effect in a script file, much like Microsoft's DirectX effects files. Using NSF files allowed rapid, data-driven iteration to occur on the shaders. This rapid feedback cycle produced more refined shaders without consuming significant amounts of time rebuilding programs. The NSF files were parsed at run time, making changes to the NSF files instantly apparent in the application.

Industry Standard Formats

The Gamebryo Shader System is designed to be compatible with major industry standards while still adding information specific to Gamebryo where necessary. With this fact in mind, effects for Eturnum were often built initially in ATI's RenderMonkey program. Although the library to directly import RenderMonkey XML files directly into Gamebryo was not complete at the time the demo was authored, translating the information from a RenderMonkey file to NSF was trivial given the compatible setup of the Gamebryo Shader System.

Simple Access to Shader Collections

Parsing the NSF files at run time for Eturnum provided a strong, data-driven shader model for the application. Additionally, it fulfilled another requirement for the shader system — providing simple access to shader collections for all members of the development team. Throughout Eturnum, the shaders for each member of the development team could be updated with a simple text file that was parsed at run time.

Art Pipeline Integration

The Gamebryo plug-ins for 3ds max and Maya both support the use of shader libraries at run time, and they ship with libraries to parse NSF files and load the associated NSB files. This fact was invaluable to the development of Eturnum. It was possible for artists to create the assets, assign shaders to assets, and preview those assets before even considering exporting for use in the application. Additionally, the use of custom attributes to hold shader parameters in both plug-ins allowed the artists rather than the programmers to modify shader effects.

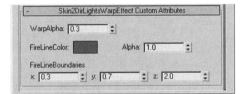

Figure 5: The original artist interface

Ease of Use without Sacrificing Power or Flexibility

Of all the design requirements for the Gamebryo Shader System, generating an easy-to-use system without limiting the creativity of artists and programmers was the most difficult and the most important. In the end, the system showed its strength by demonstrating just this capability in the development of Eturnum. For our alien, the initial shader effect implemented matrix palette skinning with a base map and two per-vertex directional lights. This effect was satisfactory, but the demo called for more. We needed to add a warp effect to the alien for use when he teleports in and out of the temple. Because the system was designed to allow almost any imaginable effect, the warp effect was easily coded with a change to the NSF file and changes to the accompanying shader programs.

Once the alien was teleporting into the temple, however, the art staff wanted per-pixel lighting and dot3 bump mapping on the character. Again, these features were not a problem to add since the system was designed for easy use and powerful expansion. Changes to the NSF file were instantly recognized in the art packages, and the art team did not have to redesign any art to fit the new shaders. Additional custom attributes in the art packages were transparently added and set to default values without disrupting the art production pipeline in the slightest.

Lessons Learned

Although the development of Eturnum reinforced the design goals of the Gamebryo Shader System, some important lessons were learned regarding the shader system and shader-driven development in general.

First, although distributing NSF files to our art staff allowed easy access to shaders, this solution was still not optimal. It was always possible that a single NSF file out of the group was not synchronized. Ideally, all shaders would be collected into a single file that represented the current database for use in the application. Much like a source control database, this file would always contain the most current version of all the shader effects.

We also found that understandable, artist-editable parameters must be available in the art development packages to provide the necessary customizability and creativity. An initial version of the warp effect used hard-coded values to control the waves of color that washed over our character. When the shader was changed to use the custom attributes shown in Figure 5, artists had the ability to control the effect but also had difficulty understanding how the various numerical parameters affected the shader. To address this confusion, the effect was changed to use a texture map for the effect rather than numeric inputs. For this texture, the U coordinate of lookups was calculated from the normal dotted with the view vector and the V coordinate was the current value of the WarpAlpha parameter. When presented with this change, one artist stayed three extra hours to play with the effect because he was having so much fun with it.

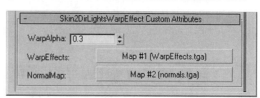

Figure 6: The more artist-friendly interface

Wrap-Up and Future Plans

A fully configurable and programmable pipeline can provide huge benefits to a game's overall visual impact. Such a pipeline allows the flexibility for very creative effects but cannot stand alone. For artists to create these effects, they must be provided with an environment that makes the authoring of shader-driven assets simple and understandable. During the development of Eturnum, we discovered that a programmer-centric interface to shaders was not enough to enable the full abilities of the artist efficiently. The Gamebryo tools team created an artist-centric integration that leveraged the user interface components provided by the SDKs of the art tools themselves, ensuring that the controls looked and behaved in ways that were familiar to the artist. This increased the artist's shader-tweaking productivity significantly, an important factor as project milestones approached.

The Gamebryo Shader System was designed with a clear set of requirements that we at NDL felt were needed to provide a complete shader solution to our developers. The system met or exceeded most of the goals we set, but like any software development project, additional features are in the process of being integrated or are planned for future integration. These include:

- Allowing the constant mapping technique for per-object and global attributes to be used for other values, such as render state and texture stage settings

- Adding shader constant register management to minimize SetShaderConstant calls

- High-level shader language support is currently only available via the DirectX effect, RenderMonkey, and CgFX support. A method for supporting this in the NDL Shader Format should also be developed.

- Implementing a method for integrating render-to-texture effects into the data-driven system

- Adding a WAD-type system for packaging binary shaders as well as their associated pixel and vertex shader files

- Developing analysis tools that analyze a scene with the default pipeline and generate custom, per-object shaders that contain only the effects required to render them

- Developing and supporting a cross-platform shader language that provides support on all Gamebryo platforms

Due to the constant advancement of graphics hardware, shader integration is never truly complete in a graphics engine. While the Gamebryo Shader System is full-featured with respect to our list of requirements, we are looking forward to its continued development.

Vertex Shader Compiler

David Pangerl

Introduction

The Vertex Shader Compiler (VSC) is a free, C-based, DirectX vertex shader (VS) compiler. It is a high-level programming language (HLPL) for the DirectX VS assembler programming. The result of the VSC is an optimized VS assembler with the additional run-time information. This article describes what VSC can do for a VS programmer and how it can be used for simpler and efficient high-level writing of vertex shaders.

Current Features

The VSC is a fast, robust, and stable compiler. It was designed to divide the vertex shader pipeline into several parts. It has a powerful plug-in system, built-in optimization, and a precompiler. Its features include:

- Compilation of a program provided via string or file
- Same code for different mesh vertex types
- Function swapping
- Fast compilation
- Good optimization
- Handling register restrictions
- VS array support
- Small and simple C++ code (~3300 lines) with a very simple interface

VSC License

The VSC is copyrighted by ZootFly. This library is free software. You can redistribute it and/or modify it under the terms of the BSD-style license, which is included in this library in the file licence_bsd.txt.

Concept

DirectX Vertex Shader Assembler

The DirectX VS assembler is a direct way of programming the vertex processing. It is very powerful and useful, although using it requires knowledge from a variety of fields:

- Basic assembler knowledge
- Instruction specifications (DirectX documentation)
- Instruction restrictions (DirectX documentation)
- Register usage (DirectX documentation)
- Register per instruction restrictions (DirectX documentation)

Even the simplest function (length, sin, cos, etc.) requires a lot of assembler instructions. It also requires a slightly different approach than the HLPL. Furthermore, the maintenance, debugging, and upgrades of the assembler code are very hard and demanding tasks.

This is why we decided to develop a custom HLPL, which eliminates all the tedious tasks of assembler programming.

Language

The VSC language is based on the C syntax with some simplifications and modifications, as shown in the following example:

```
//first.cvs

#include <standard.hvs>

float sqr(float a)
{
    return a*a;
}

void vsmain(float param)
{
    out.Pos=m4x4(in.Pos * sqr(param) + 10,  FinalMatrix.x);
}
```

Because of the DirectX VS assembler specifics, there are some architectural differences from classic C:

- All functions are compiled inline (due to no stack).
- All function parameters are treated as references.
- Only float and vector types are supported (the VS register consists of four floats).

- There are no if, while, for, and switch statements (DirectX 8 VS has no branching instructions; this will be implemented in DirectX 9 VS).

Furthermore, some simplifications have been made due to the relative simplicity of the VS programs:

- No scopes
- No user-defined types and structures
- Much simpler precompiler

The nature of VS leads to some grammar additions:

- VS input and output structure definition
- Plug-in introduction
- Constant register reservation introduction

Types

- The float type is IEEE single-precision (32 bits) floating point.
- A vector is a structure of four floats (see the following C definition of a vector structure).

```
struct vector {
    float x;
    float y;
    float z;
    float w;
};
```

Variables

Local variables can be defined at any point in the program as in C++. The VSC doesn't support global variables.

Constants

The VSC supports two types of constants: float and vector constants. Float constants are defined by a single float number. Vector constants are defined as an array of one to four float numbers in brackets. Note the following examples:

```
// float constant
float a=10;
float b=1.234;
//
a=a*0.5+b*0.2;

// vector constants
vector x=(1);
vector y=(1,1,1,0);
//
x=in.Pos + (0,1,0);
```

The constant definition table contains additional data exported with the program assembly, as shown below. It can be used to set the constants within a user program.

```
//Result of first.cvs with constant definition table export (first.vs)


vs.1.1
mov    r0.x, c4.x                    // max reg per ins. salvage
mul    r0.y, c4.x, r0.x
mad    r0, inPos, r0.y, c5.x         // |  (o2.1)
m4x4   outPos, r0, c0               // assignment|  (o1.1)


// Plugin: FinalMatrix::x=c0
// Plugin: FinalMatrix::y=c1
// Plugin: FinalMatrix::z=c2
// Plugin: FinalMatrix::w=c3
// Constant: c5=(10.000,?,?,?)
```

Functions

All functions in the VSC are compiled in-line. All function parameters are treated as references (modifying the parameter within a function will modify the value of the variable that was passed to the function).

The program entry function is vsmain. Parameters can be passed to the vsmain function, as shown below.

```
//vsmain.cvs
output vertexshader {
    vector      Pos;
};


void vsmain(float a, vector b)
{
    out.Pos=a*b;
}
```

Here is the output:

```
vs.1.0
// vsmain parameter assignment:
//     parameter 'a'=c0.x.
//     parameter 'b'=c1.
mov    r0, c1                 // max reg per ins. salvage
mul    outPos, c0.x, r0       // assignment||max reg per ins. salvage (o1 failed) (o1.1)
```

All DirectX VS instructions and macros are added as VSC functions, as shown in the following table:

Functions
add(anytype a, anytype b)
dp3(anytype a, anytype b)
dp4(anytype a, anytype b)
dst(anytype a, anytype b)

Functions
exp(anytype a)
expp(anytype a)
frc(anytype a)
lit(anytype a)
log(anytype a)
logp(anytype a)
m3x2(anytype a, anytype b)
m3x3(anytype a, anytype b)
m3x4(anytype a, anytype b)
m4x3(anytype a, anytype b)
m4x4(anytype a, anytype b)
mad(anytype a, anytype b, anytype c)
max(anytype a, anytype b)
min(anytype a, anytype b)
mov(anytype a, anytype b)
mul(anytype a, anytype b)
rcp(anytype a)
rsq(anytype a)
sge(anytype a, anytype b)
slt(anytype a, anytype b)
sub(anytype a, anytype b)

VSC also supports some comparison expressions:

Syntax	Description
(a>=b?c)	Returns c if a>=b; otherwise returns 0.
(a<b?c)	Returns c if a<b; otherwise returns 0.
(a>=b?c:d)	Returns c if a>=b; otherwise returns d.
(a<b?c:d)	Returns c if a<b; otherwise returns d.

Input and Output Definition

The VSC input and output definition provides VS with information on the VS input vertex structure and output vertex structure. The program input is defined as the predefined variable in and the program output is defined as the predefined variable out. Input and output variable members are accessible as C structure/class members. All output members are write only, while all input members are read only.

Here is the input/output structure grammar:

```
input_definition    : input vertexshader '{' member_list '}' ';'
output_definition   : output vertexshader '{' member_list '}' ';'
member_list         : member
                    | member ';' member_list
member              : type name
type                : float
                    | vector
```

Here is an example of the input/output structure definition:

```
output vertexshader {
    vector          Pos;            // vertex position
    vector          DColor;         // diffuse color
    vector          SColor;         // specular color
    float           PointSize;      // sprite point size
    float           Fog;            // fog value
    vector          Tex0;           // texture [0..7] coordinates
    vector          Tex1;
    vector          Tex2;
    vector          Tex3;
    vector          Tex4;
    vector          Tex5;
    vector          Tex6;
    vector          Tex7;
};

input vertexshader {
    vector          Pos;
    vector          Normal;
    vector          Color;
    vector          Tex0;
    vector          Tex1;
    vector          Tex2;
    vector          Tex3;
};
```

Plug-ins

Plug-ins are the VSC substitutes for structures in the C language. They are the main link between the VS and the main program and are used to provide the VS with the main program data (i.e., object matrix, camera matrix, final matrix, lighting information, soft binding, etc.) and to manipulate the constants in the VS.

There are two types of plug-ins: simple and radical. The simple plug-in optimizes its variable space usage. It reserves space in the VS constant variable space only for those variables that are actually used, while the radical plug-in reserves the constant space for all the plug-in variables defined in the plug-in, if any of them is being used (see the first .cvs example in the "Constants" section).

All of the plug-in variables are read-only.

Here is the plug-in grammar:

```
plugin_definition    : [radical] plugin '(' argument_list ')' ';'
argument_list        : argument
                     | argument ',' argument_list
argument             : type name array_definition
array_definition     :
                     | '[' number ']'
type                 : float
                     | vector
```

This is an example of a plug-in:

```
// plugins.cvs
input vertexshader {
    vector        Pos;
};

output vertexshader {
    vector        Pos;
    vector        DColor;
};

radical plugin FinalMatrix(vector x, vector y, vector z, vector w);

plugin Light(vector Color, vector Direction, float Range);

void vsmain()
{
    out.Pos=m4x4(in.Pos,  FinalMatrix.x);
    out.DColor=Light.Color;
}
```

The radical plug-in FinalMatrix reserves constant space for all variables x, y, z, and w, while the simple plug-in Light reserves constant space only for the variable Color that is used in the shader (see below).

```
vs.1.0
m4x4    outPos, inPos, c0            // assignment| (o1.1)
mov     outDColor, c4                // assignment

// Plugin: FinalMatrix::x=c0
// Plugin: FinalMatrix::y=c1
// Plugin: FinalMatrix::z=c2
// Plugin: FinalMatrix::w=c3
// Plugin: Light::Color=c4
```

Reservation of Constant Registers

The VSC allows you to reserve temporary and constant registers. This is useful when you want to use the VSC output with user modifications. Below are examples of the constant reservation grammar and the use of the constant reservation:

```
define_reservation    : reserve register_type '(' reserve_register_list ')' ';'
register_list         : register
                      | register ',' register_list
register              : number
                      : number '.' '.' number
                      : number ',' register
register_type         : temp
                      | const

reserve const (10,11,12,20..30);    // reserve register c10, c11, c12, and c20 through c30
reserve temp (0..4);                // reserve register r0, r1, r2, r3, and r4
```

Arrays

The VSC supports arrays as plug-in variables (see the "Plug-ins" section). As the array parameter type, only vector type can be used.

Here is an example:

```
// softbind.cvs
input vertexshader {
    vector      JointIndex;
    vector      JointWeight;
    //
    vector      PosOffset0;
    vector      PosOffset1;
};

output vertexshader {
    vector      Pos;
};

plugin Skeleton(vector mat[78]);   // max 26 bones per one mesh

void vsmain()
{
    vector t=in.JointIndex*768;    // 256 * 3 (3 vectors per matrix)
    //
    out.Pos=m4x3(in.PosOffset0, Skeleton.mat[ t.x ]) * in.JointWeight.x +
            m4x3(in.PosOffset1, Skeleton.mat[ t.y ]) * in.JointWeight.y;
}
```

Precompiler

The VSC has a simple built-in precompiler, which uses the grammar shown in the following table:

Grammar	Description
#include '"' filename '"'	The file "filename" is inserted. File uses the search path from the source file directory.
#include '<' filename '>'	The file "filename" is inserted. File uses the include search path.
#define name	Define precompiler variable name
#undefine name	Undefine precompiler variable name
#O0	Set optimization level 0 (no optimization)
#O1	Set optimization level 1
#O2	Set optimization level 2
#On	Set optimization level Max
#ifdef name statements [#else statements] #endif	If precompiler variable name exists, statements will be compiled; otherwise, if else statements exist, they will be compiled.
#ifndef name statements [#else statements] #endif	If precompiler variable name doesn't exist, statements will be compiled; otherwise, if else statements exist, they will be compiled.

Function Swapping

The VS program is required to do several VS calculations, like matrix transformations, lighting, etc. To write a specific VS, we need to write a VS for all the combinations of different transformations and lighting methods.

The number of shaders we have to write for each new shader is multiplied by the number of different transformation methods (normal transformation, soft binding, wobbly effect, teleport effect, etc.) and different lighting methods (ambient light, directional light, light with attenuation, light map, etc.).

For example, we have transformations T_1 and T_2, lighting methods L_1 and L_2, and we want to write a VS to do effect E. We need to write VS T_1+L_1+E, T_1+L_2+E, T_2+L_1+E, T_2+L_2+E.

With the VSC, you can divide the VS pipeline and avoid a large number of required shaders.

In the transformation example below, you can see an instance of how to use function swapping for dividing transformation types. First, we introduce the virtual function vstransfrom. This function will transform the input position and normal. Then we write all the different transformations we need.

At compile time, we specify the appropriate function swap: If we want a normal transformation, we specify vstransform, vstransform_normal; however, if we want a wobbly effect, we specify vstransform, vstransform_wobbly (see included file compileall.bat).

```
// transformation.cvs

// softbind.cvs
input vertexshader {
    vector      Pos;
    vector      Normal;
};

output vertexshader {
    vector      Pos;
    vector      Normal;
};

// normal mesh vertex type transformation
void vstransform_normal(vector pos,vector nor)
{
    pos=in.Pos;
    nor=in.Normal;
}

void vstransform_wobly(vector pos, vector nor)
{
    pos=in.Pos * in.Pos;
    nor=in.Normal * 2;
}
```

```
radical plugin FinalMatrix(vector x, vector y, vector z, vector w);

void vsmain()
{
    // position and normal transformation
    vector pos,nor;
    vstransform(pos, nor);

    // transform position into world space
    out.Pos=m4x4(pos, FinalMatrix.x);
}
```

Optimization

VSC uses very simple optimization techniques, described in this section. Although they are simple, they produce very optimized assembler code.

Register Scope Optimization

Within the register A scope (the register scope starts at the instruction at which register A has been set and ends at the instruction that overwrites it with a new value), all occurrences of register A are replaced with register B.

Instruction	Register 1	Register 2	Register 3
Mov	A	B	
ins1	*	A	*
ins2	*	*	A

...is replaced with:

Instruction	Register 1	Register 2	Register 3
ins1	*	B	*
ins2	*	*	B

A set instruction (all instructions except mov) followed by the mov instruction into the target register are replaced with the set instruction directly to the target register (if the target register scope allows it).

Instruction	Register 1	Register 2	Register 3
ins1	A	*	*
Mov	B	A	

...is replaced with:

Instruction	Register 1	Register 2	Register 3
ins1	B	*	*

All instructions for setting the registers that are not used are removed (output registers are excluded).

Additional Optimizations

The combination of multiplication and addition is replaced with a single instruction.

Instruction	Register 1	Register 2	Register 3
Mul	A	B	C
add	D	A	E

...is replaced with:

Instruction	Register 1	Register 2	Register 3	Register 4
mad	D	B	C	E

And:

Instruction	Register 1	Register 2	Register 3
mul	A	B	C
add	D	E	A

...is replaced with:

Instruction	Register 1	Register 2	Register 3	Register 4
mad	D	B	C	E

VSC Standard Library

The VSC provides a small set of built-in functions to simplify VS programming. These functions are similar to the C standard library functions and include mathematical, geometric, and VSC functions.

Mathematical Functions

Table 1 lists the mathematical functions provided in the VSC Standard Library. The list includes functions useful in trigonometry, exponentiation, and rounding. Functions change the parameters only where noted.

Table 1: Mathematical functions

Function	Description
float abs(float a)	Absolute value of a.
float acos(float a)	Arccosine of x in range [–1,1]; result is in range [–pi/2,pi/2].
float all(vector x)	Returns 0 if any component of x is equal to 0; returns 1 otherwise.
float any(vector x)	Returns 1 if any component of x is equal to 1; returns 0 otherwise.
float asin(float a)	Arcsine of a in range [–1,1]; result is in range [0,pi].
float atan(float a)	Arctangent of a in range [–pi/2,pi/2].
float atan2(float a, float b)	Arctangent of b/a in range [–pi,pi].

Function	Description
float ceil(float a)	Smallest integer not less than a.
float clamp(float a, float b, float c)	a clamped to the range [b,c] as follows: Returns b if a < b. Returns c if a > c. Otherwise returns a.
float cos(float a)	Cosine of a in range [–pi,pi].
float cross(vector x, vector y)	Cross product of x and y.
float exp(float a)	Exponential function e ^ a.
float exp2(float a)	Exponential function 2 ^ a.
float floor(float a)	Largest integer not greater than a.
float fmod(float a, float b)	Reminder of a/b with the same sign as a. b must not be equal to 0.
float frac(float a)	Fractional part of a.
float ldexp(float a, float b)	a * 2 ^ b.
float lerp(float a, float b, float f)	(1–f)*a + f*b.
float log(float a)	Natural logarithm ln(a). a must be greater than 0.
float log2(float a)	Base 2 logarithm of a. a must be greater than 0.
float log10(float a)	Base 10 logarithm of a. a must be greater than 0.
float max(float a, float b)	Maximum of a and b.
float min(float a, float b)	Minimum of a and b.
float pow(float a, float b)	a ^ b.
float round(float a)	Closest integer to a.
float rsqrt(float a)	Reciprocal square root of a.
float sign(float a)	Returns 1 if a > 0. Returns –1 if a< 0. Otherwise returns 0.
float sin(float a)	Sine of a in range [–pi,pi].
float sqrt(float a)	Square root of a. a must be greater than 0.
void fsplit(float a, float b, float c)	Splits a into integral part b and fractional part c.
void sincos(float a, float sin, float cos)	sin is set to sin(a), and cos is set to cos(a).

Geometric Functions

Table 2 lists the geometric functions provided in the VSC Standard Library.

Table 2: Geometric functions

Function	Description
float distance(vector x, vector y)	Euclidean distance between points x and y.
float length(vector x)	Euclidean length of vector x.
float normalize(vector x)	Returns a vector of length 1 that points in the same direction as vector x.
vector reflect(vector n, vector i)	Returns reflection vector for surface normal n and eye to position vector direction i.

VSC Functions

Table 3 lists the VSC functions provided in the VSC Standard Library.

Table 3: VSC functions

Function	Description
vector bumpmapuv(vector lightdir)	Bump map vector calculation for uv output.
vector bumpmapcolor(vector lightdir)	Bump map vector calculation for color output.
vector light(vector pos, 　　　　vector normal, 　　　　vector lightpos, 　　　　vector lightcolor)	Simple lighting calculation.
vector lightadvanced 　　　　(vector pos, 　　　　vector normal, 　　　　vector lightpos, 　　　　vector lightcolor, 　　　　vector lightrange)	Advanced lighting calculation with light fallout.
vector lightattenuation 　　　　(vector pos, 　　　　vector normal, 　　　　vector lightpos, 　　　　vector lightcolor, 　　　　vector tex0, 　　　　vector tex1)	Lighting calculation with texture attenuation lookup. Function returns the texture uv for stage0 int tex0 and texture uv for stage1 in tex1.

Examples

This section includes example programs written in VSC.

Lighting

Lighting shaders:

- Light attenuation
- Per-pixel specularity

Light attenuation:

```
#include <standard.hvs>
void vsmain()
{
    // position transformation
    vector pos,nor;
    vstransform(pos, nor);

    // std output
    out.Pos=m4x4(pos, FinalMatrix.x);

    // attenuation texture coordinates
    lightattenuation(pos, nor, SelectedLight.Pos, SelectedLight.Color,
```

```
                    SelectedLight.Range, out.Tex0, out.Tex1)

   // light intensity
   out.DColor=light(pos, nor, SelectedLight.Pos, SelectedLight.Color);

   // base texture for alpha
   #ifdef inTex0
      out.Tex2=in.Tex0;
   #endif
}
```

Per-pixel specularity:

```
#include <standard.hvs>
void vsmain()
{
   vector pos,nor;
   vstransform(pos, nor);

   // std output
   out.Pos=m4x4(pos, FinalMatrix.x);

   //
   vector lightdir=normalize(SpecularLight.Pos - pos);
   vector half    =normalize(normalize(CameraMatrix.Pos - pos) + lightdir);
   //
   out.DColor.xyzw=SpecularLight.Color;

   // color cube normal color
   out.Tex0=bumpmapuv(half);
   //
   #ifdef inLightMapUV
      out.Tex1=in.LightMapUV;
   #else
      out.Tex1=(0,0,0,0);
   #endif
}
```

Base Shaders

Base shaders:

- bump mapping
- multi-texture blending

Bump mapping:

```
#include <standard.hvs>
void vsmain()
{
   // position transformation
   vector pos,nor;
   vstransform(pos, nor);
```

```
// std output
out.Pos=m4x4(pos, FinalMatrix.x);
#ifdef inTex1
    out.Tex0=in.Tex1;
#else
    out.Tex0=in.Tex0;
#endif

// normal map
vector lightdir=normalize(SelectedLight.Pos - pos);
out.Tex1=bumpmapuv(lightdir);

// attenuation texture coordinates
lightattenuation(pos, nor, SelectedLight.Pos, SelectedLight.Color,
                SelectedLight.Range, out.Tex2, out.Tex3)

// light color
out.SColor=SelectedLight.Color;
}
```

Multi-texture blending:

```
#include <standard.hvs>
void vsmain()
{
    vector pos,nor;
    vstransform(pos, nor);
    out.Pos=m4x4(pos, FinalMatrix.x);

    // define color
    out.DColor=in.Color.zwxy;
    out.SColor=in.Color.xyzw;

    // define as many texure outputs as given
#ifdef inTex1
    out.Tex0=in.Tex0;
    out.Tex1=in.Tex1;
    out.Tex2=in.Tex1;
#else
    out.Tex0=in.Tex0;
    out.Tex1=in.Tex0;
    out.Tex2=in.Tex0;
#endif
}
```

Effects

Effects:

■ Volumetric shadows

Volumetric shadows:

```
#include <standard.hvs>
void vsmain(float projectionlength)
{
    // in Tex0.x is plane D parameter
    // test if face normal is facing towards light
    vector pos,nor;
    vstransform(pos, nor);
    //
    vector lightdir=pos - Light1.Pos;
    lightdir=normalize(lightdir);
    float test=dp3(nor, lightdir).x;
    pos.xyz=pos + (test < 0 ? lightdir*projectionlength);
    //
    out.Pos=m4x4(pos, FinalMatrix.x);
}
```

Gallery

The following figures demonstrate the VSC example programs.

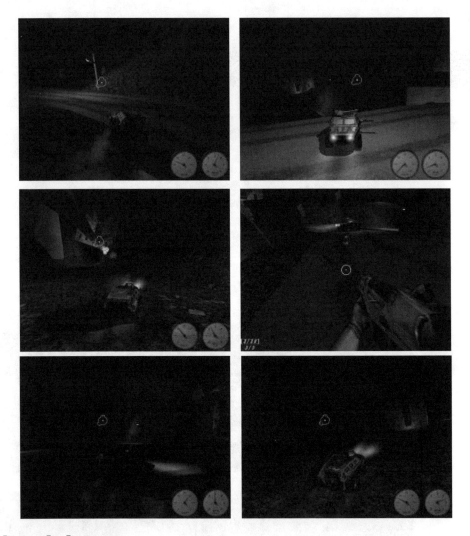

Acknowledgments

I am very grateful to Gregor Grlj for proofreading. I am also thankful to Helena Smigoc and Mladen Zagorac for lecturing.

Shader Disassembler

Jean-Sebastian Luce

Nadeo

 NOTE In this article, the word "shader" refers to programs for both the vertex and pixel pipelines.

Microsoft DirectX 9 introduces a new shading language, High Level Shading Language (HLSL), which is much easier to use compared to shader assembler. However, since the video driver understands nothing but shader byte code, both HLSL and assembler shader code have to be respectively compiled and assembled by the DirectX runtime. Unlike shader assembler, shader byte code is not "readable" by humans. This article gives a solution for converting shader byte code (back) into assembly instructions.

A Shader Disassembler: What Is It Useful For?

Although HLSL has many benefits for the programmer, its main drawback is that generated code is not always as optimal as hand-written assembly code. Sometimes, when coding in HLSL, if the programmer forgets to use fully vectorized operations, a non-optimal binary program can still result. For instance, the following code scales a 2D vector by two uniform constants:

```
struct VS_OUTPUT {float4 Position : POSITION; float2 TcO : TEXCOORDO;};
vs_1_1 VS_OUTPUT vsMain(float4 Position : POSITION, uniform float4x4 ObjectPrCamera,
                        uniform float ScaleU, uniform float ScaleV)
{
        VS_OUTPUT Output = (VS_OUTPUT) 0;
        Output.Position = mul(Position, ObjectPrCamera);
        Output.TcO.x = Position.x*ScaleU;
        Output.TcO.y = Position.y*ScaleV;
        return Output;
}
```

This results in the HLSL compiler generating the equivalent of the following assembly:

```
vs_1_1
dcl_position0    v0
m4x4      oPos, v0,   c0; c0-c3 = ObjectPrCamera
mul       oT0.x, v0.x, c4.x; c4 = ScaleU
```

```
mul        oT0.y, v0.y, c5.x; c5 = ScaleV
```

An obvious improvement is to scale by a 2D vector instead of two scalar constants:

```
struct VS_OUTPUT {float4 Position : POSITION; float2 Tc0 : TEXCOORD0;};
vs_1_1 VS_OUTPUT vsMain(float4 Position : POSITION, uniform float4x4 ObjectPrCamera,
                        uniform float2 ScaleUV)
{
        VS_OUTPUT Output = (VS_OUTPUT) 0;
        Output.Position = mul(Position, ObjectPrCamera);
        Output.Tc0 = Position*ScaleUV;
        return Output;
}
```

...which is compiled to the following (note that one less instruction is generated):

```
vs_1_1
dcl_position0    v0
m4x4       oPos, v0, c0 ; c0-c3 = ObjectPrCamera
mul        oT0.xy, v0, c4 ; c4 = ScaleUV
```

Moreover, early pixel shader hardware (ps_1_x) is very limited in its capabilities compared to later versions (few address operations and arithmetic instructions, small number of available instruction slots). Therefore, HLSL coding for these platforms should be done with care. Even ps_2_0-compliant hardware has important limitations (like the lack of arbitrary swizzling), which can force the compiler to use more instruction slots. An HLSL programmer should at least know the limitations of the target platform, and getting a look at the generated assembly would be helpful in writing optimal code. For this reason, reading and checking the generated shader assembly of an HLSL program is important. In the DirectX 9 SDK, the only way to view the assembly code generated by the HLSL compiler is to use the external compiler fxc.exe with the -Fc flag. Because this tool is not suited to be called from another program, and since we can get clearer assembly, as we see later in the "Disassembler Integration and Customization" section, let's implement a vertex/pixel shader disassembler. In addition, this disassembler can be used to view shaders where you don't have the source assembly.

Shader Byte Code Description

To understand how a shader byte code disassembler works, we start by describing the byte code itself: the elements of the byte code (called tokens) and their formatting. The DirectX 9 shader byte code is simpler than, for instance, the 80x86 code; instructions are always made of 32-bit aligned, little-endian byte-ordered *tokens*.

The first token in a compiled shader program is always a *version token*, corresponding to vs_x_y and ps_x_y assembler instructions.

Version Token		
Bits 31-16	Bits 15-8	Bits 7-0
• 0xFFFF=pixel pipeline • 0xFFFE=vertex pipeline	major version	minor version

For 1_x vertex and pixel shader targets, the minor version field contains a sub-version. For instance, 0xFFFF0103 is a version token meaning ps_1_3. But for DirectX 9 targets ($>=2\_0$), the minor version has another meaning:

0x00: normal target (for instance, 0xFFFF0200 means ps_2_0)

0x01: extended target (for instance, 0xFFFF0201 means ps_2_x)

0xFF: software target (for instance, 0xFFFF02FF means ps_2_sw)

Each assembler instruction generates one *instruction token* (even if this instruction is a macro like "m4x4," which uses four instruction slots in the graphic chip), containing the following information:

Instruction Token						
Bit 31	Bit 30	Bit 29	Bit 28	Bits 27-14	Bits 23-16	Bits 15-0
0	Co-issue	0	Predicate	Tokens count (excluding this one)	Specific controls	Operation code

The *co-issue* bit has meaning only on pixel shader versions earlier than 2_0. When this bit is set, the corresponding instruction is executed simultaneously with the preceding instruction. The two instructions can be paired only if they are executed concurrently in the RGB and alpha pipes.

The *predicate* bit has meaning only on vertex and pixel shader versions 2_0 and later. When this bit is set, the value of the predicate register (p0) is used to control, at run time, the instruction write per component. For instance:

```
if p0=(true, true, false, false)
"(p0) add r1, r2, r3" only writes r1.xy.
```

When the predicate bit is set, an extra predicate source token is inserted between the destination token and the first source token. This extra token describes the predicate register used and is formatted like the source register token, which will be seen later.

The *specific controls* field has meaning only for the ifc, breakc, and setp instructions, with values from 1 to 6 corresponding to gt, eq, ge, lt, ne, and le, respectively.

The *operation code* value is one of the values in the D3DSHADER_IN-STRUCTION_OPCODE_TYPE enum and is defined for all vertex and pixel assembler instructions (for instance, the nop operation code is 0, and mov is 1).

Depending on the precise operation that an instruction token specifies (defined by the *operation code* field), *destination/source parameter tokens* can follow the instruction token. For example, if the instruction token specifies an add operation, one destination and two source parameter tokens would follow. The following table outlines the description of the parameter token:

Destination Parameter Token								
Bit 31	Bits 30-28	Bits 27-24	Bits 23-20	Bits 19-16	Bits 15-14	Bit 13	Bits 12-11	Bits 10-0
1	Register type (1)	Shift scale	Result modifier	Write mask	0	Relative addressing	Register type (2)	Register number

In the destination parameter token, the *register type* is split into two parts: (1) = bits 0-2 and (2) = bits 3 and 4. The final value is one of those defined in the D3DSHADER_PARAM_REGISTER_TYPE enum. Using this field, we can determine if the register is a constant, a temporary, a texture, etc. This field is used with the *register number* field to get the full register name (for instance, c21).

There are a few special cases for register type/index:

- The registers an and tn share the same register type value (i.e., D3DSPR_ADDR=D3DSPR_TEXTURE), since addressing and texture registers are valid only in the vertex and pixel pipelines, respectively.

- The registers oPos, oFog, and oPts have the same type D3DSPR_RASTOUT but are distinguished by the register number, ranging from 0 to 2.

- Similarly, the registers vPos and vFace have the same type D3DSPR_MISC-TYPE but are distinguished by register numbers 0 and 1.

- The *relative addressing* bit is meaningful only on vertex shader versions 3_0 and later.

- The *write mask* field contains a bit per destination channel, set to 1 if the component is written to (bit 16=X, bit 17 = Y, ...).

The final two fields modify certain instructions rather than the destination register itself.

- The *shift scale* field is a 4-bit signed scale (0x00=none, 0x01=_x2, 0x0F=_d2, for instance mul_x2 r0, r1, t0).

- The *result modifier* field can be a combination of _sat, _pp (partial precision), and _centroid.

The format of the source parameter token is similar to the destination parameter token, with the exception that the write mask, result modifier, and shift scale are replaced by swizzle and source modifiers.

Source Parameter Token								
Bit 31	Bits 30-28	Bits 27-24	Bits 23-16	Bits 15-14	Bit 13	Bits 12-11	Bits 10-0	
1	Register type (1)	Source modifier	Swizzle	0	Relative addressing	Register type (2)	Register number	

- The *register type* field works identically to the field in the destination parameter token.

- The *source modifier* field is one of the values in the D3DSHADER_PARAM_SRCMOD_TYPE enum.

- The *swizzle* field contains (for each of the four destination components) two bits selecting the source component (0=X, 1=Y, 2=Z, and 3=W). For instance, if bits 17-16 hold 0x1, this means that the source component Y is swizzled into the destination component X.

- The *relative addressing* flag has meaning for all vertex shader versions and pixel shader versions 3_0 and later. Relative addressing enables constant register index selection at run time, depending on the value of an address register (a0 or aL) component. The actual constant register index selected is the sum of the token's constant register number and the (run-time) value of the address register component. For instance:

```
mov    r0,    c16[a0.x]
```

copies the value of the constant register n "16+a0.x" into r0.

On the vs_1_1 target, only a0.x is available. On vs_2_0 and ps_3_0 or later targets, a0.x/y/z/w and aL are available.

When *relative addressing* is enabled and when the shader version is at least 2_0 (vs_1_1 always implicitly uses the unique address register a0.x), a relative-addressing token follows this parameter token.

Relative-Addressing Token							
Bit 31	Bits 30-28	Bits 27-20	Bits 19-16	Bits 15-14	Bit 13	Bits 12-11	Bits 10-0
1	Register type (1)	Unused	Component index	0	Unused	Register type (2)	Register number

The special assembler instructions def, defi, and defb, respectively, require floating-point number, integer, or Boolean source parameters, which represent immediate values written in the assembly.

The assembler instruction dcl is followed by a special parameter token giving (in addition to the register type and number) a usage and usage index, or a texture type (for a sampler register).

A comment token may also be used by the compiler to store debug information (we read it only to compute the jump offset to the next instruction token).

Comment token		
Bit 31	Bits 30-16	Bits 15-0
0	Length in DWORD count (not including the comment token)	0xFFFE

An end token (identified by the value 0x0000FFFF) terminates the shader byte code stream.

Additional information about DirectX 9 shader byte code can be found at [1].

Disassembly Algorithm

Since each instruction is followed by one or more parameter tokens before reaching the next instruction token, to disassemble the shader byte code, all we have to do is parse each instruction token and then, depending on the instruction found, parse its expected parameter tokens, output the disassembly, and loop for the next instruction.

The first thing to do with a new token is check it against the special tokens (namely, the version token, comment tokens, and the end token). If we are not processing one of those tokens, we have to check the *operation code* of the instruction. Then we come to the first difficult part of the task; there are a lot of different instructions with various prototypes (type and number of arguments of the instruction).

To solve that issue, we use C preprocessor macros. If you read the Dx9-ShaderBCode_Instr.h file, you'll notice that (almost) every instruction is described by a line giving its OpCode_ID (for instance, D3DSIO_NOP) and then its parameters (RegSrc/Dst for source/destination register, Real/Bool/Integer for immediate values). A switch is done on the opcode, and for each instruction, the macros expand the parameters with calls to instruction/parameters disassembly methods. A few instruction opcodes have to be handled in a specific way because they have a unique syntax (like the dcl instruction) or a behavior that depends on the vertex/pixel shader target version (like texcoord/texcrd and tex/texld).

We now look, in further detail, at how each instruction is disassembled. First, the CatInstr method outputs the instruction name in lowercase, appends an optional specific control text for some comparison instructions (ifc, breakc, and setp), and then appends an optional shift text and a destination modifier text (both are taken from the next destination parameter token, if applicable).

Then, the destination and source parameters are disassembled by the CatParamRegSrc and CatParamRegDst methods. These two methods are based upon the CatRegister method, which outputs the register name and an optional index. CatParamRegSrc begins to write the start of a possible source modifier (for example, negation or bias), followed by the register name, an optional address text with the right swizzle (in this case, an address register token would follow the current source parameter token), and the end of the modifier if necessary. Finally, a swizzle specifier (".x" will be written for ".xxxx") is finally added. CatParamRegDst is simpler, since only a write mask has to be appended to the register.

CoIssue and Predicated instruction modifiers are handled before the OpCode switch. The predicated case is the more difficult one, since the predicate register token is inserted between the first and second parameter tokens (InstrToken, Param1Token, PredicateToken, Param2Token, ...), so the idea is to jump over the predicate token in order to make the following instruction disassembly work.

Disassembler Integration and Customization

This disassembler is easily integrated with C++ code; as an example, in the DisAsm.cpp file, only one DisAssemble call is required, passing the byte code data as input parameters. The disassembly is returned in an allocated string (valid until another DisAssemble call).

In addition, symbol information taken from constant tables (for example, the fact that the constant ObjectPrCamera uses c0 to c3 registers) can be incorporated to help in understanding the assembly.

A callback method pointer can be set to override constant and sampler register name disassembly. This callback is called with the register index and a "user data" in parameters. If the user returns a valid string pointer, the constant will be displayed as "cMyConstantName" or "sMySamplerName" in the output asm (returning 0 selects the normal register name, which is defined by the DirectX shader assembler reference as when no callback is installed). Here is a sample of how to implement a constant name callback:

```
struct SConstantTable {
    D3DXCONSTANT_DESC*Constants;
    Natural           Count;
};
const char* GetRegisterNameC(Natural _iRegister, void* _UserData)
{
    SConstantTable* Table = (SConstantTable*)_UserData;
    for (Natural i=0; i<Table->Count; i++)
    {
        const D3DXCONSTANT_DESC & Constant = Table->Constants[i];
        if (Constant.RegisterSet!=D3DXRS_FLOAT4)
            continue;
        Integer iRegisterRel = _iRegister-Constant.RegisterIndex;
        if (iRegisterRel<0 || iRegisterRel>=Constant.RegisterCount)
            continue;
        char    Name[128];
        if (Constant.RegisterCount==1)
            strcpy(Name, Constant.Name);
        else
            sprintf(Name, "%s_%d", Constant.Name, iRegisterRel);
        return Name;
    }
    return Null;          // index out of bounds
}

SConstantTable Table;    // to fill
CDx9ShaderDisasm::UserData = & Table;
CDx9ShaderDisasm::CallbackGetRegisterNameC = & GetRegisterNameC;
```

The input and ouput (vs_3_0 only) registers can be displayed using their declaration semantic (usage and usage index) rather than their register index (again, this helps in understanding the assembly). There is a special case for the vs_3_0 output register since several semantics can be linked to the same register.

In this case, we get back to the register index naming convention to remove any ambiguity. Because these registers cannot be understood by DirectX assembler, there is the possibility of disabling this (enabled by default) semantic register naming behavior by changing two booleans' values (one for the input registers and one for the output registers).

References

[1] Direct3D Driver Shader Codes (MSDN Library, Direct3D DDK) http://msdn.microsoft.com/library/default.asp? url=/library/en-us/graphics/hh/graphics/d3denum-9o6f.asp.

Index

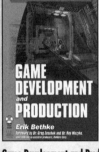

POWERVR

Visionary IP

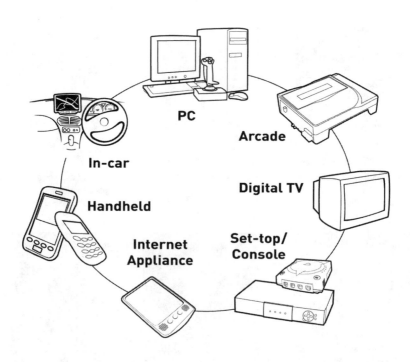

PC

Arcade

In-car

Digital TV

Handheld

Internet
Appliance

Set-top/
Console

Get **Deep** into 3D!

Search, View, Translate, Animate, Render and Publish!

Deep Exploration™ provides easy navigation tools that let you search and view your 2D graphics and 3D models. It gives artists everywhere a production edge, including the ability to quickly translate 2D and 3D file formats with animation included. Deep Exploration creates high quality fast renderings of 3D objects and scenes for use in many graphic applications. It is also a powerful web publication tool, ideal for creating interactive 3D content for web-based presentations.

3D Painting and Texturing

Deep Paint 3D® provides artists with an intuitive, easy to use tool to paint and texture 3D models interactively in 3D! It uses textures or natural media paints which can be brushed directly or projected onto 3D models and scenes. This creative environment supports an integrated workflow with 3ds max®, Maya®, SoftImage® and LightWave 3D®. Deep Paint 3D comes complete with a bi-directional interface to Photoshop® and special support for the Wacom® Intuos™ pressure sensitive tablet.

Ultimate UV Mapping

Deep UV™ is a superior set of tools for the creation and modification of UV mapping for polygonal and sub-division surface models within an interactive 2D and 3D UV mapping environment. Deep UV includes fast and easy to use tools such as soft selection, relax and 3D UV selection. Whether you're a beginner or a professional 3D artist, you'll have the most efficient UV mapping possible with both automatic and advanced features. Deep UV can be used standalone, or with Deep Paint 3D.

RIGHT ⟨ HEMISPHERE.

www.righthemisphere.com

ONLY 100
WILL BE CHOSEN
FOR THE QUEST
of a
LIFETIME

Twice a year the challenge is raised — and 100 of the best
are admitted to the Hart eCenter at SMU Digital Games
Guildhall. The Guildhall is designed to train talented
students to become immediately productive digital games
developers. The program is just like the industry — intense,
results oriented, and only for the dedicated few.

The Guildhall grants membership to those who complete
the 18-month certificate program, designed by industry
professionals to train the next generation of game developers.
High-profile industry leaders from top name development
companies have designed the courses and take special interest
in the Guildhall as teachers, mentors, and craft experts.

For more information and details on how to apply, contact
David Najjab at **214-768-9903** or email **najjab@smu.edu.**

Check out the website at **guildhall.smu.edu.**

About the CD

The companion CD contains examples and source code discussed in the articles. There are folders for each section and subfolders for each article within the sections, although there may not be an example for some articles. Many folders include a readme.txt document that explains the examples, contains instructions, and lists hardware requirements.

Simply place the CD in your CD drive and select the folder for which you would like to see the example.

 Warning: By opening the CD package, you accept the terms and conditions of the CD/Source Code Usage License Agreement on the following page.

Additionally, opening the CD package makes this book nonreturnable.

CD/Source Code Usage License Agreement

Please read the following CD/Source Code usage license agreement before opening the CD and using the contents therein:

1. By opening the accompanying software package, you are indicating that you have read and agree to be bound by all terms and conditions of this CD/Source Code usage license agreement.

2. The compilation of code and utilities contained on the CD and in the book are copyrighted and protected by both U.S. copyright law and international copyright treaties, and is owned by Wordware Publishing, Inc. Individual source code, example programs, help files, freeware, shareware, utilities, and evaluation packages, including their copyrights, are owned by the respective authors.

3. No part of the enclosed CD or this book, including all source code, help files, shareware, freeware, utilities, example programs, or evaluation programs, may be made available on a public forum (such as a World Wide Web page, FTP site, bulletin board, or Internet news group) without the express written permission of Wordware Publishing, Inc. or the author of the respective source code, help files, shareware, freeware, utilities, example programs, or evaluation programs.

4. You may not decompile, reverse engineer, disassemble, create a derivative work, or otherwise use the enclosed programs, help files, freeware, shareware, utilities, or evaluation programs except as stated in this agreement.

5. The software, contained on the CD and/or as source code in this book, is sold without warranty of any kind. Wordware Publishing, Inc. and the authors specifically disclaim all other warranties, express or implied, including but not limited to implied warranties of merchantability and fitness for a particular purpose with respect to defects in the disk, the program, source code, sample files, help files, freeware, shareware, utilities, and evaluation programs contained therein, and/or the techniques described in the book and implemented in the example programs. In no event shall Wordware Publishing, Inc., its dealers, its distributors, or the authors be liable or held responsible for any loss of profit or any other alleged or actual private or commercial damage, including but not limited to special, incidental, consequential, or other damages.

6. One (1) copy of the CD or any source code therein may be created for backup purposes. The CD and all accompanying source code, sample files, help files, freeware, shareware, utilities, and evaluation programs may be copied to your hard drive. With the exception of freeware and shareware programs, at no time can any part of the contents of this CD reside on more than one computer at one time. The contents of the CD can be copied to another computer, as long as the contents of the CD contained on the original computer are deleted.

7. You may not include any part of the CD contents, including all source code, example programs, shareware, freeware, help files, utilities, or evaluation programs in any compilation of source code, utilities, help files, example programs, freeware, shareware, or evaluation programs on any media, including but not limited to CD, disk, or Internet distribution, without the express written permission of Wordware Publishing, Inc. or the owner of the individual source code, utilities, help files, example programs, freeware, shareware, or evaluation programs.

8. You may use the source code, techniques, and example programs in your own commercial or private applications unless otherwise noted by additional usage agreements as found on the CD.

 **Warning:** By opening the CD package, you accept the terms and conditions of the CD/Source Code Usage License Agreement.

Additionally, opening the CD package makes this book nonreturnable.